T0143075

Lecture Notes in Artificial Intelligence   **13562**

Subseries of Lecture Notes in Computer Science

More information about this subseries at https://link.springer.com/bookseries/1244

Florence Dupin de Saint-Cyr ·
Meltem Öztürk-Escoffier · Nico Potyka (Eds.)

Scalable Uncertainty Management

15th International Conference, SUM 2022
Paris, France, October 17–19, 2022
Proceedings

Springer

Editors
Florence Dupin de Saint-Cyr 🄳
IRIT-Université Toulouse
Toulouse, France

Meltem Öztürk-Escoffier
Université Paris-Dauphine - PSL
Paris, France

Nico Potyka 🄳
Imperial College London
London, UK

ISSN 0302-9743   ISSN 1611-3349 (electronic)
Lecture Notes in Artificial Intelligence
ISBN 978-3-031-18842-8   ISBN 978-3-031-18843-5 (eBook)
https://doi.org/10.1007/978-3-031-18843-5

LNCS Sublibrary: SL7 – Artificial Intelligence

This Springer imprint is published by the registered company Springer Nature Switzerland AG
The registered company address is: Gewerbestrasse 11, 6330 Cham, Switzerland

Preface

These are the proceedings of the 15th International Conference on Scalable Uncertainty Management (SUM 2022) held during October 17–19, 2022, at Université Paris-Dauphine - PSL, in Paris, France. The SUM conferences are annual events which aim to gather researchers with a common interest in managing and analyzing imperfect information from a wide range of fields, such as artificial intelligence and machine learning, databases, information retrieval and data mining, the semantic web, and risk analysis, and with the aim of fostering collaboration and cross-fertilization of ideas from the different communities.

The first SUM conference was held in Washington DC in 2007. Since then, the SUM conferences have successively taken place in Naples in 2008, Washington DC in 2009, Toulouse in 2010, Dayton in 2011, Marburg in 2012, Washington DC in 2013, Oxford in 2014, Québec in 2015, Nice in 2016, Granada in 2017, Milano in 2018, and Compiègne in 2019. SUM 2020 was initially planned to be held in Bolzano, Italy, during September 2020. Unfortunately, the COVID-19 pandemic forced it to be fully virtual. For the same reasons, there was no SUM conference in 2021.

SUM 2022 solicited three types of paper submissions. Long papers report on original research, or provide a survey that synthesizes some current research trends. Short papers describe promising work in progress, systems, or positions on controversial issues. Finally, extended abstracts, which did not go into the proceedings, allowed participants to present their recently published work or preliminary ideas at SUM to discuss them with the community.

We received a small number of submissions (21 long and four short papers), mostly by reputed research groups. We assigned three to four reviewers from the Program Committee per paper, and only accepted papers with an overall positive evaluation. This resulted in 19 long and four short papers that went into the proceedings.

The conference also included three invited talks by Gabriele Kern-Isberner (Technische Universität Dortmund), Silja Renooij (Universiteit Utrecht), and Francesca Toni (Imperial College London) and eight tutorials by Denis Bouyssou (CNRS, Université Paris Dauphine - PSL), Tanya Braun (University of Münster), Anne Laurent (Université de Montpellier), Jean-Guy Mailly (Université Paris Cité), Michael Poss (CNRS, Université de Montpellier), Jeremy Rohmer (BRGM, Paris), Diedrich Wolter (University of Bamberg) and Christophe Gonzales (Aix Marseille Université). Two tutorials were accompanied by a tutorial article that can be found in the proceedings.

We would like to thank all authors, invited speakers, and tutorial speakers for their valuable contributions to the conference program, the members of the Program Committee and the external reviewers for their constructive reviews, and the Local Organization and the SUM Steering Committee for their support in organizing the event. We are particularly grateful to Henri Prade and Didier Dubois for their constant support and advice during the organization of the conference and to Lluis Godo and Leopoldo Bertossi for the extra effort that they put into advertising the conference. We also want to thank Lamsade and the Université Paris-Dauphine - PSL for funding and hosting the conference and Springer for their ongoing support and sponsoring this year's Best Student Paper Award. Finally, we would like to thank all participants of SUM 2022 for attending the conference and making it a success.

September 2022

Florence Dupin de Saint-Cyr
Meltem Öztürk-Escoffier
Nico Potyka

Organization

General Chair

Meltem Öztürk-Escoffier   Université Paris-Dauphine - PSL, France

Program Committee Chairs

Florence Dupin de Saint-Cyr   IRIT-Université Toulouse 3, France
Nico Potyka   Imperial College London, UK

Local Organization Committee

Lucie Galand   Université Paris-Dauphine - PSL, France
Brice Mayag   Université Paris-Dauphine - PSL, France
Stefano Moretti   CNRS, Université Paris-Dauphine - PSL, France
Meltem Öztürk-Escoffier   Université Paris-Dauphine - PSL, France
Sonia Toubaline   Université Paris-Dauphine - PSL, France
Paolo Viappiani   CNRS, Université Paris-Dauphine - PSL, France

Steering Committee

Salem Benferhat   Artois University, France
Didier Dubois   IRIT-CNRS, France
Lluis Godo   IIIA-CSIC, Spain
Eyke Hüllermeier   Universität Paderborn, Germany
Anthony Hunter   University College London, UK
Henri Prade   IRIT-CNRS, France
Steven Schockaert   Cardiff University, UK
V. S. Subrahmanian   University of Maryland, USA

Program Committee

Leila Amgoud   IRIT - CNRS, France
Alessandro Antonucci   IDSIA, Switzerland
Nahla Ben Amor   Institut Supérieur de Gestion de Tunis, Tunisia
Salem Benferhat   Artois University, France
Leopoldo Bertossi   Skema Business School, Canada
Fernando Bobillo   University of Zaragoza, Spain

Imen Boukhris	Université de Tunis, ISG Tunis, Tunisia
Rafika Boutalbi	University of Stuttgart, Germany
Tanya Braun	University of Münster, Germany
Fabio Cozman	University of São Paulo, Brazil
Davide Ciucci	University of Milano-Bicocca, Italy
Thierry Denoeux	Université de Technologie de Compiègne, France
Sylvie Doutre	University of Toulouse 1 - IRIT, France
Zied Elouedi	Institut Supérieur de Gestion de Tunis, Tunisia
Lluis Godo	IIIA-CSIC, Spain
Manuel Gómez-Olmedo	University de Granada, Spain
Christophe Gonzales	Aix-Marseille Université, LIS, France
John Grant	Towson University, USA
Arjen Hommersom	Open Universiteit, The Netherlands
Eric Lefevre	Artois University, France
Philippe Leray	Nantes University, France
Thomas Lukasiewicz	University of Oxford, UK
Francesca Mangili	IDSIA, Switzerland
Silviu Maniu	Université Paris-Sud, France
Thomas Meyer	University of Cape Town and CAIR, South Africa
Serafin Moral	University de Granada, Spain
Francesco Parisi	DIMES, University of Calabria, Italy
Henri Prade	IRIT-CNRS, France
Andrea Pugliese	University of Calabria, Italy
Benjamin Quost	Université de Technologie de Compiègne, France
Steven Schockaert	Cardiff University, UK
Umberto Straccia	ISTI-CNR, Italy
Andrea Tettamanzi	University of Nice Sophia Antipolis, France
Matthias Thimm	FernUniversität in Hagen, Germany
Maurice van Keulen	University of Twente, The Netherlands
Barbara Vantaggi	La Sapienza University of Rome, Italy

Additional Reviewers

| Xiaolong Liu | Xiangtan University, China |
| Kai Sauerwald | FernUniversität in Hagen, Germany |

Abstracts of Invited Talks

Cognitive Logics, and the Relevance of Nonmontonic Formal Logics for Human-Centred AI

Gabriele Kern-Isberner

Technische Universität Dortmund, Germany

Abstract. Classical logics like propositional or predicate logic have been considered as the gold standard for rational human reasoning, and hence as a solid, desirable norm on which all human knowledge and decision making should be based, ideally. For instance, Boolean logic was set up as kind of an arithmetic framework that should help make rational reasoning computable in an objective way, similar to the arithmetics of numbers. Computer scientists adopted this view to (literally) implement objective knowledge and rational deduction, in particular for AI applications. Psychologists have used classical logics as norms to assess the rationality of human commonsense reasoning. However, both disciplines could not ignore the severe limitations of classical logics, e.g., computational complexity and undecidedness, failures of logic-based AI systems in practice, and lots of psychological paradoxes. Many of these problems are caused by the inability of classical logics to deal with uncertainty in an adequate way. Both disciplines have used probabilities as a way out of this dilemma, hoping that numbers and the Kolmogoroff axioms can do the job (somehow). However, psychologists have been observing also lots of paradoxes here (maybe even more).

So then, are humans hopelessly irrational? Is human reasoning incompatible with formal, axiomatic logics? In the end, should computer-based knowledge and information processing be considered as superior in terms of objectivity and rationality?

Cognitive logics aim at overcoming the limitations of classical logics and resolving the observed paradoxes by proposing logic-based approaches that can model human reasoning consistently and coherently in benchmark examples. The basic idea is to reverse the normative way of assessing human reasoning in terms of logics resp. probabilities, and to use typical human reasoning patterns as norms for assessing the cognitive quality of logics. Cognitive logics explore the broad field of logic-based approaches between the extreme points marked by classical logics and probability theory with the goal to find more suitable logics for AI applications, on the one hand, and to gain more insights into the rational structures of human reasoning, on the other.

Surfing the Waves of Explanation

Silja Renooij

Utrecht University, The Netherlands

Abstract. The need for explaining black box machine learning models has revived the interest in explainability in AI more in general. One of the ideas underlying explainable AI is to use (new) models that are inherently explainable to replace or complement black box models in machine learning. Explainable or interpretable models exist and have existed for quite some time, and different aspects of these models and their outputs can be explained. In this talk I will focus on explanation of probabilistic graphical models, with an emphasis on Bayesian networks. From their very first introduction in the late 1980s, explanation of Bayesian networks has been a topic of interest: sometimes receiving a lot of attention, sometimes a seemingly forgotten topic, but now resurfacing again, riding on the waves of explainable AI.

Learning Argumentation Frameworks

Francesca Toni

Imperial College London, UK

Abstract. Argumentation frameworks are well studied as concerns their support for various forms of reasoning. Amongst these, abstract argumentation and assumption-based argumentation framworks can be used to support various forms of defeasible, non-monotonic reasoning. In this talk I will focus on methods for learning these frameworks automatically from data. Specifically, I will overview two recent methods to obtain, respectively, abstract argumentation frameworks from past cases and assumption-based argumentation frameworks from examples of concepts. In both cases, the learnt frameworks can be naturally used to obtain argumentative explanations for predictions drawn from the data (past cases or examples) in the form of disputes, thus supporting the vision of data-centric explainable AI.

Contents

Short Papers: Non-classical Reasoning

Short Papers: Explanation

Tutorial Articles

A Glimpse into Statistical Relational AI: The Power of Indistinguishability

Tanya Braun$^{(\boxtimes)}$ (iD)

Computer Science Department, University of Münster, Münster, Germany
`tanya.braun@uni-muenster.de`

Abstract. Statistical relational artificial intelligence, StaRAI for short, focuses on combining reasoning in uncertain environments with reasoning about individuals and relations in those environments. An important concept in StaRAI is indistinguishability, where groups of individuals behave indistinguishably in relation to each other in an environment. This indistinguishability manifests itself in symmetries in a propositional model and can be encoded compactly using logical constructs in relational models. Lifted inference then exploits indistinguishability for efficiency gains. This article showcases how to encode indistinguishability in models using logical constructs and highlights various ways of using indistinguishability during probabilistic inference.

1 Introduction

Artificial intelligence (AI) at its core is about building agents acting rationally in an environment [34]. The nature of the environment plays a crucial part in how complex this task is. In a more simple world, the environment is (i) deterministic, i.e., there is no uncertainty about the state of the environment or the outcome of an action, (ii) fully observable, i.e., the agent can fully determine the state, (iii) discrete, i.e., there are a finite number of labels, which characterise a feature of the state, and (iv) episodic, i.e., the state and an agent's decision on an action does not depend on previous states or actions, with a single agent acting in it. However, the real world contains multiple agents acting in an environment characterised by uncertainty, due to non-deterministic behaviour, noise, or system failures, with parts of the environment being hidden from the agent, features carrying continuous characteristics, or actions influencing future decisions (sequential setting). Additionally, a world usually has more structure than a collection of feature values. It contains various objects or individuals that are in relation with each other.

To represent such a world, one can model uncertainty using probabilistic graphical models (PGMs), possibly with a temporal or decision-making dimension. To focus on the relational part, one may turn to first-order logics. *Statistical Relational AI*, or StaRAI for short, concentrates on combining reasoning under uncertainty and reasoning about individuals and relations [7]. To do so, one can extend first-order logics with probabilities and utilities, like ProbLog [8,48] to

F. Dupin de Saint-Cyr et al. (Eds.): SUM 2022, LNAI 13562, pp. 3–18, 2022.
https://doi.org/10.1007/978-3-031-18843-5_1

name a well-known representative. This article focuses on the other direction, extending a PGM with logical constructs. Specifically, it highlights so-called parfactor models [31] as well as Markov logic networks (MLNs) [33]. Such probabilistic relational models follow the grounding semantics [9,37], which turns a relational model back into a propositional one through grounding, where standard probabilistic inference methods apply. These grounded models usually show symmetries in the graph structure and distributions associated with it. These symmetries are used for efficiency gains in so called *lifted inference*.

These symmetries come from groups of individuals forming identical relations and being represented by the same distributions, encoding indistinguishable behaviour, which leads to identical calculations during inference. Working with representatives for those groups of indistinguishable individuals allows for those efficiency gains during inference, avoiding grounding the relational structures. Therefore, this article showcases various points where indistinguishability helps to gain efficiency. Specifically, we look at probabilistic query answering in probabilistic relational models, the effect of a temporal dimension, and which parts of decision making can be lifted. Along the way, we highlight a way to get from a propositional model to a relational representation, discuss what completeness and tractability means for lifted inference, and take a look at leaving behind a universe of known individuals.

Due to space limitations, this article focuses on one specific aspect, namely indistinguishability and its potential for lifted probabilistic inference. Hopefully, it provides inspiration and starting points for further readings. Unfortunately, it cannot cover all the wonderful work in the field of StaRAI. Apologies to those whose work does not make into this article! For a more general introduction to StaRAI or lifted inference, please refer to [7] and [45], respectively.

2   Probabilistic Relational Models (PRMs)

This section shows how to combine probabilistic and relational modelling as done in parfactor models [31], also briefly highlighting MLNs [33].

Figure 1 depicts an example parfactor model, which is an extension of the epidemic-sick benchmark by de Salvo Braz et al. [35]. Please ignore the grey parts for now. Let us concentrate on the elliptical nodes. They represent parameterised random variables, PRVs for short, which are random variables parameterised with logical variables. E.g., PRV $Sick(X)$ has a name $Sick$ and a logical variable X as a parameter. Replacing the logical variables of a PRV with specific constants, also called *grounding*, leads to propositional random variables, which form nodes in Bayesian networks, factor graphs, or Markov networks. Grounding $Sick(X)$ yields $Sick(x_1)$, $Sick(x_2)$, and so on, considered indistinguishable without further evidence. Lifting works with representatives for the indistinguishable random variables, aiming to avoid grounding logical variables. PRVs have discrete range values like the Boolean range of *true* and *false*. The example model contains PRVs to represent people X being sick, travelling, and being treated with treatments T as well as a random variable $Epid$ for an epidemic.

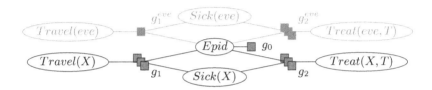

Fig. 1. Graphical representation of a parfactor model (grey part: shattered off for *eve*)

PRVs are linked through parfactors, short for parametric factors, which are functions that take PRVs as arguments and return a real number, called potential. A potential can be thought of as a measure of compatibility between the argument states. In the figure, parfactors are depicted by boxes, with edges to those PRVs that are arguments to the parfactor. A set of such parfactors forms a model G. When grounding such a model, symmetries in the grounded network become apparent as the grounded parts coming from the same parfactor form isomorphic subgraphs. Joining all grounded parfactors through multiplication using a join over the arguments and multiplication for the potentials leads to a full joint probability distribution after normalising the join result (distribution semantics [9,37]). Formally, the semantics is defined as follows, which boils down to a grounded Markov random field.

Definition 1 (Parfactor Semantics). *With Z as normalising constant, a parfactor model G represents the full joint distribution $P_G = \frac{1}{Z} \prod_{f \in gr(G)} f$, where $gr(G)$ refers to the grounding of G.*

MLNs explicitly contain first-order logics. An MLN M consist of a set of weighted (function-free) first-order logical formulas, i.e., a set of pairs (F_i, w_i), where F_i is an FOL formula and $w_i \in \mathbb{R}$, which can be considered weighted constraints, with an infinite weight denoting a hard constraint. A common example is the smokers benchmark [47]:

$$2 \quad friends(X,Y) \wedge smokes(X) \Rightarrow smokes(Y)$$

MLNs also follow the grounding semantics, representing a full joint probability distribution in the following way:

Definition 2 (MLN Semantics). *With Z as normalising constant, an MLN M represents the full joint distribution $P_M = \bigcup_{r \in asgn(R)} \frac{1}{Z} \exp\left(\sum_i w_i n_i(r)\right)$, where R is the set of all grounded random variables in M, w_i the weight of formula F_i, and $n_i(r)$ the number of true groundings of F_i in assignment r.*

Grounded formulas coming from the same first-order formula are also considered indistinguishable if they receive the same valuation in a given world. MLNs require first-order logical formulas, providing specific descriptions about the connection between atoms in a formula. Parfactors do not require those formulas, allowing for more general distributions describing a connection between PRVs. However, general distributions make it harder for humans to interpret them.

One can transform parfactor models with Boolean PRVs into an MLN by translating each input-output mapping of each parfactor into a logical formula with universal quantifiers for the logical variables [42]. Depending on local symmetries within a parfactor (multiple input-output pairs with the same potential), it might be possible to reduce the number of formulas by finding at best one logical formula to represent the mappings [21]. One can also transform an MLN into a parfactor model, setting up parfactors for the weighted constraint [42].

Given a propositional model learned from data in a relational domain, symmetries are set to occur. This model can be lifted, e.g., using the colour passing algorithm [1], which works like a belief propagation scheme, passing colours around. The same colours for random variables at the beginning denote identical observations if available (otherwise all have the same one colour). The same colours for factors mean the same potentials in the potential function. Colours are passed from variables to factors, which send the colours received back after adding their own colour, Then, each node and factor is recoloured according to the colour signature received. This procedure continues until no new colour is created. Nodes with the same colours can then be compactly encoded using logical variables. While going from the propositional to the lifted model is possible, the propositional model might be prohibitively large. The idea is to directly use a relational model, whether it is the result of a learning method given data, an expert setting up the model by hand, or a combination of both.

Given a probabilistic relational model, one can ask queries for probability distributions or the probability of an event, possibly given a set of observations as evidence, like $P(Sick(x_1))$, $P(Treat(x_1, t_1) = true)$, or $P(Epid \mid Sick(x_1) = true, Sick(x_2) = true)$. Formally, a query can be defined as follows:

Definition 3 (Query). *The term $P(Q \mid e)$ denotes a query in a model with Q a grounded PRV or atom and e a set of events $\{E_j = e_j\}_{j=1}^m$, $e_j \in ran(E_j)$, ran referring to the range (possible values) of E_j, as evidence. The query answering problem refers to the problem of computing an answer to a query.*

Answering a query would require eliminating all PRVs occurring in the model that do not occur in the query (non-query terms) after absorbing given evidence. To answer a query, one could always ground the model, yielding a propositional model, and use any fitting inference algorithm. Looking at those eliminations in the grounded model however reveals that the computations among indistinguishable parts are identical. So, instead of grounding, one could do the computations once for a representative and reuse the result for all indistinguishable instances. For MLNs, the query answering problem may also be transformed into a weighted model counting problem, where one has to count the models in which $q \wedge e$ holds, yielding a weighted model count (WMC), to compute an answer to a query $P(q \mid e)$, i.e., $\frac{WMC(M \wedge q \wedge e)}{WMC(M \wedge e)}$. Again, the idea is the consider one representative grounding of a first-order formula when counting. Both formulations showcase the basic idea of lifting in probabilistic inference: to not ground the model but try to work with the lifted representation, specifically with representatives, for as long as possible when computing an answer. The following section sketches how one can accomplish that for query answering in more detail.

3   Using Indistinguishability in Episodic PRMs

This section looks into indistinguishability in query answering, which involves the model itself, the query terms, and the evidence. Specifically, this section considers lifting for those three aspects and its effect on complexity and completeness.

3.1   Lifted Model

Let us consider the first lifted inference algorithm proposed, which is lifted variable elimination (LVE) [31], which has been extended repeatedly over the years [5,23,35,39]. For a query of Definition 3, using lifting means that LVE, instead of eliminating each instance individually, can eliminate a PRV as a whole using a representative and then account for all instances represented. Let us consider $P(Travel(eve))$ as an example. The first step is to split the PRVs w.r.t. eve in the model. This procedure is called shattering [35], the result of which can be seen in Fig. 1 including the grey parts. Then, LVE eliminates all non-query terms, starting with PRV $Treat(X, T)$, $X \neq eve$, which fulfils the preconditions of lifted summing out: it appears in only one parfactor g, contains all logical variables of g, and contains for each X constant the same number of T constants (called count-normalised; assumed here), denoted by $\#_{T|X}$. Mathematically, the following happens:

$$\left(\sum_{v \in ran(Treat(X,T))} g_2(Epid = e, Sick(X) = s, Treat(X, T) = v) \right)^{\#_{T|X}} \tag{1}$$

The following shows an arbitrary specification of g_2, with $\tilde{g}_2$ the result of the representative sum-out and g'_2 the result of the exponentiation, assuming $\#_{M|X} = 2$, meaning two treatments available for each person:

$Epid$	$Sick(X)$	$Treat(X, T)$	g_2	$\tilde{g}_2$	g'_2
$false$	$false$	$false$	5	$5 + 1$	6^2
$false$	$false$	$true$	1		
$false$	$true$	$false$	3	$3 + 2$	5^2
$false$	$true$	$true$	2		
$true$	$false$	$false$	5	$5 + 4$	9^2
$true$	$false$	$true$	4		
$true$	$true$	$false$	1	$1 + 7$	8^2
$true$	$true$	$true$	7		

In the ground model, each $Treat(x, t)$ would be eliminated individually in identical calculations. The results would be multiplied for each x, leading to the exponentiation. PRV $Travel(X)$ can be eliminated in a similar fashion with $\#_{\emptyset|X} = 1$ (no logical variable eliminated), yielding g'_1. Afterwards, g'_2 and g'_1 can be multiplied (in a lifted way) and $Sick(X)$ can be eliminated with $\#_{X|\emptyset} = n$, n the domain size of X without eve. $Treat(eve, M)$ is eliminated in the same way as $Treat(X, T)$, since $\#(T \mid eve) = 2$. Then, the model is ground and LVE proceeds like propositional variable elimination, summing out the remaining random variables, multiplying if necessary, and normalising the result.

The example shows how LVE uses the explicit encoding of indistinguishability for efficiency gains, using a suite of lifted operators [39]. Other lifted inference algorithms that incorporate helper structures for efficient multi-query answering include (i) first-order knowledge compilation (FOKC) [44], building a first-order circuit representation of an MLN and solving a first-order weight model counting problem, (ii) the lifted junction tree algorithm (LJT) [4], building a parametric junction tree, on which messages calculated by LVE are sent, and (iii) probabilistic theorem proving [14], also solving a first-order weight model counting problem. Lifted belief propagation [1] is a deterministic approximate algorithm, using message passing directly on the structure of the model. There also exist various sampling-based algorithms using indistinguishability to their advantage such as lifted importance sampling [15], lifted Gibbs and Metropolis-Hastings sampling [28,46], and a weighted model sampler [49].

3.2   Complexity, Tractability, Completeness

Given the grounding semantics, there is an equivalence between exact lifted inference and exact propositional inference, which implies the worst case for lifted inference is propositional inference. The inference problem is *tractable* if it is solved by an algorithm running in time polynomial in the number of random variables. Inference in general is intractable. However, given a model that allows for lifted calculations without groundings, solving an instance of the inference problem is possible in time polynomial in the domain sizes of the logical variables. We call such a model *liftable* and an algorithm that can solve a problem instance in polynomial time *domain-lifted* [41]. So, when the number of random variables is characterised by the domain sizes of the logical variables, then solving an inference problem in a liftable model is tractable with a domain-lifted algorithm. For a detailed discussion, please refer to Niepert and Van den Broeck [29].

Of course, it would be advantageous to know in advance whether a model is liftable or not, based solely on the model specification. While it is not possible to determine liftability in advance in general, one can identify classes of models (and in extension, evidence and queries) that are guaranteed to be liftable, investigated under the notion of *completeness*.

There are two classes characterised as liftable that have at least one domain-lifted algorithm solving problem instances in them in a lifted way without grounding. The first class refers to those models that contain at most two universally quantified logical variables per parfactor or weighted constraint in MLNs (*two-logvar* class/fragment). Examples of parfactors falling into this class are:

$$g(R(X,Y), S(Y,X)) \tag{2}$$
$$g(R(X,X'), T(X), T(X')), X \neq X' \tag{3}$$
$$g(R(X,Y), T(X), U(Y)) \tag{4}$$

The second class refers to those models that contain at most one logical variable per PRV or atom (universally quantified), e.g.,

$$g(R(X), S(Y), T(Z)).$$

LVE, FOKC, and LJT are all domain-lifted algorithms [2,40,41]. In LVE, for example, completeness stems from the fact that there exist lifted operators to handle each possible setting of logical variables in a lifted way when eliminating PRVs. The weighted model sampler mentioned above is also a domain-lifted algorithm for the first class [49]. There may be liftable models in classes that are not liftable. E.g., LVE in its current form is not complete for the class of three logical variables per parfactor:

$$g(R(X,Y,Z), S(Y), T(Z)) \rightarrow \text{liftable} \tag{5}$$
$$g(R(X,Y), S(Y,Z), T(X,Z)) \rightarrow \text{not liftable} \tag{6}$$

In Eq. 5, LVE would eliminate $R(X,Y,Z)$, count-convert $S(Y)$ (or $T(Z)$; no PRV contains all logical variables but there is a logical variable occurring only once that can be counted if it is count-normalised w.r.t. the other logical variables), eliminate $T(Z)$ ($S(Y)$), and then eliminate the count-converted $S(Y)$ ($T(Z)$) (see [23] for details on counting). In Eq. 6, no LVE operator apart from grounding is applicable as no PRV contains all logical variables of the parfactor and no PRV is count-convertible (no logical variable occurs only once). Equation 6 encodes transitivity. For FOKC, a lifted approach exists to solve models that exhibit transitivity [19].

3.3 Lifted Evidence

Normally, evidence is considered a distinguishing factor. In the discrete setting however, since there is only a finite number of values a PRV can take, there again is indistinguishability between individuals sharing the same evidence.

Assume for the example in Fig. 1 with n constants for X that we observe $Sick(x_1) = \cdots = Sick(x_{10}) = true$, $Sick(x_{11}) = \cdots = Sick(x_{20}) = false$, and no value for the rest, yielding three disjoint sets of constants, which we could represent using logical variables X^T, X^F, and X' for example:

$Sick(X^T)$	g_e^T
$false$	0
$true$	1

$Sick(X^F)$	g_e^F
$false$	1
$true$	0

The model is then shattered on the evidence, leading to copies of the parfactors containing the original X, i.e., g_1 and g_2, for the three sets of constants.

Those copies for X^T absorb g_e^T and those for X^F absorb g_e^F in a lifted way [39]. Absorption means selecting the input-output mappings that match the observation and projecting the result onto the parfactor arguments minus the evidence PRV, here $Sick(X)$, which is actually equivalent to multiplying with g_e and then dropping the lines with zeroes and the evidence PRV (dimension reduction).

Van den Broeck and Davis [44] have shown that evidence is liftable if observations are for propositional random variables or PRVs with one logical variable. The problem of having evidence for PRVs with two logical variables is no longer liftable in general. The proof uses reduction, reducing a #2SAT problem to conditioning on evidence and model counting. Nonetheless, not all evidence on PRVs with two logical variables leads to groundings and groups of indistinguishable constants might still be identifiable, allowing for lifted calculations for those groups. There is further work on using lifting in asymmetrical models or for binary evidence [43, 46].

3.4 Lifted Queries

Having looked at indistinguishability in models and evidence, the next step is to consider queries. So far, we have only considered queries for single grounded query terms Q. With marginal queries over sets of grounded query terms $\boldsymbol{Q}$, there also arises the potential for indistinguishability in queries, namely, when grounded query terms come from the same PRV, e.g., $P(Sick(alice), Sick(eve), Sick(bob))$. One might even be interested over distributions over all possible groundings, e.g., $P(gr(Sick(X)))$.

When shattering a model on query terms from the same PRV, logical variables get grounded for those constants in the query. Subsequent calculations might then again be identical. Consider the model in Fig. 1 after shattering on the above query, which leads to copies of g_1 for $alice$, eve, bob, and the rest, in which each $Travel$ variable is eliminated in the same way. On-demand shattering may help such that the model is shattered later. However, not all identical calculations may be eliminated using on-demand shattering. In addition, if the queried groundings are truly indistinguishable, i.e., not made distinguishable through inner workings fo the model or evidence, the result shows a symmetry itself. The following illustrates the point with potentials $1, 2, 3, 4$ on the left:

$Sick(alice)$	$Sick(eve)$	$Sick(bob)$	g'		$\#_X Sick(X)$	g'
$false$	$false$	$false$	1		$[0,3]$	1
$false$	$false$	$true$	2		$[1,2]$	2
$false$	$true$	$false$	2		$[2,1]$	3
$false$	$true$	$true$	3		$[3,0]$	4
$true$	$false$	$false$	2			
$true$	$false$	$true$	3			
$true$	$true$	$false$	3			
$true$	$true$	$true$	4			

The lines with two times *false* and one time *true* map to one number, here 2, and the lines with one time *false* and two times *true* map to another number, here 3. The whole distribution can be represented by four lines, using counting random variables (CRVs) with histograms as range (see [23] for details on CRVs), as shown above on the right.

To efficiently handle queries with indistinguishable query terms, yielding a compact encoding, logical variables are introduced into queries. The standard LVE procedure changes in the way that at the end, if there are logical variables remaining in the result, the logical variables are counted to get the compact encoding from the above illustration. In terms of complexity, as lifted queries can be solved using existing lifted operators, the complexity of query answering does not change. In terms of completeness, only queries with at most one logical variable are liftable as otherwise, groundings might be unavoidable, e.g., $P(R(X,Y))$ in Eq. 4. As a corollary, one can note that a liftable query can always be encoded compactly using CRVs [2].

After looking at indistinguishability in episodic models, the question becomes what happens once we introduce another dimension, namely, time into the mix. The next section offers a peek into what happens with indistinguishability when dealing with sequences of model states and evidence.

4 Keeping Indistinguishability in Sequential PRMs

A common extension of PGMs comes in the form of time, using an episodic model, indexed by t, as a template over discrete (time) steps. In many cases, this sequential dimension is referred to as time but it can just mean a sequence of, e.g., words, signals, or nucleotides. A standard specification of a sequential model contains an episodic model for $t = 0$ and a so-called two-time slice model for $t-1$ and t, with an episodic model for t and transition distributions from $t-1$ to t. Given a relational context, the episodic template model is a parfactor model or MLN [1,11]. Figure 2 shows a small example sequential parfactor model.

The semantics of a sequential PGM is given by unrolling for T steps (copying the template T times, connected accordingly), leading to one large episodic model with semantics of Definition 1, 2. With evidence $e^{(0:t)}$ and query terms $Q^{(\pi)}$, typical query types are *filtering* for $\pi = t$, *prediction* for $\pi > t$, and *hindsight* for $\pi < t$. Exact inference algorithms follow the idea of the interface algorithm [25], which calculates a set of random variables or PRVs I that make individual

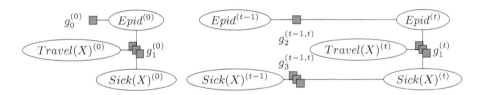

Fig. 2. Graphical representation of a sequential parfactor model

steps independent from each other, e.g., those PRVs from a two-time slice model with index $t - 1$. The independence allows for calculating a message from the present to the future over I to ensure all information is available at the next step. A relational model enables reducing the interface size in a liftable model from $|gr(I)|$ to $|I|$, on which the complexity depends exponentially [10].

Given a sequential *relational* model, a significant problem comes with seeing evidence over time, which can ground a model even with liftable evidence each time step [12]. Consider observing $Sick = true$ for $x_1, \ldots, x_{10}$ at $t = 0$, observing $Sick = true$ for $x_1, \ldots, x_{12}$ at $t = 1$, and $Sick = true$ for $x_3, \ldots, x_{14}$ at $t = 2$. Shattering the model at $t = 0$ leads to two groups for X, then another group forms for x_{11}, x_{12} at $t = 1$ as those two had different observations at $t = 0$ than the other x. In $t = 2$, two more groups form, one for x_{13}, x_{14} and one for x_1, x_2, bringing it to a total of five groups. Over time, logical variables become grounded as the interface carries over the splits from one step to the next.

To *keep reasoning polynomial*, i.e., to not revert to grounded inference, we use the fact that each step, the model behaviour is added, overwriting evidence with expected behaviour over time. Determining similar groups using clustering with cosine similarity enables merging similar parfactors over small domains into parfactors over larger domains. Due to the model behaviour of the template model added each step, one can show that approximating inference in this way exhibits an indefinitely bounded error [12]. That is an error bounded over all time steps with the largest deviation at the point of the approximation and declining afterwards, which applies to all approximations done over time in the presence of the other approximations. Without evidence, the model would even move back towards the template behaviour, eventually yielding an error of 0 again.

Yet another dimension to introduce into PGMs comes in the form of actions and utilities, i.e., decision making capabilities, which the next section highlights.

5   Decision Making and Indistinguishability

Decision theory as the basis to decision making in PGMs can be considered a combination of utility and probability theory [34]. The central principle is that of maximum expected utility (MEU), where a rational agent should decide on an action that is expected to maximise its utility or reward, which encodes preferences over outcomes or outcome states as values of random variables V after performing an action. There can also be further random variables R in a model to describe other aspects of the environment influencing V.

In PGMs, these ideas are incorporated by introducing decision nodes D, whose ranges are possible actions [16], and a utility node U, which gets the overall utility assigned. The utility can be the result of a utility function $\phi_U(V)$ that maps argument values of V to utilities. In case of (the simplifying assumption of) preference independence between the random variables in V, the utility function can be decomposed into a set of one-dimensional utility functions $\phi_u(V_u)$ that are combined using summation, i.e.,

$$\phi_U(\boldsymbol{V}) = \sum_{V_u \in \boldsymbol{V}} \phi_u(V_u). \tag{7}$$

Formally, an MEU problem for some model G and evidence $\boldsymbol{e}$ is given by:

$$meu[G \mid \boldsymbol{e}] = (\boldsymbol{d}^*, eu(\boldsymbol{e}, \boldsymbol{d}^*)), \boldsymbol{d}^* = \arg\max_{\boldsymbol{d}} eu(\boldsymbol{e}, \boldsymbol{s}).$$

where eu refers to the expected utility of decisions $\boldsymbol{d} \in \boldsymbol{D}$ in G, i.e.,

$$eu(\boldsymbol{e}, \boldsymbol{d}) = \sum_{\boldsymbol{v} \in ran(\boldsymbol{V})} P(\boldsymbol{v} \mid \boldsymbol{e}, \boldsymbol{d}) \cdot \phi_U(\boldsymbol{v}) \tag{8}$$

Under preference independence, ϕ_U can be replaced by Eq. 7 but note that preference independence does not imply stochastic independence. So, simplifying $P(\boldsymbol{v} \mid \boldsymbol{e}, \boldsymbol{d})$ into a product of $P(v_u \mid \boldsymbol{e}, \boldsymbol{d})$ that can be moved into the sum of Eq. 7 is only correct if stochastic independence holds as well between the random variables in $\boldsymbol{V}$, which might not hold in presense of $\boldsymbol{R}$. Independent of these considerations, solving an MEU problem depends on $|\boldsymbol{D}|$ exponentially.

Approaches to decision making, which includes solving an MEU problem, can be divided into online and offline approaches. Online approaches look a certain number of steps (horizon) into the future to determine the best course of action, which allows for reacting to extreme evidence and unlikely states. Offline approaches work towards finding a steady state solution in form of a policy, which requires close to no computation time online as acting boils down to looking up an action in the policy. However, a policy is fixed and cannot easily be manipulated to changed circumstances or extreme situations.

In terms of relational models and online decision making, there exist decision-theoretic versions of parfactor models [13] as well as MLNs [26], both extended with decision PRVs and utility nodes. Figure 3 shows a decision-theoretic parfactor model (decision PRV: rectangle, utility node: diamond), which is a variant of Fig. 1 where $Treat$ is turned into a decision on treatments and $Epid$ and $Sick(X)$ determine the utility U. An extension to the LJT algorithm solves MEU problems in such parfactor models [13] in a lifted way. For MLNs, a partially lifted algorithm exists [27]. The upside of having decision PRVs is that one can solve parts of an MEU problem instance by looking at representatives, in addition to having a relational description of the environment and outcome states through PRVs. In terms of offline decision making, the standard problem formalisation of a (partially observable) Markov decision problem ((PO)MPD) has been lifted to

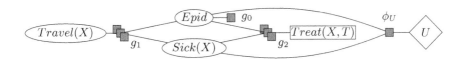

Fig. 3. Graphical representation of a decision-theoretic parfactor model

include relational descriptions of the state space in which the agent acts, forming first-order (PO)MDPs (FO (PO) MDPs) [17,36].

Another dimension that has become the focus of analysis for its lifting potential are multi-agent systems. Decentralised POMDPs [30] contain s set of agents. Assuming (a small number of) types of agents, it is reasonable to further assume that the set of agents can be partitioned into subsets, in which the agents have the same set of actions and observations available and the same behaviour encoded in the transition and sensor model as well as reward function that make up a DecPOMDP. Adding independence assumptions between the agents of a partition, a reduction from exponential to logarithmic dependence on the number of agents is possible in exchange for an exponential dependence on the number of agent types, which is assumed to be much smaller [3].

A Note on Domains. The models and approaches presented here rely on a closed-world assumption where the domains of logical variables are known, hence allowing for grounding semantics to apply. The existing domains also imply that the potentials in the model make sense w.r.t. the domain sizes. However, one might want to look at models under increasing domain sizes. When keeping a model as is and increasing domain sizes, one can investigate whether implicit modelling assumptions hold like more people in a domain requires more people to be sick for an epidemic to happen. Yet, when letting domain sizes increase too much, extreme behaviour occurs where query answers tend towards a distribution of $\langle 0, 1 \rangle$ [32]. To avoid such extreme behaviour, domain-size aware MLNs scale the weights in an MLN according to relative changes in domain sizes [24].

An investigation of what happens to a lifted model with unknown domains leads to an approach that again works with grounding semantics by discussing how a meta-program can set up different plausible sets of domains [6]. Another approach extends domains based on incoming evidence [22]. Unknown domains blur the line towards models under open-world assumption where a domain might be initially known but it is unknown whether other constants exist, which for example is investigated for FO POMDPs [38].

6   Conclusion

StaRAI as a field comprises research that combines reasoning under uncertainty and reasoning with individuals and relations. With individuals and relations in a model, groups of individuals emerge that behave indistinguishably. This indistinguishability is a powerful tool for probabilistic inference in standard PGMs as well as sequential and decision-theoretic models. It allows for handling groups of indistinguishable individuals through representatives, enabling efficiency gains up to tractable inference w.r.t. domain sizes under certain conditions.

Even though StaRAI and lifted probabilistic inference has come a long way since its first appearance in the scientific world, there is still so much to explore. Next to further improvements of existing algorithms and optimisations for inference tasks, there are other dimensions coming into play: Causality moves beyond correlation, investigating cause-effect relations where relational domains pose interesting challenges [20]. Explainability takes into account that an agent should exhibit explainable behaviour to the humans interacting with it [18]. In a more general setting, human-aware AI not only includes explainability but may also cover aspects such as transparency, accountability, ethics, or privacy.

Note: Any material used during the tutorial is available at https://www.uni-muenster.de/Informatik.AGBraun/en/research/tutorials/sum-2022.html.

Acknowledgements. The author wishes to thank the SUM 2022 organisers for the invitation to give a tutorial on StaRAI and for the opportunity to write this article. The author also wishes to thank Marcel Gehrke and Ralf Möller for their continued collaboration and, with regards to this article, for collaborating on a tutorial at ECAI 2020, out of which this article grew.

References

1. Ahmadi, B., Kersting, K., Mladenov, M., Natarajan, S.: Exploiting symmetries for scaling loopy belief propagation and relational training. Mach. Learn. **92**(1), 91–132 (2013)
2. Braun, T.: Rescued from a sea of queries: exact inference in probabilistic relational models. Ph.D. thesis, University of Lübeck (2020)
3. Braun, T., Gehrke, M., Lau, F., Möller, R.: Lifting in multi-agent systems under uncertainty. In: UAI-22 Proceedings of the 38th Conference on Uncertainty in Artificial Intelligence, pp. 1–8. AUAI Press (2022)
4. Braun, T., Möller, R.: Preventing groundings and handling evidence in the lifted junction tree algorithm. In: Kern-Isberner, G., Fürnkranz, J., Thimm, M. (eds.) KI 2017. LNCS (LNAI), vol. 10505, pp. 85–98. Springer, Cham (2017). https://doi.org/10.1007/978-3-319-67190-1_7
5. Braun, T., Möller, R.: Counting and conjunctive queries in the lifted junction tree algorithm. In: Croitoru, M., Marquis, P., Rudolph, S., Stapleton, G. (eds.) GKR 2017. LNCS (LNAI), vol. 10775, pp. 54–72. Springer, Cham (2018). https://doi.org/10.1007/978-3-319-78102-0_3
6. Braun, T., Möller, R.: Exploring unknown universes in probabilistic relational models. In: Liu, J., Bailey, J. (eds.) AI 2019. LNCS (LNAI), vol. 11919, pp. 91–103. Springer, Cham (2019). https://doi.org/10.1007/978-3-030-35288-2_8
7. De Raedt, L., Kersting, K., Natarajan, S., Poole, D.: Statistical Relational Artificial Intelligence: Logic, Probability, and Computation. Morgan & Claypool, San Rafael (2016)
8. De Raedt, L., Kimmig, A., Toivonen, H.: ProbLog: A probabilistic prolog and its application in link discovery. In: IJCAI-07 Proceedings of 20th International Joint Conference on Artificial Intelligence, pp. 2062–2467. IJCAI Organization (2007)
9. Fuhr, N.: Probabilistic datalog - a logic for powerful retrieval methods. In: SIGIR-95 Proceedings of the 18th Annual International ACM SIGIR Conference on Research and Development in Information Retrieval, pp. 282–290. ACM (1995)
10. Gehrke, M.: Taming exact inference in temporal probabilistic relational models. Ph.D. thesis, University of Lübeck (2021)
11. Gehrke, M., Braun, T., Möller, R.: Lifted dynamic junction tree algorithm. In: Chapman, P., Endres, D., Pernelle, N. (eds.) ICCS 2018. LNCS (LNAI), vol. 10872, pp. 55–69. Springer, Cham (2018). https://doi.org/10.1007/978-3-319-91379-7_5

12. Gehrke, M., Braun, T., Möller, R.: Taming reasoning in temporal probabilistic relational models. In: ECAI-20 Proceedings of the 24th European Conference on Artificial Intelligence (2020)
13. Gehrke, M., Braun, T., Möller, R., Waschkau, A., Strumann, C., Steinhäuser, J.: Lifted maximum expected utility. In: Koch, F., et al. (eds.) AIH 2018. LNCS (LNAI), vol. 11326, pp. 131–141. Springer, Cham (2019). https://doi.org/10.1007/978-3-030-12738-1_10
14. Gogate, V., Domingos, P.: Probabilistic theorem proving. In: UAI-11 Proceedings of the 27th Conference on Uncertainty in Artificial Intelligence, pp. 256–265. AUAI Press (2011)
15. Gogate, V., Jha, A., Venugopal, D.: Advances in lifted importance sampling. In: AAAI-12 Proceedings of the 26th AAAI Conference on Artificial Intelligence, pp. 1910–1916. AAAI Press (2012)
16. Howard, R.A., Matheson, J.E.: Influence diagrams. In: Readings on the Principles and Applications of Decision Analysis, pp. 721–762. Strategic Decision Group (1984)
17. Joshi, S., Kersting, K., Khardon, R.: Generalized First Order Decision Diagrams for First Order Markov Decision Processes. In: IJCAI-09 Proceedings of the 21st International Joint Conference on Artificial Intelligence, pp. 1916–1921. Morgan Kaufmann Publishers Inc. (2009)
18. Kambhampati, S.: Synethesizing explainable behavior for human-AI collaboration. In: AAMAS-19 Proceedings of the 18th International Conference on Autonomous Agents and Multiagent Systems, pp. 1–2. IFAAMAS (2019). Keynote talk
19. Kazemi, S.M., Kimmig, A., Van den Broeck, G., Poole, D.: New liftable classes for first-order probabilistic inference. In: NIPS-16 Advances in Neural Information Processing Systems 29, pp. 1–9 (2016)
20. Lee, S., Honavar, V.: On learning causal models from relational data. In: AAAI-16 Proceedings of the 30th AAAI Conference on Artificial Intelligence, pp. 3263–3270. AAAI Press (2016)
21. Marwitz, F., Braun, T., Möller, R.: A first step towards even more sparse encodings of probability distributions. In: ILP-21 Proceedings of the 30th International Conference on Inductive Logic Programming (2021)
22. Milch, B.: Probabilistic models with unknown objects. Ph.D. thesis, University of California, Berkeley (2006)
23. Milch, B., Zettelmoyer, L.S., Kersting, K., Haimes, M., Kaelbling, L.P.: Lifted probabilistic inference with counting formulas. In: AAAI-08 Proceedings of the 23rd AAAI Conference on Artificial Intelligence, pp. 1062–1068. AAAI Press (2008)
24. Mittal, H., Bhardwaj, A., Gogate, V., Singla, P.: Domain-size aware Markov logic networks. In: AISTATS-19 Proceedings of the 22nd International Conference on Artificial Intelligence and Statistics, pp. 3216–3224. PMLR (2019)
25. Murphy, K.P.: Dynamic Bayesian networks: representation, inference and learning. Ph.D. thesis, University of California, Berkeley (2002)
26. Nath, A., Domingos, P.: A language for relational decision theory. In: Proceedings of the 6th International Workshop on Statistical Relational Learning (2009)
27. Nath, A., Domingos, P.: Efficient lifting for online probabilistic inference. In: AAAI-10 Proceedings of the 24th AAAI Conference on Artificial Intelligence, pp. 64–69. AAAI Press (2010)
28. Niepert, M.: Markov chains on orbits of permutation groups. In: UAI-12 Proceedings of the 28th Conference on Uncertainty in Artificial Intelligence, pp. 624–633. AUAI Press (2012)

29. Niepert, M., Van den Broeck, G.: Tractability through exchangeability: A new perspective on efficient probabilistic inference. In: AAAI-14 Proceedings of the 28th AAAI Conference on Artificial Intelligence, pp. 2467–2475. AAAI Press (2014)
30. Oliehoek, F.A., Amato, C.: A Concise Introduction to Decentralised POMDPs. Springer, Cham (2016). https://doi.org/10.1007/978-3-319-28929-8
31. Poole, D.: First-order probabilistic inference. In: IJCAI-03 Proceedings of the 18th International Joint Conference on Artificial Intelligence, pp. 985–991. IJCAI Organization (2003)
32. Poole, D., Buchman, D., Kazemi, S.M., Kersting, K., Natarajan, S.: Population size extrapolation in relational probabilistic modelling. In: Straccia, U., Calì, A. (eds.) SUM 2014. LNCS (LNAI), vol. 8720, pp. 292–305. Springer, Cham (2014). https://doi.org/10.1007/978-3-319-11508-5_25
33. Richardson, M., Domingos, P.: Markov logic networks. Mach. Learn. **62**(1–2), 107–136 (2006)
34. Russell, S., Norvig, P.: Artificial Intelligence: A Modern Approach. Pearson, London (2020)
35. de Salvo Braz, R., Amir, E., Roth, D.: Lifted first-order probabilistic inference. In: IJCAI-05 Proceedings of the 19th International Joint Conference on Artificial Intelligence, pp. 1319–1325. IJCAI Organization (2005)
36. Sanner, S., Kersting, K.: Symbolic dynamic programming for first-order POMDPs. In: AAAI-10 Proceedings of the 24th AAAI Conference on Artificial Intelligence, pp. 1140–1146. AAAI Press (2010)
37. Sato, T.: A statistical learning method for logic programs with distribution semantics. In: Proceedings of the 12th International Conference on Logic Programming, pp. 715–729. MIT Press (1995)
38. Srivastava, S., Russell, S., Ruan, P., Cheng, X.: First-order open-universe POMDPs. In: UAI-14 Proceedings of the 30th Conference on Uncertainty in Artificial Intelligence, pp. 742–751. AUAI Press (2014)
39. Taghipour, N., Fierens, D., Davis, J., Blockeel, H.: Lifted variable elimination: decoupling the operators from the constraint language. J. Artif. Intell. Res. **47**(1), 393–439 (2013)
40. Taghipour, N., Fierens, D., Van den Broeck, G., Davis, J., Blockeel, H.: Completeness results for lifted variable elimination. In: AISTATS-13 Proceedings of the 16th International Conference on Artificial Intelligence and Statistics, pp. 572–580. AAAI Press (2013)
41. Van den Broeck, G.: On the completeness of first-order knowledge compilation for lifted probabilistic inference. In: NIPS-11 Advances in Neural Information Processing Systems 24, pp. 1386–1394. Curran Associates, Inc. (2011)
42. Van den Broeck, G.: Lifted inference and learning in statistical relational models. Ph.D. thesis, KU Leuven (2013)
43. Van den Broeck, G., Darwiche, A.: On the complexity and approximation of binary evidence in lifted inference. In: NIPS-13 Advances in Neural Information Processing Systems 26, pp. 2868–2876. Curran Associates, Inc. (2013)
44. Van den Broeck, G., Davis, J.: Conditioning in first-order knowledge compilation and lifted probabilistic inference. In: AAAI-12 Proceedings of the 26th AAAI Conference on Artificial Intelligence, pp. 1961–1967. AAAI Press (2012)
45. Van den Broeck, G., Kersting, K., Natarajan, S., Poole, D.: An Introduction to Lifted Probabilistic Inference. MIT Press, Cambridge (2021)
46. Van den Broeck, G., Niepert, M.: Lifted probabilistic inference for asymmetric graphical models. In: AAAI-15 Proceedings of the 29th AAAI Conference on Artificial Intelligence, pp. 3599–3605. AAAI Press (2015)

47. Van den Broeck, G., Taghipour, N., Meert, W., Davis, J., De Raedt, L.: Lifted probabilistic inference by first-order knowledge compilation. In: IJCAI-11 Proceedings of the 22nd International Joint Conference on Artificial Intelligence, pp. 2178–2185. IJCAI Organization (2011)
48. Van den Broeck, G., Thon, I., van Otterlo, M., Raedt, L.D.: DTProbLog: a decision-theoretic probabilistic prolog. In: AAAI-10 Proceedings of the 24th AAAI Conference on Artificial Intelligence, pp. 1217–1222. AAAI Press (2010)
49. Wang, Y., van Bremen, T., Wang, Y., Kuželka, O.: Domain-lifted sampling for universal two-variable logic and extensions. In: AAAI-22 Proceedings of the 36th AAAI Conference on Artificial Intelligence, pp. 10070–10079. AAAI Press (2022)

On Incompleteness in Abstract Argumentation: Complexity and Expressiveness

Jean-Guy Mailly[(✉)] [iD]

Université Paris Cité, LIPADE, 75006 Paris, France
`jean-guy.mailly@u-paris.fr`

Abstract. One of the recent trends in research about abstract argumentation is the study of how incomplete knowledge can be integrated to argumentation frameworks (AFs). In this paper, we survey main results on Incomplete AFs (IAFs), following two directions: how hard is it to reason with IAFs? And what can be expressed with IAFs? We show that two generalizations of IAFs, namely Rich IAFs and Constrained IAFs, despite having a higher expressive power than IAFs, have the same complexity regarding classical reasoning tasks.

Keywords: Abstract argumentation · Uncertainty · Incomplete knowledge · Computational complexity

1 Introduction

Abstract argumentation [18] has been a prominent formalism in the domain of Knowledge Representation and Reasoning, allowing an elegant representation of conflicting information. Classically, an argumentation framework (AF) is a directed graph where the nodes are *arguments* and the edges are *attacks* between these arguments. Reasoning is then based on the selection of sets of arguments that can be collectively accepted, named *extensions*. Since the seminal paper by Dung, various generalizations of the original framework have been proposed (using weights on attacks [20] or arguments [34], preferences [1], collective attacks [32], . . .) as well as new reasoning methods [8].

We focus on one such generalization of Dung's framework, namely Incomplete Argumentation Frameworks (IAFs) [3,6,26], where both arguments and attacks can have two different natures: either they are *certain* or they are *uncertain*. While there exists models where this uncertainty is quantified (mainly, with probabilities of existence attached to the elements [25]), in IAFs the uncertainty is purely qualitative: uncertain elements are maybe actually there, maybe not, but the agent reasoning with such an IAF does no have more information about the uncertain elements. This kind of uncertainty in abstract argumentation can be intuitively justified in various ways. An argument or attack can be uncertain, for instance, in multi-agent contexts where one agent tries to model the knowledge of other agents. Then, it is a reasonable assumption that an agent does

F. Dupin de Saint-Cyr et al. (Eds.): SUM 2022, LNAI 13562, pp. 19–33, 2022.
https://doi.org/10.1007/978-3-031-18843-5_2

not perfectly know the internal state of other agents. This means that an argument can be uncertain in situations where the agent is not sure whether other agents know this argument (or whether they will choose to use it). Similarly, an agent usually does not perfectly know the preferences of other agents. So, if an agents knows that there is a conflict between two arguments a and b, but she does not know whether her opponent prefers a to b, or b to a, then she does not know whether there is actually an attack between these arguments in her opponent's internal knowledge (in the spirit of Preference-based AFs, where attacks are somehow "cancelled" when they are contradicted by preferences [1]). This has motivated the use of IAFs (or more precisely, Control AFs [15,28], a generalization of IAFs) for defining automated negotiation protocols where agents have partial knowledge about their opponent [16,17].

In this paper, we present the main results in the literature about the complexity of reasoning with IAFs. We describe two families of approaches for defining the acceptable arguments with respect to an IAF. The first one is based on the notion of *completion* (*i.e.* standard AFs that represent, roughly speaking, the possible worlds compatible with the uncertain information encoded in the IAF), and the second one is based on adaptation to IAFs of the basic principles underlying classical AF semantics, namely conflict-freeness and defense. We show how hard it is to reason with IAFs, compared to the classical reasoning approach for standard AFs. Then, we focus on the expressivity of IAFs. More precisely, we answer the question "Can any set of AFs correspond to the set of completions of an IAF?". We show that it is not the case. A partial solution to increase the expressivity of the formalism is to add another kind of uncertainty in the model: uncertainty about the direction of attacks. This model is called Rich IAF [27]. However, even this solution does not allow to represent any set of completions. Then, we propose the Constrained IAFs [29], where an IAF is attached with a propositional formula describing the "valid" completions, *i.e.* any completion not complying with the formula is not used for defining reasoning methods. We show that this model allows to represent any set of completions, and in turn this is a powerful tool for solving representation problems about extensions, in the context of belief revision or belief merging applied to abstract argumentation [11,14]. Finally, we describe some challenges about the CIAF model, regarding the construction of an optimal CIAF for representing a given set of completions (or extensions), where optimality can concern either the graph part of the CIAF, or the syntax of the propositional constraint.

2 Background: Abstract Argumentation Frameworks

Roughly speaking, abstract argumentation [18] is the study of how one can conclude a reasonable point of view about conflicting pieces of information. Usually, an *abstract argumentation framework* is simply a directed graph where the nodes represent the pieces of information and the edges represent the conflicts between them. The exact nature of these pieces of information is ignored. We follow this approach in this paper, and we assume the existence of a finite set **A** of atomic entities called arguments. An argumentation framework is then a directed graph whose nodes are a subset of **A**.

Definition 1 (Argumentation Framework [18]). *An argumentation framework (AF) is a pair* $\mathcal{F} = \langle \mathcal{A}, \mathcal{R} \rangle$ *with* $\mathcal{A} \subseteq \mathbf{A}$ *the set of arguments and* $\mathcal{R} \subseteq \mathcal{A} \times \mathcal{A}$ *the set of attacks.*

For $a, b \in \mathcal{A}$, we say that a *attacks* b if $(a, b) \in \mathcal{R}$. If b attacks some $c \in \mathcal{A}$, then a *defends* c against b. Similarly, a set $S \subseteq \mathcal{A}$ attacks an argument b if there is some $a \in S$ that attacks b. Finally, S defends some $b \in \mathcal{A}$ if S attacks all the attackers of b.

Example 1. In the AF $\mathcal{F} = \langle \mathcal{A}, \mathcal{R} \rangle$, with $\mathcal{A} = \{a, b, c, d, e, f, g\}$ and $\mathcal{R} = \{(a, b), (b, c), (c, d), (d, c), (d, e), (e, f), (f, g), (g, e)\}$ (see Fig. 1), c is attacked by b and d, and it is defended by $\{a, c\}$ (because $\{a, c\}$ attacks b and d, more precisely a attacks b and c attacks d).

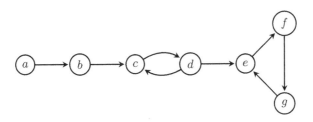

Fig. 1. An example of AF $\mathcal{F}$

In the seminal paper on abstract argumentation [18], Dung proposes a family of methods to reason with an AF, based on the notion of *extension*. An extension is a set of arguments that can be jointly accepted. The methods for determining the extensions are called *semantics*, and they are usually based on two principles: conflict-freeness and admissibility.

Definition 2 (Conflict-freeness and Admissibility). *Given* $\mathcal{F} = \langle \mathcal{A}, \mathcal{R} \rangle$ *an AF, the set* $S \subseteq \mathcal{A}$ *is*

- conflict-free *iff* $\forall a, b \in S$, $(a, b) \notin \mathcal{R}$;
- admissible *iff it is conflict-free and* $\forall a \in S$, $\forall b \in \mathcal{A}$ *s.t.* $(b, a) \in \mathcal{R}$, $\exists c \in S$ *s.t.* $(c, b) \in \mathcal{R}$.

Intuitively, a set of arguments is admissible if it is a point of view on the AF which is internally coherent and can defend itself against all the attacks it receives. We use $\mathsf{cf}(\mathcal{F})$ (respectively $\mathsf{ad}(\mathcal{F})$) to denote the set of conflict-free (respectively admissible) sets of an AF $\mathcal{F}$. These basic principles are used to define admissibility-based semantics as follows:

Definition 3 (Admissibility-based Semantics). *Given* $\mathcal{F} = \langle \mathcal{A}, \mathcal{R} \rangle$ *an AF, the admissible set* $S \subseteq \mathcal{A}$ *is*

- a complete *extension iff S contains all the arguments that it defends;*
- a preferred *extension iff S is a $\subseteq$-maximal admissible set;*
- a grounded *extension iff S is a $\subseteq$-minimal complete extension.*

A fourth semantics is defined by Dung, that does not directly rely on the notion of admissibility:

Definition 4 (Stable Semantics). *Given $\mathcal{F} = \langle \mathcal{A}, \mathcal{R} \rangle$ an AF, the conflict-free set $S \subseteq \mathcal{A}$ is a stable extension iff $\forall a \in \mathcal{A} \setminus S$, S attacks a.*

We use $\mathsf{co}(\mathcal{F})$, $\mathsf{pr}(\mathcal{F})$, $\mathsf{gr}(\mathcal{F})$ and $\mathsf{st}(\mathcal{F})$ for the sets of (respectively) complete, preferred, grounded and stable extensions. Notice that, for any $\mathcal{F}$, $\mathsf{st}(\mathcal{F}) \subseteq \mathsf{pr}(\mathcal{F}) \subseteq \mathsf{co}(\mathcal{F})$, $\mathsf{pr}(\mathcal{F}) \neq \emptyset$, and $|\mathsf{gr}(\mathcal{F})| = 1$.

Example 2. The extensions of $\mathcal{F}$ from Example 1 are provided in the second column of Table 1.

For further details about these semantics, as well as other semantics that have been defined subsequently, we refer the reader to [2,18].

From the set of extensions of an AF, we can determine the acceptability status of an argument. Two classical reasoning modes have been defined, namely $\mathsf{Cred}_\sigma(\mathcal{F}) = \bigcup \sigma(\mathcal{F})$ (respectively $\mathsf{Skep}_\sigma(\mathcal{F}) = \bigcap \sigma(\mathcal{F})$) which denotes the set of credulously (respectively skeptically) accepted arguments of $\mathcal{F}$.

Example 3. The credulously and skeptically accepted arguments in $\mathcal{F}$ from Example 1 are given in Table 1 (third and fourth columns).

Table 1. Extensions and acceptable arguments of $\mathcal{F}$, for $\sigma \in \{\mathsf{gr}, \mathsf{st}, \mathsf{co}, \mathsf{pr}\}$.

Semantics σ	$\sigma(\mathcal{F})$	$\mathsf{Cred}_\sigma(\mathcal{F})$	$\mathsf{Skep}_\sigma(\mathcal{F})$
gr	$\{\{a\}\}$	$\{a\}$	$\{a\}$
st	$\{\{a,d,f\}\}$	$\{a,d,f\}$	$\{a,d,f\}$
co	$\{\{a,d,f\},\{a,c\},\{a\}\}$	$\{a,c,d,f\}$	$\{a\}$
pr	$\{\{a,d,f\},\{a,c\}\}$	$\{a,c,d,f\}$	$\{a\}$

The corresponding decision problems are defined by:

σ-CA Given $\mathcal{F} = \langle \mathcal{A}, \mathcal{R} \rangle$ and $a \in \mathcal{A}$, does a belong to some σ-extension of $\mathcal{F}$?
σ-SA Given $\mathcal{F} = \langle \mathcal{A}, \mathcal{R} \rangle$ and $a \in \mathcal{A}$, does a belong to each σ-extension of $\mathcal{F}$

3   Incomplete Argumentation Frameworks

This section introduces formal definitions related to Incomplete AFs, as well a complexity results and short description of SAT-based computational approaches for the main reasoning problems.

3.1   Formal Definitions

Definition 5 (Incomplete Argumentation Framework). *An incomplete argumentation framework (IAF) is a tuple* $\mathcal{I} = \langle \mathcal{A}, \mathcal{A}^?, \mathcal{R}, \mathcal{R}^? \rangle$ *with* $\mathcal{A}, \mathcal{A}^? \subseteq \mathbf{A}$ *disjoint sets of* arguments *and* $\mathcal{R}, \mathcal{R}^? \subseteq \mathcal{A} \times \mathcal{A}$ *disjoint sets of* attacks.

The partition of arguments and attacks in two sets correspond to the two possible natures of elements in an incomplete AF: $\mathcal{A}$ and $\mathcal{R}$ correspond to arguments and attacks for which it is sure that they exist. On the contrary, $\mathcal{A}^?$ and $\mathcal{R}^?$ are uncertain arguments and attacks.

Example 4. In $\mathcal{I}$ from Fig. 2, $\mathcal{A} = \{a, b\}$ is the set of certain arguments, and $\mathcal{A}^? = \{c\}$ is the set of uncertain arguments. Plain arrows represent the certain attacks, *i.e.* $\mathcal{R} = \{(c, b)\}$, and dotted arrows represent the uncertain attacks, *i.e.* $\mathcal{R}^? = \{(b, a)\}$.

Fig. 2. An example of IAF $\mathcal{I}$

Classical reasoning methods for IAFs are based on the notion of *completion*, which are standard AFs that somehow correspond to a possible way to solve the uncertainty encoded in the IAF.

Definition 6 (Completion). *Given an IAF* $\mathcal{I} = \langle \mathcal{A}, \mathcal{A}^?, \mathcal{R}, \mathcal{R}^? \rangle$, *a completion is an AF* $\mathcal{F}^* = \langle \mathcal{A}^*, \mathcal{R}^* \rangle$ *such that* $\mathcal{A} \subseteq \mathcal{A}^* \subseteq \mathcal{A} \cup \mathcal{A}^?$ *and* $\mathcal{R}_{|\mathcal{A}^*} \subseteq \mathcal{R}^* \subseteq (\mathcal{R} \cup \mathcal{R}^?)_{|\mathcal{A}^*}$.[1]

Example 5. Continuing the previous example, we see that $\mathcal{I}$ has four completions (Fig. 3). In $\mathcal{F}_1^*$, none of the uncertain element is included, while on the contrary $\mathcal{F}_4^*$ includes all the uncertain elements. In the middle, $\mathcal{F}_2^*$ and $\mathcal{F}_3^*$ include either the argument c, or the attack (b, a).

3.2   Reasoning with IAFs

Completion-Based Reasoning. The main approach for reasoning with IAFs consists in verifying whether some property of interest (*e.g.* the credulous or skeptical acceptability of a given argument, or the fact that a given set of arguments is an extension) is true in some completion (*possible reasoning*) or in each completion (*necessary reasoning*). This means that each decision problem studied

---

[1] For R a set of attacks and A a set of arguments, we define the projection of R on A by $R_{|A} = R \cap (A \times A)$.

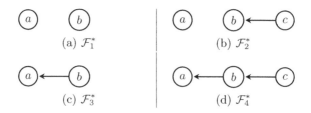

Fig. 3. The completions of $\mathcal{I}$

in the literature on AFs can be adapted in two ways when IAFs are considered. This approach was first studied for subclasses of IAFs, namely Attack-Incomplete AFs [4] (IAFs where only attacks can be uncertain, *i.e.* $\mathcal{A}^? = \emptyset$) and Argument-Incomplete AFs [7] (IAFs where only arguments can be uncertain, *i.e.* $\mathcal{R}^? = \emptyset$). These first works have been generalized to the full IAF model in [3,6].

In this paper, we focus on acceptability problems studied in [5], *i.e.*[2]

σ-PCA Given $\mathcal{I} = \langle \mathcal{A}, \mathcal{A}^?, \mathcal{R}, \mathcal{R}^? \rangle$ an IAF and $a \in \mathcal{A}$, is there a completion $\mathcal{F}^* = \langle \mathcal{A}^*, \mathcal{R}^* \rangle$ such that a is credulously accepted in $\mathcal{F}^*$ under σ?

σ-NCA Given $\mathcal{I} = \langle \mathcal{A}, \mathcal{A}^?, \mathcal{R}, \mathcal{R}^? \rangle$ an IAF and $a \in \mathcal{A}$, for each completion $\mathcal{F}^* = \langle \mathcal{A}^*, \mathcal{R}^* \rangle$, is a a credulously accepted in $\mathcal{F}^*$ under σ?

σ-PSA Given $\mathcal{I} = \langle \mathcal{A}, \mathcal{A}^?, \mathcal{R}, \mathcal{R}^? \rangle$ an IAF and $a \in \mathcal{A}$, is there a completion $\mathcal{F}^* = \langle \mathcal{A}^*, \mathcal{R}^* \rangle$ such that a is skeptically accepted in $\mathcal{F}^*$ under σ?

σ-NSA Given $\mathcal{I} = \langle \mathcal{A}, \mathcal{A}^?, \mathcal{R}, \mathcal{R}^? \rangle$ an IAF and $a \in \mathcal{A}$, for each completion $\mathcal{F}^* = \langle \mathcal{A}^*, \mathcal{R}^* \rangle$, is a a skeptically accepted in $\mathcal{F}^*$ under σ?

Example 6. Continuing the previous example, observe that a is possibly credulously accepted, as well as possible skeptically accepted, under most classical semantics. Indeed, a belongs to the single (grounded, stable, preferred, complete) extension of $\mathcal{F}_1^*$, $\mathcal{F}_2^*$ and $\mathcal{F}_4^*$, but it is not accepted in $\mathcal{F}_3^*$. No argument is necessarily accepted: a is not accepted in $\mathcal{F}_3^*$, b is not accepted in $\mathcal{F}_2^*$ and $\mathcal{F}_4^*$, and c is not accepted in $\mathcal{F}_1^*$ and $\mathcal{F}_3^*$.

Direct Reasoning. It is possible to propose reasoning methods for IAFs which do not require to consider the notion of completion. It was first proposed for so-called Partial AFs (which correspond to Attack-Incomplete AFs, and were first defined in [10] where they are used during a process of merging several AFs), the main idea is that basic notions of conflict-freeness and defense can be re-defined to take into account uncertain knowledge. These basic notions can be combined to obtain various versions of admissibility [9]. It has been proposed recently to generalize this approach to IAFs [30].

One can summarize the approach from [30] by saying that conflicts where uncertainty is involved can either be considered as serious or not. This yields two families of semantics.

---

[2] See [31] for an overview of other relevant decision problems.

Definition 7 (Weak Admissibility [30]). *Given an IAF $\mathcal{I} = \langle \mathcal{A}, \mathcal{A}^?, \mathcal{R}, \mathcal{R}^? \rangle$, a set $S \subseteq \mathcal{A} \cup \mathcal{A}^?$ is weakly conflict-free if $\forall a, b \in S \cap \mathcal{A}$, $(a, b) \notin \mathcal{R}$. Then, given $a \in \mathcal{A} \cup \mathcal{A}^?$, S weakly defends a if $\forall b \in \mathcal{A}$ such that $(b, a) \in \mathcal{R}$, $\exists c \in S \cap \mathcal{A}$ s.t. $(c, b) \in \mathcal{R}$. Finally, S is weakly admissible if it is weakly conflict-free and it weakly defends all its elements.*

Weak conflict-freeness means that two arguments can be accepted together when there is an uncertain conflict between them, *i.e.* either one of the arguments involved in the conflict is uncertain, or the attack between them is uncertain. If we consider that uncertain conflicts are not serious threats in the reasoning, then there is no need to defend an argument against uncertain attacks and uncertain attackers, hence the definition of weak defense.

Definition 8 (Strong Admissibility [30]). *Given an IAF $\mathcal{I} = \langle \mathcal{A}, \mathcal{A}^?, \mathcal{R}, \mathcal{R}^? \rangle$, a set $S \subseteq \mathcal{A} \cup \mathcal{A}^?$ is strongly conflict-free if $\forall a, b \in S$, $(a, b) \notin \mathcal{R} \cup \mathcal{R}^?$. Then, given $a \in \mathcal{A} \cup \mathcal{A}^?$, S strongly defends a if $\forall b \in \mathcal{A} \cup \mathcal{A}^?$ such that $(b, a) \in \mathcal{R} \cup \mathcal{R}^?$, $\exists c \in S \cap \mathcal{A}$ s.t. $(c, b) \in \mathcal{R}$. Finally, S is strongly admissible if it is strongly conflict-free and it strongly defends all its elements.*

Contrary to the weak version, strong admissibility assumes that all internal conflicts are bad, and all attackers must be counter-attacked (even the uncertain ones). [30] then defines the weak and strong versions of the preferred and complete semantics, and proposes also an adaptation of the stable semantics to this setting. For $\sigma \in \{\mathsf{cf}, \mathsf{ad}, \mathsf{co}, \mathsf{pr}, \mathsf{st}\}$, we use respectively σ_S and σ_W to denote the strong and weak counter-parts of these semantics.

Example 7. Consider again the IAF from Fig. 2. The set of arguments $S = \{a, b, c\}$ is weakly admissible. Indeed, none of the conflicts is certain (either the attack is uncertain, namely (b, a), or the attacker is uncertain, namely c). So S is weakly conflict-free, and moreover, none of the arguments requires to be defended, so they are (trivially) weakly defended as well. Notice that this set is not strongly conflict-free. Now assume the existence of a certain argument $d \in \mathcal{A}$, such that $(d, c) \in \mathcal{R}$. This time, c is not weakly defended because it has one certain attacker which is not counter-attacked. But $S' = \{a, b, d\}$ is weakly conflict-free, and weakly admissible.

Complexity and Algorithms. Table 2 presents the complexity for the various decision problems discussed earlier. See [31] for an overview of other complexity results regarding IAFs. Given a semantics σ, σ-CA (respectively σ-SA) corresponds to credulous (respectively skeptical) acceptability for AFs, while σ_X-CA (respectively σ_X-SA) is the corresponding problem for the σ_X semantics of IAFs (where $X \in \{S, W\}$).

For $\mathcal{C}$ a complexity class of the polynomial hierarchy, $\mathcal{C}$-c means $\mathcal{C}$-complete, *i.e.* the corresponding problem is one of the hardest problem of the class $\mathcal{C}$. "Trivial" means that the answer to the question is trivially "no" for all instance. It comes from the fact that $\emptyset$ is always an admissible set, hence there is no

Table 2. Complexity of acceptability for AFs and IAFs.

σ	σ-CA	σ-SA	σ-PCA	σ-NCA	σ-PSA	σ-NSA	σ_X-CA	σ_X-SA
ad	NP-c	trivial	NP-c	Π_2^P-c	trivial	trivial	NP-c	trivial
st	NP-c	coNP-c	NP-c	Π_2^P-c	Σ_2^P-c	coNP-c	NP-c	coNP-c
co	NP-c	P	NP-c	Π_2^P-c	NP-c	coNP-c	NP-c	in coNP
gr	P	P	NP-c	coNP-c	NP-c	coNP-c	?	?
pr	NP-c	Π_2^P-c	NP-c	Π_2^P-c	Σ_3^P-c	Π_2^P-c	NP-c	Π_2^P-c

skeptically accepted argument with respect to ad. Finally, the question marks indicate open questions.

For the various reasoning tasks described previously, computational approaches based on SAT have been proposed, and experimental studies have shown their scalability [3, 30].

4   Constrained Incomplete Argumentation Frameworks

4.1   The Disjunction Problem

An important question with reasoning formalisms is "What can be represented with this formalism?". In the case of abstract argumentation, this question has arisen in a context of belief revision and belief merging, adapted for argumentation frameworks [11, 14]. These works propose two step processes to revise or merge argumentation frameworks: first revise (or merge) the extensions, using an adaptation of propositional belief revision (or merging) operators [23, 24]. Then, from the revised (or merged) extensions, generate a set of argumentation frameworks that correspond to these extensions. Indeed, it is necessary to use a set instead of a single AF, because it is known that some sets of extensions cannot be represented by a single AF [19]. However, from a purely logical point of view, it is not surprising: the result of a revision (or merging) can be a disjunction of several (equally plausible) pieces of information. In the case of AFs, if the result of the first step is $\{\{a\}, \{a, b\}\}$, then it makes sense to have two AFs, one where a attacks b, and one where this attack does not exist. This set of AFs can be seen as a "disjunction" of its elements. We have thus been interested in the question whether IAFs would be a suitable formalism for representing any set of extensions, or any set of AFs, i.e. given $\mathfrak{F}$ a set of AFs, is there an IAF $\mathcal{I}$ such that $\mathtt{comp}(\mathcal{I}) = \mathfrak{F}$. The answer to this question is negative, as shown in this example (borrowed from [29]).

Example 8. Suppose that the result of revising an AF is the set $\mathfrak{F} = \{\mathcal{F}_1 = \langle\{a, b\}, \{(b, a)\}\rangle, \mathcal{F}_2 = \langle\{a, c\}, \{(c, a)\}\rangle\}$. The question is to determine whether this set can be compactly represented by a single IAF. Towards a contradiction, suppose that there is an IAF $\mathcal{I} = \langle\mathcal{A}, \mathcal{A}^?, \mathcal{R}, \mathcal{R}^?\rangle$ s.t. $\mathtt{comp}(\mathcal{I}) = \mathfrak{F}$. Since a belongs to both $\mathcal{F}_1$ and $\mathcal{F}_2$, it must belong to the certain arguments $\mathcal{A}$. On the contrary, the uncertain arguments are $\mathcal{A}^? = \{b, c\}$, each of them belongs to some (but not all) completions. $\mathcal{A} = \{a\}$ and $\mathcal{A}^? = \{b, c\}$ imply the existence of some completions that only contain a, and some completions that contain the three arguments a, b, c. This is not the case in $\mathfrak{F}$. So $\mathcal{I}$ does not exist.

4.2 Towards Higher Expressiveness: Rich IAFs

Control Argumentation Frameworks (CAFs) [15, 28] introduce several novelties to IAFs. One of them is a new kind of uncertain information, namely conflicts with uncertain direction. In [27], we borrow this new kind of uncertainty and add it to IAFs, thus defining Rich IAFs (RIAFs).

Definition 9. *A Rich Incomplete Argumentation Framework (RIAF) is a tuple* $r\mathcal{I} = \langle \mathcal{A}, \mathcal{A}^?, \mathcal{R}, \mathcal{R}^?, \leftrightarrow^? \rangle$, *where $\mathcal{A}$ and $\mathcal{A}^?$ are disjoint sets of arguments, and* $\mathcal{R}, \mathcal{R}^?, \leftrightarrow^? \subseteq (\mathcal{A} \cup \mathcal{A}^?) \times (\mathcal{A} \cup \mathcal{A}^?)$ *are disjoint sets of attacks, such that $\leftrightarrow^?$ is symmetric.*

The new relation $\leftrightarrow^?$ borrowed from CAFs [15] is a symmetric (uncertain) conflict relation: if $(a, b) \in \leftrightarrow^?$, then we are sure that there is a conflict between a and b, but not of the direction of the attack. This new relation impacts the definition of completions.

Definition 10 (Completion of a RIAF). *Given $r\mathcal{I} = \langle \mathcal{A}, \mathcal{A}^?, \mathcal{R}, \mathcal{R}^?, \leftrightarrow^? \rangle$, a completion of $r\mathcal{I}$ is $\mathcal{F}^* = \langle \mathcal{A}^*, \mathcal{R}^* \rangle$, such that*

- $\mathcal{A} \subseteq \mathcal{A}^* \subseteq \mathcal{A} \cup \mathcal{A}^?$;
- $\mathcal{R}_{|\mathcal{A}^*} \subseteq \mathcal{R}^* \subseteq \mathcal{R}_{|\mathcal{A}^*} \cup \mathcal{R}^?_{|\mathcal{A}^*} \cup \leftrightarrow^?_{|\mathcal{A}^*}$;
- *if $(a, b) \in \leftrightarrow^?_{|\mathcal{A}^*}$, then $(a, b) \in \mathcal{R}^*$ or $(b, a) \in \mathcal{R}^*$ (or both).*

Example 9. Assume the RIAF $r\mathcal{I} = \langle \mathcal{A}, \mathcal{A}^?, \mathcal{R}, \mathcal{R}^?, \leftrightarrow^? \rangle$, described by Fig. 4. Its completions are shown at Fig. 5.

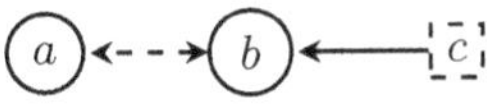

Fig. 4. The RIAF $r\mathcal{I}$

In [27] we also proved that RIAFs are strictly more expressive than IAFs, in the sense that there are sets of AFs that can be the completions of a RIAF, but not of an IAF.

Proposition 1 (Relative Expressivity of IAFs and RIAFs). *RIAFs are strictly more expressive than IAFs, i.e.*

- *for any IAF $\mathcal{I}$, there exists a RIAF $r\mathcal{I}$ such that $\mathsf{comp}(\mathcal{I}) = \mathsf{comp}(r\mathcal{I})$;*
- *there exists a RIAF $r\mathcal{I}$ such that there is no IAF $\mathcal{I}$ with $\mathsf{comp}(\mathcal{I}) = \mathsf{comp}(r\mathcal{I})$.*

However, one can also prove that some sets of AFs cannot be represented by a RIAF. Indeed, the additional expressiveness of RIAFs does not solve the problem illustrated by Example 8.

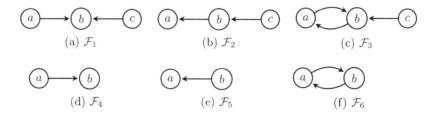

Fig. 5. The completions of $r\mathcal{I}$

4.3 Constrained IAFs

To improve the expressiveness of the formalism, instead of adding different types of attacks, we add a propositional formula which serves as a constraint over the set of completions. The idea is to restrict the set of completions of the IAF which can be used for possible and necessary reasoning.

Definition 11 (Constraint). *Given $\mathcal{A}$ a set of arguments, we define the set of propositional atoms $Prop_{\mathcal{A}} = Arg_{\mathcal{A}} \cup Att_{\mathcal{A}}$ where $Arg_{\mathcal{A}} = \{\arg_a \mid a \in \mathcal{A}\}$ and $Att_{\mathcal{A}} = \{\text{att}_{a,b} \mid (a,b) \in \mathcal{A} \times \mathcal{A}\}$. Then, $\mathcal{L}_{\mathcal{A}}$ is the propositional language built from $Prop_{\mathcal{A}}$ with classical connectives $\{\neg, \vee, \wedge\}$.*

The satisfaction of a constraint by an AF is defined as follows.

Definition 12 (Constraint Satisfaction). *Given $\mathcal{A}$ a set of arguments, and $\phi \in \mathcal{L}_{\mathcal{A}}$ a formula, the set of models of ϕ is denoted $\text{mod}(\phi)$. An AF $\mathcal{F} = \langle \mathcal{A}', \mathcal{R} \rangle$ with $\mathcal{A}' \subseteq \mathcal{A}$ and $\mathcal{R} \subseteq \mathcal{A}' \times \mathcal{A}'$ satisfies ϕ iff there is a model $\omega \in \text{mod}(\phi)$ s.t. $\mathcal{A}' = \{a \in \mathcal{A} \mid \omega(\arg_a) = \top\}$, and $\mathcal{R} = \{(a,b) \in \mathcal{A} \times \mathcal{A} \mid \omega(\text{att}_{a,b}) = \top)\}$.*

Definition 13 (Constrained IAF). *A Constrained Incomplete Argumentation Framework (CIAF) is a tuple $c\mathcal{I} = \langle \mathcal{A}, \mathcal{A}^?, \mathcal{R}, \mathcal{R}^?, \phi \rangle$, where $\langle \mathcal{A}, \mathcal{A}^?, \mathcal{A}, \mathcal{A}^? \rangle$ is an IAF, and $\phi \in \mathcal{L}_{\mathcal{A} \cup \mathcal{A}^?}$ is a constraint.*

The constraint ϕ is used to select a subset of the completions of the IAF $\mathcal{I}_{c\mathcal{I}} = \langle \mathcal{A}, \mathcal{A}^?, \mathcal{R}, \mathcal{R}^? \rangle$. The completions of a CIAF are then defined as follows.

Definition 14 (Completions of a CIAF). *Given $c\mathcal{I} = \langle \mathcal{A}, \mathcal{A}^?, \mathcal{R}, \mathcal{R}^?, \phi \rangle$ a CIAF, we define its set of completions by $\text{comp}(c\mathcal{I}) = \{c \in \text{comp}(\mathcal{I}_{c\mathcal{I}}) \mid c \text{ satisfies } \phi\}$ where $\mathcal{I}_{c\mathcal{I}} = \langle \mathcal{A}, \mathcal{A}^?, \mathcal{R}, \mathcal{R}^? \rangle$.*

Example 10. Let $c\mathcal{I} = \langle \mathcal{A}, \mathcal{A}^?, \mathcal{R}, \mathcal{R}^?, \phi \rangle$ be a CIAF s.t. $\mathcal{I}_{c\mathcal{I}} = \langle \mathcal{A}, \mathcal{A}^?, \mathcal{R}, \mathcal{R}^? \rangle$ is the IAF from Fig. 6, and $\phi = \text{att}_{e,a} \wedge \arg_f$. The completions of $\mathcal{I}_{c\mathcal{I}}$ are given in Fig. 7. Only two of them satisfy ϕ, namely $\mathcal{F}_5$ (Fig. 7c) and $\mathcal{F}_6$ (Fig. 7f). So $\text{comp}(c\mathcal{I}) = \{\mathcal{F}_5, \mathcal{F}_6\}$. This means, for instance, that f is necessary skeptically accepted with respect to $c\mathcal{I}$, while it is not with respect to $\mathcal{I}_{c\mathcal{I}}$.

Now we recall the result from [29] about the expressiveness of CIAFs. This result is based on Definition 15, which introduces a constraint satisfied by only one AF.

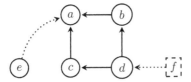

Fig. 6. The IAF $\mathcal{I}$

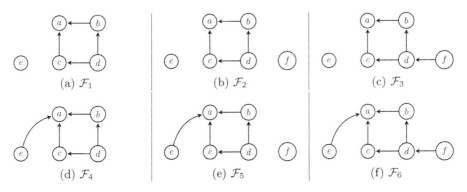

Fig. 7. The completions of $\mathcal{I}$

Definition 15. *Given $\mathcal{A}$ a set of arguments, and $\mathcal{F} = \langle \mathcal{A}', \mathcal{R} \rangle$ with $\mathcal{A}' \subseteq \mathcal{A}$, and $\mathcal{R} \subseteq \mathcal{A}' \times \mathcal{A}'$, we define $\psi_{\mathcal{F}} \in \mathcal{L}_{\mathcal{A}}$ as*

$$\psi_{\mathcal{F}} = \left(\bigwedge_{a \in \mathcal{A}'} \text{arg}_a \right) \wedge \left(\bigwedge_{a \in \mathcal{A} \backslash \mathcal{A}'} \neg \text{arg}_a \right) \wedge \left(\bigwedge_{(a,b) \in \mathcal{R}} \text{att}_{a,b} \right) \wedge \left(\bigwedge_{(a,b) \in (\mathcal{A} \times \mathcal{A}) \backslash \mathcal{R}} \neg \text{att}_{a,b} \right)$$

Proposition 2. *Let $\mathfrak{F} = \{\mathcal{F}_1 = \langle \mathcal{A}_1, \mathcal{R}_1 \rangle, \ldots, \mathcal{F}_n = \langle \mathcal{A}_n, \mathcal{R}_n \rangle\}$ be a set of AFs. There is a CIAF $c\mathcal{I} = \langle \mathcal{A}, \mathcal{A}^?, \mathcal{R}, \mathcal{R}^?, \phi \rangle$ s.t. $\text{comp}(c\mathcal{I}) = \mathfrak{F}$.*

Intuitively, a simple CIAF that does the job consists of all the arguments and attacks from $\mathfrak{F}$ defined as uncertain, and then ϕ is the disjunction of the $\psi_{\mathcal{F}}$ formulas, for $\mathcal{F} \in \mathfrak{F}$. Let us prove this result with a simple illustration of a well suited CIAF.

Proof. Let us build a CIAF $c\mathcal{I} = \langle \mathcal{A}, \mathcal{A}^?, \mathcal{R}, \mathcal{R}^?, \phi \rangle$ s.t. $\text{comp}(c\mathcal{I}) = \mathfrak{F}$. To do that, we first choose $\mathcal{A} = \emptyset$ and $\mathcal{A}^? = \bigcup_{i=1}^{n} \mathcal{A}_i$, *i.e.* all the arguments that appear in an AF from $\mathfrak{F}$ are uncertain. Similarly, all the attacks are uncertain, *i.e.* $\mathcal{R} = \emptyset$ and $\mathcal{R}^? = \bigcup_{i=1}^{n} \mathcal{R}_i$. With all these choices, we define an IAF that has all the possible completions on arguments and attacks from $\mathfrak{F}$. In order to restrict the completions to exactly the AFs in $\mathfrak{F}$, we define $\phi = \bigvee_{i=1}^{n} \psi_{\mathcal{F}_i}$, where $\psi_{\mathcal{F}_i}$ is the formula that is only satisfied by the AF $\mathcal{F}_i$, following Definition 15. The AFs that satisfy ϕ are exactly the ones in $\mathfrak{F}$, so we have $\text{comp}(c\mathcal{I}) = \mathfrak{F}$.

A consequence of this result is that any set of extensions can be represented by an IAF.

Proposition 3. *Let $\mathfrak{E} = \{E_1, \ldots, E_n\}$ be a set of non-empty extensions, and $\sigma \in \{\mathsf{co}, \mathsf{pr}, \mathsf{st}, \mathsf{gr}\}$. There is a CIAF $c\mathcal{I} = \langle \mathcal{A}, \mathcal{A}^?, \mathcal{R}, \mathcal{R}^?, \phi \rangle$ s.t. $\bigcup_{c \in \mathsf{comp}(c\mathcal{I})} \sigma(c) = \mathfrak{E}$.*

Proof. First, let us define $\mathcal{A} = \bigcup_{i=1}^{n} E_i$, *i.e.* it is the set of all the arguments that appear in some extension. Then, for each $E_i \in \mathfrak{E}$, we define $\mathcal{F}_i = \langle \mathcal{A}, \mathcal{R}_i \rangle$ s.t. $\mathcal{R}_i = \{(a, b) \mid a \in E_I, b \in \mathcal{A} \setminus E_i\}$, *i.e.* each argument in E_i is unattacked, and it attacks all the arguments that are not in the extension. For any σ defined in this paper,[3] E_i is the only extension of $\mathcal{F}_i$. Thus, $\bigcup_{i=1}^{n} \sigma(\mathcal{F}_i) = \mathfrak{E}$. From Proposition 2, there is $c\mathcal{I}$ s.t. $\mathsf{comp}(c\mathcal{I}) = \{\mathcal{F}_1, \ldots, \mathcal{F}_n\}$. This concludes the proof.

Corollary 1. *Let $\mathfrak{E} = \{E_1, \ldots, E_n\}$ be a set of extensions, and $\sigma \in \{\mathsf{co}, \mathsf{pr}, \mathsf{gr}\}$. There is a CIAF $c\mathcal{I} = \langle \mathcal{A}, \mathcal{A}^?, \mathcal{R}, \mathcal{R}^?, \phi \rangle$ s.t. $\bigcup_{c \in \mathsf{comp}(c\mathcal{I})} \sigma(c) = \mathfrak{E}$.*

Proof. For non-empty extensions, Proposition 3 can be applied. If some $E_i \in \mathfrak{E}$ is empty, then simply build $\mathcal{F}_i = \langle \mathcal{A}, \mathcal{R}_i \rangle$ where $\mathcal{R}_i = \{(a, a) \mid a \in \mathcal{A}\}$, *i.e.* each argument is self-attacking. The unique σ-extension of $\mathcal{F}_i$ is $E_i = \emptyset$.

From Propositions 2 and 3 and Corollary 1, we deduce that the result of any revision or merging operator from [11,14] can be represented by a CIAF, or said otherwise any set of extensions is realizable [19] when CIAFs are used as the knowledge representation formalism instead of AFs. The same result has been demonstrated independently in [22].

Besides the interest of CIAFs for representing the result of revision or merging operators, more generally they allow to represent the epistemic state of any agent about the current and future states of a debate. Assume than agent A is debating with agent B regarding two arguments a and b which are mutually exclusive. Agent A knows that agent B has some preferences over these arguments, but she does not know exactly agent B's preferences. This means that in agent B's state of mind, either a attacks b, or b attacks a, but not both. These two possible AFs corresponding to agent A's knowledge about B cannot be encoded into a single (R)IAF, but the result described in this section show that they can be represented by a single CIAF.

4.4   Complexity

In the previous section, we have shown that RIAFs are strictly more expressive than IAFs, and CIAFs even more, since any set of AFs (or extensions) can be represented by a CIAF. However, this expressiveness does not come at the price of an increased complexity, compared to the complexity of standard IAFs. More precisely, [29] has shown that the complexity of the decision problems PCA and NSA are the same as in the case of IAFs. The complexity of other decision problems for CIAFs remains an open question.

---

[3] And arguably most semantics defined in the literature.

5   Related Work

As mentioned previously, Control Argumentation Frameworks [15,28] are a generalization of IAFs (or more precisely, of RIAFs). The additional component, namely the *control part* of the CAF, represents arguments and attacks that can be used by an agent to influence the outcome of the argumentation process. Complexity and algorithms were provided in [15,28,33], and an application of this framework to automated negotiation was proposed in [16,17]. CAFs are intrinsically made for strategic applications of argumentation (and in this sense, they are more general than IAFs), but they do not have the maximal expressiveness of CIAFs regarding their set of completions. For this reason, combining CIAFs and CAFs is an interesting future work.

In IAFs (and the related frameworks discussed in this paper), uncertainty is purely qualitative, in the sense that the agent knows that some argument or attack may exist or not, but without a possibility to quantify how plausible is the existence of this element. Probabilistic Argumentation Frameworks (PrAFs) [25] can be seen as an enriched version of IAFs, where the existence of each element is associated with a probability. In the case where such a probability is available, it allows to have more precise inference, for instance because some completions are more probable than other ones. A probabilistic version of CAFs has also been defined [21]. The relation between PrAFs and IAFs has been discussed in [3].

6   Conclusion

There are interesting research tracks regarding CIAFs. In particular, the method described in this paper to exhibit a CIAF corresponding to a set of AFs (or extensions) only works for proving the existence of this CIAF, but it may not be suited to real application of this formalism. For instance, in the case of belief revision or merging, a classical principle is minimal change: we expect the result to be as close as possible to the initial knowledge. To ensure that the graph structure of the CIAF (*i.e.* the sets $\mathcal{A}$, $\mathcal{A}^?$, $\mathcal{R}$ and $\mathcal{R}^?$) is as close as possible to the input graph, one can use techniques similar to distance minimization used in the literature [10,12]. Regarding the constraint, there are two aspects. The first one applies in the case where the initial knowledge of the agent is a CIAF, and not simply an AF. In this case, one can expect that the constraint in the revised CIAF is close to the constraint in the initial CIAF. Then, we can see that the formula defined in the proof of Proposition 2 can be exponentially large in the worst case. To avoid this kind of issue, one can apply techniques from knowledge compilation, in order to obtain an equivalent formula that would be more succinct [13]. Among other future works, one can mention the combination of CIAFs with CAFs or PrAFs, which would allows better representation of the epistemic states of agents participating in a negotiation [16,17,21].

References

1. Amgoud, L., Cayrol, C.: A reasoning model based on the production of acceptable arguments. Ann. Math. Artif. Intell. **34**(1–3), 197–215 (2002)

2. Baroni, P., Caminada, M., Giacomin, M.: Abstract argumentation frameworks and their semantics. In: Baroni, P., Gabbay, D., Giacomin, M., van der Torre, L. (eds.) Handbook of Formal Argumentation, pp. 159–236. College Publications (2018)
3. Baumeister, D., Järvisalo, M., Neugebauer, D., Niskanen, A., Rothe, J.: Acceptance in incomplete argumentation frameworks. Artif. Intell. **295**, 103470 (2021)
4. Baumeister, D., Neugebauer, D., Rothe, J.: Verification in attack-incomplete argumentation frameworks. In: Walsh, T. (ed.) ADT 2015. LNCS (LNAI), vol. 9346, pp. 341–358. Springer, Cham (2015). https://doi.org/10.1007/978-3-319-23114-3_21
5. Baumeister, D., Neugebauer, D., Rothe, J.: Credulous and skeptical acceptance in incomplete argumentation frameworks. In: 7th International Conference on Computational Models of Argument (COMMA 2018), pp. 181–192 (2018)
6. Baumeister, D., Neugebauer, D., Rothe, J., Schadrack, H.: Verification in incomplete argumentation frameworks. Artif. Intell. **264**, 1–26 (2018)
7. Baumeister, D., Rothe, J., Schadrack, H.: Verification in argument-incomplete argumentation frameworks. In: Walsh, T. (ed.) ADT 2015. LNCS (LNAI), vol. 9346, pp. 359–376. Springer, Cham (2015). https://doi.org/10.1007/978-3-319-23114-3_22
8. Bonzon, E., Delobelle, J., Konieczny, S., Maudet, N.: A comparative study of ranking-based semantics for abstract argumentation. In: Proceedings of the Thirtieth AAAI Conference on Artificial Intelligence, pp. 914–920. AAAI Press (2016)
9. Cayrol, C., Devred, C., Lagasquie-Schiex, M.C.: Handling ignorance in argumentation: semantics of partial argumentation frameworks. In: Mellouli, K. (ed.) ECSQARU 2007. LNCS (LNAI), vol. 4724, pp. 259–270. Springer, Heidelberg (2007). https://doi.org/10.1007/978-3-540-75256-1_25
10. Coste-Marquis, S., Devred, C., Konieczny, S., Lagasquie-Schiex, M., Marquis, P.: On the merging of Dung's argumentation systems. Artif. Intell. **171**(10–15), 730–753 (2007)
11. Coste-Marquis, S., Konieczny, S., Mailly, J.G., Marquis, P.: On the revision of argumentation systems: minimal change of arguments statuses. In: Proceedings of the Fourteenth International Conference on Principles of Knowledge Representation and Reasoning (KR 2014). AAAI Press (2014)
12. Coste-Marquis, S., Konieczny, S., Mailly, J.G., Marquis, P.: Extension enforcement in abstract argumentation as an optimization problem. In: Proceedings of the Twenty-Fourth International Joint Conference on Artificial Intelligence (IJCAI 2015), pp. 2876–2882 (2015)
13. Darwiche, A., Marquis, P.: A knowledge compilation map. J. Artif. Intell. Res. **17**, 229–264 (2002). https://doi.org/10.1613/jair.989
14. Delobelle, J., Haret, A., Konieczny, S., Mailly, J.G., Rossit, J., Woltran, S.: Merging of abstract argumentation frameworks. In: Proceedings of the Fifteenth International Conference on Principles of Knowledge Representation and Reasoning (KR 2016), pp. 33–42 (2016)
15. Dimopoulos, Y., Mailly, J.G., Moraitis, P.: Control argumentation frameworks. In: 32nd AAAI Conference on Artificial Intelligence (AAAI 2018), pp. 4678–4685 (2018)
16. Dimopoulos, Y., Mailly, J.G., Moraitis, P.: Argumentation-based negotiation with incomplete opponent profiles. In: 18th International Conference on Autonomous Agents and MultiAgent Systems (AAMAS 2019), pp. 1252–1260 (2019)
17. Dimopoulos, Y., Mailly, J.G., Moraitis, P.: Arguing and negotiating using incomplete negotiators profiles. Auton. Agents Multi-Agent Syst. **35**(2), 18 (2021). https://doi.org/10.1007/s10458-021-09493-y

18. Dung, P.M.: On the acceptability of arguments and its fundamental role in non-monotonic reasoning, logic programming and n-person games. Artif. Intell. **77**(2), 321–358 (1995)
19. Dunne, P.E., Dvořák, W., Linsbichler, T., Woltran, S.: Characteristics of multiple viewpoints in abstract argumentation. Artif. Intell. **228**, 153–178 (2015)
20. Dunne, P.E., Hunter, A., McBurney, P., Parsons, S., Wooldridge, M.J.: Weighted argument systems: basic definitions, algorithms, and complexity results. Artif. Intell. **175**(2), 457–486 (2011)
21. Gaignier, F., Dimopoulos, Y., Mailly, J.G., Moraitis, P.: Probabilistic control argumentation frameworks. In: Proceedings of the 20th International Conference on Autonomous Agents and MultiAgent Systems (AAMAS 2021), pp. 519–527 (2021)
22. Herzig, A., Yuste-Ginel, A.: Abstract argumentation with qualitative uncertainty: an analysis in dynamic logic. In: Baroni, P., Benzmüller, C., Wáng, Y.N. (eds.) CLAR 2021. LNCS (LNAI), vol. 13040, pp. 190–208. Springer, Cham (2021). https://doi.org/10.1007/978-3-030-89391-0_11
23. Katsuno, H., Mendelzon, A.O.: On the difference between updating a knowledge base and revising it. In: 2nd International Conference on Principles of Knowledge Representation and Reasoning (KR 1991), pp. 387–394 (1991)
24. Konieczny, S., Pérez, R.P.: Merging information under constraints: a logical framework. J. Log. Comput. **12**(5), 773–808 (2002)
25. Li, H., Oren, N., Norman, T.J.: Probabilistic argumentation frameworks. In: Proceedings of the First International Workshop on Theory and Applications of Formal Argumentation (TAFA 2011), pp. 1–16 (2011)
26. Mailly, J.G.: Yes, no, maybe, I don't know: complexity and application of abstract argumentation with incomplete knowledge. Argum. Comput. (2021, to appear). https://doi.org/10.3233/AAC-210010
27. Mailly, J.G.: A note on rich incomplete argumentation frameworks. CoRR abs/2009.04869 (2020). https://arxiv.org/abs/2009.04869
28. Mailly, J.G.: Possible controllability of control argumentation frameworks. In: 8th International Conference on Computational Models of Argument (COMMA 2020), pp. 283–294 (2020)
29. Mailly, J.-G.: Constrained incomplete argumentation frameworks. In: Vejnarová, J., Wilson, N. (eds.) ECSQARU 2021. LNCS (LNAI), vol. 12897, pp. 103–116. Springer, Cham (2021). https://doi.org/10.1007/978-3-030-86772-0_8
30. Mailly, J.-G.: Extension-based semantics for incomplete argumentation frameworks. In: Baroni, P., Benzmüller, C., Wáng, Y.N. (eds.) CLAR 2021. LNCS (LNAI), vol. 13040, pp. 322–341. Springer, Cham (2021). https://doi.org/10.1007/978-3-030-89391-0_18
31. Mailly, J.G.: Yes, no, maybe, I don't know: complexity and application of abstract argumentation with incomplete knowledge. Argum. Comput. (2022, to appear). https://doi.org/10.3233/AAC-210010
32. Nielsen, S.H., Parsons, S.: A generalization of Dung's abstract framework for argumentation: arguing with sets of attacking arguments. In: Maudet, N., Parsons, S., Rahwan, I. (eds.) ArgMAS 2006. LNCS (LNAI), vol. 4766, pp. 54–73. Springer, Heidelberg (2007). https://doi.org/10.1007/978-3-540-75526-5_4
33. Niskanen, A., Neugebauer, D., Järvisalo, M.: Controllability of control argumentation frameworks. In: Proceedings of the Twenty-Ninth International Joint Conference on Artificial Intelligence, IJCAI 2020, pp. 1855–1861 (2020)
34. Rossit, J., Mailly, J.G., Dimopoulos, Y., Moraitis, P.: United we stand: accruals in strength-based argumentation. Argum. Comput. **12**(1), 87–113 (2021)

Full Papers: Non-classical Reasoning

Towards a Principle-Based Approach for Case-Based Reasoning

Leila Amgoud[1(✉)] and Vivien Beuselinck[2]

[1] CNRS – IRIT, Toulouse, France
amgoud@irit.fr
[2] Toulouse University, Toulouse, France
vivien@beuselinck.fr

Abstract. Case-based reasoning (CBR) is an experience-based app-roach to solving problems; it adapts previously successful cases to new problems following the key assumption: *the more similar the cases, the more similar their solutions.* Despite its popularity, there are few works on foundations, or properties, that may underlie CBR models.

This paper bridges this gap by defining various notions capturing the above assumption, and proposing a set of principles that a CBR system would satisfy. We discuss their properties and show that the principles that are founded on the CBR assumption are incompatible with some axioms underlying non-monotonic reasoning (NMR). This shows that CBR and NMR are different forms of reasoning, and sheds light on the reasons behind their disagreements.

Keywords: Case-based reasoning · Non-monotonic reasoning · Principles

1 Introduction

Case-based reasoning (CBR) is an experience-based approach to solving problems. It uses stored cases describing similar prior problem-solving episodes and adapts their solutions to fit new needs (or new cases). For example, a car dealer would guess the price of a given car by comparing its characteristics with those of cars that have been sold. This form of reasoning has been used in the literature for solving various practical problems including some in the medical (e.g. [10,13,14]) and legal (e.g. [2–4,15]) domains.

Several works have been devoted to modeling CBR, and various approaches can be distinguished including logic-based [5,6,16] and argumentation-based [9, 11] approaches (see [1,7,12] for surveys). However, despite its popularity, there are few works on foundations, or properties, that may underlie CBR models. Foundations are important not only for a better understanding of case-based reasoning in general, but also for clarifying the basic assumptions underlying models, comparing different models, and also for comparing case-based reasoning with other kinds of reasoning like defeasible reasoning.

© The Author(s), under exclusive license to Springer Nature Switzerland AG 2022
F. Dupin de Saint-Cyr et al. (Eds.): SUM 2022, LNAI 13562, pp. 37–46, 2022.
https://doi.org/10.1007/978-3-031-18843-5_3

This paper bridges this gap. It starts by analysing the basic assumption behind case-based reasoning, namely *"the more similar the cases, the more similar their outcomes"*. It discusses three independent notions that capture (in different ways) the assumption. Then, the paper proposes principles that a case-based reasoning model would satisfy and analyses their properties. Some principles ensure the three forms of the CBR assumption, and we show that they are incompatible with some axioms underlying non-monotonic reasoning (NMR) [8], namely cautious monotonicity. This shows that CBR and NMR are different forms of reasoning, and sheds light on the reasons behind their differences.

The paper is organized as follows: Sect. 2 introduces CBR problems, Sect. 3 discusses various formalizations of the key assumption behind CBR, Sect. 4 introduces basic principles that a model would satisfy. The last section concludes.

2   Background

Before introducing formally the basic notions of a CBR problem, let us consider the following illustrative example borrowed from [5].

Example 1. Consider the problem of identifying the price of second-hand cars. A car is described with five attributes, namely years old, power, mileage, the state of equipment, and shape. Knowing the characteristics and the prices of four cars (C_1, C_2, C_3, C_4) (summarized in the table below), the problem is to identify the price of the new car (C_n) whose characteristics are also known.

Cases	Years old	Power	Mileage	Equipment	Shape	Price
C_1	1	1300	20 000	poor	good	8000
C_2	2	1600	30 000	excellent	poor	7000
C_3	2	1600	40 000	good	good	5000
C_4	3	1500	60 000	excellent	poor	5000
C_n	2	1600	50 000	poor	good	?

To identify the price of C_n, any CBR model would compare the characteristics of cars as well as their prices. Hence, it would use two similarity measures: one for comparing prices ($\mathbf{S}^o$) and another for comparing attributes-values ($\mathbf{S}^i$). In [5], $\mathbf{S}^o$ is defined as follows:

$$\mathbf{S}^o(u, v) = \begin{cases} 1 & \textit{if } |u - v| \leq 500 \\ 0 & \textit{if } |u - v| \geq 2000 \\ 1 - \frac{1}{1500} * (|u - v| - 500) & \textit{if } 500 < |u - v| < 2000 \end{cases}$$

It is easy to check that $\mathbf{S}^o(x, x) = 1$, $\mathbf{S}^o(5000, 7000) = \mathbf{S}^o(5000, 8000) = 0$ and $\mathbf{S}^o(7000, 8000) = \frac{2}{3}$.

Regarding $\mathbf{S}^i$, it combines five measures, each of which compares the values of an attribute. $\mathbf{S}^1$ compares years old (respectively mileage) as follows: $\mathbf{S}^1(u, v) = \frac{\min(u,v)}{\max(u,v)}$. For instance, $\mathbf{S}^1(1, 2) = \frac{1}{2}$ and $\mathbf{S}^1(20000, 30000) = \frac{2}{3}$. The measure that compares the powers of two cars is defined as follows: $\mathbf{S}^2(u, v) = 1 - (\frac{|u-v|}{1000})$. For instance, $\mathbf{S}^2(1300, 1600) = \frac{7}{10}$. Finally, equipment and shape are compared using the measure $\mathbf{S}^3$, which assumes the ordering bad $<$ poor $<$ good $<$ excellent.

$$\mathbf{S}^3(v, v') = \begin{cases} 1 & \text{if} & v = v' \\ \frac{2}{3} & \text{if} & \text{v and v' are consecutive} \\ \frac{1}{3} & \text{if} & \text{there is exactly one element between v and v'} \\ 0 & \text{otherwise.} \end{cases}$$

The similarity between (the characteristics of) two cars is the minimal similarity of the characteristics. For instance, $\mathbf{S}^i(C_1, C_2) = \min(\mathbf{S}^1(1, 2), \mathbf{S}^2(1300, 1600),$ $\mathbf{S}^1(20000, 30000), \mathbf{S}^3(\text{poor}, \text{excellent}), \mathbf{S}^3(\text{good}, \text{poor})) = \min(\frac{1}{2}, \frac{7}{10}, \frac{2}{3}, \frac{1}{3}, \frac{2}{3}) = \frac{1}{3}$. The table below summarises the values returned by $\mathbf{S}^i$ for each pair of cars.

Cases	C_1	C_2	C_3	C_4	C_n
C_1	1	$\frac{1}{3}$	$\frac{1}{2}$	$\frac{1}{3}$	$\frac{2}{5}$
C_2	$\frac{1}{3}$	1	$\frac{2}{3}$	$\frac{1}{2}$	$\frac{1}{3}$
C_3	$\frac{1}{2}$	$\frac{2}{3}$	1	$\frac{2}{3}$	$\frac{2}{3}$
C_4	$\frac{1}{3}$	$\frac{1}{2}$	$\frac{2}{3}$	1	$\frac{1}{3}$
C_n	$\frac{2}{5}$	$\frac{1}{3}$	$\frac{2}{3}$	$\frac{1}{3}$	1

Throughout the paper, we assume a finite and non-empty set $\mathcal{F} = \{f_1, \ldots, f_n, f\}$ of *features*, where $f_1, \ldots, f_n$ describe the cases (e.g. Power, Mileage, Shape) and f is the feature being solved (price in the example). Let dom be a function on $\mathcal{F}$ which returns the domain of every $f \in \mathcal{F}$. Hence, $\text{dom}(f)$ is the set of possible outcomes of a CBR problem, which is finite in classification tasks. In addition to this set, we assume the special symbols ? and Und, which denote respectively that the value of f is *pending* and *undecided* by a CBR model. We call *literal* every pair (f, v) such that $f \in \mathcal{F} \setminus \{f\}$ and $v \in \text{dom}(f)$, and *instance* every set of literals, where each feature $f_1, \ldots, f_n$ appears exactly once. We denote by Inst the set of all possible instances, and call it *input space*. The latter is endowed with a similarity measure $\mathbf{S}^i$, which assesses how close are instances. The set $\text{dom}(f)$ is endowed with a similarity measure $\mathbf{S}^o$, which compares outcomes. Recall that a similarity measure $\mathbf{S}$ on a set X is a function $\mathbf{S} : X \times X \to [0, 1]$ where:

- $\forall x \in X, \mathbf{S}(x, x) = 1$
- $\forall x, y \in X, \mathbf{S}(x, y) = \mathbf{S}(y, x)$

We consider two additional parameters $0 < \delta^i \leq 1$ and $0 < \delta^o \leq 1$, which represent the *thresholds* for considering respectively two instances and two outcomes as somewhat similar. More precisely, for $x, y \in \text{Inst}$, x is dissimilar to y iff $\mathbf{S}^i(x, y) < \delta^o$ and for $v, v' \in \text{dom}(f)$, v is dissimilar to v' iff $\mathbf{S}^o(v, v') < \delta^o$.

Let us now introduce the backbone of a CBR problem, the notion of *case*. It is an instance labelled with an outcome.

Definition 1 (Case). *A case is a pair* $c = \langle I, v \rangle$ *such that* $I \in \text{Inst}$ *and* $v \in \text{dom}(f) \cup \{?\}$. *We call* c *a past case when* $v \in \text{dom}(f)$, *and a new case when* $v = ?$. *A case base is a sample that consists of n past cases* $c_i = \langle I_i, v_i \rangle$ $(1 \leq i \leq n)$.

In [5], a case base is said to be *consistent* if identical cases in the base have identical outcomes (i.e., for all cases $\langle I, v \rangle$ and $\langle I', v' \rangle$ in a base, if $I = I'$ then $v = v'$). In some problems like the one described in the above example, this constraint may be strong as the same instances may have different but similar outcomes. It is also possible that similar instances have the same or similar outcomes. Imagine a second-hand car $C*$ which has the same characteristics as C_1, but its price is 8400. Note that $\mathbf{S}^o(8000, 8400) = 1$, which means that the difference between the two prices is negligible. In what follows, we generalize this notion of consistency using similarity measures. The idea is that fully similar instances get fully similar outcomes.

Definition 2 (Consistency). *A case base Σ is* consistent *iff $\forall \langle I, v \rangle, \langle I', v' \rangle \in \Sigma$, if $\mathbf{S}^i(I, I') = 1$ then $\mathbf{S}^o(v, v') = 1$. It is* inconsistent *otherwise.*

It is easy to see that in a consistent case base, identical instances may receive different but fully similar outcomes.

Property 1. If a case base Σ is consistent, then $\forall \langle I, v \rangle, \langle I', v' \rangle \in \Sigma$, if $I = I'$, then $\mathbf{S}^o(v, v') = 1$.

Proof. Let Σ be a consistent case base. Assume that $\langle I, v \rangle, \langle I', v' \rangle \in \Sigma$ such that $I = I'$. Since $\mathbf{S}^i$ is a similarity measure, then $\mathbf{S}^i(I, I') = 1$. From Consistency of Σ, $\mathbf{S}^o(v, v') = 1$.

Throughout the paper, we call CBR theory, or theory for short, a tuple containing a set of attributes, their domains, two similarity measures $\mathbf{S}^i, \mathbf{S}^o$ and their thresholds.

Definition 3 (Theory). *A theory is a tuple* $\mathbf{T} = \langle \mathcal{F}, \mathrm{dom}, \mathbf{S}^i, \mathbf{S}^o, \delta^i, \delta^o \rangle$.

3   CBR Basic Assumption

Case-based reasoning is heavily based on similarities between cases. It looks for the most similar past cases to the new case, then adapts their outcomes following the key rule:

The more similar the cases (in the sense of $\mathbf{S}^i$), the more similar their outcomes (in the sense of $\mathbf{S}^o$).

Formalizing this rule is important for developing reasonable CBR models and also for checking whether existing models obey the rule. In [5], it has been formalized as a *fuzzy gradual* rule, which states that the similarity of two instances should be lower or equal to the similarity of their outcomes. Throughout the paper, we refer to this notion as *strong coherence*.

Definition 4 (Strong Coherence). *A case base Σ is strongly coherent iff $\forall \langle I, v \rangle, \langle I', v' \rangle \in \Sigma$, $\mathbf{S}^i(I, I') \leq \mathbf{S}^o(v, v')$.*

Example 1 (Cont). The case base $\Sigma_1 = \{C_i = \langle I_i, v_i \rangle, i = 1, \ldots, 4\}$ is not strongly coherent. For instance, $\mathbf{S}^i(I_1, I_3) = \frac{1}{2}$ while $\mathbf{S}^o(v_1, v_3) = 0$.

Example 2. Consider the case base $\Sigma_2 = \{C = \langle I, v \rangle, C' = \langle I', v' \rangle\}$. If $\mathbf{S}^i(I, I') = 0.7$ and $\mathbf{S}^o(v, v') \geq 0.7$, then Σ is strongly coherent. Assume now that $\mathbf{S}^i(I, I') = 0.1$ and $\mathbf{S}^o(v, v') = 1$. Again, Σ_2 is strongly coherent even if the two cases are dissimilar (let $\delta^i = 0.5$).

It is easy to show that fully similar cases in a strongly coherent case base have fully similar outcomes.

Property 2. Let Σ be a strongly coherent case base. For all $\langle I, v \rangle, \langle I', v' \rangle \in \Sigma$, if $\mathbf{S}^i(I, I') = 1$, then $\mathbf{S}^o(v, v') = 1$.

Proof. Let Σ be a strongly coherent case base. Let $\langle I, v \rangle, \langle I', v' \rangle \in \Sigma$ such that $\mathbf{S}^i(I, I') = 1$. Strong coherence of Σ implies $\mathbf{S}^i(I, I') \leq \mathbf{S}^o(v, v')$. Since $\mathbf{S}^o(v, v') \in [0, 1]$, then $\mathbf{S}^o(v, v') = 1$.

It is also easy to show that any strongly coherent case base is consistent. The converse is false as shown in Example 1 (the base Σ_1 is consistent but not strongly coherent).

Property 3. If a case base is strongly coherent, then it is consistent. The converse does not hold.

Proof. Let Σ be a case base and assume it is strongly coherent. Let $\langle I, v \rangle, \langle I', v' \rangle \in \Sigma$ such that $\mathbf{S}^i(I, I') = 1$. From Property 2, it follows that $\mathbf{S}^o(v, v') = 1$.

By directly linking the similarity of outcomes with the similarity of instances, the property of strong coherence ensures that the former is proportional to the latter. However, the similarity measures $\mathbf{S}^i$ and $\mathbf{S}^o$ as well as their corresponding thresholds (δ^i and δ^o) may be different and not necessarily commensurate. This makes the satisfaction of the property difficult in case of such measures. Let us illustrate the issue with the following example.

Example 3. Suppose we have a case base Σ_3 on student grades. There are 4 attributes corresponding to courses and which take values from the interval $[0, 20]$; the outcome is a global appreciation whose range consists of 4 qualitative levels: bad < poor < good < excellent. Let $\mathbf{S}^o$ be the similarity measure $\mathbf{S}^3$ in Example 1. Similarity between any pair of grades obtained in a course is defined by $\mathbf{S}(u, v) = 1 - (\frac{|u-v|}{20})$. The similarity measure $\mathbf{S}^i$ takes the minimal value returned by $\mathbf{S}$ on the four courses. Assume Σ_3 contains two students who got respectively $I = \langle 20, 20, 20, 20 \rangle$ and $v =$ "excellent" as global appreciation, and $I' = \langle 20, 20, 15, 15 \rangle$ with appreciation $v' =$ "good". Hence, $\mathbf{S}^i(I, I') = 0.75$ and $\mathbf{S}^o(v, v') = \frac{2}{3}$. Note that the base is not strongly coherent. In order to be coherent, $\mathbf{S}^o(v, v')$ should be equal to 1, which is not reasonable in the example as the two instances are different and deserve different appreciations. Furthermore, the scale of $\mathbf{S}^o$ does not have an intermediate value between $\frac{2}{3}$ and 1.

In what follows, we introduce a novel notion of *weak coherence*, which makes use of the two thresholds for judging similar instances/outcomes. It states that similar cases should receive similar outcomes.

Definition 5 (Weak Coherence). *A case-base Σ is* weakly coherent *iff $\forall \langle I, v \rangle, \langle I', v' \rangle \in \Sigma$, if $\mathbf{S}^i(I, I') \geq \delta^i$, then $\mathbf{S}^o(v, v') \geq \delta^o$.*

Example 3 (Cont). If $\delta^i \geq 0.75$ and $\delta^o \geq \frac{2}{3}$, then Σ_2 is weakly coherent.

The above example shows that a case base may be weakly but not strongly coherent. However, weak coherence follows from the strong version when $\delta^i \geq \delta^o$.

Proposition 1. *Let Σ be a case base and $\delta^i \geq \delta^o$. If Σ is strongly coherent, then Σ is also weakly coherent.*

Proof. Assume $\delta^i \geq \delta^o$. Let Σ be a strongly coherent case base, and $\langle I, v \rangle$, $\langle I', v' \rangle \in \Sigma$. Assume $\mathbf{S}^i(I, I') \geq \delta^i$. From strong coherence, $\delta^i \leq \mathbf{S}^i(I, I') \leq \mathbf{S}^o(v, v')$. Hence, $\mathbf{S}^o(v, v') \geq \delta^o$.

It is worth mentioning that consistency does not follow from weak coherence. Indeed, it is possible to find a weakly coherent case base which contains two cases such that $\mathbf{S}^i(I, I') = 1$, thus $\mathbf{S}^i(I, I') \geq \delta^i$, while $\delta^o \leq \mathbf{S}^o(v, v') < 1$.

The two versions of coherence compare pairs of cases of a case base. Our next notion, called *regularity*, is defined on the whole set of cases and ensures that the closest instances receive the closest outcomes. Indeed, if an instance I is closer to I' than to I'', then its outcome should be closer to that of I'.

Definition 6 (Regularity). *A case-base Σ is* regular *iff $\forall \langle I, v \rangle, \langle I', v' \rangle, \langle I'', v'' \rangle \in \Sigma$, if $\mathbf{S}^i(I, I') \geq \mathbf{S}^i(I, I'')$ then $\mathbf{S}^o(v, v') \geq \mathbf{S}^o(v, v'')$.*

Example 1 (Cont). The case base $\Sigma_1 = \{C_i = \langle I_i, v_i \rangle, i = 1, \ldots, 4\}$ is not regular. For instance, $\mathbf{S}^i(I_1, I_3) > \mathbf{S}^i(I_1, I_2)$ while $\mathbf{S}^o(v_1, v_3) < \mathbf{S}^o(v_1, v_2)$.

Regularity is different from the two forms of coherence, and thus it does not imply or follow from them. It is also independent from consistency.

4   Axioms for CBR

A CBR model is a function, which takes as input a theory and a new case, and returns possible outcomes of the latter. Since every instance is assigned exactly one label, one expects that a model provides a single solution. However, this is not always possible since the new case may be close to several differently labelled cases, and the model cannot discriminate between those labels. So, each of label is considered as a *candidate* outcome. It is also possible that the new case is dissimilar to all past cases of a base. Hence, instead of returning an arbitrary outcome, we assume that a model may rerun the symbol Und (for undecided), meaning no solution is proposed.

Definition 7 (CBR Model). *Let* $\mathbf{T} = \langle \mathcal{F}, \mathrm{dom}, \mathbf{S}^i, \mathbf{S}^o, \delta^i, \delta^o \rangle$ *be a theory. A CBR model is a function* R *mapping every case base* Σ *and new case* $\langle I, ? \rangle$ *into a set* $O \subseteq \mathrm{dom}(\mathsf{f}) \cup \{\mathtt{Und}\}$ *such that* $O \neq \emptyset$ *and either* $O = \{\mathtt{Und}\}$ *or* $O \subseteq \mathrm{dom}(\mathsf{f})$. *We write* $\Sigma \oplus \langle I, ? \rangle \mathrel{|\!\sim}_{\mathbf{T},\mathsf{R}} O$.

In what follows, we assume arbitrary but fixed theory $\mathbf{T}$, case base Σ, new case $\langle I, ? \rangle$ and CBR model $\mathbf{R}$. We introduce some principles (or properties) that a reasonable CBR model would satisfy. The first two principles concern the situation where the new case is dissimilar to all the past cases of the base. There are two possibilities. The first consists of proposing outcomes of the closest cases. This may be undesirable in applications like medical diagnosis, where a CBR model looks for a diagnosis of patients of the basis of their symptoms.

Principle 1 (Strong Completeness). $\Sigma \oplus \langle I, ? \rangle \mathrel{|\!\sim}_{\mathbf{T},\mathsf{R}} O$ *with* $O \subseteq \mathrm{dom}(\mathsf{f})$.

The second possibility consists of abstaining from choosing an arbitrary outcome, and ensures that the model returns the symbol $\mathtt{Und}$.

Principle 2 (Weak Completeness). $\Sigma \oplus \langle I, ? \rangle \mathrel{|\!\sim}_{\mathbf{T},\mathsf{R}} \{\mathtt{Und}\}$ *iff* $\forall \langle I, v \rangle \in \Sigma$, $\mathbf{S}^i(I_n, I) < \delta^i$.

Note that any model which satisfies weak completeness returns $\mathtt{Und}$ when the case base is empty. This is reasonable as arbitrariness is avoided.

Proposition 2. *If a model* R *satisfies weak completeness, then* $\emptyset \oplus \langle I, ? \rangle \mathrel{|\!\sim}_{\mathbf{T},\mathsf{R}} \{\mathtt{Und}\}$.

The strong and weak versions of completeness are incompatible, i.e., there is no CBR model which can satisfies both at the same time. Indeed, they recommend different outcomes in the above mentioned particular case.

Proposition 3. *Strong completeness and weak completeness are incompatible*

The third principle ensures that the model preserves the consistency of the case base. Of course, this therefore assumes that the base is consistent.

Principle 3 (Consistency). *Let* Σ *be consistent and* $\Sigma \oplus \langle I, ? \rangle \mathrel{|\!\sim}_{\mathbf{T},\mathsf{R}} O$ *such that* $O \neq \{\mathtt{Und}\}$. *For any* $v \in O$, $\Sigma \cup \{\langle I_n, v \rangle\}$ *is consistent.*

The three next principles are those that capture the CBR rule discussed previously. Strong coherence states that adding the new case labelled with any of its candidate outcomes to a strongly coherent base would preserve coherence.

Principle 4 (Strong Coherence). *Let* Σ *be strongly coherent and* $\Sigma \oplus \langle I, ? \rangle \mathrel{|\!\sim}_{\mathbf{T},\mathsf{R}} O$ *such that* $O \neq \{\mathtt{Und}\}$. *For any* $v \in O$, $\Sigma \cup \{\langle I_n, v \rangle\}$ *is strongly coherent.*

In the same way, weak coherence ensures that a CBR model preserves the weak coherence of a case base.

Principle 5 (Weak Coherence). *Let Σ be weakly coherent and $\Sigma \oplus \langle I, ? \rangle$ $\vdash_{T,R} O$ such that $O \neq \{\text{Und}\}$. For any $v \in O$, $\Sigma \cup \{\langle I_n, v \rangle\}$ is weakly coherent.*

Proposition 4. *Let $\mathbf{T} = \langle \mathcal{F}, \text{dom}, \mathbf{S}^i, \mathbf{S}^o, \delta^i, \delta^o \rangle$ be a theory such that $\delta^i \geq \delta^o$. If a CBR model satisfies strong coherence, then it satisfies weak coherent.*

Proof. Let $\delta^i \geq \delta^o$, $\langle I, ? \rangle$ a new case, and a CBR model which satisfies strong coherence. Let $\Sigma \oplus \langle I, ? \rangle \vdash_{T,R} O$. It holds that for any $v \in O$, $\Sigma \cup \{\langle I_n, v \rangle\}$ is strongly coherent. From Proposition 1, since $\delta^i \geq \delta^o$, then $\Sigma \cup \{\langle I_n, v \rangle\}$ is weakly coherent.

Regularity principle ensures that a CBR model preserves the regularity of a case base.

Principle 6 (Regularity). *Let Σ be regular and $\Sigma \oplus \langle I, ? \rangle \vdash_{T,R} O$ such that $O \neq \{\text{Und}\}$. For any $v \in O$, $\Sigma \cup \{\langle I_n, v \rangle\}$ is regular.*

In what follows, we show that case-based reasoning is non-monotonic as its conclusions can be revised when a base is extended with additional cases. Let us first define formally the principle of non-monotonicity.

Principle 7 (Non-Monotonicity).

$$\begin{cases} \Sigma \oplus \langle I, ? \rangle \vdash_{T,R} O \\ \\ \Sigma \subseteq \Sigma' \end{cases} \not\Rightarrow \Sigma' \oplus \langle I, ? \rangle \vdash_{T,R} O$$

The following result shows that non-monotonicity follows from weak completeness.

Proposition 5. *If a CBR model satisfies weak completeness, then it satisfies non-monotonicity.*

Proof. Assume a CBR model $\mathbf{R}$ which satisfies weak completeness. Let Σ be a case base and $\langle I, ? \rangle$ a new case. Assume $\Sigma = \emptyset$, then $\emptyset \oplus \langle I, ? \rangle \vdash_{T,R} \{\text{Und}\}$. Let now $\Sigma' = \{\langle I, v \rangle\}$ such that $I = I_n$. Obviously, $\mathbf{S}^i(I, I_n) = 1$ and $\mathbf{S}^i(I, I_n) \geq \delta^i$ (since $0 < \delta^i \leq 1$). So, $\Sigma' \oplus \langle I, ? \rangle \not\vdash_{T,R} \{\text{Und}\}$.

We show next that one of the principles capturing the basis assumption of CBR, namely strong coherence, is incompatible with cautious monotonicity from [8]. This means there in no CBR model which can satisfy the two properties.

Definition 8 (Cautious Monotonicity).

$$\begin{cases} \Sigma \oplus \langle I, ? \rangle \vdash_{T,R} \{v\} \\ \\ \Sigma \oplus \langle I', ? \rangle \vdash_{T,R} \{v'\} \end{cases} \implies \Sigma \cup \{\langle I, v \rangle\} \oplus \langle I', ? \rangle \vdash_{T,R} \{v'\}$$

Proposition 6. *Strong coherence and cautious monotonicity are incompatible.*

5   Conclusion

The paper presented a preliminary contribution on foundations of case-based reasoning. It started by formalizing the key rule behind this form of reasoning, then proposed a set of principles that any model would satisfy. We have shown that CBR is non-monotonic in that conclusion could be revised in light of additional information (cases). However, some of its principles are incompatible with some axioms describing nonmonotonic reasoning in [8].

This work can be extended in several ways. First, we plan to investigate the properties of the principles, their consequences, and properties of models satisfying them. We also plan to develop models satisfying the axioms. Finally, we will analyse existing CBR models against the axioms.

Acknowledgements. Support from the ANR-3IA Artificial and Natural Intelligence Toulouse Institute is gratefully acknowledged.

References

1. Aamodt, A., Plaza, E.: Case-based reasoning: foundational issues, methodological variations, and system approaches. AI Commun. **7**(1), 39–59 (1994)
2. Ashley, K.D.: Case-based reasoning and its implications for legal expert systems. Artif. Intell. Law **1**(2–3), 113–208 (1992)
3. Ashley, K.D.: The case-based reasoning approach: ontologies for analogical legal argument. In: Sartor, G., Casanovas, P., Biasiotti, M.A., Fernández-Barrera, M. (eds.) Approaches to Legal Ontologies. Law, Governance and Technology Series, vol. 1, pp. 99–115. Springer, Dordrecht (2011). https://doi.org/10.1007/978-94-007-0120-5_6
4. Atkinson, K., Bench-Capon, T.J.M.: Legal case-based reasoning as practical reasoning. Artif. Intell. Law **13**(1), 93–131 (2005)
5. Dubois, D., Esteva, F., Garcia, P., Godo, L., De Màntaras, R.L., Prade, H.: Case-based reasoning: a fuzzy approach. In: Ralescu, A.L., Shanahan, J.G. (eds.) FLAI 1997. LNCS, vol. 1566, pp. 79–90. Springer, Heidelberg (1999). https://doi.org/10.1007/BFb0095072
6. Greco, S., Matarazzo, B., Slowinski, R.: Dominance-based rough set approach to case-based reasoning. In: Torra, V., Narukawa, Y., Valls, A., Domingo-Ferrer, J. (eds.) MDAI 2006. LNCS (LNAI), vol. 3885, pp. 7–18. Springer, Heidelberg (2006). https://doi.org/10.1007/11681960_3
7. Hüllermeier, E.: Case-Based Approximate Reasoning. Springer, Netherlands (2007). https://doi.org/10.1007/1-4020-5695-8_2
8. Kraus, S., Lehmann, D., Magidor, M.: Nonmonotonic reasoning, preferential models and cumulative logics. Artif. Intell. **44**(1–2), 167–207 (1990)
9. Paulino-Passos, G., Toni, F.: Monotonicity and noise-tolerance in case-based reasoning with abstract argumentation. In: Proceedings of the 18th International Conference on Principles of Knowledge Representation and Reasoning, KR, pp. 508–518 (2021)
10. Perez, B., Lang, C., Henriet, J., Philippe, L., Auber, F.: Risk prediction in surgery using case-based reasoning and agent-based modelization. Comput. Biol. Med. **128**, 104040 (2021)

11. Prakken, H., Wyner, A., Bench-Capon, T., Atkinson, K.: A formalization of argumentation schemes for legal case-based reasoning in ASPIC+. J. Log. Comput. **25**(5), 1141–1166 (2013)

12. Richter, M., Weber, R.: Case-Based Reasoning. Springer, Heidelberg (2013). https://doi.org/10.1007/978-3-642-40167-1

13. Schnell, M.: Using case-based reasoning and argumentation to assist medical coding. Assistance au codage médical par du raisonnement à partir de cas argumentatif. Ph.D. thesis, University of Lorraine, Nancy, France (2020)

14. Smiti, A., Nssibi, M.: Case based reasoning framework for COVID-19 diagnosis. Ingénierie des Systèmes d Inf. **25**(4), 469–474 (2020)

15. Zhang, H., Zhang, Z., Zhou, L., Wu, S.: Case-based reasoning for hidden property analysis of judgment debtors. Mathematics **9**(13) (2021). https://www.mdpi.com/2227-7390/9/13/1559

16. Zheng, H., Grossi, D., Verheij, B.: Case-based reasoning with precedent models: preliminary report. In: Prakken, H., Bistarelli, S., Santini, F., Taticchi, C. (eds.) Computational Models of Argument - Proceedings of COMMA, vol. 326, pp. 443–450 (2020)

Iterated Conditionals, Trivalent Logics, and Conditional Random Quantities

Lydia Castronovo$^{(\boxtimes)}$ and Giuseppe Sanfilippo$^{(\boxtimes)}$

Department of Mathematics and Computer Science,
University of Palermo, Palermo, Italy
{lydia.castronovo,giuseppe.sanfilippo}@unipa.it

Abstract. We consider some notions of iterated conditionals by checking the validity of some desirable basic logical and probabilistic properties, which are valid for simple conditionals. We consider de Finetti's notion of conditional as a three-valued object and as a conditional random quantity in the betting framework. We recall the notions of conjunction and disjunction among conditionals in selected trivalent logics. Then, we analyze the two notions of iterated conditional introduced by Calabrese and de Finetti, respectively. We show that the compound probability theorem and other basic properties are not preserved by these objects, by also computing some probability propagation rules. Then, for each trivalent logic we introduce an iterated conditional as a suitable random quantity which satisfies the compound prevision theorem and some of the desirable properties. Finally, we remark that all the basic properties are satisfied by the iterated conditional mainly developed in recent papers by Gilio and Sanfilippo in the setting of conditonal random quantities.

Keywords: Coherence · Conditional events · Conditional random quantities · Conditional previsions · Conjoined and disjoined conditionals · Iterated conditionals · Compound probability theorem · Lower and upper bounds · Import-export principle

1 Introduction

The study of conditionals is a relevant research topic in many fields, like philosophy of science, psychology of uncertain reasoning, probability theory, conditional logics, knowledge representation (see, e.g., [1,2,11–13,15,16,18,31,32,35–37]). Usually, conjunctions and disjunctions among conditionals have been introduced in tri-valued logics (see, e.g., [1,4,8,9,31]) In particular, de Finetti in 1935 ([17]) proposed a three-valued logic (which coincides with Kleen-Lukasiewicz-Heyting

L. Castronovo and G. Sanfilippo—Both authors contributed equally to the article and are listed alphabetically.

G. Sanfilippo—Supported by the FFR project of University of Palermo and by the INdAM-GNAMPA Research Group, Italy.

F. Dupin de Saint-Cyr et al. (Eds.): SUM 2022, LNAI 13562, pp. 47–63, 2022.
https://doi.org/10.1007/978-3-031-18843-5_4

logic [9]) for conditional events by also introducing suitable notions of conjunction and disjunction. Calabrese in [5] introduced an algebra of conditionals by using the notions of quasi conjunction and quasi disjunction also studied in ([1]). Both, de Finetti and Calabrese, introduced a notion of iterated conditional as a suitable conditional event with the requirement, among other properties, that the Import-Export principle be satisfied, which means that the iterated conditional $(B|K)|A$ coincides with the conditional event $B|AK$. The validity of such a principle, jointly with the requirement of preserving the classical probabilistic properties, leads to the well-known Lewis' triviality results ([34]). Moreover, by defining conjunctions and disjunctions as conditional events (in a trivalent-logic) it follows that some classical probabilistic properties are lost; for instance, the lower and upper probability bounds for the conjunction are no more the Fréchet-Hoeffding bounds ([39]). A different approach to compound conditionals has been given in [32,35]. A related approach has been developed in the setting of coherence in recent papers by Gilio and Sanfilippo (see, e.g., [24–28]), where compound conditionals are defined as suitable conditional random quantities with a finite number of possible values in the interval $[0, 1]$. The advantage of this approach is that all the basic logical and probabilistic properties are preserved, for instance De Morgan's Laws and Fréchet-Hoeffding bounds; for a synthesis see [28]. The iterated conditional, named here $|_{gs}$, is defined by means of the structure $\square|\bigcirc = \square \wedge \bigcirc + \mathbb{P}(\square|\bigcirc)\overline{\bigcirc}$ (where $\mathbb{P}$ is the symbol of prevision) and hence satisfies the compound prevision theorem. Moreover, Lewis' triviality results are avoided because the Import-Export Principle is not satisfied (see [24,40,41]).

The purpose of this paper is to investigate some of the basic properties valid for events and conditional events with a view to different notions of iterated conditionals. Indeed, things get more problematic when we replace events with conditional events and we move to the properties of iterated conditionals. After recalling some trivalent logics (Kleene-Lukasiewicz-Heyting-de Finetti, Lukasiewicz, Bochvar-Kleene, and Sobocinski) we study basic properties for the notions of iterated conditional introduced by Calabrese and by de Finetti. We also compute some sets of coherent assessments on families of conditional events involving the previous two iterated conditionals. Among other things, we observe that the compound probability theorem is not preserved by these objects. Then, by exploiting the structure $\square|\bigcirc = \square \wedge \bigcirc + \mathbb{P}(\square|\bigcirc)\overline{\bigcirc}$, for each trivalent logic we introduce a suitable notion of iterated conditional which satisfies the compound prevision theorem and some (but not all) of the selected basic properties. Finally, we remark that, among the selected iterated conditionals, $|_{gs}$ is the only one which satisfies all the basic properties.

The paper is organized as follows. In Sect. 2 we first recall some preliminary notions and results on coherence, conditional events and conditional random quantities; then, we recall the logical operations in some trivalent logics and in the context of conditional random quantities. In Sect. 3 we check the validity of some logical and probabilistic properties satisfied by events and conditional events for the iterated conditional defined by Calabrese (Sect. 3.1) and by de

Finetti (Sect. 3.2). We also compute the lower and upper probability bounds for both the iterated conditionals. In Sect. 4, we recall some results on $\mid_{gs}$ and for each trivalent logic, we introduce and briefly study the iterated conditional defined as a suitable conditional random quantity. We also consider a generalized version of Bayes formula and give some results on the set of coherent assessments. Finally, we give some conclusion remarks.

2   Preliminary Notions and Results

In this section we recall some basic notions and results which concern coherence and logical operations among conditional events.

Events, Conditional Events, Conditional Random Quantities and Coherence. An event A is a two-valued logical entity which is either *true* (T), or *false* (F). We use the same symbol to refer to an event and its indicator. We denote by Ω the sure event and by $\varnothing$ the impossible one. We denote by $A \wedge B$ (resp., $A \vee B$), or simply by AB, the conjunction (resp., disjunction) of A and B. By $\overline{A}$ we denote the negation of A. We simply write $A \subseteq B$ to denote that A logically implies B, i.e., $A\overline{B} = \varnothing$. Given two events A and H, with $H \neq \varnothing$, the conditional event $A|H$ is a three-valued logical entity which is *true*, or *false*, or *void* (V), according to whether AH is true, or $\overline{A}H$ is true, or $\overline{H}$ is true, respectively. We recall that, given any conditional event $A|H$, the negation $\overline{A|H}$ is defined as $\overline{A|H} = \overline{A}|H$. The notion of logical inclusion among events has been generalized to conditional events by Goodman and Nguyen in [30]. Given two conditional events $A|H$ and $B|K$, we say that $A|H$ logically implies $B|K$, denoted by $A|H \subseteq B|K$, if and only if AH logically implies BK and $\overline{B}K$ logically implies $\overline{A}H$, that is

$$A|H \subseteq B|K \iff AH \subseteq BK \text{ and } \overline{B}K \subseteq \overline{A}H. \qquad (1)$$

In the betting framework, to assess $P(A|H) = x$ amounts to say that, for every real number s, you are willing to pay an amount $s\,x$ and to receive s, or 0, or $s\,x$, according to whether AH is true, or $\overline{A}H$ is true, or $\overline{H}$ is true (bet called off), respectively. Hence, for the random gain $G = sH(A - x)$, the possible values are $s(1 - x)$, or $-s\,x$, or 0, according to whether AH is true, or $\overline{A}H$ is true, or $\overline{H}$ is true, respectively. We denote by X a *random quantity*, that is an uncertain real quantity, which has a well determined but unknown value. We assume that X has a finite set of possible values. Given any event $H \neq \varnothing$, agreeing to the betting metaphor, if you assess that the prevision of "X *conditional on H*" (or short: "X *given H*"), $\mathbb{P}(X|H)$, is equal to μ, this means that for any given real number s you are willing to pay an amount $s\mu$ and to receive sX, or $s\mu$, according to whether H is true, or false (bet called off), respectively. The random gain is $G = s(XH + \mu\overline{H}) - s\mu = sH(X - \mu)$. In particular, when X is (the indicator of) an event A, then $\mathbb{P}(X|H) = P(A|H)$. Given a conditional event $A|H$ with $P(A|H) = x$, the indicator of $A|H$, denoted by the same symbol, is

$$A|H = AH + x\overline{H} = AH + x(1 - H) = \begin{cases} 1, & \text{if } AH \text{ is true,} \\ 0, & \text{if } \overline{A}H \text{ is true,} \\ x, & \text{if } \overline{H} \text{ is true.} \end{cases} \qquad (2)$$

Notice that it holds that $\mathbb{P}(AH + x\overline{H}) = xP(H) + xP(\overline{H}) = x$. The third value of the random quantity $A|H$ (subjectively) depends on the assessed probability $P(A|H) = x$. When $H \subseteq A$ (i.e., $AH = H$), it holds that $P(A|H) = 1$; then, for the indicator $A|H$ it holds that $A|H = AH + x\overline{H} = H + \overline{H} = 1$, (when $H \subseteq A$). Likewise, if $AH = \emptyset$, it holds that $P(A|H) = 0$; then $A|H = 0 + 0\overline{H} = 0$, (when $AH = \emptyset$). For the indicator of the negation of $A|H$ it holds that $\overline{A}|H = 1 - A|H$. Given two conditional events $A|H$ and $B|K$, for every coherent assessment (x, y) on $\{A|H, B|K\}$, it holds that ([28, formula (15)])

$$AH + x\overline{H} \leq BK + y\overline{K} \iff A|H \subseteq B|K, \text{ or } AH = \emptyset, \text{ or } K \subseteq B,$$

that is, between the numerical values of $A|H$ and $B|K$, under coherence it holds that

$$A|H \leq B|K \iff A|H \subseteq B|K, \text{ or } AH = \emptyset, \text{ or } K \subseteq B. \tag{3}$$

By following the approach given in [10,24,33], once a coherent assessment $\mu = \mathbb{P}(X|H)$ is specified, the conditional random quantity $X|H$ (is not looked at as the restriction to H, but) is defined as X, or μ, according to whether H is true, or $\overline{H}$ is true; that is,

$$X|H = XH + \mu\overline{H}. \tag{4}$$

As shown in (4), given any random quantity X and any event $H \neq \emptyset$, in the framework of subjective probability, in order to define $X|H$ we just need to specify the value μ of the conditional prevision $\mathbb{P}(X|H)$. Indeed, once the value μ is specified, the object $X|H$ is (subjectively) determined. We observe that (4) is consistent because

$$\mathbb{P}(XH + \mu\overline{H}) = \mathbb{P}(XH) + \mu P(\overline{H}) = \mathbb{P}(X|H)P(H) + \mu P(\overline{H}) = \mu P(H) + \mu P(\overline{H}) = \mu.$$

By (4), the random gain associated with a bet on $X|H$ can be represented as $G = s(X|H - \mu)$, that is G is the difference between what you receive, $sX|H$, and what you pay, $s\mu$. In what follows, for any given conditional random quantity $X|H$, we assume that, when H is true, the set of possible values of X is finite. In this case we say that $X|H$ is a finite conditional random quantity. Denoting by $\mathcal{X}_H = \{x_1, \ldots, x_r\}$ the set of possible values of X restricted to H and by setting $A_j = (X = x_j)$, $j = 1, \ldots, r$, it holds that $\bigvee_{j=1}^r A_j = H$ and $X|H = XH + \mu\overline{H} = x_1 A_1 + \cdots + x_r A_r + \mu\overline{H}$. Given a prevision function $\mathbb{P}$ defined on an arbitrary family $\mathcal{K}$ of finite conditional random quantities, consider a finite subfamily $\mathcal{F} = \{X_1|H_1, \ldots, X_n|H_n\} \subseteq \mathcal{K}$ and the vector $\mathcal{M} = (\mu_1, \ldots, \mu_n)$, where $\mu_i = \mathbb{P}(X_i|H_i)$ is the assessed prevision for the conditional random quantity $X_i|H_i$, $i \in \{1, \ldots, n\}$. With the pair $(\mathcal{F}, \mathcal{M})$ we associate the random gain $G = \sum_{i=1}^n s_i H_i(X_i - \mu_i) = \sum_{i=1}^n s_i(X_i|H_i - \mu_i)$. We denote by $\mathcal{G}_{\mathcal{H}_n}$ the set of values of G restricted to $\mathcal{H}_n = H_1 \vee \cdots \vee H_n$. Then, the notion of coherence is defined as below.

Definition 1. The function $\mathbb{P}$ defined on $\mathcal{K}$ is coherent if and only if, $\forall n \geq 1$, $\forall s_1, \ldots, s_n, \forall \mathcal{F} = \{X_1|H_1, \ldots, X_n|H_n\} \subseteq \mathcal{K}$, it holds that: $\min \mathcal{G}_{\mathcal{H}_n} \leq 0 \leq \max \mathcal{G}_{\mathcal{H}_n}$.

In other words, $\mathbb{P}$ on $\mathcal{K}$ is incoherent if and only if there exists a finite combination of n bets such that, after discarding the case where all the bets are called off, the values of the random gain are all positive or all negative. In the particular case where $\mathcal{K}$ is a family of conditional events, then Definition 1 becomes the well known definition of coherence for a probability function, denoted as P.

Given a family $\mathcal{F} = \{X_1|H_1, \ldots, X_n|H_n\}$, for each $i \in \{1, \ldots, n\}$ we denote by $\{x_{i1}, \ldots, x_{ir_i}\}$ the set of possible values of X_i when H_i is true; then, we set $A_{ij} = (X_i = x_{ij})$, $i = 1, \ldots, n$, $j = 1, \ldots, r_i$. We set $C_0 = \bar{H}_1 \cdots \bar{H}_n$ (it may be $C_0 = \varnothing$) and we denote by $C_1, \ldots, C_m$ the constituents contained in $\mathcal{H}_n = H_1 \vee \cdots \vee H_n$. Hence $\bigwedge_{i=1}^{n}(A_{i1} \vee \cdots \vee A_{ir_i} \vee \bar{H}_i) = \bigvee_{h=0}^{m} C_h$. With each C_h, $h \in \{1, \ldots, m\}$, we associate a vector $Q_h = (q_{h1}, \ldots, q_{hn})$, where $q_{hi} = x_{ij}$ if $C_h \subseteq A_{ij}$, $j = 1, \ldots, r_i$, while $q_{hi} = \mu_i$ if $C_h \subseteq \bar{H}_i$; with C_0 we associate $Q_0 = \mathcal{M} = (\mu_1, \ldots, \mu_n)$. Denoting by $\mathcal{I}$ the convex hull of $Q_1, \ldots, Q_m$, the condition $\mathcal{M} \in \mathcal{I}$ amounts to the existence of a vector $(\lambda_1, \ldots, \lambda_m)$ such that: $\sum_{h=1}^{m} \lambda_h Q_h = \mathcal{M}$, $\sum_{h=1}^{m} \lambda_h = 1$, $\lambda_h \geq 0$, $\forall h$; in other words, $\mathcal{M} \in \mathcal{I}$ is equivalent to the solvability of the system (Σ), associated with $(\mathcal{F}, \mathcal{M})$,

$$(\Sigma) \quad \sum_{h=1}^{m} \lambda_h q_{hi} = \mu_i, \ i \in \{1, \ldots, n\}, \sum_{h=1}^{m} \lambda_h = 1, \ \lambda_h \geq 0, \ h \in \{1, \ldots, m\}. \quad (5)$$

Given the assessment $\mathcal{M} = (\mu_1, \ldots, \mu_n)$ on $\mathcal{F} = \{X_1|H_1, \ldots, X_n|H_n\}$, let S be the set of solutions $\Lambda = (\lambda_1, \ldots, \lambda_m)$ of system (Σ). We point out that the solvability of system (Σ) is a necessary (but not sufficient) condition for coherence of $\mathcal{M}$ on $\mathcal{F}$. When (Σ) is solvable, that is $S \neq \varnothing$, we define:

$$\Phi_i(\Lambda) = \Phi_j(\lambda_1, \ldots, \lambda_m) = \sum_{r: C_r \subseteq H_i} \lambda_r, \ ; \ \Lambda \in S, M_i = \max_{\Lambda \in S} \Phi_i(\Lambda), \ i \in \{1, \ldots, n\};$$
$$I_0 = \{i : M_i = 0\}, \mathcal{F}_0 = \{X_i|H_i, i \in I_0\}, \ \mathcal{M}_0 = (\mu_i, i \in I_0). \quad (6)$$

For what concerns the probabilistic meaning of I_0, it holds that $i \in I_0$ if and only if the (unique) coherent extension of $\mathcal{M}$ to $H_i|\mathcal{H}_n$ is zero. Then, the following theorem can be proved ([3, Theorem 3]):

Theorem 1. A conditional prevision assessment $\mathcal{M} = (\mu_1, \ldots, \mu_n)$ on the family $\mathcal{F} = \{X_1|H_1, \ldots, X_n|H_n\}$ is coherent if and only if the following conditions are satisfied: (i) the system (Σ) defined in (5) is solvable; (ii) if $I_0 \neq \varnothing$, then $\mathcal{M}_0$ is coherent.

Of course, the previous results can be used in the case of conditional events. In particular, given a probability assessment $\mathcal{P} = (p_1, \ldots, p_n)$ on a family of n conditional events $\mathcal{F} = \{E_1|H_1, \ldots, E_n|H_n\}$, we can determine the constituents $C_0, C_1, \ldots, C_m$, where $C_0 = \bar{H}_1 \cdots \bar{H}_n$, and the associated points $Q_0, Q_1, \ldots, Q_m$, where $Q_0 = \mathcal{P}$. We observe that $Q_h = (q_{h1}, \ldots, q_{hn})$, with $q_{hi} \in \{1, 0, p_i\}$, $i = 1, \ldots, n$, $h = 1, \ldots, m$.

Trivalent Logics, Logical Operations of Conditionals and Conditional Random Quantities. We recall some notions of conjunction among conditional events in some trivalent logics: Kleene-Lukasiewicz-Heyting conjunction $(\wedge_K)$, or de Finetti conjunction ([14]); Lukasiewicz conjunction $(\wedge_L)$; Bochvar internal conjunction, or Kleene weak conjunction $(\wedge_B)$; Sobocinski conjunction, or quasi conjunction $(\wedge_S)$. In all these definitions the result of the conjunction is still a conditional event with set of truth values $\{true, false, void\}$ (see, e.g., [8,9]). We also recall the notions of conjunction among conditional events, $\wedge_{gs}$, introduced as a suitable conditional random quantity in a betting-scheme context ([24,25], see also [32,35]). We list below in an explicit way the five conjunctions and the associated disjunctions obtained by De Morgan's law ([22]):

1. $(A|H) \wedge_K (B|K) = AHBK|(HK \vee \overline{A}H \vee \overline{B}K)$,
   $(A|H) \vee_K (B|K) = (AH \vee BK)|(\overline{A}H\overline{B}K \vee AH \vee BK)$;
2. $(A|H) \wedge_L (B|K) = AHBK|(HK \vee \overline{A}\,\overline{B} \vee \overline{A}\,\overline{K} \vee \overline{B}\,\overline{H} \vee \overline{H}\,\overline{K})$,
   $(A|H) \vee_L (B|K) = (AH \vee BK)|(\overline{A}H\overline{B}K \vee AH \vee BK \vee \overline{H}\,\overline{K})$;
3. $(A|H) \wedge_B (B|K) = AHBK|HK$,
   $(A|H) \vee_B (B|K) = (A \vee B)|HK$;
4. $(A|H) \wedge_S (B|K) = ((AH \vee \overline{H}) \wedge (BK \vee \overline{K}))|(H \vee K)$,
   $(A|H) \vee_S (B|K) = (AH \vee BK)|(H \vee K)$;
5. $(A|H) \wedge_{gs} (B|K) = (AHBK + P(A|H)\overline{H}BK + P(B|K)AH\overline{K})|(H \vee K)$,
   $(A|H) \vee_{gs} (B|K) = (AH \vee BK + P(A|H)\overline{H}\,\overline{B}K + P(B|K)\overline{A}H\overline{K})|(H \vee K)$.

The operations above are all commutative and associative. By setting $P(A|H) = x$, $P(B|K) = y$, $P[(A|H) \wedge_i (B|K)] = z_i$, $i \in \{K, L, B, S\}$, and $\mathbb{P}[(A|H) \wedge_{gs} (B|K)] = z_{gs}$, based on (2) and on (4) the conjunctions $(A|H) \wedge_i (B|K)$, $i \in \{K, L, B, S, gs\}$ can be also looked at as random quantities with set of possible value illustrated in Table 1. A similar interpretation can also be given for the associated disjunctions. Notice that, differently from conditional events which are three-valued objects, the conjunction $(A|H) \wedge_{gs} (B|K)$ (and the associated disjunction) is no longer a three-valued object, but a five-valued object with values in $[0, 1]$. In betting terms, the prevision $z_{gs} = \mathbb{P}[(A|H) \wedge_{gs} (B|K)]$ represents the amount you agree to pay, with the proviso that you will receive the random quantity $AHBK + x\overline{H}BK + yAH\overline{K}$, if $H \vee K$ is true, z_{gs} if $\overline{H}\,\overline{K}$ is true. In other words by paying z_{gs} you receive: 1, if both conditional events

Table 1. Numerical values (of the indicator) of the conjunctions $\wedge_i$, $i \in \{K, L, B, S, gs\}$. The triplet (x, y, z_i) denotes a coherent assessment on $\{A|H, B|K, (A|H) \wedge_i (B|K)\}$.

	$A|H$	$B|K$	$\wedge_K$	$\wedge_L$	$\wedge_B$	$\wedge_S$	$\wedge_{gs}$
$AHBK$	1	1	1	1	1	1	1
$AH\overline{B}K$	1	0	0	0	0	0	0
$AH\overline{K}$	1	y	z_K	z_L	z_B	1	y
$\overline{A}HBK$	0	1	0	0	0	0	0
$\overline{A}H\overline{B}K$	0	0	0	0	0	0	0
$\overline{A}H\,\overline{K}$	0	y	0	0	z_B	0	0
$\overline{H}BK$	x	1	z_K	z_L	z_B	1	x
$\overline{H}\,\overline{B}K$	x	0	0	0	z_B	0	0
$\overline{H}\,\overline{K}$	x	y	z_K	0	z_B	z_S	z_{gs}

are true; 0, if at least one of the conditional event is false; the probability of the conditional event that is void if one conditional event is void and the other one is true; the amount z_{gs} you paid if both conditional events are void. The notion of conjunction $\wedge_{gs}$ (and disjunction $\vee_{gs}$) among conditional events has been generalized to the case of n conditional events in [25]. For some applications see, .e.g., [21,40,41]. Developments of this approach to general compound conditionals has been given in [20]. Differently from the other notions of conjunctions, $\wedge_{gs}$ preserves the classical logical and probabilistic properties valid for uncon-ditional events (see, e.g., [28]). In particular, the Fréchet-Hoeffding bounds, i.e., the lower and upper bounds $z' = \max\{x + y - 1, 0\}, z'' = \min\{x, y\}$, obtained under logical independence in the unconditional case for the coherent extensions $z = P(AB)$ of $P(A) = x$ and $P(B) = y$, when A and B are replaced by $A|H$ and $B|K$, are only satisfied by z_{gs} (see Table 2).

Table 2. Lower and upper bounds z', z'' for the selected conjunctions $\wedge_K, \wedge_L, \wedge_B,$ $\wedge_S, \wedge_{gs}$, for the given assessment $x = P(A|H)$ and $y = P(B|K)$ ([39]).

	$\wedge_K$	$\wedge_L$	$\wedge_B$	$\wedge_S$	$\wedge_{gs}$
z'	0	0	0	$\max\{x + y - 1, 0\}$	$\max\{x + y - 1, 0\}$
z''	$\min\{x, y\}$	$\min\{x, y\}$	1	$\begin{cases} \frac{x+y-2xy}{1-xy}, & \text{if } (x,y) \neq (1,1) \\ 1, & \text{if } (x,y) = (1,1) \end{cases}$	$\min\{x, y\}$

3   Some Basic Properties and Iterated Conditionals

We recall some basic logical and probabilistic properties satisfied by events and conditional events. Notice that, from (2), $B|A = AB + P(B|A)\overline{A}$.

(P1) $B|A = AB|A$;
(P2) $AB \subseteq B|A$, and $P(AB) \leq P(B|A)$;
(P3) $P(AB) = P(B|A)P(A)$ (*compound probability theorem*);
(P4) given two logical independent events A, B, with $P(A) = x$ and $P(B) = y$, the extension $\mu = P(B|A)$ is coherent if and only if $\mu \in [\mu', \mu'']$, where (see, e.g. [41, Theorem 6])

$$\mu' = \begin{cases} \frac{\max\{x+y-1,0\}}{x}, & \text{if } x \neq 0, \\ 0, & \text{if } x = 0, \end{cases}, \quad \mu'' = \begin{cases} \frac{\min\{x,y\}}{x}, & \text{if } x \neq 0, \\ 1, & \text{if } x = 0. \end{cases} \quad (7)$$

We will check the validity of the properties above when replacing events A, B by conditional events $A|H, B|K$ for the notion of iterated conditional introduced in the trivalent logics by Calabrese and by de Finetti, respectively.

3.1   The Iterated Conditional of Calabrese

We analyze the iterated conditional, here denoted by $(B|K)|_C(A|H)$, introduced by Calabrese in [5] (see also [6,7]).

Definition 2. *Given any pair of conditional events $A|H$ and $B|K$, the iterated conditional $(B|K)|_C(A|H)$ is defined as*

$$(B|K)|_C(A|H) = B|(K \wedge (\overline{H} \vee A)). \tag{8}$$

We observe that in (8) the conditioning event is the conjunction of the conditioning event K of the consequent $B|K$ and the material conditional $\overline{H} \vee A$ associated with the antecedent $A|H$. By applying Definition 2 with $H = \Omega$, it holds that $(B|K)|_C A = ABK|AK = B|AK$, which shows that the Import-Export principle (i.e., $(B|K)|A = B|AK$, see, e.g., [35]) is satisfied by the iterated conditional $|_C$.

By recalling that the notions of conjunction and disjunction of conditionals used by Calabrese ([5]) coincide with $\wedge_S$ and $\vee_S$, respectively, we observe that

$$[(A|H) \wedge_S (B|K)]|_C(A|H) = [(AHBK \vee AH\overline{K} \vee \overline{H}BK)|(H \vee K)]|_C(A|H) =$$
$$= (AHBK \vee AH\overline{K} \vee \overline{H}BK)|(AK \vee \overline{H}K \vee AH\overline{K}). \tag{9}$$

From (8) and (9) it follows that $(B|K)|_C(A|H) \neq ((A|H) \wedge_S (B|K))|_C(A|H)$. Indeed, as illustrated by Table 3, when the constituent $AH\overline{K}$ is true, it holds that $(B|K)|_C(A|H)$ is void, while $[(A|H) \wedge_S (B|K)]|_C(A|H)$ is true. Then, property (P1) is not satisfied by the pair $(\wedge_S, |_C)$. From Table 3 we also obtain that property (P2) is not satisfied by $(\wedge_S, |_C)$. Indeed, when $AH\overline{K}$ is true, it holds that $(A|H) \wedge_S (B|K)$ is true, while $(B|K)|_C(A|H)$ is void and hence $((A|H) \wedge_S (B|K)) \not\subseteq (B|K)|_C(A|H)$.

Table 3. Truth values of $(A|H) \wedge_S (B|K)$, $(B|K)|_C(A|H)$, and $[(A|H) \wedge_S (B|K)]|_C(A|H)$.

C_h	$(A|H) \wedge_S (B|K)$	$(B|K)|_C(A|H)$	$[(A|H) \wedge_S (B|K)]|_C(A|H)$
$AHBK \vee \overline{H}BK$	True	True	True
$AH\overline{B}K \vee \overline{H}\,\overline{B}K$	False	False	False
$AH\overline{K}$	True	Void	True
$\overline{A}H$	False	Void	Void
$\overline{H}\,\overline{K}$	Void	Void	Void

Now let us focus our attention on the following results regarding the coherence of a probability assessment on $\{A|H, (B|K)|_C(A|H), (A|H) \wedge_S (B|K)\}$ (Theorem 2) and on $\{A|H, B|K, (B|K)|_C(A|H)\}$ (Theorem 3).

Theorem 2. *Let A, B, H, K be any logically independent events. A probability assessment $\mathcal{P} = (x, y, z)$ on the family of conditional events $\mathcal{F} = \{A|H, (B|K)|_C(A|H), (A|H) \wedge_S (B|K)\}$ is coherent if and only if $(x, y) \in [0, 1]^2$ and $z \in [z', z'']$, where $z' = xy$ and $z'' = max(x, y)$.*

Proof. Due to lack of space we illustrate the proof only for the lower bound $z' = xy$. The constituents C_h's and the points Q_h's associated with the assessment

$\mathcal{P} = (x, y, z)$ on $\mathcal{F}$ are $C_1 = AHBK, C_2 = \overline{A}H, C_3 = \overline{H}BK, C_4 = AH\overline{B}K, C_5 = \overline{H}\,\overline{B}K, C_6 = AH\overline{K}, C_0 = \overline{H}\,\overline{K}$ and $Q_1 = (1, 1, 1)$, $Q_2 = (0, y, 0)$, $Q_3 = (x, 1, 1), Q_4 = (1, 0, 0), Q_5 = (x, 0, 0)$, $Q_6 = (1, y, 1)$, $\mathcal{P} = Q_0 = (x, y, z)$. The system (Σ) in (5) associated with the pair $(\mathcal{F}, \mathcal{P})$ becomes

$$\begin{cases} \lambda_1 + x\lambda_3 + \lambda_4 + x\lambda_5 + \lambda_6 = x, \ \lambda_1 + y\lambda_2 + \lambda_3 + y\lambda_6 = y, \\ \lambda_1 + \lambda_3 + \lambda_6 = z, \lambda_1 + \cdots + \lambda_6 = 1, \ \lambda_i \geq 0 \ \forall i = 1, \ldots, 6. \end{cases} \quad (10)$$

We observe that, for every $(x, y) \in [0, 1]^2$, it holds that $\mathcal{P} = (x, y, xy) = xyQ_1 + (1 - x)Q_2 + x(1 - y)Q_4$. Then, $\mathcal{P} \in \mathcal{I}$, where $\mathcal{I}$ is the convex hull of $Q_1, \cdots Q_6$, with a solution of (10) given by $\Lambda = (xy, 1 - x, 0, x(1 - y), 0, 0)$. For the functions ϕ_j, as defined in (6), it holds that $\phi_1(\Lambda) = \sum_{h:C_h \subseteq H} \lambda_h = \lambda_1 + \lambda_2 + \lambda_4 + \lambda_6 = xy + (1 - x) + x(1 - y) = 1 > 0$, $\phi_2(\Lambda) = \sum_{h:C_h \subseteq (A \vee \overline{H}) \vee K} \lambda_h = x$, $\phi_3(\Lambda) = \sum_{h:C_h \subseteq H \vee K} \lambda_h = 1 > 0$. We distinguish two cases: (i) $x > 0$, (ii) $x = 0$. In the case (i) we get $\phi_1 = \phi_3 = 1 > 0$ and $\phi_2 > 0$; then $\mathcal{I}_0 = \varnothing$. By Theorem 1, the assessment (x, y, xy) is coherent $\forall (x, y) \in [0, 1]^2$. In the case (ii) we get $\mathcal{I}_0 \subseteq \{2\}$, with the sub-assessment $\mathcal{P}_0 = y$ on $\mathcal{F}_0 = \{(B|K)|_C(A|H)\}$ coherent for every $y \in [0, 1]$. Then, by Theorem 1, the assessment (x, y, xy) on $\mathcal{F}$ is coherent for every $(x, y) \in [0, 1]^2$. In order to prove that $z' = xy$ is the lower bound for $z = P((A|H) \wedge_S (B|K))$, we verify that (x, y, z), with $(x, y) \in [0, 1]^2$ and $z < z' = xy$, is not coherent because $(x, y, z) \notin \mathcal{I}$. We observe that the points Q_1, Q_2, Q_4 belong to the plane $\pi : yX + Y - Z = y$. We set $f(X, Y, Z) = yX + Y - Z$ and we obtain $f(Q_1) = f(Q_2) = f(Q_4) = y$, $f(Q_3) = f(Q_5) = xy \leq y$, $f(Q_6) = f(1, y, 1) = y + y - 1 = 2y - 1 \leq y$. Then, by considering $\mathcal{P} = (x, y, z)$, with $z < xy$, it holds that $f(\mathcal{P}) = f(x, y, z) = xy + y - z > y \geq f(Q_h), h = 1, \ldots, 6$, and hence $\mathcal{P} = (x, y, z) \notin \mathcal{I}$. Indeed, if it were $\mathcal{P} \in \mathcal{I}$, that is $\mathcal{P}$ linear convex combination of $Q_1, \ldots, Q_6$, it would follow that $f(\mathcal{P}) = f(\sum_{h=1}^{6} \lambda_h Q_h) = \sum_{h=1}^{6} \lambda_h f(Q_h) \leq y$. Thus, the lower bound for $z = P((A|H) \wedge_S (B|K))$ is $z' = xy$.

From Theorem 2 any probability assessment (x, y, z) on $\mathcal{F} = \{A|H, (B|K)|_C (A|H), (A|H) \wedge_S (B|K)\}$, with $(x, y) \in [0, 1]^2$ and $xy \leq z \leq max(x, y)$ is coherent. Thus, as $z = xy$ is not the unique coherent extension of the conjunction $(A|H) \wedge_S (B|K)$, in general the quantity $P[(A|H) \wedge_S (B|K)]$ do not coincide with the product $P[(B|K)|_C(A|H)]P(A|H)$. For example, it could be that $P[(B|K)|_C(A|H)]P(A|H) = 0 < P[(A|H) \wedge_S (B|K)] = 1$, because the assessment $(1, 0, 1)$ on $\mathcal{F}$ is coherent (while it is not coherent on $\{A, B|A, AB\}$). Then, property (P3) is not satisfied by the pair $(\wedge_S, |_C)$.

Theorem 3. *Let A, B, H, K be any logically independent events. The probability assessments $\mathcal{P} = (x, y, z)$ on the family of conditional events $\mathcal{F} = \{A|H, B|K, (B|K)|_C(A|H)\}$ is coherent for every $(x, y, z) \in [0, 1]^3$.*

Proof. The proof is omitted due to lack of space.

We observe that the probability propagation rule valid for unconditional events (property (P4)) is no longer valid for Calabrese's iterated conditional. Indeed, from Theorem 3, any probability assessment (x, y, z) on $\mathcal{F} = \{A|H, B|K, (B|K)|_C(A|H)\}$, with $(x, y, z) \in [0, 1]^3$ is coherent. For instance, the assessment $(1, 1, 0)$ on $\mathcal{F}$ is coherent, while it is not coherent on $\{A, B, B|A\}$.

3.2   The Iterated Conditional of de Finetti

We now analyze the iterated conditional introduced by de Finetti in [14].

Definition 3. *Given any pair of conditional events $A|H$ and $B|K$, de Finetti iterated conditional, denoted by $(B|K)|_{df}(A|H)$, is defined as*

$$(B|K)|_{df}(A|H) = B|(AHK). \tag{11}$$

By applying Definition 3 with $H = \Omega$, it holds that $(B|K)|_{df} A = B|AK$, which shows that the Import-Export principle [35] is satisfied by $|_{df}$. We recall that the notion of conjunction and disjunction of conditionals introduced by de Finetti in [14] coincide with $\wedge_K$ and $\vee_K$ recalled in Sect. 2. From (11) it holds that

$$[(A|H) \wedge_K (B|K)]|_{df}(A|H) = [AHBK|(HK \vee \overline{A}H \vee \overline{B}K)]|_{df}(A|H) = \\ AHBK|(AHK \vee AH\overline{B}K) = AHBK|AHK = (B|K)|_{df}(A|H). \tag{12}$$

Then, property (P1) is satisfied by the pair $(\wedge_K, |_{df})$ (see also Table 4). From Table 4 we also observe that relation (P2) is satisfied by $(\wedge_K, |_{df})$. Indeed, according to (1), if $(A|H) \wedge_K (B|K)$ is true, then $(B|K)|_{df}(A|H)$ is true; if $(B|K)|_{df}(A|H)$ is false, then $(A|H) \wedge_K (B|K)$ is false. We consider now the following results regarding the coherence of a probability assessment on $\{A|H, (B|K)|_{df}(A|H), (A|H) \wedge_K (B|K)\}$ (Theorem 4) and on $\{A|H, B|K, (B|K)|_{df}(A|H)\}$ (Theorem 5).

Table 4. Truth table of $(A|H) \wedge_K (B|K)$, $(B|K)|_{df}(A|H)$, and $[(A|H) \wedge_K (B|K)]|_{df}(A|H)$.

C_h	$(A|H) \wedge_K (B|K)$	$(B|K)|_{df}(A|H)$	$[(A|H) \wedge_K (B|K)]|_{df}(A|H)$
$AHBK$	True	True	True
$AH\overline{B}K$	False	False	False
$AH\overline{K} \vee \overline{H}BK \vee \overline{H}\,\overline{K}$	Void	Void	Void
$\overline{A}H \vee \overline{H}\,\overline{B}K$	False	Void	Void

Theorem 4. *Let A, B, H, K be any logically independent events. A probability assessment $\mathcal{P} = (x, y, z)$ on the family of conditional events $\mathcal{F} = \{A|H, (B|K)|_{df}(A|H), (A|H) \wedge_K (B|K)\}$ is coherent if and only if $(x, y) \in [0, 1]^2$ and $z \in [z', z'']$, where $z' = 0$ and $z'' = xy$.*

Proof. The proof is omitted due to lack of space.

From Theorem 4 any probability assessment (x, y, z) on $\mathcal{F} = \{A|H, (B|K)|_{df}(A|H), (A|H) \wedge_K (B|K)\}$, with $(x, y) \in [0, 1]^2$ and $0 \leq z \leq xy$, is coherent. Thus, as $z = xy$ is not the unique coherent extension of the conjunction $(A|H) \wedge_K (B|K)$, the quantity $P[(A|H) \wedge_K (B|K)]$ could not coincide with the product

$P[(B|K)|_{df}(A|H)]P(A|H)$. For example, if we choose the probability assessment $\mathcal{P} = (1, 1, 0)$, it is coherent on $\mathcal{F}$ but not on $\{A, B|A, AB\}$ because $P[(A|H) \wedge_K (B|K)] = 0 < P[(B|K)|_{df}(A|H)]P(A|H) = 1$.

Then, property (P3) is not satisfied by the pair $(\wedge_K, |_{df})$.

Theorem 5. *Let* A, B, H, K *be any logically independent events. The probability assessments* $\mathcal{P} = (x, y, z)$ *on the family of conditional events* $\mathcal{F} = \{A|H, B|K, (B|K)|_{df}(A|H)\}$ *is coherent for every* $(x, y, z) \in [0, 1]^3$.

Proof. The proof is omitted due to lack of space.

We observe that the probability propagation rule valid for unconditional events (P4) is no longer valid for de Finetti's iterated conditional. Indeed, from Theorem 5, any probability assessment (x, y, z) on $\mathcal{F} = \{A|H, B|K, (B|K)|_{df}(A|H)\}$, with $(x, y, z) \in [0, 1]^3$ is coherent. For instance, the assessment $(1, 1, 0)$ is coherent on $\mathcal{F}$ but it is not coherent on $\{A, B, B|A\}$.

4 Iterated Conditionals and Compound Prevision Theorem

In [23] (see also [40]), by using the structure

$$\square|\bigcirc = \square \wedge \bigcirc + \mathbb{P}(\square|\bigcirc)\overline{\bigcirc}, \tag{13}$$

which reduces to formula (2) when $\square = A, \bigcirc = H$, given two conditional events $A|H$, $B|K$, with $AH \neq \emptyset$, the iterated conditional $(B|K)|_{gs}(A|H)$ has been defined as the following conditional random quantity

$$(B|K)|_{gs}(A|H) = (A|H) \wedge_{gs} (B|K) + \mu_{gs}(\overline{A}|H). \tag{14}$$

We now examine the different definitions of iterated conditional (see Table 5), beyond $|_{gs}$, we can obtain by using the structure (13) and each conjunction: $\wedge_K, \wedge_L, \wedge_B, \wedge_S$.

Definition 4. *Given two conditional events* $A|H$, $B|K$, *with* $AH \neq \emptyset$, *for each* $i \in \{K, L, B, S\}$, *we define the iterated conditional* $(B|K)|_i(A|H)$ *as*

$$(B|K)|_i(A|H) = (A|H) \wedge_i (B|K) + \mu_i(\overline{A}|H), \tag{15}$$

where $\mu_i = \mathbb{P}[(B|K)|_i(A|H)]$.

Remark 1. We remind that, in agreement with [1,32] and differently from [35], for the iterated conditional $(B|K)|_{gs}(A|H)$ the Import-Export principle is not valid. As a consequence, as shown in [24] (see also [40,41]), Lewis' triviality results ([34]) are avoided by $|_{gs}$. It can be easily proved that $(B|K)|_i A \neq B|AK$, $i \in \{K, L, B, S\}$. Then, the Import-Export principle is not satisfied by any of the iterated conditional $|_K, |_L, |_B, |_S, |_{gs}$.

For each pair $(\wedge_i, |_i)$, $i \in \{K, L, B, S, gs\}$, we show the validity of properties (P1)–(P3) introduced in Sect. 3, where the events A, B are replaced by the conditional events $A|H$, $B|K$, respectively. Then, we discuss the validity of generalized versions of Bayes's Theorem and the validity of property (P4).

(P1). We recall that the pair $(\wedge_{gs}, |_{gs})$ satisfies property (P1) because $((A|H) \wedge_{gs} (B|K))|_{gs}(A|H) = (B|K)|_{gs}(A|H)$ ([29, Theorem 5]). Moreover, each pair $(\wedge_i, |_i)$, $i \in \{K, L, B, S\}$, also satisfies property (P1) as shown by the following result.

Theorem 6. *Given two conditional events $A|H$, $B|K$, with $AH \neq \emptyset$, it holds that*

$$((A|H) \wedge_i (B|K))|_i(A|H) = (B|K)|_i(A|H), \quad i \in \{K, L, B, S\}. \tag{16}$$

Proof. Let be given $i \in \{K, L, B, S\}$. We set $\mu_i = \mathbb{P}[(B|K)|_i(A|H)]$ and $\nu_i = \mathbb{P}[((A|H) \wedge (B|K))|_i(A|H)]$. By Definition 4, as $(A|H) \wedge_i (A|H) \wedge_i (B|K) = (A|H) \wedge_i (B|K)$, it holds that

$$((A|H) \wedge_i (B|K))|_i(A|H) = (A|H) \wedge_i (B|K) + \nu_i(\overline{A}|H). \tag{17}$$

From (15) and (17), in order to prove (16) it is enough to verify that $\nu_i = \mu_i$. We observe that $((A|H) \wedge_i (B|K))|_i(A|H) - (B|K)|_i(A|H) = (\nu_i - \mu_i)(\overline{A}|H)$, where $\nu_i - \mu_i = \mathbb{P}[((A|H) \wedge_i (B|K))|_i(A|H) - (B|K)|_i(A|H)]$. By setting $P(A|H) = x$, it holds that

$$(\nu_i - \mu_i)(\overline{A}|H) = \begin{cases} 0, & \text{if } A|H = 1, \\ \nu_i - \mu_i, & \text{if } A|H = 0, \\ (\nu_i - \mu_i)(1 - x), & \text{if } A|H = x, \ 0 < x < 1. \end{cases}$$

Notice that, in the betting scheme, $\nu_i - \mu_i$ is the amount to be paid in order to receive the random amount $(\nu_i - \mu_i)(\overline{A}|H)$. Then, by coherence, $\nu_i - \mu_i$ must be a linear convex combination of the possible values of $(\nu_i - \mu_i)(\overline{A}|H)$, by discarding the cases where the bet called off, that is the cases where you receive back the paid amount $\nu_i - \mu_i$, whatever $\nu_i - \mu_i$ be. In other words, coherence requires that $\nu_i - \mu_i$ must belong to the convex hull of the set $\{0, (\nu_i - \mu_i)(1 - x)\}$, that is $\nu_i - \mu_i = \alpha \cdot 0 + (1 - \alpha)(\nu_i - \mu_i)(1 - x)$, for some $\alpha \in [0, 1]$. Then, as $0 < x < 1$, we observe that the previous equality holds if and only if $\nu_i - \mu_i = 0$, that is $\nu_i = \mu_i$. Therefore, equality (16) holds.

(P2). Coherence requires that $\mu_i \geq 0$, $i \in \{K, L, B, S, gs\}$. Then, from (15) it holds that $(A|H) \wedge_i (B|K) \leq (B|K)|_i(A|H)$, $i \in \{K, L, B, S, gs\}$ and hence $P[(A|H) \wedge_i (B|K)] \leq \mathbb{P}[(B|K)|_i(A|H)]$, $i \in \{K, L, B, S, gs\}$. Therefore, each pair $(\wedge_i, |_i)$, $i \in \{K, L, B, S, gs\}$ satisfies the numerical counterpart of (P2), where, based on (3), the symbol $\subseteq$ is replaced by $\leq$.

(P3). We recall that the pair $(\wedge_{gs}, |_{gs})$ satisfies (P3) because, by exploiting the structure (13), it holds that $\mathbb{P}[(A|H) \wedge_{gs} (B|K)] = \mathbb{P}[(B|K)|_{gs}(A|H)]P(A|H)$ ([23]). Concerning the pairs $(\wedge_i, |_i)$, $i \in \{K, L, B, S\}$ we show below that (P3) is also valid. Indeed, for the linearity of prevision, from (15), we obtain that

$$\begin{aligned} \mu_i = \mathbb{P}[(B|K)|_i(A|H)] &= \mathbb{P}[(B|K) \wedge_i (A|H)] + \mu_i \mathbb{P}(\overline{A}|H) = \\ &= \mathbb{P}[(B|K) \wedge (A|H)] + \mu_i P(\overline{A}|H) = z_i + \mu_i(1 - x), \end{aligned} \tag{18}$$

Table 5. Numerical values of $(B|K)|_i(A|H)$, $i \in \{K, L, B, S, gs\}$. We denotes $x = P(A|H)$, $y = P(B|K)$, and $\mu_i = \mathbb{P}[(B|K)|_i(A|H)]$, $i \in \{K, L, B, S, gs\}$.

	$(B|K)|_K(A|H)$	$(B|K)|_L(A|H)$	$(B|K)|_B(A|H)$	$(B|K)|_S(A|H)$	$(B|K)|_{gs}(A|H)$
$AHBK$	1	1	1	1	1
$AH\overline{B}K$	0	0	0	0	0
$AH\overline{K}$	$x\mu_K$	$x\mu_L$	$x\mu_B$	1	y
$\overline{A}HK$	μ_K	μ_L	μ_B	μ_S	μ_{gs}
$\overline{A}H\,\overline{K}$	μ_K	μ_L	$\mu_B(1+x)$	μ_S	μ_{gs}
$\overline{H}BK$	μ_K	μ_L	μ_B	$1+\mu_S(1-x)$	$x+\mu_{gs}(1-x)$
$\overline{H}\,\overline{B}K$	$\mu_K(1-x)$	$\mu_L(1-x)$	μ_B	$\mu_S(1-x)$	$\mu_{gs}(1-x)$
$\overline{H}\,\overline{K}$	μ_K	$\mu_L(1-x)$	μ_B	μ_S	μ_{gs}

where $z_i = \mathbb{P}((A|H) \wedge_i (B|K))$, $i \in \{K, L, B, S\}$. As $\mu_i = z_i + \mu_i(1-x)$, it follows that $z_i = \mu_i x$, for $i \in \{K, L, B, S\}$. In other words, coherence requires that

$$\mathbb{P}[(A|H) \wedge_i (B|K)] = \mathbb{P}[(B|K)|_i(A|H)]P(A|H), \quad i \in \{K, L, B, S\}, \qquad (19)$$

which states that the compound prevision theorem (property (P3)) is valid for each pair $(\wedge_i, |_i)$, $i \in \{K, L, B, S\}$.

Remark 2. By exploiting the compound prevision theorem, we analyze generalized versions of Bayes' Theorem for the iterated conditionals $|_K, |_L, |_B, |_S, |_{gs}$. As $\mathbb{P}[(B|K) \wedge_i (A|H)] = \mathbb{P}[(B|K)|_i(A|H)]P(A|H) = \mathbb{P}[(A|H)|_i(B|K)]P(B|K)$, $i \in \{K, L, B, S, gs\}$, when $P(A|H) > 0$ it holds that

$$\mathbb{P}[(B|K)|_i(A|H)] = \frac{\mathbb{P}[(A|H)|_i(B|K)]P(B|K)}{P(A|H)}, \, i \in \{K, L, B, S, gs\}, \qquad (20)$$

which generalizes the Bayes's formula $P(B|A) = \frac{P(A|B)P(B)}{P(A)}$. We now analyze the validity of the generalization of Bayes's Theorem given in the following version: $P(B|A) = \frac{P(A|B)P(B)}{P(A|B)P(B)+P(A|\overline{B})P(\overline{B})}$. We recall that, given two events A and B, it holds that $A = AB \vee A\overline{B}$, and hence $P(A) = P(AB) + P(A\overline{B}) = P(A|B)P(B) + P(A|\overline{B})P(\overline{B})$. However, when A, B are replaced by the conditional events $A|H, B|K$, respectively, we obtain that (see [22])

- $[(A|H) \wedge_K (B|K)] \vee_K [(A|H) \wedge_K (\overline{B}|K)] = AHK|(AHK \vee \overline{A}H) \neq A|H$;
- $[(A|H) \wedge_L (B|K)] \vee_L [(A|H) \wedge_L (\overline{B}|K)] = AHK|(H \vee \overline{K}) \neq A|H$;
- $[(A|H) \wedge_B (B|K)] \vee_B [(A|H) \wedge_B (\overline{B}|K)] = A|(HK) \neq A|H$;
- $[(A|H) \wedge_S (B|K)] \vee_S [(A|H) \wedge_S (\overline{B}|K)] = (A \vee \overline{H})|(H \vee K) \neq A|H$;
- $[(A|H) \wedge_{gs} (B|K)] \vee_{gs} [(A|H) \wedge_{gs} (\overline{B}|K)] = A|H$.

Then, for each $i \in \{K, L, B, S\}$, $P(A|H)$ cannot be decomposed as $\mathbb{P}((A|H) \wedge_i (B|K)) + \mathbb{P}((A|H) \wedge_i (\overline{B}|K)) = \mathbb{P}((A|H)|_i(B|K))P(B|K) + \mathbb{P}((A|H)|_i(\overline{B}|K))P(\overline{B}|K)$, while $P(A|H) = \mathbb{P}((A|H) \wedge_{gs} (B|K)) + \mathbb{P}((A|H) \wedge_{gs} (\overline{B}|K)) =$

$\mathbb{P}((A|H)|_{gs}(B|K))P(B|K) + \mathbb{P}((A|H)|_{gs}(\overline{B}|K))P(\overline{B}|K)$. Hence, for each $i \in \{K, L, B, S\}$, $\mathbb{P}[(B|K)|_i(A|H)]$ does not in general coincide with $\mathbb{P}((A|H)|_i (B|K))P(B|K)/(\mathbb{P}((A|H)|_i(B|K))P(B|K) + \mathbb{P}((A|H)|_i(\overline{B}|K))P(\overline{B}|K))$, while

$$\mathbb{P}[(B|K)|_{gs}(A|H)] = \frac{\mathbb{P}((A|H)|_{gs}(B|K))P(B|K)}{\mathbb{P}((A|H)|_{gs}(B|K))P(B|K) + \mathbb{P}((A|H)|_{gs}(\overline{B}|K))P(\overline{B}|K)}. \tag{21}$$

Therefore, the generalization of the second version of Bayes' formula only holds for $|_{gs}$ and does not hold for $|_K, |_L, |_B$, and $|_S$.

(P4). Concerning the pair $(\wedge_K, |_K)$, we have the following result

Theorem 7. *Let A, B, H, K be any logically independent events. The set Π of all the coherent assessment (x, y, z, μ) on the family $\mathcal{F} = \{A|H, B|K, (A|H) \wedge_K (B|K), (B|K)|_K(A|H)\}$ is $\Pi = \Pi' \cup \Pi''$, where $\Pi' = \{(x, y, z, \mu) : x \in (0, 1], y \in [0, 1], z \in [z', z''], \mu = \frac{z}{x}\}$ with $z' = 0$, $z'' = min\{x, y\}$, and $\Pi'' = \{(0, y, 0, \mu) : (y, \mu) \in [0, 1]^2\}$.*

Proof. The proof is omitted due to lack of space.

Based on Theorem 7, as the assessment $(1, 1, 0, 0)$ on $\{A|H, B|K, (A|H) \wedge_K (B|K), (B|K)|_K(A|H)\}$ is coherent, it follows that the sub-assessment $(1, 1, 0)$ on $\{A|H, B|K, (B|K)|_K(A|H)\}$ is coherent too. However, the assessment $(1, 1, 0)$ on $\{A, B, B|A\}$ is not coherent because by (7) it holds that $0 = \mu < \mu' = \frac{max\{1+1-1, 0\}}{1} = 1$. Then, formula (P4) is not satisfied by $|_K$.

Concerning the pair $(\wedge_L, |_L)$ it can be easily shown that statement of Theorem 7 also holds when $\wedge_K, |_K$ are replaced by $\wedge_L, |_L$, respectively. Then, also $|_L$ does not satisfy property (P4).

We now focus on the pair $(\wedge_B, |_B)$. We recall that the assessment $(x, y, 1)$ on $\{A|H, B|K, (A|H) \wedge_B (B|K)\}$ is coherent for every $(x, y) \in [0, 1]^2$ (see Table 2). Then, when $0 < x < 1$, the extension $\mu = \mathbb{P}[(B|K)|_B(A|H)] = \frac{\mathbb{P}[(A|H) \wedge_B (B|K)]}{P(A|H)} = \frac{1}{x} > 1$ is coherent and hence property (P4) is not satisfied by $|_B$, because by (7) it holds that $\mu > 1 \geq \mu''$.

Likewise, we observe that the assessment $(x, 1, 1)$ on $\{A|H, B|K, (A|H) \wedge_S (B|K)\}$ is coherent for every $x \in [0, 1]$ (see Table 2). Then, when $0 < x < 1$, as $\mathbb{P}[(B|K)|_S(A|H)] = \frac{1}{x}$, the extension $\mu = \frac{1}{x} > 1$ on $(B|K)|_S(A|H)$ is coherent. That is, it is coherent to assess $\mathbb{P}[(B|K)|_S(A|H)] > 1$ and hence property (P4) is not satisfied by $|_S$.

Finally, differently from the other iterated conditionals, we recall that $|_{gs}$ satisfies (P4) ([41, Theorem 4]). Indeed, given a coherent assessment (x, y) on $\{A|H, B|K\}$, under logical independence, for the iterated conditional $(B|K)|_{gs}(A|H)$ the extension $\mu = \mathbb{P}((B|K)|_{gs}(A|H))$ is coherent if and only if $\mu \in [\mu', \mu'']$, where $\mu' = \begin{cases} \frac{max\{x+y-1, 0\}}{x}, & \text{if } x \neq 0, \\ 0, & \text{if } x = 0, \end{cases}$, $\mu'' = \begin{cases} \frac{min\{x, y\}}{x}, & \text{if } x \neq 0, \\ 1, & \text{if } x = 0. \end{cases}$

5 Conclusions

We recalled some trivalent logics (Kleene-Lukasiewicz-Heyting-de Finetti, Lukasiewicz, Bochvar-Kleene, and Sobocinski) and the notion of compound conditional as conditional random quantity. We considered some basic logical and probabilistic properties, valid for events and conditional events, by checking their validity for selected notions of iterated conditional. In particular, we studied the iterated conditionals introduced in trivalent logics by Calabrese and by de Finetti, by also focusing on the numerical representation of the truth-values. For both the iterated conditionals we computed the lower and upper bounds and we showed that some basic properties are not satisfied. Then, for each trivalent logic, we introduced the iterated conditional $(|_K, |_L, |_B, |_S)$ defined by exploiting the same structure used in order to define $|_{gs}$, that is as a suitable random quantity which satisfies the compound prevision theorem. We observed that all the basic properties are satisfied only by the iterated conditional $|_{gs}$. Future work will concern the deepening of other logical and probabilistic properties of the iterated conditionals $|_K, |_L, |_B$, and $|_S$ in the framework of nonmonotonic reasoning, Boolean algebras of conditionals ([18,19]), and in other non-classical logics, like connexive logic ([38]).

Acknowledgements. We thank the three anonymous reviewers for their useful comments and suggestions. We also thank the Gugino Prize committee of University of Palermo.

References

1. Adams, E.W.: The Logic of Conditionals. Reidel, Dordrecht (1975)
2. Benferhat, S., Dubois, D., Prade, H.: Nonmonotonic reasoning, conditional objects and possibility theory. Artif. Intell. **92**, 259–276 (1997)
3. Biazzo, V., Gilio, A., Sanfilippo, G.: Generalized coherence and connection property of imprecise conditional previsions. In: Proceedings of IPMU 2008, Malaga, Spain, 22–27 June 2008, pp. 907–914 (2008)
4. Calabrese, P.G.: An algebraic synthesis of the foundations of logic and probability. Inf. Sci. **42**(3), 187–237 (1987)
5. Calabrese, P.G.: Reasoning with uncertainty using conditional logic and probability. In: Proceedings of ISUMA 1990, pp. 682–688 (1990)
6. Calabrese, P.G.: Logic and Conditional Probability: A Synthesis. College Publications, Pompton Lakes (2017)
7. Calabrese, P.G.: Deduction with uncertain conditionals (revised & simplified, with examples). Heliyon **7**(11), e08328 (2021)
8. Ciucci, D., Dubois, D.: Relationships between connectives in three-valued logics. In: Advances on Computational Intelligence, CCIS, vol. 297, pp. 633–642 (2012)
9. Ciucci, D., Dubois, D.: A map of dependencies among three-valued logics. Inf. Sci. **250**, 162–177 (2013)
10. Coletti, G., Scozzafava, R.: Conditioning and inference in intelligent systems. Soft Comput. **3**(3), 118–130 (1999)

11. Coletti, G., Scozzafava, R., Vantaggi, B.: Coherent conditional probability, fuzzy inclusion and default rules. In: Soft Computing: State of the Art Theory and Novel Applications, pp. 193–208. Springer, Heidelberg (2013). https://doi.org/10.1007/978-3-642-34922-5_14
12. Coletti, G., Scozzafava, R., Vantaggi, B.: Possibilistic and probabilistic logic under coherence: default reasoning and System P. Mathematica Slovaca **65**(4), 863–890 (2015)
13. Cruz, N.: Deduction from uncertain premises? In: Logic and Uncertainty in the Human Mind: A Tribute to David E. Over, pp. 27–41. Routledge, Oxon (2020)
14. de Finetti, B.: La Logique de la Probabilité. In: Actes du Congrès International de Philosophie Scientifique, Paris, 1935, pp. IV 1–IV 9. Hermann et C.ie, Paris (1936)
15. Douven, I., Elqayam, S., Singmann, H., van Wijnbergen-Huitink, J.: Conditionals and inferential connections: toward a new semantics. In: Thinking & Reasoning, pp. 1–41 (2019)
16. Dubois, D., Prade, H.: Conditional objects as nonmonotonic consequence relationships. IEEE Trans. Syst. Man Cybern. **24**(12), 1724–1740 (1994)
17. de Finetti, B.: La logique de la probabilité. In: Actes du Congrès International de Philosophie Scientifique, Paris, 1935, pp. IV 1–IV 9 (1936)
18. Flaminio, T., Godo, L., Hosni, H.: Boolean algebras of conditionals, probability and logic. Artif. Intell. **286**, 103347 (2020)
19. Flaminio, T., Gilio, A., Godo, L., Sanfilippo, G.: Canonical extensions of conditional probabilities and compound conditionals. In: Proceedings of IPMU 2022, CCIS, vol. 1602, pp. 584–597. Springer, Heidelberg (2022). https://doi.org/10.1007/978-3-031-08974-9_47
20. Flaminio, T., Gilio, A., Godo, L., Sanfilippo, G.: Compound conditionals as random quantities and Boolean algebras. In: Proceedings of KR2022, pp. 141–151 (2022)
21. Gilio, A., Pfeifer, N., Sanfilippo, G.: Probabilistic entailment and iterated conditionals. In: Logic and Uncertainty in the Human Mind: A Tribute to David E. Over, pp. 71–101. Routledge, Oxon (2020)
22. Gilio, A., Sanfilippo, G.: Subjective probability, trivalent logics and compound conditionals. Submitted
23. Gilio, A., Sanfilippo, G.: Conjunction, disjunction and iterated conditioning of conditional events. In: Synergies of Soft Computing and Statistics for Intelligent Data Analysis. AISC, vol. 190, pp. 399–407. Springer, Heidelberg (2013). https://doi.org/10.1007/978-3-642-33042-1_43
24. Gilio, A., Sanfilippo, G.: Conditional random quantities and compounds of conditionals. Studia Logica **102**(4), 709–729 (2014)
25. Gilio, A., Sanfilippo, G.: Generalized logical operations among conditional events. Appl. Intell. **49**(1), 79–102 (2019)
26. Gilio, A., Sanfilippo, G.: Algebraic aspects and coherence conditions for conjoined and disjoined conditionals. Int. J. Approx. Reason. **126**, 98–123 (2020)
27. Gilio, A., Sanfilippo, G.: Compound conditionals, Fréchet-Hoeffding bounds, and Frank t-norms. Int. J. Approx. Reason. **136**, 168–200 (2021)
28. Gilio, A., Sanfilippo, G.: On compound and iterated conditionals. Argumenta **6**(2), 241–266 (2021)
29. Gilio, A., Sanfilippo, G.: Iterated conditionals and characterization of p-entailment. In: Vejnarová, J., Wilson, N. (eds.) ECSQARU 2021. LNCS (LNAI), vol. 12897, pp. 629–643. Springer, Cham (2021). https://doi.org/10.1007/978-3-030-86772-0_45
30. Goodman, I.R., Nguyen, H.T.: Conditional objects and the modeling of uncertainties. In: Gupta, M.M., Yamakawa, T. (eds.) Fuzzy Computing, pp. 119–138. North-Holland (1988)

31. Goodman, I.R., Nguyen, H.T., Walker, E.A.: Conditional Inference and Logic for Intelligent Systems: A Theory of Measure-Free Conditioning. North-Holland (1991)
32. Kaufmann, S.: Conditionals right and left: probabilities for the whole family. J. Phil. Logic **38**, 1–53 (2009)
33. Lad, F.: Operational Subjective Statistical Methods: A Mathematical, Philosophical, and Historical Introduction. Wiley, New York (1996)
34. Lewis, D.: Probabilities of conditionals and conditional probabilities. Phil. Rev. **85**(3), 297–315 (1976)
35. McGee, V.: Conditional probabilities and compounds of conditionals. Phil. Rev. **98**(4), 485–541 (1989)
36. Nguyen, H.T., Walker, E.A.: A history and introduction to the algebra of conditional events and probability logic. IEEE Trans. Syst. Man Cybern. **24**(12), 1671–1675 (1994)
37. Petturiti, D., Vantaggi, B.: Modeling agent's conditional preferences under objective ambiguity in dempster-shafer theory. Int. J. Approx. Reason. **119**, 151–176 (2020)
38. Pfeifer, N., Sanfilippo, G.: Interpreting connexive principles in coherence-based probability logic. In: Vejnarová, J., Wilson, N. (eds.) ECSQARU 2021. LNCS (LNAI), vol. 12897, pp. 672–687. Springer, Cham (2021). https://doi.org/10.1007/978-3-030-86772-0_48
39. Sanfilippo, G.: Lower and upper probability bounds for some conjunctions of two conditional events. In: Ciucci, D., Pasi, G., Vantaggi, B. (eds.) SUM 2018. LNCS (LNAI), vol. 11142, pp. 260–275. Springer, Cham (2018). https://doi.org/10.1007/978-3-030-00461-3_18
40. Sanfilippo, G., Gilio, A., Over, D., Pfeifer, N.: Probabilities of conditionals and previsions of iterated conditionals. Int. J. Approx. Reason. **121**, 150–173 (2020)
41. Sanfilippo, G., Pfeifer, N., Over, D., Gilio, A.: Probabilistic inferences from conjoined to iterated conditionals. Int. J. Approx. Reason. **93**(Supplement C), 103–118 (2018)

Using Atomic Bounds to Get Sub-modular Approximations

Sébastien Destercke[1($\boxtimes$)], Agnes Rico[2], and Olivier Strauss[3]

[1] UMR CNRS 7253, Heudiasyc, Sorbonne Université,
Université de Technologie de Compiègne, Compiègne, France
sebastien.destercke@hds.utc.fr
[2] ERIC, Claude Bernard Université Lyon 1, Lyon, France
Agnes.Rico@univ-lyon1.fr
[3] LIRMM, Univ. Montpellier, CNRS, Montpellier, France
Olivier.Strauss@umontpellier.fr

Abstract. Set functions and inferences over them play an important role in many AI-related problems. They are commonly used in kernel-based methods, game theory, uncertainty representation and preference modelling. Of particular importance are additive set-functions and their associated expectation operator, as well as sub-modular functions. However, specifying precisely and completely such set functions can be a daunting task as well as a lot of data and knowledge. When time or information is missing, it may be handy to have approximating tools of such set-functions, that require less information and possibly enjoy nice mathematical properties. In this paper, we show that if the only information we have are atomic bounds of such functions, we can build conservative approximations that are either sub- or super-modular. We then illustrate the potential use of our approximation on a convolution-based signal processing problem.

1 Introduction

Set functions or measures play an important role in many aspects of artificial intelligence. The most well-known are undoubtedly probability measures, i.e., additive, normalised positive set functions. Increasing set functions, called capacities or fuzzy measures, generalise such probability measures. They appeared in 50's, and have been extensively used in areas related to decision [1]. In particular, they can represent the weights of coalitions in cooperative games, or measures of uncertainty such as lower probabilities or belief functions (see [12]). Particular fuzzy measures that are maxitive rather than additive are possibility measures [22], the basic building blocks of possibility theory [4,5].

Other capacities that have attracted a lot of attention are sub-modular functions, as they have taken a very important role in many aspects of artificial intelligence. They are used in numerous problems of machine learning and signal processing [11,18], in social choice theory where they can be used to induce fairness in the obtained solutions [3], and in modelling preferences in item selection problems [19]. Indeed, the sub-modularity property comes with many advantages, notably the one to be able to use greedy optimisation algorithms with good guaranteed approximation properties.

© The Author(s), under exclusive license to Springer Nature Switzerland AG 2022
F. Dupin de Saint-Cyr et al. (Eds.): SUM 2022, LNAI 13562, pp. 64–78, 2022.
https://doi.org/10.1007/978-3-031-18843-5_5

There are good reasons to consider set functions that are not necessarily increasing with respect to set inclusion, nor that are normalized as probability or possibility measures can be. A question that follows is whether approximation tools allowing for efficient inferences are still valid in such contexts. This is the question we address in this paper, where we focus on approximation obtained by considering atomic bounds (i.e., lower/upper bounds over singletons).

The paper is structured as follows. Section 2 is a brief recall of set-functions and their use. We will focus on additive set functions and sub-modular set functions. Section 3 is devoted to the approximation of set of additive set-functions and sub-modular functions. Section 4 presents an application to signal convolution.

2   Set-Functions and Their Use

In this paper, we are concerned with approximating (sets) of discrete set-functions. By set function κ over a finite space $\mathcal{X} = \{x_1, \ldots, x_n\}$, we understand a bounded real-valued function $\kappa : 2^{\mathcal{X}} \to \mathbb{R}$ from the power set of $\mathcal{X}$ to the reals. We furthermore assume that $\kappa(\emptyset) = 0$. The *conjugate* κ^c of a set function κ is $\kappa^c(A) = \kappa(\mathcal{X}) - \kappa(A^c)$.

2.1   Additive Set-Functions and Expectation

One of the most widespread set functions are additive ones, i.e., set functions defined from a mass distribution $\psi : \mathcal{X} \to \mathbb{R}$ assigning a mass to each element, from which we have $\kappa_\psi(A) = \sum_{x \in A} \psi(x)$ (in the rest of the paper, we denote by κ_ψ additive measures derived from the mass distribution ψ).

Once we are given such a set-function, a very common operator applied to them to make inferences is the linear expectation operator. If we have a real valued bounded function $f : \mathcal{X} \to \mathbb{R}$, such an operator is

$$\mathbb{E}_{\kappa_\psi}(f) = \sum_{x \in \mathcal{X}} f(x)\psi(x) \tag{1}$$

$$= \sum_{i=1}^{n} (f(x_{[i]}) - f(x_{[i-1]}))\kappa_\psi(A_{[i]}), \tag{2}$$

where $[.]$ is the permutation such that $(f(x_{[1]}) \leq \cdots \leq f(x_{[N]}))$, $A_{[i]} = \{x_{[i]}, \ldots, x_{[N]}\}$ with, by convention, $x_{[0]} = 0$ and $A_{[N+1]} = \emptyset$. Equations (2) will be helpful when considering sub-modular functions later on.

If we assume that ψ is non-negative, $\psi \geq 0$, and that $\kappa_\psi(\mathcal{X}) = \sum_{x \in \mathcal{X}} \psi(x) = 1$, we retrieve classical probabilities and (1) is just standard expectations. Also, ψ being positive ensures that the obtained function κ is monotonic with respect to inclusion, i.e., $\kappa_\psi(A) \geq \kappa_\psi(B)$ whenever $B \subseteq A$.

In this paper, however, we make neither of these two assumptions, i.e., $\kappa_\psi(\mathcal{X})$ can be any real value, as well as $\psi(x)$ that can be negative. This latter relaxation implies that we may have $B \subseteq A$ but $\kappa_\psi(A) > \kappa_\psi(B)$.

While the latter property may seem odd to some readers, there are good reasons to consider such a relaxation. For instance, deriving a signal through convolution (the application of Sect. 4 is of this kind), we are considering a non-null function ψ such that $\kappa(\mathcal{X}) = 0$, meaning that some values of ψ must be negative. Similarly, in social ranking problems [14], the elements x_i can be individuals and one search to assess/order the performances of groups or subsets of individuals. In this case, it can be that two groups $A \subset B$ are such that B performs worse than A ($A \succ B$), for instance because B contains individuals that do not get along together and worsen the whole group performance. Should such a statement be numerically encoded as a set function, we should have $\kappa_\psi(A) > \kappa_\psi(B)$.

Example 1. Consider a digital signal f taking values on two successive points:

$$f(x_1) = 3, f(x_2) = 5$$

computing its derivative in x_2 comes down to compute $\mathbb{E}_{\kappa_\psi}$ with $\psi(x_1) = -1, \psi(x_2) = 1$, giving $\mathbb{E}_{\kappa_\psi} = 2$.

2.2 Sub-modular Set Functions

Another kind of set functions that are widely used in artificial intelligence are sub-modular set functions. Sub-modularity means that, for any pair $A, B \subseteq \mathcal{X}$ of event, κ is such that

$$\kappa(A \cup B) + \kappa(A \cap B) \leq \kappa(A) + \kappa(B), \tag{3}$$

or equivalently [15, Ch. 44] that, for any $A \subseteq B$ and any $x \notin B$, we have

$$\kappa(A \cup \{x\}) - \kappa(A) \geq \kappa(B \cup \{x\}) - \kappa(B). \tag{4}$$

This latter formulation is sometimes referred as the property of *diminishing return*, modelling the fact that element $\{x\}$ has a higher value when added to a smaller subset.

However, in contrast with the additive case, specifying a sub-modular set-function requires in general to specify or to work with $2^{|\mathcal{X}|}$ values, a daunting quantity. In practice, it may be useful to have approximations requiring to collect and work with a limited number of values. In this paper, we will see that this can be done by simply considering $2|\mathcal{X}|$ values of κ. Note that the idea of non-monotonic (w.r.t. inclusion), non-additive set functions already appears in [10], precisely to model numerically rankings of subsets.

Sub-modular set functions have many interesting properties, but we will only mention those useful for our purpose, and proved in [7]. A first property is that its *core*

$$\mathcal{C}_\kappa = \{\psi : \forall A \subseteq \mathcal{X}, \kappa_\psi(A) \leq \kappa(A), \psi(\mathcal{X}) = \kappa(\mathcal{X})\}, \tag{5}$$

that is the set of additive measures that is dominated by it is never empty. In particular, this means that sub-modular set functions can be useful to describe or approximate sets of additive set functions, e.g., in convolution problems where the convolution filter is ill-known.

A second property one can also show [7] that applying the Choquet integral to a bounded function $f : \mathcal{X} \to \mathbb{R}$ gives

$$\overline{\mathbb{E}}_\kappa(f) = \sum_{i=1}^n (f(x_{[i]}) - f(x_{[i-1]}))\kappa(A_{[i]}), \tag{6}$$

$$= \sup_{\psi \in \mathcal{C}_\kappa} \mathbb{E}_{\kappa_\psi}(f) \tag{7}$$

Similar properties apply to the super-modular κ^c

$$\underline{\mathbb{E}}_\kappa(f) = \sum_{i=1}^{n}(f(x_{[i]}) - f(x_{[i-1]}))\kappa^c(A_{[i]}), \tag{8}$$

$$= \inf_{\psi \in \mathcal{C}_\kappa} \mathbb{E}_{\kappa_\psi}(f) \tag{9}$$

3 Approximating Set-Functions with Atomic Bounds

In this section, we provide our main results concerning non-additive set functions, that show that one can build sub-modular approximations by only focusing on atomic bounds of some sets of additive measures or of some initial sub-modular function. This provides a very easy way to get approximations by focusing on only $2n$ values.

3.1 Approximating Sets of Additive Set-Functions

We first consider the case where we have a set $\mathcal{M}$ of possible additive measures. In signal processing, those may come from the fact that the convoluting kernel has an ill-known bandwidth, while in preference modelling they may represent the doubt an agent has about the strength or rankings of coalitions. $\mathcal{M}$ may also be a neighbourhood around some initial distribution ψ_0, used for instance to make a sensitivity/robustness study around ψ_0.

However, working with general sets $\mathcal{M}$ is highly inconvenient, whether they are discrete or continuous. We will now show that we can easily obtain a sub-modular approximation of $\mathcal{M}$. To do this, we will denote by

$$\underline{\psi}(x) = \inf_{\psi \in \mathcal{M}} \psi(x),$$

$$\overline{\psi}(x) = \sup_{\psi \in \mathcal{M}} \psi(x).$$

Let us now define the two set functions

$$\underline{\mu}_{\mathcal{M}}(A) = \max\left(\sum_{x \in A} \underline{\psi}(x), \kappa_\psi(\mathcal{X}) - \sum_{x \in A^c} \overline{\psi}(x)\right), \tag{10}$$

$$\overline{\mu}_{\mathcal{M}}(A) = \min\left(\sum_{x \in A} \overline{\psi}(x), \kappa_\psi(\mathcal{X}) - \sum_{x \in A^c} \underline{\psi}(x)\right), \tag{11}$$

with $\kappa_\psi(\mathcal{X})$ the value for any $\psi \in \mathcal{M}$. The subscript $\mu_{\mathcal{M}}$ denotes that μ originates from a set of additive measures.

Example 2. Let us assume that some group of persons want to pack some food before going on a hike. They can choose between (a)pples, (b)ananas, (c)horizo and (d)anish pastries, so that $\mathcal{X} = \{a, b, c, d\}$. In order to know what to take (it is impossible to take all four types of food), members of the group are allowed to distribute 10 points between all food types to express their individual preferences. They can also give negative scores (up to -5) if they really dislike a food. We assume that food values are additive. So we know that $\kappa_\psi(\mathcal{X}) = 10$, and the span of scores given by the group to each type of food is summarised in Table 1. Everyone likes apples as even the lower score $\underline{\psi}$ is positive (some more than others), but some dislikes bananas (e.g., because of their taste) while some dislikes chorizo (e.g., as they are vegetarian). We can now try to assess the possible values of various packages to compare them. For instance, evaluating the set $\{a, b, c\}$, we get

Table 1. Table of scores of example 2.

Food ($\mathcal{X}$)	a	b	c	d
$\overline{\psi}$	5	7	4	4
$\underline{\psi}$	1	-3	-3	-2

$$\overline{\mu}(\{a, b, c\}) = \min(5 + 7 + 4, 10 - (-2)) = 12$$

$$\underline{\mu}(\{a, b, c\}) = \max(1 - 3 - 3, 10 - 4) = 6$$

so that this package is clearly interesting, for instance compared to $\{b, c, d\}$ for which $\overline{\mu}(\{b, c, d\}) = 9$.

We will now study the properties of the set functions given by Eqs. 10–11. Let us first show that the two set functions are conjugate ones.

Proposition 1. *For any $\mathcal{M}$, $\underline{\mu}_\mathcal{M}$ and $\overline{\mu}_\mathcal{M}$ are conjugate.*

Proof.

$$\underline{\mu}_\mathcal{M}(A) = \underline{\mu}_\mathcal{M}(\mathcal{X}) - \underline{\mu}_\mathcal{M}(A^c)$$
$$= \kappa_\psi(\mathcal{X}) - \max\{\sum_{x \notin A} \underline{\psi}(x), \kappa_\psi(\mathcal{X}) - \sum_{x \in A} \overline{\psi}(x)\}$$
$$= \min\{\kappa_\psi(\mathcal{X}) - \sum_{x \notin A} \underline{\psi}(x), \sum_{x \in A} \overline{\psi}(x)\} = \overline{\mu}_\mathcal{M}(A).$$

We can then show that $\overline{\mu}_\mathcal{M}$ can be used as a conservative approximation of $\mu_\mathcal{M}$, by the following proposition.

Proposition 2. *We have $\mathcal{M} \subseteq \mathcal{C}_{\overline{\mu}_\mathcal{M}}$.*

Proof. The proof simply consists in showing that for any $\psi \in \mathcal{M}$, we have $\psi(A) \leq \overline{\mu}(A)$ for any $A \subseteq \mathcal{X}$. To see this, observe that for any ψ, we have $\overline{\psi} \geq \psi$. This means that $\sum_{x \in A} \overline{\psi}(x) \geq \sum_{x \in A} \psi(x)$. Similarly, since $\underline{\psi} \leq \psi$, we have $\sum_{x \notin A} \underline{\psi}(x) \leq \sum_{x \notin A} \psi(x)$, hence $\kappa_\psi(\mathcal{X}) - \sum_{x \in A^c} \underline{\psi}(x) \geq \kappa_\psi(\mathcal{X}) - \sum_{x \in A^c} \psi(x) = \sum_{x \in A} \psi(x)$ where the last equality comes from ψ being additive and $\sum_{x \in \mathcal{X}} \psi(x) = \kappa_\psi(\mathcal{X})$.

We now demonstrate that $\underline{\mu}_{\mathcal{M}}$ is a super-modular set function. Among other things, this ensures that applying Eq. (8) (that is computationally cheap to evaluate) to a function f will yield bounds that correspond to an expectation operator applied to an additive measure.

Proposition 3. $\overline{\mu}_{\mathcal{M}}$ *is a sub-modular set function.*

Proof. Following the ideas of [6] that prove super-modularity of $\underline{\mu}_{\mathcal{M}}$ when ψ are probabilities, we will demonstrate the super-modularity of $\underline{\mu}_{\mathcal{M}}$, which by Proposition 1 is the same as proving sub-modularity of $\overline{\mu}_{\mathcal{M}}$. To do so, we consider arbitrary subsets $A, B \subseteq \mathcal{X}$ and we define the sets $C = A \cap B$ and $D = (A \cup B) \setminus (A \cap B)$. We have $C \cap D = \emptyset$ and $C \cup D = A \cup B$, as well as $\mu_{\mathcal{M}}(A \cap B) + \mu_{\mathcal{M}}(A \cup B) = \mu_{\mathcal{M}}(C) + \mu_{\mathcal{M}}(C \cup D)$. So we are going to prove the property considering C and D subsets such that $C \cap D = \emptyset$.

The idea of the proof is to define an additive set function $\kappa_{\psi} : 2^{\mathcal{X}} \to \mathbb{R}$ and its mass function ψ such that $\underline{\mu}_{\mathcal{M}}(C) = \kappa_{\psi}(C)$ and $\underline{\mu}_{\mathcal{M}}(C \cup D) = \kappa_{\psi}(C \cup D)$ and $\underline{\psi} \leq \psi \leq \overline{\psi}$.

This is sufficient to prove sub-modularity of $\underline{\mu}_{\mathcal{M}}$, since $\kappa_{\psi}(C) + \kappa_{\psi}(C \cup D) = \kappa_{\psi}(B) + \kappa_{\psi}(A)$ due to its additivity, and $\kappa_{\psi}(A) \geq \underline{\mu}_{\mathcal{M}}(A)$ and $\kappa_{\psi}(B) \geq \underline{\mu}_{\mathcal{M}}(B)$, follows from $\underline{\psi} \leq \psi \leq \overline{\psi}$.

There are four possible cases to study (two possible values for $\underline{\mu}_{\mathcal{M}}(C)$ and two for $\underline{\mu}_{\mathcal{M}}(C \cup D)$). All the cases are similar since the sets C and D are such that $C \cap D = \emptyset$. We will therefore provide the details for only one of them.

Let us consider the specific case $\underline{\mu}_{\mathcal{M}}(C) = \sum_{x \in C} \underline{\psi}(x)$ and $\underline{\mu}_{\mathcal{M}}(C \cup D) = \kappa(\mathcal{X}) - \sum_{x \notin C \cup D} \overline{\psi}(x)$. On each $x \in \mathcal{X}$ we are going to define the weights $\psi(x)$ as follows:

- $\forall x \in C, \psi(x) = \underline{\psi}(x)$,
- $\forall x \notin C \cup D, \psi(x) = \overline{\psi}(x)$,

This ensures that κ_{ψ} coincide with $\underline{\mu}_{\mathcal{M}}(C \cup D)$ and $\underline{\mu}_{\mathcal{M}}(C)$

We are now going to see how we can assign masses $d_x := \psi(x)$ on elements of the subset D so that that $\underline{\psi}(x) \leq \psi(x) = d_x \leq \overline{\psi}(x)$ and $\sum_{x \in \mathcal{X}} = \kappa(\mathcal{X})$. Observe that we still have to assign a total (potentially negative) mass $\kappa(\mathcal{X}) - \sum_{x \notin C \cup D} \overline{\psi}(x) - \sum_{x \in C} \underline{\psi}(x)$ on elements of D. To do so, consider first that, given the considered case, we have

$$\underline{\mu}_{\mathcal{M}}(C \cup D) - \underline{\mu}_{\mathcal{M}}(C) =$$
$$\kappa(\mathcal{X}) - \sum_{x \notin C \cup D} \overline{\psi}(x) - \sum_{x \in C} \underline{\psi}(x).$$

As, $\underline{\mu}_{\mathcal{M}}(C) = \sum_{x \in C} \underline{\psi}(x) \geq \kappa(\mathcal{X}) - \sum_{x \notin C} \overline{\psi}(x)$, we have

$$\underline{\mu}_{\mathcal{M}}(C \cup D) - \underline{\mu}_{\mathcal{M}}(C) \leq$$
$$\kappa(\mathcal{X}) - \sum_{x \notin C \cup D} \overline{\psi}(x) - \kappa(\mathcal{X}) + \sum_{x \notin C} \overline{\psi}(x) \leq \sum_{x \in D} \overline{\psi}(x).$$

Similarly, as $\underline{\mu}_{\mathcal{M}}(C \cup D) = \kappa(\mathcal{X}) - \sum_{x \notin C \cup D} \overline{\psi}(x) \geq \sum_{x \in C \cup D} \underline{\psi}(x)$, we have

$$\underline{\mu}_{\mathcal{M}}(C \cup D) - \underline{\mu}_{\mathcal{M}}(C)$$
$$\geq \sum_{x \in C \cup D} \underline{\psi}(x) - \sum_{x \in C} \underline{\psi}(x) = \sum_{x \in D} \underline{\psi}(x).$$

So $\sum_{x \in D} \underline{\psi}(x) \leq \underline{\mu}_{\mathcal{M}}(C \cup D) - \underline{\mu}_{\mathcal{M}}(C) \leq \sum_{x \in D} \overline{\psi}(x)$. This means that we can divide the difference $\underline{\mu}_{\mathcal{M}}(C \cup D) - \underline{\mu}_{\mathcal{M}}(C)$ (equal to the remaining mass to assign) on D and choose a real d_x for all $x \in D$ such that $\underline{\psi}(x) \leq d_x \leq \overline{\psi}(x)$ and $\sum_{x \in D} d_x = \underline{\mu}_{\mathcal{M}}(C \cup D) - \underline{\mu}_{\mathcal{M}}(C)$.

What Propositions 2 and 3 show is that previous results obtained for the probabilistic case (summative functions ψ summing up to one) readily extend to more general and complex cases, opening up new areas of applications such as the signal treatment one described in Sect. 4 and already suggested in Example 1.

3.2 Approximating Sub-modular Functions

We will now show that our approximation also works when one starts from a sub-modular function κ to approximate. There are at least two ways in which our proposed results can be useful: as an upper bound[1], it can be useful in Branch and Bound techniques applied to sub-modular optimization [20]; as a trace on the singletons of a potentially unknown κ, it allows to build an approximation of κ while collecting only a $2n$ of its values.

We consider a sub-modular $\kappa : 2^{\mathcal{X}} \to \mathbb{R}$. Recall that the conjugate set-function κ^c of κ is $\forall A, \kappa^c(A) = \kappa(\mathcal{X}) - \kappa(A^c)$. It is easy to check that for any pair $A, B \subseteq \mathcal{X}, \kappa^c$ is such that

$$\kappa^c(A \cup B) + \kappa^c(A \cap B) \geq \kappa^c(A) + \kappa^c(B),$$

it is super-modular. κ is sub-modular so we have $\kappa^c \leq \kappa$. Now let us assume that we know only κ and κ^c on each element $x \in \mathcal{X}$. This is equivalent to know κ on each x and $\{x\}^c$. In Example 2, this could amount to ask group member the value of every single food element, as well as the value of packages if we remove each food element, assuming that they aggregate values in a sub-modular way. By Eq. (4), it means that adding a food element to an existing package is all the less interesting as the package grows bigger, which seems a reasonable assumption.

For all $x \in \mathcal{X}$ let us define[2] $\underline{\psi}^\kappa(x) = \kappa^c(\{x\})$ and $\overline{\psi}^\kappa(x) = \kappa(\{x\})$. The knowledge of $\underline{\psi}^\kappa(x)$ and $\overline{\psi}^\kappa(x)$ entails the following property:

Proposition 4. $\sum_{x \in \mathcal{X}} \underline{\psi}^\kappa(x) \leq \kappa(\mathcal{X}) \leq \sum_{x \in \mathcal{X}} \overline{\psi}^\kappa(x)$.

Proof. $\underline{\psi}^k(x) \leq \overline{\psi}^k(x) = \kappa(\{x\}) = \kappa(\mathcal{X}) - \kappa^c(\{x\}^c) \leq \kappa(\mathcal{X}) - \sum_{x' \neq x} \underline{\psi}^k(x')$, so we have $\sum_{x \in \mathcal{X}} \underline{\psi}^k(x) \leq \kappa(\mathcal{X})$.

---

[1] Or lower bound if we consider the complementary measure.
[2] The reason for also calling them ψ is clarified in the proof of Proposition 6.

$\overline{\psi}^k(x) \geq \underline{\psi}^k(x) = \kappa^c(\{x\}) = \kappa(\mathcal{X}) - \kappa(\{x\}^c) \geq \kappa(\mathcal{X}) - \sum_{x' \neq x} \overline{\psi}^k(x')$, so we have
$\kappa(\mathcal{X}) \leq \sum_{x \in \mathcal{X}} \overline{\psi}^k(x)$. $\qquad\qquad\qquad\qquad\qquad\qquad\qquad\qquad\qquad\qquad$ □

As in the previous section, we now define two set functions

$$\underline{\mu}_\kappa(A) = \max\{\sum_{x \in A} \underline{\psi}^k(x), \kappa(\mathcal{X}) - \sum_{x \notin A} \overline{\psi}^k(x)\}, \qquad (12)$$

$$\overline{\mu}_\kappa(A) = \min\{\sum_{x \in A} \overline{\psi}^k(x), \kappa(\mathcal{X}) - \sum_{x \notin A} \underline{\psi}^k(x)\}, \qquad (13)$$

with the subscript κ denoting that they come from an initial sub-modular set function. We will now proceed to show that $\underline{\mu}_\kappa$ and $\overline{\mu}_\kappa$ approximate κ and that they are respectively sub-and super-modular. Indeed, even if κ has a non-empty core $\mathcal{C}_\kappa$, we are not especially interested in positioning $\underline{\mu}_\kappa$ and $\overline{\mu}_\kappa$ with respect to this core, but with respect to the initial κ. Let us first show that $\underline{\mu}_\kappa$ and $\overline{\mu}_\kappa$ can act as lower/upper bounds.

Proposition 5. $\underline{\mu}_\kappa \leq \kappa^c \leq \overline{\mu}_\kappa$.

Proof. Let us first prove that $\underline{\mu}_\kappa \leq \kappa^c$. There are two possible values for $\underline{\mu}_\kappa(A)$:

- If $\underline{\mu}_\kappa(A) = \sum_{x \in A} \underline{\psi}^k(x)$ then $\underline{\mu}_\kappa(A) \leq \kappa^c(A)$ since κ is a sub-modular set function.
- If $\underline{\mu}_\kappa(A) = \kappa(\mathcal{X}) - \sum_{x \notin A} \overline{\psi}^k(x)$ then $\sum_{x \notin A} \overline{\psi}^k(x) \geq \kappa(A^c) = \kappa(\mathcal{X}) - \kappa^c(A)$ which entails $\underline{\mu}_\kappa(A) \leq \kappa(\mathcal{X}) - \kappa(\mathcal{X}) + \kappa^c(A) = \kappa^c(A)$.

The proof of $\kappa^c \leq \overline{\mu}_\kappa$ is similar.

Note that Proposition 1 also applies here, from which follows that $\underline{\mu}_\kappa$ and $\overline{\mu}_\kappa$ can also be used to approximate κ, as we can reproduce Proposition 5 proof for κ.

Corollary 1. $\underline{\mu}_\kappa \leq \kappa^c \leq \kappa \leq \overline{\mu}_\kappa$

We can now prove that $\underline{\mu}_\kappa$ enjoys the same interesting property as the function κ it approximates.

Proposition 6. $\overline{\mu}_\kappa$ is a sub-modular set function i.e.,

$$\forall A, B \subseteq \mathcal{X}, \overline{\mu}_\kappa(A \cup B) + \overline{\mu}_\kappa(A \cup B) \leq \overline{\mu}_\kappa(A) + \overline{\mu}_\kappa(B).$$

Proof. The proof is quite simple once we notice that $\mathcal{C}_\kappa$ is not empty and that

$$\underline{\psi}^\kappa(x) = \inf_{\psi \in \mathcal{C}_\kappa} \psi(x)$$
$$\overline{\psi}^\kappa(x) = \sup_{\psi \in \mathcal{C}_\kappa} \psi(x),$$

which can be obtained by applying Eqs. (9) and (7) to the indicator function $\mathbb{I}_x$ ($= 1$ on x and zero everywhere else). Since the bounds $\underline{\psi}^\kappa$ and $\overline{\psi}^\kappa$ are atomic bounds over the set of additive measures $\mathcal{C}_\kappa$, one can apply Proposition 3.

Corollary 2. $\overline{\mu}_\kappa$ *is super-modular.*

Our results demonstrate that $\underline{\mu}_\kappa$ and $\overline{\mu}_\kappa$ are interesting approximations of a sub-modular function κ, possibly partially unknown. They are tight outer approximations, in the sense that as $\underline{\psi}^\kappa(x) = \kappa^c(\{x\})$ and $\overline{\psi}^\kappa(x) = \kappa(\{x\})$, any smaller intervals would not be outer approximations on the singletons. Finally, we can show an interesting link between the precision of the intervals $[\underline{\psi}^\kappa, \overline{\psi}^\kappa]$ and the functions $\overline{\mu}_\kappa, \underline{\mu}_\kappa$.

Proposition 7. *For all $A \subseteq \mathcal{X}$,*

$$|\overline{\mu}_\kappa(A) - \underline{\mu}_\kappa(A)| \leq card(A)\|u - l\|_{A,\infty}$$

where $\|u - l\|_{A,\infty} = \max_{x \in A} |\overline{\psi}(x) - \underline{\psi}(x)|$ and $card(A)$ is the cardinality of A.

Proof. According to the definition of $\underline{\mu}_\kappa$ and $\overline{\mu}_\kappa$, we have for possible cases.
$\overline{\mu}_\kappa(A) - \underline{\mu}_\kappa(A) =$

- $\overline{\mu}_\kappa(A) = \sum_{x \in A} \overline{\psi}^k(x) \leq \kappa(\mathcal{X}) - \sum_{x \notin A} \underline{\psi}^k(x)$
  $\underline{\mu}_\kappa(A) = \sum_{x \in A} \underline{\psi}^k(x) \geq \kappa(\mathcal{X}) - \sum_{x \notin A} \overline{\psi}^k(x).$
  $\overline{\mu}_\kappa(A) - \underline{\mu}_\kappa(A) = \sum_{x \in A}(\overline{\psi}^k(x) - \underline{\psi}^k(x)).$
- $\overline{\mu}_\kappa(A) = \sum_{x \in A} \overline{\psi}^k(x) \leq \kappa(\mathcal{X}) - \sum_{x \notin A} \underline{\psi}^k(x)$
  $\underline{\mu}_\kappa(A) = \kappa(\mathcal{X}) - \sum_{x \notin A} \overline{\psi}^k(x) \geq \sum_{x \in A} \underline{\psi}^k(x).$
  $\overline{\mu}_\kappa(A) - \underline{\mu}_\kappa(A) = \sum_{x \in A} \overline{\psi}^k(x) - \kappa(\mathcal{X}) + \sum_{x \notin A} \overline{\psi}^k(x) \leq \sum_{x \in A}(\overline{\psi}^k(x) - \underline{\psi}^k(x)).$
- $\overline{\mu}_\kappa(A) = \kappa(\mathcal{X}) - \sum_{x \notin A} \underline{\psi}^k(x) \leq \sum_{x \in A} \overline{\psi}^k(x)$
  $\underline{\mu}_\kappa(A) = \sum_{x \in A} \underline{\psi}^k(x) \geq \kappa(\mathcal{X}) - \sum_{x \notin A} \overline{\psi}^k(x).$
  $\overline{\mu}_\kappa(A) - \underline{\mu}_\kappa(A) = \kappa(\mathcal{X}) - \sum_{x \notin A} \underline{\psi}^k(x) - \sum_{x \in A} \underline{\psi}^k(x) \leq \sum_{x \in A}(\overline{\psi}^k(x) - \underline{\psi}^k(x)).$
- $\overline{\mu}_\kappa(A) = \kappa(\mathcal{X}) - \sum_{x \notin A} \underline{\psi}^k(x) \leq \sum_{x \in A} \overline{\psi}^k(x)$
  $\underline{\mu}_\kappa(A) = \kappa(\mathcal{X}) - \sum_{x \notin A} \overline{\psi}^k(x) \geq \sum_{x \in A} \underline{\psi}^k(x).$
  $\overline{\mu}_\kappa(A) - \underline{\mu}_\kappa(A) = \kappa(\mathcal{X}) - \sum_{x \notin A} \underline{\psi}^k(x) - \kappa(\mathcal{X}) + \sum_{x \notin A} \overline{\psi}^k(x) \leq \sum_{x \in A}(\overline{\psi}^k(x) - \underline{\psi}^k(x)).$

So we have $|\overline{\mu}_\kappa(A) - \underline{\mu}_\kappa(A)| \leq card(A)\|u - l\|_{A,\infty}$.

Note that if κ is linear the previous result proves that $\overline{\mu}_\kappa = \underline{\mu}_\kappa$ which is trivially true. More over, the further κ is from additivity, the greater the difference $|\overline{\mu}_\kappa(A) - \underline{\mu}_\kappa(A)|$ can be. This result also seems to connect our approximation with the total variation distance, routinely used in statistics [8].

Finally, let us remark that in Example 2, we would have derived the same bounds if we assumed that the group computed the utility of a subset A according to a sub-modular aggregation function. In particular, this means that if we concentrate on atomic bounds only, it does not really matter whether μ and $\overline{\mu}$ approximate a set $\mathcal{M}$ of additive set functions or a sub-modular set function (which itself can be considered as a non-empty set of dominated additive set functions), as both approximations will coincide if the bounds $\underline{\psi}, \overline{\psi}$ are the same.

4   An Application to Signal Convolution

We illustrate our approximation technique on an application in signal processing, as signal processing is strongly based on the notion of linear system, i.e. additive set functions.

4.1   Signal Processing and Additive Set Functions

We speak of continuous systems when the signals are continuous and of discrete systems when the signals are discrete. However, a signal is rarely discrete by nature. Discrete signals are generally continuous signals that have been discretized. For example, natural digital images are discretizations, by the retina of a camera, of continuous luminance images in real space. When they are naturally discrete, signals are often produced to mimic a discretized signal (synthetic images and sounds) with the aim of being used in the real world (special effects, electronic music, etc.).

Except in very rare cases, signal processing only really makes sense in continuous space. When the processing of the sound signal is used to recognize a sound for example (voice dictation) it is indeed recognition of the continuous signal that is involved via the recognition of the discrete signal from which it originates. So, doing digital signal processing generally means digitally performing a modification or analysis of the continuous signal from which it is being sampled. We limit ourselves here to linear signal processing.

The classical view consists in supposing that the processing of the signal, for which it is a question of finding a digital equivalent, is obtained thanks to a known continuous linear system (e.g. noise reduction filter (sound), texture modification (images), ...).

When a system (continuous or discrete) is linear, then the relation between input and output is completely defined by a continuous (φ) or discrete (ψ) signal called *impulse response of the system* and a linear operation called *convolution*. If the system is continuous, s the output of the system is written as a function of e the input:

$$s(t) = (e * \varphi)(t) = \int_{-\infty}^{\infty} e(u).\varphi(t-u)du, \tag{14}$$

and in the discrete case:

$$s(y) = (e * \psi)(y) = \sum_{x=-\infty}^{\infty} e(x).\psi(y-x). \tag{15}$$

Most signal processing being inherently continuous, one needs to go from the continuous ideal impulse response $\varphi(t), t \in \mathbb{R}$ to a corresponding discrete impulse response $\psi(x)$ $x \in \mathbb{Z}$. One standard way to do that is to consider $\psi(x) = \beta.\varphi(k.\Delta)$, Δ being the sampling period, and β a normalization coefficient allowing to respect the dynamics of the system, i.e. $\int_{\mathbb{R}} \varphi(t)dt = \sum_{x \in \mathbb{Z}} \psi(x)$. This approach is based on a modeling of the sampling by a Dirac impulse, which is very far from reality.

A more reasonable way to see the problem is to assume that the sampling was performed by a real system allowing to go from continuous space to discrete space whose impulse response η is of finite support and bound to the sampling period Δ. This is written $\psi(x) = (\varphi * \eta)(x.\Delta)$ (see Figure (1)). η is called the summative *sampling kernel*, summative meaning that it integrates to one ($\int_{\mathbb{R}} \eta(t)dt = 1$) and its support is included in $[-\Delta, \Delta]$ (i.e. $\forall t \notin [-\Delta, \Delta]$, $\eta(t) = 0$).

Note that the input signal e being generally finite, i.e. it is made of n samples, the expression (15) is generally written:

$$s(y) = (e * \psi)(y) = \sum_{x=1}^{n} e(x).\psi(y - x) = \mathbb{E}_{\kappa_{\psi_y}}(e), \tag{16}$$

with $\forall y \in \mathbb{Z}$, $\psi_y(y) = \psi(y - x)$. When the operation of the Eq. (16) does not represent a system but a mathematical operation aimed at modifying a signal, ψ is more generally named *convolution kernel*.

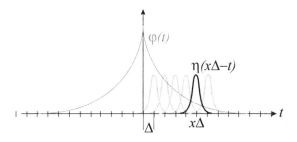

Fig. 1. Sampling of the impulse response φ with the kernel η.

4.2   Sampling and Fuzzy Transformation

A major problem posed by this approach is that the values of ψ strongly depend on the arbitrary choice of the chosen sampling kernel. For the discrete-continuous approach to be valid, the continuous convolution kernel must be digitized with the same sampling kernel as the discrete signal to be filtered. In most applications, this kernel is at best unknown or even, in the case of image processing, non-existent because the sampling is not invariant by translation: each pixel has its own impulse response.

To overcome this problem, Loquin et al. [13] propose to replace the summative sampling kernel by a family of continuous sampling kernels (which are formally equivalent to probability distributions) represented by a possibility distribution π [9], and called maxitive kernels. Within the framework of this theory, the triangular maxitive kernel plays a particular role since it allows to represent all the symmetric monomodal sampling kernels of lesser granularity [2].

This technique has been used in [17] under the name of imprecise fuzzy transformation to obtain an interval-valued impulse response $[\underline{\psi}(x), \overline{\psi}(x)]$ ($x \in \mathbb{Z}$) of all the values that could have been obtained by considering a family of sampling kernels represented by π.

We propose to extend the convolution operation defined in Eq. (16) to the interval-valued impulse response $[\underline{\psi}, \overline{\psi}]$ by:

$$[\underline{s}(y), \overline{s}(y)] = (e * [\underline{\psi}, \overline{\psi}])(y) = [\mathbb{E}_{\underline{\mu}_{\mathcal{M}_y}}(e), \overline{\mathbb{E}}_{\overline{\mu}_{\mathcal{M}_y}}(e)], \tag{17}$$

with $\underline{\mu}_{\mathcal{M}_y}$ being defined by Eqs. (10), considering $\forall x \in \mathbb{Z}$, $\underline{\psi}_y(x) = \underline{\psi}(y - x)$ and likewise for $\overline{\mu}_{\mathcal{M}_y}$.

4.3 Derivation of a Discrete Signal

The derivation of a discrete signal does not make sense. Indeed, only continuous signals can be differentiable. However, many signal analysis techniques are based on their derivation (extraction of contours or particular points in images, extraction of patterns in physiological signals, ...). In this context, it is not the discrete signal that we want to derive. What we want to do is to find an operation equivalent to a derivation of the continuous signal (before digitization) then sampling of the derivative obtained. It has been shown in [21] that this succession of operations is equivalent to convoluting the discrete signal with the sampling of the derivative of the kernel used for the reconstruction. One of the kernels often used to perform this operation is the Shen-Castan kernel [16]

$$\forall t \in \mathbb{R}, \quad \phi(t) = -\frac{\ln(\beta)}{2} . \beta^{|t|}, \tag{18}$$

where $\beta \in]0, 1[$ is a form factor of the kernel. The derivation of the kernel ϕ leads to the continuous kernel

$$\forall t \in \mathbb{R}, \quad \varphi(t) = -\text{sign}(t) . \frac{\ln(\beta)^2}{2} . \beta^{|t|}$$

Let us assume, without any loss of generality, that the sampling step $\Delta = 1$. Then, sampling φ as proposed in Sect. 4.2 by using a possibility distribution π leads to the interval-valued impulse response of the form $[\underline{\psi}, \overline{\psi}]$:

$$\text{if } x > 0, \ \overline{\psi}(x) = -\frac{\ln(\beta).(\beta^{|x+1|} - \beta^{|x|})}{2},$$

$$\underline{\psi}(x) = -\frac{\ln(\beta).(\beta^{|x|} - \beta^{|x-1|})}{2},$$

$$\text{and if } x < 0, \ \overline{\psi}(x) = \frac{\ln(\beta).(\beta^{|x|} - \beta^{|x-1|})}{2},$$

$$\underline{\psi}(x) = \frac{\ln(\beta).(\beta^{|x|} - \beta^{|x|})}{2}.$$

It is interesting to note that, in this application, $\underline{\mu}_{\mathcal{M}_y}(\mathcal{X}) = \overline{\mu}_{\mathcal{M}_y}(\mathcal{X}) \approx 0$. Figure 2 shows the corresponding bounds, together with some discrete ψ obtained by the use of sampling kernels that are within the family represented by π, that is symmetric kernels with support $[-\delta, \delta]$ ($\delta \in]0, 1]$). Such kernels includes, e.g., linear and quadratic kernels, as well as the Dirac kernel (whose result is in black in Fig. 2).

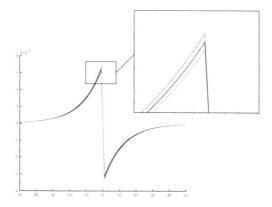

Fig. 2. $\overline{\psi}$ (in blue), $\underline{\psi}$ (in red), 8 impulse responses for different kernels within the family represented by π (in magenta), and the response of the Dirac kernel (in black). (Color figure online)

Figure 3 and Fig. 4 respectively show a time-attenuated signal and its derivative bounds obtained by our approach, together with some sampled filters. We can see on Fig. 4 that our approach makes a good job, providing wide bounds when variations are important (bottom box in Fig. 4), while providing very tight bounds when variation decreases along time (upper box).

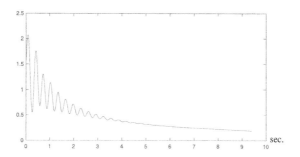

Fig. 3. Synthesis signal composed of a sum of attenuated sinusoids.

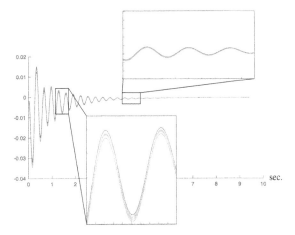

Fig. 4. Original signal derived by the imprecise Shen filter (lower bound in red, upper bound in blue) superimposed with derived signals obtained by various sampled Shen filters. (Color figure online)

5   Conclusion

In this paper, we have discussed how having only atomic bounds can be used to efficiently approximate very generic sets of very generic additive or sub-modular measures (i.e., non-monotonic with arbitrary bounds).

We have shown how they can successfully be applied to perform robust signal processing. Our next step will be to investigate how our results regarding sub-modular and super-modular set functions can be instrumental to represent non-monotonic rankings of sets or as approximation tools in optimisation problems using sub-modular functions.

References

1. Cohen, M., Chateauneuf, A.: Cardinal extensions of the Eu model based on the Choquet integral. In: Bouyssou, D., et al. (eds.) Decision-making Process–Concepts and Methods, chapter 9, pp. 401–434. Wiley (2009)
2. Baudrit, C., Dubois, D.: Practical representations of incomplete probabilistic knowledge. Comput. Stat. Data Anal. **51**(1), 86–108 (2006)
3. Benabbou, N., Leroy, C., Lust, T., Perny, P.: Interactive optimization of submodular functions under matroid constraints. In: Fotakis, D., Ríos Insua, D. (eds.) ADT 2021. LNCS (LNAI), vol. 13023, pp. 307–322. Springer, Cham (2021). https://doi.org/10.1007/978-3-030-87756-9_20
4. Prade, H., Dubois, D.: Possibility theory. an approach to computerized processing of uncertainty. New York and London (1988)
5. Dubois, D., Prade, H.: Possibility Theory and Its Applications: Where Do We Stand? In: Kacprzyk, J., Pedrycz, W. (eds.) Springer Handbook of Computational Intelligence, pp. 31–60. Springer, Heidelberg (2015). https://doi.org/10.1007/978-3-662-43505-2_3
6. De Campos, L.M., Huete, J.F., Moral, S.: Probability intervals: a tool for uncertain reasoning. Int. J. Uncertain. Fuzziness Knowl. Based Syst. **2**(02), 167–196 (1994)

7. De Waegenaere, A., Wakker, P., et al.: Choquet integrals with respect to non-monotonic set functions. Center for Economic Research, Tilburg University (1997)
8. Devroye, L., Gyorfi, L.: No empirical probability measure can converge in the total variation sense for all distributions. Ann. Stat. **18**, 1496–1499 (1990)
9. Dubois, D., Prade, H.: When upper probabilities are possibility measures. Fuzzy Sets Syst. **49**(1), 65–74 (1992)
10. Fishburn, P.C., LaValle, I.H.: Binary interactions and subset choice. Eur. J. Oper. Res. **92**(1), 182–192 (1996)
11. Gabillon, V., Kveton, B., Wen, Z., Eriksson, B., Muthukrishnan, S.: Adaptive submodular maximization in bandit setting. In: NIPS, pp. 2697–2705. Citeseer (2013)
12. Grabisch, M.: Set Functions, Games and Capacities in Decision-Making. Springer, Cham (2016). https://doi.org/10.1007/978-3-319-30690-2
13. Loquin, K., Strauss, O.: On the granularity of summative kernels. Fuzzy Sets Syst. **159**(15), 1952–1972 (2008)
14. Moretti, S., Öztürk, M.: Some axiomatic and algorithmic perspectives on the social ranking problem. In: Rothe, J. (ed.) ADT 2017. LNCS (LNAI), vol. 10576, pp. 166–181. Springer, Cham (2017). https://doi.org/10.1007/978-3-319-67504-6_12
15. Schrijver, A., et al.: Combinatorial optimization: polyhedra and efficiency. In: Algorithms and Combinatorics, vol. 24. Springer, Berlin (2003)
16. Shen, J., Castan, S.: Towards the unification of band-limited derivative operators for edge detection. Signal Process. **31**(2), 103–119 (1993)
17. Strauss, O.: Non-additive interval-valued f-transform. Fuzzy Sets Syst. **270**, 1–24 (2015)
18. Tohidi, E., Amiri, R., Coutino, M., Gesbert, D., Leus, G., Karbasi, A.: Submodularity in action: from machine learning to signal processing applications. IEEE Signal Process. Mag. **37**(5), 120–133 (2020)
19. Tschiatschek, S., Singla, A., Krause, A.: Selecting sequences of items via submodular maximization. In: Thirty-First AAAI Conference on Artificial Intelligence (2017)
20. Uematsu, N., Umetani, S., Kawahara, Y.: An efficient branch-and-cut algorithm for submodular function maximization. J. Oper. Res. Soc. Jpn. **63**(2), 41–59 (2020)
21. Unser, M., Aldroubi, A., Eden, M.: B-spline signal processing. I. theory. IEEE Trans. Signal Process. **41**(2), 821–833 (1993)
22. Zadeh, L.A.: Fuzzy sets as a basis for a theory of possibility. Fuzzy Sets Syst. **100**, 9–34 (1978)

Characterizing Multipreference Closure
with System W

Jonas Haldimann$^{(\boxtimes)}$ and Christoph Beierle

Faculty of Mathematics and Computer Science, FernUniversität in Hagen,
58084 Hagen, Germany
{jonas.haldimann,christoph.beierle}@fernuni-hagen.de

Abstract. System W is an approach to reasoning from conditional
beliefs that exhibits many properties desirable for nonmonotonic reasoning like extending rational closure, avoiding the drowning problem, and
complying with syntax splitting. Multipreference closure, initially considered for reasoning in description logics with exceptions, has recently
been reconstructed as a method for reasoning with conditionals based on
propositional logic by Giordano and Gliozzi; this reconstruction is rather
involved and complex. In this paper, we show how system W can be used
to obtain a significantly less involved semantical characterization of MP-
closure. To do this, we first present a representation theorem for system
W using a canonical preferential model $\mathcal{M}^{w}(\Delta)$ for a belief base Δ that
is obtained straightforwardly from system W. We then prove our main
result, stating that $\mathcal{M}^{w}(\Delta)$ also induces the MP-closure of Δ; furthermore, this implies that MP-closure coincides with system W inference.

1 Introduction

There are many different approaches for reasoning with conditional beliefs.
Established examples include p-entailment [18] which coincides inference according to the axioms of system P [1], system Z [11,22] which coincides with rational
closure [20], or lexicographic inference [21]. Further examples include possibilistic approaches [6] or various versions of inference based on c-representations
which are ranking functions of a conditional belief base obtained by observing
the property of conditional indifference [2,14].

System W, introduced by Komo and Beierle in [16], is an approach to reasoning from conditional belief bases that has been shown to exhibit many desirable
properties put forward for nonmonotonic reasoning with conditionals [16,17]:
For instance, system W fulfils the axioms of system P [1,18], it captures and
strictly extends system Z [22] and thus rational closure [20], it also captures
and strictly extends c-inference [2,4], and avoids the drowning problem [7]. Furthermore, recently it has been shown that, in contrast to e.g. p-entailment and
system Z, system W fully complies with syntax splitting [12,13,15].

Inspired by the rational closure construction of a conditional belief base [20],
multipreference closure (MP-closure) has been proposed for reasoning in description logics with exceptions [9]. Giordano and Gliozzi [9] present a reconstruction

F. Dupin de Saint-Cyr et al. (Eds.): SUM 2022, LNAI 13562, pp. 79–91, 2022.
https://doi.org/10.1007/978-3-031-18843-5_6

of MP-closure for the case of conditionals based on propositional logic. The characterization of MP-closure presented in [9] is rather involved and complex, using among other notations, canonical models, the ordering $<_{FIMS}$ on sets of conditionals, minimal canonical models, MP-bases, and a functor mapping minimal canonical ranked models to preferential models.

In this paper we develop a simpler, gentle reconstruction of MP-closure with system W. First we present a construction assigning to every consistent belief base Δ a unique model $\mathcal{M}^w(\Delta)$, called the system W preferential model, and show that the inference induced by $\mathcal{M}^w(\Delta)$ coincides with system W inference. Using $\mathcal{M}^w(\Delta)$, we prove the main theorem of this paper stating that for every consistent belief base Δ and all formulas A, B the entailment from A to B is in the MP-closure of Δ iff the model $\mathcal{M}^w(\Delta)$ licences the entailment from A to B. This also shows that for any consistent conditional belief base Δ the inferences according to MP-closure coincide with the inferences according to system W.

The rest of this paper is structured as follows. In Sect. 2, we present the required background on conditional logic and preferential models. In Sect. 3, we give the definition of system W and provide the construction of $\mathcal{M}^w(\Delta)$. Section 4 recalls the definition of MP-closure given in [9]. In Sect. 5, the main theorem connecting system W and MP-closure is proved before we conclude in Sect. 6.

2   Reasoning with Conditional Beliefs

2.1   Conditional Logic

A *(propositional) signature* is a finite set Σ of propositional variables. For a signature Σ, we denote the propositional language over Σ by $\mathcal{L}_\Sigma$. Usually, we denote elements of signatures with lowercase letters $a, b, c, \ldots$ and formulas with uppercase letters $A, B, C, \ldots$. We may denote a conjunction $A \wedge B$ by AB and a negation $\neg A$ by $\overline{A}$ for brevity of notation. The set of interpretations over a signature Σ is denoted as Ω_Σ. Interpretations are also called *worlds* and Ω_Σ is called the *universe*. An interpretation $\omega \in \Omega_\Sigma$ is a *model* of a formula $A \in \mathcal{L}_\Sigma$ if A holds in ω. This is denoted as $\omega \models A$. The set of models of a formula (over a signature Σ) is denoted as $Mod_\Sigma(A) = \{\omega \in \Omega_\Sigma \mid \omega \models A\}$ or sometimes as Ω_A. The Σ in Ω_Σ or in $Mod_\Sigma(A)$ can be omitted if the signature is clear from the context. A formula A *entails* a formula B if $Mod_\Sigma(A) \subseteq Mod_\Sigma(B)$. By slight abuse of notation we sometimes interpret worlds as the corresponding complete conjunction of all elements in the signature in either positive or negated form.

A *conditional* $(B|A)$ connects two formulas A, B and represents the rule "If A then usually B", where A is called the *antecedent* and B the *consequent* of the conditional. The conditional language over a signature Σ is denoted as $(\mathcal{L}|\mathcal{L})_\Sigma = \{(B|A) \mid A, B \in \mathcal{L}_\Sigma\}$. A finite set of conditionals is called a *conditional belief base*. We use a three-valued semantics of conditionals in this paper [8]. For a world ω a conditional $(B|A)$ is either *verified* by ω if $\omega \models AB$, *falsified* by ω if $\omega \models A\overline{B}$, or *not applicable* to ω if $\omega \models \overline{A}$. The set of propositional variables occurring in a conditional belief base Δ is denoted as $Sig(\Delta)$.

2.2   Preferential Models

Preferential models have been introduced as semantic models for conditional belief bases.

Definition 1 (smoothness [20]). *A set S with a strict partial ordering $\prec$ is called* smooth *if for every $t \in S$ either t is minimal in S or there is a $s \in S$ such that s is minimal in S and $s \prec t$.*

Definition 2 (preferential model [20]). *A preferential model is a triple $\mathcal{M} = \langle S, l, \prec \rangle$ consisting of a set S of states, a function $l : S \to \Omega$, and a strict partial order (i.e., a transitive and antireflexive binary relation) on S such that*

$$\text{for every } A \in \mathcal{L}_\Sigma : \quad \hat{A} = \{s \mid s \in S, l(s) \models A\} \text{ is smooth.}$$
$$\text{(smoothness condition)}$$

A preferential model is called finite *if S is finite. A preferential model is called* well-founded *if $\langle S, \prec \rangle$ is well-founded.*

Obviously, every finite preferential model is well-founded. If $\langle S, \prec \rangle$ is well-founded then $\langle S, l, \prec \rangle$ satisfies the smoothness condition [20]. Note that in this paper we use the terms *world* and *state* as in [20], deviating from the wording used in [9]. Every preferential model induces an inference relation.

Definition 3 (inference relation induced by a preferential model [20]). *Let $\mathcal{M} = \langle S, l, \prec \rangle$ be a preferential model. The inference relation $\succvdash_\mathcal{M}$ induced by $\mathcal{M}$ is defined by, for $A, B \in \mathcal{L}_\Sigma$,*

$$A \succvdash_\mathcal{M} B \quad \text{iff} \quad \text{for any } s \text{ minimal in } S \text{ it holds that } l(s) \models B.$$

A conditional $(B|A)$ is *accepted* by a preferential model $\mathcal{M}$ if $A \succvdash_\mathcal{M} B$. A preferential model $\mathcal{M}$ is a model for a belief base Δ if $\mathcal{M}$ accepts all conditionals in Δ. Preferential models can be used to define preferential entailment.

Definition 4 (preferential entailment $\succvdash^p_\Delta$ [18,20]). *The conditional $(B|A)$ is preferentially entailed by Δ, denoted as $A \succvdash^p_\Delta B$, if $(B|A)$ is accepted by all models of Δ.*

The following definitions present special preferential models that are used in the characterization of MP-closure.

Definition 5 (ranked model (adapted from [20])). *A ranked model is a preferential model $\mathcal{M} = \langle S, l, \prec \rangle$ with*

$$\text{if } x \prec y \text{ then either } z \prec y \text{ or } x \prec z \text{ for any } x, y, z \in S. \quad \text{(modularity)}$$

Definition 6 (rank of a state/formula in a model [10]). *Let $\mathcal{M} = \langle S, l, \prec \rangle$ be a finite preferential model. The* rank *of a state $s \in S$, denoted by $\mathbf{k}_\mathcal{M}(s)$, is the length of the longest chain of states $s_0 \prec \cdots \prec s$ from a minimal s_0 to s. The rank of a formula $A \in \mathcal{L}_\Sigma$ is $\mathbf{k}_\mathcal{M}(A) = \min\{\mathbf{k}_\mathcal{M}(s) \mid s \in S, l(s) \models A\}$.*

Definition 7 ($<_{FIMS}$, minimal ranked model [9,10]). *Let $\mathcal{M} = \langle S, l, \prec \rangle$, $\mathcal{M}' = \langle S', l', \prec' \rangle$ be preferential models. $\mathcal{M}$ is preferred to $\mathcal{M}'$ (in the fixed interpretations minimal semantics, FIMS), denoted as $\mathcal{M} <_{FIMS} \mathcal{M}'$, if*

- *$S = S'$,*
- *$l = l'$,*
- *$\mathbf{k}_{\mathcal{M}}(s) \leq \mathbf{k}_{\mathcal{M}'}(s)$ for every $s \in S$, and*
- *there is an $s \in S$ such that $\mathbf{k}_{\mathcal{M}}(s) < \mathbf{k}_{\mathcal{M}'}(s)$.*

A ranked model $\mathcal{M}$ is a minimal ranked model *of a belief base Δ if $\mathcal{M}$ is minimal with respect to $<_{FIMS}$ among the models of Δ.*

Definition 8 (canonical model [10]). *A canonical model of a belief base Δ is a preferential model $\mathcal{M} = \langle S, l, \prec \rangle$ of Δ such that for every world ω over $Sig(\Delta)$ there is a state $s \in S$ with $l(s) \models \omega$.*

Definition 9 (minimal canonical ranked model [9]). *A minimal canonical ranked model of a belief base Δ is a canonical ranked model of Δ that is minimal with respect to $<_{FIMS}$ among the canonical ranked models of Δ. The set of minimal canonical ranked models of Δ is denoted as $Min_{RC}(\Delta)$.*

3 System W and its Characterization with Preferential Models

In this section, we briefly recall the definition of system W, illustrate it with an example, and present a representation theorem for system W employing a single preferential model.

3.1 Definition of System W

System W is an inductive inference operator [16,17] that takes into account the inclusion maximal tolerance partition of a belief base Δ, which is also used for the definition of system Z [22].

Definition 10 (inclusion maximal tolerance partition [22]). *A conditional $(B|A)$ is tolerated by $\Delta = \{(B_i|A_i) \mid i = 1, \ldots, n\}$ if there exists a world $\omega \in \Omega_\Sigma$ such that ω verifies $(B|A)$ and ω does not falsify any conditional in Δ, i.e., $\omega \models AB$ and $\omega \models \bigwedge_{i=1}^{n}(\overline{A_i} \vee B_i)$. The inclusion maximal tolerance partition $OP(\Delta) = (\Delta^0, \ldots, \Delta^k)$ of a consistent belief base Δ is the ordered partition of Δ where each Δ^i is the inclusion maximal subset of $\bigcup_{j=i}^{n}\Delta^j$ that is tolerated by $\bigcup_{j=i}^{n}\Delta^j$.*

It is well-known that $OP(\Delta)$ exists iff Δ is consistent; moreover, because the Δ^i are chosen inclusion-maximal, the tolerance partitioning is unique [22].

In addition to $OP(\Delta)$, system W also takes into account the structural information which conditionals are falsified. System W is based on a binary relation called *preferred structure on worlds* $<_{\Delta}^{w}$ over Ω_Σ induced by every consistent belief base Δ.

Definition 11 (ξ^j, ξ, preferred structure $<_\Delta^w$ on worlds [17]). *Consider a consistent belief base $\Delta = \{r_i = (B_i|A_i) \mid i \in \{1,\ldots,n\}\}$ with the tolerance partition $OP(\Delta) = (\Delta^0,\ldots,\Delta^k)$. For $j = 0,\ldots,k$, the functions ξ^j and ξ are the functions mapping worlds to the set of falsified conditionals from the set Δ^j in the tolerance partition and from Δ, respectively, given by*

$$\xi^j(\omega) := \{r_i \in \Delta^j \mid \omega \models A_i\overline{B_i}\}, \tag{1}$$

$$\xi(\omega) := \{r_i \in \Delta \mid \omega \models A_i\overline{B_i}\}. \tag{2}$$

The preferred structure on worlds is given by the binary relation $<_\Delta^w \subseteq \Omega \times \Omega$ defined by, for any $\omega, \omega' \in \Omega$,

$$\omega <_\Delta^w \omega' \text{ iff there exists an } m \in \{0,\ldots,k\} \text{ such that}$$
$$\xi^i(\omega) = \xi^i(\omega') \quad \forall i \in \{m+1,\ldots,k\} \text{ and} \tag{3}$$
$$\xi^m(\omega) \subsetneq \xi^m(\omega'). \tag{4}$$

Thus, $\omega <_\Delta^w \omega'$ if and only if ω falsifies strictly fewer conditionals than ω' in the partition with the biggest index m where the conditionals falsified by ω and ω' differ. Note, that $<_\Delta^w$ is a strict partial order [17, Lemma 3].

Definition 12 (system W, $\models_\Delta^w$ [17]). *Let Δ be a consistent belief base and A, B be formulas. Then B is a system W inference from A (in the context of Δ), denoted $A\models_\Delta^w B$, if for every $\omega' \in \Omega_{A\overline{B}}$ there is an $\omega \in \Omega_{AB}$ such that $\omega <_\Delta^w \omega'$.*

System W fulfils system P, extends both system Z [22] and c-inference [3], and enjoys further desirable properties for nonmonotonic reasoning like avoiding the drowning problem [7,17] and fully complying with syntax splitting [12,13,15]. We illustrate system W with an example.

Example 1 (from [13]). Consider the belief base $\Delta_{ve} = \{(m|e), (g|m), (\overline{g}|me), (t|b)\}$ over the signature $\Sigma = \{m,b,e,t,g\}$ with the intended meaning

m being a *motorized vehicle*
b being a *bike*
e having an *electric motor*
t having *two wheels*
g requiring *gasoline*.

The inclusion maximal tolerance partition of Δ is $OP(\Delta_{ve}) = (\Delta^0, \Delta^1)$ with $\Delta^0 = \{(g|m), (t|b)\}$ and $\Delta^1 = \{(m|e), (\overline{g}|me)\}$. The resulting preferred structure $<_{\Delta_{ve}}^w$ is given in Fig. 1. Using $<_{\Delta_{ve}}^w$ we can verify that for each world ω' with $\omega' \models be\overline{t}$ there is a world ω with $\omega \models bet$ such that $\omega <_{\Delta_{ve}}^w \omega'$. Therefore, with system W we can infer $be\models_{\Delta_{ve}}^w t$, i.e., that electric bikes have usually two wheels. Note that $be\models t$ is not a valid inference from Δ_{ve} with p-entailment or system Z/rational closure.

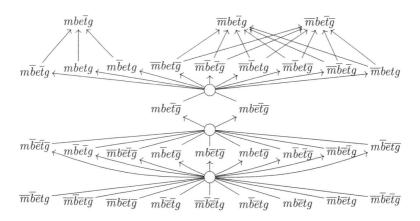

Fig. 1. The preferred structure on worlds induced by the belief base Δ_{ve} from Example 1. Edges that can be obtained from transitivity are omitted.

3.2 A Preferential Model for System W

In the remainder of this section we will construct a preferential model $\mathcal{M}^w(\Delta)$ that induces system W inference. Relying on the fact that the preferential structure on worlds $<^w_\Delta$ is a strict partial order [17], the following definition assigns to every belief base Δ a unique preferential model based on $<^w_\Delta$.

Definition 13 (system W preferential model $\mathcal{M}^w(\Delta)$). *For a belief base Δ the* system W preferential model *(for Δ) is $\mathcal{M}^w(\Delta) = \langle \Omega, \mathrm{id}, <^w_\Delta \rangle$.*

For every consistent belief base the inference relation induced by the system W preferential model $\mathcal{M}^w(\Delta)$ coincides with system W inference yielding the following representation theorem for system W.

Proposition 1. *Let Δ be a consistent belief base. For $A, B \in \mathcal{L}_\Sigma$ we have*

$$A \mathrel{\mathop{\sim}\limits_{\mathcal{M}^w(\Delta)}} B \quad \textit{iff} \quad A \mathrel{\mathop{\sim}\limits^w_\Delta} B. \tag{5}$$

Proof. We prove the proposition by proving both directions of (5).

Direction $\Leftarrow$ of (5) Assume that $A \mathrel{\mathop{\sim}\limits^w_\Delta} B$ for $A, B \in \mathcal{L}_\Sigma$. Let $\omega \in \Omega_A$ minimal, i.e., there is no $\omega' \in \Omega_A$ s.t. $\omega' <^w_\Delta \omega$.

Towards a contradiction assume $\omega \not\models B$. Then $A \mathrel{\mathop{\sim}\limits^w_\Delta} B$ requires the existence of a model $\omega' \in \Omega_{A\overline{B}}$ with $\omega' <^w_\Delta \omega$. This contradicts that ω is minimal in Ω_A, therefore $\omega \models B$. Hence, $A \mathrel{\mathop{\sim}\limits_{\mathcal{M}^w(\Delta)}} B$.

Direction $\Rightarrow$ of (5)   Assume that $A \mathrel{\mathop{\sim}\limits_{\mathcal{M}^w(\Delta)}} B$ for $A, B \in \mathcal{L}_\Sigma$. Let $\omega' \in \Omega_{A\overline{B}}$. Because of $A \mathrel{\mathop{\sim}\limits_{\mathcal{M}^w(\Delta)}} B$ the world ω' is not minimal in Ω_A. Let ω be minimal among the worlds in Ω_A that satisfy $\omega <^w_\Delta \omega'$. As $<^w_\Delta$ is transitive, ω is also minimal in Ω_A. With $A \mathrel{\mathop{\sim}\limits_{\mathcal{M}^w(\Delta)}} B$ it follows that $\omega \models AB$. Hence, $A \mathrel{\mathop{\sim}\limits^w_\Delta} B$.   □

Note that given $<^w_\Delta$, the model $\mathcal{M}^w(\Delta)$ is a simple and straightforwardly defined preferential model: Its set of states coincides with the set of worlds and the labelling function is the identity. Moreover, $\mathcal{M}^w(\Delta)$ is also a canonical model in the sense of Definition 8.

Proposition 2. *The system W preferential model $\mathcal{M}^w(\Delta)$ is a canonical model of Δ.*

Proof. Let Σ be the signature underlying Δ. By construction, $\mathcal{M}^w(\Delta)$ has a state s with $l(s) \models \omega$ for every world $\omega \in \Omega_\Sigma$. We have $Sig(\Delta) \subseteq \Sigma$ and therefore for every $\omega' \in \Omega_{Sig(\Delta)}$ there is an $\omega \in \Omega_\Sigma$ such that $\omega' \models \omega$. Therefore, $\mathcal{M}^w(\Delta)$ is a canonical model. Proposition 1 implies that $\mathcal{M}^w(\Delta)$ is a model of Δ because system W satisfies direct inference, i.e., if $(B|A) \in \Delta$ then $A \hspace{1pt}\vdash^w_\Delta B$. $\hfill\square$

4   Definition of MP-closure

In this section we recall the definition of MP-closure as presented in [9]. This requires the definition of some other concepts first.

Definition 14 (exceptionality of a formula/conditional [20]). *Let Δ be a belief base. A formula $A \in \mathcal{L}_\Sigma$ is exceptional for Δ if $\top \hspace{1pt}\vdash^p_\Delta \neg A$. A conditional $(B|A)$ is exceptional for Δ if A is exceptional for Δ. The set of exceptional conditionals for Δ is denoted as $E(\Delta)$.*

Definition 15 (rank of a formula/conditional [20], order of a belief base [9]). *Let Δ be belief base. We define a sequence of sets $C_0, C_1, \ldots$ by $C_0 = \Delta$ and $C_i = E(C_{i-1})$ for $i > 0$. The least finite k with $C_k = C_{k+1}$ is called the order of Δ.*

The rank of a formula A (with respect to Δ) is the smallest i such that A is not exceptional for C_i. If A is exceptional for all C_i it has rank ∞. The rank of a conditional is the rank of its antecedent.

Note that a belief base Δ with order k does not contain conditionals with rank k. For $k > 0$ the highest finite rank of a conditional in Δ is $k - 1$.

Definition 16 (MP-seriousness ordering $\prec^{MP}_\Delta$ [9]). *Let Δ be a belief base with order k. For $X \subseteq \Delta$ let $(X_\infty, X_k, \ldots, X_0)_X$ be a tuple of sets such that X_i is the set of conditionals in X with rank i.*
For two tuples $(X_n, \ldots, X_1)$ and $(Y_n, \ldots, Y_1)$ we define

$$(X_1) \ll (Y_1) \qquad \text{iff} \quad X_1 \subsetneq Y_1$$
$$\text{and } (X_k, \ldots, X_1) \ll (Y_k, \ldots, Y_1) \qquad \text{iff} \quad X_k \subsetneq Y_k \text{ or}$$
$$X_k = Y_k \text{ and } (X_{k-1} \ll Y_{k-1}).$$

The MP-seriousness ordering $\prec^{MP}_\Delta$ on subsets of Δ is defined by

$$C \prec^{MP}_\Delta D \quad \text{iff} \quad (C^\infty, C^k, \ldots, C^0)_C \ll (D^\infty, D^k, \ldots, D^0)_D.$$

MP-closure is defined in terms of MP-bases in [9].

Definition 17 (MP-basis [9]). *Let Δ be a belief base. Let $A \in \mathcal{L}_\Sigma$ be a formula with finite rank with respect to Δ. A set $D \subseteq \Delta$ is an MP-basis for A if*

- *A is consistent with $\tilde{D} = \{B \rightarrow C \mid (C|B) \in D\}$, and*
- *D is maximal with respect to the MP-seriousness ordering among the subsets of Δ with this property.*

Definition 18 (MP-closure [9]). *Let Δ be a belief base. $A \hspace{1pt} \vdash\hspace{-9pt}\sim_\Delta^{MP} B$ is in the MP-closure $MP(\Delta)$ of Δ if for all MP-bases D of A it holds that $\tilde{D} \cup \{A\} \models B$.*

This definition for MP-closure is similar to the definition of lexicographic inference in [21]; MP-closure utilizes the MP-ordering $\prec_\Delta^{MP}$ instead of the seriousness ordering defined by Lehmann.

5   A Reconstruction of MP-closure with System W

In this section we prove our main theorem of this paper, stating that for every consistent belief base Δ, the MP-closure of Δ coincides with the inference relation induced by $\mathcal{M}^w(\Delta)$. As a consequence, the MP-closure of Δ coincides with system W inference from Δ. To prove this theorem we use the characterization of MP-closure with preferential models presented in [9]. In Sect. 5.1 we recall this characterization, and in Sect. 5.2 we present and prove our main theorem.

5.1   Characterization of MP-closure with Preferential Models

The characterization of MP-closure utilizes certain preferential models called *MP-models*. These are defined using the following functor $\mathcal{F}_\Delta$.

Definition 19 (functor $\mathcal{F}_\Delta$ [9]). *Let Δ be a belief base. The functor $\mathcal{F}_\Delta$ is a mapping from minimal canonical ranked models of Δ to preferential models defined by*

$$\mathcal{F}_\Delta((S, l, \prec)) = (S, l, \prec_F)$$

with $s \prec_F t$ iff $\xi(s) \prec_\Delta^{MP} \xi(t)$ for $s, t \in S$.

$\mathcal{F}_\Delta$ is extended to sets P of minimal canonical ranked models of Δ by $\mathcal{F}_\Delta(P) = \{\mathcal{F}_\Delta(\mathcal{M}) \mid \mathcal{M} \in P\}$.

Definition 20 (MP-model [9]). *Let Δ be a belief base. An MP-model of Δ is any model in $\mathcal{F}_\Delta(Min_{RC}(\Delta))$.*

Proposition 3 (MP-closure representation theorem [9]). *Let Δ be a belief base. A conditional $(B|A)$ is accepted by every MP-model of Δ iff $A \hspace{1pt}\vdash\hspace{-9pt}\sim_\Delta^{MP} B$.*

The MP-closure representation uses skeptical inference over all MP-models of a belief base. Giordano and Gliozzi [9] showed that all MP-models induce the same inference relation.

Proposition 4 ([9]). *Let $\mathcal{N}, \mathcal{N}'$ be two MP-models of a belief base Δ. For any $A, B \in \mathcal{L}_\Sigma$ we have $A \hspace{1pt}\vdash\hspace{-9pt}\sim_\mathcal{N} B$ iff $A \hspace{1pt}\vdash\hspace{-9pt}\sim_{\mathcal{N}'} B$.*

5.2   Characterization of MP-closure with System W

As a first step we show that a belief base Δ tolerating a conditional $(B|A)$ is the opposite of $(B|A)$ being exceptional for Δ.

Proposition 5. *Let Δ be a consistent belief base and $(B|A)$ be a conditional. Δ tolerates $(B|A)$ iff $(B|A)$ is not exceptional for Δ.*

Proof. Let Δ be a consistent belief base and $(B|A) \in \Delta$.

Direction $\Rightarrow$ of "iff": Assume $(B|A)$ is tolerated by Δ. By definition there is a world $\omega \in \Omega_\Sigma$ such that $\omega \models AB$ and ω does not falsify any conditional in Δ. Now take a preferential model $\mathcal{M}$ of Δ (which exists because Δ is consistent) and obtain a new model $\mathcal{M}'$ by adding a minimal state associated with ω. Because ω does not falsify any conditional in Δ the new model $\mathcal{M}'$ is also accepted by Δ. It also has a minimal state that does not accept $\neg A$; therefore $\top \not\hspace{-1pt}\vdash^p_\Delta \neg A$. Hence $(B|A)$ is not exceptional for Δ.

Direction $\Leftarrow$ of "iff": Assume $(B|A)$ is not exceptional for Δ. Then $\top \not\hspace{-1pt}\vdash^p_\Delta \neg A$, i.e., there is a preferential model $\mathcal{M} = \langle S, l, \prec \rangle$ of Δ and a state $s \in S$ such that s is minimal and $l(s) \models A$. Because $\mathcal{M}$ accepts all conditionals in Δ including $(B|A)$, state s is minimal, and $l(s) \models A$, we have $l(s) \models AB$. As s is minimal, it cannot falsify any of the conditionals in Δ. All in all, the world $l(s)$ verifies $(B|A)$ and falsifies none of the other conditionals in Δ, yielding that $(B|A)$ is tolerated by Δ. □

Using Proposition 5 we can show that the ordered partition on worlds partitions the worlds according to their rank.

Lemma 1. *Let Δ be a consistent belief base of order k and $OP(\Delta) = (\Delta^0, \ldots, \Delta^l)$ be the inclusion maximal tolerance partition of Δ. Then for $i = 0, \ldots, l$ the conditionals $(B|A) \in \Delta^i$ have rank i, and furthermore $l = k - 1$. Especially, no conditional in Δ has rank k or rank ∞.*

Proof. For $i = 0, \ldots, l$ the conditionals in Δ_i are those that are tolerated by $\bigcup_{j \geq i} \Delta^j$ but not tolerated by $\bigcup_{j \geq i-1} \Delta^j$. Let the sets $C_0, C_1, \ldots$ be constructed from Δ as in Definition 15. We proof that $\Delta^i = C_i \backslash C_{i-1}$ by induction on i.

Base Case: We have $C_0 = \Delta$ and $C_1 = E(\Delta)$. $C_0 \backslash C_1 = \Delta \backslash E(\Delta)$ is the set of conditionals in Δ that is not exceptional for Δ. By Proposition 5 this is the maximal set of conditionals that are tolerated by Δ. Therefore, $\Delta_0 = C_0 \backslash C_1$ which is the set of conditionals from Δ with rank 0.

Induction Step: Let $i > 0$. With the induction hypothesis we have $C_i = \Delta \backslash \bigcup_{j < i} \Delta^j = \bigcup_{j \geq i} \Delta^j$. Analogously to the base case we show that $C_i \backslash C_{i+1}$ is the set of conditionals from C_i that are tolerated by C_i. By construction of $OP(\Delta)$ this is Δ^i.

Because $OP(\Delta)$ is a partition of Δ we have $C_i = \emptyset$ for $i > l$. Hence, the order of Δ is $k = l + 1$ and no conditional has rank k. We have shown that the conditionals $C_i \backslash C_{i-1}$ of rank i are those in Δ^i. As every conditional in Δ has a finite rank, there are no conditionals with rank ∞ in Δ. □

Based on Lemma 1, the next lemma states that the preferred structure on worlds of system W coincides with the MP-seriousness ordering of the conditionals falsified by the corresponding worlds.

Lemma 2. *Let Δ be a consistent belief base. For all $\omega, \omega' \in \Omega$ it holds that*

$$\xi(\omega) \prec^{MP}_\Delta \xi(\omega') \quad iff \quad \omega <^{\mathsf{w}}_\Delta \omega'.$$

Proof. Let Δ, ω, ω' be as in the lemma. Let k be the order of Δ, let $D = \xi(\omega)$, and let $D' = \xi(\omega')$. Let $(D_\infty, D_k, \ldots, D_0)_D$ be the tuple of sets such that D_i is the set of conditionals in D with rank i; and let $(D'_\infty, D'_k, \ldots, D'_0)_{D'}$ be the corresponding tuple of subsets of D'. Lemma 1 implies that $D_\infty = D'_\infty = \emptyset$ and that $D_k = D'_k = \emptyset$. Using Lemma 1 again, for $i = 0, \ldots, k-1$ we have that the set D_i of conditionals that are falsified by ω and have rank i equals the set $\xi^i(\omega)$ of conditionals that are falsified by ω and are in Δ_i. Analogously, $D'_i = \xi^i(\omega')$ for $i = 0, \ldots, k-1$. It holds that

$$D \prec^{MP}_\Delta D'$$

$$\text{iff} \quad (D_\infty, D_k, \ldots, D_0)_D \ll (D'_\infty, D'_k, \ldots, D'_0)_{D'}$$

$$\text{iff} \quad (\emptyset, \emptyset, \xi^{k-1}(\omega), \ldots, \xi^0(\omega)) \ll (\emptyset, \emptyset, \xi^{k-1}(\omega'), \ldots, \xi^0(\omega'))$$

$$\text{iff} \quad \text{there is an } m \in \{0, \ldots, k-1\} \text{ such that}$$

$$\xi^i(\omega) = \xi^i(\omega') \quad \forall i \in \{m+1, \ldots, k-1\} \text{ and}$$
$$\xi^m(\omega) \subsetneqq \xi^m(\omega')$$

$$\text{iff} \quad \omega <^{\mathsf{w}}_\Delta \omega'.$$

$\square$

Now, we can show that the system W preferential model of a belief base is also an MP-model.

Proposition 6. *For every consistent belief base Δ the system W preferential model $\mathcal{M}^w(\Delta)$ is an MP-model of Δ.*

Proof. Let $<_Z$ be the ordering on Ω_Σ that is induced by the system Z ranking function κ^Z of Δ (see [22]) given by $\omega <_Z \omega'$ iff $\kappa^Z(\omega) < \kappa^Z(\omega')$ for $\omega, \omega' \in \Omega_\Sigma$. Consider the preferential model $\mathcal{U} = \langle \Omega_\Sigma, \mathrm{id}, <_Z \rangle$. The model $\mathcal{U}$ is a canonical ranked model of Δ as the ordering $<_Z$ is compatible with Δ. As $<_{FIMS}$ only relates models with the same set of states and the same valuation function and because there are only finitely many ranked models with the set of states S_V and the valuation function l_V, there is a state $\mathcal{V} = \langle \Omega_\Sigma, \mathrm{id}, \prec_V \rangle$ that is a minimal canonical ranked model of Δ.

Now let $\mathcal{W} = \langle S_W, l_W, \prec_W \rangle = \mathcal{F}_\Delta(\mathcal{V})$. Hence, $\mathcal{W}$ is an MP-model of Δ. By the definition of $\mathcal{F}_\Delta$ it holds that $\omega \prec_W \omega'$ iff $\xi(\omega) \prec^{MP}_\Delta \xi(\omega')$. Using Lemma 2 yields that $\omega \prec_W \omega'$ iff $\omega <^{\mathsf{w}}_\Delta \omega'$. As $\mathcal{F}_\Delta$ leaves the set of states and the valuation function unchanged, we have $S_W = \Omega_\Sigma$ and $l_W = \mathrm{id}$. Hence $\mathcal{W} = \mathcal{M}^w(\Delta)$. Because $\mathcal{W}$ is an MP-model and $\mathcal{W} = \mathcal{M}^w(\Delta)$ we have that the $\mathcal{M}^w(\Delta)$ is an MP-model of Δ.

$\square$

Finally, we can show that the MP-closure of Δ coincides with the inference relation induced by $\mathcal{M}^w(\Delta)$. This entails that the MP-closure of Δ coincides with system W inference from Δ.

Theorem 1. *For every consistent belief base Δ and formulas $A, B \in \mathcal{L}_\Sigma$ it holds that:*

$$- A \mathrel{\mathop{\mid\!\sim}\limits_{\Delta}^{MP}} B \quad \textit{iff} \quad A \mathrel{\mid\!\sim}_{\mathcal{M}^w(\Delta)} B.$$
$$- A \mathrel{\mathop{\mid\!\sim}\limits_{\Delta}^{MP}} B \quad \textit{iff} \quad A \mathrel{\mathop{\mid\!\sim}\limits_{\Delta}^{w}} B.$$

Proof. As all MP-models of Δ induce the same inference relation (see Proposition 4), a conditional is accepted by every MP-model if and only if it is accepted by an arbitrary MP-model of Δ.

Using this, we have that $\mathrel{\mid\!\sim}_{\mathcal{M}^w(\Delta)}$ is the MP-closure of Δ because $\mathcal{M}^w(\Delta)$ is an MP-model of Δ (see Proposition 6). As $\mathrel{\mid\!\sim}_{\mathcal{M}^w(\Delta)}$ coincides with system W (see Proposition 1), MP-closure coincides with system W. $\square$

6 Conclusions and Further Work

In this paper, we show that system W provides a semantic definition of MP-closure that is less complex than the reconstruction of MP-closure given in [9]. To do this, for a consistent belief base Δ we construct a preferential model $\mathcal{M}^w(\Delta)$ inducing the system W inference from Δ. In the main theorem of this paper, we show that this model also induces the MP-closure of Δ, implying also that system W and MP-closure coincide.

The coincidence of the two reasoning approaches allows transferring properties proven for system W (e.g., syntax splitting) to MP-closure and vice versa. Additionally, whenever we consider system W or MP-closure, of the two rather different definitions one can now use the definition that is more suitable for a given context.

In our current work, we further investigate properties of system W. Additionally, we are extending the reasoning platform InfOCF-Web [19] by a web-based implementation of system W [5], and we work on more efficient algorithms for reasoning with system W. Given the results of this paper, any findings on such algorithms and implementations of them cover MP-closure as well.

Acknowledgements. We thank the anonymous reviewers for their detailed and helpful comments. This work was supported by the Deutsche Forschungsgemeinschaft (DFG, German Research Foundation), grant BE 1700/10-1 awarded to Christoph Beierle as part of the priority program "Intentional Forgetting in Organizations" (SPP 1921).

References

1. Adams, E.: The logic of conditionals. Inquiry **8**(1–4), 166–197 (1965)
2. Beierle, C., Eichhorn, C., Kern-Isberner, G., Kutsch, S.: Skeptical, weakly skeptical, and credulous inference based on preferred ranking functions. In: Kaminka, G.A., et al. (eds.) Proceedings 22nd European Conference on Artificial Intelligence, ECAI-2016. Frontiers in Artificial Intelligence and Applications, vol. 285, pp. 1149–1157. IOS Press (2016)
3. Beierle, C., Eichhorn, C., Kern-Isberner, G., Kutsch, S.: Properties of skeptical c-inference for conditional knowledge bases and its realization as a constraint satisfaction problem. Ann. Math. Artif. Intell. **83**(3–4), 247–275 (2018)
4. Beierle, C., Eichhorn, C., Kern-Isberner, G., Kutsch, S.: Properties and interrelationships of skeptical, weakly skeptical, and credulous inference induced by classes of minimal models. Artif. Intell. **297**, 103489 (2021)
5. Beierle, C., Haldimann, J., Kollar, D., Sauerwald, K., Schwarzer, L.: An implementation of nonmonotonic reasoning with system W. In: Bergmann, R., Malburg, L., Rodermund, S.C., Timm, I.J. (eds.) KI 2022: Advances in Artificial Intelligence. KI 2022. Lecture Notes in Computer Science, vol. 13404, pp. 1–8 Springer, Cham (2022). https://doi.org/10.1007/978-3-031-15791-2_1
6. Benferhat, S., Dubois, D., Prade, H.: Possibilistic and standard probabilistic semantics of conditional knowledge bases. J. of Logic Comput. **9**(6), 873–895 (1999)
7. Benferhat, S., Cayrol, C., Dubois, D., Lang, J., Prade, H.: Inconsistency management and prioritized syntax-based entailment. In: Proceedings of the Thirteenth International Joint Conference on Artificial Intelligence (IJCAI 1993), vol. 1, pp. 640–647. Morgan Kaufmann Publishers, San Francisco, CA, USA (1993)
8. de Finetti, B.: La prévision, ses lois logiques et ses sources subjectives. Ann. Inst. H. Poincaré **7**(1), 1–68 (1937). Engl. transl. Theory of Probability, J. Wiley & Sons, 1974
9. Giordano, L., Gliozzi, V.: A reconstruction of multipreference closure. Artif. Intell. **290**, 103398 (2021). https://doi.org/10.1016/j.artint.2020.103398
10. Giordano, L., Gliozzi, V., Olivetti, N., Pozzato, G.L.: Semantic characterization of rational closure: From propositional logic to description logics. Artif. Intell. **226**, 1–33 (2015). https://doi.org/10.1016/j.artint.2015.05.001
11. Goldszmidt, M., Pearl, J.: Qualitative probabilities for default reasoning, belief revision, and causal modeling. Artif. Intell. **84**(1–2), 57–112 (1996)
12. Haldimann, J., Beierle, C.: Inference with system W satisfies syntax splitting. In: Kern-Isberner, G., Lakemeyer, G., Meyer, T. (eds.) Proceedings of the 19th International Conference on Principles of Knowledge Representation and Reasoning, KR 2022, Haifa, Israel. 31 July–5 August 2022, pp. 405–409 (2022)
13. Haldimann, J., Beierle, C.: Properties of system W and its relationships to other inductive inference operators. In: Varzinczak, I. (ed.) Foundations of Information and Knowledge Systems - 12th International Symposium, FoIKS 2022, Lecture Notes in Computer Science, vol. 13388, pp. 206–225. Springer, Cham (2022). https://doi.org/10.1007/978-3-031-11321-5_12
14. Kern-Isberner, G.: A thorough axiomatization of a principle of conditional preservation in belief revision. Ann. Math. Artif. Intell. **40**(1–2), 127–164 (2004)
15. Kern-Isberner, G., Beierle, C., Brewka, G.: Syntax splitting = relevance + independence: new postulates for nonmonotonic reasoning from conditional belief bases. In: Calvanese, D., Erdem, E., Thielscher, M. (eds.) Principles of Knowledge Representation and Reasoning: Proceedings of the 17th International Conference, KR 2020, pp. 560–571. IJCAI Organization (2020)

16. Komo, C., Beierle, C.: Nonmonotonic inferences with qualitative conditionals based on preferred structures on worlds. In: Schmid, U., Klügl, F., Wolter, D. (eds.) KI 2020. LNCS (LNAI), vol. 12325, pp. 102–115. Springer, Cham (2020). https://doi.org/10.1007/978-3-030-58285-2_8

17. Komo, C., Beierle, C.: Nonmonotonic reasoning from conditional knowledge bases with system W. Ann. Math. Artif. Intell. **90**(1), 107–144 (2022)

18. Kraus, S., Lehmann, D., Magidor, M.: Nonmonotonic reasoning, preferential models and cumulative logics. Artif. Intell. **44**(1–2), 167–207 (1990)

19. Kutsch, S., Beierle, C.: InfOCF-Web: An online tool for nonmonotonic reasoning with conditionals and ranking functions. In: Zhou, Z. (ed.) Proceedings of the Thirtieth International Joint Conference on Artificial Intelligence, IJCAI 2021, Virtual Event / Montreal, Canada, August 19–27 2021, pp. 4996–4999. ijcai.org (2021)

20. Lehmann, D., Magidor, M.: What does a conditional knowledge base entail? Artif. Intell. **55**, 1–60 (1992)

21. Lehmann, D.: Another perspective on default reasoning. Ann. Math. Artif. Intell. **15**(1), 61–82 (1995). https://doi.org/10.1007/BF01535841

22. Pearl, J.: System Z: A natural ordering of defaults with tractable applications to nonmonotonic reasoning. In: Proceedings of the 3rd Conference on Theoretical Aspects of Reasoning About Knowledge (TARK'1990), pp. 121–135. Morgan Kaufmann Publication Inc., San Francisco, CA, USA (1990)

From Forgetting Signature Elements to Forgetting Formulas in Epistemic States

Kai Sauerwald[1]([⊠]) [iD], Gabriele Kern-Isberner[2] [iD], Alexander Becker[2],
and Christoph Beierle[1] [iD]

[1] FernUniversität in Hagen, Hagen, Germany
{kai.sauerwald,christoph.beierle}@fernuni-hagen.de
[2] TU Dortmund University, Dortmund, Germany
{gabriele.kern-isberner,alexander2.becker}@tu-dortmund.de

Abstract. In this paper, we bring together marginalization and forgetting of signature elements in the framework of epistemic states. Marginalization of epistemic states is a specific approach to actively reduce signatures, also aiming at forgetting atoms which are very well known from probability theory. On the other hand, rooted in Boole's variable elimination, Delgrande's knowledge level account of forgetting provides a general approach to forgetting syntax elements from sets of formulas with links to many other forgetting operations. We generalize Delgrande's axioms to epistemic states and show that marginalization is the most specific and informative forgetting operator that satisfies these axioms. Moreover, we propose rephrasing Delgrande's postulates suitable for forgetting formulas by transferring the basic ideas of the axioms to forgetting formulas in epistemic states.

1 Introduction

Forgetting has become recently an emerging topic in AI and there exist several approaches to forgetting with different aims and unique viewpoints on forgetting. Some works understand forgetting as a technical procedure for removing signature elements. Examples are Boole's variable elimination [6], fact forgetting in first-order logic [8], and forgetting in modal logic [2]. However, none of these specific approaches argues about a general notion of forgetting; they rather provide a way to compute the result of forgetting. Delgrande [7] provides a general forgetting approach with the goal to unify many of the hitherto existing logic-specific approaches. Moreover, he states a set of properties he refers to as *right* and *desirable* when it comes to the notion of forgetting [7].

In contrast to the above-mentioned approaches, Beierle et al. [5] argue that forgetting should also be considered as a process of everyday life, which plays an important role in the organization of an agent's mind. The general framework for cognitively different kinds of forgetting proposed by Beierle et al. [5] takes into account the common-sense understanding of forgetting and its realization by means of ordinal conditional functions.

F. Dupin de Saint-Cyr et al. (Eds.): SUM 2022, LNAI 13562, pp. 92–106, 2022.
https://doi.org/10.1007/978-3-031-18843-5_7

This paper contributes results to the clarification of the overall landscape of different forgetting approaches. We state that Delgrande's forgetting approach [7] is included in and even generalized by the cognitively different kinds of forgetting given by Beierle et al. [5], concretely by means of marginalization. Moreover, we present results that give a reason for questioning Delgrande's claim that his forgetting properties are the *"right"* and *"desirable"* properties to axiomatise the general properties of all kinds of forgetting; it seems that Delgrande's properties merely only capture forgetting of signature elements. Thus, the results presented here form another step towards a general framework for different kinds of forgetting, and provide a deeper understanding of their properties and inherent differences. This paper provides the following main contributions:

- an adoption of Delgrande's postulates for forgetting to epistemic states,
- an adoption of Delgrande's postulates for forgetting to formulas, and
- several formal results regarding these postulates, including proof that marginalization satisfies Delgrande's postulates.

Due to space reasons, we omit the proofs and refer to our workshop paper [3], which contains proofs for all results presented here.

This paper is organized as follows. In Sect. 2, we give all the preliminaries needed in the later sections including model theoretical basics and ordinal conditional functions. Then we present both of the above-mentioned general forgetting approaches in Sect. 3 and show that marginalization extends Delgrande's forgetting to epistemic states, in the sense that both approaches always result in the same posterior beliefs. In Sect. 4, we will then generalize and extend the properties stated by Delgrande to epistemic states, and show that marginalization satisfies all of them. Moreover, we conclude that marginalization is the most specific approach satisfying these properties. Finally, we extend the same properties to forgetting formulas in epistemic states. It will turn out that this yields only an approach to forgetting formulas that is trivial. In Sect. 6, we present our conclusions as well as some outlook for future work.

2   Formal Basics

In the following, we introduce the formal basics as needed in this work. With $\mathcal{L}_\Sigma$ we denote a propositional language over the finite signature Σ with formulas $\varphi, \psi \in \mathcal{L}_\Sigma$. We abbreviate conjunctions $\varphi \wedge \psi$ by the juxtaposition $\varphi\psi$, and instead of writing $\neg\varphi$ we often abbreviate the negation of a formula φ by an overline, i.e., we write $\overline{\varphi}$. The corresponding interpretations are denoted as Ω_Σ. The interpretations $\omega \in \Omega_\Sigma$ that satisfy a formula $\varphi \in \mathcal{L}_\Sigma$, i.e., $\omega \models \varphi$, are called models of φ and the set of all models of φ is denoted by $[\![\varphi]\!]_\Sigma$. If the signature of a model set is unambiguously given by the context, we also write $[\![\varphi]\!]$ instead. The explicit declaration of the corresponding signature is of particular importance when arguing about different signatures. Moreover, each model $\omega \in \Omega_\Sigma$ can also be considered as a conjunction of literals corresponding to the truth values ω assigns to each signature element $\rho \in \Sigma$.

When we specifically want to argue about some signature elements in an interpretation $\omega \in \Omega_\Sigma$, we denote those signature elements $\rho \in \Sigma$ as $\dot\rho$ for which the concrete truth assignment is not needed, e.g. $p\dot b\dot f \in \Omega_\Sigma$ with $\Sigma = \{p, b, f\}$. For two formulas $\varphi, \psi \in \mathcal{L}_\Sigma$, we say that φ entails ψ, denoted as $\varphi \models_\Sigma \psi$, if $\llbracket\varphi\rrbracket \subseteq \llbracket\psi\rrbracket$. In case that both model sets are equal, φ and ψ are equivalent, i.e., $\varphi \equiv \psi$, if both, $\varphi \models \psi$ and $\psi \models \varphi$, hold. Furthermore, the deductively closed set of all formulas that can be inferred from a formula $\varphi \in \mathcal{L}_\Sigma$ is given by $Cn_\Sigma(\varphi) = \{\psi \in \mathcal{L}_\Sigma \mid \varphi \models_\Sigma \psi\}$. Again, the signature in the index of the Cn operator as well as for $\models$ can be omitted when it is clearly given by the context. Notice that a formula $\varphi \in \mathcal{L}_\Sigma$ is always equivalent to its deductive closure, since their models are equal. The deductive closure $Cn_\Sigma(\varphi)$ of a formula $\varphi \in \mathcal{L}_\Sigma$ can also be expressed by means of the theory $Th(\llbracket\varphi\rrbracket) = \{\psi \in \mathcal{L}_\Sigma \mid \llbracket\varphi\rrbracket \models \psi\}$ of its models $\llbracket\varphi\rrbracket$. All the above-mentioned notions extend naturally to sets of formulas $\Gamma \subseteq \mathcal{L}_\Sigma$.

For $\omega \in \Omega_\Sigma$ and $\omega' \in \Omega_{\Sigma'}$ with $\Sigma' \subseteq \Sigma$, with often consider whether $\omega \models \omega'$ holds. In this context, ω' is understood as the conjunction of literals corresponding to the interpretation ω', hence ω' is considered as a formula over Σ. We will make use of this notation several times in this paper.

The following definition considers the reduction and expansion of sets of models, which allows us to argue about models in subsignatures or supersignatures as well.

Definition 1 ([7]). *Let $\Sigma' \subseteq \Sigma$ be signatures and let $\varphi \in \mathcal{L}_\Sigma$ and $\varphi' \in \mathcal{L}_{\Sigma'}$ be formulas. The* reduction to Σ' *of models $\llbracket\varphi\rrbracket_\Sigma$ is defined as*

$$(\llbracket\varphi\rrbracket_\Sigma)_{|\Sigma'} = \{\omega' \in \Omega_{\Sigma'} \mid \text{there is } \omega \in \llbracket\varphi\rrbracket_\Sigma \text{ s.t. } \omega \models_\Sigma \omega'\}.$$

The expansion to Σ *of models $\llbracket\varphi'\rrbracket_{\Sigma'}$ is defined as*

$$(\llbracket\varphi'\rrbracket_{\Sigma'})_{\uparrow\Sigma} = \bigcup_{\omega' \in \llbracket\varphi'\rrbracket_{\Sigma'}} \omega'_{\uparrow\Sigma},$$

where $\omega'_{\uparrow\Sigma} = \{\omega \in \Omega_\Sigma \mid \omega \models_\Sigma \omega'\}$.

Note that $\omega \models_\Sigma \omega'$, intuitively, denotes that $\omega \in \Omega_\Sigma$ is more specific than $\omega' \in \Omega_{\Sigma'}$ with respect to Σ, which holds if and only if $\omega_{|\Sigma'} = \omega'$ holds. Furthermore, notice that multiple subsequently performed reductions $(\llbracket\varphi\rrbracket_{|\Sigma'})_{|\Sigma''}$ can be reduced to a single reduction $\llbracket\varphi\rrbracket_{|\Sigma''}$, if the signature Σ'' is a subset of Σ'.

In this work, we generally argue about epistemic states in the form of ordinal conditional functions (OCFs) introduced in a more general form by Spohn [9]. An OCF κ is a ranking function that assigns a rank $r \in \mathbb{N}_0$ to each interpretation $\omega \in \Omega_\Sigma$ with $\kappa^{-1}(0) \neq \emptyset$. The rank of an interpretation can be understood as a degree of plausibility, where $\kappa(\omega) = 0$ means that ω is most plausible. The interpretations with rank 0, according to an OCF κ, are also called models of κ, and are therefore denoted by $\llbracket\kappa\rrbracket_\Sigma$. The rank of a formula $\kappa(\varphi) = \min\{\kappa(\omega) \mid \omega \in \llbracket\varphi\rrbracket\}$ is given by the minimal rank of its models, where $\kappa(\varphi \vee \psi) = \min\{\kappa(\varphi), \kappa(\psi)\}$. The beliefs of an OCF

$Bel_\Sigma(\kappa) = \{\varphi \in \mathcal{L}_\Sigma \mid [\![\kappa]\!] \models \varphi\}$ is the deductively closed set of formulas $\varphi \in \mathcal{L}_\Sigma$ that are satisfied by the OCF's models $[\![\kappa]\!]_\Sigma$. Instead of $Bel_\Sigma(\kappa) \models \varphi$, we also write $\kappa \models \varphi$.

3 Delgrande's Forgetting and Marginalization

In this section, we will first recall Delgrande's general forgetting approach [7] as well as some of its most important properties. Afterwards, we consider the OCF marginalization as a kind of forgetting [5] and show that it generalizes Delgrande's definition to epistemic states.

3.1 Delgrande's General Forgetting Approach

Delgrande [7] defines a general forgetting approach with the goal to unify many of the hitherto existing logic-specific forgetting definitions, e.g. forgetting in propositional logic [6], first-order logic [8], or answer set programming [10,11]. While most of these logic-specific approaches depend on the syntactical structure of the knowledge, Delgrande defines forgetting on the knowledge level itself, which means that it is independent of any syntactic properties, and only argues about the beliefs that can be inferred. Concretely, this is realized by arguing about the deductive closure $Cn_\Sigma(\Gamma)$ of a set of formulas Γ.

Definition 2 ([7]). *Let Σ and P be signatures, let $\mathcal{L}_\Sigma$ be a language with corresponding consequence operator Cn_Σ, and let $\mathcal{L}_{\Sigma \setminus P} \subseteq \mathcal{L}_\Sigma$ be a sublanguage of $\mathcal{L}_\Sigma$. Forgetting a signature P in a set of formulas $\Gamma \subseteq \mathcal{L}_\Sigma$ is defined as $\mathcal{F}(\Gamma, P) = Cn_\Sigma(\Gamma) \cap \mathcal{L}_{\Sigma \setminus P}$.*

By intersecting the prior knowledge $Cn_\Sigma(\Gamma)$ with the sublanguage $\mathcal{L}_{\Sigma \setminus P}$ all formulas that mention any signature element $\rho \in P$ will be removed. Therefore, forgetting according to Definition 2 results in those consequences of Γ that are included in the reduced language $\mathcal{L}_{\Sigma \setminus P}$. However, since many of the logic-specific forgetting approaches do not result in a sublanguage, Delgrande provides a second definition of forgetting that results in the original language instead. This allows comparing the results of the different forgetting approaches more easily.

Definition 3 ([7]). *Let Σ and P be signatures and let $\mathcal{L}_\Sigma$ be a language with corresponding consequence operator Cn_Σ. Forgetting a signature P in the original language $\mathcal{L}_\Sigma$ in a set of formulas $\Gamma \subseteq \mathcal{L}_\Sigma$ is defined as $\mathcal{F}_O(\Gamma, P) = Cn_\Sigma(\mathcal{F}(\Gamma, P))$.*

Thereby, forgetting in the original language $\mathcal{L}_\Sigma$ is defined as the deductive closure of $\mathcal{F}(\Gamma, P)$ with respect to Σ. Due to the syntax independent nature of Delgrande's forgetting definition, it is theoretically applicable to each logic with a well-defined consequence operator.

Note that $\mathcal{F}_O(\Gamma, P)$ contains formulas mentioning the forgotten signature elements P, as $\mathcal{F}_O(\Gamma, P)$ is deductively closed with respect to Σ. However, we know that these formulas do not provide any information about P. The following theorem captures this property of Delgrands's definition of forgetting from a model theoretical point of view.

Theorem 4 ([7]). *Let $\Gamma \subseteq \mathcal{L}_\Sigma$ be a set of formulas and let P be a signature, then the following equations hold:*

1. $[\![\mathcal{F}(\Gamma, P)]\!]_{\Sigma \setminus P} = ([\![\Gamma]\!]_\Sigma)_{|(\Sigma \setminus P)}$
2. $[\![\mathcal{F}(\Gamma, P)]\!]_\Sigma = (([\![\Gamma]\!]_\Sigma)_{|(\Sigma \setminus P)})_{\uparrow \Sigma}$

As a direct consequence of Theorem 4, we obtain that the models of forgetting in the original language are equal to those of forgetting in the reduced language with respect to Σ.

Corollary 5. *Let $\Gamma \subseteq \mathcal{L}_\Sigma$ be a set of formulas and P a signature, then it holds that $[\![\mathcal{F}_O(\Gamma, P)]\!]_\Sigma = ([\![\mathcal{F}(\Gamma, P)]\!]_{\Sigma \setminus P})_{\uparrow \Sigma} = [\![\mathcal{F}(\Gamma, P)]\!]_\Sigma$.*

We illustrate the relations of both forgetting definitions stated by Delgrande, forgetting in the reduced as well as in the original language, and its effects on the semantic level.

Example 6. Consider the knowledge base $\Gamma = \{p \to b, f \to \overline{p}, f \to b, \overline{f} \to (p \vee \overline{b})\} \subseteq \mathcal{L}_\Sigma$ with $\Sigma = \{p, b, f\}$, where the signature elements can be read as:

$$p - \text{the observed animal is a penguin,}$$
$$b - \text{the observed animal is a bird,}$$
$$f - \text{the observed animal can fly.}$$

Thus, $\overline{f} \to (p \vee \overline{b})$ for example reads *if the observed animal cannot fly, then it is a penguin or not a bird at all.* In the following, we want to forget the subsignature $\{p\} \subseteq \Sigma$. Forgetting $\{p\}$ in the reduced language $\mathcal{L}_{\Sigma \setminus \{p\}}$ results in

$$\mathcal{F}(\Gamma, \{p\}) = Cn_\Sigma(\Gamma) \cap \mathcal{L}_{\Sigma \setminus \{p\}} = Th_\Sigma([\![\Gamma]\!]_\Sigma) \cap \mathcal{L}_{\Sigma \setminus \{p\}},$$

where $[\![\Gamma]\!]_\Sigma = \{\overline{p}\overline{b}\overline{f}, p b \overline{f}, \overline{p} b f\}$. Concretely, $\mathcal{F}(\Gamma, \{p\})$ consists of all conclusions that can be drawn from Γ and are part of the reduced language $\mathcal{L}_{\Sigma \setminus \{p\}}$, i.e., those conclusions that do not argue about penguins (p). According to Theorem 4, we know that the models after forgetting $\{p\}$ from Γ correspond to the prior models $[\![\Gamma]\!]_\Sigma$ reduced to $\Sigma \setminus \{p\}$:

$$[\![\mathcal{F}(\Gamma, \{p\})]\!]_{\Sigma \setminus \{p\}} = ([\![\Gamma]\!]_\Sigma)_{|\Sigma \setminus \{p\}}$$
$$= \{\overline{p}\overline{b}\overline{f}, p b \overline{f}, \overline{p} b f\}_{|\Sigma \setminus \{p\}} = \{\overline{b}\overline{f}, b\overline{f}, bf\}.$$

Thus, the posterior models after forgetting $\{p\}$ are obtained by mapping each interpretation $\dot{p}b\dot{f}$ to $\dot{b}\dot{f}$.

If we forget $\{p\}$ in the original language $\mathcal{L}_\Sigma$ instead, we obtain

$$\mathcal{F}_O(\Gamma, \{p\}) = Cn_\Sigma(\mathcal{F}(\Gamma, \{p\})) = Th([\![\mathcal{F}(\Gamma, \{p\})]\!]_\Sigma)$$
$$= Th(([\![\mathcal{F}(\Gamma, \{p\})]\!]_{\Sigma \setminus \{p\}})_{\uparrow \Sigma}) = Th((([\![\Gamma]\!]_\Sigma)_{|\Sigma \setminus \{p\}})_{\uparrow \Sigma}).$$

Table 1. Models of Γ, $\mathcal{F}(\Gamma, \{p\})$, and $\mathcal{F}_O(\Gamma, \{p\})$ with respect to the corresponding signatures of the languages, where $\Gamma = \{p \rightarrow b, f \rightarrow \overline{p}, f \rightarrow b, \overline{f} \rightarrow (p \vee \overline{b})\} \subseteq \mathcal{L}_\Sigma$ and $\Sigma = \{p, b, f\}$.

$[\![\Gamma]\!]_\Sigma$	$[\![\mathcal{F}(\Gamma, \{p\})]\!]_{\Sigma \setminus \{p\}}$	$[\![\mathcal{F}_O(\Gamma, \{p\})]\!]_\Sigma$
$\overline{p}b\overline{f},\ pb\overline{f},\ \overline{p}bf$	$\overline{b}\overline{f},\ b\overline{f},\ bf$	$\overline{p}\overline{b}\overline{f},\ p\overline{b}\overline{f},\ \overline{p}b\overline{f},$
		$pb\overline{f},\ \overline{p}bf,\ pbf$

By means of the deductive closure of $\mathcal{F}(\Gamma, \{p\})$ with respect to Σ, the result of forgetting in the reduced language is extended by those formulas $\varphi \in \mathcal{L}_\Sigma$ in the original language that can be inferred by it. However, due to the relations of the prior models $[\![\Gamma]\!]_\Sigma$ and those after forgetting $\{p\}$ in the reduced and the original language

$$[\![\mathcal{F}_O(\Gamma, \{p\})]\!]_\Sigma = (([\![\Gamma]\!]_\Sigma)_{|\Sigma \setminus \{p\}})_{\uparrow\Sigma}$$
$$= (\{\overline{p}\overline{b}\overline{f}, pb\overline{f}, \overline{p}bf\}_{|\Sigma \setminus \{p\}})_{\uparrow\Sigma} = \{\overline{b}\overline{f}, b\overline{f}, bf\}_{\uparrow\Sigma}$$
$$= \{\overline{p}\overline{b}\overline{f}, p\overline{b}\overline{f}, pb\overline{f}, \overline{p}b\overline{f}, \overline{p}bf, pbf\},$$

we see that $\mathcal{F}_O(\Gamma, \{p\})$ can only contain trivial proposition about penguins (p), since we know that if $p\overline{b}\overline{f} \in [\![\mathcal{F}_O(\Gamma, \{p\})]\!]$, then $\overline{p}\overline{b}\overline{f} \in [\![\mathcal{F}_O(\Gamma, \{p\})]\!]$ must hold as well. This way non-trivial propositions about penguins are prevented, which is why forgetting in the original language can still be considered as forgetting p. We provide an overview of the different models in Table 1.

Besides defining a general forgetting approach, Delgrande also states several properties of his definition, which he refers to as *right* and *desirable* [7]. The following theorem lists these properties as **(DFP-1)-(DFP-7)**.

Theorem 7 ([7]). *Let $\mathcal{L}_\Sigma$ be a language over a signature Σ and let Cn_Σ be the corresponding consequence operator. The following postulates are satisfied by $\mathcal{F}$ for all sets of formulas $\Gamma, \Gamma' \subseteq \mathcal{L}_\Sigma$ and signatures P, P':*

(DFP-1) $\Gamma \models \mathcal{F}(\Gamma, P)$
(DFP-2) If $\Gamma \models \Gamma'$, then $\mathcal{F}(\Gamma, P) \models \mathcal{F}(\Gamma', P)$
(DFP-3) $\mathcal{F}(\Gamma, P) = Cn_{\Sigma \setminus P}(\mathcal{F}(\Gamma, P))$
(DFP-4) If $P' \subseteq P$, then $\mathcal{F}(\Gamma, P) = \mathcal{F}(\mathcal{F}(\Gamma, P'), P)$
(DFP-5) $\mathcal{F}(\Gamma, P \cup P') = \mathcal{F}(\Gamma, P) \cap \mathcal{F}(\Gamma, P')$
(DFP-6) $\mathcal{F}(\Gamma, P \cup P') = \mathcal{F}(\mathcal{F}(\Gamma, P), P')$
(DFP-7) $\mathcal{F}(\Gamma, P) = \mathcal{F}_O(\Gamma, P) \cap \mathcal{L}_{\Sigma \setminus P}$

(DFP-1) states the monotony of forgetting, which means that it is not possible to obtain new knowledge by means of forgetting. **(DFP-2)** states that any consequence relation $\Gamma \models \Gamma'$ of prior knowledge sets is preserved after forgetting a signature P in both. **(DFP-3)** describes that forgetting always results in deductively closed knowledge set with respect to the reduced signature. This also corresponds to Delgrande's idea of defining forgetting on the knowledge level – forgetting is applied to a deductively closed set and results in such. In **(DFP-4)**, Delgrande states that forgetting two signatures P' and P consecutively always equals the forgetting of P, if P' is included in P. Thus, forgetting a signature twice has no effect on the prior knowledge. **(DFP-5)** provides that the forgetting of multiple signature elements is decomposable to multiple forgetting operations. Moreover, due to **(DFP-6)** the order of forgetting does not affect the result. Finally, **(DFP-7)** describes the relation between forgetting in the original and the reduced language by stating that the result of forgetting in the reduced language can always be obtained by intersecting the result of forgetting in the original language with the reduced language. Note that we changed the notation of **(DFP-7)** in order to make it more explicit. For more information on **(DFP-1)**-**(DFP-7)**, we refer to Delgrande [7].

3.2   Marginalization

A general framework of forgetting and its instantiation to an approach using OCFs is given by Beierle et al. [5]. For the purpose of this paper, we concentrate on marginalization, which on a cognitive level corresponds to the notion of focusing and can briefly be summarized as:

1. Focusing on relevant aspects retains our beliefs about them.
2. Focusing on relevant aspects (temporarily) changes our beliefs such that they do not contain any information about irrelevant aspects anymore.

In practice, this notion of forgetting is useful when it comes to efficient and focused query answering by means of abstracting from irrelevant details, e.g. marginalization is crucially used in all inference techniques for probabilistic networks. At this point, we consider the relevant aspects to be given and focus on the marginalization (Definition 8) as a kind of forgetting as such.

Definition 8 ([5]). *Let κ be an OCF over a signature Σ and let $\omega' \in \Omega_{\Sigma'}$ be an interpretation with respect to the signature $\Sigma' \subseteq \Sigma$. The OCF $\kappa_{|\Sigma'}$ is called the* marginalization of κ to Σ' *with*

$$\kappa_{|\Sigma'}(\omega') = \min\{\kappa(\omega) \mid \omega \in \Omega_\Sigma \text{ with } \omega \models \omega'\}.$$

By marginalizing an OCF to a subsignature Σ', we consider interpretations over Σ' as conjunctions and assign the corresponding rank to them. Note that the marginalization for OCFs presented here is a special case of the general *forgetful functor* $\mathrm{Mod}(\sigma)$ from Σ-models to Σ'-models given by Beierle and Kern-Isberner [4] where σ is the inclusion from Σ' to Σ.

The first notion of focusing corresponds to Lemma 9, which states that a formula over the reduced signature is believed after the marginalization if and only if it is also believed by the prior OCF. Thus, the beliefs that only argue about the relevant aspects Σ' are retained.

Lemma 9. *Let κ be an OCF over a signature Σ and let $\Sigma' \subseteq \Sigma$ be a subsignature of Σ. For each $\varphi \in \mathcal{L}_{\Sigma'}$ the following holds:*

$$\kappa_{|\Sigma'} \models \varphi \Leftrightarrow \kappa \models \varphi$$

Note that Lemma 9 is a special case of the effect of marginalization on conditional beliefs [5, Prop. 1]. In the following, we provide that, similarly to Delgrande's forgetting, marginalization reduces beliefs to a subsignature.

Proposition 10. *Let κ be an OCF over a signature Σ and let $\Sigma' \subseteq \Sigma$ be a subsignature of Σ.*

$$Bel(\kappa_{|\Sigma'}) = Bel(\kappa) \cap \mathcal{L}_{\Sigma'}$$

Thereby, Proposition 10 also corresponds to the second notion of focusing given in the beginning of Sect. 3.2, due to the intersection with reduced language $\mathcal{L}_{\Sigma'}$. The above-stated relations of the prior and posterior beliefs further imply that the models of the posterior beliefs are equal to the those of the prior when reducing them to Σ' (Proposition 11). This rather technical property allows us to freely switch between the models of the marginalized and the prior OCF.

Proposition 11. *Let κ be an OCF over a signature Σ and let $\Sigma' \subseteq \Sigma$ be a subsignature of Σ. Then $[\![\kappa_{|\Sigma'}]\!] = [\![\kappa]\!]_{|\Sigma'}$ holds.*

Similar to Delgrande's idea of forgetting in the original language, we might be interested in arguing about the original signature after focusing , e.g. for reasons of comparability. Thus, we define the concept of lifting an OCF in Definition 12 below.

Definition 12. *Let κ' be an OCF over a signature $\Sigma' \subseteq \Sigma$. A lifting of κ' to Σ, denoted by $\kappa'_{\uparrow\Sigma}$, is uniquely defined by $\kappa'_{\uparrow\Sigma}(\omega) = \kappa'(\omega_{|\Sigma'})$ for all $\omega \in \Omega_\Sigma$.*

By means of lifting an OCF κ' over signature Σ' to a signature Σ with $\Sigma' \subseteq \Sigma$, we (re-)introduce new signature elements to κ' in a way that $\kappa'_{\uparrow\Sigma}$ acts invariantly towards them. This is guaranteed by the fact that all interpretations $\omega \in \Omega_\Sigma$ that only differ in the truth value they assign to the new signature elements $\Sigma \setminus \Sigma'$ are assigned to the same rank. Analogously to Proposition 11, note that that the models of a lifted OCF are equal to the prior models when expanded to the super-signature.

Proposition 13. *Let κ' be an OCF over a signature $\Sigma' \subseteq \Sigma$. Then the models of the lifted κ' are the expanded models of κ', i.e., $[\![\kappa'_{\uparrow\Sigma}]\!] = [\![\kappa']\!]_{\uparrow\Sigma}$.*

Therefore, we also know that the beliefs after lifting are equivalent to the prior with respect to Σ, which can also be denoted as the deductive closure of the prior beliefs with respect to Σ.

Proposition 14. *Let κ' be an OCF over a signature $\Sigma' \subseteq \Sigma$ and let $\kappa'_{\uparrow\Sigma}$ be a lifting of κ' to Σ, then the beliefs of $\kappa'_{\uparrow\Sigma}$ are given by $Bel(\kappa'_{\uparrow\Sigma}) = Cn_\Sigma(Bel(\kappa'))$.*

Proposition 14 clearly shows that the beliefs of a marginalized OCF relate to those after lifting it to the original signature again in the same way Delgrande's forgetting in the original language relates to forgetting in the reduced language (see Definition 3).

Finally, we state that marginalization generalizes Delgrande's forgetting definition to epistemic states, since both forgetting approaches result in equivalent posterior beliefs when applied to the same prior knowledge.

Theorem 15. *Let $\Gamma \subseteq \mathcal{L}_\Sigma$ be a set of formulas and let κ be an OCF over a signature Σ with $Bel(\kappa) \equiv \Gamma$. Then $\mathcal{F}(\Gamma, P) = Bel(\kappa_{|(\Sigma \setminus P)})$ for each signature P.*

Notice that the precondition $Bel(\kappa) \equiv \Gamma$ expresses that both forgetting approaches are applied to equivalent prior beliefs, i.e., the set of formulas Delgrande's forgetting is applied to is equivalent to the prior beliefs $Bel(\kappa)$. Furthermore, note that Delgrande's forgetting definition argues about the elements that should be forgotten, while the marginalization argues about the remaining subsignature.

In the following, we illustrate the marginalization of an OCF and the subsequently performed lifting thereof. Moreover, we demonstrate how marginalization and lifting correspond to Delgrande's forgetting definitions. For this, we reconsider the scenario provided in Example 6, illustrating Delgrande's notions of forgetting.

Example 16. We illustrate a marginalization and a consecutively performed lifting of the OCF κ over $\Sigma = \{p, b, f\}$ (see Example 6) given in Table 2, as well as the relations to Delgrande's forgetting definitions. In the following, we want to forget the subsignature $\{p\} \subseteq \Sigma$.

First, we want to note that the beliefs of κ are equivalent to the knowledge base Γ (Example 6), since their corresponding models are the same:

$$Bel_\Sigma(\kappa) = Th(\llbracket \kappa \rrbracket_\Sigma) = Th(\{\overline{pb}\overline{f}, pb\overline{f}, \overline{p}bf\})$$
$$= Th(\llbracket \Gamma \rrbracket_\Sigma) = Cn_\Sigma(\Gamma) \equiv \Gamma$$

Marginalizing κ to $\Sigma \setminus P$ results in $\kappa_{|(\Sigma \setminus P)}$ as given in Table 2. There it can be seen that the posterior most plausible interpretation correspond to those of κ when omitting p, i.e., each interpretation $\dot{p}bf \in \llbracket \kappa \rrbracket$ is mapped to $\dot{b}f \in \llbracket \kappa_{|(\Sigma \setminus \{p\})} \rrbracket$. This exactly corresponds to the way Delgrande's forgetting in the reduced language affects the models of the given knowledge base Γ:

$$\llbracket \kappa_{|(\Sigma \setminus \{p\})} \rrbracket_{\Sigma \setminus P} = \llbracket \kappa \rrbracket_{|(\Sigma \setminus \{p\})} = \{\overline{pb}\overline{f}, pb\overline{f}, \overline{p}bf\}_{|(\Sigma \setminus \{p\})}$$
$$= \{\overline{b}\overline{f}, b\overline{f}, bf\} = \llbracket \mathcal{F}(\Gamma, \{p\}) \rrbracket_{\Sigma \setminus \{p\}}$$

We obtain that the posterior beliefs of the marginalization and the result of Delgrande's forgetting must be equal:

$$Bel(\kappa_{|(\Sigma \setminus \{p\})}) = Th(\llbracket \kappa_{|(\Sigma \setminus \{p\})} \rrbracket_{\Sigma \setminus \{p\}})$$
$$= Th(\{\overline{b}\overline{f}, b\overline{f}, bf\}) = Th(\llbracket \mathcal{F}(\Gamma, \{p\}) \rrbracket_{\Sigma \setminus P}) = \mathcal{F}(\Gamma, \{p\})$$

When we lift the marginalized OCF $\kappa_{|(\Sigma \setminus \{p\})}$ back to the original signature Σ, the posterior most plausible interpretations can be obtained by mapping each interpretation $\dot{b}f \in \llbracket \kappa_{|(\Sigma \setminus \{p\})} \rrbracket_{\Sigma \setminus \{p\}}$ to $\{p\dot{b}f, \overline{p}\dot{b}f\} \subseteq \llbracket (\kappa_{|(\Sigma \setminus \{p\})})_{\uparrow \Sigma} \rrbracket_\Sigma$ (see Table 2). Just as for the marginalization, this exactly corresponds to the way Delgrande's forgetting in the original language affects the prior models of the knowledge base Γ:

$$\llbracket (\kappa_{|(\Sigma \setminus \{p\})})_{\uparrow \Sigma} \rrbracket_\Sigma = \{\overline{b}\overline{f}, b\overline{f}, bf\}_{\uparrow \Sigma}$$
$$= \{\overline{pb}\overline{f}, p\overline{b}\overline{f}, pb\overline{f}, \overline{p}b\overline{f}, \overline{p}bf, pbf\} = \llbracket \mathcal{F}_O(\Gamma, \{p\}) \rrbracket_\Sigma$$

Table 2. OCFs κ over signature $\Sigma = \{p, b, f\}$, as well as its marginalization $\kappa_{|(\Sigma \setminus \{p\})}$ and the corresponding lifting $(\kappa_{|(\Sigma \setminus \{p\})})_{\uparrow \Sigma}$.

	κ	$\kappa_{|(\Sigma \setminus \{p\})}$	$(\kappa_{|(\Sigma \setminus \{p\})})_{\uparrow \Sigma}$
2	pbf, $\overline{p}b\overline{f}$	–	–
1	$p\overline{b}\,\overline{f}$, $\overline{p}\overline{b}f$, $p\overline{b}f$	$\overline{b}f$	$p\overline{b}f$, $\overline{p}\overline{b}f$
0	$\overline{p}\overline{b}\,\overline{f}$, $pb\overline{f}$, $\overline{p}bf$	$\overline{b}\,\overline{f}$, $b\overline{f}$, bf	$\overline{p}\overline{b}\,\overline{f}$, $p\overline{b}\,\overline{f}$, $pb\overline{f}$, $\overline{p}b\overline{f}$, $\overline{p}bf$, pbf

Therefore, the result of Delgrande's forgetting in the original language is equal to the beliefs after marginalizing and lifting κ:

$$Bel_\Sigma((\kappa_{|(\Sigma \setminus \{p\})})_{\uparrow \Sigma}) = Th([\![(\kappa_{|(\Sigma \setminus \{p\})})_{\uparrow \Sigma}]\!]_\Sigma)$$
$$= Th(\{\overline{p}\overline{b}\,\overline{f}, p\overline{b}\,\overline{f}, pb\overline{f}, \overline{p}b\overline{f}, \overline{p}bf, pbf\})$$
$$= Th([\![\mathcal{F}_O(\Gamma, \{p\})]\!]_\Sigma) = \mathcal{F}_O(\Gamma, \{p\})$$

From the equivalence stated in Theorem 15, we know that all relations of the logic-specific forgetting approaches and Delgrande's general approach that can be traced back to the equivalence of the results must hold for the marginalization as well. In the following, we exemplarily state this for Boole's atom forgetting in propositional logic, of which we know that it can also be described by means of $\mathcal{F}$.

Definition 17 ([6]). *Let $\varphi \in \mathcal{L}_\Sigma$ be a formula and let $\rho \in \mathcal{L}_\Sigma$ be an atom. Forgetting ρ in φ is then defined as*

$$forget(\varphi, \rho) = \varphi[\rho/\top] \vee \varphi[\rho/\bot],$$

where $\varphi[\rho/\top]$ denotes the substitution of ρ by $\top$, and $\varphi[\rho/\bot]$ the substitution by $\bot$.

Theorem 18 ([7]). *Let $\mathcal{L}_\Sigma$ be the propositional language over a signature Σ and let $\rho \in \Sigma$ be an atom. The following holds:*

$$forget(\varphi, \rho) \equiv \mathcal{F}(\varphi, \{\rho\})$$

From Theorem 15 and Theorem 18, we can directly conclude that Boole's forgetting definition can also be realized by means of a marginalization.

Corollary 19. *Let κ be an OCF over signature Σ and let $\varphi \in \mathcal{L}_\Sigma$ be a formula with $Bel(\kappa) \equiv \varphi$, then*

$$forget(\varphi, \rho) \equiv Bel(\kappa_{|\Sigma \setminus \{\rho\}})$$

holds for each atom $\rho \in \Sigma$.

4 Postulates for Forgetting Signatures in Epistemic States

Delgrande argues [7] that the properties **(DFP-1)-(DFP-7)** (see Theorem 7) of his forgetting definition are *right* and *desirable* for describing the general notions of forgetting. Since we already proved that his definition can be generalized to epistemic states by means of the marginalization, we also present an extended and generalized form of **(DFP-1)-(DFP-7)**, namely **(DFPes-1)$_\Sigma$**-**(DFPes-6)$_\Sigma$**, and show that the marginalization satisfies all of them. In the following, let Ψ, Φ be epistemic states, let P, P', P_1, P_2 be signatures, and let $\circ_f^\Sigma$ be an arbitrary operator that maps an epistemic state together with a signature to a new epistemic state:

(DFPes-1)$_\Sigma$ $Bel(\Psi) \models Bel(\Psi \circ_f^\Sigma P)$

(DFPes-2)$_\Sigma$ If $Bel(\Psi) \models Bel(\Phi)$, then $Bel(\Psi \circ_f^\Sigma P) \models Bel(\Phi \circ_f^\Sigma P)$

(DFPes-3)$_\Sigma$ If $P' \subseteq P$, then $Bel((\Psi \circ_f^\Sigma P') \circ_f^\Sigma P) \equiv Bel(\Psi \circ_f^\Sigma P)$

(DFPes-4)$_\Sigma$ $Bel(\Psi \circ_f^\Sigma (P_1 \cup P_2)) \equiv Bel(\Psi \circ_f^\Sigma P_1) \cap Bel(\Psi \circ_f^\Sigma P_2)$

(DFPes-5)$_\Sigma$ $Bel(\Psi \circ_f^\Sigma (P_1 \cup P_2)) \equiv Bel((\Psi \circ_f^\Sigma P_1) \circ_f^\Sigma P_2)$

(DFPes-6)$_\Sigma$ $Bel(\Psi \circ_f^\Sigma P) \equiv Bel((\Psi \circ_f^\Sigma P)_{\uparrow\Sigma}) \cap \mathcal{L}_{\Sigma \setminus P}$

For a detailed explanation of the above-stated postulates (**DFPes-1)$_\Sigma$**-**(DFPes-6)$_\Sigma$**, we refer to the explanations of the postulates **(DFP-1)-(DFP-7)** as originally stated by Delgrande. However, there are a few points we want to emphasise in particular. First, since the beliefs of an epistemic state are deductively closed by definition, it is not necessary to maintain **(DFP-3)**. Notice that due to omitting **(DFP-3)** the postulates **(DFP-4)-(DFP-7)** correspond to **(DFPes-3)$_\Sigma$**-**(DFPes-6)$_\Sigma$**. Furthermore, we expressed the forgetting in the original signature $\mathcal{F}_O(\Gamma, P)$ in **(DFP-7)** as the beliefs after forgetting P and lifting the posterior epistemic state back to the original signature. The models of $\mathcal{F}_O(\Gamma, P)$ are equal to the models of forgetting P in Γ in the reduced signature lifted back to the original signature, i.e., $[\![\mathcal{F}(\Gamma, P)]\!]_{\uparrow\Sigma}$ (Corollary 5). When we consider the models of $Bel((\Psi \circ_f^\Sigma P)_{\uparrow\Sigma})$, i.e., $[\![\Psi \circ_f^\Sigma P]\!]_{\uparrow\Sigma}$, we see that this also describes the models after forgetting P lifted back to the original signature. Therefore, **(DFPes-6)$_\Sigma$** exactly matches the property originally stated by **(DFP-7)**. In the following, we refer to those operators satisfying **(DFPes-1)$_\Sigma$**-**(DFPes-6)$_\Sigma$** as signature forgetting operators.

Marginalization satisfies **(DFPes-1)$_\Sigma$**-**(DFPes-6)$_\Sigma$**, and therefore not only yields results equivalent to those of Delgrande's forgetting definition, but also corresponds to the notions of forgetting stated by Delgrande by means of **(DFP-1)-(DFP-7)**.

Theorem 20. *Let κ be an OCF over signature Σ and let P be a signature. The marginalization $\kappa_{|(\Sigma \setminus P)}$ to a subsignature $(\Sigma \setminus P) \subseteq \Sigma$ satisfies (***DFPes-1***)$_\Sigma$-(***DFPes-6***)$_\Sigma$.*

Note that there exist forgetting approaches that yield results semantically equivalent to those of Delgrande's approach, but do not satisfy **(DFP-1)**-**(DFP-7)**. An example is Boole's atom forgetting (Definition 17), which violates **(DFP-3)**. From Theorem 20 above, we can also conclude that the marginalization forms the signature forgetting operator that only induces minimal changes to the prior beliefs.

Proposition 21. *Let κ be an OCF over a signature Σ, let $P \subseteq \Sigma$ be a subsignature of Σ, and let $\circ_f^\Sigma$ be an operator satisfying (**DFPes-1**)$_\Sigma$-(**DFPes-6**)$_\Sigma$, where $\kappa \circ_f^\Sigma P$ is an OCF over the reduced signature $\Sigma \setminus P$, then the following relation holds:*

$$Bel(\kappa_{|\Sigma \setminus P}) \models Bel(\kappa \circ_f^\Sigma P)$$

Thus, we know that any signature forgetting operator other than the marginalization must induce further belief changes for some epistemic states and signatures. Such signature forgetting operators could for example depend on some model prioritization in addition to the epistemic state and the signature itself.

5 Delgrand's Postulates for Forgetting Formulas

Following the overview of cognitively different kinds of forgetting given by Beierle et al. [5], there are different kinds of forgetting that, unlike marginalization, constitute forgetting with respect to formulas. Thus, to investigate Delgrande's forgetting properties for those kinds of forgetting that argue about formulas instead, we have to generalize and extend **(DFP-1)**-**(DFP-7)** such that they not only argue about arbitrary epistemic states and operators, but also about formulas. We refer to them as **(DFPes-1)**$_\mathcal{L}$-**(DFPes-6)**$_\mathcal{L}$. In the following, let Ψ, Φ be epistemic states, let $\varphi, \psi \in \mathcal{L}$ be formulas, and let $\circ_f^\mathcal{L}$ be an arbitrary belief change operator:

(DFPes-1)$_\mathcal{L}$ $Bel(\Psi) \models Bel(\Psi \circ_f^\mathcal{L} \varphi)$

(DFPes-2)$_\mathcal{L}$ If $Bel(\Psi) \models Bel(\Phi)$, then $Bel(\Psi \circ_f^\mathcal{L} \varphi) \models Bel(\Phi \circ_f^\mathcal{L} \varphi)$

(DFPes-3)$_\mathcal{L}$ If $\varphi \models \psi$, then $Bel(\Psi \circ_f^\mathcal{L} \varphi) \equiv Bel((\Psi \circ_f^\mathcal{L} \psi) \circ_f^\mathcal{L} \varphi)$

(DFPes-4)$_\mathcal{L}$ $Bel(\Psi \circ_f^\mathcal{L} (\varphi \vee \psi)) \equiv Bel(\Psi \circ_f^\mathcal{L} \varphi) \cap Bel(\Psi \circ_f^\mathcal{L} \psi)$

(DFPes-5)$_\mathcal{L}$ $Bel(\Psi \circ_f^\mathcal{L} (\varphi \vee \psi)) \equiv Bel((\Psi \circ_f^\mathcal{L} \varphi) \circ_f^\mathcal{L} \psi)$

(DFPes-6)$_\mathcal{L}$ If $\varphi \not\equiv \top$, then $Bel(\Psi \circ_f^\mathcal{L} \varphi) \not\models \varphi$

While the extension of **(DFP-1)**-**(DFP-7)** to (**DFPes-1)**$_\mathcal{L}$-**(DFPes-6)**$_\mathcal{L}$ works almost analogously to the extension of **(DFP-1)**-**(DFP-7)** to (**DFPes-1)**$_\Sigma$-**(DFPes-6)**$_\Sigma$, there exist some crucial differences, which we will address in the following.

In **(DFP-4)**, Delgrande argues about forgetting signature P, P' for which we assume that P' is fully included in P. In order to extend and generalize this property, we have to examine how this notion can be described with respect to formulas. We found it most accurate to generalize this relation of the information we would like to forget by means of the specificity of formulas, i.e., $\varphi \models \psi$. Thereby, we say that the knowledge described by ψ is fully included in that of φ, if and only if ψ can be inferred from φ. More formally, this can be stated by means of the deductive closures of φ and ψ, i.e., $\varphi \models \psi \Leftrightarrow Cn(\psi) \subseteq Cn(\varphi)$.

In **(DFP-5)** and **(DFP-6)**, Delgrande argues about forgetting two signatures P, P' at once, which is described as forgetting $P \cup P'$. On a more intuitive level this can be viewed as only forgetting a single piece of information that consist of both the information we actually like to forget. When arguing about formulas instead of signatures, this can be expressed by means of a disjunction $\varphi \vee \psi$, where φ and ψ are the two formulas we want to forget. Even though it might seem more appropriate to describe this idea by means of a conjunction $\varphi \wedge \psi$, it is not sufficient to forget the conjunction in order to forget both φ and ψ, since it is generally sufficient to forget one of the formulas to forget the conjunction as well. Thus, describing the unification of two pieces of information by means of a disjunction guarantees that both formulas can no longer be inferred after forgetting.

Just as for the postulates for forgetting signatures, we omit **(DFP-3)**, since a belief set is already deductively closed by definition. Furthermore, we omit **(DFP-7)** since it argues about the relation of forgetting in the reduced and in the original language, which is not applicable in case of forgetting formulas. Instead, we introduce an additional postulate **(DFPes-6)**$_\mathcal{L}$ that explicitly states the success of the forgetting operator, i.e., after forgetting a non-tautologous formula φ, we are no longer able to infer φ.

When extending **(DFP-1)**-**(DFP-7)** to forgetting formulas, Delgrande's idea that forgetting should be performed on the knowledge level, and therefore should be independent of the syntactic structure of the given knowledge also extends to the knowledge we want to forget. The following theorem establishes that syntax independence is implied by **(DFPes-1)**$_\mathcal{L}$-**(DFPes-6)**$_\mathcal{L}$.

Theorem 22. (Syntax Independence). *Let Ψ be an epistemic state and let $\circ_f^\mathcal{L}$ be a belief change operator satisfying **(DFPes-1)**$_\mathcal{L}$-**(DFPes-6)**$_\mathcal{L}$. The following holds for all formulas $\varphi, \psi \in \mathcal{L}$:*

$$\text{If } \varphi \equiv \psi, \text{ then } Bel(\Psi \circ_f^\mathcal{L} \varphi) \equiv Bel(\Psi \circ_f^\mathcal{L} \psi).$$

While Theorem 22 reveals satisfaction of a desirable property, our investigations show that the only forgetting operator satisfying **(DFPes-1)**$_\mathcal{L}$-**(DFPes-6)**$_\mathcal{L}$ must always forget all prior beliefs except for tautologies.

Theorem 23. (Triviality Result). *Let Ψ be an epistemic state. A belief change operator $\circ_f^\mathcal{L}$ satisfies **(DFPes-1)**$_\mathcal{L}$-**(DFPes-6)**$_\mathcal{L}$ if and only if $Bel(\Psi \circ_f^\mathcal{L} \varphi) \equiv \top$ holds for each $\varphi \in \mathcal{L}$.*

Delgrande's principles seem not to apply directly to forgetting formulas, since simply generalizing these properties to **(DFPes-1)**$_\mathcal{L}$-**(DFPes-6)**$_\mathcal{L}$ implies the triviality result stated in Theorem 23.

In the following, we discuss this observation. We still think that **(DFP-1)**-**(DFP-7)**, or **(DFPes-1)**$_\Sigma$-**(DFPes-6)**$_\Sigma$ respectively, describe properties that are *right* and *desirable* as long as we consider the forgetting of signature elements. Moreover, we agree with Delgrande insofar that belief change operators like contraction [1] are essentially different from the notion of forgetting as it is implemented by Delgrande's approach. However, we argue that Delgrande's approach and in general, approaches based on variable elimination, are too narrow to cover cognitive forgetting in its full generality. As our triviality result shows, (a direct translation of) Delgrande's postulates seem to be unsuitable for describing the forgetting of formulas. Nevertheless, as the works of Beierle et al. [5] show, very different kinds of forgetting are realizable in a common framework, distinguishable by different properties. So, as part of our future work, we pursue the research question which of Delgrande's postulates (which all seem very rational at first sight) need to be modified or omitted to make the idea of forgetting by variable elimination reconcilable to other forms of forgetting and how Delgrande's forgetting definition itself could be amended to satisfy the adapted postulates.

6   Conclusion

We discussed two of the existing approaches towards a general forgetting framework. The first approach was that of Delgrande [7] in which he gives a general forgetting definition that argues about forgetting on the knowledge level, and is capable of representing several of the hitherto existing logic-specific forgetting approaches, such as Boole's atom forgetting in propositional logic [6]. The second approach was that of Beierle et al. [5]. In contrast to Delgrande's approach, Beierle et al. define several cognitively different kinds of forgetting in a general OCF framework, which is generally more expressive than just arguing about knowledge sets. Thereby, we concretely focused on the marginalization or the concept of focusing as one kind of forgetting, respectively, which is of importance when it comes to efficient and focused query answering.

We showed that the marginalization generalizes Delgrande's forgetting definition to epistemic states by resulting in equivalent posterior beliefs, as well as holding the same properties, which Delgrande referred to as *right* and *desirable*. Furthermore, this implies that the relations Delgrande elaborated between his and the logic-specific approaches also hold for the marginalization. We exemplary showed this by means of Boole's atom forgetting in propositional logic.

Finally, we provide an adaption of Delgrande's postulates to forgetting of formulas. Our results give doubts about Delgrande's claim that his postulates are *right* and *desirable* for describing forgetting at the whole, which is mainly supported by our triviality result given in Theorem 23. This yields the interesting challenge of capturing forgetting in its full breadth. In our current work, we address this problem from an axiomatic point of view.

Acknowlegements. We would like to thank the reviewers for their fruitful, detailed, and helpful comments. This work was supported by the Deutsche Forschungsgemeinschaft (DFG, German Research Foundation), grant KE 1413/12-1 awarded to Gabriele Kern-Isberner and grant BE 1700/10-1 awarded to Christoph Beierle as part of the priority program "Intentional Forgetting in Organizations" (SPP 1921). Kai Sauerwald was supported by the grant BE 1700/10-1.

References

1. Alchourrón, C.E., Gärdenfors, P., Makinson, D.: On the logic of theory change: partial meet contraction and revision functions. J. Symbolic Logic **50**(2), 510–530 (1985)
2. Baral, C., Zhang, Y.: Knowledge updates: semantics and complexity issues. Artif. Intell. **164**(1–2), 209–243 (2005)
3. Becker, A., Kern-Isberner, G., Sauerwald, K., Beierle, C.: Forgetting formulas and signature elements in epistemic states. In: Amgoud, L., Booth, R. (eds.) 19th International Workshop on Non-Monotonic Reasoning (NMR 2021), Hanoi, Vietnam, 2–5 November 2021, Proceedings, pp. 233–242 (2021)
4. Beierle, C., Kern-Isberner, G.: Semantical investigations into nonmonotonic and probabilistic logics. Ann. Math. Artif. Intell. **65**(2–3), 123–158 (2012)
5. Beierle, C., Kern-Isberner, G., Sauerwald, K., Bock, T., Ragni, M.: Towards a general framework for kinds of forgetting in common-sense belief management. KI-Künstliche Intelligenz **33**(1), 57–68 (2019)
6. Boole, G.: An Investigation of The Laws of Thought: On Which are Founded the Mathematical Theories of Logic and Probabilities. Dover Publications, New York (1854)
7. Delgrande, J.P.: A knowledge level account of forgetting. J. Artif. Intell. Res. **60**, 1165–1213 (2017)
8. Lin, F., Reiter, R.: Forget it. In: Working Notes of AAAI Fall Symposium on Relevance, pp. 154–159 (1994)
9. Spohn, W.: Ordinal conditional functions: a dynamic theory of epistemic states. In: Causation in decision belief change, and statistics, vol. 42, pp. 105–134. Springer, Dordrecht (1988). https://doi.org/10.1007/978-94-009-2865-7_6
10. Wong, K.S.: Forgetting in logic programs. Ph.D. thesis, Ph. D. thesis, The University of New South Wales (2009)
11. Zhang, Y., Foo, N.Y.: Solving logic program conflict through strong and weak forgettings. Artif. Intell. **170**(8–9), 739–778 (2006)

Full Papers: Inconsistency

A Capacity-Based Semantics
for Inconsistency-Tolerant Inferences

Didier Dubois$^{(\boxtimes)}$ and Henri Prade

IRIT, CNRS & Université Paul Sabatier, Toulouse, France
{dubois,prade}@irit.fr

Abstract. Classical logic can deal with uncertainty caused by incomplete information and, beside the standard interpretation-based semantics, also has a semantics in terms of modalities expressing "known to be true", "known to be false", where binary-valued possibility theory and necessity measures are instrumental. When uncertainty is caused by inconsistency, the standard semantics of classical logic collapses, but the other one survives provided that we replace necessity measures by more general set functions. This is the topic of this paper where we show that various inconsistency-tolerant inferences for propositional bases, some of which defined at the syntactic level only, have a semantics in terms of binary-valued capacities.

1 Introduction

It is well-known that two major causes of uncertainty are the lack of sufficient information, on the one hand, but also the excess of information leading to conflict and inconsistency. Classical logic can deal with uncertainty due to incomplete information. Indeed, given a knowledge base in propositional logic, a given proposition can be inferred from it (hence known to be true), or its negation can be inferred, or yet neither can be inferred (the truth of the proposition is then unknown). The statement that a proposition is unknown can even be encoded in logic using a modality in the language, as done in the logic MEL [1], and more generally in modal logic.

In contrast, classical logic can hardly deal with inconsistency. When it is present in a knowledge base, mathematically any proposition can be inferred. However, inconsistent knowledge bases naturally occur in practice, for instance when a knowledge base is fed by several sources of information that may not be totally reliable and contradict each other. In that case, inconsistency-tolerant inference methods have been proposed for a long time (at least since 1970 [22]). One difficulty with these approaches comes from the fact that the usual model-based semantics of classical logic (whereby propositions are evaluated in each interpretation) collapses in the presence of inconsistency (an inconsistent knowledge base has no standard model). As a consequence many existing inconsistency-tolerant inferences are syntax-based, and no clear semantics are provided.

© The Author(s), under exclusive license to Springer Nature Switzerland AG 2022
F. Dupin de Saint-Cyr et al. (Eds.): SUM 2022, LNAI 13562, pp. 109–123, 2022.
https://doi.org/10.1007/978-3-031-18843-5_8

One way out of this difficulty is to notice that propositional logic has an alternative semantics in terms of states of information, or epistemic states, which can be called its epistemic semantics; this is justified when a set of formulas is understood as a knowledge (or belief) base. An epistemic state is a non-empty set of interpretations, and a proposition is believed to be true in an epistemic state whenever it is true in any interpretation in the epistemic state. In such a semantics, the use of possibility theory is instrumental to define the closure of a knowledge base: they are all formulas that have necessity degree equal to 1. In other words, the epistemic semantics of a (consistent) knowledge base can be explained in terms of (all-or-nothing) necessity measures.

The aim of this paper is to show that the epistemic semantics of classical logic survive in the presence of inconsistency, if we replace necessity measures by more general all-or-nothing set-functions known as capacities, expressing supported belief. Our purpose differs from the one of numerous recent works aiming at quantifying the amount of inconsistency in a classical knowledge base by means of suitable inconsistency measures (see [17] for references).

The paper is structured as follows. Section 2 recalls epistemic semantics of propositional logic, and the notion of Boolean capacity. Section 3 introduces a very basic and weak approach to inconsistent reasoning, called EIT, with epistemic semantics in terms of Boolean capacities. Section 4 recalls a modal framework for Boolean capacities, that captures the EIT logic. Section 5 shows that the Boolean capacity framework unifies several known inconsistency-tolerant inferences.

2   From Epistemic Semantics of Classical Logic to Capacities

Consider a standard propositional language $\mathcal{L}$, based on a set $\mathbb{V}$ of variables. Let $\mathcal{I}$ be the corresponding set of interpretations. In the Artificial Intelligence literature, a set of formulas $K = \{p_1, \cdots, p_n\}$ is often called a knowledge or belief base. It is supposed to contain all that an agent knows or believes about an actual state of facts. Under this view, one may argue that propositions should be evaluated on epistemic states, that is, non-empty sets $E \subset \mathcal{I}$ of interpretations, each representing all states of the world considered possible for an agent.

Usually, a formula p_i in K is evaluated on an interpretation w: w is said to satisfy p_i (denoted by $w \models p_i$) if $w \in [p_i]$ where $[p_i]$ is the set of models of p_i. In the epistemic semantics, we say that an epistemic state E satisfies a formula p if p is true in all interpretations considered possible according to E (i.e., $E \subseteq [p]$), which we denote by $E \models p$; and E satisfies a belief base K if all propositions in K are true in all interpretations considered possible according to E, formally $E \subseteq [K]$ (where $[K]$ is the set of models of K). Likewise a set of formulas K implies p if $\forall w, w \models p_i \forall p_i \in K$, then $w \models p$. This is the standard semantics we can call "objective".

We can define an epistemic counterpart of semantic consequence:

$$K \models_E p \iff \forall E \neq \emptyset \subseteq \mathcal{I}, (\forall p_i \in K, E \models p_i) \Rightarrow E \models p$$

It is easy to see that the standard and the epistemic semantics are equivalent. Indeed, there is a least informative epistemic state satisfying K, which is precisely $[K] = \bigcap_i [p_i]$. So, we have

$$K \models p \iff K \models_E p \iff [K] \subset [p]$$

In particular $K \models \neg p \iff K \models_E \neg p \iff [K] \subset [\neg p]$.[1]

In fact, using epistemic semantics, we retrieve the three epistemic statuses of propositions under incomplete information, as captured by possibility theory [12]. Let N and Π be the necessity and possibility functions induced by the non-empty disjunctive set $E \subseteq \mathcal{I}$, and such that $N(A) = 1$ if and only if $E \subseteq A$, and $\Pi(A) = 1 - N(A^c)$, where A^c is the complement of A. We extend the domain of these set-functions from sets of interpretations to the whole language, letting $N(p) = N([p])$, $\Pi(p) = \Pi([p])$, etc. Note that:

- $E \models p$ means that p is certain and corresponds to $N(p) = 1$, hence $\Pi(p) = 1$;
- $E \models \neg p$ means that p is certainly false ($\Pi(p) = 0$, hence $N(p) = 0$).
- $E \not\models p$ means that p is not certain and corresponds to $N(p) = 0$. If moreover, $E \not\models \neg p$ holds, it corresponds to the state of ignorance about p ($N(p) = N(\neg p) = 0$ or equivalently, $\Pi(p) = \Pi(\neg p) = 1$).

In this approach, it is clear that assuming $N(p_i) = 1, \forall p_i \in K$ the set of consequences of K are precisely all p such that $N(p) = 1$, i.e., they are characterized by means of the set function N, since $N(A \cap B) = \min(N(A), N(B))$.

The above epistemic semantics makes sense provided that $E \neq \emptyset$, i.e., K is consistent. For otherwise, there is no necessity measure that represents the consequences of K (all subsets $[p]$ of $\mathcal{I}$ receive the value 1 since $[K] = \emptyset$).

In order to grasp the inconsistent knowledge base case, we can replace necessity measures by a more general class of set functions: capacities. Capacities (the name was coined by Gustave Choquet [8] on the basis of an electrical analogy), also called "fuzzy measure" by Michio Sugeno [24] are increasing set functions used for representing uncertainty when they are valued on the unit interval $[0, 1]$ (probability measures, belief and plausibility functions, possibility and necessity measures, for mentioning the most usual ones only). A capacity is a set-function g with domain $2^{\mathcal{I}}$ and ranging in the unit interval, such that

- g is monotonic with inclusion;
- g satisfies the limit conditions $g(\mathcal{I}) = 1$, $g(\emptyset) = 0$.

In the following we focus on Boolean capacities that are valued on $\{0, 1\}$. The family of sets $\{A : g(A) = 1\}$ is closed under inclusion and possesses minimal elements called *focal sets*. The set $\mathcal{F}_g$ of focal sets of a Boolean capacity g forms an anti-chain (none of the focal sets is included in the other). It is clear that $g(A) = 1$ if and only if $\exists F \in \mathcal{F}_g, F \subseteq A$. We show that Boolean capacities provide semantics for several inconsistency-tolerant reasoning methods.

---

[1] *BUT we cannot express the situation when $E \not\subseteq [p]$ (i.e. $K \not\models_E p$) in the language $\mathcal{L}$. Likewise, we do not have that $K \models_E p \vee q$ if and only if $K \models_E p$ or $K \models_E q$ (only the if part holds). To fully capture the epistemic semantics, the syntax needs a modality $\square$ in front of $\mathcal{L}$-formulas so as to properly express the statement $E \subseteq [p]$ as $N(p) = 1$ [1].*

3   An Elementary Inconsistency Handling Approach

Given an inconsistent propositional knowledge base K, an elementary inconsistency-tolerant consequence relation, can be defined as follows:

$$K \models_{eit} p \iff \exists p_i \in K, p_i \text{ consistent, such that } p_i \models p.$$

It supposes basic information chunks p_i in K come from different sources. But it does not presuppose that consistent pieces of information coming from several sources can be combined to improve knowledge. It has the advantage of preserving the basic information chunks p_i in K.

This inference is thus much weaker than classical logic inference, but it remains non-trivial even if K is inconsistent. Denoting $\mathbb{C}_{eit}(K)$ the set of eit-consequences (while C_{PrL} stands for propositional logic consequences), we have that $\mathbb{C}_{eit}(K) = \bigcup_{p_i \in K} \mathbb{C}_{PrL}(\{p_i\})$. In particular, we have $\mathbb{C}_{eit}(\{p, \neg p\}) \neq \mathcal{L}$. This logic does not obey the contradiction law. It is clear that Modus Ponens is not a valid inference rule (since $\mathbb{C}_{eit}(\{p, \neg p \lor q\}) = \mathbb{C}_{PrL}(\{p\}) \cup \mathbb{C}_{PrL}(\{\neg p \lor q\})$ generally does not contain q).

We can compute the status of all propositions with respect to the knowledge base K, using the eit-inference, i.e., we can decide that any proposition p is

- *supported* if $K \models_{eit} p$ and $K \not\models_{eit} \neg p$;
- *rejected* if $K \models_{eit} \neg p$ and $K \not\models_{eit} p$;
- *unknown* if p is neither supported nor rejected, i.e., $K \not\models_{eit} p$ and $K \not\models_{eit} \neg p$;
- *conflicting* if p is both supported and rejected, i.e., $K \models_{eit} p$ and $K \models_{eit} \neg p$.

Note that if K is consistent, only the three first cases can occur. To rule out the third case we need that K contains a formula p_i having a single model w that satisfies none of the other formulas in K.

Example 1. It is inspired by one proposed by Revesz [23] in the literature on knowledge base merging. There are three variables $\{a, b, c\}$. Models are denoted by triples of truth-values for a, b, c in this order. K is made of three formulas:

- $p_1 = (a \lor c) \land \neg b$ with models $E_1 = \{100, 001, 101\}$
- $p_2 = \neg a \land (b \lor \neg c) \land (c \lor \neg b)$ with models $E_2 = \{000, 011\}$
- $p_3 = a \land b$ with models $E_3 = \{110, 111\}$.

It can be checked that, in our approach, c is unknown (implied by none of the bases), $a \land b$ is conflicting (implied by p_3 but $\neg a \lor \neg b$ is implied by p_2), $a \land b \land c$ is rejected (implied by none of the bases but its negation is implied by p_1 and p_2) as well as $a \land \neg b$ (implied by none of the bases but its negation is implied by p_2 and p_3), $a \lor b$ and $a \lor c$ are supported (implied by p_3, but rejected by none). □

At the semantic level, it comes down to defining a Boolean capacity g_K on $\mathcal{I}$ such that $g_K = \max_{p_i \in K} N_{[p_i]}$, where $N_{[p_i]}$ is the necessity measure with unique focal set focused on $[p_i]$. Now the Boolean capacity g_K has focal sets defined by $\mathcal{F}_K = \{[p_i] : p_i \in K, \nexists q \in K, q \models p_i\}$. The set $\mathcal{F}_K$ reflects the set of non-directly redundant propositions in K. In this sense, the handling of inconsistency is still resorting to possibility theory, considering each formula in K as an epistemic state for a given source of information. Since for any p, $g_K([p]) = \max_{p_i \in K} N_{[p_i]}([p])$, it is clear that

$$K \models_{eit} p \iff g_K([p]) = 1.$$

More generally a capacity g is an eit-model of K if and only if $g([p_i]) = 1, \forall p_i \in K$. It is clear that $g \geq g_K$. The four epistemic statuses of a given a proposition p based on the information provided by K, listed above, can be expressed by means of the capacity g_K, letting $A = [p]$:

– *Support*: $g_K(A) = 1$ and $g_K(A^c) = 0$. *Rejection*: $g_K(A^c) = 1$ and $g_K(A) = 0$.
– *Ignorance*: $g_K(A) = g_K(A^c) = 0$. *Conflict*: $g_K(A) = g_K(A^c) = 1$.

Important special cases of Boolean capacities are associated to various assumptions about the base K [14]:

– when there is a single proposition $K = \{p_1\}$ hence a single focal set: $\mathcal{F}_g = \{E\}$. This is equivalent to having g *minitive*, i.e., a *necessity measure*. There is only one source of information and its information is incomplete (if E is not a singleton), but there is no conflict. The general case when there is no conflict, but possible ignorance is captured by Boolean capacities such that $\min(g(A), g(A^c)) = 0$. It is easy to check that their focal sets overlap, which comes down to assuming that K is consistent. Such capacities are said to be *pessimistic* because they are less than their conjugates ($g(A) \leq 1 - g(A^c)$); see more details in [10,13].
– when all formulas in K have a single model: the focal sets are singletons $\{w_1\}, \{w_2\}, \ldots, \{w_n\}$. This is equivalent to having g is *maxitive*, i.e., a possibility measure. All sources have complete information, so there are conflicts, but no ignorance. The general case of this kind is captured by Boolean capacities such that $\max(g(A), g(A^c)) = 1$. It is easy to check that their focal sets must contain a singleton not contained in any other focal set, which comes down to assuming that K contains a formula p_i having a single model. Such capacities are said to be *optimistic* because they are not less than their conjugates ($g(A) \geq 1 - g(A^c)$); see more details in [10,13].

There is a universal counterpart to the *eit* inference, namely:

$$K \models_{\forall eit} p \iff \forall p_i \in K, p_i \models p \iff \vee_i p_i \models p.$$

Considering the capacity $g_{\forall K}(A) = \min_{p_i \in K} N_{[p_i]}(A)$, we have that $K \models_{\forall eit} p \iff g_{\forall K}([p]) = 1$. It is easy to see that $K \models_{\forall eit} p \iff \vee_{p_i \in K} p_i \models p$, since $g_{\forall K}$ is a necessity measure. This inference is very conservative (much less productive than the *eit*-consequence), but it is classical deduction from $\vee_{p_i \in K} p_i$.

4 Boolean Capacity Logic

We can embed the elementary inconsistency logic $EITL$ based on $\models_{eit}$ in a modal framework as done for PrL by the logic MEL in [1]. This is the logical framework for multiple source information, proposed in [11,14], which accounts for the above capacity-based framework. Consider a two-tiered propositional modal-like language $\mathcal{L}_{\Box}$ (the one of MEL), containing atoms of the form $\Box p$ for all formulas p in a propositional language $\mathcal{L}$, plus conjunctions and negations of such modal atoms.

A minimal epistemic logic with conflicts called MELC [11] using the language $\mathcal{L}_{\Box}$ has been proposed as a two-tiered propositional logic augmented with modal axioms weaker than the ones of MEL [14]:

1. (PrL): All axioms of propositional logic for $\mathcal{L}_{\Box}$-formulas.
2. (RM): $\Box p \to \Box q$ if $\vdash p \to q$ in PrL;
3. (N): $\Box p$, whenever p is a propositional tautology;
4. (P): $\Diamond p$ (i.e., $\neg\Box\neg p$), whenever p is a propositional tautology.

The only inference rule is modus ponens: If ϕ and $\phi \to \psi$ then ψ.

This is a fragment of the non-normal logic EMN [7]. In particular the axiom (RE): $\Box p \equiv \Box q$ if and only if $\vdash p \equiv q$ is valid. Note that the two dual modalities $\Box$ and $\Diamond$ play the same role (in particular, we can replace $\Box$ by $\Diamond$ in (RM)). Namely the above axioms remain valid if we exchange $\Box$ and $\Diamond$. So these modalities are not distinguishable.

Semantics of non-normal logics are usually expressed in terms of neighborhoods, which attach a family of subsets of interpretations to each possible world [7]. Here we do not need this complex semantics since modalities are not nested. We use Boolean capacities g on the set of interpretations $\mathcal{I}$ of the language $\mathcal{L}$. They encode a set of subsets A such that $g(A) = 1$, which is a special case of world-independent neighborhood containing $\mathcal{I}$ and closed under inclusion (after axiom RM).

We call this formalism BC $logic$, where BC stands for Boolean capacities.[2] A BC-model of an atomic formula $\Box p$ for this modal logic is then a Boolean capacity g such that $g([p]) = 1$. The satisfaction of BC-formulas $\phi \in \mathcal{L}_{\Box}$ is then defined recursively as usual:

- $g \models \Box p$, if and only if $g([p]) = 1$;
- $g \models \neg\phi$ if $g \not\models \phi$;
- $g \models \phi \wedge \psi$ if $g \models \phi$ and $g \models \psi$.

Satisfiability can be equivalently expressed in terms of the focal sets of g, as follows:

$$g \models \Box p \quad \text{iff} \quad \exists E \in \mathcal{F}_g, E \subseteq [p]. \tag{1}$$

So one might as well define a model in this logic as any antichain of subsets that form a family of focal sets of a capacity, thus laying bare the multiple-source

---

[2] In [14], it is called QC logic, where QC stands for qualitative capacities.

nature of this logic. The antichain condition can be relaxed to any n-tuple of non-empty subsets $(E_1, \ldots, E_n), \forall n > 0$. However, such tuples will generate the same Boolean capacity as the minimal subsets among them (focal sets).

Semantic entailment is defined classically, and syntactic entailment is classical propositional entailment taking RM, N, P as axiom schemata: $\Gamma \vdash_{BC} \phi$ if and only if $\Gamma \cup \{\text{all instances of } RM, N, P\} \vdash \phi$ (classically defined). It has been proved that BC logic is sound and complete wrt Boolean capacity models [14]. In fact, axiom RM clearly expresses the monotonicity of capacities, and it is easy to realize that a classical propositional interpretation of $\mathcal{L}_\square$ that respects the axioms of BC can be precisely viewed as a Boolean capacity.

The elementary inconsistency-tolerant logic EITL can be cast in BC, like propositional logic is cast in MEL. Namely a knowledge base K can be viewed as a model of $\square p$ in BC logic if, in (1), we define the subsets $E_i, i = 1, \ldots, n$ as $E_i = [p_i], p_i \in K$. Then we do have that $K \models_{eit} p$ if and only if $g_K \models \square p$. Or equivalently $\{\square p_i : p_i \in K\} \vdash_{BC} \square p$.

Note that adding standard modal logic axioms K (i.e., $\square(p \to q) \to (\square p \to \square q)$) and D (i.e., $\square p \to \Diamond p$) to BC yields the logic MEL [1]. Adding only (D) comes down to assuming $\square p \wedge \square \neg p$ false, i.e., capacities that are pessimistic.

5   Capacity Semantics for Some Known Inconsistency-Tolerant Logics

In this section, we reinterpret some known approaches to cope with inconsistency in propositional logics, such as the ones based on maximal consistent subsets, and the ones related to Belnap logic.

5.1   Reasoning with Maximal Consistent Subsets of Formulas

The oldest approach to inconsistency handling is mainly due to Rescher and Manor [22]. Suppose a propositional knowledge base $K = \{p_i : i = 1, \cdots, n\}$ is inconsistent, A maximal consistent subset (MCS) MC of K is a maximal family of formulas in K such that $\wedge_{p_i \in K}[p_i] \neq \emptyset$. To define a non-trivial consequence relation, the idea is to consider classical consequences of MCSs of K. There are two extreme possible consequence relations [22] ($\vdash_{PrL}$ is the propositional logic consequence relation):

Definition 1. *A formula p is said to be a universal (or inevitable) consequence of an inconsistent knowledge base K, denoted $K \vdash_\forall p$ if and only if $\forall MC \subseteq K, MC \vdash_{PrL} p$; p is said to be an existential (or weak) consequence of an inconsistent knowledge base K, denoted $K \vdash_\exists p$ if and only if $\exists MC \subseteq K, MC \vdash_{PrL} p$.*

The two consequence relations $\vdash_\forall$ and $\vdash_\exists$ coincide to the classical inference if K is consistent. The set of existential consequences of K is equal to $\mathbb{C}_\exists(K) = \cup_k \mathbb{C}(MC_k)$, where $\mathbb{C}(B)$ denotes the set of classical consequences of B. The existential consequence is very liberal in the sense that the set of existential consequences of K is generally inconsistent (since there may be two consistent subsets MC_1 and MC_2 such that $MC_1 \vdash_{PrL} p$ and $MC_2 \vdash_{PrL} \neg p$). In fact, the existential inference can be related to the EITL logic as follows: Let q_k be the conjunction of formulas in the maximal consistent subset MC_k, and assume there are m of them. The propositions q_i are mutually inconsistent with each other. Now,

$$K \vdash_\exists p \iff \{q_1, \dots, q_m\} \models_{eit} p.$$

The set of existential consequences $\mathbb{C}_\exists(K)$ of K can thus be associated to a Boolean capacity $g_{K\exists}$ on the set of interpretations $\mathcal{I}$. Namely define $g_{K\exists}$ as $g_{K\exists}([p_i]) = 1, \forall p_i \in K$, and $\forall C$ consistent subset of formulas in K, set $g_{K\exists}([\wedge_{p_i \in C} p_i]) = \min_{p_i \in C} g_{K\exists}([p_i]) = 1$. It is easy to see that $g_{K\exists}([p]) = 1$ if and only if $p \in \mathbb{C}_\exists(K)$. The capacity $g_{K\exists}$ has disjoint focal sets $[q_k]$.

In contrast, the set of universal consequences $\mathbb{C}_\forall(K)$ of K is consistent and deductively closed in the usual sense. It is the set of consequences of the disjunction of formulas equivalent to the MCSs: $\bigvee_k \wedge_{p_i \in MC_k} p_i$. This non-trivial consequence relation is very conservative since we can check that $\mathbb{C}_\forall(K) = \bigcap_k \mathbb{C}(MC_k)$. It is associated to the Boolean capacity of the form $g_{K\forall}([p]) = \min_{MC_k \subseteq K} N_k([p])$,[3] which is a necessity measure based on the epistemic state $[\bigvee_k \wedge_{p_i \in MC_k} p_i]$.

5.2   Belnap's Approach

At the opposite of the Rescher-Manor inconsistency-tolerant approach, the logic of Dunn-Belnap [2,3,15] does not presuppose that consistent pieces of information coming from several sources can be combined to improve knowledge. Moreover, like tri-valued Kleene logic [18], it is a multiple-valued logic with an epistemic flavor. However it is strictly weaker than Kleene logic, adding a truth-value expressing inconsistency.

Belnap [2,3] considers an artificial information processor, fed from a variety of sources, and capable of answering queries on propositions of interest. In this context, inconsistency threatens, all the more so as the information processor is supposed never to subtract information. The basic assumption is that the computer receives information about *atomic propositions* in a cumulative way from outside sources, each asserting for each atomic proposition whether it is true, false, or being silent (hence ignorant) about it.

Consider a Belnap set-up where each source i provides a set T_i of atoms considered true, a set F_i of atoms considered false, where $T_i \cap F_i = \emptyset$. This information would correspond to a *partial model*, which is a conjunction of literals, namely:

$$p_i = (\bigwedge_{a \in T_i} a) \wedge (\bigwedge_{b \in F_i} \neg b).$$

---

[3] N_k is the necessity measure associated with MC_k.

As there are n sources, we can model information coming to the processor as a knowledge base $K_B = \{p_1, \cdots, p_n\}$ containing only conjunctions of literals, aka cubes.

The notion of *epistemic set-up* is defined as an assignment, of one of four so-called *epistemic truth-values*, here denoted by $\mathbf{T}, \mathbf{F}, \mathbf{C}, \mathbf{U}$, to each atomic proposition $a, b, \ldots$:

1. Assigning $\mathbf{T}$ to a means the computer has only been told that a is true by at least one source, and false by none, which can be expressed as $K_B \models_{eit} a$ and $K_B \not\models_{eit} \neg a$.
2. Assigning $\mathbf{F}$ to a means the computer has only been told that a is false by at least one source, and true by none, which can be expressed as $K_B \models_{eit} \neg a$ and $K_B \not\models_{eit} a$.
3. Assigning $\mathbf{C}$ to a means the computer has been told at least that a is true by one source and false by another, which can be expressed as $K_B \models_{eit} a$ and $K_B \models_{eit} \neg a$.
4. Assigning $\mathbf{U}$ to a means the computer has been told nothing about a, which can be expressed as $K_B \not\models_{eit} a$ and $K_B \not\models_{eit} \neg a$.

It is clear that the above assignment of the four Belnap truth-values to atoms can be captured by the EIT logic inference for special knowledge bases containing only logical cubes. It makes it clear that Belnap truth-values express states of knowledge about the truth or falsity of Boolean atomic propositions.

Having attached an epistemic truth-value to all atoms of the language $\mathcal{L}$, this assignment is extended to all formulas in $\mathcal{L}$ using the truth tables in Table 1.

Table 1. Belnap-Dunn negation, disjunction and conjunction.

	$\neg$		$\vee$	F	U	C	T		$\wedge$	F	U	C	T
F	**T**		**F**	F	U	C	T		**F**	F	F	F	F
U	**U**		**U**	U	U	T	T		**U**	F	U	F	U
C	**C**		**C**	C	T	C	T		**C**	F	F	C	C
T	**F**		**T**	T	T	T	T		**T**	F	U	C	T

Belnap's approach relies on two orderings in $\mathbf{V}_4 = \{\mathbf{T}, \mathbf{F}, \mathbf{C}, \mathbf{U}\}$, equipping it with two lattice structures, thus yielding a bilattice:

- *The information ordering*, $\sqsubseteq$ whose meaning is "less informative than", such that $\mathbf{U} \sqsubseteq \mathbf{T} \sqsubseteq \mathbf{C}; \mathbf{U} \sqsubseteq \mathbf{F} \sqsubseteq \mathbf{C}$. It intends to reflect the amount of (possibly conflicting) data provided by the sources. $\mathbf{U}$ is at the bottom because (to quote) "it gives no information at all". $\mathbf{C}$ is at the top because (following Belnap) it gives too much information.
- *The truth ordering*, $<_t$, representing "more true than" according to which $\mathbf{F} <_t \mathbf{C} <_t \mathbf{T}$ and $\mathbf{F} <_t \mathbf{U} <_t \mathbf{T}$, each chain reflecting the truth-set of Kleene's logic. In other words, ignorance and conflict play the same role with respect to $\mathbf{F}$ and $\mathbf{T}$ according to this ordering.

The information ordering is in agreement with the specificity ordering of possibility theory [11], if we interpret Belnap truth-values as epistemic states (disjunctive subsets) on the classical logic truth-values $\{0, 1\}$:[4]

$$\mathbf{T} : \{1\}; \quad \mathbf{F} : \{0\}; \quad \mathbf{C} : \emptyset; \quad \mathbf{U} : \{0, 1\}.$$

The truth-ordering yields *the logical lattice*, which coincides with the interval extension of classical connectives, $\wedge$, $\vee$ and $\neg$ from $\{0, 1\}$ to $2^{\{0,1\}} \setminus \{\emptyset\}$. In this lattice, the maximum of $\mathbf{U}$ and $\mathbf{C}$ is $\mathbf{T}$ and their minimum is $\mathbf{F}$, as appears in Tables 1.

A valuation in Belnap logic is thus a mapping v_4 from the Pr-language to the bilattice $v_4 : \mathcal{L} \rightarrow \mathbf{V_4} = \{\mathbf{T}, \mathbf{F}, \mathbf{U}, \mathbf{C}\}$ defined according to Belnap set-up and the above truth-tables. It can be checked that no formula p in $\mathcal{L}$ is a contradiction (i.e., has value $v_4(p) = \mathbf{F}$)) nor a tautology (i.e., has value $v_4(p) = \mathbf{T}$)). In particular $a \wedge \neg a$ is not a contradiction nor is $a \vee \neg a$ a tautology. Belnap logic thus has no axiom, and has only inference rules that correspond to describing a structure of De Morgan algebra [16,21]. The designated truth-values that determine the semantic consequence in Belnap logic are $\mathbf{T}$ and $\mathbf{B}$.

This four-valued logic is not in total agreement with inferences that can be drawn from the base K_B using the EIT-consequence. The latter does sanction the a priori surprizing item $\mathbf{C} \wedge \mathbf{U} = \mathbf{F}$. Namely the Belnap truth assignment $v_4(a) = \mathbf{C}$ means $p_i \models a$ for some i and $p_j \models \neg a$ for some j, while $v_4(b) = \mathbf{U}$ means that no p_i classically infers b nor $\neg b$. It is then clear that no p_i can infer the conjunction $a \wedge b$ while $p_i \models \neg(a \wedge b)$. So $v_4(a \wedge b) = \mathbf{F}$.

However we cannot justify the (at first sight obvious) equality $\mathbf{T} \wedge \mathbf{T} = \mathbf{T}$. Indeed $v_4(a) = \mathbf{T}$ means $p_i \models a$ for some i, but $\neg a$ cannot be inferred from any p_i, and likewise for b, possibly inferred from another p_j. As a consequence, there is generally no p_k that infers the conjunction $a \wedge b$ in the sense of EITL.

In contrast, Belnap logic can be embedded in the logic BC of Boolean capacities [10]. Indeed, Belnap-Dunn truth-values described above can be expressed by means of pairs of values $(g(A), g(A^c))$ for a Boolean capacity g, restricting the set A to the set of classical models $[a]$ of an atomic formula a. Namely, in conformity with the EIT inference:

- $v_4(a) = \mathbf{T}$ is interpreted as $g([a]) = 1$ and $g([\neg a]) = 0$
- $v_4(a) = \mathbf{F}$ is interpreted as $g([a]) = 0$ and $g([\neg a]) = 1$
- $v_4(a) = \mathbf{U}$ is interpreted as $g([a]) = 0$ and $g([\neg a]) = 0$
- $v_4(a) = \mathbf{C}$ is interpreted as $g([a]) = 1$ and $g([\neg a]) = 1$

Based on this intuition, the translation of Belnap-Dunn logic into BC naturally follows.

As mentioned in Sect. 4, the modal sentence $\Box p$, where p is a propositional formula in PrL, is encoding the statement $g([p]) = 1$ for a Boolean capacity g,

---

[4] The convention for representing epistemic states is in agreement with possibility theory, but it is opposite to Dunn-Belnap's for whom the (now conjunctive) set $\{0, 1\}$ represents $\mathbf{C}$ (at the same time true and false) and the empty set represents $\mathbf{U}$ understood as the lack of information.

which clearly means that at least one source (corresponding to a focal set in $\mathcal{F}_g$) asserts p. The case where $g([\neg p]) = 0$ thus corresponds to $\Diamond p = \neg\Box\neg p$, which clearly means that no source is asserting $\neg p$. Hence, formulas in BC can be related to Belnap-Dunn truth-values [11]:

- $\Box p \wedge \Diamond p$ holds when $g([p]) = 1$ and $g([\neg p]) = 0$ (related to the epistemic truth-value **T**).
- $\Box\neg p \wedge \Diamond\neg p$ holds when $g([\neg p]) = 1$ and $g([p]) = 0$ (related to the epistemic truth-value **F**).
- $\Diamond p \wedge \Diamond\neg p$ holds when $g([p]) = 0$ and $g([\neg p]) = 0$ (related to the epistemic truth-value **U**).
- $\Box p \wedge \Box\neg p$ holds when $g([p]) = 1$ and $g([\neg p]) = 1$ (related to the epistemic truth-value **C**).

Belnap-Dunn approach first assigns epistemic truth-values to atomic propositions only. We can encode these truth-qualified atoms into the modal language of BC as follows. Let $\mathcal{T}$ denote the translation operation that takes a partial Belnap-Dunn truth-value assignment of the form $v_4(a) \in \Theta \subseteq \mathbb{V}_4$ to atomic propositional formulas, (indicating their epistemic status w.r.t. a set of sources), and turns it into a modal formula in the logic BC. For instance:

$$\mathcal{T}(v_4(a) = \mathbf{T}) = \Box a \wedge \Diamond a \qquad\qquad \mathcal{T}(v_4(a) = \mathbf{F}) = \Box\neg a \wedge \Diamond\neg a \qquad (2\text{a})$$

$$\mathcal{T}(v_4(a) = \mathbf{U}) = \Diamond a \wedge \Diamond\neg a \qquad\qquad \mathcal{T}(v_4(a) = \mathbf{C}) = \Box a \wedge \Box\neg a \qquad (2\text{b})$$

$$\mathcal{T}(v_4(a) \geq_t \mathbf{C}) = \Box a \qquad\qquad\qquad\quad \mathcal{T}(v_4(a) \leq_t \mathbf{C}) = \Box\neg a \qquad\qquad (2\text{c})$$

$$\mathcal{T}(v_4(a) \geq_t \mathbf{U}) = \Diamond a \qquad\qquad\qquad\quad \mathcal{T}(v_4(a) \leq_t \mathbf{U}) = \Diamond\neg a \qquad\qquad (2\text{d})$$

(where $\geq_t$ refers to the truth ordering). In Belnap-Dunn logic, since valuations of propositions other than elementary ones are obtained via truth tables, the translation of $\mathbb{V}_4$-truth-qualified formulas will be carried out by respecting the truth tables of the logic.

There are two designated values: **T** and **C** in Belnap-Dunn logic. So, asserting a formula p in this logic means $v_4(p) \geq \mathbf{C}$. So, for inference purposes, we only have to consider the translation of expressions of the form $\mathcal{T}(v_4(p) \geq_t \mathbf{C})$. Since $\mathcal{T}(v_4(a) \geq_t \mathbf{C}) = \Box a$, and $\mathcal{T}(v_4(\neg a) \geq_t \mathbf{C}) = \Box\neg a$ for literals, the other formulas being translated via Belnap-Dunn truth tables. It can be shown that $\mathcal{T}(v_4(a \vee b) \geq_t \mathbf{C}) = \Box a \vee \Box b$, and $\mathcal{T}(v_4(a \wedge b) \geq_t \mathbf{C}) = \Box a \wedge \Box b$ [10]. This translation sends Belnap-Dunn logic into the following fragment of the language of BC:

$$\mathcal{L}_\Box^B = \Box a | \Box\neg a | \phi \wedge \psi | \phi \vee \psi$$

where no negation appears in front of $\Box$. This is the same sublanguage as the one for the translation of Kleene logic into MEL [10]. So, the translation of a formula p from Belnap-Dunn logic (in fact, the *PrL* language) consists in adding $\Box$ in front of each literal in p. Conversely, any formula in $\mathcal{L}_\Box^B$ can be translated back to a formula in Belnap-Dunn logic.

At the inferential level, it can be shown that all inference rules of Belnap logic, once the involved formulas translated into $\mathcal{L}_\Box^B$, remain valid in BC. In fact we have a perfect coincidence between inferences in Belnap-Dunn logic, and in BC within the restricted language. Interestingly at the semantic levels the Boolean capacities equivalent to Belnap valuations v_4 are so-called atomic capacities, whose focal sets are of the form $[a], [\neg a]$, for atoms a. More details can be found in [10].

5.3   Priest Logic of Paradox

It is a 3-valued paraconsistent logic that has the same syntax as propositional logic, and the same truth tables as Kleene logic [19,20]. The truth-set of Dunn-Belnap logic is restricted to the three linearly ordered truth-values $\mathbb{P}_3 = \{\mathbf{F}, \mathbf{C}, \mathbf{T}\}$, and the designated set of truth-values is $\{\mathbf{C}, \mathbf{T}\}$, as opposed to Kleene logic where only $\mathbf{T}$ is designated; it comes down to merging $\mathbf{U}$ and $\mathbf{F}$ in Belnap $\mathbb{V}_4$. The truth tables for conjunction, disjunction and negation are obtained from the restriction of Belnap-Dunn truth tables to $\mathbb{P}_3$.[5] It is then clear that, letting v_3 denote a three-valued truth assignment ranging on $\mathbb{P}_3$, we have $\forall a \in V, v_3(a \vee \neg a) \in \{\mathbf{C}, \mathbf{T}\}$, which gives intuition for the following result by Pynko [21]:

Proposition 1. *A Hilbert system for* Priest Logic of Paradox *is obtained by Belnap-Dunn logic inference rules plus axiom* $a \vee \neg a$.

Semantic inference $\vDash_P$ from a knowledge base Γ in the Logic of Paradox is then defined by:

$$\Gamma \vDash_P p \text{ iff } \forall v_3, \text{ if } v_3(p_i) \in \{\mathbf{C}, \mathbf{T}\}, \forall p_i \in \Gamma \text{ then } v_3(p) \in \{\mathbf{C}, \mathbf{T}\}$$

Any sentence of the form $p \vee \neg p$ is then clearly a tautology, since $v_3(p \vee \neg p) \in \{\mathbf{C}, \mathbf{T}\}$ for any proposition p in the Logic of Paradox. In fact all tautologies of propositional calculus can be recovered, but modus ponens does not hold in this logic, where there is no contradiction (formulas that always take truth-value $\mathbf{F}$).

Like Kleene logic, Priest Logic of Paradox has been translated into MEL [9]. We can also get it from the translation of Belnap-Dunn logic into BC. To this end, we must add to BC an axiom that is the translation of the axiom $a \vee \neg a$ that has been added to Belnap-Dunn logic. Based on our translation principles for Belnap-Dunn logic, it follows that $\mathcal{T}(v_4(a \vee \neg a) \geq_t \mathbf{C}) = \Box a \vee \Box \neg a$, which must be added as an (unusual) axiom to the Belnap fragment of BC.

More generally, we can strengthen BC by adding the converse D^d of axiom D: $\Diamond p \rightarrow \Box p$. Translating formulas of Priest logic (Belnap-Dunn's plus axiom $a \vee \neg a$) to BC + D^d yields:

$$\mathcal{T}(v_4(a) = \mathbf{T}) = \Diamond a; \qquad\qquad \mathcal{T}(v_4(a) = \mathbf{F}) = \Diamond \neg a; \qquad (3a)$$

$$\mathcal{T}(v_4(a) = \mathbf{C}) = \Box a \wedge \Box \neg a; \qquad\qquad\qquad\qquad (3b)$$

$$\mathcal{T}(v_4(a) \geq_t \mathbf{C}) = \Box a; \qquad\qquad \mathcal{T}(v_4(a) \leq_t \mathbf{C}) = \Box \neg a. \qquad (3c)$$

---

[5] Remember that values $\mathbf{U}$ and $\mathbf{C}$ play strictly equivalent roles for the truth ordering in $\mathbb{V}_4$.

while $\mathcal{T}(v_4(a) = \mathbf{U}) = \Diamond a \vee \Diamond \neg a = \bot$ in BC + D^d. Stating elementary formula a in Priest logic is translated into $\Box a$ in BC. But since $\Box a \wedge \Box \neg a$ is no longer a contradiction, we cannot use modus ponens in BC $+\mathrm{D}^d$ in order to infer $\Box b$ from $\{\Box a, \Box \neg a \vee \Box b\}$.

We thus get, for the translation of Priest logic, the logic BC restricted to language $\mathcal{L}_{\Box}^B$ with the supplementary axiom $\Box a \vee \Box \neg a$. But this axiom is not in the spirit of modal logics. Due to the symmetric roles of $\mathbf{C}$ and $\mathbf{U}$ in the bilattice, and the corresponding symmetry of modalities $\Box$ and $\Diamond$ in BC, we can modify our translation principles by switching the modalities $\Box$ and $\Diamond$ and express Priest logic inference inside BC + D. It comes down, as pointed out in [9], to replacing $\mathbf{C}$ by $\mathbf{U}$, assuming the same conventions as for the translation of Kleene logic, albeit now considering both $\mathbf{U}$ and $\mathbf{T}$ as designated truth-values. It forces to changing the target sublanguage $\mathcal{L}_{\Box}^B$ of $\mathcal{L}_{\Box}$ into $\mathcal{L}_{\Diamond}^B$ containing only atoms $\Diamond a, \Diamond \neg a$ and their combinations via $\wedge$ and $\vee$. Note that $\mathcal{L}_{\Box}^B \cap \mathcal{L}_{\Diamond}^B = \emptyset$. It leads to translating the assertion of a proposition p in Priest logic as $\mathcal{T}(v_3(p) \in \{\mathbf{T}, \mathbf{U}\})$ and adding axiom $\Diamond a \vee \Diamond \neg a$ (an avatar of axiom D) to be used in $\mathcal{L}_{\Diamond}^B$.

This is summarized by a theorem in [9], (resp. reformulated in [10]), saying that there is a consequence-preserving translation into MEL (resp. BC + D) of Priest logic, viewed as Kleene logic with designated truth-values $\mathbf{T}, \mathbf{U}$.

Just like in the target language of Belnap logic in BC, it is not possible to write axiom (K) in the target propositional language for Priest logic. Using it in BC enforces a semantics in terms of Boolean possibility measures whose focal sets are singletons corresponding to an arbitrary number of completely informed hence inconsistent sources. The above results show that pure paraconsistency already prevails when only one of the sources is completely informed and disagree with the other ones. Indeed, capacities that are models of the translation of axiom $a \vee \neg a$ are optimistic, i.e., such that $\max(g(A), g(A^c)) = 1$. It is known from the literature on qualitative capacities [14] (see also [10]) that the focal sets of such an optimistic capacity g include a singleton disjoint from other focal sets, which comes down to letting the truth-value $\mathbf{U}$ disappear in Belnap-Dunn logic, since the case of a proposition being ignored by the set of sources ($g(A) = g(A^c) = 0$) cannot happen: it is ruled out by the presence of a focal singleton.

5.4 Argumentative Inference

A definition of inconsistency-tolerant inference, named argumentative inference, has been proposed in [4]. In some sense, it puts together the existential inference of Rescher and Manor described in Sect. 5.1, and ideas from Belnap-Dunn logic.

Namely, a proposition p is said to be an *argued consequence* from a possibly inconsistent propositional knowledge base K if and only if there is a consistent subset C of K that infers p ($C \vdash p$), but no consistent subset of K that infers $\neg p$. Here the consistent subset C is viewed as an argument for p.

This inference, denoted by $\vdash_A$, can be expressed in terms of the existential inference $\vdash_\exists$ as follows: $K \vdash_A p$ if and only if $K \vdash_\exists p$ and $K \nvdash_\exists \neg p$.

It is easy to see that if K is consistent, the argumentative inference reduces to classical propositional inference (as does the existential inference). Two consequences obtained by $\vdash_A$ cannot be in contradiction (it follows from the definition). However a set of at least three consequences obtained by $\vdash_A$ may be inconsistent [4].

The argumentative inference can be semantically modelled by the capacity $g_{K\ni}$ as $K \vdash_A p$ if and only if $g_{K\ni}([p]) = 1$ and $g_{K\ni}([\neg p]) = 0$, which is the capacity encoding of Belnap-Dunn epistemic truth-value $\mathbf{T}$.

6   Conclusion

We have shown that Boolean capacities provide a natural epistemic semantics for a number of inconsistency-tolerant inferences from a set of propositional formulas, thus offering a unified framework for various, although quite different, approaches to the handling of inconsistency ranging from the use of maximal consistent subsets of formulas, to Belnap and Priest paraconsistent logics. The capacity semantics extends the epistemic semantics of classical inference from consistent bases based on possibility theory.

Still there are some syntactic inconsistency-tolerant inferences which are not covered here, especially those involving the cardinality of subsets of formulas, and that are very much syntax-sensitive [5] nor approaches consisting in restoring consistency prior to inferring classically. An obvious direction for further research would be to investigate the case of stratified inconsistent knowledge bases (typically, possibilistic logic) and see whether graded capacities (valued in a bounded chain) can provide a natural semantics to existing inconsistency-tolerant inferences, as surveyed in [6].

References

1. Banerjee, M., Dubois, D.: A simple logic for reasoning about incomplete knowledge. Int. J. Approx. Reason. **55**(2), 639–653 (2014)
2. Belnap, N.D.: How a computer should think. In: Contemporary Aspects of Philosophy, pp. 30–56. Oriel Press, Boston (1977)
3. Belnap, N.D.: A useful four-valued logic. In: Epstein, G. (ed.) Modern Uses of Multiple-valued Logic, pp. 8–37. Reidel (1977)
4. Benferhat, S., Dubois, D., Prade, H.: Argumentative inference in uncertain and inconsistent knowledge bases. In: Heckerman, D., Mamdani, E.H. (eds.) Proceedings of 9th Annual Conference on Uncertainty in AI (UAI 1993), pp. 411–419. Morgan Kaufmann (1993)
5. Benferhat, S., Dubois, D., Prade, H.: Some syntactic approaches to the handling of inconsistent knowledge bases: a comparative study. Part 1: The flat case. Stud. Log. **58**, 17–45 (1997)
6. Benferhat, S., Dubois, D., Prade, H.: An overview of inconsistency-tolerant inferences in prioritized knowledge bases. In: Dubois, D., Prade, H., Klement, E. (eds.) Fuzzy Sets, Logic and Reasoning about Knowledge, pp. 395–417. Kluwer (1999)
7. Chellas, B.F.: Modal Logic: An Introduction. Cambridge University Press, Cambridge (1980)
8. Choquet, G.: Theory of capacities. Ann. l'Inst. Fourier **5**, 131–295 (1953)

9. Ciucci, D., Dubois, D.: From possibility theory to paraconsistency. In: Beziau, J.-Y., Chakraborty, M., Dutta, S. (eds.) New Directions in Paraconsistent Logic. SPMS, vol. 152, pp. 229–247. Springer, New Delhi (2015). https://doi.org/10.1007/978-81-322-2719-9_10

10. Ciucci, D., Dubois, D.: A capacity-based framework encompassing Belnap-Dunn logic for reasoning about multisource information. Int. J. Approx. Reason. **106**, 107–127 (2019)

11. Dubois, D.: Reasoning about ignorance and contradiction: many-valued logics versus epistemic logic. Soft. Comput. **16**(11), 1817–1831 (2012)

12. Dubois, D., Prade, H.: Possibility Theory: An Approach to Computerized Processing of Uncertainty. Plenum Press (1988)

13. Dubois, D., Prade, H., Rico, A.: On the informational comparison of qualitative fuzzy measures. In: Laurent, A., Strauss, O., Bouchon-Meunier, B., Yager, R.R. (eds.) IPMU 2014. CCIS, vol. 442, pp. 216–225. Springer, Cham (2014). https://doi.org/10.1007/978-3-319-08795-5_23

14. Dubois, D., Prade, H., Rico, A.: Representing qualitative capacities as families of possibility measures. Int. J. Approx. Reason. **58**, 3–24 (2015)

15. Dunn, J.M.: Intuitive semantics for first-degree entailment and coupled trees. Philos. Stud. **29**(3), 149–168 (1976)

16. Font, J.: Belnap's four-valued logic and De Morgan lattices. Log. J. IGPL **5**(3), 1–29 (1997)

17. Grant, J., Parisi, F.: General information spaces: measuring inconsistency, rationality postulates, and complexity. Ann. Math. Artif. Intell. **90**(2–3), 235–269 (2022)

18. Kleene, S.C.: Introduction to Metamathematics. D. Van Nostrand Co. (1952)

19. Priest, G.: The logic of paradox. J. Philos. Log. **8**(1), 219–241 (1979)

20. Priest, G.: The logic of paradox revisited. J. Philos. Log. **13**, 153–179 (1984)

21. Pynko, A.: Characterizing Belnap's logic via De Morgan's laws. Math. Log. Q. **41**, 442–454 (1995)

22. Rescher, N., Manor, R.: On inference from inconsistent premises. Theor. Decis. **1**, 179–219 (1970)

23. Revesz, P.Z.: On the semantics of theory change: arbitration between old and new information. In: 12th ACM SIGACT-SIGMOD-SIGART Symposium on Principles of Databases, pp. 71–92 (1993)

24. Sugeno, M.: Theory of fuzzy integrals and its applications. Tokyo Institute of Technology (1974)

An Approach to Inconsistency-Tolerant Reasoning About Probability Based on Łukasiewicz Logic

Tommaso Flaminio⬤, Lluis Godo[✉]⬤, and Sara Ugolini⬤

IIIA - CSIC, 08193 Bellaterra, Spain
{tommaso,godo,sara}@iiia.csic.es

Abstract. In this paper we consider the probability logic over Łukasiewicz logic with rational truth-constants, denoted FP(RPL), and we explore a possible approach to reason from inconsistent FP(RPL) theories in a non-trivial way. It basically consists of suitably weakening the formulas in an inconsistent theory T, depending on the degree of inconsistency of T. We show that such a logical approach is in accordance with other proposals in the literature based on distance-based and violation-based inconsistency measures.

1 Introduction

Nowadays, there are huge amounts of available data and information and it is likely to encounter inconsistencies among different pieces of information. Thus, finding a suitable way of handling inconsistent information has become a challenge for both logicians and computer scientists working on knowledge representation techniques and reasoning models, see e.g. [2,4,13] among many others.

From a logical point of view, inconsistency is ubiquitous in many contexts in which, regardless of the given information being contradictory, one is still expected to extract inferences in a sensible way. In this work we aim at exploring a fuzzy logic-based approach to the handling of conflicts when the information is of probabilistic nature. Reasoning with inconsistent probabilistic information is indeed a research topic that has received growing attention in the last years, in particular with respect to inconsistency measurement of probabilistic knowledge bases, and to how inconsistency measures can be used to devise paraconsistent inference methods, see e.g. the survey [9].

The approach we follow here is based on a logical formalization of probabilistic reasoning on classical propositions as a modal theory over Łukasiewicz fuzzy logic, called FP(Ł), as developed by Hájek et al. [14,15]. The idea is to understand the probability of a classical proposition φ as the truth-degree of a fuzzy modal proposition $P\varphi$, standing for the statement "φ is probable", in such a way that the higher (resp. lower) is the probability of φ, the more (resp. less) true is $P\varphi$. Then, the $[0, 1]$-based semantics of Łukasiewicz connectives, heavily relying

F. Dupin de Saint-Cyr et al. (Eds.): SUM 2022, LNAI 13562, pp. 124–138, 2022.
https://doi.org/10.1007/978-3-031-18843-5_9

on the usual addition and subtraction operations, make it possible to capture the postulates of probability measures (in particular the additivity property) with formulas in the language of FP(L). This idea has been explored in depth in the last years and several systems to reason about the uncertainty of classical and non-classical events have been proposed, see for instance [1,7,10,11]. By expanding Łukasiewicz logic with rational truth-constants, yielding the logic called Rational Pavelka logic (RPL), it is possible to encode purely quantitative expressions like "the probability of φ is at least 0.4" as the modal formula $\overline{0.4} \to P\varphi$ in the language of FP(RPL), the probability logic obtained by replacing Ł by RPL in FP(Ł).

In this paper we explore a possible approach to reason from inconsistent FP(RPL) theories in a non-trivial way by suitably weakening formulas of an inconsistent theory T depending on a logical degree of inconsistency of T. The paper is then structured as follows. After this introduction, in the next section we recall main definitions and properties of Łukasiewicz logic Ł, as well as Rational Pavelka logic (RPL), its expansion with rational truth-constants, while in Sect. 3 we recap the probability logics based on Ł and on RPL. Section 4 is devoted to our proposal to deal with inconsistent probability theories over FP(RPL), and in Sect. 5 we relate our approach based on measuring the consistency of theories to those in the literature based on distance-based and violation-based inconsistency measures. We end with some conclusions and ideas for future work.

2   Łukasiewicz Logic and Rational Pavelka Logic

Łukasiewicz infinite-valued logic is one of the most prominent systems falling under the umbrella of Mathematical Fuzzy Logic (see e.g. [6]) although it was defined much before fuzzy logic was born. The interested reader is referred to the monographs [5,14,17] for full details.

The language of Łukasiewicz logic is built in the usual way from a set of propositional variables, one binary connective $\to$ (that is, Łukasiewicz implication) and the truth constant $\overline{0}$, that we will also denote as $\perp$. An *evaluation* e maps every propositional variable to a real number from the unit interval $[0, 1]$ and extends to all formulas in the following way:

$$e(\overline{0}) = 0, \qquad e(\varphi \to \psi) = \min(1 - e(\varphi) + e(\psi), 1).$$

Other interesting connectives can be defined from them,

$\overline{1}$ is $\varphi \to \varphi$, $\neg\varphi$ is $\varphi \to \overline{0}$, $\varphi \oplus \psi$ is $\neg\varphi \to \psi$,
$\varphi \& \psi$ is $\neg(\neg\varphi \oplus \neg\psi)$, $\varphi \ominus \psi$ is $\varphi \& \neg\psi$, $\varphi \equiv \psi$ is $(\varphi \to \psi) \& (\psi \to \varphi)$,
$\varphi \wedge \psi$ is $\varphi \& (\varphi \to \psi)$, $\varphi \vee \psi$ is $\neg(\neg\varphi \wedge \neg\psi)$,

and they have the following interpretations:

$$
\begin{aligned}
e(\neg\varphi) &= 1 - e(\varphi), & e(\varphi \oplus \psi) &= \min(1, e(\varphi) + e(\psi)), \\
e(\varphi \& \psi) &= \max(0, e(\varphi) + e(\psi) - 1), & e(\varphi \ominus \psi) &= \max(0, e(\varphi) - e(\psi)), \\
e(\varphi \equiv \psi) &= 1 - |e(\varphi) - e(\psi)|, & e(\varphi \wedge \psi) &= \min(e(\varphi), e(\psi)), \\
e(\varphi \vee \psi) &= \max(e(\varphi), e(\psi)).
\end{aligned}
$$

An evaluation e is called a *model* of a set of formulas T whenever $e(\varphi) = 1$ for each formula $\varphi \in T$. Axioms and rules of Łukasiewicz Logic are the following [5,14]:

(L1) $\varphi \rightarrow (\psi \rightarrow \varphi)$
(L2) $(\varphi \rightarrow \psi) \rightarrow ((\psi \rightarrow \chi) \rightarrow (\varphi \rightarrow \chi))$
(L3) $(\neg \varphi \rightarrow \neg \psi) \rightarrow (\psi \rightarrow \varphi)$
(L4) $((\varphi \rightarrow \psi) \rightarrow \psi) \rightarrow ((\psi \rightarrow \varphi) \rightarrow \varphi)$
(MP) Modus ponens: from φ and $\varphi \rightarrow \psi$ derive ψ

From this axiomatic system, the notion of proof from a theory (a set of formulas), denoted $\vdash$ L, is defined as usual.

The above axioms are tautologies or valid (i.e., they are evaluated to 1 by any evaluation), and the rule of modus ponens preserves validity. Moreover, the following completeness result holds.

Theorem 1. *The logic L is complete for deductions from finite theories. That is, if T is a finite theory, then $T \vdash_L \varphi$ iff $e(\varphi) = 1$ for each Łukasiewicz evaluation e model of T.*

In the rest of this section we briefly recall the expansion of Łukasiewicz logic with rational truth-constants that will be used later on. Following Hájek [14], the language of *Rational Pavelka logic*, denoted RPL, is the language of Łukasiewicz logic expanded with countably-many truth-constants $\bar{r}$, one for each rational $r \in [0,1]$. The evaluation of RPL formulas is as in Łukasiewicz logic, with the proviso that evaluations evaluate truth-constants to their intended value, that is, for any rational $r \in [0,1]$ and any evaluation e, $e(\bar{r}) = r$. Note that, for any evaluation e, $e(\bar{r} \rightarrow \varphi) = 1$ iff $e(\varphi) \geq r$, and $e(\bar{r} \equiv \varphi) = 1$ iff $e(\varphi) = r$.

Axioms and rules of RPL are those of L plus the following countable set of bookkeeping axioms for truth-constants:

$$(BK) \ \bar{r} \rightarrow \bar{s} \equiv \overline{\min(1, 1 - r + s)}, \text{ for any rationals } r, s \in [0,1].$$

The notion of proof is defined as in Łukasiewicz logic, and the deducibility relation will be denoted by $\vdash_{RPL}$. Moreover, completeness of Łukasiewicz logic smoothly extends to RPL as follows: if T is finite theory over RPL, then $T \vdash_{RPL} \varphi$ iff $e(\varphi) = 1$ for any RPL-evaluation e model of T.

It is customary in RPL to introduce the following notions: for any set of RPL formulas $T \cup \{\varphi\}$, define:

- the *truth degree* of φ in T: $\|\varphi\|_T = \inf\{e(\varphi) : e \text{ is a RPL-evaluation model of } T\}$,
- the *provability degree* of φ from T: $|\varphi|_T = \sup\{r \in [0,1]_{\mathbb{Q}} \mid T \vdash_{RPL} \bar{r} \rightarrow \varphi\}$.

Then, the so-called *Pavelka-style completeness* for RPL refers to the result that

$$|\varphi|_T = \|\varphi\|_T$$

holds for any arbitrary (non necessarily finite) theory T [14]. However, if T is finite, we can restrict ourselves to rational-valued Łukasiewicz evaluations and get the following result, proved in [14].

Proposition 1. *If T is a finite theory over RPL, then:*

- $\|\varphi\|_T = 1$ *iff* $T \vdash_{RPL} \varphi$.
- $\|\varphi\|_T$ *is rational, hence* $\|\varphi\|_T = r$ *iff* $T \vdash_{RPL} \bar{r} \to \varphi$.

3 FP(RPL): A Logic to Reason About Probability as Modal Theories over RPL

In this section we first describe the fuzzy modal logic FP(RPL) to reason qualitatively about probability, built upon Łukasiewicz logic RPL described in the previous section. We basically follow [14]. The language of FP(RPL) is defined in two layers:

Non-modal Formulas: built from a set V of propositional variables, that will be assumed here to be finite, using the classical binary connectives $\wedge$ and $\neg$. Other connectives like $\vee$, $\to$ and $\leftrightarrow$ are defined from them in the usual way.[1] Non-modal formulas, or Boolean propositions, will be denoted by lower case Greek letters φ, ψ, etc. The set of non-modal formulas will be denoted by $\mathcal{L}$.

Modal Formulas: built from elementary modal formulas of the form $P\varphi$, where φ is a non-modal formula, using the connectives and truth constants of Rational Pavelka logic. We shall denote them by upper case Greek letters Φ, Ψ, etc. Notice that we do not allow nested modalities of the form $P(P(\psi) \oplus P(\varphi))$, nor mixed formulas of the kind $\psi \to P\varphi$.

Definition 1. *The axioms of the logic FP(RPL) are the following:*

  (i) Axioms of classical propositional logic for non-modal formulas
 (ii) Axioms of RPL for modal formulas
(iii) Probabilistic modal axioms:[2]

(FP0) $P\varphi$, *for φ being a theorem of CPL*
(FP1) $P(\varphi \to \psi) \to (P\varphi \to P\psi)$
(FP2) $P(\neg\varphi) \equiv \neg P\varphi$
(FP3) $P(\varphi \vee \psi) \equiv (P\varphi \to P(\varphi \wedge \psi)) \to P\psi$

The only deduction rule of FP(RPL) is that of L (i.e. modus ponens)

---

[1] Although we are using the same symbols $\wedge, \neg, \vee, \to$ as in Łukasiewicz logic to denote the conjunction, negation, disjunction and implication, the context will help in avoiding any confusion. In particular classical logic connectives will appear only under the scope of the operator P, see below.
[2] An equivalent formulation of (FP3) is $P(\varphi \vee \psi) \equiv P\varphi \oplus (P\psi \ominus P(\varphi \wedge \psi))$.

The notion of proof for modal formulas is defined as usual from the above axioms and rule. We will denote by the expression $T \vdash_{FP} \Phi$ that in FP(RPL) a modal formula Φ follows from a theory (set of modal formulas) T. Note that FP(RPL) preserves (classical) logical equivalence. Indeed, due to axioms (FP0) and (FP1), FP(RPL) proves the formula $P\varphi \equiv P\psi$ whenever φ and ψ are (classically) logically equivalent.

The semantics for FP(RPL) is basically given by probability functions on classical (i.e. non-modal) formulas of $\mathcal{L}$, or equivalently, assuming $\mathcal{L}$ is built up from a finite set of variables V, by probability functions on the set Ω of classical interpretations of $\mathcal{L}$. If $\mu : 2^{\Omega} \to [0,1]$ is a probability, we will simply write $\mu(\varphi)$ to denote $\mu(\{w \in \Omega \mid w(\varphi) = 1\})$. We will denote by $\mathcal{P}(\mathcal{L})$ the set of probabilities on $\mathcal{L}$. Then every probability $\mu \in \mathcal{P}(\mathcal{L})$ determines an evaluation e_{μ} of modal formulas as follows: for a basic modal $P\varphi$,

$$e_{\mu}(P\varphi) = \mu(\varphi),$$

and it is extended to arbitrary modal formulas according to the semantics of Rational Pavelka logic: $e_{\mu}(\bar{r}) = r$, $e_{\mu}(\Phi \to_L \Psi) = \min(1 - e_{\mu}(\Phi) + e_{\mu}(\Psi), 1)$. Then we say that a probability $\mu \in \mathcal{P}(\mathcal{L})$ is a *model* of a theory T of modal formulas if $e_{\mu}(\Phi) = 1$ for every $\Phi \in T$.

FP(RPL) can be used to reason in a purely qualitative way about comparative probability statements by exploiting the fact a FP(RPL)-formula of the form $P\psi \to P\varphi$ is 1-true in a model defined by a probability μ iff $\mu(\psi) \leqslant \mu(\varphi)$. However, FP(RPL) also allows one to explicitly reason about numerical statements, like "the probability of φ is 0.8", "the probability of φ is at least 0.8", or "the probability of φ is at most 0.8". Indeed, the above statements can be easily expressed in FP(RPL):

- "the probability of φ is 0.8" as $P\varphi \equiv \overline{0.8}$,
- "the probability of φ is at least 0.8" as $\overline{0.8} \to P\varphi$, and
- "the probability of φ is at most 0.8" as $P\varphi \to \overline{0.8}$.

The following general Pavelka-style completeness result for FP(RPL) was presented in [14,15].

Theorem 2 (Probabilistic completeness of FP(RPL)). *Let T be a modal theory over FP(L) and Φ a modal formula. Then,*

$$\mid \Phi \mid_T = \|\Phi\|_T,$$

where now $\mid \Phi \mid_T = \sup\{r \in [0,1]_{\mathbb{Q}} \mid T \vdash_{FP} \bar{r} \to \Phi\}$ and $\|\varphi\|_T = \inf\{e_{\mu}(\Phi) : \mu \in \mathcal{P}(\mathcal{L})$ is a model of $T\}$.

As in the case of RPL, if the modal theory T is finite, we can get a standard completeness result, that follows from [14, Th. 8.4.14].

Theorem 3 (Probabilistic completeness of FP(RPL)). *Let T be a finite modal theory over FP(RPL) and Φ a modal formula. Then $T \vdash_{FP} \Phi$ iff $e_{\mu}(\Phi) = 1$ for each probability $\mu \in \mathcal{P}(\mathcal{L})$ model of T.*

Similarly to RPL, for deductions from finite theories FP(RPL) is still complete for rational-valued probabilities.

Corollary 1. *Let T be a finite modal theory over FP(RPL) and Φ a modal formula. Then $T \vdash_{FP} \Phi$ iff $e_\mu(\Phi) = 1$ for each rational-valued probability $\mu \in \mathcal{P}(\mathcal{L})$ model of T.*

Moreover, since deductions in FP(RPL) from a finite theory can be encoded as deductions from a (larger) finite theory in RPL, as a direct corollary of Proposition 1, we get the following.

Corollary 2. *If T is finite, for any FP(RPL)-formula Φ, $\|\Phi\|_T$ is rational.*

4 Reasoning with Inconsistent Probabilistic Information in FP(RPL)

If we want to reason in a non-trivial way from inconsistent probabilistic theories over FP(RPL), we need to devise possible ways to define paraconsistent reasoning inference relations in a meaningful form. The way we approach this issue is to compute what we will call the "degree of inconsistency" of a modal theory T, and use that value to suitably weaken the formulas in T so that the obtained weaker theory is consistent.

Let us recall from Sect. 3 that, from a semantical point of view, the logic FP(RPL) is defined as follows: for any set of FP(RPL)-formulas $T \cup \{\Phi\}$,

$$T \models_{FP} \Phi \quad \text{if,} \quad \text{for every probability } \mu \in \mathcal{P}(\mathcal{L}) \text{ on Boolean formulas,}$$
$$\text{if } \mu \text{ is a model of } T \text{ then } e_\mu(\Phi) = 1.$$

We will denote by $[\![T]\!]$ the set probabilities that are models of T. In other words, $[\![T]\!] = \{\text{probability } \mu \in \mathcal{P}(\mathcal{L}) \mid \text{for all } \Psi \in T, e_\mu(\Psi) = 1\}$.

Of course, the above definition trivializes in the case T is inconsistent, i.e. when $[\![T]\!] = \varnothing$. However, in FP(RPL) one can take advantage of its fuzzy component and consider the notion of (in)consistency as being fuzzy as well. Indeed, if a probabilistic theory T has no models, it makes sense to distinguish, for instance, cases where: (1) for every probability μ there is a formula $\Phi \in T$ such that $e_\mu(\Phi) = 0$; and (2) there exists a probability μ such that, for all $\Phi \in T$, $e_\mu(\Phi)$ is close to 1. In the former case T is clearly inconsistent, while in the latter case one could say that T is *close* to being consistent.

This observation justifies to introduce, for a given threshold $\alpha \in [0,1]$, the set of α-*generalised models* (or just α-models) of a theory T defined as follows:

$$[\![T]\!]_\alpha = \{\mu \in \mathcal{P}(\mathcal{L}) \mid \text{for all } \Psi \in T, e_\mu(\Psi) \geqslant \alpha\}.$$

Note that the set $[\![T]\!]_1$ coincides with the set $[\![T]\!]$ of usual models of T, while $[\![T]\!]_0 = \mathcal{P}(\mathcal{L})$. Moreover, for any α, $[\![T]\!]_\alpha$ is a convex set of probabilities.

This in turn allows us to define the degree of consistency of a theory as the highest value α for which T has at least one α-generalised model.

Definition 2. *Let T be a theory of FP(RPL). The consistency degree of T is defined as*

$$Con(T) = \sup\{\beta \in [0,1] \mid [\![T]\!]_\beta \neq \varnothing\}.$$

Dually, the inconsistency degree of T is defined as

$$Incon(T) = 1 - Con(T) = \inf\{1 - \beta \in [0,1] \mid [\![T]\!]_\beta \neq \varnothing\}.$$

For every finite modal theory T, by completeness of FP(RPL) with respect to probability models (Theorem 3), we can also express $Con(T)$ and $Incon(T)$ as follows:

$$Con(T) = \sup\{\beta \in [0,1] \mid T_\beta \nvdash_{FP} \bot\} \quad \text{and} \quad Incon(T) = \inf\{1 - \beta \in [0,1] \mid T_\beta \nvdash_{FP} \bot\},$$

where $T_\beta = \{\bar{\beta} \to \varPhi \mid \varPhi \in T\}$. A somewhat different, yet equivalent, formulation for the degrees of consistency and inconsistency is as follows:

$$Con(T) = \sup\{\bigwedge_{\varPhi \in T} e_\mu(\varPhi) \mid \mu \in \mathcal{P}(\mathcal{L})\}, \quad Incon(T) = \inf\{\bigvee_{\varPhi \in T} e_\mu(\neg\varPhi) \mid \mu \in \mathcal{P}(\mathcal{L})\}.$$

It can be shown that, if T is finite, the suprema and the infima in the above definition and expressions of $Con(T)$ and $Incon(T)$, are in fact maxima and minima. And not only this, in fact, $Con(T)$ and $Incon(T)$ are always rational numbers.

Lemma 1. *Let T be a finite theory of FP(RPL). Then:*

$$Con(T) = \max\{\bigwedge_{\varPhi \in T} e_\mu(\varPhi) \mid \mu \text{ probability}\} = \max\{\beta \in [0,1] \mid T_\beta \nvdash_{FP} \bot\},$$

$$Incon(T) = \min\{\bigvee_{\varPhi \in T} e_\mu(\neg\varPhi) \mid \mu \text{ probability}\} = \min\{1 - \beta \in [0,1] \mid T_\beta \nvdash_{FP} \bot\}.$$

Moreover, $Con(T)$ and $Incon(T)$ are rational.

In particular, from the previous lemma it follows that for a finite theory T, if $Con(T) = \alpha$, then $[\![T]\!]_\alpha \neq \varnothing$. Moreover:

(i) If $Con(T) = 1$ then T has a model, while if $Con(T) = 0$ then, for any probability μ there is a formula $\varPsi \in T$ such that $e_\mu(\varPsi) = 0$.
(ii) If $T' \subseteq T$ then $Con(T') \geqslant Con(T)$.

Let us clarify what the degree of consistency represents in the case of some very simple examples.

Example 1. Let us consider the following theory of precise probability assignments $T = \{\bar{r}_i \equiv P\varphi_i\}_{i=1,\dots,n}$ to a set of events $\mathcal{E} = \{\varphi_1, \dots, \varphi_n\}$. If μ is a probability, then $e_\mu(\bar{r}_i \equiv P\varphi_i) = 1 - |\mu(\varphi_i) - r_i|$. Then,

$$Con(T) = \sup_\mu \bigwedge_{i=1,\dots,n} 1 - |\mu(\varphi_i) - r_i|, \quad Incon(T) = \inf_\mu \bigvee_{i=1,\dots,n} |\mu(\varphi_i) - r_i|.$$

That is to say, $Incon(T)$ is nothing but the Chebyshev distance of the point $(r_1, \ldots, r_n) \in [0,1]^n$ to the convex set of *consistent* probability assignments $\mathscr{C}_{\mathcal{E}}$ on the events $\mathcal{E}$, i.e., the set of values that probabilities assign to the events in $\mathcal{E}$.

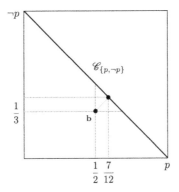

Fig. 1. $Con(T^{\mathbf{b}})$ is computed as 1 minus the Chebyshev distance between the point **b** that represents the partial assignment on p and $\neg p$, and the set of consistent assignments on p and $\neg p$.

For instance, consider the theory $T^{\mathbf{b}} = \{P(p) \equiv \overline{1/2}, P(\neg p) \equiv \overline{1/3}\}$ given by the inconsistent assignment $\mathbf{b} : p \mapsto 1/2; \neg p \mapsto 1/3$. The set of all consistent assignments on events p and $\neg p$ is the set $\mathscr{C}_{\{p, \neg p\}} = \{(x, 1-x) \mid x \in [0,1]\}$, i.e. the segment in $[0,1]^2$ with endpoints $(1,0)$ and $(0,1)$ (see Fig. 1), and the inconsistent assignment $\mathbf{b}$ is displayed as the point $(1/2, 1/3) \notin \mathscr{C}_{\{p, \neg p\}}$. As mentioned above, $Con(T^{\mathbf{b}})$ can be computed as 1 minus the Chebyshev distance between $(1/2, 1/3)$ and $\mathscr{C}_{\{p, \neg p\}}$. This value is attained at the point of coordinates $(7/12, 5/12)$ and then we have:

$$1 - |\mathbf{b}(p) - 7/12| = 1 - |\mathbf{b}(\neg p) - 5/12| = 1 - 1/12 = 11/12 = Con(T^{\mathbf{b}}).$$

Example 2. Let us now consider a theory representing an imprecise probability assignment to the set of events $\mathcal{E} = \{\varphi_1, \ldots, \varphi_n\}$:

$$T = \{(\overline{r_i - \epsilon_i} \to P\varphi_i) \wedge (P\varphi_i \to \overline{r_i + \epsilon_i})\}_{i=1,\ldots,n}$$

where, for each i, $r_i - \epsilon_i \geqslant 0$ and $r_i + \epsilon_i \leqslant 1$, that is $\epsilon_i \leqslant r_i \leqslant 1 - \epsilon_i$. Then, using that $\min((x - y) \to z, z \to (x + y)) = y \to (x \equiv z)$, if $y \leqslant x \leqslant 1 - y$ (where here and below we also use $\to$ and $\equiv$ to denote the truth-functions for Lukasiewicz implication and equivalence connectives), the degree of inconsistency of T can be computed as follows:

$$Incon(T) = 1 - Con(T) = 1 - \sup_{\mu} \bigwedge_{i=1,\ldots,n} e_{\mu}((\overline{r_i - \epsilon_i} \to P\varphi_i) \wedge (P\varphi_i \to \overline{r_i + \epsilon_i}))$$

$$= 1 - \sup_{\mu} \bigwedge_{i=1,\ldots,n} ((1 - \epsilon_i) \to |r_i - \mu(\varphi_i)| = \inf_{\mu} \bigvee_{i=1,\ldots,n} (1 - \epsilon_i) \otimes |r_i - \mu(\varphi_i)|.$$

As for paraconsistently reasoning from an inconsistent theory in FP(RPL), the idea we explore here is to use α-generalised models instead of usual models to define a context-dependent inconsistent-tolerant notion of probabilistic entailment.

Definition 3. *Let T be a theory such that $Con(T) = \alpha > 0$. We define:*

$$T \approx^* \Phi \ \text{if} \ e_\mu(\Phi) = 1 \ \text{for all probabilities} \ \mu \in [\![T]\!]_\alpha.$$

Note that for a finite theory T, $T \not\approx^* \bot$, hence $\approx^*$ does not trivialize even if T is inconsistent $(Con(T) < 1)$. Moreover, observe that if $Con(T) = 0$, then $T \approx^* \Phi$ iff Φ is a theorem of FP(RPL). The following are some further interesting properties of the consequence relation $\approx^*$:

- Clearly, $\approx^*$ does not satisfy monotonicity. For instance, if $T' = \{P\varphi \equiv 0.4, P\varphi \rightarrow P\psi\}$, then $Con(T') = 1$ and trivially $T' \approx^* 0.4 \equiv P\varphi$, but $T \not\approx^* 0.4 \equiv P\varphi$, where $T = T' \cup \{0.3 \equiv P\varphi\}$.
- $\approx^*$ is idempotent, that is, if $S \approx^* \Phi$ and $T \approx^* \Psi$ for all $\Psi \in S$, then $T \approx^* \Phi$.

The next proposition shows that paraconsistent reasoning from an inconsistent theory T by means of the inference relation $\approx^*$ can be reduced to usual reasoning in FP(RPL) by suitably weakening the formulas in the initial theory T.

Proposition 2. *Given a finite theory T, with $Con(T) = \alpha$, let $T_\alpha = \{\overline{\alpha} \rightarrow \Psi \mid \Psi \in T\}$. Then the following condition holds:*

$$T \approx^* \Phi \ \text{iff} \ T_\alpha \vdash_{FP} \Phi.$$

Proof. If μ is a probability such that $e_\mu(\overline{\alpha} \rightarrow \Psi) = 1$, i.e. such that $e_\mu(\Psi) \geq \alpha$, for all $\Psi \in T$, then $\mu \in [\![T]\!]_\alpha$. But if we assume $T \approx^* \Phi$, then it follows that $e_\mu(\Phi) = 1$. Hence $T_\alpha \vdash_{FP} \Phi$.

Conversely, assume $T_\alpha \vdash_{FP} \Phi$ with $Con(T) = \alpha$ and that $\mu \in \|T\|_\alpha$. The latter means that $e_\mu(\Psi) \geq \alpha$ for all $\Psi \in T$, i.e. $e_\mu(\alpha \rightarrow \Psi) = 1$ for all $\Psi \in T$. But then, since $T_\alpha \vdash_{FP} \Phi$, it follows that $e_\mu(\Phi) = 1$, that is, $T \approx^* \Phi$.

The weakened theory T_α, that is consistent, can be seen as a *repair* of T. In the case the theory represents a precise probability assignment of the form $T = \{\overline{r_i} \equiv P\varphi_i\}_{i=1,\ldots,n}$, then $T_\alpha = \{(\overline{\alpha \otimes r_i} \rightarrow P\varphi_i) \wedge (P\varphi_i \rightarrow \overline{\alpha \Rightarrow r_i})\}_{i=1,\ldots,n}$, that is, it becomes a theory of an imprecise assignment. On the other hand, in the case the theory already represents an imprecise probability assignment of the form $T = \{(\overline{r_i} \rightarrow P\varphi_i) \wedge (P\varphi_i \rightarrow \overline{s_i})\}_{i=1,\ldots,n}$, then $T_\alpha = \{(\overline{\alpha \otimes r_i} \rightarrow P\varphi_i) \wedge (P\varphi_i \rightarrow \overline{\alpha \Rightarrow s_i})\}_{i=1,\ldots,n}$, that is, it represents a more imprecise assignment.

The consequence relation $\approx^*$ introduced above has some nice features, but it may also have a counter-intuitive behaviour in some cases. For instance, let $T = \{\overline{0.3} \equiv P\varphi, \overline{0.4} \equiv P\varphi, \overline{0.6} \equiv P\psi\}$, where φ and ψ are assumed to be propositional variables. Then it is easy to check that $Con(T) = 0.95$, and hence $T \approx^* \overline{0.35} \equiv P\varphi$. But strangely enough, $T \not\approx^* \overline{0.6} \equiv P\psi$, since we can only derive $T \models^* \overline{0.95} \rightarrow (\overline{0.6} \equiv P\psi)$, even though the formula $\overline{0.6} \equiv P\psi$ is not involved in the conflict in T. The reason is that $Con(T)$ is a global measure that does not take into account individual formulas. Actually, if $T' = T \cup \{\overline{0.7} \equiv P\psi\}$, we still have $Con(T) = Con(T') = 0.95$.

The above example motivates the following iterative procedure to come up with a more suitable repair of an inconsistent theory T. The idea is to first identify minimal inconsistent subtheories S of T that are responsible for the degree of consistency of T, i.e. such that $Con(S) = Con(T) = \alpha$. Then we only repair the formulas of these subtheories by using the degree α. In a next step, one proceeds with the rest of the initial theory T by repeating the same process. This procedure stops when all the formulas have been dealt with in some previous step.

Step 1: Let $Con(T) = \alpha_1$. Then we know that the set of probabilities $[\![T]\!]_{\alpha_1}$ is non-empty. Hence, we can partition T in the following two disjoint subtheories:
- $T^= = \bigcup\{S \subseteq T \mid S \text{ minimal such that } Con(S) = \alpha_1\}$
- $T^> = T \setminus T^=$

Note that $T^= \neq \varnothing$ and if $T^> \neq \varnothing$ then $Con(T^>) > \alpha_1$. By definition $T^= \cap T^> = \varnothing$ and $T = T^= \cup T^>$.

Then we proceed to weaken only those formulas in $T^=$, so we define:

$$T^{(1)} = \{\overline{\alpha_1} \rightarrow \Phi \mid \Phi \in T^=\}.$$

If $T^> = \varnothing$, then we stop and we define the repaired theory as $T^w = T^{(1)}$. Otherwise we follow to the next step to repair $T^>$.

Step 2: Restrict the set of possible probability models to those of $[\![T]\!]_{\alpha_1}$ to compute the consistency degree of $T^>$.
Let $Con_T(T^>) = \max\{\beta \mid \text{there exists } \mu \in [\![T]\!]_{\alpha_1}, e_\mu(\Phi) \geq \beta \text{ for all } \Phi \in T^>\} = \alpha_2$.
By definition, $\alpha_2 > \alpha_1$. And we proceed similarly as above, but restricting the set of models to those in $[\![T]\!]_{\alpha_1}$, and we partition $T^>$ into the following two subtheories:
- $(T^>)^= = \bigcup\{S \subseteq T^> \mid S \text{ minimal such that } Con_T(S) = \alpha_2\}$
- $(T^>)^> = T^> \setminus (T^>)^=$

Again note that $(T^>)^= \neq \varnothing$, and if $(T^>)^> \neq \varnothing$ then $Con((T^>)^>) > \alpha_2$. We proceed to the weakening of the subtheory $(T^>)^=$ and define:

$$T^{(2)} = \{\overline{\alpha_2} \rightarrow \Phi \mid \Phi \in (T^>)^=\}.$$

If $(T^>)^> = \varnothing$, then we stop and we define the repaired theory as $T^w = T^{(1)} \cup T^{(2)}$. Otherwise we follow to the next step to repair $(T^>)^>$.

Step 3: Restrict the set of possible probabilistic models to those of $[\![T]\!]_{\alpha_1} \cap [\![T^>]\!]_{\alpha_2}$ to compute the consistency degree of $(T^>)^>$:
Let $Con_{T,T^>}((T^>)^>) = \max\{\beta \mid \text{there exists } \mu \in [\![T]\!]_{\alpha_1} \cap [\![T^>]\!]_{\alpha_2}, e_\mu(\Phi) \geq \beta \text{ for all } \Phi \in (T^>)^>\} = \alpha_3$.
By definition, $\alpha_3 > \alpha_2 > \alpha_1$. we then follow the same procedure as above, but restricting the set of models to those in $[\![T]\!]_{\alpha_1} \cap [\![T^>]\!]_{\alpha_2}$, and we partition $(T^>)^>$ into the following two subtheories:

- $((T^>)^>)^= = \cup\{S \subseteq (T^>)^> \mid S \text{ minimal such that } Con_{T,T^>}(S) = \alpha_3\}$
- $((T^>)^>)^> = (T^>)^> \setminus ((T^>)^>)^=$

Now we proceed to weaken the subtheory $((T^>)^>)^=$ and define:

$$T^{(3)} = \{\overline{\alpha_3} \to \Phi \mid \Phi \in ((T^>)^>)^=\}.$$

If $((T^>)^>)^> = \varnothing$, then we stop and we define the repaired theory as $T^w = T^{(1)} \cup T^{(2)} \cup T^{(3)}$. Otherwise we follow to the next step to repair $((T^>)^>)^>$.

... ...

This procedure goes on until, for a first m, $(...(T^>) \overset{m}{...})^>) = \varnothing$. Then the procedure stops and as a result we get a (finite) sequence of subtheories $T^{(1)}, T^{(2)}, \ldots, T^{(m)}$, with associated consistency values $\alpha_1 < \ldots < \alpha_m$. By construction, the theory

$$T^w = T^{(1)} \cup \ldots \cup T^{(m)}$$

is consistent.

This allows us to define a refined variant of the $\approx^*$ consequence relation.

Definition 4. *Let T be a theory over FP(RPL). Then we define a refinement $\approx^\circ$ of the consequence relation $\approx^*$ as follows:*

$$T \approx^\circ \Phi \text{ if } T^w \vdash_{FP} \Phi.$$

Compare this definition with the characterisation of $\approx^*$ in Proposition 2. It is clear that $\approx^\circ$ is stronger than $\approx^*$ while still paraconsistent.

Example 3. Let $T = \{\overline{0.3} \equiv P\varphi, \overline{0.4} \equiv P\varphi, \overline{0.6} \equiv P\psi, \overline{0.8} \equiv P\psi, \overline{0.7} \equiv P\chi\}$, where φ, ψ, χ are propositional variables. Since $Con(T) = 0.9$, we have

$$T_{0.9} = \{\overline{0.9} \to (\overline{0.3} \equiv P\varphi), \overline{0.9} \to (\overline{0.4} \equiv P\varphi), \overline{0.9} \to (\overline{0.6} \equiv P\psi),$$
$$\overline{0.9} \to (\overline{0.8} \equiv P\psi), \overline{0.9} \to (\overline{0.7} \equiv P\chi)\}$$

Models of $T_{0.9}$ are probabilities μ such that $\mu(\varphi) \in [0.2, 0.4] \cap [0.3, 0.5] = [0.3, 0.4]$, $\mu(\psi) \in [0.5, 0.7] \cap [0.7, 0.9] = \{0.7\}$ and $\mu(\chi) \in [0.6, 0.8]$. However, using the refinement procedure, we get

$$T^w = \{\overline{0.9} \to (\overline{0.6} \equiv P\psi), \overline{0.9} \to (\overline{0.8} \equiv P\psi), \overline{0.95} \to (\overline{0.3} \equiv P\varphi),$$
$$\overline{0.95} \to (\overline{0.4} \equiv P\varphi), \overline{0.7} \equiv P\chi\},$$

that is equivalent to the theory

$$T'^w = \{\overline{0.5} \to P\psi, P\psi \to \overline{0.7}, \overline{0.7} \to P\psi, P\psi \to \overline{0.9}, \overline{0.25} \to P\varphi,$$
$$P\varphi \to \overline{0.35}, \overline{0.35} \to P\varphi, P\varphi \to \overline{0.45}, \overline{0.7} \equiv P\chi\}.$$

In this case, models of T^w are probabilities μ such that $\mu(\varphi) = 0.35$, $\mu(\psi) = 0.7$ and $\mu(\chi) = 0.7$, and hence the refined consequence relation $\approx^\circ$ is such that:

$$T \approx^\circ \overline{0.7} \equiv P\psi, \overline{0.35} \equiv P\varphi, \overline{0.7} \equiv P\chi.$$

5   Related Approaches

In the literature there has been quite a lot of interest on measuring the inconsistency of probabilistic knowledge bases, see for instance [8,16,18–23]. In particular, there is a nice overview by De Bona, Finger, Potyka and Thimm in [9] on which we will base the comparison with our approach.

First of all, by a probabilistic knowledge base it is usually understood a finite set of (conditional) probability constraints on classical propositional formulas (from a given finitely generated language $\mathcal{L}$), of the form $KB = \{(\varphi_i \mid \psi_i)[\underline{q}_i, \overline{q}_i] \mid i = 1, \ldots n\}$, where $\underline{q}_i$ and $\overline{q}_i$ are rational values from the unit interval $[0,1]$. Such an expression $(\varphi_i \mid \psi_i)[\underline{q}_i, \overline{q}_i]$ intuitively expresses the constraint (or belief) that the conditional probability of φ_i given ψ_i lies in the interval $[\underline{q}_i, \overline{q}_i]$.

Then, a probability on formulas μ satisfies a conditional expression $(\varphi_i \mid \psi_i)[\underline{q}_i, \overline{q}_i]$, written $\mu \models (\varphi_i \mid \psi_i)[\underline{q}_i, \overline{q}_i]$, whenever $\mu(\varphi_i \wedge \psi_i) \geq \underline{q}_i \cdot \mu(\psi_i)$ and $\mu(\varphi_i \wedge \psi_i) \leq \overline{q}_i \cdot \mu(\psi_i)$. Such a probability is called a *model* of the formula. Of course, if $\mu(\psi_i) > 0$, these conditions amount to state that $\mu \models (\varphi_i \mid \psi_i)[\underline{q}_i, \overline{q}_i]$ when the conditional probability $\mu(\varphi_i \mid \psi_i)$ belongs to the interval $[\underline{q}_i, \overline{q}_i]$.

In the case a probabilistic knowledge base KB is inconsistent, a number of *inconsistency measures* have been proposed in the literature to measure how much inconsistent KB is, some of them generalising to the probabilistic case inconsistency measures already proposed for the propositional case, and some of them specifically tailored to deal with probabilistic expressions. Among these, there are the so-called distance-based measures and violation-based measures. Very roughly speaking, the former look for consistent knowledge bases that *minimize the distance* (for some suitable notion of distance) to the original inconsistent KB, while the latter look for probabilities that *minimize the violation* (for some suitable notion of violation) of the knowledge base [18,23].

According to [9], when it comes to reasoning with an inconsistent probabilistic KB, there are two sensible ways to proceed: either repair the inconsistent knowledge base and then apply classical probabilistic reasoning, or apply paraconsistent reasoning models that can deal with inconsistent knowledge bases. For the first approach, distance-based measures are well-suited while for the second approach violation-based measures (together with so-called fuzzy-based measures) seem to be the most suitable ones.

We can show here that our approach to reason with inconsistent probabilistic theories over FP(RPL), when restricted to theories of the form $T = \{\overline{r_i} \equiv P\varphi_i\}_{i=1,\ldots,n}$, can be seen both as a distance-based approach and as violation-based approach. Note that here we do not deal with conditional probability expressions as most of the approaches in the literature, thus our case is simpler.

Indeed, in the distance-based approach, given a distance d on $\mathbb{R}^n$, and two theories $T = \{\overline{r_i} \equiv P\varphi_i\}_{i=1,\ldots,n}$ and $T' = \{\overline{r'_i} \equiv P\varphi_i\}_{i=1,\ldots,n}$, one can define the distance between T and T' as the distance between their corresponding vectors of truth-constants:

$$d(T, T') = d((r_1, \ldots, r_n), (r'_1, \ldots, r'_n))$$

Then, if $T = \{\overline{r_i} \equiv P\varphi_i\}_{i=1,\ldots,n}$ is an inconsistent theory, the aim is to look for a consistent theory (a *repair*), by minimally modifying the truth-constants r_i's such that the resulting new theory is at a minimum distance from T. Note that all possible repairs of T that are precise-assignments theories are of the form

$$T^\mu = \{\overline{\mu(\varphi_i)} \equiv P\varphi_i\}_{i=1,\ldots,n}$$

for μ being a rational-valued probability on formulas. In our approach, the degree of inconsistency of T can be seen as providing the minimum Chebyshev distance from T to the set of all its repairs, indeed we have:

$$Incon(T) = \inf_\mu \bigvee_{i=1,\ldots,n} |\mu(\varphi_i) - r_i|$$

$$= \inf_\mu d_c((\mu(\varphi_1),\ldots,\mu(\varphi_n)),(r_1,\ldots,r_n)) = \inf_\mu d_c(T,T^\mu),$$

where d_c is the well-known Chebyshev distance in $\mathbb{R}^n$.

Suppose now that T represents an imprecise probability assignment

$$T = \{(\overline{r_i - \epsilon_i} \to P\varphi_i) \wedge (P\varphi_i \to \overline{r_i + \epsilon_i})\}_{i=1,\ldots,n}$$

where, for each i, $r_i - \epsilon_i \geq 0$ and $r_i + \epsilon_i \leq 1$, that is $\epsilon_i \leq r_i \leq 1 - \epsilon_i$. Then, as shown in Example 2, the degree of inconsistency of T is:

$$Incon(T) = \inf_\mu \bigvee_{i=1,\ldots,n} (1 - \epsilon_i) \otimes |r_i - \mu(\varphi_i)|.$$

Therefore, by defining $d_c^*(T,T^\mu) = \bigvee_{i=1,\ldots,n}(1 - \epsilon_i) \otimes |r_i - \mu(\varphi_i)|$, we can write

$$Incon(T) = \inf_\mu d_c^*(T,T^\mu).$$

Note that the definition of $d_c^*(T,T^\mu)$ is similar to the one of $d_c(T,T^\mu)$ that takes into account the width of the probability intervals assigned to the events in T. However, d_c^* is not symmetric in its arguments since T is in general an imprecise assignment theory, while T^μ is a precise assignment theory. The question is then whether d_c^* can still be considered as a kind of distance. What we can say in this respect is that: i) in the particular case T is a precise assignment theory, then all the ϵ_i's are zero, and thus $d_c^*(T,T^\mu) = d_c(T,T^\mu)$; and ii) it is not hard to check that the following restricted form of the triangle inequality holds for any $\mu, \sigma \in \mathcal{P}(\mathcal{L})$: $d_c^*(T,T^\mu) \leq d_c^*(T,T^\sigma) + d_c^*(T^\sigma,T^\mu)$. From all the above, we could claim that $Incon(\cdot)$ belongs (to a high degree) to the family of distance-based inconsistency measures.

On the other hand, in our setting, for a given inconsistent theory T over FP(RPL), a violation-based inconsistency measure should aim at, first, estimating how far every interpretation (i.e. every probability) is from satisfying every formula in T (violation degrees), and then, minimising a suitable aggregation of those degrees. We can show that $Incon(\cdot)$ can be seen as well as a violation-based measure in this sense. Indeed, given a probability μ, we define the violation degree of a formula $\Phi \in T$ by μ as the satisfaction degree of its negation, i.e.

$$vd_\mu(\Phi) = e_\mu(\neg\Phi) = 1 - e_\mu(\Phi),$$

and then we define the global violation degree of T as $vd_\mu(T) = \max_{\Phi \in T} vd_\mu(\Phi)$. Finally, according to Lemma 1, it is straightforward to check that

$$Incon(T) = \inf_\mu dv_\mu(T),$$

that is, $Incon(T)$ is nothing but the infimum of the violation degrees of T by all possible probabilities, and the set of *generalised models* of T are those probabilities yielding a minimum violation degree:

$$GMod(T) = \{\mu \in \mathcal{P}(\mathcal{L}) \mid dv_\mu(T) = Incon(T)\} = \|T\|_{Con(T)}.$$

Finally, we can show that, in our particular case, the set of consequences entailed by the set of generalised models in fact coincides with the common consequences of all theories in $Repairs(T)$. Namely, for a precise-assignment theory T, we have:

$$GMod(T) \subseteq \llbracket \Phi \rrbracket \quad \text{iff} \quad \text{for all } T^\mu \in Repairs(T),\ T^\mu \vdash_{RPL} \Phi.$$

6   Conclusions and Future Work

We have presented some initial steps towards an approach to reason with inconsistent probabilistic theories in the setting of a probabilistic logic defined on top of the $[0,1]$-valued Łukasiewicz fuzzy logic enriched with rational truth-constants, and have put it into relation with other approaches in the literature based on distance-based and violation-based inconsistency measures.

There is a lot of future work to be done, in particular to generalise the approach to deal with inconsistent theories about conditional probabilities. This would need to replace the underlying Łukasiewicz logic by a more powerful one like the $\text{Ł}\Pi\frac{1}{2}$ logic, which combines connectives from Łukasiewicz logic and Product fuzzy logics, as it was done in e.g. [12] to define a logic of conditional probability. Another venue to explore is to replace classical logic as a logic of events by a paraconsistent logic and then define probability on top of that paraconsistent logic, in the line of [3].

Acknowledgments. The authors are grateful to the anonymous reviewers for their helpful comments. The authors also acknowledge partial support by the MOSAIC project (EU H2020- MSCA-RISE-2020 Project 101007627). Flaminio and Godo also acknowledge support by the Spanish project ISINC (PID2019-111544GB-C21) funded by MCIN/AEI/10.13039/501100011033, while Ugolini also acknowledges the Marie Sklodowska-Curie grant agreement No. 890616 (H2020-MSCA-IF-2019).

References

1. Baldi, P., Cintula, P., Noguera, C.: Classical and fuzzy two-layered modal logics for uncertainty: translations and proof-theory. Int. J. Comput. Intell. Syst. **13**(1), 988–1001 (2020)

2. Bertossi, L., Hunter, A., Schaub, T. (eds.): Inconsistency Tolerance. Lecture Notes in Computer Science, vol. 3300. Springer, Heidelberg (2005). https://doi.org/10.1007/b104925
3. Bueno-Soler, J., Carnielli, W.: Paraconsistent Probabilities: consistency, contradictions and Bayes' theorem. Entropy **18**(9), 325 (2016)
4. Carnielli, W., Coniglio, M.E., Marcos, J.: Logics of formal inconsistency. In: Gabbay, D., Guenthner, F. (eds.) Handbook of Philosophical Logic. Handbook of Philosophical Logic, vol. 14, pp. 1–93. Springer, Dordrecht (2007). https://doi.org/10.1007/978-1-4020-6324-4_1
5. Cignoli, R., D'Ottaviano, I.M.L., Mundici, D.: Algebraic Foundations of Many-valued Reasoning. Kluwer, Dordrecht (2000)
6. Cintula, P., Hájek, P., Noguera, C., Fermüller, C. (eds.): Handbook of Mathematical Fuzzy Logic - volumes 1, 2 and 3. Studies in Logic, Mathematical Logic and Foundations, vol. 37, 38, 58. College Publications, London (2011, 2016)
7. Cintula, P., Noguera, C.: Modal logics of uncertainty with two-layer syntax: a general completeness theorem. In: Kohlenbach, U., Barceló, P., de Queiroz, R. (eds.) WoLLIC 2014. LNCS, vol. 8652, pp. 124–136. Springer, Heidelberg (2014). https://doi.org/10.1007/978-3-662-44145-9_9
8. De Bona, G., Finger, M.: Measuring inconsistency in probabilistic logic: rationality postulates and Dutch book interpretation. Artif. Intell. **227**, 140–164 (2015)
9. De Bona, G., Finger, M., Potyka, N., Thimm, M.: Inconsistency measurement in probabilistic logic. In: Grant, J., Martinez, M.V. (eds.) Measuring Inconsistency in Information. Studies in Logic, vol. 73, pp. 235–269. College Publications (2018)
10. Flaminio, T., Godo, L.: A logic for reasoning about the probability of fuzzy events. Fuzzy Sets Syst. **158**(6), 625–638 (2007)
11. Flaminio, T., Godo, L., Marchioni, E.: Reasoning about uncertainty of fuzzy events: an overview. In: Cintula, P. et al. (eds.) Understanding Vagueness - Logical, Philosophical, and Linguistic Perspectives, pp. 367–400. College Publications (2011)
12. Godo, L., Marchioni, E.: Coherent conditional probability in a fuzzy logic setting. Log. J. IGPL **14**(3), 457–481 (2006)
13. Grant, J., Martinez, M.V. (eds.): Measuring Inconsistency in Information. Studies in Logic, vol. 73. College Publications (2018)
14. Hájek, P.: Metamathematics of Fuzzy Logic. Kluwer Academy Publishers (1998)
15. Hájek, P., Godo, L., Esteva, F.: Fuzzy logic and probability. In: Proceedings of the 11th Conference on Uncertainty in Artificial Intelligence (UAI 1995), pp. 237–244 (1995)
16. Muiño, D.P.: Measuring and repairing inconsistency in probabilistic knowledge bases. Int. J. Approx. Reason. **52**(6), 828–840 (2011)
17. Mundici, D.: Advanced Łukasiewicz Calculus and MV-Algebras. Springer, Dordrecht (2011). https://doi.org/10.1007/978-94-007-0840-2
18. Potyka, N.: Linear programs for measuring inconsistency in probabilistic logics. In: Proceedings of KR 2014, pp. 568–577 (2014)
19. Potyka, N., Thimm, M.: Consolidation of probabilistic knowledge bases by inconsistency minimization. In: Proceedings of ECAI 2014, pp. 729–734 (2014)
20. Potyka, N., Thimm, M.: Probabilistic reasoning with inconsistent beliefs using inconsistency measures. In: Proceedings of IJCAI 2015, pp. 3156–3163 (2015)
21. Potyka, N., Thimm, M.: Inconsistency-tolerant reasoning over linear probabilistic knowledge bases. Int. J. Approx. Reason. **88**, 209–236 (2017)
22. Thimm, M.: Measuring inconsistency in probabilistic knowledge bases. In: Proceedings of UAI 2009, pp. 530–537. AUAI Press (2009)
23. Thimm, M.: Inconsistency measures for probabilistic logics. Artif. Intell. **197**, 1–24 (2013)

A Comparison of ASP-Based and SAT-Based Algorithms for the Contension Inconsistency Measure

Isabelle Kuhlmann[✉], Anna Gessler, Vivien Laszlo, and Matthias Thimm

Artificial Intelligence Group, University of Hagen, Hagen, Germany
{isabelle.kuhlmann,vivien.laszlo,matthias.thimm}@fernuni-hagen.de,
anna.gessler.work@gmail.com

Abstract. We propose an algorithm based on satisfiability problem (SAT) solving for determining the contension inconsistency degree in propositional knowledge bases. In addition, we present a revised version of an algorithm based on answer set programming (ASP), which serves the same purpose. In an experimental analysis, we compare the two algorithms to each other, as well as to a naive baseline method. Our results demonstrate that both the SAT and the ASP approach expectedly outperform the baseline algorithm. Further, the revised ASP method is not only superior to the SAT approach, but also to its predecessors from the literature. Hence, it poses a new state of the art.

Keywords: Inconsistency measurement · Answer set programming · Satisfiability solving

1 Introduction

The ubiquitous presence of conflicting information and the handling thereof constitutes a major challenge in Artificial Intelligence. The field of *inconsistency measurement* (see the seminal work by Grant [14], and the book by Grant and Martinez [15]) allows for an analytical perspective on the subject of inconsistency in formal knowledge representation formalisms. In inconsistency measurement, the aim is to quantitatively assess the *severity* of inconsistency in order to both guide automatic reasoning mechanisms and to help human modelers to identify issues and compare different alternative formalizations. For example, inconsistency measures have been used to estimate reliability of agents in multi-agent systems [9], to analyze inconsistencies in news reports [17], to support collaborative software requirements specifications [21], to allow for inconsistency-tolerant reasoning in probabilistic logic [23], and to monitor and maintain quality in database settings [4]. Hence, there is clearly a need for practically applicable approaches.

There are numerous inconsistency measures, based on different concepts, such as minimal inconsistent subsets (see, e.g., [16]) or maximal consistent sets (see,

F. Dupin de Saint-Cyr et al. (Eds.): SUM 2022, LNAI 13562, pp. 139–153, 2022.
https://doi.org/10.1007/978-3-031-18843-5_10

e.g., [3]), or non-classical semantics (see, e.g., [13]); see [26] for an overview. A number of problems related to these measures lies on the first level of the polynomial hierarchy, which renders them complexity-wise most likely to be suitable for practical applications, compared to other measures where the associated problems are located higher up the polynomial hierarchy [29]. Further, a natural approach to computing these measures is using *satisfiability problem* (SAT) solving, which is widely used in applications such as the automatic verification of hardware specifications [31], or cryptanalysis [22]. Moreover, there exist highly optimized SAT solvers (see the results of the annual SAT competition[1] for an overview). In this paper, we present a SAT-based approach for inconsistency measurement. To be precise, we develop a SAT encoding for determining the *contension inconsistency measure* (which we also simply refer to as *contension measure*) [13] via binary search.

There already exist a couple of works that take an algorithmic perspective on inconsistency measurement. In [18] and [19], the authors present approaches for computing a number of inconsistency measures based on reductions to *answer set programming* (ASP). A total of three inconsistency measures [5,13,27], where the corresponding decision problems are all on the first level of the polynomial hierarchy, were selected. The three measures were implemented and compared to naive baseline implementations in an experimental analysis. As anticipated, the results showed that the ASP-based implementations were clearly superior.

We compare the newly proposed SAT-based approach with a revised version of the ASP approach that was presented in [19]. In an extensive experimental evaluation, we additionally compare the two methods to a naive baseline method, which is, to the best of our knowledge, the only other existing implementation of the contension measure. Yet, we focus our analysis on the comparison between the SAT approach and the ASP approach, as those are the more promising—and, in terms of performance, more comparable—methods. The results reveal that, as expected, the SAT approach is clearly superior to the naive one, however, it cannot compete with the ASP approach. In addition, we draw a comparison between the previous versions of the ASP-based method [18,19] and the newly proposed one. We demonstrate that the latter is superior, and thus represents a new state of the art.

The remainder of this paper is organized as follows. In Sect. 2, we explain fundamental definitions regarding inconsistency measurement, ASP, and SAT solving. Sections 3 and 4, respectively, provide descriptions of the SAT-based and ASP-based approaches for the contension inconsistency measure. In Sect. 5, we describe our experimental evaluation, including an in-depth discussion of the results, and we conclude in Sect. 6. Due to space restrictions, all proofs are omitted in the main paper, but are provided in an appendix[2].

---

[1] http://www.satcompetition.org/.
[2] https://e.feu.de/sum2022-appendix.

2 Preliminaries

We define At to be a fixed set of propositions (also referred to as (propositional) *atoms*), and $\mathcal{L}(\mathsf{At})$ to be the corresponding propositional language. $\mathcal{L}(\mathsf{At})$ is constructed by applying the usual connectives, i.e., $\wedge$ (*conjunction*), $\vee$ (*disjunction*), and $\neg$ (*negation*). A finite set of (propositional) formulas $\mathcal{K} \subseteq \mathcal{L}(\mathsf{At})$ is called a (propositional) *knowledge base* (KB). Let $\mathbb{K}$ denote the set of all KBs. Let F be a formula or a set of formulas. We denote the set of propositions appearing in F, i.e., the *signature* of F, as $\mathsf{At}(F)$. Semantics of a propositional language is determined by *interpretations*.

Definition 1. A propositional *interpretation* is a function $\omega : \mathsf{At} \to \{\mathsf{true}, \mathsf{false}\}$. Let $\Omega(\mathsf{At})$ be the set of all interpretations.

An interpretation *satisfies* an atom $x \in \mathsf{At}$ if and only if $\omega(x) = \mathsf{true}$. This is also denoted as $\omega \models x$, and ω is also referred to as a *model* of x. We extend this concept to formulas and sets of formulas in the usual manner.

2.1 Inconsistency Measurement

If there exists no model for a formula or a set of formulas F, i.e., if $\neg \exists \omega \models F$, then F is *inconsistent*. The intuition behind an *inconsistency measure* is that a higher value indicates a more severe inconsistency than a lower one. Besides, the minimal value (0) is supposed to model the absence of inconsistency, i.e., consistency. Let $\mathbb{R}_{\geq 0}^{\infty}$ be the set of non-negative real numbers, including infinity.

Definition 2. An *inconsistency measure* $\mathcal{I}$ is a function $\mathcal{I} : \mathbb{K} \to \mathbb{R}_{\geq 0}^{\infty}$ that satisfies $\mathcal{I}(\mathcal{K}) = 0$ if and only if $\mathcal{K}$ is consistent, for all $\mathcal{K} \in \mathbb{K}$.

We further define $\mathrm{UPPER}_{\mathcal{I}}$ to be the decision problem of deciding whether a given value $u \in \mathbb{R}_{\geq 0}^{\infty}$ is an upper bound of $\mathcal{I}(\mathcal{K})$ wrt. a given KB $\mathcal{K}$, and we define $\mathrm{VALUE}_{\mathcal{I}}$ to be the functional problem of determining the value of $\mathcal{I}(\mathcal{K})$.

The *contension inconsistency measure* $\mathcal{I}_{\mathrm{c}}$ [13] is based on Priest's three-valued propositional logic [24], which extends the two classical truth values true (t) and false (f) by a third value, which indicates *paradoxical*, or *both true and false* (b). The truth tables of this logic are presented in Table 1. A *three-valued interpretation* $\omega^3 : \mathsf{At}(\mathcal{K}) \mapsto \{t, f, b\}$ assigns one of the three truth values to each atom in a KB $\mathcal{K}$. An interpretation ω^3 is a *three-valued model* of an atom, if it evaluates to either t or b. Again, we extend this concept to formulas, and sets of formulas. We denote the set of all three-valued models wrt. an arbitrary KB $\mathcal{K}$ as $\mathsf{Models}(\mathcal{K}) = \{\omega^3 \mid \forall \alpha \in \mathcal{K}, \omega^3(\alpha) = t \text{ or } \omega^3(\alpha) = b\}$.

Furthermore, we can divide the domain of an interpretation ω^3 into two sets, of which one contains those atoms that are assigned a classical truth value (t, f), and the other one contains those atoms that are assigned truth value b. The latter is defined as $\mathsf{Conflictbase}(\omega^3) = \{x \in \mathsf{At}(\mathcal{K}) \mid \omega^3(x) = b\}$. Consider the interpretation ω_B^3 which sets all atoms in a KB $\mathcal{K}$ to b. Such an interpretation will

Table 1. Truth tables for Priest's propositional three-valued logic.

x	y	$x \wedge y$	$x \vee y$
t	t	t	t
t	b	b	t
t	f	f	t
b	t	b	t
b	b	b	b
b	f	f	b
f	t	f	t
f	b	f	b
f	f	f	f

x	$\neg x$
t	f
b	b
f	t

always satisfy $\mathcal{K}$ (i.e., $\omega_B^3 \in \mathsf{Models}(\mathcal{K})$). However, if we minimize the number of b assignments (i.e., $|\mathsf{Conflictbase}(\omega^3)|$), it becomes evident which atoms are involved in a conflict, because they are exactly those atoms that cannot be set to t or f without rendering $\mathcal{K}$ unsatisfiable.

Definition 3. We define the *contension inconsistency measure* $\mathcal{I}_c$ wrt. a knowledge base $\mathcal{K}$ as $\mathcal{I}_c(\mathcal{K}) = \min\{|\mathsf{Conflictbase}(\omega^3)| \mid \omega^3 \in \mathsf{Models}(\mathcal{K})\}$.

The minimal number of atoms that are assigned b corresponds exactly to the number of atoms which are involved in a conflict, as the following example illustrates.

Example 1. Consider $\mathcal{K}_1 = \{x \wedge y, \neg x, y \vee z\}$. Let ω_1^3 be an interpretation with $\omega_1^3(y) = \omega_1^3(z) = t$, and $\omega_1^3(x) = b$, i.e., ω_1^3 is a model of $\mathcal{K}$, and $\mathsf{Conflictbase}(\omega_1^3) = \{x\}$. It is easy to see that x must be assigned b in order to make $\mathcal{K}_1$ satisfiable, and that no lower number of atoms being assigned b could achieve this. Hence, $\mathcal{I}_c(\mathcal{K}_1) = |\mathsf{Conflictbase}(\omega_1^3)| = |\{x\}| = 1$.

2.2   Satisfiability Solving

One of the major problems of propositional logic is the *Boolean Satisfiability Problem*, which is one of the most-studied problems of computer science, and which is NP-complete [7].

Definition 4. The *Boolean Satisfiability Problem* (SAT) is the problem of deciding if there exists an interpretation that satisfies a given propositional formula.

A *SAT solver* is a program that solves SAT for a given formula. There exist numerous high-performance SAT solvers (see [10] for a recent overview). Note that the input formula of a SAT solver must be in Conjunctive Normal Form (CNF), i.e., it must be a conjunction of clauses. Although every propositional formula can be transformed to CNF, a naive conversion using Boolean transformation rules may result in a formula which is exponentially larger than the original formula. For this reason, in this work we use the Tseitin method [30] for converting formulas to CNF, which yields an equisatisfiable formula in CNF, with only a linear increase in size. We further have a concept of modeling *cardinality constraints* in SAT, which represent that at least, at most, or exactly some number k out of a set of propositional atoms are allowed to be true. Using the formal definition of Abio et al. [1], we define a cardinality constraint to be of the form $a_1 + \ldots + a_n \bowtie k$, where $a_1, \ldots, a_n$ are propositional atoms with $|\mathsf{At}| = n$, k is a natural number, and $\bowtie \in \{<, \leq, =, \geq, >\}$. The meaning of the $+$ operator is that for every true atom the number 1 is added and for every false atom the number 0 is added, thereby counting the number of true atoms. To encode $\mathcal{I}_c$, we merely require *at-most-k constraints*, i.e., constraints of the form $a_1 + \ldots + a_n \leq k$. A straightforward approach to realize at-most-k constraints is to add all clauses which are disjunctions of subsets $A_i \subseteq \{\neg a_1, \ldots, \neg a_n\}$ with $|A_i| = k+1$ to the SAT encoding. Since this method creates $\binom{n}{k+1}$ clauses (*binomial encoding*), it does not scale well, and it is often not suitable for practical applications. There are, however, more efficient approaches, such as the *sequential counter encoding* [25], which is used in our experiments (see Sect. 5).

2.3   Answer Set Programming

Answer set programming (ASP) [8,11,20] is a declarative problem solving approach targeted at difficult search problems. Thus, rather than modeling instructions on how to solve a problem, a representation of the problem itself is modeled. More precisely, a problem is modeled as an *extended logic program* which consists of a set of *rules* of the form

$$r = H \text{:- } A_1, \ldots, A_n, \text{not } B_1, \ldots, \text{not } B_m. \tag{1}$$

where H, A_i with $i \in \{1, \ldots, n\}$, and B_j with $j \in \{1, \ldots, m\}$ are classical literals. ASP rules consist of a *head* and a *body*, separated by ":-", of which one may be empty. Wrt. a rule r, we denote the sets of literals contained in the head and body as $\mathsf{head}(r)$, and $\mathsf{body}(r)$, respectively. In Eq. (1), $\mathsf{head}(r) = \{H\}$, and $\mathsf{body}(r) = \{A_1, \ldots, A_n, B_1, \ldots, B_m\}$. We refer to a rule with an empty body as *fact*, and to one with an empty head as *constraint*. An extended logic program is *positive* if it does not contain any default negation (**not**). A set of literals L is called *closed under* a positive program P if and only if for any rule $r \in P$, $\mathsf{head}(r) \in L$ whenever $\mathsf{body}(r) \subseteq L$. A set L is consistent if it does not contain both A and $\neg A$ for some literal A. We denote the smallest of such sets wrt. a positive program P, which is always uniquely defined, as $\mathsf{Cn}(P)$. Wrt. an arbitrary program P, a set L is called an *answer set* of P if $L = \mathsf{Cn}(P^L)$, with

$$P^L = \{H \text{:- } A_1, \ldots, A_n \mid$$
$$H \text{:- } A_1, \ldots, A_n, \text{not } B_1, \ldots, \text{not } B_m. \in P, \{B_1, \ldots, B_m\} \cap L = \emptyset\}.$$

In addition to the "basic" rules (as described above), modern ASP dialects allow for more complex structures. An example of such is the *cardinality constraint*, which is of the form

$$l\{A_1, \ldots, A_n, \text{not } B_1, \ldots, \text{not } B_m\}u,$$

where l is a lower bound, u is an upper bound, and $A_1, \ldots, A_n, B_1, \ldots, B_m$ are literals. It can be interpreted as follows: if at least l and at most u of the literals are included in an answer set, the cardinality rule is satisfied by that answer set. ASP solvers also offer the option to express cost functions involving minimization and/or maximization in order to solve optimization problems [11]. In this work, we only require a specific type of optimization statements of the form #minimize$\{A_1, \ldots, A_n\}$. Such a *minimize statement* instructs the ASP solver to include only a minimal number of the literals $A_1, \ldots, A_n$ in any answer set. We refer to an answer set that corresponds to the minimization (i.e., that contains a minimal number of $A_1, \ldots, A_n$) as an *optimal answer set*.

As of yet, we introduced a basic *propositional* syntax and semantics of ASP, in order to define the different language concepts in a concise manner. Note, however, that we model $\mathcal{I}_c$ in ASP using *first-order* predicates and functions. This serves the purpose of a) easing readability, and b) facilitating an improved automated grounding process. The use of first-order concepts allows us to set variables which range over constant symbols. Following the Clingo syntax [20], we use capitalized identifiers for variables and non-capitalized ones for constants. Replacing the variables in a rule by the corresponding constant symbols is referred to as *grounding*. In addition, we express the arity n of a predicate or function f as f$/n$.

Example 2. Our aim is to model a KB $\mathcal{K}_2$ with $\mathsf{At}(\mathcal{K}_2) = \{a, b\}$ in ASP. To represent the concept of an atom, we introduce the predicate atom/1. We also use the constant symbols a and b to represent the atoms a and b, and create the facts atom(a) and atom(b). If we now wish to use atom/1 in a rule, we do not have to explicitly state atom(a) and atom(b), but we can simply use a variable, e.g., X, and write atom(X). During the grounding process, X will then be replaced by a and b.

3   An Algorithm for $\mathcal{I}_c$ Based on SAT

In order to compute the value of $\mathcal{I}_c(\mathcal{K})$ wrt. a KB $\mathcal{K}$, i.e., in order to solve $\text{VALUE}_{\mathcal{I}_c}$, we use the standard approach to solve the functional problem $\text{VALUE}_{\mathcal{I}_c}$ by iterative calls to a SAT solver which determines the answers to the decision problem $\text{UPPER}_{\mathcal{I}_c}$ [29]. The range of $\mathcal{I}_c(\mathcal{K})$ is clearly defined (with 0 being the minimal and $|\mathsf{At}(\mathcal{K})|$ the maximal value), which enables us to use binary search to find the exact value. To be precise, we start with $u = \lfloor |\mathsf{At}(\mathcal{K})|/2 \rfloor$, and determine a SAT encoding for $\text{UPPER}_{\mathcal{I}_c}$ wrt. the KB $\mathcal{K}$ and the value u as the upper bound. If u is in fact an upper bound of $\text{UPPER}_{\mathcal{I}_c}$, we continue the binary search in the lower interval, if it is not, we continue in the upper interval. After $\log_2(|\mathsf{At}(\mathcal{K})|)$ iterative calls to a SAT solver, we know the lowest possible value for which $\text{UPPER}_{\mathcal{I}_c}$ returns true, i.e., we know the solution to $\text{VALUE}_{\mathcal{I}_c}$.

In the following, we illustrate how to construct a set of formulas $S(\mathcal{K}, u)$ wrt. a KB $\mathcal{K}$ and a non-negative integer value u, which is satisfied if and only if u is an upper bound of $\mathcal{I}_c(\mathcal{K})$. To encode Priest's tree-valued logic in propositional logic, we require additional variables. To begin with, for every atom x in the original signature $\mathsf{At}(\mathcal{K})$, we introduce three new atoms x_t, x_b, x_f (S1) to represent the three truth values t, b, f. In order to ensure that only one of such atoms is true wrt. some $x \in \mathsf{At}(\mathcal{K})$, we add the following rule:

$$(x_t \vee x_f \vee x_b) \wedge (\neg x_t \vee \neg x_f) \wedge (\neg x_t \vee \neg x_b) \wedge (\neg x_b \vee \neg x_f) \tag{S2}$$

In addition, we must model the evaluation of formulas in three-valued logic (see Table 1). We introduce three variables v_ϕ^t, v_ϕ^f, v_ϕ^b (S3) for every sub-formula ϕ of every formula $\alpha \in \mathcal{K}$ to represent when each of the three possible valuations of ϕ occurs. For each of these atoms we add an equivalence relation which defines the evaluations based on the operator of the sub-formula. Thus, we need to model conjunction, disjunction, and negation. To encode a conjunction $\phi_c = \psi_{c,1} \wedge \psi_{c,2}$, we need to model that ϕ_c is t if both conjuncts are t, ϕ_c is f if at least one of the conjuncts is f, and ϕ_c is b if at least one of the conjuncts is b and the other one is not f:

$$v_{\phi_c}^t \leftrightarrow v_{\psi_{c,1}}^t \wedge v_{\psi_{c,2}}^t \tag{S4}$$

$$v_{\phi_c}^f \leftrightarrow v_{\psi_{c,1}}^f \vee v_{\psi_{c,2}}^f \tag{S5}$$

$$v_{\phi_c}^b \leftrightarrow (v_{\psi_{c,1}}^b \vee v_{\psi_{c,2}}^b) \wedge \neg v_{\psi_{c,1}}^f \wedge \neg v_{\psi_{c,2}}^f \tag{S6}$$

In the same fashion, we can encode that a disjunction is f if both of its disjuncts are f, it is t if at least one of the disjuncts is t, and it is b if at least one disjunct is b and the other one is not t:

$$v_{\phi_d}^t \leftrightarrow v_{\psi_{d,1}}^t \vee v_{\psi_{d,2}}^t \tag{S7}$$

$$v_{\phi_d}^f \leftrightarrow v_{\psi_{d,1}}^f \wedge v_{\psi_{d,2}}^f \tag{S8}$$

$$v_{\phi_d}^b \leftrightarrow (v_{\psi_{d,1}}^b \vee v_{\psi_{d,2}}^b) \wedge \neg v_{\psi_{d,1}}^t \wedge \neg v_{\psi_{d,2}}^t \tag{S9}$$

Negations $\phi_n = \neg \psi_n$ are encoded as follows:

$$v_{\phi_n}^t \leftrightarrow v_{\psi_n}^f \qquad v_{\phi_n}^f \leftrightarrow v_{\psi_n}^t \qquad v_{\phi_n}^b \leftrightarrow v_{\psi_n}^b \tag{S10–12}$$

Further, we add variables for each sub-formula ϕ_a which represents an individual atom x:

$$v_{\phi_a}^t \leftrightarrow x_t \qquad v_{\phi_a}^f \leftrightarrow x_f \qquad v_{\phi_a}^b \leftrightarrow x_b \tag{S13–15}$$

Moreover, we need to represent a formula $\alpha \in \mathcal{K}$ being satisfied in three-valued logic. This is the case when the sub-formula which contains the entire formula evaluates to t or b. Thus, we add the formula $v_\alpha^t \vee v_\alpha^b$ (S16). Finally, we add a cardinality constraint representing that at most u of the b-atoms can be true: $\mathtt{at\_most\_u}(\mathsf{At}_b)$ (S17). We define $S(\mathcal{K}, u)$ to be comprised of (S1–17).

Theorem 1. *For a given value u, the encoding $S(\mathcal{K}, u)$ is satisfiable if and only if $\mathcal{I}_c(\mathcal{K}) \leq u$.*

4   An Algorithm for $\mathcal{I}_c$ Based on ASP

There already exist two ASP-based approaches for computing $\mathcal{I}_c$ in the literature. In [18], the authors introduce a method similar to our SAT approach (see
Sect. 3), which uses ASP encodings for the problem $\text{UPPER}_{\mathcal{I}_c}$, in order to find
$\text{VALUE}_{\mathcal{I}_c}$ via binary search. A revised version of this approach is proposed in [19],
which calculates $\text{VALUE}_{\mathcal{I}_c}$ directly within ASP by means of a minimize statement. Note that in both versions, only propositional language concepts are used,
which leads to a program that is already ground (i.e., the program is essentially
ground manually, instead of by a grounder). In the present work, we demonstrate yet another revision of the ASP approach, which is very similar to the one
in [19], but makes use of first-order predicates and variables, which enables an
automated, and internally optimized, grounding procedure.

We address the problem of computing $\mathcal{I}_c(\mathcal{K})$ wrt. a KB $\mathcal{K}$ by constructing an
extended logic program as follows. First, we define some facts that describe the
composition of $\mathcal{K}$. Every atom $x \in \text{At}(\mathcal{K})$ is represented in ASP as `atom(x)` (A1),
and every formula $\alpha \in \mathcal{K}$ as `kbMember(α)` (A2). Further, every conjunction $\phi_c =
\psi_{c,1} \wedge \psi_{c,2}$ is encoded as `conjunction(φc,ψc,1,ψc,2)` (A3). In the same fashion,
every disjunction $\phi_d = \psi_{d,1} \vee \psi_{d,2}$ is encoded as `disjunction(φd,ψd,1,ψd,2)`
(A4). Each negation, i.e., each $\phi_n = \neg\psi_n$, is represented as `negation(φn,ψn)`
(A5). Further, each formula ϕ_a that consists of an individual atom x is encoded as
`formulaIsAtom(φa,x)` (A6). Moreover, we represent the truth values of Priest's
three-valued logic (t, f, b) as `tv(t)`, `tv(f)`, and `tv(b)` (A7).

To encode the actual functionality of the contension measure, we need to
create a rule which "guesses" a three-valued interpretation. To achieve this, we
model that each atom is assigned exactly one truth value by using the cardinality
constraint

$$1\{\texttt{truthValue(A,T)}: \texttt{tv(T)}\}1:\texttt{- atom(A)}. \tag{A8}$$

As with the SAT approach, we need to represent the role of the operators $\wedge$, $\vee$,
and $\neg$ in three-valued logic. In order for a conjunction $\phi_c = \psi_{c,1} \wedge \psi_{c,2}$ to be t,
both of its conjuncts need to be t:

$$\texttt{truthValue(F},t)\texttt{:- conjunction(F,G,H)}, \tag{A9}$$
$$\texttt{truthValue(G},t)\texttt{, truthValue(H},t)\texttt{.}$$

For a conjunction to be f, on the other hand, it is sufficient if only one of the
conjuncts is f:

$$\texttt{truthValue(F},f)\texttt{:- conjunction(F,G,H)}, \tag{A10}$$
$$1\{\texttt{truthValue(G},f)\texttt{, truthValue(H},f)\}\texttt{.}$$

Finally, a conjunction is b if it is neither t nor f:

$$\texttt{truthValue(F},b)\texttt{:- conjunction(F,\_,\_)}, \tag{A11}$$
$$\texttt{not truthValue(F},t)\texttt{, not truthValue(F},f)\texttt{.}$$

In the same fashion, a disjunction $\phi_d = \psi_{d,1} \vee \psi_{d,2}$ is only f if both of its disjuncts are f (A12), it is t if at least one disjunct is t (A13), and it is b if it is neither t nor f (A14). A negation is t in three-valued logic if its base formula is f, i.e.,

$$\texttt{truthValue(F,}t\texttt{):- negation(F,G), truthValue(G,}f\texttt{).} \qquad \text{(A15)}$$

and vice versa, and it is b if its base formula is also b. Hence, the other two cases (A16–17) follow accordingly. Moreover, if a (sub-)formula consists of a single atom, it must have the same truth value as the referred atom:

$$\texttt{truthValue(F,T):- formulaIsAtom(F,G),} \qquad \text{(A18)}$$
$$\texttt{truthValue(G,T), tv(T).}$$

In order to compute $\mathcal{I}_c$, we still need to ensure that the ASP solver finds an interpretation that satisfies all formulas $\alpha \in \mathcal{K}$. Consequently, every $\alpha \in \mathcal{K}$ must evaluate to either t or b—in other words, no formula must evaluate to f. We realize this using the following integrity constraint:

$$\texttt{:- truthValue(F,}f\texttt{), kbMember(F).} \qquad \text{(A19)}$$

Finally, as our aim is to find the minimal number of atoms being evaluated to b, we add

$$\texttt{\#minimize\{1,A: truthValue(A,}b\texttt{), atom(A)\}.} \qquad \text{(A20)}$$

We define P_c to be the union of all rules (A1–20) defined above. Further, let ω_M^3 be the three-valued interpretation represented by an answer set M of $P_c(\mathcal{K})$.

Theorem 2. *Let M be an optimal answer set of $P_c(\mathcal{K})$. Then $|(\omega_M^3)^{-1}(b)| = \mathcal{I}_c(\mathcal{K})$.*[3]

5   Experimental Analysis

The central aspect of our experimental evaluation is a comparison between the SAT-based and ASP-based approaches introduced in Sects. 3 and 4, as well as a naive baseline algorithm. The latter, which is provided by *TweetyProject*[4], is implemented by first converting the KB to CNF, followed by iterating through all subsets of atoms (with increasing cardinality), deleting all clauses in which one of the atoms of the current set appears (thus, effectively setting their three-valued truth value to b). At each interation we check whether the resulting KB is consistent by means of a SAT solver (here, CaDiCal sc2021[5] [6]). If it is, the cardinality of the current set of atoms is returned.

---

[3] For any function $\varphi : X \mapsto Y$ and $y \in Y$ we define $\varphi^{-1}(y) = \{x \in X \mid f(x) = y\}$.
[4] https://e.feu.de/tweety-contension.
[5] https://github.com/arminbiere/cadical.

Although the ASP approach has been proven to be clearly superior to the naive one in terms of runtime (see [19]), and we can expect the same for the SAT approach, we still draw this comparison in order to concretely quantify this assumption. Besides, the naive algorithm is, to the best of our knowledge, the only existing alternative to compute $\mathcal{I}_c$. However, as the result of comparing the SAT and ASP approaches is far less predictable (both SAT and ASP are established formalisms for dealing with problems on the first level of the polynomial hierarchy), we examine the two methods more closely. We consider how the runtimes of the approaches are composed, e.g., how much time the respective solvers require, or the time it takes to compute the encodings. Moreover, we draw a comparison between previous versions of the ASP approach [18,19] and the newly proposed one.

5.1   Experimental Setup

As there is, to the best of our knowledge, no dedicated benchmark dataset for inconsistency measurement, we need to compile our own dataset. One option to achieve this is to generate completely synthetic data; another one is to "translate" benchmark data from a different research field. Therefore, we use both a synthetic and a "translated" dataset. The **SRS** dataset[6] consists of synthetic KBs generated by the *SyntacticRandomSampler*[7] provided by TweetyProject. This dataset corresponds exactly to the union of datasets A and B in [19]. Hence, the SRS dataset contains a total of 1800 KBs of varying complexity. The smallest instances have a signature size of 3, and contain between 5 and 15 formulas, the biggest ones have a signature size of 30, and contain between 50 and 100 formulas. As the formulas are created randomly, and independently of one another, most KBs are highly inconsistent[8]. The **ML** dataset[9] consists of a total of 1920 KBs learned from the *Animals with Attributes*[10] (AWA) dataset, which is widely used in the area of machine learning. It describes 50 types of animals using 85 binary attributes. Following [28], we used the Apriori algorithm [2] to mine association rules from the AWA dataset for a given minimal confidence value c and minimal support value s. These rules were then interpreted as propositional logic implications. We finally selected one animal at random and added all its attributes as facts, likely making the KB inconsistent, as even rules with low confidence values were interpreted as strict implications. We set

$$c \in \{0.6, 0.65, 0.70, 0.75, 0.8, 0.85, 0.90, 0.95\},$$
$$s \in \{0.6, 0.65, 0.70, 0.75, 0.8, 0.85, 0.90, 0.95\},$$

and allowed a maximum of 4 literals per rule.

---

[6] Download: https://e.feu.de/srs-dataset.
[7] https://e.feu.de/tweety-syntactic-random-sampler.
[8] Overview of inconsistency values: https://e.feu.de/sum2022-tables.
[9] Download: https://e.feu.de/ml-dataset.
[10] http://attributes.kyb.tuebingen.mpg.de.

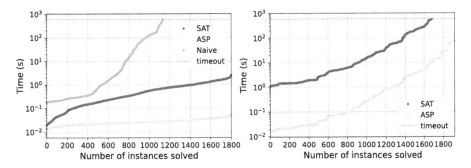

Fig. 1. Runtime comparison of the ASP-based, SAT-based, and naive approach on the SRS dataset (left). Further runtime comparison of the ASP-based and SAT-based methods on the ML dataset (right). Timeout: 10 min.

Both the SAT-based and the ASP-based approach are implemented in C++. The SAT solver we use is CaDiCal sc2021 (as with the naive method), and the ASP solver we use is Clingo 5.5.1[11] [12]. For the computation of cardinality constraints in SAT we use sequential counter encoding, and for transforming formulas to CNF we use Tseitin's method. All experiments were run on a computer with 125 GB RAM and an Intel Xeon E5-2690 CPU which has a basic clock frequency of 2.90 GHz.

5.2   Results

We first consider the overall runtime per KB of all three approaches wrt. the SRS dataset. Figure 1 (left) shows a *cactus plot* of the measured runtimes, i.e., wrt. each method it shows the runtimes wrt. each KB of the dataset, sorted from low to high, with a timeout set to 10 min. We can see that both the SAT and the ASP approach fare quite well compared to the naive method. While the latter produces a total of 664 timeouts, the former are able to compute all inconsistency values easily within the time limit. However, even though the SAT method clearly outperforms the naive method, it cannot match the ASP approach. A comparison of the SAT method and the ASP method wrt. the more challenging ML dataset shows the same pattern (see the right part of Fig. 1). Here, the SAT method actually times out in 237 cases.

We now proceed to a more detailed examination of how the SAT and ASP runtimes are composed. To achieve this, we measure the amount of time required to compute the SAT/ASP encoding, the respective solving time, and, in the SAT case, the time required to transform the formulas to CNF. Note that wrt. SAT, we measure the *total* time needed for encoding, solving, and transforming, as the iterative nature of the approach requires multiple calls. Further, in the ASP case, "solving" includes the grounding process, and in both the ASP and the SAT case, it includes initializing the solver, and feeding it the program/clauses.

---

[11] https://potassco.org/clingo/.

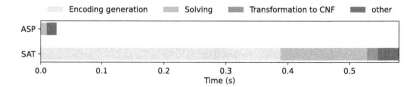

Fig. 2. Overview of the average runtime composition of the ASP-based and SAT-based approaches wrt. the SRS dataset.

Figure 2 visualizes how the runtimes of both approaches are composed on average (regarding the SRS dataset). The category "other" included in the figure covers factors such as loading the KB. As the cactus plot in Fig. 1 (left) already indicates, the average runtime of the ASP-based method is several times shorter than the runtime of the SAT-based method (0.026 s vs. 0.580 s). With regard to the ASP approach, it is noticeable that the encoding generation only takes up a tiny fraction of the overall runtime (with 0.0008 s it is barely even visible in Fig. 2), while the "other" category takes up more than half the runtime. However, since the average total runtime of this method is very low in general, this observation should be taken with a grain of salt, as the ratio of the different runtime shares could shift with an increasing size and complexity of the KBs at hand. One striking observation wrt. the SAT approach is that the encoding generation represents the largest fraction of the overall runtime. This is mainly due to the fact that a new cardinality constraint is required for each iteration, and its calculation can be costly even when using a non-trivial method. The transformation to CNF, on the other hand, hardly contributes to the overall runtime. It should also be noted that the pure solving time (excluding any preprocessing) is only 0.0064 s on average, which demonstrates the extent to which modern SAT solvers are optimized. Hence, we see that SAT solvers are in fact able to solve $\text{UPPER}_{\mathcal{I}_c}$ quite fast, however, the iterative nature of the approach leads to a large overhead, in particular wrt. the generation of cardinality constraints.

Yet another aspect we aim to investigate is how well the newly proposed revision of the ASP approach performs in comparison to its predecessors in [18] and [19] (see Sect. 4 for an overview of the two approaches). We apply exactly those Java implementations which were used in the two corresponding papers. To conduct our analysis, we use the SRS dataset. The results of this experiment, which are illustrated in Fig. 3, show that the new version of the method in fact outperforms the older ones. The first ASP approach [18], which is based on a binary search procedure, clearly performs the poorest, and hits the timeout of 10 min in 600 cases. The second version of the approach [19] yields more consistent results, nevertheless it performs on average roughly 7 times slower than the newest version (0.266 vs. 0.037 s). Although the new version might have an advantage by being implemented in C++, both rely on the same ASP solver. In fact, the solving time itself is around 3 times shorter wrt. the new ASP version compared to the previous one (0.010 vs. 0.028 s on average).

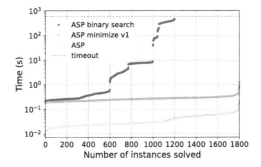

Fig. 3. Runtime comparison of the different versions of the ASP approach on the SRS dataset. "ASP binary search" refers to the version from [18], "ASP minimize v1" to the version from [19], and "ASP" to the new version. Timeout: 10 min.

6   Conclusion

In the course of this work, we addressed the problem of computing the contension inconsistency measure from an algorithmic perspective. To be specific, we introduced a SAT-based approach, as well as a revised version of an ASP-based approach. We have subjected the two methods to extensive experimental analysis and have learned the following. SAT is generally a suitable formalism to compute $\mathcal{I}_c$ (as our SAT-based method clearly outperforms a naive baseline approach), however, due to its iterative nature, it cannot compete with the ASP-based method. In particular, our new version of the ASP approach outperforms not only the SAT-based one, but also its previous two versions from the literature. Besides, the performance of the ASP approach can now be more accurately assessed—a comparison with a SAT-based method is more appropriate than merely with a naive algorithm.

There are still numerous aspects to be examined in future work. For instance, wrt. SAT, one can compare different SAT solvers, different methods of converting formulas to CNF, different techniques of generating cardinality constraints, or exploit approaches to MaxSAT. Furthermore, both SAT and ASP approaches for other inconsistency measures could be developed and compared. Moreover, other formalisms, such as *Quantified Boolean Formulas* (QBF), might be interesting for computing inconsistency measures. One could also consider measures of higher complexity.

References

1. Abío, I., Nieuwenhuis, R., Oliveras, A., Rodríguez-Carbonell, E.: A parametric approach for smaller and better encodings of cardinality constraints. In: 19th International Conference on Principles and Practice of Constraint Programming, pp. 80–96. CP 2013 (2013). https://doi.org/10.1007/978-3-642-40627-0_9
2. Agrawal, R., Srikant, R.: Fast algorithms for mining association rules in large databases. In: Proceedings VLDB 1994, pp. 487–499 (1994)

3. Ammoura, M., Raddaoui, B., Salhi, Y., Oukacha, B.: On measuring inconsistency using maximal consistent sets. In: European Conference on Symbolic and Quantitative Approaches to Reasoning and Uncertainty, pp. 267–276. Springer (2015). https://doi.org/10.1007/978-3-319-20807-7_24

4. Bertossi, L.: Measuring and computing database inconsistency via repairs. In: 12th International Conference on Scalable Uncertainty Management, pp. 368–372 (2018). https://doi.org/10.1007/978-3-030-00461-3_26

5. Besnard, P.: Forgetting-based inconsistency measure. In: 10th International Conference on Scalable Uncertainty Management, pp. 331–337. Springer (2016). https://doi.org/10.1007/978-3-319-45856-4_23

6. Biere, A., Fazekas, K., Fleury, M., Heisinger, M.: CaDiCaL, Kissat, Paracooba, Plingeling and Treengeling entering the SAT competition 2020. In: Proceeding of SAT Competition 2020 - Solver and Benchmark Descriptions. Department of Computer Science Report Series B, vol. B-2020-1, pp. 51–53. University of Helsinki (2020)

7. Biere, A., Heule, M., Maaren, H., Walsh, T.: Handbook of Satisfiability. Frontiers in Artificial Intelligence and Applications. IOS Press (2009)

8. Brewka, G., Eiter, T., Truszczynski, M.: Answer set programming at a glance. Commun. ACM **54**(12), 92–103 (2011)

9. Cholvy, L., Perrussel, L., Thevenin, J.M.: Using inconsistency measures for estimating reliability. Int. J. Approximate Reasoning **89**, 41–57 (2017)

10. Department of Computer Science, University of Helsinki, Helsinki: Proceedings of SAT Competition 2021: Solver and Benchmark Descriptions (2021)

11. Gebser, M., Kaminski, R., Kaufmann, B., Schaub, T.: Answer set solving in practice. Synth. Lect. Artif. Intell. Mach. Learn. **6**(3), 1–238 (2012)

12. Gebser, M., Kaminski, R., Kaufmann, B., Schaub, T.: Multi-shot ASP solving with clingo. Theory Pract. Logic Program. **19**(1), 27–82 (2019)

13. Grant, J., Hunter, A.: Measuring consistency gain and information loss in stepwise inconsistency resolution. In: Proceedings ECSQARU 2011, pp. 362–373 (2011). https://doi.org/10.1007/978-3-642-22152-1_31

14. Grant, J.: Classifications for inconsistent theories. Notre Dame J. Formal Logic **19**(3), 435–444 (1978)

15. Grant, J., Martinez, M.V. (eds.): Measuring Inconsistency in Information, Studies in Logic, vol. 73. College Publications (2018)

16. Hunter, A., Konieczny, S.: Measuring inconsistency through minimal inconsistent sets. In: Proceedings KR 2008, pp. 358–366 (2008)

17. Hunter, A.: How to act on inconsistent news: ignore, resolve, or reject. Data Knowl. Eng. **57**(3), 221–239 (2006)

18. Kuhlmann, I., Thimm, M.: An algorithm for the contension inconsistency measure using reductions to answer set programming. In: 14th International Conference on Scalable Uncertainty Management, pp. 289–296. Springer (2020). https://doi.org/10.1007/978-3-030-58449-8_23

19. Kuhlmann, I., Thimm, M.: Algorithms for inconsistency measurement using answer set programming. In: 19th International Workshop on Non-Monotonic Reasoning (NMR), pp. 159–168 (2021)

20. Lifschitz, V.: Answer Set Programming. Springer, Berlin (2019). https://doi.org/10.1007/978-3-030-24658-7

21. Martinez, A.B.B., Arias, J.J.P., Vilas, A.F.: On measuring levels of inconsistency in multi-perspective requirements specifications. In: Proceedings of the 1st Conference on the Principles of Software Engineering (PRISE 2004), pp. 21–30 (2004)

22. Mironov, I., Zhang, L.: Applications of SAT solvers to cryptanalysis of hash functions. In: International Conference on Theory and Applications of Satisfiability Testing, pp. 102–115. Springer (2006). https://doi.org/10.1007/11814948_13
23. Potyka, N., Thimm, M.: Inconsistency-tolerant reasoning over linear probabilistic knowledge bases. Int. J. Approximate Reason. **88**, 209–236 (2017)
24. Priest, G.: The logic of paradox. J. Philos. Logic, 219–241 (1979)
25. Sinz, C.: Towards an optimal cnf encoding of boolean cardinality constraints. In: International Conference on Principles and Practice of Constraint Programming, pp. 827–831. Springer (2005). https://doi.org/10.1007/11564751_73
26. Thimm, M.: On the evaluation of inconsistency measures. In: Measuring Inconsistency in Information, vol. 73. College Publications (2018)
27. Thimm, M.: Stream-based inconsistency measurement. Int. J. Approximate Reason. **68**, 68–87 (2016)
28. Thimm, M., Rienstra, T.: Approximate reasoning with ASPIC+ by argument sampling. In: Proceedings of the Third International Workshop on Systems and Algorithms for Formal Argumentation (SAFA 2020), pp. 22–33 (2020)
29. Thimm, M., Wallner, J.P.: On the complexity of inconsistency measurement. Artif. Intell. **275**, 411–456 (2019)
30. Tseitin, G.S.: On the complexity of derivation in propositional calculus. Structures in Constructive Mathematics and Mathematical Logic, pp. 115–125 (1968)
31. Vizel, Y., Weissenbacher, G., Malik, S.: Boolean satisfiability solvers and their applications in model checking. Proc. IEEE **103**(11), 2021–2035 (2015)

Full Papers: Decision Making and Social Choice

A Non-utilitarian Discrete Choice Model for Preference Aggregation

Martin Durand(iD), Fanny Pascual(iD), and Olivier Spanjaard$^{(\boxtimes)}$(iD)

Sorbonne Université, LIP6, CNRS, Paris, France
{martin.durand,fanny.pascual,olivier.spanjaard}@lip6.fr

Abstract. We study in this paper a non-utilitarian discrete choice model for preference aggregation. Unlike the Plackett-Luce model, this model is not based on the assignment of utility values to alternatives, but on probabilities p_i to choose the best alternative (according to a ground truth ranking r^*) in a subset of i alternatives. We consider $k-1$ parameters p_i (for $i = 2$ to k) in the model, where k is bounded by the number m of alternatives. We study the application of this model to voting, where we assume that the input is a set of choice functions provided by voters. If $k = 2$, our model amounts to the model used by Young [25] in his statistical analysis of Condorcet's voting method, and a maximum likelihood ranking is a consensus ranking for the Kemeny rule [12]. If $k > 2$, we show that, under some restrictive assumptions about probabilities p_i, the maximum likelihood ranking is a consensus ranking for the k-wise Kemeny rule [10]. In the general case, we provide a characterization result for the maximum likelihood ranking r and probabilities p_i. We propose an exact and a heuristic algorithm to compute both ranking r and probabilities p_i. Numerical tests are presented to assess the efficiency of these algorithms, and measure the model fitness on synthetic and real data.

1 Introduction

Preference aggregation is ubiquitous in multiple fields, among which are social choice [2,22], information retrieval [7], collaborative filtering [17], or peer grading [20]. The aggregation problem is formulated as follows: given n agents (or voters) and m alternatives (or candidates), each agent's preferences are specified by a ranking (permutation) of the alternatives, and the aim is to determine a single *consensus* ranking. Alternatively, preferences can also be expressed as choice functions instead of rankings [1], i.e., each agent chooses her preferred candidate among various subsets of candidates. A choice function allows more possibilities for the voters (cyclic preferences are even possible), and may be easier to elicit if only a few subsets of candidates are considered. However, if all subsets of candidates are considered, their number becomes quickly very large (2^m). The procedure producing a consensus ranking from the n agents' preferences (expressed as rankings or choice functions) is called a *voting rule*.

A stream of research aims to rationalize voting rules by using statistical models for rank data, whose characteristics depend on the application domain (see

F. Dupin de Saint-Cyr et al. (Eds.): SUM 2022, LNAI 13562, pp. 157–171, 2022.
https://doi.org/10.1007/978-3-031-18843-5_11

e.g. [24]). This assumption of a statistical model behind the agents' preferences dates back to Condorcet. As emphasized by Young [25], "Condorcet argued that if the object of voting is to determine the 'best' decision for society but voters sometimes make mistakes in their judgments, then the majority alternative (if it exists) is statistically most likely to be the best choice".

Young's examination of Condorcet's work through the lens of modern statistics leads him to put forward the Kemeny rule [12]. This well-known rule consists of producing a consensus ranking r that minimizes the number of disagreements between r and the pairwise preferences of the agents on the candidates. Young shows that a consensus ranking for the Kemeny rule is a Maximum Likelihood Estimate (MLE) of a "ground truth" ranking r^* of the alternatives if one assumes that the pairwise preferences of the voters follow a statistical model parameterized by r^* under specific assumptions. The assumptions (already made by Condorcet) are: 1) in every pairwise comparison, each voter chooses the better alternative in r^* with some fixed probability p, with $p > \frac{1}{2}$; 2) each voter's judgment on every pair of alternatives is independent of her judgment on every other pair[1]; 3) each voter's judgment is independent of the other voters' judgments.

When voters' preferences are expressed as rankings, it is also known that a consensus ranking for the Kemeny rule is an MLE of a ground truth ranking r^* for a distance-based statistical model for ranking data [5]. Consider indeed the conditional probability distribution Pr on rankings r' of candidates defined by $Pr(r'|r^*) \propto 2^{-\delta(r^*, r')}$, where $\delta(r^*, r')$ is the Kendall tau distance between r^* and r' (number of pairwise disagreements between r^* and r'). Assuming that each voter's judgment is independent of the other voters' judgments, it is easy to show that the Kemeny rule returns a ranking r maximizing $Pr(r_1, \ldots, r_n|r) = \prod_{j=1}^{n} Pr(r_j|r) = 2^{-\sum_j \delta(r, r_j)}$, i.e., an MLE of r^*.

Other works about the use of MLE for preference aggregation explore the estimation of the parameters of *discrete choice models* from voting data. A discrete choice model consists of predicting the probabilities, called *choice probabilities*, of choosing $c \in S$ when presented with a subset S of alternatives, for each possible subset S [14]. A set of agents' rankings can be seen as choice data by considering that each ranking rationalizes a *choice function*. A choice function f picks a favorite alternative in any subset S of alternatives. For instance, the ranking $1 \succ 2 \succ 3$ (where "$\succ$" stands for "is preferred to") rationalizes the choice function $f(\{1, 2\}) = 1$, $f(\{1, 3\}) = 1$, $f(\{2, 3\}) = 2$, and $f(\{1, 2, 3\}) = 1$. The most famous discrete choice model is due to Plackett-Luce. It consists of assigning a utility u_c to each alternative c, and setting the probability $Pr(f(S) = c)$ to choose c in S equal to $u_c / \sum_{d \in S} u_d$. The corresponding voting rule returns the ranking of alternatives by decreasing order of maximum likelihood utilities. Unlike most discrete choice model, the model we propose hereafter does not rely on the assignment of utility values (or utility distributions) to alternatives. Like the Plackett-Luce model, and unlike the model we will propose and study, most discrete choice models rely on the assignment of utility values (or utility distributions) to alternatives.

---

[1] Note that this assumption allows the preferences to be cyclic.

The use of discrete choice models based on utilities for preference aggregation deviates from Young's point of view. Indeed, Young uses distinct parameters to model, *on the one hand*, the respective "objective" skills of the candidates, namely the parameter r^* (ground truth ranking), and *on the other hand*, the "reliability" of the judgments of the voters, namely the parameter p (the closer the probability p is to 1, the more consistent the preferences are with the ground truth ranking). In discrete choice models based on utilities, the utilities are used *both* for modeling the objective skills of the candidates and the reliability of the judgments (the greater the differences in utilities, the more reliable the voters' judgments). Besides, unlike Young's model, that is related to the Kemeny rule, the consensus rankings obtained by sorting the candidates by decreasing order of maximum likelihood utilities are not related to well-identified voting rules.

Our contributions. We propose a discrete choice model inspired by Young's model for the Kemeny rule. Given a ground truth ranking r^* of the alternatives, the choice of an agent in a subset of i alternatives is consistent with r^* with a probability p_i (p_i is $\alpha_i > 1$ times greater than the probability to choose any other given candidate in a subset of size i). Unlike many discrete choice models used for social choice, the model is thus *non-utilitarian*, i.e., not based on the assignment of utility scores to alternatives. While the introduction of utility scores is appealing because the cardinal data are richer than the ordinal ones, the interpretation of such utility scores is not always obvious, e.g., when comparing artworks. We show the following results regarding the model we propose:

- Proposition 1 states that, if the value of α_i does not depend on i, then a maximum likelihood ranking is a consensus ranking for the k-wise Kemeny rule, a recently introduced voting rule [10].
- If values α_i depend on i, we provide a characterization result (Proposition 2) for a maximum likelihood estimation of the ground truth ranking r^* and α_i's. The characterization involves a weighted variant of the k-wise Kemeny rule.
- Based on Proposition 2, we provide an exact algorithm and a heuristic algorithm for determining a maximum likelihood couple in the general case.
- Finally, using synthetic and real data, we present numerical tests to assess the efficiency of these algorithms, as well as the model fitness to data.

2   Related Work

The related work concerns either the maximum likelihood approach to voting, or set extensions of the Kemeny rule.

The Maximum Likelihood Approach to Voting. In this approach, we make the assumption that a true "objective" ranking of the candidates exists, and that the preferences expressed by the voters are noisy observations of this true ranking. If the preferences are rankings drawn i.i.d. from a distribution, the probability of observing a set $\mathcal{P} = \{r_1, \ldots, r_n\}$ is then $Pr(\mathcal{P}|r) = \prod_{j=1}^n Pr(r_j|r)$. Each probability model for $Pr(r_j|r)$ induces a voting rule where a ranking maximizing $Pr(\mathcal{P}|r)$ (the likelihood) is a consensus ranking. Drissi-Bakhkhat and Truchon [8] investigate a setting in which the probability of comparing two alternatives consistently with a ground truth ranking r^* is increasing with the distance between them in r^*. This leads to a new voting rule that the authors examined from an axiomatic point of view. While every noise model on the votes[2] induces a voting rule, Conitzer and Sandholm [6] study the opposite direction, using it as a way to rationalize voting rules. They identify noise models for which an MLE ranking is a consensus ranking of well-known voting rules (scoring rules and single transferable vote), and on the contrary, for other rules (Bucklin, Copeland, maximin), they show that no such noise model can be constructed. Conitzer et al. [5] pursue this line of work, providing an exact characterization of the class of voting rules for which a noise model can be constructed. More recently, Caragiannis et al. [4] study how many votes are needed by a voting rule to reconstruct the true ranking. Another line of research focuses on the use of discrete choice models in social choice. Souani et al. [23] study an extension of the Plackett-Luce model. This model can be viewed as a random utility model in which the utilities of alternatives are drawn i.i.d. from a Gumbel distribution. They propose a random utility model based on distributions in the exponential family (to which Gumbel distributions belong), as well as inference methods for the parameters.

Set Extensions of the Kemeny Rule. Gilbert et al. [10] introduce the k-wise Kemeny rule, show that the computation of a consensus ranking according to this rule is NP-hard, and provide a dynamic programming procedure for this purpose. At least two other set extensions of the Kemeny rule have been proposed. Both extensions consider a setting in which, although the voters have preferences over a set $\mathcal{C}$, the election will in fact occur on a subset $S \subseteq \mathcal{C}$ drawn according to a probability distribution on $2^{\mathcal{C}}$ [3,13]. A consensus ranking r is then one that minimizes, in expectation, the number of voters' disagreements with the chosen candidate in S (a voter disagrees with r on S if $t_r(S)$ is not her most preferred candidate in S). Baldiga and Green study a setting in which the probability $Pr(S)$ only depends on the cardinality of S. Lu and Boutilier study a special case of the previous setting, where each candidate is unavailable in S with a probability p, independently of the others, i.e., $Pr(S) = p^{|C \setminus S|}(1-p)^{|S|}$. Proposition 2 later in the paper uses a weighted sum of disagreements δ_α^k on subsets of size at most k that is formally equivalent to the rule used by Baldiga and Green for $k = m$: the weights $\log \alpha_i$ assigned to disagreements on subsets S of size $i = |S|$ play the role of $Pr(S)$. However, the viewpoint we take here is completely different, as the values α_i are not given, but inferred from the choice data. In addition, to determine a maximum likelihood ranking for our model, we do not minimize δ_α^k only, but the sum of δ_α^k and another term.

---

[2] When the votes are viewed as noisy perceptions of a ground truth ranking r^*, a noise model is the mathematical description of the probabilities of the votes based on r^*.

3   Preliminaries

In the following, we will consider that the preferences of the agents are expressed as choice functions. A first possibility to elicit these choice functions is by asking each agent to give her most preferred alternative for each subset of size at most k – this may be a good solution if there are few candidates and k is not too large, or when the agents are not able to give their preferences as rankings. Another possibility is to ask for rankings, and infer choice functions from them (the choice in a subset S of candidates is the highest ranked candidate among S) – a ranking can be seen as a compact representation of a choice function.

Example 1. Let us consider 3 candidates $\{c_1, c_2, c_3\}$ and 10 voters with preferences, expressed as rankings, as follows: 3 voters of type I have preferences $c_1 \succ c_2 \succ c_3$; 3 voters of type II have preferences $c_3 \succ c_1 \succ c_2$; 2 voters of type III have preferences $c_2 \succ c_1 \succ c_3$; 2 voters of type IV have preferences $c_3 \succ c_2 \succ c_1$.

This preference profile yields the choice function profile given in Table 1, where each cell gives the favorite alternative $f_j(S)$ in S for voter j of the type corresponding to the row. Considering the rightmost column, one sees that c_1 (resp. c_3) is the preferred candidate in $\{c_1, c_2, c_3\}$ for voters of type I (resp. II and IV).

Table 1. The choice function profile in Example 1.

	$S=\{c_1,c_2\}$	$S=\{c_1,c_3\}$	$S=\{c_2,c_3\}$	$S=\{c_1,c_2,c_3\}$
$f_j(S)$ (j of type I)	c_1	c_1	c_2	c_1
$f_j(S)$ (j of type II)	c_1	c_3	c_3	c_3
$f_j(S)$ (j of type III)	c_2	c_1	c_2	c_2
$f_j(S)$ (j of type IV)	c_2	c_3	c_3	c_3

Let $\mathcal{V} = \{1, \ldots, n\}$ be a set of n agents (or voters) and $\mathcal{C}$ a set of m alternatives (or candidates). We denote by R the set of the $m!$ possible rankings of $\mathcal{C}$. For $k \in \{2, \ldots, m\}$, we denote by Δ_k the set of all subsets S of $\mathcal{C}$ such that $2 \leq |S| \leq k$. Given a value $k \in \{2, \ldots, m\}$, each agent $j \in \mathcal{V}$ has a choice function $f_j : \Delta_k \to \mathcal{C}$ which gives, for each subset S of alternatives of size at most k, her preferred alternative in S (assuming that each agent has only one favorite alternative per subset). We denote by $\mathcal{F}_k$ the set of all possible choice functions on sets of size at most k. A *choice function profile* $\mathcal{P} = (f_1, \ldots, f_n) \in \mathcal{F}_k^n$ is a tuple of n choice functions f_j, one per agent. In this setting, the purpose of preference aggregation is to determine a *consensus ranking* from the choice functions in $\mathcal{P}$. A voting rule $\mathcal{R} : \mathcal{F}_k^n \to (2^R \setminus \{\emptyset\})$ in which ballots are choice functions, maps each choice function profile to a non-empty set of consensus rankings.

The statistical model for choice functions studied in this paper will reveal closely related to a recently proposed voting rule, namely the k-wise Kemeny rule [10]. To compute a consensus rankings for the k-wise Kemeny rule, one needs only the information from the *choice matrix* derived from $\mathcal{P}$, denoted by $\mathcal{M}_\mathcal{P}$. The choice matrix gives, for each subset S of candidates and each candidate c, the number of voters for which c is the preferred candidate in S. If only subsets of size at most k matter, the choice matrix can be restricted to these subsets.

Example 2. The choice matrix synthesizing the results of all setwise contests for the choice functions of Table 1 is given in Table 2. The matrix reads as follows: for instance, considering the rightmost column, one sees that c_1 is the most preferred candidate in $\{c_1, c_2, c_3\}$ for 3 voters, c_2 is the most preferred candidate for 2 voters, and c_3 is the most preferred candidate for 5 voters.

Table 2. The choice matrix for the instance of Example 1.

S	$\{c_1, c_2\}$	$\{c_1, c_3\}$	$\{c_2, c_3\}$	$\{c_1, c_2, c_3\}$
c_1	6	5	–	3
c_2	4	–	5	2
c_3	–	5	5	5

We now formally describe the k-wise Kemeny rule. Given a ranking r and a subset $S \in \Delta_k$ of candidates, let $t_r(S) \in S$ denote the most preferred candidate in S for r (i.e., for each candidate $c \neq t_r(S) \in S$, $t_r(S)$ is ranked at a higher position in r than c – is preferred to c). The k-wise distance $\delta^k(r, f)$ between a ranking r and a choice function $f \in \mathcal{F}_k$ is the number of disagreements between r and f on sets of candidates of size between 2 and k:

$$\delta^k(r, f) = \sum_{S \in \Delta_k} \mathbb{1}_{t_r(S) \neq f(S)}$$

where $\mathbb{1}_{t_r(S) \neq f(S)} = 1$ if $t_r(S) \neq f(S)$, 0 otherwise. Note that when $k = 2$, $\delta^2(r, f)$ is the well-known Kendall tau distance between r and $f \in \mathcal{F}_2$ (which associates a winner to each pair of candidates). We may also express δ^k by splitting Δ_k into sets of subsets of the same cardinality. Let us denote by $\mathcal{C}_i$ the set of subsets of $\mathcal{C}$ of cardinality equal to i. We have thus $\bigcup_{i=2}^{k} \mathcal{C}_i = \Delta_k$ and δ^k can be written:

$$\delta^k(r, f) = \sum_{i=2}^{k} \sum_{S \in \mathcal{C}_i} \mathbb{1}_{t_r(S) \neq f(S)}$$

Given a profile $\mathcal{P}$, the cost of a ranking r is the sum of the k-wise distances between r and each choice function f_j ($j \in \{1, \ldots, n\}$) in the choice function profile. It is thus the total number of disagreements between r and the voters on all the possible subsets of candidates of size at most k:

$$\delta^k(r, \mathcal{P}) = \sum_{j=1}^{n} \delta^k(r, f_j) = \sum_{j=1}^{n} \sum_{i=2}^{k} \sum_{S \in \mathcal{C}_i} \mathbb{1}_{t_r(S) \neq f_j(S)}$$

The k-wise Kemeny rule determines a ranking minimizing $\delta^k(r, \mathcal{P})$ among all the rankings $r \in R$. To compute such a consensus ranking, one needs only the information from the choice matrix $\mathcal{M_P}$. It indeed minimizes $\delta^k(r, \mathcal{P})$:

$$\delta^k(r, \mathcal{P}) = \sum_{i=2}^{k} \sum_{S \in \mathcal{C}_i} d(\mathcal{M_P}, S, r) \tag{1}$$

where $d(\mathcal{M_P}, S, r)$ is the number of voters whose most preferred candidate in S is *not* $t_r(S)$ (number of disagreements between r and $\mathcal{M_P}$ for S). That is, a consensus ranking for the k-wise Kemeny rule minimizes the number of disagreements with the agents' choice functions on subsets of cardinality at most k (a disagreement occurs between a ranking r and choice function f on a subset S of candidates if $f(S) \neq t_r(S)$). The k-wise Kemeny rule generalizes the Kemeny rule, as it amounts to the usual Kemeny rule if $k = 2$. Increasing k allows to overcome a well-known drawback of the Kemeny rule, namely that very different consensus rankings may coexist. The example below illustrates this.

Example 3. In Example 1, there are two consensus rankings for the Kemeny rule, namely $c_1 \succ c_2 \succ c_3$ and $c_3 \succ c_1 \succ c_2$ since both of them induce 14 pairwise disagreements with the preference profile. Candidate c_3 is thus ranked last in the former, and first in the latter. In contrast, for the 3-wise Kemeny rule, the only consensus ranking is $c_3 \succ c_1 \succ c_2$, with $14 + 5 = 19$ disagreements (14 on pairs, and 5 on $\{c_1, c_2, c_3\}$), while there are $14 + 7 = 21$ disagreements for $c_1 \succ c_2 \succ c_3$.

4   A Non-utilitarian Discrete Choice Model

We now present the statistical model on choice functions that we will study in the remainder of the paper. The sample space (i.e., the possible observed outcomes from which the parameter of the statistical model are inferred) is the set of choice matrices. In this framework, the assumptions made by Condorcet and Young (see the introduction) need to be adapted, as we consider not only choices on pairs of candidates but also on subsets. Given a true ranking r^* of $\mathcal{C}$, the following assumptions are made on random variables $f_j(S)$ for all voters j:

1. for every $i \in \{2, \ldots, k\}$, $S \in \mathcal{C}_i$, $c \in S \setminus \{t_{r^*}(S)\}$, the probability that $f_j(S) = t_{r^*}(S)$ is $\alpha_i > 1$ times greater than the probability that $f_j(S) = c$: $Pr(f_j(S) = t_{r^*}(S)) = \alpha_i \cdot Pr(f_j(S) = c)$; that is, it is $\alpha_{|S|}$ more likely to choose the highest ranked candidate of S in r^* than any other given candidate of S.
2. for every pair $\{S, S'\}$ of subsets in Δ_k, $f_j(S)$ and $f_j(S')$ are independent.

For any pair $\{j, j'\}$ of voters, we also assume that each voter's preferred choice on each subset of candidates is independent of the other voters' preferences, i.e.:

3. for every $\{j, j'\} \subseteq V$ and $(S, S') \in \Delta_k^2$, $f_j(S)$ and $f_{j'}(S')$ are independent.

For $k = 2$, these assumptions amount to those made by Young on pairwise judgments in his analysis of Condorcet's theory of voting. If $k > 2$, the additional parameters $\alpha_{|S|}$ (for $|S| > 2$) give more flexibility to fit the observed choice data, at the cost of a greater computational load. Note that Assumption 1 means that the probability that voter j agree with ranking r^* on the preferred candidate in S depends only on the size of S, and not on the members of S.

Assumptions 1 and 2 yield the following statistical model for choice functions f, that we call k-*wise Young's model*, parameterized by a ranking r and choice probabilities $p_i = \alpha_i/(\alpha_i + i - 1)$ (conversely, $\alpha_i = (i-1)p_i/(1-p_i)$), where p_i represents $Pr(f(S) = t_r(S))$ for $|S| = i$:

Definition 1 (k-wise Young's Model). *Given a set $\mathcal{C}$ of m alternatives, the k-wise Young's model is defined as follows:*

- *the parameter space is $R \times \Theta$, where R is the set of rankings on $\mathcal{C}$ and $\Theta = (\frac{1}{2}, 1] \times \ldots \times (\frac{1}{k}, 1]$ is the set of choice probabilities $\overrightarrow{p} = (p_2, \ldots, p_k)$,*
- *for any $(r, \overrightarrow{p}) \in R \times \Theta$, the probability $Pr(f|r, \overrightarrow{p})$ is*

$$\prod_{i=2}^{k} \prod_{S \in \mathcal{C}_i} p_i^{1 - \mathbb{1}_{t_r(S) \neq f(S)}} \left(\frac{1 - p_i}{i - 1}\right)^{\mathbb{1}_{t_r(S) \neq f(S)}}$$

where $\mathbb{1}_{t_r(S) \neq f(S)} = 1$ *if* $t_r(S) \neq f(S)$, *0 otherwise.*

If $r = r^*$, we have indeed $Pr(f(S) = c) = (1 - p_i)/(i - 1)$ for $c \neq t_r(S)$ by Assumption 1, and the products in the formula for $Pr(f|r, \overrightarrow{p})$ follow from Assumption 2.

As the preferences revealed by the choices may be cyclic, sampling a choice function according to this model can be decomposed into independent draws for each subset $S \subseteq \mathcal{C}$. Given a choice function profile $\mathcal{P}$ with n voters, if one assumes the functions in $\mathcal{P}$ are *independently* sampled (in line with Assumption 3) from a k-wise Young's model of parameters r and $\overrightarrow{p}$, the probability $Pr(\mathcal{M}_\mathcal{P}|r, \overrightarrow{p})$ follows a multinomial distribution:

$$\prod_{i=2}^{k} \prod_{S \in \mathcal{C}_i} \frac{n!}{\prod_{c \in S} n_c!} p_i^{n - d(\mathcal{M}_\mathcal{P}, S, r)} \left(\frac{1 - p_i}{i - 1}\right)^{d(\mathcal{M}_\mathcal{P}, S, r)} \tag{2}$$

where n_c denotes the number of voters that choose candidate c in subset S.

From Eq. 2, it is clear that the likelihood of $(r, \overrightarrow{p})$ given $\mathcal{M}_\mathcal{P}$, denoted by $\mathcal{L}(r, \overrightarrow{p}|\mathcal{M}_\mathcal{P})$, is proportional to

$$\prod_{i=2}^{k} \prod_{S \in \mathcal{C}_i} p_i^{n - d(\mathcal{M}_\mathcal{P}, S, r)} \left(\frac{1 - p_i}{i - 1}\right)^{d(\mathcal{M}_\mathcal{P}, S, r)} \tag{3}$$

because the coefficients $n!/(\prod_{c \in S} n_c!)$ depend neither on r nor on $\overrightarrow{p}$. Let us now study different voting rules arising from Eq. 3. Depending on whether or not restrictive assumptions are made about probabilities p_i, we show that a maximum likelihood ranking r is a consensus ranking for the k-wise Kemeny rule, or for a weighted variant whose parameters vary with $\mathcal{M}_\mathcal{P}$ and r.

5   MLE of the Parameters of the k-Wise Young's Model

A consensus ranking for the k-wise Kemeny rule is an MLE of a ground truth ranking r^* if one assumes that the choice function profile is sampled according to the k-wise Young's model when $\alpha_2 = \ldots = \alpha_k = \alpha > 1$, i.e., in a subset S, candidate $t_{r^*}(S)$ is the most likely to be chosen, with a probability α times greater than any other given member of S, whatever the size of S. More formally:

Proposition 1. *If there exists $\alpha > 1$ such that $\alpha_2 = \ldots = \alpha_k = \alpha$, then, given a choice matrix $\mathcal{M}_\mathcal{P}$, a ranking r has maximum likelihood for the k-wise Young's model iff it minimizes $\delta^k(r, \mathcal{P})$, i.e., ranking r is a consensus ranking for the k-wise Kemeny rule.*

Proof. Maximizing Eq. 3 amounts to maximizing:

$$\log \left(\prod_{i=2}^{k} \prod_{S \in \mathcal{C}_i} p_i^{n - d(\mathcal{M}_\mathcal{P}, S, r)} \cdot \left(\frac{1 - p_i}{i - 1} \right)^{d(\mathcal{M}_\mathcal{P}, S, r)} \right)$$

$$= \sum_{i=2}^{k} \sum_{S \in \mathcal{C}_i} \left((n - d(\mathcal{M}_\mathcal{P}, S, r)) \cdot \log p_i + d(\mathcal{M}_\mathcal{P}, S, r) \cdot \log \left(\frac{1 - p_i}{i - 1} \right) \right)$$

$$= \sum_{i=2}^{k} \sum_{S \in \mathcal{C}_i} n \log p_i - \sum_{i=2}^{k} \sum_{S \in \mathcal{C}_i} d(\mathcal{M}_\mathcal{P}, S, r) \cdot \log \left(\frac{p_i}{\frac{1 - p_i}{i - 1}} \right)$$

For a given set of values p_i, determining a ranking r that maximizes the above formula is equivalent to minimizing:

$$\sum_{i=2}^{k} \sum_{S \in \mathcal{C}_i} d(\mathcal{M}_\mathcal{P}, S, r) \cdot \log \left(\frac{p_i}{\frac{1 - p_i}{i - 1}} \right)$$

As p_i is the probability to choose $t_r(S)$ and $(1 - p_i)/(i - 1)$ the probability to choose any other member of S, we have $p_i/(1 - p_i/(i - 1)) = \alpha_i$. Furthermore, by assumption, $\alpha_i = \alpha \; \forall i \in \{2, \ldots, k\}$. Consequently, the expression simplifies to:

$$(\log \alpha) \cdot \sum_{i=2}^{k} \sum_{S \in \mathcal{C}_i} d(\mathcal{M}_\mathcal{P}, S, r)$$

The coefficient $\log \alpha$ is strictly positive because $\alpha > 1$ by assumption, and it can therefore be omitted when minimizing according to r. From Eq. 1, we have:

$$\sum_{i=2}^{k} \sum_{S \in \mathcal{C}_i} d(\mathcal{M}_\mathcal{P}, S, r) = \delta^k(r, \mathcal{P})$$

Therefore, whatever the vector $\overrightarrow{p}$ of choice probabilities, a ranking r that maximizes $\mathcal{L}(r, \overrightarrow{p} | \mathcal{M}_\mathcal{P})$ minimizes $\delta^k(r, \mathcal{P})$, which concludes the proof. □

For $k = 2$, this proposition amounts to the result of Young regarding the interpretation of the Kemeny rule as an MLE of a ground truth ranking.

If we do not assume that the α_i are equal, then the maximum likelihood ranking may depend on $\overrightarrow{\alpha} = (\alpha_2, \ldots, \alpha_k)$, and we need to determine[3] a *couple* $(r, \overrightarrow{\alpha})$ of maximum likelihood $\mathcal{L}(r, \overrightarrow{\alpha}|\mathcal{M}_\mathcal{P})$, even if we are only interested in r. Determining such a couple $(r, \overrightarrow{\alpha})$ defines a new voting rule in itself, which returns r as a consensus ranking. The following result shows that it can be formulated as a discrete optimization problem on the space of rankings, because, for each ranking r, there exists a closed-form expression to determine the corresponding maximum likelihood values α_i.

Proposition 2. *Given a choice matrix $\mathcal{M}_\mathcal{P}$, a couple $(r, \overrightarrow{\alpha})$ has maximum likelihood for the k-wise Young's model if and only if ranking r minimizes*

$$\delta_\alpha^k(r, \mathcal{P}) - \sum_{i=2}^{k} \sum_{S \in \mathcal{C}_i} n \log \frac{\alpha_i}{\alpha_i + i - 1}, \tag{4}$$

$$\text{where } \delta_\alpha^k(r, \mathcal{P}) = \sum_{i=2}^{k} (\log \alpha_i) \sum_{S \in \mathcal{C}_i} d(\mathcal{M}_\mathcal{P}, S, r) \tag{5}$$

$$\text{and } \alpha_i = ((i-1) \cdot \sum_{S \in \mathcal{C}_i} (n - d(\mathcal{M}_\mathcal{P}, S, r))) / (\sum_{S \in \mathcal{C}_i} d(\mathcal{M}_\mathcal{P}, S, r)). \tag{6}$$

Proof. From the proof of Proposition 1, we know that a couple $(r, \overrightarrow{p})$ has maximum likelihood iff, for a given choice matrix $\mathcal{M}_\mathcal{P}$ and ranking r, it maximizes:

$$f(\overrightarrow{p}) = \sum_{i=2}^{k} \sum_{S \in \mathcal{C}_i} n \log p_i - \sum_{i=2}^{k} \sum_{S \in \mathcal{C}_i} d(\mathcal{M}_\mathcal{P}, S, r) \cdot \log \left(\frac{p_i}{\frac{1-p_i}{i-1}} \right) \tag{7}$$

To determine an optimum of function f, each component p_i can be optimized independently from the others, because each one appears in a different term of the sum from $i = 2$ to k. Noting that $\sum_{C \in \mathcal{C}_i} n = \binom{m}{i} \cdot n$ as there are $\binom{m}{i}$ different subsets $C \in \mathcal{C}_i$, the partial derivative of order 1 is written as:

$$\frac{\partial f}{\partial p_i}(\overrightarrow{p}) = \frac{\binom{m}{i} \cdot n - \sum\limits_{S \in \mathcal{C}_i} d(\mathcal{M}_\mathcal{P}, S, r)}{p_i} - \frac{\sum\limits_{S \in \mathcal{C}_i} d(\mathcal{M}_\mathcal{P}, S, r)}{(1 - p_i)}.$$

For $p_i \in [0, 1]$, the derivative vanishes for:

$$p_i = \left(\binom{m}{i} \cdot n - \sum_{S \in \mathcal{C}_i} d(\mathcal{M}_\mathcal{P}, S, r) \right) / \left(\binom{m}{i} \cdot n \right).$$

---

[3] From now on, we use indifferently $\overrightarrow{p}$ or $\overrightarrow{\alpha}$, because one vector can be inferred from the other.

It is easy to prove that $\frac{\partial^2 f}{\partial p_i^2}(\overrightarrow{p}) < 0$ for $p_i \in [0, 1]$, thus the corresponding stationary point of f is a maximum. From the values p_i of maximum likelihood we derive the values α_i of maximum likelihood:

$$\alpha_i = \frac{p_i}{\frac{1-p_i}{(i-1)}} = (i-1) \cdot \frac{\sum_{S \in \mathcal{C}_i} (n - d(\mathcal{M}_{\mathcal{P}}, S, r))}{\sum_{S \in \mathcal{C}_i} d(\mathcal{M}_{\mathcal{P}}, S, r)}$$

The result is obtained by expressing Eq. 7 in function of α_i instead of p_i, and turning the maximization into a minimization of the opposite expression.   □

Note that, according to Proposition 2, the maximum likelihood value of each p_i given r corresponds to the observed proportion of agreements between r and $\mathcal{P}$ on subsets of size i, which is consistent with intuition. The formula of the likelihood of a couple $(r, \overrightarrow{\alpha})$ is written as the sum of two terms:

- the term $\delta_\alpha^k(r, \mathcal{P})$ is a weighted sum of disagreements between r and $\mathcal{P}$, where the disagreements on subsets of size i are weighted by $\log \alpha_i$;
- the term $-\sum_{i=2}^k \sum_{S \in \mathcal{C}_i} n \log(\alpha_i/(\alpha_i + i - 1)) = -\log \prod_{j=1}^n \prod_{i=2}^k \prod_{S \in \mathcal{C}_i} p_i$; as $\prod_{j=1}^n \prod_{i=2}^k \prod_{S \in \mathcal{C}_i} p_i \leq 1$, the opposite of its logarithm is positive, and the term is all the greater as the empirical probability that the n choice functions in $\mathcal{P}$ coincide with r is low.

Let us now present algorithms (an exact one and a heuristic one) to compute a maximum likelihood couple $(r, \overrightarrow{\alpha})$ given a choice matrix $\mathcal{M}_{\mathcal{P}}$.

6   Algorithms for Determining an MLE

A brute force method for determining a couple $(r, \overrightarrow{\alpha})$ of maximum likelihood given $\mathcal{P}$ consists of computing a vector $\overrightarrow{\alpha}$ of maximum likelihood for each ranking r (thanks to Proposition 2), and, turning $\overrightarrow{\alpha}$ into $\overrightarrow{p}$, retaining the couple $(r, \overrightarrow{p})$ that maximizes Eq. 3.

A Faster Exact Algorithm. It is possible to improve this procedure by considering only a *subset* of rankings r on the candidates. We know indeed from Proposition 2 that, for any given $\overrightarrow{\alpha}$, the corresponding maximum likelihood ranking r minimizes $\delta_\alpha^k(r, \mathcal{P})$ (see Eq. 5). Minimizing $\delta_\alpha^k(r, \mathcal{P})$ can be seen as a multi-objective optimization problem, by associating to each r the vector:

$$\overrightarrow{d}_{\mathcal{P}}(r) = \left(\sum_{S \in \mathcal{C}_2} d(\mathcal{M}_{\mathcal{P}}, S, r), \ldots, \sum_{S \in \mathcal{C}_k} d(\mathcal{M}_{\mathcal{P}}, S, r) \right)$$

In multi-objective optimization problems, the goal is often to enumerate all the Pareto optimal solutions, i.e., in our setting, the rankings r such that there does not exist another ranking r' for which $\overrightarrow{d}_{\mathcal{P}}(r') \leq \overrightarrow{d}_{\mathcal{P}}(r)$, where $\overrightarrow{x} \leq \overrightarrow{y}$ if $\forall i \in \{2, \ldots, k\}$ $x_i \leq y_i$, and $\exists i \in \{2, \ldots, k\}$ $x_i < y_i$. A ranking r minimizing $\delta_\alpha^k(r, \mathcal{P})$ is obviously Pareto optimal. Such a ranking actually belongs to a more restricted set: the set of *supported* solutions, i.e., those that optimizes a weighted sum of the objectives [9]. The weight assigned to each objective i is here $\log \alpha_i$. An even more restricted set can be considered: the set of *extreme* rankings. A Pareto optimal ranking r is *extreme* if $\overrightarrow{d}_{\mathcal{P}}(r)$ is a vertex of the convex hull of $\{\overrightarrow{d}_{\mathcal{P}}(r) : r \in R\}$ in the $(k-1)$-dimensional objective space, where R is the set of all rankings. Indeed, it is well-known in multi-objective optimization that, for each supported ranking r', there exists an extreme ranking r such that $\delta_\alpha^k(r, \mathcal{P}) = \delta_\alpha^k(r', \mathcal{P})$.

A recent work presents a method for enumerating the extreme solutions in multi-objective optimization problems [19]. Based on such a method, we design an exact procedure for determining a maximum likelihood pair $(r, \overrightarrow{\alpha})$ by Proposition 2:

1. Determine all the extreme rankings by using Przybylski et al.'s method [19];
2. For each extreme ranking r, compute by Eq. 6 the vector $\overrightarrow{\alpha}_r$ such that $(r, \overrightarrow{\alpha})$ has maximum likelihood;
3. Return a couple $(r, \overrightarrow{\alpha}_r)$ that minimizes Eq. 4.

Although this procedure allows us to reduce the number of rankings we need to consider, there are still many of them, especially when the value of k increases. For this reason, we now propose a faster heuristic giving a very good approximation of an optimal couple $(r, \overrightarrow{\alpha})$.

A Heuristic Algorithm. Instead of considering all the extreme rankings, we propose an Iterative Optimization (IO) heuristic, which alternates two steps:

- α-step: compute an $\overrightarrow{\alpha}$ of maximum likelihood given r by Eq. 6;
- r-step: compute an r of maximum likelihood given $\overrightarrow{\alpha}$ by minimizing $\delta_\alpha^k(r, \mathcal{P})$ (see Eq. 5).

The minimization of $\delta_\alpha^k(r, \mathcal{P})$ is performed thanks to a weighted variant of the dynamic programming algorithm proposed by Gilbert et al. [10] for the k-wise Kemeny rule. The two steps are alternated until the same ranking is found in two consecutive r-steps. The complexity of the dynamic programming algorithm that computes a ranking r minimizing $\delta_\alpha^k(r, \mathcal{P})$ is $O(2^m m^2 n)$, thus the heuristic is not polynomial time (but much faster than the exact algorithm, as will be seen later). We launch the algorithm from a given vector $\overrightarrow{\alpha}$ for the r-step (in the numerical tests, we have set the values α_i corresponding to $p_i = 1/i + (i-1)/(10i)$).

7   Numerical Tests

We report here the results of several experiments[4] to test the performance of our heuristic and the fitness of the k-wise Young's (k-wise) model compared to that of the Plackett-Luce (PL) model on synthetic and real-world data.

---

[4] All algorithms have been implemented in C++, and the tests have been carried out on an Intel Core I5-8250 1.6 GHz processor with 8 GB of RAM.

Instances. The tests are carried out both on real data sets from the Preflib library [16], and on three types of synthetic instances. The first type of synthetic instances are *uniform instances*, in which the preferences of each voter is a random ranking in the set R of all permutations. The second type of instances, called *PL instances*, are preference profiles generated thanks to the PL model [14,18]. The third type of instances, called *k-wise instances*, are choice matrices generated with our model. Given a ground truth ranking r^*, the choice function of a voter is generated as follows: for each subset S of size i, the voter chooses the winner in S w.r.t. r^* with probability p_i, and chooses any other candidate in S with probability $(1 - p_i)/(i - 1)$. We set $k = m$ in all tests.

Performance of the Heuristic. In order to evaluate the performance of the IO heuristic, we compare the log-likelihood (LL) of the returned pair $(r, \overrightarrow{\alpha})$ with the one obtained by the exact method. Denoting by $OPT(I)$ the value of the LL of an optimal pair for a given instance I and by $IO(I)$ the value of the LL of the pair returned by the IO method, we calculate the ratio $q = IO(I)/OPT(I)$. For all the real instances from the PrefLib library, and for all tested PL instances, the heuristic always returns an optimal pair $(r, \overrightarrow{\alpha})$. On uniform instances, the result is not always optimal, but it is very close to the optimal LL: the ratio q is above 0.9999 on average. The heuristic provides an excellent approximation of an optimal pair $(r, \overrightarrow{\alpha})$. Regardless of the type of instance, the IO method is much faster than the exact multi-objective algorithm. For example, for $m = k = 8$, the IO method takes 260 (resp. 185) s on average to return a solution for uniform (resp. PL) instances whereas the exact algorithm requires 30 000 (resp. 1000) s on average to determine an optimal pair for the same instances.

Model Fitness. We now compare our model with the PL model in terms of fitness with real-world data. We use instances from the sushi dataset [11], in which 5000 voters give their ranking over 10 kinds of sushis. We randomly draw $n \in \{50, 100\}$ voters among the 5000. We apply the exact solution procedure proposed above, and compare the results with those of the PL model. The likelihood of a choice matrix w.r.t. the PL model for choice functions is written as follows: $\prod_{i=2}^{k} \prod_{S \in \mathcal{C}_i} \frac{n!}{\prod_{c \in S} n_c!} \prod_{c \in S} \left(\frac{u_c}{\sum_{d \in S} u_d} \right)^{n_c}$ where n_c denotes the number of voters choosing candidate c in S, and u_c the utility of c. To compare the fitness of the models, we use the Bayesian Information Criterion –BIC– [21]. Regarding the k-wise model, we consider the case of constant α_i's (model α) and the general case where the α_i may vary (model α_i). We compute the ratio $BIC(\mu)/BIC(PL)$ for $\mu \in \{\alpha, \alpha_i\}$. For 50 voters, the obtained ratio is 1.054 (resp. 1.047) for model α (resp. α_i). This improves to 1.052 (resp. 1.045) for 100 voters. This shows that for this dataset, the fitness of models α and α_i is close to the PL model, although the fitness of the latter is slightly better (by 5% at most).

Cross Comparison. We now compare the PL model and the k-wise model on PL instances and k-wise instances. In both cases, we compute a correlation factor ρ between the returned ranking and the ground truth ranking used for generation. The factor ρ is the Kendall-Tau distance normalized between 0 and

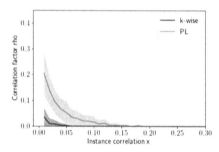 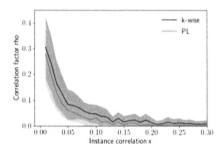

Fig. 1. Mean ρ (and 68% confidence interval) between the returned ranking and the ground truth on k-wise instances (left) and PL instances (right).

1–0 indicates that the two rankings are identical while 1 means that they are opposite. Figure 1 shows the mean value of ρ in function of the level of correlation of the voters' preferences, for k-wise instances (left) and PL instances (right). For k-wise instances, the correlation between the choice functions is controlled by setting $p_i = 1/i + x(1 - 1/i)$ for $x \in [0, 1]$: all choice functions are equally likely and independent from the ground truth ranking for $x = 0$, while all choice functions are perfectly consistent with the ground truth ranking for $x = 1$. For PL instances, the correlation between the rankings is controlled by setting $u_p = 1 + (m - p)x$ as utility of the candidate in position p in the ground truth ranking: the higher x, the stronger the correlation. As one would expect, the MLE ranking for the k-wise (resp. PL) model is closer to the ground truth ranking on k-wise (resp. PL) instances. Interestingly, the k-wise model performs better on PL instances than the PL model on k-wise instances. When instances are correlated enough, the MLE ranking for both models always correspond to the ground truth.

8   Conclusion

We have studied here an extension of Young's model for pairwise preferences to choices in subsets of size at most k, showing that the maximum likelihood ranking w.r.t. this model coincides with a consensus ranking for the k-wise Kemeny rule under certain assumptions on the choice probabilities. Relaxing these assumptions, we have proposed inference algorithms for the model, learning the choice probabilities from the data. The fitness of the model on real data is comparable with the Plackett-Luce model, although no utilities are embedded in our model. This is a first step towards the use of non-utilitarian discrete choice models for preference aggregation. For future work, correlating the choice probabilities with the ranks of the candidates within the considered subset (according to the ground truth ranking) is a natural research direction. Another direction is to investigate if the k-wise Young's model can be related to a k-wise distance-based statistical model for *rankings*, similarly to the connection between Young's model for pairwise preferences and Mallows' model [15] for rankings.

Acknowledgements. We acknowledge a financial support from the project THEMIS ANR20-CE23-0018 of the French National Research Agency (ANR).

References

1. Aleskerov, F.: Arrovian Aggregation Models. Kluwer Academic (1999)
2. Arrow, K.J.: Social Choice and Individual Values (1951)
3. Baldiga, K.A., Green, J.R.: Assent-maximizing social choice. Soc. Choice Welfare **40**(2), 439–460 (2013). https://doi.org/10.1007/s00355-011-0614-6
4. Caragiannis, I., Procaccia, A.D., Shah, N.: When do noisy votes reveal the truth? ACM Trans. Econ. Comput. (TEAC) **4**(3), 1–30 (2016)
5. Conitzer, V., Rognlie, M., Xia, L.: Preference functions that score rankings and maximum likelihood estimation. In: IJCAI, pp. 109–115 (2009)
6. Conitzer, V., Sandholm, T.: Common voting rules as maximum likelihood estimators. In: Proceedings of UAI 2005, pp. 145–152 (2005)
7. Cormack, G.V., Clarke, C.L., Buettcher, S.: Reciprocal rank fusion outperforms condorcet and individual rank learning methods. In: SIGIR, pp. 758–759 (2009)
8. Drissi-Bakhkhat, M., Truchon, M.: Maximum likelihood approach to vote aggregation with variable probabilities. Soc. Choice Welfare **23**(2), 161–185 (2004). https://doi.org/10.1007/s00355-003-0242-x
9. Ehrgott, M.: Multicriteria Optimization, vol. 491. Springer (2005). https://doi.org/10.1007/3-540-27659-9
10. Gilbert, H., Portoleau, T., Spanjaard, O.: Beyond pairwise comparisons in social choice: a setwise Kemeny aggregation problem. In: AAAI, pp. 1982–1989 (2020)
11. Kamishima, T.: Nantonac collaborative filtering: recommendation based on order responses. In: SIGKDD, pp. 583–588 (2003)
12. Kemeny, J.G.: Mathematics without numbers. Daedalus **88**(4), 577–591 (1959)
13. Lu, T., Boutilier, C.: The unavailable candidate model: a decision-theoretic view of social choice. In: Proceedings of EC 2010, pp. 263–274 (2010)
14. Luce, R.D.: Individual Choice Behavior: A Theoretical analysis. Wiley (1959)
15. Mallows, C.L.: Non-null ranking models. I. Biometrika **44**(1/2), 114–130 (1957)
16. Mattei, N., Walsh, T.: Preflib: a library of preference data http://preflib.org. In: ADT 2013, Lecture Notes in Artificial Intelligence, Springer (2013). https://doi.org/10.1007/978-3-642-41575-3_20
17. Pennock, D.M., Horvitz, E., Giles, C.L., et al.: Social choice theory and recommender systems: analysis of the axiomatic foundations of collaborative filtering. In: AAAI/IAAI, pp. 729–734 (2000)
18. Plackett, R.L.: The analysis of permutations. Appl. Stat. **24**(2), 193–202 (1975)
19. Przybylski, A., Klamroth, K., Lacour, R.: A simple and efficient dichotomic search algorithm for multi-objective mixed integer linear programs. arXiv (2019)
20. Raman, K., Joachims, T.: Methods for ordinal peer grading. In: SIGKDD, pp. 1037–1046 (2014)
21. Schwarz, G.: Estimating the dimension of a model. Ann. Stat. 461–464 (1978)
22. Sen, A.: The possibility of social choice. Am. Eco. Rev. **89**(3), 349–378 (1999)
23. Soufiani, H.A., Parkes, D.C., Xia, L.: Random utility theory for social choice. In: NeurIPS, pp. 126–134, NIPS 2012, Curran Associates Inc. (2012)
24. Xia, L.: Learning and decision-making from rank data. Synth. Lect. Artif. Intell. Mach. Learn. **13**(1), 1–159 (2019)
25. Young, H.P.: Condorcet's theory of voting. Am. Polit. Sci. Rev. **82**(4), 1231–1244 (1988)

Selecting the Most Relevant Elements from a Ranking over Sets

Sébastien Konieczny[1] ⓘ, Stefano Moretti[2](✉) ⓘ, Ariane Ravier[2](✉),
and Paolo Viappiani[2] ⓘ

[1] CRIL - CNRS, Université d'Artois, Lens, France
konieczny@cril.fr
[2] LAMSADE, CNRS, Université Paris-Dauphine, Université PSL,
75016 Paris, France
{stefano.moretti,ariane.ravier,paolo.viappiani}@lamsade.dauphine.fr

Abstract. In this paper we study the problem of selecting the most relevant elements of a finite set N of elements from a ranking of non-empty subsets of N, that represents the performance of different coalitions. To solve this problem, we first introduce the notion of coalitional social choice function (*i.e.*, a map that associates each total preorder of the non-empty subsets of N with a subset of N). Then, we provide four basic properties that a coalitional social choice function should satisfy to select the most relevant elements. Finally, we prove that the unique coalitional social choice function that satisfies such properties is the one selecting the elements ranked in the highest position of the lexicographic excellence ranking, which is computed according to a social ranking solution from the literature.

Keywords: Social ranking · Power relation · Coalitions · Social choice function

1 Introduction

The problem of defining a ranking of individual elements based on their contribution in establishing the position of groups or coalitions within a society has been recently introduced in the literature related to the notion of social ranking [6,8]. Taking as input a ranking of sets of objects like, for instance, a ranking over all possible research groups of a department, or over alternative combinations of attackers in a football team, or even a dichotomous order of winning or losing coalitions within a voting body, a social ranking generates a ranking of the individuals (researchers, football players, voters...) reflecting the overall relevance of individuals within the rank of coalitions [1,2,6].

In [6], for example, the individuals are ranked according to their frequency in the highest positions in the ranking of sets and a special social ranking function, called *lexicographic excellence* (*lex-cel*), has been identified as the unique one satisfying a set of appealing properties. A generalization of the lex-cel has been

© The Author(s), under exclusive license to Springer Nature Switzerland AG 2022
F. Dupin de Saint-Cyr et al. (Eds.): SUM 2022, LNAI 13562, pp. 172–185, 2022.
https://doi.org/10.1007/978-3-031-18843-5_12

introduced in papers [2,5] considering the size of coalitions, in addition to their positions in the ranking of sets. For other notions of social ranking solutions see also the papers [3,5,9] (for a software implementation of social ranking solutions from the literature, the interested reader is referred to the R package [7]).

Sometimes, however, we are not interested in generating an entire ranking of the individual elements, but instead just want to select the most important ones. Consider for instance the problem of identifying the most influential scientists within an Academic Association (AA) based on the number and the quality of their publications. One of the major difficulties in comparing scientists is taking into account their contributions to multi-authored publications [4,12]. Several bibliometric indices exist to compare the impact of research activity of individual scientists and of research groups, and the choice of the appropriate index goes beyond the scope of this paper (see, for instance, the paper [11] for an in-depth analysis of the problem). Nevertheless, each group of scientists can be characterized by a record of jointly published papers (possibly with other authors who do not belong to the AA). So, in principle, a ranking of groups of scientists can be established according to a predefined bibliometric criterion for the comparison of the overall influence of research groups (see Example 1 for a toy situation illustrating some naive approaches aimed at ranking groups starting from records of papers published in journals). Starting from such a ranking of groups, which scientists can be identified as the most influential in a way that the scientists' ranking positions over different groups are considered?

In this paper we provide an answer to this question following a property-driven approach. We first single out a set of reasonable properties that a method selecting the set of most relevant elements (namely, a *coalitional social choice function*) from a ranking over groups should satisfy. Then we prove that the unique method satisfying those properties is the one which selects the best elements according to the ranking produced by the lex-cel.

As a first property, we consider the *All-Indifferent-All-Winners* axiom, which indicates that all the elements should be treated in the same way; so, if all groups are equally powerful and there is no reason to distinguish among the roles played by the elements, then all the elements should be selected. The second axiom we introduce is a *Monotonicity for Winners* property stating that if some elements are selected as the most relevant in a ranking of groups, and a new ranking over groups is produced improving the position of groups in the last equivalence class (but without affecting the comparison with groups in the other equivalence classes), then the most frequent elements over the improved groups should be considered as the most relevant ones also in the new ranking of groups. The third property, called the *Dominance* axiom, deals with the same kind of improvements described for the monotonicity axiom, but in this case it rules out the elements that are less represented among the improved groups. Finally, the *Independence for Losers from the Worst Set* axiom, prevents the elements that are excluded from being the most relevant ones in an original ranking of groups to become the most relevant in any other ranking of groups obtained from the original one by partitioning the last equivalence class. In other words, once the decision to exclude an element from the most relevant set is taken, the decision shall not be affected by changes involving the worst groups.

The roadmap of the paper is as follows. In the next section we introduce some preliminary definitions and a motivational example for the computation of the lex-cel. In Sect. 3, we formally introduce the four axioms and we illustrate them along the lines of the example introduced in Sect. 2. Section 4 is devoted to the axiomatic characterization of the lex-cel coalitional social choice function using the axioms introduced in Sect. 3, and to establishing their logical independence. Section 5 concludes with some comments and directions for future research.

2   Preliminaries

Let $N = \{1, \ldots, n\}$ be a finite set of *elements* (individuals, items, etc.) and let $\mathcal{P}(N)$ be the set of the non-empty subsets of N (also called *coalitions* or *groups*). A binary relation $R \subseteq N \times N$ is said to be: *reflexive*, if for each $i \in N$, iRi; *transitive*, if for each $i, j, k \in N$, iRj and $jRk \Rightarrow iRk$; *total*, if for each $i, j \in N$, iRj or jRi; *antisymmetric*, if for each $i, j \in N$, iRj and $jRi \Rightarrow i = j$. A *total preorder* (also called a *ranking*) is a reflexive, transitive and total binary relation. A *total order* is a reflexive, transitive, total and antisymmetric binary relation. $\mathcal{R}(N)$ denotes the set of rankings (or total preorders) on a given set N.

A total preorder $\succeq \in \mathcal{R}(\mathcal{P}(N))$ is called a *power relation*. Given $S, T \in \mathcal{P}(N)$, $S \succeq T$ means that "S is at least as powerful as T with respect to the power relation $\succeq$". We denote by $\sim$ the symmetric part of $\succeq$ (*i.e.* $S \sim T$ if $S \succeq T$ and $T \succeq S$) and by $\succ$ its asymmetric part (*i.e.* $S \succeq T$ and not $T \succeq S$). So, for each pair of subsets $S, T \in \mathcal{P}(N)$, $S \succ T$ means that S is *strictly more powerful* than T, whereas $S \sim T$ means that S and T are *are equally powerful*.

Let $\succeq \in \mathcal{R}(\mathcal{P}(N))$ be a power relation of the form $S_1 \succeq S_2 \succeq \cdots \succeq S_{|\mathcal{P}(N)|}$. The *quotient order* of $\succeq$ is denoted as $\Sigma_1 \succ \Sigma_2 \succ \cdots \succ \Sigma_l$ in which the subsets S_j are grouped in the *equivalence classes* Σ_k generated by the symmetric part of $\succeq$. This means that all the sets in Σ_1 are equally powerful to S_1 and are strictly better than the sets in Σ_2 and so on.

Given a power relation $\succeq$ and its associated quotient order $\Sigma_1 \succ \Sigma_2 \succ \cdots \succ \Sigma_l$, we denote by $i_k = |\{S \in \Sigma_k : i \in S\}|$ the number of sets in Σ_k containing i for $k = 1, \ldots, l$. Now, let $\theta^{\succeq}(i)$ be the l-dimensional vector $\theta^{\succeq}(i) = (i_1, \ldots, i_l)$ associated to $\succeq$. Consider the lexicographic order $\geq_L$ among vectors $\mathbf{i}$ and $\mathbf{j}$: $\mathbf{i} \geq_L \mathbf{j}$ if either $\mathbf{i} = \mathbf{j}$ or there exists t such that $i_t > j_t$ and $i_r = j_r$ for all $r \in \{1, \ldots, t-1\}$.

Let $\succeq \in \mathcal{R}(\mathcal{P}(N))$. The *lexicographic excellence (lex-cel)* [6] is the binary relation $R_{le}^{\succeq}$ such that for all $\succeq \in \mathcal{R}(\mathcal{P}(N))$ and all $i, j \in N$:

$$i \; R_{le}^{\succeq} \; j \iff \theta^{\succeq}(i) \; \geq_L \; \theta^{\succeq}(j).$$

(in the remaining $I_{le}^{\succeq}$ and $P_{le}^{\succeq}$ stand for the symmetric part and the asymmetric part of $R_{le}(\succeq)$, respectively.)

We illustrate the computation of the lex-cel via the following toy example.

Example 1. Consider an AA formed by three scientists $N = \{1, 2, 3\}$ and the problem of identifying the most influential scientist(s) within the AA based on the number of papers published in journals ranked according to the SCImago Journal Rank (SJR) and awarding the publication in the highest position of the SJR. Suppose that the three scientists never worked all together on a research project, so there is no paper co-authored by the three scientists together. Instead, some published papers exist which were co-authored by pairs of authors. Moreover, while scientists 1 and 2 are more experienced and they published some papers without the help of the others, 3 is a young researcher and he never published a paper alone. Journals related to the AA discipline are grouped into four quartiles Q_1, Q_2, Q_3 and Q_4, where Q_1 is the first quartile formed by the top 25% of journals in the SJR list, Q_2 is the second quartile (from 25% to 50%), Q_3 the third one (from 50% to 75%) and Q_4 the last one (from 75% to 100%). The number of papers co-authored by each group of scientists is summarized in Table 1.

Table 1. Number of published papers co-authored by groups of scientists in each SJR quartile.

Groups	Q_1	Q_2	Q_3	Q_4
$\{1, 2, 3\}$	0	0	0	0
$\{1, 2\}$	5	0	0	15
$\{1, 3\}$	0	10	5	0
$\{2, 3\}$	5	0	5	0
$\{1\}$	5	0	0	15
$\{2\}$	0	0	10	5
$\{3\}$	0	0	0	0

To reward the publications in the highest-ranked journals in the SJR, one may argue that the performance of the above groups may be ranked according to the lexicographic comparison (from the first quartile to the fourth one) of the rows of Table 1. As a result, we obtain the following power relation $\succeq$ (in the following, to avoid cumbersome notation, commas and parentheses for sets are omitted, e.g., we use 123 instead of $\{1, 2, 3\}$):

$$23 \succ 1 \sim 12 \succ 13 \succ 2 \succ 3 \sim 123.$$

So, the quotient order $\succ$ of $\succeq$ is

$$\Sigma_1 = \{23\} \succ \Sigma_2 = \{1, 12\} \succ \Sigma_3 = \{13\} \succ \Sigma_4 = \{2\} \succ \Sigma_5 = \{3, 123\}.$$

Assume that the lex-cel is adopted to rank the scientists according to their influence over the ranking of groups. To compute the lex-cel on $\succeq$, we need to lexicographically compare the vectors $\theta^{\succeq}(i)$, $i \in N$, defined earlier in this section. So,

$$\theta^{\succeq}(2) = (1,1,0,1,1) >_L \theta^{\succeq}(3) = (1,0,1,0,2) >_L \theta^{\succeq}(1) = (0,2,1,0,1)$$

and therefore the lex-cel $R_{le}^{\succeq}$ gives a total order over N such that $2P_{le}^{\succeq}3P_{le}^{\succeq}1$.

Notice that alternative approaches, less oriented to rewarding the highest positions in the SJR, might be adopted. Therefore, a different power relation could be generated from Table 1. For instance, the use of the total number of publications as bibliometric index would produce the power relation $\sqsupseteq$

$$1 \sim 12 \sqsupseteq 2 \sim 13 \sqsupseteq 23 \sqsupseteq 3 \sim 123.$$

It is easy to verify that the lex-cel in this case gives the ranking $1P_{le}^{\sqsupseteq}2P_{le}^{\sqsupseteq}3$.

3   Properties for Coalitional Social Choice Functions

We define the notion of *coalitional social choice function* (cscf) as a map

$$B : \mathcal{R}(\mathcal{P}(N)) \to \mathcal{P}(N)$$

that associates to each power relation $\succeq \in \mathcal{R}(\mathcal{P}(N))$ a non-empty subset $B(\succeq)$ $\in \mathcal{P}(N)$ which is interpreted as the set of *most relevant elements* or *winners* in $\succeq$. We now introduce some properties for a cscf.

The first axiom states a principle of neutrality for elements: if all coalitions are indifferent then there is no way to distinguish a major contribution of any element and all the elements should be considered winners.

Axiom 1 (All-Indifferent-All-Winners (AIAW)). Consider a power relation $\succeq \in \mathcal{R}(\mathcal{P}(N))$ such that for all $S, T \in \mathcal{P}(N)$:

$$S \sim T. \tag{1}$$

Then a cscf B satisfies the property *All-Indifferent-All-Winners* if it holds that $B(\succeq) = N$.

Example 2. Consider again an AA with $N = \{1, 2, 3\}$, as in Example 1, but suppose now that all non-empty subsets of the set N of scientists have published precisely the same number of papers in each SJR quartile. Based on such information, all coalitions may be considered equally powerful. So, we have a power relation $\succeq$ such that.

$$1 \sim 2 \sim 3 \sim 12 \sim 13 \sim 23 \sim 123.$$

A cscf B satisfying Axiom 1 selects as winners $B(\succeq) = \{1, 2, 3\}$.

The second axiom is a particular monotonicity condition for winners: improving the position of some coalitions in the worst equivalence class, but keeping the same relation among coalitions in the other equivalence classes, should not affect the status of most represented winners (over the improved coalitions). In the following, given a family of coalitions $\Sigma \subseteq \mathcal{P}(N)$ and any element $i \in N$, we use the notation i_Σ to denote the number of coalitions in Σ to which i belongs, *i.e.* $i_\Sigma = |\{S \in \Sigma : i \in S\}|$.

Axiom 2 (Monotonicity for Winners (MW)). Consider two power relations $\succeq, \sqsupseteq \in \mathcal{R}(\mathcal{P}(N))$ and their respective quotient orders $\succ$ and $\sqsupset$ such that:

- $\Sigma_1 \succ \Sigma_2 \succ \cdots \succ \Sigma_l$,
- $\Sigma_1 \sqsupset \Sigma_2 \sqsupset \cdots \sqsupset \Sigma_{l-1} \sqsupset \Sigma \sqsupset \Sigma_l \setminus \Sigma$,
- with $\Sigma \subseteq \Sigma_l$.

Take a cscf B and let $T \subseteq B(\succeq)$ be the set of most represented winners over Σ, *i.e.*

$$T = \{i \in B(\succeq) : i_\Sigma \geq j_\Sigma \ \forall j \in B(\succeq)\}. \tag{2}$$

We say that B satisfies the *Monotonicity for Winners* property if it holds that

$$T \subseteq B(\sqsupseteq).$$

Example 3. Consider again the power relation $\succeq$ of Example 2. Now, suppose that, after an update of the publication records, it turns out the number of joint-papers published by scientists 2 and 3 together (and without author 1) improves with respect to SJR. As a consequence, a new power relation $\sqsupseteq$ is considered where coalition 23 is the most powerful coalition:

$$23 \sqsupset 1 \sim 2 \sim 3 \sim 12 \sim 13 \sim 123.$$

According to relation (2), the set of most represented winners is $T = \{2, 3\}$. So, a cscf B satisfying Axiom 2 is such that $2, 3 \in B(\sqsupseteq)$. Notice that, based on Axiom 2, we cannot affirm whether element 1 belongs to $B(\sqsupseteq)$ or not.

The third axiom states that after making an improvement to coalitions in the worst equivalence class (as in the previous axiom), the winners that are now strictly less represented than other winners over the improved coalitions (*i.e.*, they are dominated by other winners) become losers (no longer winners).

Axiom 3 (Dominance (D)). Consider two power relations $\succeq, \sqsupseteq \in \mathcal{R}(\mathcal{P}(N))$ and their respective quotient orders $\succ$ and $\sqsupset$ such that:

- $\Sigma_1 \succ \Sigma_2 \succ \cdots \succ \Sigma_l$,
- $\Sigma_1 \sqsupset \Sigma_2 \sqsupset \cdots \sqsupset \Sigma_{l-1} \sqsupset \Sigma \sqsupset \Sigma_l \setminus \Sigma$,
- with $\Sigma \subseteq \Sigma_l$.

Take a cscf B and let $L \subseteq B(\succeq)$ be the set of winners that are strictly less represented than other winners over Σ, *i.e.*

$$L = \{j \in B(\succeq) : \exists i \in B(\succeq) \text{ with } i_\Sigma > j_\Sigma\}. \tag{3}$$

We say that B satisfies the *Dominance* property if it holds that

$$B(\sqsupseteq) \subseteq N \setminus L.$$

Remark 1. Notice that the set L in Axiom 3 is the complement in the set of winners of the set T in Axiom 2, so $T \cup L = B(\succeq)$ and $T \cap L = \emptyset$.

Example 4. Consider again the power relation $\succeq$ of Example 2 and the power relation $\sqsupseteq$ of Example 3. According to Remark 1, we have $L = N \setminus \{2,3\} = \{1\}$. So, a cscf B satisfying Axiom 3 is such that scientist 1 does not belong to the set $B(\sqsupseteq)$ of most important elements.

Finally, the last axiom states that once an element becomes a loser it remains a loser over all possible power relation obtained fractioning the worst equivalence class of the quotient order.

Axiom 4 (Independence for Losers from the Worst Set (ILWS)). We say that a cscf B satisfies the property of *Independence for Losers from the Worst Set* if for any power relation $\succeq \in \mathcal{R}(\mathcal{P}(N))$ with the associated quotient order $\succ$ such that

$$\Sigma_1 \succ \Sigma_2 \succ \cdots \succ \Sigma_l$$

and $i \in N$ such that

$$i \notin B(\succeq),$$

then for any partition $T_1, \ldots, T_m$ of Σ_l and for any power relation $\sqsupseteq \in \mathcal{R}(\mathcal{P}(N))$ with the associated quotient order $\sqsupset$ such that

$$\Sigma_1 \sqsupset \Sigma_2 \sqsupset \cdots \sqsupset \Sigma_{l-1} \sqsupset T_1 \sqsupset \cdots \sqsupset T_m,$$

it holds that

$$i \notin B(\sqsupseteq).$$

Example 5. Consider $\sqsupseteq$ of Example 3 and its quotient order $\sqsupset$ such that $\Sigma_1 = \{23\}$ and $\Sigma_2 = \mathcal{R}(\mathcal{P}(N)) \setminus \{23\}$. Now, suppose that after an update in the publications records of groups of scientists, we obtain a new power relation $\sqsupseteq'$ obtained from $\sqsupseteq$ via a partition of Σ_2 and such that

$$23 \sqsupset' 1 \sim' 12 \sqsupset' 13 \sqsupset' 2 \sqsupset' 3 \sim' 123.$$

Notice that $\sqsupseteq'$ coincides with $\succeq$ of Example 1. Consider a cscf B satisfying Axiom 4 and suppose $1 \notin B(\sqsupseteq)$ (like in Example 4). A direct consequence of Axiom 4 is that 1 does not even belong to $B(\sqsupseteq')$.

4   The Lex-Cel Coalitional Social Choice Function

A particular cscf denoted as B_{le} is based on the lex-cel and it associates to a each power relation $\succeq \in \mathcal{R}(\mathcal{P}(N))$ the set of elements in the highest positions in the ranking $R_{le}^{\succeq}$ provided by the lex-cel.

Definition 1 (Lex-cel cscf). *Let $\succeq \in \mathcal{R}(\mathcal{P}(N))$. The lex-cel cscf is the map $B_{le} : \mathcal{R}(\mathcal{P}(N)) \to \mathcal{P}(N)$ such that for all $\succeq \in \mathcal{R}(\mathcal{P}(N))$:*

$$B_{le}(\succeq) = \{i \in N : i\ R_{le}^{\succeq}\ j\ \forall j \in N\}.$$

Example 6. Consider the power relation $\succeq$ of Example 1 and the lex-cel ranking computed over $\succeq$ in the same example. Then, $B_{le}(\succeq) = \{2\}$.

To axiomatically characterize the lex-cel cscf we first need to introduce the following lemma.

Lemma 1. *Consider two power relations $\succeq, \sqsupseteq \in \mathcal{R}(\mathcal{P}(N))$ and their respective quotient orders $\succ$ and $\sqsupset$ such that:*

- $\Sigma_1 \succ \Sigma_2 \succ \cdots \succ \Sigma_l,$
- $\Sigma_1 \sqsupset \Sigma_2 \sqsupset \cdots \sqsupset \Sigma_{l-1} \sqsupset \Sigma \sqsupset \Sigma_l \setminus \Sigma,$
- *with $\Sigma \subseteq \Sigma_l$.*

Then, $B_{le}(\sqsupseteq) = T = \{i \in B_{le}(\succeq) : i_\Sigma \geq j_\Sigma\ \forall j \in B_{le}(\succeq)\}.$

Proof. First, notice that for each $i \in N$

$$\boldsymbol{\theta}^{\sqsupseteq}(i) = (i_1, \ldots, i_{l-1}, i_\Sigma, i_l - i_\Sigma). \tag{4}$$

where $i_k = |\{S \in \Sigma_k : i \in S\}|$ is the number of sets in Σ_k containing i for $k = 1, \ldots, l$. We prove that, for each $i \in T$, we have $i \in B_{le}(\sqsupseteq)$ or, equivalently by the definitions of lex-cel, that

$$\boldsymbol{\theta}^{\sqsupseteq}(i)\ \geq_L\ \boldsymbol{\theta}^{\sqsupseteq}(j)\ \forall j \in N.$$

We distinguish three cases:

i) $j \in T$: since $i, j \in T$, we have that $i_\Sigma = j_\Sigma$; moreover, $i, j \in B_{le}(\succeq)$ implies that $\boldsymbol{\theta}^{\succeq}(i) = \boldsymbol{\theta}^{\succeq}(j)$). Then, by relation (4), $\boldsymbol{\theta}^{\sqsupseteq}(i) = \boldsymbol{\theta}^{\sqsupseteq}(j)$;

ii) $j \in B_{le}(\succeq) \setminus T$: since $i, j \in B_{le}(\succeq)$, we have that $i_k = j_k$ for all $k = 1, \ldots, l$; moreover, $j \in B_{le}(\succeq) \setminus T$ implies that $i_\Sigma > j_\Sigma$. Then, by relation (4), $\boldsymbol{\theta}^{\sqsupseteq}(i) >_L \boldsymbol{\theta}^{\sqsupseteq}(j)$

iii) $j \in N \setminus B_{le}(\succeq)$: since $i \in B_{le}(\succeq)$ but $j \notin B_{le}(\succeq)$, it must exist $k = 1, \ldots, l-1$ such that $i_k > j_k$. Then, by relation (4), $\boldsymbol{\theta}^{\sqsupseteq}(i) >_L \boldsymbol{\theta}^{\sqsupseteq}(j)$.

So, $T \subseteq B_{le}(\sqsupseteq)$. Moreover, by the the above points $ii)$ and $iii)$ for each $j \in N \setminus T$ we have that $\boldsymbol{\theta}^{\sqsupseteq}(i) >_L \boldsymbol{\theta}^{\sqsupseteq}(j)$ for all $i \in T$. So $B_{le}(\sqsupseteq) \subseteq T$, which concludes the proof.

We are now ready to introduce the main result of this section.

Theorem 5. *The cscf B_{le} is the unique cscf fulfilling Axioms 1, 2, 3 and 4.*

Proof. We first prove that the cscf B_{le} satisfies the four axioms.

To see that B_{le} satisfies Axiom 1, consider a power relation $\succeq \in \mathcal{R}(\mathcal{P}(N))$ such that $S \sim T$ for all $S, T \in \mathcal{P}(N)$. We have that $\theta^{\succeq}(i) = (2^{n-1})$ for any $i \in N$ since any element i belongs to precisely 2^{n-1} coalitions in the same equivalence class $\Sigma_1 = \mathcal{P}(N)$ of the quotient order $\succ$.

The fact that B_{le} satisfies Axiom 2 immediately follows from Lemma 1, for $B(\sqsupseteq) = T$ for any $\succeq, \sqsupseteq \in \mathcal{R}(\mathcal{P}(N))$ with the properties considered in Axiom 2.

The fact that B_{le} satisfies Axiom 3 immediately follows from Lemma 1 and Remark 1, for $B(\sqsupseteq) = T = B(\succeq) \setminus L \subseteq N \setminus L$ for any $\succeq, \sqsupseteq \in \mathcal{R}(\mathcal{P}(N))$ with the properties considered in Axiom 3.

Finally, to see that B_{le} satisfies Axiom 4, consider any power relation $\succeq \in \mathcal{R}(\mathcal{P}(N))$ with quotient order $\succ$ such that

$$\Sigma_1 \succ \Sigma_2 \succ \cdots \succ \Sigma_l$$

and $i \in N$ such that $i \notin B(\succeq)$. For any partition $T_1, \ldots, T_m$ of Σ_l and for any power relation $\sqsupseteq \in \mathcal{R}(\mathcal{P}(N))$ with quotient order $\sqsupset$ such that

$$\Sigma_1 \sqsupset \Sigma_2 \sqsupset \cdots \sqsupset \Sigma_{l-1} \sqsupset T_1 \sqsupset \cdots \sqsupset T_m,$$

we have that

$$\boldsymbol{\theta}^{\sqsupseteq}(i) = (i_1, \ldots, i_{l-1}, i_{T_1}, \ldots, i_{T_m}), \tag{5}$$

where $i_{T_p} = |\{S \in T_p : i \in S\}|$ is the number of sets in T_p containing i for $p = 1, \ldots, m$.

Since $i \notin B(\succeq)$, by Definition 1 there must exist $j \neq i$ such that $\boldsymbol{\theta}^{\succeq}(j) >_L \boldsymbol{\theta}^{\succeq}(i)$. So, for the sum $\sum_{k=1}^{l} i_k = 2^{n-1}$ for all $i \in N$, there must exist $s \in \{1, \ldots, l-1\}$ such that $i_k = j_k$ for all $k \in \{1, \ldots, s-1\}$ and $i_s < j_s$. Consequently, by relation (5), $\boldsymbol{\theta}^{\sqsupseteq}(j) >_L \boldsymbol{\theta}^{\sqsupseteq}(i)$; so $i \notin B_{le}(\sqsupseteq)$.

We now prove that if a cscf B satisfies the four axioms then $B = B_{le}$.

Consider a cscf B that satisfies Axioms 1, 2, 3 and 4. We want to prove that for any power relation $\succeq \in \mathcal{R}(\mathcal{P}(N))$ (and its quotient order $\succ$ such that $\Sigma_1 \succ \Sigma_2 \succ \cdots \succ \Sigma_l$) it holds that $B(\succeq) = B_{le}(\succeq)$. The proof is by induction to the number l of equivalence classes in the quotient order $\succ$.

If $l = 1$ (therefore the power relation $\succeq \in \mathcal{R}(\mathcal{P}(N))$ is such that $S \sim T$ for all $S, T \in \mathcal{P}(N)$), by Axiom 1 and the first part of this proof, we have that $B(\succeq) = N = B_{le}(\succeq)$.

Now, let $l \geq 1$ and suppose that the assertion $B(\succeq) = B_{le}(\succeq)$ has been proven for any power relation $\succeq$ such that the quotient order $\succ$ contains precisely l equivalence classes.

Let $\sqsupseteq \in \mathcal{R}(\mathcal{P}(N))$ be such that the quotient order $\sqsupset$ is $\Sigma_1 \sqsupset \cdots \sqsupset \Sigma_{l+1}$. Consider a new power relation $\succeq \in \mathcal{R}(\mathcal{P}(N))$ such that the quotient order $\succ$ is

$\Sigma_1 \succ \cdots \succ \Sigma_l \cup \Sigma_{l+1}$, containing precisely l equivalence classes. By Lemma 1 with Σ_l in the role of Σ, we have that

$$B_{le}(\sqsupseteq) = T = \{i \in B_{le}(\succeq) : i_l \geq j_l \; \forall j \in B_{le}(\succeq)\}. \tag{6}$$

Application of the induction hypothesis on $\succeq$ yields $B(\succeq) = B_{le}(\succeq)$.

Now, by Axioms 2 and 3 on B, with Σ_l in the role of Σ, it follows that

$$T \subseteq B(\sqsupseteq) \subseteq N \setminus L, \tag{7}$$

where $L = \{j \in B(\succeq) : \exists i \in B(\succeq) \text{ with } i_l \geq j_l\}$. Then, by Axiom 4, with partition $T_1 = \Sigma_l, T_2 = \Sigma_{l+1}$ of the last equivalence class $\Sigma_l \cup \Sigma_{l+1}$ in $\succ$, we have

$$B(\sqsupseteq) \subseteq B_{le}(\succeq) = L \cup T. \tag{8}$$

Finally, by relations (7) and (8) we have that $T \subseteq B(\sqsupseteq) \subseteq T$. So, by relation (6), we have proven that $B(\sqsupseteq) = T = B_{le}(\sqsupseteq)$.

We now show that Axioms 1, 2, 3 and 4 are logically independent, which means that they are necessary for the axiomatic characterization of the lex-cel cscf provided in Theorem 5 .

Proposition 1. *Axioms 1, 2, 3 and 4 are logically independent.*

Proof. We want to prove that axioms 1, 2, 3 and 4 are necessary in order to uniquely characterize the cscf B_{le}. Therefore, we show that for any combination of three out of the four axioms, a cscf $B : \mathcal{R}(\mathcal{P}(N)) \rightarrow \mathcal{P}(N)$, with $N = \{1, \ldots, n\}$, that satisfies such three axioms does not necessarily satisfies the fourth one.

Axiom 1 is not satisfied:

Let $i \in N$ and consider a cscf $B^1 : \mathcal{R}(\mathcal{P}(N)) \rightarrow \mathcal{P}(N)$ such that $B^1(\succeq) = \{i\}$ for all $\succeq \in \mathcal{R}(\mathcal{P}(N))$.

- Clearly B^1 does not satisfy Axiom 1 if $|N| \geq 2$.
- B^1 trivially satisfies Axiom 2, since $T = \{i\} = B^1(\sqsupseteq)$ for all power relations $\succeq, \sqsupseteq \in \mathcal{R}(\mathcal{P}(N))$ as in Axiom 2.
- B^1 trivially satisfies Axiom 3, since $L = \emptyset$ and $B^1(\sqsupseteq) = \{i\} \subseteq N$ for all power relations $\succeq, \sqsupseteq \in \mathcal{R}(\mathcal{P}(N))$ as in Axiom 3.
- B^1 also satisfies Axiom 4, for all $j \in N \setminus \{i\}$, $j \notin B^1(\succeq)$ and $j \notin B^1(\sqsupseteq)$ for all power relations $\succeq, \sqsupseteq \in \mathcal{R}(\mathcal{P}(N))$ as in Axiom 4.

Axiom 2 is not satisfied:

For any $S \in \mathcal{P}(N)$, let $b(S) = \min\{i \in S\}$ and consider a cscf $B^2 : \mathcal{R}(\mathcal{P}(N)) \rightarrow \mathcal{P}(N)$ such that for all $\succeq \in \mathcal{R}(\mathcal{P}(N))$

$$B^2(\succeq) = \begin{cases} N, & \text{if } \succeq = \succeq^0, \\ \{b(B_{le}(\succeq))\}, & \text{otherwise.} \end{cases} \tag{9}$$

where $\succeq^0 \in \mathcal{R}(\mathcal{P}(N))$ is a power relation with quotient order $\succ^0$ having a unique equivalence class $\Sigma_1 = \mathcal{P}(N)$ (all coalitions are indifferent in $\succeq^0$).

– B^2 does not satisfy Axiom 2: take for instance the power relations $\succeq, \sqsupseteq \in$ $\mathcal{R}(\mathcal{P}(N))$ such that the quotient order $\succ$ is

$$\Sigma_1 = \mathcal{P}(N)$$

and the quotient order $\sqsupset$ is

$$\{12\} \sqsupset \mathcal{P}(N) \setminus \{12\}.$$

Taking $\Sigma = \{12\}$, with the notations of Axiom 2, we have $T = \{1,2\}$, but $B^2_{le}(\sqsupseteq) = \{1\}$, which violates the axiom.
– Clearly B^2 satisfies Axiom 1.
– Since B_{le} satisfies Axiom 3, the same holds for B^2, as the set L in Axiom 3 remains precisely the same for both cscfs.
– Finally, since all elements that do not belong to $B_{le}(\succeq)$, $\succeq \in \mathcal{R}(\mathcal{P}(N))$, do not neither belong to $B^2(\succeq)$, it follows that B^2 also satisfies Axiom 4.

Axiom 3 is not satisfied
Consider a cscf $B^3 : \mathcal{R}(\mathcal{P}(N)) \to \mathcal{P}(N)$ such that $B^3(\succeq) = N$ for all $\succeq \in$ $\mathcal{R}(\mathcal{P}(N))$.

– B^3 does not satisfy Axiom 3: take for instance two power relations $\succeq, \sqsupseteq \in$ $\mathcal{R}(\mathcal{P}(N))$ such that the quotient order $\succ$ is

$$\Sigma_1 = \mathcal{P}(N)$$

and the quotient order $\sqsupset$ is

$$\{1, 12\} \sqsupset \mathcal{P}(N) \setminus \{12, 1\}.$$

Taking $\Sigma = \{1, 12\}$, with the notation of Axiom 3 we have $L = \{2\}$, but $B^3_{le}(\sqsupseteq) = N \nsubseteq N \setminus \{2\}$, which violates the axiom.
– On the other hand, B^3 clearly satisfies Axiom 1.
– B^3 trivially satisfies Axiom 2, as we have $T \subseteq N$.
– B^3 also satisfies Axiom 4, as the set of elements not in $B^3(\succeq)$ is empty, for all $\succeq \in \mathcal{R}(\mathcal{P}(N))$.

Axiom 4 is not satisfied:
To define the last solution $B^4 : \mathcal{R}(\mathcal{P}(N)) \to \mathcal{P}(N)$, we first need to introduce the notion of dual lex-cel (see [6]). Consider the lexicographic* order $\geq_{L^*}$ among vectors $\mathbf{i}$ and $\mathbf{j}$: $\mathbf{i} \geq_{L^*} \mathbf{j}$ if either $\mathbf{i} = \mathbf{j}$ or there exists t such that $i_t < j_t$ and $i_r = j_r$ for all $r \in \{t+1, \ldots, l\}$. The *dual lex-cel* is the binary relation $R^{\succeq}_{\bar{d}}$ such that for all $\succeq \in \mathcal{R}(\mathcal{P}(N))$ and all $i, j \in N$:

$$i \; R^{\succeq}_{\bar{d}} \; j \Longleftrightarrow \theta^{\succeq}(i) \; \geq_{L^*} \; \theta^{\succeq}(j).$$

Consider the *dual lex-cel* cscf $B^4 : \mathcal{R}(\mathcal{P}(N)) \to \mathcal{P}(N)$ such that for all $\succeq \in$ $\mathcal{R}(\mathcal{P}(N))$:

$$B^4(\succeq) = \{i \in N : i \; R^{\succeq}_{\bar{d}} \; j \; \forall j \in N\}.$$

– B^4 does not satisfy Axiom 4: take for instance two power relations $\succeq, \sqsupseteq \in$ $\mathcal{R}(\mathcal{P}(N))$ such that the quotient order $\succ$ is

$$\{1, 12\} \succ \mathcal{P}(N) \setminus \{1, 12\}$$

and the quotient order $\sqsupset$ is

$$\{1, 12\} \sqsupset \{2, 23\} \sqsupset 13 \sqsupset \mathcal{P}(N) \setminus \{1, 12, 2, 23, 13\}.$$

Notice that the conditions of Axiom 4 for $\succ$ and $\sqsupset$ apply with the partition of the worst equivalence class in $\succ$ into the three disjoint sets $T_1 = \{2, 23\}$, $T_2 = \{13\}$ and $T_3 = \mathcal{P}(N) \setminus (T_1 \cup T_2)$.
However, it easy to check that $1P_d(\succeq)i$ for all $i \in N \setminus \{1\}$, so, $2 \notin B^4(\succeq)$, whereas $2P_d(\sqsupseteq)j$ for all $j \in N \setminus \{2\}$ and so, $2 \in B^4(\sqsupseteq)$.
– We leave to the reader to verify that B^4 satisfies Axioms 1, 2 and 3 by following the same steps as in the proof of Theorem 5 where we proved that B_{le} satisfies those axioms.

We have therefore proven that the cscf B_{le} is the unique solution satisfying the four proposed axioms and that these four axioms are logically independent. So we obtained a full characterization of this method.

As already noticed in [6], the dual lex-cel R_d (cf. to its definition in the proof of Proposition 1) penalizes elements appearing many times in the worst coalitions of a power relation. As a consequence, the dual lex-cel cscf B^4 shows a similar behaviour for the selection of the most relevant elements, as illustrated in the following example.

Example 7. Consider again the power relation $\succeq$ of Example 1. It is easy to verify that the dual lex-cel ranking $R_d^\succeq$ is such that $1P_d^\succeq 2P_d^\succeq 3$. So, the corresponding dual lex-cel cscf B^4 yields the most relevant element $B^4(\succeq) = \{1\}$. In contrast with the lex-cel cscf, which rewards the excellence of element 2 as a member of the best coalitions (specifically, coalitions 23 and 12) according to the power relation $\succeq$, the dual lex-cel csfc punishes the presence of element 2 in the worst coalitions (specifically, coalitions 123 and 2) according to $\succeq$.

5   Conclusion and Future Work

There are many situations where sets of elements are compared; for instance, in sports, in job performance evaluations, etc. A common task in these situations is to reason about the elements in order to assess the performance; typically one might want to compare elements based on their performance when part of different teams. An approach that has been recently proposed is the *lexicographic excellence (lex-cel)* method [6], that provides a full ranking of the elements given the full ranking of all possible coalitions (called power relation). The peculiar characteristic of the lex-cel is its qualitative nature and the fact that is a relatively simple rule to use.

In this work we addressed the problem of determining the most relevant element(s) given in input the ranking over coalitions. We define a coalitional social choice function (cscf) as a mapping from a power relation to a (typically small) subset of "winners". We adopted an axiomatic approach and stated four axioms that we believe constitute reasonable behaviors of the desired cscf. We then showed that the cscf which returns the first element(s) in the ranking obtained by lex-cel is the only cscf compatible with the four axioms. So we proposed the first, as far as we know, method for determining the most relevant elements given a ranking of coalitions, as well as its corresponding characterization in terms of four intuitive axioms. Although there are similarities between some of the axioms introduced in this paper and those for social rankings introduced in [6], we would like to point out some important differences suggesting a novel interpretation of the lex-cel ranking when it is applied to select the most relevant elements from a power relation. First, our axiomatic characterization of the lex-cel cscf does not use any property directly related to the *Coalitional Anonymity* axiom proposed in [6], which is a strong property requiring that the relative ranking of two individual elements should exclusively depend on the relative positions of groups containing just one of them and disregarding the structure or the size of those groups. Second, our axioms highlight the fundamental mechanism driving the selection of the most relevant elements, which is essentially based on changes (i.e., improvements or partitioning) in the structure of the worst equivalence class of a power relation (in [6], only the *Independence from the Worst Set* axiom concerned the worst equivalence class). In conclusion, we believe that the set of (easy to understand) axioms used in this paper reveals in an explicit way the crucial role of the worst equivalence class in determining the most relevant elements according to the lex-cel method.

Concerning future works, we believe that an important direction is to deal with situations where there is uncertainty about the preference order over the coalitions. Preference uncertainty can arise because of a lack of information on how certain coalitions compare, or because of the user's reluctance to rank an exponential number of coalitions (due to cognitive cost or time constraints).

Indeed, the main obstacle to the adoption of lex-cel lies in the exponential size of its input (the exponential number of elements in a power relation). Therefore, we think it is worth studying the application of the lex-cel (and as well of similar methods) when a partial order of the coalitions is given as an input. This partial order can be interpreted in the sense of "strict uncertainty" [10]: we can assume that there exists a "true" complete ranking $\succeq^* \in \mathcal{R}(\mathcal{P}(N))$, but that it is unknown to us and only a reduction of the ranking is given. We can then design methods to reason about all possible completion of the partial ranking given as input, and view these methods as coalitional social choice functions taking *partial* orders as input. Considering the running example dealing with the determination of the most influential scientists with an AA, this could lead to simplification of the process of comparison of collaborations: for instance, it could be possible to have m sub-committees tasked with ranking certain subsets of $\mathcal{P}(N)$, *i.e.* the work of comparing all potential collaborations is divided between these m committees. From their conclusions, the application of a cscf equipped to work with missing information will be used to determine the ranking over the researchers' influence. In this way, it will be possible to deal with real-life situations, where a complete order is seldom given.

Acknowledgments. We acknowledge a financial support from the project THEMIS ANR-20-CE23-0018 of the French National Research Agency (ANR).

References

1. Aleandri, M., Dall'Aglio, M., Fragnelli, V., Moretti, S.: Minimal winning coalitions and orders of criticality. Ann. Oper. Res., 1–17 (2021). https://doi.org/10.1007/s10479-021-04199-6
2. Algaba, E., Moretti, S., Rémila, E., Solal, P.: Lexicographic solutions for coalitional rankings. Social Choice Welfare, 1–33 (2021). https://doi.org/10.1007/s00355-021-01340-z
3. Allouche, T., Escoffier, B., Moretti, S., Öztürk, M.: Social ranking manipulability for the cp-majority, banzhaf and lexicographic excellence solutions. In: Proceedings of the Twenty-Ninth International Joint Conference on Artificial Intelligence (IJCAI-2020), pp. 17–23 (2020)
4. Ausloos, M.: A scientometrics law about co-authors and their ranking: the co-author core. Scientometrics **95**(3), 895–909 (2013)
5. Béal, S., Rémila, E., Solal, P.: Lexicographic solutions for coalitional rankings based on individual and collective performances. J. Math. Econ., 102738 (2022). https://doi.org/10.1016/j.jmateco.2022.102738
6. Bernardi, G., Lucchetti, R., Moretti, S.: Ranking objects from a preference relation over their subsets. Social Choice Welfare **52**, 589–606 (2019)
7. Fritz, F., Staudacher, J., Moretti, S.: socialranking: Social Ranking Solutions for Power Relations on Coalitions (2022). https://CRAN.R-project.org/package=socialranking, r package version 0.1.1
8. Haret, A., Hossein, K., Moretti, S., Öztürk, M.: Ceteris paribus majority for social ranking. In: Proceedings of the 27th International Joint Conference on Artificial Intelligence (IJCAI-2018), pp. 303–309 (2018)
9. Khani, H., Moretti, S., Ozturk, M.: An ordinal banzhaf index for social ranking. In: 28th International Joint Conference on Artificial Intelligence (IJCAI 2019), pp. 378–384 (2019)
10. Konczak, K., Lang, J.: Voting procedures with incomplete preferences. In: Proceedings of the Multidisciplinary IJCAI-2005 Workshop on Advances in Preference Handling (2005)
11. Rubem, A.P.d.S., de Moura, A.L., Soares de Mello, J.C.C.B.: Comparative analysis of some individual bibliometric indices when applied to groups of researchers. Scientometrics **102**(1), 1019–1035 (2015)
12. Vavryčuk, V.: Fair ranking of researchers and research teams. PloS One **13**(4), e0195509 (2018)

Decision Making Under Severe Uncertainty on a Budget

Nawapon Nakharutai[1] , Sébastien Destercke[2(✉)] ,
and Matthias C. M. Troffaes[3]

[1] Data Science Research Center, Department of Statistics, Faculty of Science,
Chiang Mai University, Chiang Mai 50200, Thailand
`nawapon.nakharutai@cmu.ac.th`
[2] UMR CNRS 7253 Heudiasyc, Sorbonne Université,
Université de Technologie de Compiègne, Compiègne, France
`sebastien.destercke@hds.utc.fr`
[3] Department of Mathematical Sciences, Durham University, Durham, UK
`matthias.troffaes@durham.ac.uk`

Abstract. Convex sets of probabilities are general models to describe
and reason with uncertainty. Moreover, robust decision rules defined for
them enable one to make cautious inferences by allowing sets of optimal
actions to be returned, reflecting lack of information. One caveat of such
rules, though, is that the number of returned actions is only bounded by
the number of possibles actions, which can be huge, such as in combinatorial optimisation problems. For this reason, we propose and discuss
new decision rules whose number of returned actions is bounded by a
fixed value and study their consistency and numerical behaviour.

Keywords: Imprecise probabilities · Decision · Regret

1 Introduction

Imprecise probability theories [1] provide very general tools to handle uncertainty, encompassing many existing uncertainty representations, including for
instance classical probability, lower and upper previsions, sets of probability
measures, choice functions, n-monotone capacities, and sets of desirable gambles. Imprecise probability theories often use convex sets of probability measures
(or equivalent mathematical representations) as basic uncertainty models. They
are used in practical applications that involve severe uncertainty, including for
example wind-farm design [2] or machine learning [13].

Classical imprecise probability decision rules either deliver a single[1] optimal
alternative as output, or a set of such alternatives whose size is unconstrained,
apart from the trivial bounds that are 1 and the total number of alternatives.
While such rules have been widely used and have strong theoretical properties,

---

[1] up to indifference.

F. Dupin de Saint-Cyr et al. (Eds.): SUM 2022, LNAI 13562, pp. 186–201, 2022.
https://doi.org/10.1007/978-3-031-18843-5_13

there are situations where one may want more than one decision, but still limit the number of proposed alternatives by, e.g., specifying an upper bound on the number of alternatives to return. This can arise for instance in situations where one has to account for natural human cognitive limits (a decision maker cannot inspect dozens of possible alternatives), or where inspecting more closely the different proposed alternatives represents a high monetary cost. Presenting set-valued recommendations or predictions with a limited budget is already treated in preference learning [14] and in standard machine-learning [4]. Hence, treating it in the setting of decisions under uncertainty appears as a natural next step.

We say that a decision rule is *budgeted* or *on a budget* if it limits the number of decisions it outputs. In Sect. 2, we present some basic ideas and notations about budgeted decision rules. We then propose an study two such rules in Sects. 3 and 4, one based on the idea of minmax regret, the other on maximising diversity. We then discuss them in the light of numerical experiments as well as with respect to the previously proposed properties in Sect. 5.

2 Preliminaries and Definitions

We start with a finite set $\mathcal{X} = \{x_1, \ldots, x_m\}$ of possible states of nature about which we are uncertain. We assume this is uncertainty is represented by a credal set $\mathcal{P}$, i.e. $\mathcal{P}$ is a closed convex set of probability mass functions on $\mathcal{X}$ and this set represents our knowledge about the unknown true value $x \in \mathcal{X}$.

An *act* $a\colon \mathcal{X} \to \mathbb{R}$ is a real-valued function on $\mathcal{X}$ that is interpreted as an uncertain reward, i.e. $a(x)$ represents the reward (in utiles) if $x \in \mathcal{X}$ is the true state of nature. We denote by $\mathcal{A}$ the set of all finite non-empty sets of acts. Each element of $\mathcal{A}$ represents a decision problem with a finite number of options. We set ourselves in the basic decision theoretic setting where we have to make a single decision [12], that is recommend once options from an element of $\mathcal{A}$, yet we consider that when information is lacking, we can return or recommend as a decision multiple options. This contrasts, for instance, with sequential problems where one should recommend a policy over multiple time-steps and for large state spaces [6].

A *decision rule* D is a function

$$D\colon \mathcal{A} \to \mathcal{A}.$$

satisfying $D(A) \subseteq A$ for every $A \in \mathcal{A}$. For example, maximising expected utility for a given $p \in \mathcal{P}$ is a decision rule. In case one allows for sets of possibly optimal decisions, maximality with respect to a credal set $\mathcal{P}$ is one of the most used rules. It works as follows: an act a maximally dominates a', denote $a \succ_\mathcal{M} a'$, if and only if $\underline{\mathbb{E}}(a - a') > 0$, where $\underline{\mathbb{E}}(f) := \inf_{p \in \mathcal{P}} \mathbb{E}_p(f)$, $\mathbb{E}_p$ denoting the expectation operator with respect to f. The corresponding decision rule D_M then collects all maximal elements according to $\succ_\mathcal{M}$, i.e.,

$$D_M(A) := \{a \in A \colon \nexists a' \in A \text{ s.t. } a' \succ_\mathcal{M} a\},$$

that is all the undominated elements in A with respect to $\succ_{\mathcal{M}}$. While this rule has strong theoretical appeal, it can deliver any subset of A, from a single decision to the whole set [10].

As argued in the introduction, one could want to limit the number of returned decisions. To do so, we introduce the notion of a budgeted decision rule. If we now denote by $\mathcal{A}_k := \{A \in \mathcal{A} : |A| \leq k\}$ the non-empty finite sets of acts with at most k alternatives, we define a k-*budgeted decision rule* D^k as a rule

$$D^k : \mathcal{A} \to \mathcal{A}_k,$$

meaning that $D^k(A)$ returns *at most* k alternatives. Once one accepts the need for such rules, it is natural to look which properties they should follow, as well as look how computable they are.

A property we may want is such rules to be partially consistent with well-known, and theoretically well-justified rules producing non-bounded recommendation sets (maximality, E-admissibility). We define two such consistency properties, a strong one and a weak one:

Definition 1. *A k-budgeted rule D^k is said to be* strongly consistent *with a rule D if for all $A \in \mathcal{A}$*

$$D^k(A) \subseteq D(A)$$

Definition 2. *A k-budgeted rule D^k is said to be* weakly consistent *with a rule D if for all $A \in \mathcal{A}$*

$$D^k(A) \cap D(A) \neq \emptyset$$

While strong consistency requires $D^k(A)$ to be a subset of $D(A)$, weak consistency merely requires $D^k(A)$ to contain some elements that are also in $D(A)$, while others may not belong to it. Note that a natural way to ensure strong consistency with a rule $D(A)$ is simply to first compute exactly $D(A)$, and then to apply $D^k(D(A))$. However, this requires first computing $D(A)$. This may be impossible in problems where $|A|$ is extremely large, such as in machine learning problems like multi-label ones [5] or in combinatorial optimisation problems [2,3].

Next, we will introduce two rules where with each $A \in \mathcal{A}$ a value is associated, either considered as a loss or as a utility. One can then see the problem of selecting k decisions as either picking the set within $\mathcal{A}$ that has at most k decisions and that either tries to minimize a loss or to maximize a utility. The first rule is based on the idea of regret, while the second is based on the idea of maximising the spread of selected alternatives in terms of a pseudometric.

3   Regret-Based Budgeted Decision Rule

3.1   Definition

For any two acts a and a', $\overline{\mathbb{E}}(a' - a) = \sup_{p \in \mathcal{P}} \mathbb{E}_p(a' - a) = -\underline{\mathbb{E}}(a - a')$ represents the maximal expected gain in exchanging a' for a, or alternatively the worst possible loss we would incur by keeping a instead of exchanging it for

a'. It is negative only if a is better than a' in terms of expected utility under all $p \in \mathcal{P}$. The maximal loss of retaining only a from A is then

$$ML(\{a\}, A) := \max_{a' \in A \setminus \{a\}} \overline{\mathbb{E}}(a' - a).$$

Note that this is negative if and only if a dominates (in the sense of $\succ_{\mathcal{M}}$) all other actions in A, and is therefore the unique optimum. Otherwise, it is positive and something we want to miminize, since it is a loss function. Therefore, if we have to pick exactly one action, we can define a minmax[2] loss of A as follows:

$$mML(A) := \min_{a \in A} ML(\{a\}, A) \tag{1}$$

and the associated decision rule as

$$D^1_{mML}(A) := \arg\min_{a \in A} ML(\{a\}, A). \tag{2}$$

This is a kind of minmax regret criterion. We can now turn it into a set-valued criterion. Consider a solution set $S \subseteq A$, then the maximal loss associated with this set of alternatives, considering that we can pick any alternative within S as our choice but that the opponent is then free to choose the worst adversary (we first pick $a \in A$, then the adversary picks the worst alternatives according to $ML(\{a\}, A)$), can be defined for any $\emptyset \neq S \subseteq A$ as

$$mML(S, A) := \min_{a \in S} ML(\{a\}, A \setminus S) = \min_{a \in S} \max_{a' \in A \setminus S} \overline{\mathbb{E}}(a' - a). \tag{3}$$

We will use (3) to define a budgeted decision rule, yet before doing so we provide two properties of $mML(S, A)$.

Lemma 1. *For any* $\emptyset \neq S \subseteq S' \subseteq A \in \mathcal{A}$, *we have that* $mML(S, A) \geq mML(S', A)$.

Proof. Indeed,

$$
\begin{aligned}
mML(S', A) &= \min_{a \in S'} ML(\{a\}, A \setminus S') \\
&\leq \min_{a \in S} ML(\{a\}, A \setminus S') && (\text{since } S \subseteq S') \\
&= \min_{a \in S} \max_{a' \in A \setminus S'} \overline{\mathbb{E}}(a' - a) \\
&\leq \min_{a \in S} \max_{a' \in A \setminus S} \overline{\mathbb{E}}(a' - a) && (\text{since } S \subseteq S') \\
&= mML(S, A)
\end{aligned}
$$

$\square$

---

[2] as it minimizes a maximal loss that is $\overline{\mathbb{E}}(a' - a)$.

Lemma 1 tells us that as $mML(S, A)$ decreases with set inclusion, any rule that tries to find a set S minimizing it will search for the biggest possible set. In particular, among the sets of $\mathcal{A}_k$, it will always pick a set of size k. The next property shows that $mML(S, A)$ is negative if only if every alternative outside of S is dominated (in the sense of maximality) by some alternative within S.

Theorem 1. $mML(S, A) < 0$ if only if there is an $a \in S$ such that for all $a' \in A \setminus S$ we have that $a \succ_{\mathcal{M}} a'$.

Proof. By the definition, we have

$$mML(S, A) < 0 \iff \min_{a \in S} ML(\{a\}, A \setminus S) < 0$$
$$\iff \exists a \in S, \ ML(\{a\}, A \setminus S) < 0$$
$$\iff \exists a \in S, \ \max_{a' \in A \setminus S} \overline{\mathbb{E}}(a' - a) < 0$$
$$\iff \exists a \in S, \ \forall a' \in A \setminus S, \ \overline{\mathbb{E}}(a' - a) < 0$$
$$\iff \exists a \in S, \ \forall a' \in A \setminus S, \ \underline{\mathbb{E}}(a - a') > 0$$

$\square$

Corollary 1. If $mML(S, A) < 0$ then $D_M(A) \subseteq S$.

Proof. By Theorem 1, all $a' \in A \setminus S$ are dominated, hence $A \setminus S$ contains no maximal elements, so all maximal elements must be in S. $\square$

Let us now denote by $S_k^*(A)$ the optimal subset of size k w.r.t. mML criterion (that we want to minimize) within A, i.e.

$$S_k^*(A) := \arg \min_{S \in \mathcal{A}_k} mML(S, A)$$

We can now define the mML budgeted decision rule as

$$D_{mML}^k(A) := \begin{cases} D_M(A) & \text{if } mML(S_k^*(A), A) < 0 \\ S_k^*(A) & \text{otherwise} \end{cases}$$

3.2   Example and Computation

The next example illustrates some behaviour of $mML(S, A)$, as well as of $S_k^*(A)$.

Example 1. Let us consider the space $\mathcal{X} = \{x_1, x_2, x_3\}$ and the acts of Table 1. Suppose furthermore that the uncertainty on the states are specified by

$$\mathcal{P} = \{p \in \mathbb{P} : p(x_1) + 2p(x_2) + 3p(x_3) \leq 2, \ p(x_3) \leq 0.3\} \tag{4}$$

Table 2 gives the values of $\overline{\mathbb{E}}(a_j - a_i), \forall j \neq i$. According to this table, we have $D_M(A) = \{a_1, a_2, a_3, a_4\}$ and

Table 1. Acts of Example 1.

	x_1	x_2	x_3
a_1	6	3	1
a_2	2	7	4
a_3	5	1	8
a_4	5	4	3
a_5	1	2	6

Table 2. Values of $\overline{\mathbb{E}}(a_j - a_i)$.

$\overline{\mathbb{E}}(a_j - a_i)$	$i = 1$	$i = 2$	$i = 3$	$i = 4$	$i = 5$
$j = 1$	–	4.0	2.0	1.0	5.0
$j = 2$	4.0	–	6.0	3.0	5.0
$j = 3$	1.4	3.3	–	1.5	4.0
$j = 4$	1.0	3.0	3.0	–	4.0
$j = 5$	−0.4	−0.1	1.0	−1.1	–

- $S_1^*(A) = \{a_4\}$ with $mML\,(S_1^*) = 3$,
- $S_2^*(A) = \{a_1, a_2\}$ with $mML\,(S_2^*) = 1.4$,
- $S_3^*(A) = \{a_1, a_2, a_3\}$ or $\{a_2, a_3, a_4\}$ with $mML\,(S_3^*) = 1$ and
- $S_4^*(A) = \{a_1, a_2, a_3, a_4\}$ with $mML\,(S_4^*) = -1.1$.

From Example 1, we have that $S_k^*(A) \not\subseteq S_{k+1}^*(A)$, therefore showing that a greedy approach iteratively picking the next best option to build $S_{k+1}(A)$ from $S_k(A)$ will not be optimal in general which is unfortunate, as such property might help constructing efficient computational algorithms that for instance iteratively increase k. Also, $S_3^*(A)$ is not unique. The result also agrees with Theorem 1 that once $S_k(A)$ reaches the negative value of mML, then $S_k(A)$ is a superset of $D_M(A)$. Suppose we want to find $S_k^*(A)$ with respect to the mML criteria within a given set of acts A of size $n \geq k$. One may then wonder whether we have to verify all possible sets S of size k, of which there are $\binom{n}{k}$, to obtain the minimum of $mML(S, A)$. Fortunately, we can do it without checking all such sets. Let us consider the previous example and see how it can be obtained, with the formal procedure provided by Algorithm 1. Basically, it relies on the fact that the minimum of $mML(S, A)$ is reached at a specific alternative.

Example 2. From Example 1, recall the values of $\overline{\mathbb{E}}(a_j - a_i)$ for all $a_j \neq a_i$ that are given in Table 2. For $k = 1$, we notice that $S_1^*(A) = \{a_{i*}\}$, where

$$i^* = \arg \min_{i=1}^{5} \max_{j=1, j\neq i}^{5} \overline{\mathbb{E}}(a_j - a_i)$$

which can be simply obtained by searching, for each i, the maximal value of $\overline{\mathbb{E}}(a_j - a_i)$ over $j \neq i$ and then finding the minimal value among maximal values that we have. In this case, $i^* = 4$ so $S_1^*(A) = \{a_4\}$

For $k = 2$, even though there are $\binom{5}{2} = 10$ sets of size 2 that we have to consider, we do not need to search all these sets. Let $a_{i*} \in S_2^*(A)$ be such that

$$a_{i*} = \arg \min_{a_i \in S_2^*(A)} \max_{a_j \in A \setminus S_2^*(A)} \overline{\mathbb{E}}(a_j - a_i).$$

We observe that a_{i*} is obtained at the minimal value of the second highest value of $\overline{\mathbb{E}}(a_j - a_i)$ (circled values in Table 3). This is because we are looking at the a_i that attains the minimal value of $\overline{\mathbb{E}}(a_j - a_i)$ for which a_j is different from a_i.

Table 3. Second highest values of $\overline{\mathbb{E}}(a_j - a_i)$ for each a_i (values in circle).

$\overline{\mathbb{E}}(a_j - a_i)$	$i = 1$	$i = 2$	$i = 3$	$i = 4$	$i = 5$
$j = 1$	–	4.0	2.0	1.0	5.0
$j = 2$	[4.0]	–	6.0	3.0	(5.0)
$j = 3$	(1.4)	(3.3)	–	(1.5)	4.0
$j = 4$	1.0	3.0	(3.0)	–	4.0
$j = 5$	−0.4	−0.1	1.0	−1.1	–

Table 4. Third highest values of $\overline{\mathbb{E}}(a_j - a_i)$ for each a_i (values in circle).

$\overline{\mathbb{E}}(a_j - a_i)$	$i = 1$	$i = 2$	$i = 3$	$i = 4$	$i = 5$
$j = 1$	–	4.0	(2.0)	(1.0)	5.0
$j = 2$	[4.0]	–	6.0	[3.0]	5.0
$j = 3$	[1.4]	3.3	–	[1.5]	(4.0)
$j = 4$	(1.0)	(3.0)	3.0	–	4.0
$j = 5$	−0.4	−0.1	1.0	−1.1	–

In this case we have $a_{i^*} = a_1$ which can be obtained only if a_2 is also in $S_2^*(A)$. Otherwise, a_1 will not attain the minimum, as $\overline{\mathbb{E}}(a_2 - a_1) > 1.4$. Therefore, once we find the a_{i^*} that attains the minimal value of the second highest value of $\overline{\mathbb{E}}(a_j - a_i)$, the a_j such that $\overline{\mathbb{E}}(a_j - a_{i^*})$ is larger than the second highest values of a_{i^*} is also in $S_2^*(A)$ (boxed value in Table 3).

We can use the same argument for $S_3^*(A)$, and in fact $S_k^*(A)$ for any k. Specifically, for each a_i, we look at the kth highest value of $\overline{\mathbb{E}}(a_j - a_i)$, find the minimum of these values say achieved at a_{i^*}, and then take all a_j such that $\overline{\mathbb{E}}(a_j - a_{i^*})$ is larger than this minimum. For instance, in this case, for $k = 3$, $a_{i^*} = a_1$ or a_4. Again, these a_{i^*} can attain the minimum of $S_3^*(A)$ if all a_j such that $\overline{\mathbb{E}}(a_j - a_{i^*})$ is larger than the third highest values of a_{i^*} are also in $S_3^*(A)$. Thus, for selecting $a_{i^*} = a_1$, we have $S_3^*(A) = \{a_1, a_2, a_3\}$ and for selecting $a_{i^*} = a_4$, we have $S_3^*(A) = \{a_2, a_3, a_4\}$ (Table 4).

We now translate this argument into an algorithm that can find $S_k^*(A)$. Specifically, for each $a_i \in A$, we first compute $e_{ij} := \overline{\mathbb{E}}(a_j - a_i), \forall j \neq i$, and assign set $S[i]$ such that for all $j \in S[i]$, e_{ij} are the k largest elements of $\{e_{ij} : j \neq i\}$. Then, we calculate $M[i] = \min_{j \in S[i]} e_{ij}$ and $J[i] = \arg\min_{j \in S[i]} e_{ij}$. Next, we compute $i^* = \arg\min_{i=1}^{n} M[i]$. Finally, we have $S_k^*(A) = \{a_{i^*}\} \cup \{a_j : S[i^*] \setminus \{J[i^*]\}\}$. This process is summarised in Algorithm 1.

The set $S[i]$ can be obtained through a partial sort, which can be much faster than a regular sort especially for small values of k. A partial sorting

Algorithm 1. Finding $S_k^*(A)$

Input: $A = \{a_1, a_2, \ldots, a_n\}$, $\mathcal{P}$, k
Output: $S_k^*(A)$, $mML(S_k^*(A), A)$
1: **for** $i = 1: n$ **do**
2:    **for** $j = 1: n$, $j \neq i$ **do**
3:       compute $e_{ij} := \overline{\mathbb{E}}(a_j - a_i)$
4:    **end for**
5: **end for**
6: **for** $i = 1: n$ **do**
7:    $S[i] \leftarrow$ set such that $\{e_{ij} : j \in S[i]\}$ are the k largest elements of $\{e_{ij} : j \neq i\}$
8:    $M[i] \leftarrow \min_{j \in S[i]} e_{ij}$
9:    $J[i] \leftarrow \arg\min_{j \in S[i]} e_{ij}$
10: **end for**
11: $i^* \leftarrow \arg\min_{i=1}^{n} M[i]$
12: **return** $\{a_j : j \in \{i^*\} \cup S[i^*] \setminus \{J[i^*]\}\}$, $M[i^*]$

algorithm will normally also immediately give $M[i]$ (i.e. the value of the kth largest element). The algorithm can be easily adapted to perform a full sort instead of just finding the k largest elements. A full sorting can then be used to find $S_k^*(A)$ for all possible values of k simultaneously, with very little additional computational effort.

The process could be sped up further by presorting the acts a_j first by expectation with respect to $\mathbb{E}_p(a_j)$ for some $p \in \mathcal{P}$. A similar technique was shown to be very effective in the context of maximality [11].

Provided upper natural extensions $\overline{\mathbb{E}}(a_j - a_i)$ for all $j \neq i$ are all available, the (partial) sorting in Algorithm 1 is much faster (a full sort of n elements typically takes $\mathcal{O}(n \log(n))$ comparisons, and we need to do this n times) than directly searching throughout all possibilities sets of choosing. However the task to evaluate $n(n-1)$ upper natural extensions $\overline{\mathbb{E}}(a_j - a_i)$ for all $j \neq i$ may still be challenging if n is quite high, which is particularly true for combinatorial problems, where adding an element (e.g., a node to a graph) may lead to an exponential increase of $|A|$.

One way to circumvent this needs is to be able to find $\max_{a_j \in A \setminus S_2^*} \overline{\mathbb{E}}(a_j - a_i)$ without a complete enumeration, something that is sometimes doable in structured problems [3]. In this case, one solution could either be to simply sample a reasonable number of alternatives from A, and use the fact that $\max_{a_j \in A \setminus S_2^*} \overline{\mathbb{E}}(a_j - a_i)$ can be evaluated without enumerating the whole set A to greedily add sampled alternatives to the set of k returned alternatives. This is why in further experiments, we include results of the greedy algorithm, denoted by $S_k^g(A)$, and compare them with the non-greedy, global optimal solution.

3.3 Weak Consistency of S_k^* and D_{mML}^k

Let us now show that S_k^* (and consequently, also D_{mML}^k) is weakly consistent with maximality. Weak consistency for A that satisfy $mML(S_k^*(A), A) < 0$

follows from Corollary 1, so we are left to consider the case $mML\left(S_k^*(A),\ A\right) \geq 0$. The proof uses the observations we have made to obtain Algorithm 1.

Theorem 2. *For any k and A, if $mML\left(S_k^*(A),\ A\right) \geq 0$ then $S_k^*(A) \cap D_M(A) \neq \emptyset$.*

Proof. For brevity, define $S := S_k^*(A)$ and $S' := A \setminus S_k^*(A)$. Suppose that $mML(S,\ A) \geq 0$. Let

$$a_{i*} := \arg \min_{a_i \in S}\ \max_{a_j \in S'} \overline{\mathbb{E}}\left(a_j - a_i\right), \tag{5}$$

$$a_{j*} := \arg \max_{a_j \in S'} \overline{\mathbb{E}}\left(a_j - a_{i*}\right). \tag{6}$$

Note that

$$0 \leq mML\left(S,\ A\right) = \min_{a_i \in S}\ \max_{a_j \in S'} \overline{\mathbb{E}}(a_j - a_i) = \overline{\mathbb{E}}\left(a_{j*} - a_{i*}\right), \tag{7}$$

and it follows that

$$\overline{\mathbb{E}}\left(a_{j*} - a_{i*}\right) \geq 0, \tag{8}$$

$$\forall a_j \in S',\ \overline{\mathbb{E}}\left(a_j - a_{i*}\right) \leq \overline{\mathbb{E}}\left(a_{j*} - a_{i*}\right) \tag{9}$$

$$\forall a_i \in A,\ \forall j \in S[i],\ \overline{\mathbb{E}}\left(a_j - a_i\right) \geq \overline{\mathbb{E}}\left(a_{j*} - a_{i*}\right) \tag{10}$$

where $S[i]$ is defined as in the algorithm. Equation (10) holds because, from the algorithm, we know that

$$M[i] = \min_{j \in S[i]} \overline{\mathbb{E}}\left(a_j - a_i\right) \geq M[i^*] = \overline{\mathbb{E}}\left(a_{j*} - a_{i*}\right) \tag{11}$$

We have now everything in place to show that a_{i*} is maximal, i.e. $\overline{\mathbb{E}}\left(a_{i*} - a_\ell\right) \geq 0$ for all $a_\ell \in A$. Fix any $a_\ell \in A$ and consider the set

$$B := \{a_m : \overline{\mathbb{E}}\left(a_m - a_\ell\right) \geq \overline{\mathbb{E}}\left(a_{j*} - a_{i*}\right)\} \tag{12}$$

This set has at least k elements by Eq. (10). If $a_{i*} \in B$, then we are done, by Eq. (8). Otherwise, B must contain at least one element outside of S and thus in S', since S has exactly k elements and $a_{i*} \in S$. Choose $a_m \in B \cap S'$. Then

$$\overline{\mathbb{E}}\left(a_{i*} - a_\ell\right) \geq \overline{\mathbb{E}}\left(a_m - a_\ell\right) - \overline{\mathbb{E}}\left(a_m - a_{i*}\right)$$

$$= \underbrace{\overline{\mathbb{E}}\left(a_m - a_\ell\right) - \overline{\mathbb{E}}\left(a_{j*} - a_{i*}\right)}_{\text{non-negative by Eq. (12)}} + \underbrace{\overline{\mathbb{E}}\left(a_{j*} - a_{i*}\right) - \overline{\mathbb{E}}\left(a_m - a_{i*}\right)}_{\text{non-negative by Eq. (9)}} \geq 0.$$

and thus, in this case, the desired inequality also holds.   □

We then have the following corollaries from Theorem 2 and Corollary 1.

Corollary 2. S_k^* *and* D_{mML}^k *are weakly consistent with* D_M.

Corollary 3. S_1^* *and* D_{mML}^1 *are strongly consistent with* D_M.

4   Metric-Based Budgeted Decision Rule

We now discuss an alternative to regret-based rules, by considering a metric argument according to which one selects alternatives that are the most dissimilar to one another. However, a naive application of this criterion may actually selects options without any considerations for their possible optimality, as will demonstrate our experiments in Sect. 5. For this reason, metric-based budgeted decision rule should only be used once good options have already been selected, typically by first applying a decision rule filtering sub-optimal options, e.g., by first applying D_M to $\mathcal{A}$.

4.1   Definition

We now consider a different angle, where we want retained alternatives to cover as much as possible the space of all possible alternatives. The underlying idea is that retained alternatives should be as diverse as possible, so as to expose the decision maker to varied options. For this, we will try to maximise the distances between alternatives, given our knowledge represented by $\mathcal{P}$. The underlying idea is close to the one of space filling designs [8], where one tries to find samples that provide maximal coverage of a given space.

For easy of notation, for any act a, let $|a|$ be the act defined by $|a|(x) := |a(x)|$ for all $x \in \mathcal{X}$. For any pair of alternatives a and a', $\overline{\mathbb{E}}(|a - a'|)$ as a function of a and a' defines a pseudo-metric between alternatives. It is clearly non-negative and symmetric. Moreover, it satisfies the triangle inequality since $\overline{\mathbb{E}}(|a - a''|) \leq \overline{\mathbb{E}}(|a - a'|) + \overline{\mathbb{E}}(|a' - a''|)$ [15, Sect. 2.6.1]. Thus, $\overline{\mathbb{E}}(|a - a'|)$ is a pseudometric on the set of all acts.

Note that, for all $p \in \mathcal{P}$,

$$|\mathbb{E}_p(a) - \mathbb{E}_p(a')| \leq \overline{\mathbb{E}}(|a - a'|)$$

Thus, $\overline{\mathbb{E}}(|a - a'|)$ is a measure of how different a and a' are with respect to expectation. Usually, maximizing dispersion only makes sense as a security criterion, i.e. in practice we want to apply it after we have already calculated the set of optimal decisions, to reduce the size of the optimal set whilst maximizing dispersion. Finding the pair of alternatives in A that are the most different according to this pseudometric comes down to find a pair of a_{i*} and a_{j*} such that

$$\overline{\mathbb{E}}(|a_{i*} - a_{j*}|) = \max_{a_i, a_j \in A, \ i<j} \overline{\mathbb{E}}(|a_i - a_j|)$$

A value function for a given set S could then be the sum of the pairwise distances, i.e.,

$$MS(S) = \sum_{a_i, a_j \in S, \ i<j} \overline{\mathbb{E}}(|a_i - a_j|)$$

that we would like to maximise, in order to select those alternatives that are far apart from each other. Consider a decision rule D returning k alternatives such that these k alternatives are spread over the set of acts.

$$D_{MS}^k(A) = \arg \max_{S \in \mathcal{A}_k} MS(S) \tag{13}$$

Table 5. Acts of Example 3.

	x_1	x_2	x_3
a_1	8	9	3
a_2	1	5	4
a_3	8	2	6
a_4	3	1	2
a_5	5	4	9

Table 6. Pairwise distance for Example 3.

$\overline{\mathbb{E}}\left(\lvert a_i - a_j\rvert\right)$	$j=2$	$j=3$	$j=4$	$j=5$
$i=1$	7.0	7.0	8.0	5.0
$i=2$	–	7.0	4.0	4.3
$i=3$	–	–	5.0	6.0
$i=4$	–	–	–	3.9

One can readily see that MS is an increasing function, meaning that if we restrict ourselves to sets of size k, the maximum of (13) will be reached for a set of size k. We can therefore restrict our attention to those. Note that this rule cannot handle the case $k = 1$, for which one can simply take S_1^* as a solution.

4.2   Example and Computation

Example 3. Consider a space $\mathcal{X} = \{x_1, x_2, x_3\}$ together with the actions provided in Table 5 and the credal set given by Eq. (4). The values $\overline{\mathbb{E}}\left(\lvert a_i - a_j\rvert\right)$ for all $i < j$ are given in Table 6.

According to the result, we find that

- $D_{MS}^2 = \{a_1, a_4\}$ with $MS(D_{MS}^2) = 8$,
- $D_{MS}^3 = \{a_1, a_2, a_3\}$ with $MS(D_{MS}^3) = 21$ and
- $D_{MS}^4 = \{a_1, a_2, a_3, a_4\}$ with with $MS(D_{MS}^4) = 38$.

We see that $D_{MS}^2 \not\subseteq D_{MS}^3$. Therefore, $D_{MS}^k \not\subseteq D_{MS}^{k+1}$, from which we can conclude that a greedy algorithm will again not be optimal in general. However, unlike the regret-based approach, we were unable to find an efficient algorithm to directly find D_{MS}^k, and it is therefore quite relevant to study the quality of the answer provided by a greedy approach, summarised in Algorithm 2. Note that for $k = 2$, $D_{MS}^k = D_{gMS}^k$. Also note that only a_1 and a_3 are maximal, so this example also verifies the behaviour that maximizing dispersion captures non-maximal options too. Despite seeing this result, we would like to see how much D_{MS}^k and its greedy approximation can capture the maximal elements or being consistency with maximality, which will be investigate in Sect. 5.

4.3   On Some Properties of D_{gMS}^k

When maximising a value function (here MS) under cardinality constraint (here k), submodularity is a property guaranteeing the quality of greedy approximation [9]. Recall that a set function f is submodular iff $f(S \cup \{v\}) - f(S) \geq f(T \cup \{v\}) - f(T)$ whenever $S \subseteq T$. Unfortunately, we can show that MS has the reverse, supermodularity property.

Algorithm 2. Greedy approximation of D_{MS}^k

Input: A, $\mathcal{P}$, k, where $k \geq 2$
Output: an approximate solution of $D_{MS}^k(A)$
1: $D_{gMS}^k \leftarrow \emptyset$
2: **for** $i = 1: n - 1$ **do**
3:     **for** $j = 2: n$ **do**
4:        compute $\overline{\mathbb{E}}\left(|a_i - a_j|\right), \forall i < j$
5:     **end for**
6: **end for**
7: $D_{gMS}^k \leftarrow \arg\max_{a_i, a_j \in A} \overline{\mathbb{E}}\left(|a_i - a_j|\right), \forall i < j$
8: **while** $|D_{gMS}^k| < k$ **do**
9:     $a^* \leftarrow \arg\max_{a_j \in A \setminus D_{gMS}^k} \left(\sum_{a_i \in D_{gMS}^k} \overline{\mathbb{E}}\left(|a_i - a_j|\right)\right), \forall i < j$
10:     $D_{gMS}^k \leftarrow D_{gMS}^k \cup \{a^*\}$
11: **end while**
12: **return** D_{gMS}^k ▷ an approximate solution of D_{MS}^k

---

Lemma 2. *If $S_1 \subseteq S_2$, then*

$$MS(S_2 \cup \{a_k\}) - MS(S_2) \geq MS(S_1 \cup \{a_k\}) - MS(S_1) \tag{14}$$

Proof. Without loss of generality, let's k be an index such that $k > j$ for all $a_j \in S_2$.

$$(MS(S_2 \cup \{a_k\}) - MS(S_2)) - (MS(S_1 \cup \{a_k\}) - MS(S_1)) =$$
$$\sum_{a_i \in S_2} \overline{\mathbb{E}}\left(|a_i - a_k|\right) - \sum_{a_i \in S_1} \overline{\mathbb{E}}\left(|a_i - a_k|\right) = \sum_{a_i \in S_2 \setminus S_1} \overline{\mathbb{E}}\left(|a_i - a_k|\right) \geq 0.$$

□

Since MS is positive, monotone increasing but supermodular, there is no guarantee on polynomial-time constant approximating algorithm for maximizing MS with respect to a maximum cardinality of size k. Nevertheless, in the next section, we will perform an experiment to see how close the outcomes of the greedy algorithm are to the optimal solutions.

5 First Experimentation

In this section, we will perform some first experiments to compare S_k^*, D_{MS}^k and their greedy approximations S_k^g and D_{gMS}^k. Each set will be checked for consistency with respect to maximality. Specifically, we would like to find out how much S_k^*, S_k^g, D_{MS}^k and D_{gMS}^k can capture maximal alternatives in the set D_M. In addition, we will measure the quality of the greedy approximations. Note that we do not consider case $k = 1$ since by Corollaries 2 and 3, S_1^* is weakly and strongly consistent with D_M while the size of D_{MS}^k requires $k \geq 2$.

We fix $|A| = 20$, $|\mathcal{X}| = 5$ and $k \in \{2, \ldots, 6\}$. Throughout the experiment, we consider the credal set $\mathcal{P}$ that satisfies the following condition:

$$p(x_1) + p(x_2) + p(x_3) + p(x_4) + p(x_5) = 1$$
$$3p(x_1) + 2p(x_2) + p(x_3) + p(x_4) + p(x_5) \leq 1$$
$$p(x_1) \leq 0.3, 0.1 \leq p(x_2), 0.2 \leq p(x_3) \leq 0.4$$

We generate a set of alternatives A on $\mathcal{X}$ as follows. For each x_j, we sample $a_i(x_j)$ uniformly from $(0, 1)$. Then, we compute $\overline{\mathbb{E}}(a_j - a_i)$ for all $a_i, a_j \in A$ with respect to the credal set $\mathcal{P}$. Next, for each A, we find D_M and check whether $|D_M| > k$ or not. If $|D_M| \leq k$, then we regenerate A since we are not interested in this case due to S_k^* simply returning D_M. Otherwise, we compute S_k^*, S_k^g, D_{MS}^k and D_{gMS}^k with respect to A. Next, we verify whether S_k^*, S_k^g, D_{MS}^k and D_{gMS}^k are weakly consistent or strongly consistent with D_M or not. As being weakly (having only one maximal element in the set) and strongly (having all elements in the set being maximal) consistent are two extreme situations, we also calculate the proportion of alternatives in S_k^*, S_k^g, D_{MS}^k and D_{gMS}^k that are in D_M. The process was repeated 500 times. The percentages of these sets that satisfy the properties and the average percentages of elements in these sets that are in D_M are presented in the 3rd-5th columns of Table 7. As expected from the result, unlike S_k^* and S_k^g, D_{MS}^k and D_{gMS}^k are not guaranteed to be weakly consistency and rarely strongly consistency with D_M. In addition, the average percentages of maximal elements in D_{MS}^k and D_{gMS}^k are much smaller than in S_k^* and S_k^g. This result confirms our earlier comment that applying D_{MS}^k and D_{gMS}^k to obtain sets of size k makes little sense if we do not start with an optimal set, and that maximizing dispersion should only serve as a refinement of another rule.

To see how S_k^g is close to S_k^* and D_{gMS}^k is close to D_{MS}^k, we also compare the optimal solution with their greedy approximations. Specifically, for each iteration, we count how many time $S_k^g = S_k^*$ and $D_{gMS}^k = D_{MS}^k$. The percentages of these sets that satisfy this condition is presented in the 6th column. We also calculate the proportion of elements in S_k^g that are in S_k^* and the proportion of elements in D_{gMS}^k that are in D_{MS}^k and present the average of the proportions in the 7th column. Finally, we calculate $mML(S_k^g)/mML(S_k^*)$ and $MS(D_{gMS}^k)/MS(D_{MS}^k)$ and present the averages of these ratios in the last column of Table 7. While the greedy approximation of S_k^* quickly degrade as k increases, this is not the case for D_{MS}^k, with the greedy set often being pretty close in terms of quality to the optimal set. This is rather good news, as we do not have an efficient algorithm at our disposal to compute D_{MS}^k.

Table 7. Percentages and averages of S_k^*, S_k^g, D_{MS}^k and D_{gMS}^k that satisfy different conditions.

D^k	k	w.c	s.c	$\dfrac{|D^k \cap D_M|}{|D^k|}$			
S_k^*	2	100%	100%	100%	$S_k^* = S_k^g$	$\dfrac{|S_k^g \cap S_k^*|}{|S_k^g|}$	$\dfrac{mML(S_k^g)}{mML(S_k^*)}$
	3	100%	92.6%	97.5%			
	4	100%	81.0%	97.5%			
	5	100%	68.4%	94.9%			
	6	100%	55.8%	91.1%			
S_k^g	2	100%	90.2%	95.1%	24.8%	60.9%	0.841
	3	100%	74.2%	90.1%	5.2%	52.7%	0.721
	4	100%	60.8%	88.1%	1.8%	52.9%	0.651
	5	100%	44.8%	84.8%	0.4%	53.2%	0.569
	6	100%	33.2%	83.0%	0.4%	56.3%	0.509
D_{MS}^k	2	86.4%	15.4%	50.9%	$D_{MS}^k = D_{gMS}^k$	$\dfrac{|D_{gMS}^k \cap D_{MS}^k|}{|D_{gMS}^k|}$	$\dfrac{MS(D_{gMS}^k)}{MS(D_{MS}^k)}$
	3	96.6%	6.0%	51.9%			
	4	99.8%	1.8%	54.2%			
	5	100%	0.2%	52.4%			
	6	100%	0.4%	55.0%			
D_{gMS}^k	2	86.4%	15.4%	50.9%	100%	100%	1.000
	3	95.2%	5.0%	51.5%	52.4%	71.9%	0.986
	4	99.8%	1.8%	53.7%	44.4%	75.1%	0.987
	5	99.8%	0.6%	52.4%	41.0%	79.9%	0.991
	6	99.8%	1.0%	52.2%	36.4%	82.1%	0.993

6   Discussion and Conclusion

In this study, we have introduced k-budgeted decision rules that return an optimal subset of size k according to some value function. We have adopted two different views: one where we consider a regret-based argument, and the other where we want to have alternatives that are well-dispersed in the space of alternatives. This second approach is very close in spirit to some recent work bearing on E-admissibility (another well-known decision rule) [7] as well as to space-filling designs.

Concerning future work, we could look at other possibilities in each direction drafted in this paper. For instance, one could look for an alternative to Eq. (3) where the maximisation is done before the minimisation (i.e., the opponent chooses the alternative within $A \setminus S$ before we pick our alternative within S).

Similarly, one could replace the sum with a minimum in Eq. (13). Finally, as we hinted already in the paper, it would be interesting to look at situations where the alternatives are too numerous to be explicitly listed/treated, and where even estimating $\overline{\mathbb{E}}\,(a_i - a_j)$ for every pair would be computationally prohibitive.

From a more practical perspective, it would be useful to do more complete and varied experiments, even if those we conducted already allowed us to highlight several aspects of our proposals. In addition, it would be interesting to apply those rules to actual problems such as uncertainty elicitation or system design, where the decision maker can only scrutinise and analyse a limited number of options.

Acknowledgements. Work by NN was supported by CMU Junior Research Fellowship Program, and the SAFE AI chair funded by the Fondation UTC pour l'innovation. This work was also supported by ANR grant PreServe (ANR-18-CE23-0008).

References

1. Augustin, T., Coolen, F.P., de Cooman, G., Troffaes, M.C.: Introduction to Imprecise Probabilities. Wiley (2014)
2. Bains, H., Madariaga, A., Troffaes, M.C., Kazemtabrizi, B.: An economic model for offshore transmission asset planning under severe uncertainty. Renew. Energy **160**, 1174–1184 (2020)
3. Benabbou, N., Perny, P.: Interactive resolution of multiobjective combinatorial optimization problems by incremental elicitation of criteria weights. EURO J. Decis. Process. **6**(3), 283–319 (2018)
4. Chzhen, E., Denis, C., Hebiri, M., Lorieul, T.: Set-valued classification-overview via a unified framework. arXiv preprint arXiv:2102.12318 (2021)
5. Destercke, S.: Multilabel predictions with sets of probabilities: the hamming and ranking loss cases. Pattern Recogn. **48**(11), 3757–3765 (2015)
6. Huntley, N., Troffaes, M.: Normal form backward induction for decision trees with coherent lower previsions. Ann. Oper. Res. **195**(1), 111–134 (2012). https://doi.org/10.1007/s10479-011-0968-2
7. Jansen, C., Georg, S., Thomas, A.: Quantifying degrees of e-admissibility in decision making with imprecise probabilities (2018)
8. Joseph, V.R.: Space-filling designs for computer experiments: a review. Qual. Eng. **28**(1), 28–35 (2016)
9. Krause, A., Golovin, D.: Submodular function maximization. Tractability **3**, 71–104 (2014)
10. Nakharutai, N.: Algorithms for generating sets of gambles for decision making with lower previsions. In: Huynh, V.N., Entani, T., Jeenanunta, C., Inuiguchi, M., Yenradee, P. (eds.) Integrated Uncertainty in Knowledge Modelling and Decision Making, pp. 62–71. Springer International Publishing, Cham (2020). https://doi.org/10.1007/978-3-030-62509-2_6
11. Nakharutai, N., Troffaes, M.C.M., Caiado, C.C.S.: Improving and benchmarking of algorithms for decision making with lower previsions. Int. J. Approximate Reason. **113**, 91–105 (2019). https://doi.org/10.1016/j.ijar.2019.06.008
12. Troffaes, M.: Decision making under uncertainty using imprecise probabilities. Int. J. Approximate Reason. **45**, 17–29 (2007)

13. Utkin, L.V.: An imprecise extension of svm-based machine learning models. Neurocomputing **331**, 18–32 (2019)
14. Viappiani, P., Boutilier, C.: On the equivalence of optimal recommendation sets and myopically optimal query sets. Artif. Intell. **286**, 103328 (2020)
15. Walley, P.: Statistical Reasoning with Imprecise Probabilities. Chapman and Hall, New York (1991)

An Improvement of Random Node Generator for the Uniform Generation of Capacities

Peiqi Sun[1(✉)], Michel Grabisch[1,2], and Christophe Labreuche[3]

[1] Université Paris I-Panthéon-Sorbonne, Paris, France
peiqisun94@gmail.com, michel.grabisch@univ-paris1.fr
[2] Paris School of Economics, Paris, France
[3] Thales Research and Technology, Palaiseau, France
christophe.labreuche@thalesgroup.com

Abstract. Capacity is an important tool in decision-making under risk and uncertainty and multi-criteria decision-making. When learning a capacity-based model, it is important to be able to generate uniformly a capacity. Due to the monotonicity constraints of a capacity, this task reveals to be very difficult. The classical Random Node Generator (RNG) algorithm is a fast-running speed capacity generator, however with poor performance. In this paper, we firstly present an exact algorithm for generating a n elements' general capacity, usable when $n < 5$. Then, we present an improvement of the classical RNG by studying the distribution of the value of each element of a capacity. Furthermore, we divide it into two cases, the first one is the case without any conditions, and the second one is the case when some elements have been generated. Experimental results show that the performance of this improved algorithm is much better than the classical RNG while keeping a very reasonable computation time.

Keywords: Random generation · Capacity · Linear extension

1 Introduction

Capacities and the Choquet integral are widely used in decision making, especially in decision with multiple criteria, where the capacity models the importance of groups of criteria while the Choquet integral is used as a versatile aggregation operator [4,5]. It is often useful in practice to be able to randomly generate capacities, in a uniform way (measure of performance of models, learning/identification phase, etc.). This problem reveals to be surprisingly difficult, because of the monotonicity constraints defining capacities, so that naive approaches yield poor performance and give highly biased distributions.

The theoretical perfect solution to the random generation problem is however known: since the set of capacities is an order polytope, generating capacities in a uniform way amounts to generating all linear extensions of the Boolean

© The Author(s), under exclusive license to Springer Nature Switzerland AG 2022
F. Dupin de Saint-Cyr et al. (Eds.): SUM 2022, LNAI 13562, pp. 202–216, 2022.
https://doi.org/10.1007/978-3-031-18843-5_14

lattice $(2^N, \subseteq)$ [9]. However, the number of linear extensions of $(2^N, \subseteq)$ grows tremendously fast with $n := |N|$, and is even not known beyond $n = 8$. Therefore, approximate solutions have to be found. One way is to generate a sufficiently representative subset of linear extensions: this is the approach taken by Karzanov and Khachiyan using Markov Chains [8], Combarro et al. [1,2], and also the authors of this paper [6]. Another way is to find some simple heuristic for directly generating one by one all the coefficients of a capacity, for example, the random node generator of Havens and Pinar [7]. This generator is very fast but has poor performance, due to the fact that for simplicity the coefficients of a capacity are supposed to follow a uniform distribution on some interval. However, the theoretical distribution of a coefficient is very complex and relies also on linear extensions.

The aim of this paper is to provide an improvement of the random node generator of Havens and Pinar, by taking advantage of some properties of the exact distribution of the coefficients of a capacity. We show that distributions obtained by our method are much closer to the exact distributions or those obtained by the Markov Chain method, while demanding a small computation time, which is much lower than the time required by the Markov Chain method.

The paper is organized as follows: Sect. 2.1 explains the basic facts on the random generation of capacities and describes the random node generator as well as the exact method based on linear extensions. In Sect. 2.2, we investigate the theoretical distribution of the coefficients of a capacity, and in Sect. 2.3 we describe our improved random node generator. Section 3 gives experimental results on the comparison of various methods. Section 4 concludes the paper.

2 Random Node Generator Based on Beta Distribution

2.1 Background

Let P be a finite set, endowed with a partial order $\preccurlyeq$. We say that $(P, \preccurlyeq)$ is a *(finite) poset*. We recall the following notions:

- $x \in P$ is *maximal* if $x \preccurlyeq y$ with $y \in P$ implies $x = y$. We denote by $\mathsf{Max}(P, \preccurlyeq)$ (simply $\mathsf{Max}(P)$) the set of maximal elements of P.
- A *linear extension* of $(P, \preccurlyeq)$ is a total order $\leqslant$ on P which is compatible with the partial order $\preccurlyeq$ in the following sense: $x \preccurlyeq y$ implies $x \leqslant y$.
- The *order polytope* [9] associated to $(P, \preccurlyeq)$, denoted by $\mathcal{O}(P)$, is the set

$$\mathcal{O}(P) = \{f : P \longrightarrow [0,1] \mid f(x) \leqslant f(y) \text{ if } x \preccurlyeq y\}.$$

It is known from Stanley [9] that linear extensions induce a triangulation of $\mathcal{O}(P)$ into simplices of equal volume. Therefore, generating in a random uniform way an element of $\mathcal{O}(P)$ amounts to generating all linear extensions, or to generating them randomly according to a uniform distribution.

We apply this result to capacities. Let $N := \{1, 2, \ldots, n\}$ be a finite set of n elements. A *(normalized) capacity* [3,4,10] on N is a set function $\mu : 2^N \rightarrow [0,1]$

satisfying $\mu(\varnothing) = 0, \mu(N) = 1$ (normalization), and the property $S \subseteq T \Rightarrow \mu(S) \leq \mu(T)$ (monotonicity). It is easy to see that the set of capacities, denoted by $\mathcal{C}(N)$, is an order polytope, whose underlying poset is $(2^N \backslash \{\varnothing, N\}, \subseteq)$. Therefore, the problem of randomly generating capacities according to a uniform distribution amounts to generating the linear extensions of the poset $(2^N \backslash \{\varnothing, N\}, \subseteq)$. For example, for a 3 elements' capacity, $(\{1\}, \{2\}, \{3\}, \{1,2\}, \{1,3\}, \{2,3\})$ is a linear extension of the poset $(2^{\{1,2,3\}} \backslash \{\varnothing, \{1,2,3\}\}, \subseteq)$.

However, the number of linear extensions of $(2^N \backslash \{\varnothing, N\}, \subseteq)$ increases tremendously fast, and is unknown beyond $n = 8$. When $n \leq 4$, it is possible to have an exact algorithm generating all linear extensions, and therefore to generate capacities in a uniform way. We propose below such an algorithm (**Exact-capacity-generator** (ECG)), which is recursive and performs a Depth-First-Search (DFS) finding maximal elements of a poset, which will form the tail of the list describing the linear extension. The following dendrogram of Fig. 1 (right) illustrates the process of the algorithm for a 3 elements' capacity. The maximal element is $\{1, 2, 3\}$, which is the root of the dendrogram (Fig. 1, right), then we continue to find the set of maximal elements of the poset deprived of node $\{1, 2, 3\}$, which is $\{\{1, 2\}, \{1, 3\}, \{2, 3\}\}$, that is the second level of dendrogram. Next, we continue to find the set of maximal elements when each node in the second level of the dendrogram is removed. We repeat the above steps until there is only one element left in the poset to obtain the whole dendrogram.

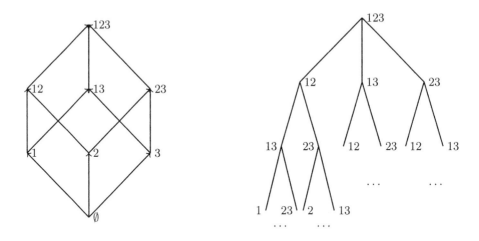

Fig. 1. Case $n = 3$. Left: representation of the poset $(2^N, \subseteq)$. Right: Dendrogram of the maximal elements when running the procedure for generating all linear extensions using the DFS algorithm.

——————————————— Algorithm 1———————————————
Exact-capacity-generator(n, k)

Input: n, k integers.
% k is the number of all linear extensions and $n = |N|$.
Output: k generated capacities on 2^N
% *AllLinear* is an empty array which will contain all linear extensions
1: $count \leftarrow 0$
   % P is an array containing the poset $2^N \setminus \{\varnothing, N\}$
2: **All-linear-extension**$(P, AllLinear, count)$
3: **repeat** k **times**
4:    Select uniformly one linear extension of *AllLinear*
5:    Generate uniformly $2^n - 2$ numbers between 0 and 1, sort them from smallest to largest, and assign them to the selected linear extension
end repeat

——————————————— Algorithm 2———————————————
All-linear-extension$(P, AllLinearExtensions, count)$

%*AllLinearExtensions* stores all linear extensions of P and *count* stores the number of linear extensions
Input: an array P containing a poset of size n, an array *AllLinearExtensions* and *count*
Output: All linear extensions of poset P
6: **If** $|P| = 1$ **then**
    % When the bottom of dendrogram is reached, add an empty linear extension to *AllLinearExtensions*.
7:    Append a zeros array of size n to *AllLinearExtensions*
8:    $AllLinearExtensions[count - 1][n - 1] \leftarrow P[0]$
9:    $count \leftarrow count + 1$
   end if
10: **For** i in Max(P) **do**
11:    Remove i from P
     % recursion algorithm
12:    **All-linear-extension**$(P, AllLinearExtensions, count)$
13:    $AllLinearExtensions[count - 1][\text{size of } P] \leftarrow$ i
14:    Re-insert i to the end of poset P
   end for

When $n > 4$, approximate methods have to be used, either generating randomly linear extensions like the Markov Chain method [8], the 2-level approximation method [6], etc., or based on other principles like the *Random Node generator (RNG) algorithm* introduced by T. C. Havens and A. J. Pinar in [7].

The core idea of this approach is to randomly select one element $S \in 2^N$ among all elements and then draw it with a uniform law between the maximum and minimum values allowed by the monotonicity constraints. This operation is repeated until all elements in 2^N have assigned values.

The most significant advantage of this method is its low complexity and fast running speed. However, theoretically, the capacities generated by it are not uniform, because firstly the range of values for $\mu(S)$ is highly dependent on the rank in which the element S is selected, and secondly the exact distribution of $\mu(S)$ is far from being a uniform distribution. Therefore, this capacity generator has a lot of theoretical undesirabilities.

As an illustration, we compare the performance of the RNG with ECG. The following figures show the distribution of $\mu(S)$ generated by the RNG and ECG.

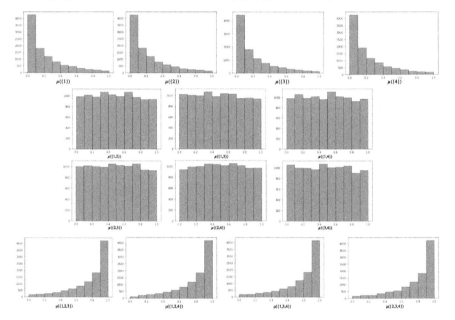

Fig. 2. Case $n = 4$. Histograms of the values of $\mu(S)$, $S \in 2^N \setminus \{N, \varnothing\}$, generated by RNG (compare with Fig. 3 where the exact generator has been used).

From Figs. 2 and 3, we notice that the discrepancy between the distribution of these two groups of μ is significant, and thus we may conclude that the uniformity of the capacity obtained by the Random-Node generator is not satisfactory. In the next subsections, we study the theoretical distribution of $\mu(S)$ and propose an improvement of the Random-Node generator.

2.2   Theoretical Distribution of μ

The main idea for improving the random node generator algorithm is to use a more realistic probabilistic distribution on the generation of the capacity of the current subset S. Let us first describe the probability distribution of such a term.

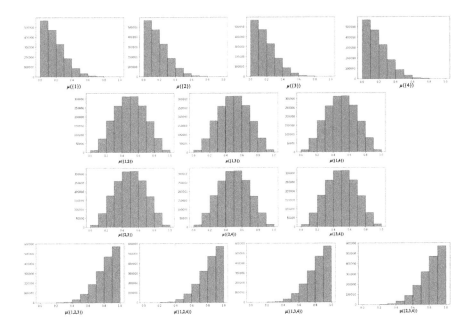

Fig. 3. Case $n = 4$. Histograms of the values of $\mu(S)$, $S \in 2^N \setminus \{N, \varnothing\}$, generated by ECG.

To this end, let us consider a set of i.i.d random variables $\mu_1, \mu_2, \ldots, \mu_m$ that follow the uniform law between 0 and 1. We sort the μ_is into the order statistics $\mu_{(1)} \leq \mu_{(2)} \cdots \leq \mu_{(m)}$. Then $\mu_{(k)}$ follows the Beta distribution $\mu_{(k)} \sim \text{Beta}(k, m - k + 1)$. If we take $\alpha = k, \beta = m - k + 1$, then the formula for the density of $\mu_{(k)}$ is as follows:

$$f_{\mu_{(k)}}(x) = \frac{\Gamma(\alpha + \beta)}{\Gamma(\alpha)\Gamma(\beta)} x^{\alpha - 1}(1 - x)^{\beta - 1},$$

where $\Gamma(\alpha) = \int_0^\infty t^{\alpha - 1}e^{-t}dt$, with $\alpha > 0$.

In order to apply this result to capacities, we need to know the rank of $\mu(S)$ within all terms of a capacity. We denote by $\mathcal{R}\hbar(S)$ the rank of element S ($S \in 2^N$) in a linear extension of poset $(2^N, \subseteq)$. Each element of 2^N has a rank in each linear extension corresponding to the poset, among them $\varnothing$ is always located at the minimal rank, i.e., $\mathcal{R}\hbar(\varnothing) = 0$ and N is always located at the maximal rank, i.e., $\mathcal{R}\hbar(N) = 2^n - 1$.

Then the cumulative distribution function of $\mu(S)$, i.e. $\mathbb{P}(\mu(S) \leq x)$ for $0 < x < 1$, considers the beta distribution over all possible rankings of $\mu(S)$

$$F_{\mu(S)}(x) = \mathbb{P}(\mu(S) \leq x) = \sum_{i=\min(\mathcal{R}k(S))}^{\max(\mathcal{R}k(S))} \mathbb{P}(\mu(S) \leq x | \mathcal{R}k(S) = i) \times \mathbb{P}(\mathcal{R}k(S) = i)$$

$$= \sum_{i=\min(\mathcal{R}k(S))}^{\max(\mathcal{R}k(S))} \mathbb{P}(\mu_{(i)} \leq x) \times \mathbb{P}(\mathcal{R}k(S) = i)$$

$$= \sum_{i=\min(\mathcal{R}k(S))}^{\max(\mathcal{R}k(S))} F_{\mu_{(i)}}(x) \times \mathbb{P}(\mathcal{R}k(S) = i),$$

with $F_{\mu_{(i)}}(x)$ the cumulative distribution function of $\mathrm{Beta}(i, 2^n - 1 - i)$, $\min(\mathcal{R}k(S))$ the smallest possible ranking of $\mu(S)$ and $\max(\mathcal{R}k(S))$ the largest possible ranking of $\mu(S)$. These bounds on the ranking of $\mu(S)$ are simply obtained by the monotonicity condition, counting the minimal number of terms ranked before and after $\mu(S)$. We obtain

$$\min(\mathcal{R}k(S)) = |\{T \subseteq S, T \neq \emptyset\}| = 2^{|S|} - 1$$

$$\max(\mathcal{R}k(S)) = 2^n - |\{T \supseteq S, T \subseteq N\}| = 2^n - 1 - 2^{|N \setminus S|}.$$

The density of $\mu(S)$ is thus:

$$f_{\mu(S)}(x) = \sum_{i=\min(\mathcal{R}k(S))}^{\max(\mathcal{R}k(S))} f_{\mu_{(i)}}(x) \times \mathbb{P}(\mathcal{R}k(S) = i) \tag{1}$$

with $\mu_{(i)} \sim \mathrm{Beta}(i, 2^n - 1 - i)$.

Density (1) is correct when $\mu(S)$ is not constrained by other terms of the capacity. When we use the RNG to generate a capacity, we should adjust the above distribution due to its monotonicity. Supposing we have already generated the elements $S_1, \ldots, S_p$ with the values $\mu(S_1) = a_1, \ldots, \mu(S_p) = a_p$, we wish to draw the distribution of $\mu(S)$ for a new subset S. Compared to (1), the knowledge of $a_1, \ldots, a_p$ provides constraints on both the numerical value of $\mu(S)$ and also its ranking. Following the monotonicity conditions, we first note that the value of $\mu(S)$ shall belong to interval $[\mathsf{Min}_\mathsf{p}\mu(S), \mathsf{Max}_\mathsf{p}\mu(S)]$ where

$$\mathsf{Min}_\mathsf{p}\mu(S) = \max_{j \in \{1,\ldots,p\}, \, S_j \subseteq S} a_j \quad \text{and} \quad \mathsf{Max}_\mathsf{p}\mu(S) = \min_{j \in \{1,\ldots,p\}, \, S_j \supseteq S} a_j.$$

Moreover, as illustrated by the following example, the smallest and largest possible rankings of $\mu(S)$ are also constrained by $a_1, \ldots, a_p$.

Example 1. Assume that we have already generated the following terms $\mu(\{1,2\}) = 0.1$, $\mu(\{1,3\}) = 0.2$ and $\mu(\{4,5\}) = 0.3$, and consider now $S = \{1,4,5\}$ with $N = \{1,2,3,4,5\}$. Subset $\{1,2\}$ and all its subsets are thus ranked before $\{4,5\}$. The same holds for $\{1,3\}$. In total, the subsets that are necessarily ranked before S are the following: $\{1\}, \{2\}, \{1,2\}, \{3\}, \{1,3\}, \{4\}, \{5\}, \{4,5\}, \{1,4\}, \{1,5\}$. Hence S has rank at least 11. □

Generalizing the previous example,

$$\underline{S}_p(S) = \{S_j \,,\, j \in \{1,\ldots,p\} \text{ s.t. } \exists i \in \{1,\ldots,p\}\,,\, S_i \subseteq S \text{ and } a_j \leq a_i\} \cup \{S\}$$

is the set of already generated subsets that are necessarily ranked before S (including S), and

$$\overline{S}_p(S) = \{S_j \,,\, j \in \{1,\ldots,p\} \text{ s.t. } \exists i \in \{1,\ldots,p\}\,,\, S_i \supseteq S \text{ and } a_j \geq a_i\} \cup \{S\}$$

is the set of already generated subsets that are necessarily ranked after S (including S). The smallest possible ranking $\mathrm{Min}_p \mathcal{R}k(S)$ of S is thus given by the number of subsets of $\underline{S}_p(S)$. It is not simply the sum of the subsets of the elements of $\underline{S}_p(S)$ as there are common subsets. In Example 1, subset $\{1\}$ is a subset of $\{1,2\}$, $\{1,3\}$ and $\{1,4,5\}$, and it shall not be counted three times. To this end, we use the Poincaré sieve formula. This formula provides the number of elements of the union of an arbitrary number of sets:

$$\left| \cup_{i=1}^q A_i \right| = \sum_{k=1}^q \left((-1)^{k-1} \sum_{1 \leq i_1 < i_2 < \cdots < i_k \leq q} |A_{i_1} \cap A_{i_2} \cap \cdots \cap A_{i_k}| \right).$$

We apply this formula to $A_j = 2^{\underline{S}_j} \setminus \{\emptyset\}$, where $\underline{S}_p(S) := \{\underline{S}_1,\ldots,\underline{S}_q\}$. As $A_{i_1} \cap \cdots \cap A_{i_k} = 2^{\underline{S}_{i_1} \cap \cdots \cap \underline{S}_{i_k}} \setminus \{\emptyset\}$, we obtain

$$\mathrm{Min}_p \mathcal{R}k(S) = \left| \{T \subseteq \underline{S}_j,\ T \neq \emptyset \text{ and } j \in \{1,\ldots,q\}\} \right|$$

$$= \sum_{k=1}^q \left((-1)^{k-1} \sum_{1 \leq i_1 < i_2 < \cdots < i_k \leq q} \left(2^{\left|\underline{S}_{i_1} \cap \underline{S}_{i_2} \cap \cdots \cap \underline{S}_{i_k}\right|} - 1 \right) \right). \quad (2)$$

Example 2. (Example 1 continued). We obtain $\mathrm{Min}_p \mu(\{1,4,5\}) = 0.3$. Moreover, we have $\underline{S}_p(\{1,4,5\}) = \{\{1,2\},\{1,3\},\{4,5\},\{1,4,5\}\}$. Applying (2), the smallest possible ranking of $\{1,4,5\}$ is

$$\left(2^{|\{1,2\}|} - 1 \right) + \left(2^{|\{1,3\}|} - 1 \right) + \left(2^{|\{4,5\}|} - 1 \right) + \left(2^{|\{1,4,5\}|} - 1 \right)$$

$$- \left(2^{|\{1\}|} - 1 \right) - \left(2^{|\{1\}|} - 1 \right) - \left(2^{|\{1\}|} - 1 \right) - \left(2^{|\{4,5\}|} - 1 \right) + \left(2^{|\{1\}|} - 1 \right)$$

$$= 3 + 3 + 3 + 7 - 1 - 1 - 1 - 3 + 1 = 11.$$

Hence we recover that S has rank at least 11.   □

Likewise, the largest possible ranking $\mathrm{Max}_p \mathcal{R}k(S)$ of S is given by

$$2^n - 1 - \left| \{T \supseteq \overline{S}_j,\ T \neq N \text{ and } j \in \{1,\ldots,q'\}\} \right|,$$

where $\overline{S}_p(S) := \{\overline{S}_1, \ldots, \overline{S}_{q'}\}$. Applying the Poincaré sieve formula to $A_j = \{T \subseteq \overline{S}_j, T \neq N\}$, we obtain $|A_{i_1} \cap \cdots \cap A_{i_k}| = |\{T \supseteq \overline{S}_{i_1}, \ldots, \overline{S}_{i_k}, T \neq N\}| = |\{T \supseteq \overline{S}_{i_1} \cup \cdots \cup \overline{S}_{i_k}, T \neq N\}| = 2^{|N \setminus (\overline{S}_{i_1} \cup \cdots \cup \overline{S}_{i_k})|} - 1$ and

$$\mathsf{Max}_p \mathcal{Rk}(S) = 2^n - 1 - |\{T \supseteq \overline{S}_j, T \neq N \text{ and } j \in \{1, \ldots, q'\}|$$

$$= 2^n - 1 - \sum_{k=1}^{q'} \left((-1)^{k-1} \sum_{1 \leq i_1 < i_2 < \cdots < i_k \leq q'} \left(2^{|N \setminus (\overline{S}_{i_1} \cup \cdots \cup \overline{S}_{i_k})|} - 1 \right) \right). \quad (3)$$

Example 3. Assume that we have already generated the following terms $\mu(\{1,2,3\}) = 0.9$, $\mu(\{1,3,4\}) = 0.8$ and $\mu(\{1,2,4,5\}) = 0.7$, and consider now $S = \{1,2,5\}$ with $N = \{1,2,3,4,5\}$. We obtain $\mathsf{Max}_p \mu(\{1,2,5\}) = 0.7$. Moreover, we have $\overline{S}_p(\{1,2,5\}) = \{\{1,2,3\}, \{1,3,4\}, \{1,2,4,5\}, \{1,2,5\}\}$. The subsets (excluding N) ranked after $\{1,2,5\}$ are $\{1,2,5\}, \{1,2,3,5\}, \{1,2,4,5\}$, $\{1,2,3\}, \{1,2,3,4\}, \{1,3,4\}, \{1,3,4,5\}$. We obtain 7 subsets.

Applying (3), the largest possible ranking of $\{1,2,5\}$ is

$$2^5 - 1 - \left(2^{|\{3,4\}|} - 1 \right) - \left(2^{|\{4,5\}|} - 1 \right) - \left(2^{|\{2,5\}|} - 1 \right) - \left(2^{|\{3\}|} - 1 \right)$$

$$+ \left(2^{|\{5\}|} - 1 \right) + \left(2^{|\{4\}|} - 1 \right) - \left(2^{|\{3\}|} - 1 \right)$$

$$= 2^5 - 1 - 3 - 3 - 3 - 1 + 3 = 2^n - 1 - 7 = 24$$

□

Summarizing, the distribution of $\mu(S)$ becomes a conditional distribution:

$$\mathbb{P}(\mu(S) \leq x | \mu(S_1) = a_1, \ldots, \mu(S_p) = a_p)$$

$$= \sum_{i=min_p \mathcal{Rk}(S)}^{max_p \mathcal{Rk}(S)} \mathbb{P}(\mathcal{Rk}(S) = i | \mu(S_1) = a_1, \ldots, \mu(S_p) = a_p)$$

$$\times \mathbb{P}(\mu(S) = \mu_{(i)} \leq x | \mu(S_1) = a_1, \ldots, \mu(S_p) = a_p) \quad (4)$$

with

$$\mathbb{P}(\mathcal{Rk}(S) = i | \mu(S_1) = a_1, \ldots, \mu(S_p) = a_p)$$
$$\approx \mathbb{P}(\mathcal{Rk}(S) = i | \mathsf{Min}_p \mathcal{Rk}(S) \leq \mathcal{Rk}(S) \leq \mathsf{Max}_p \mathcal{Rk}(S)) \quad (5)$$

and

$$\mathbb{P}(\mu(S) = \mu_{(i)} \leq x | \mu(S_1) = a_1, \ldots, \mu(S_p) = a_p)$$
$$= \mathbb{P}(\mu_{(i)} \leq x | \mathsf{Min}_p \mu(S) \leq \mu_{(i)} \leq \mathsf{Max}_p \mu(S)) \quad (6)$$

2.3   The Improved Random Node Generator

Thanks to the previous considerations and Eqs. (4), (5) and (6), we are in a position to propose an improvement of the random node generator, which we call IRNG.

As explained, our improvement consists in replacing the uniform distribution of $\mu(S)$ in the interval $[\mathrm{Min}_p\mu(S), \mathrm{Max}_p\mu(S)]$ by the distribution given by (4), computed through (5) and (6).

According to Eq. (6), when we assign a value to $\mu(S)$, it should be between $\mathrm{Min}_p\mu(S)$ and $\mathrm{Max}_p\mu(S)$. If this is not satisfied, we need to reject it and reassign a new value to $\mu(S)$.

As for Eq. (5), it is necessary to know the probability $\mathbb{P}(\mathcal{R}k(S) = i)$ for a given subset S to be ranked at ith position in a linear extension. This propability is stored in array $probability$ (where $probability[S][i] = \mathbb{P}(\mathcal{R}k(S) = i)$) in the following algorithm. As the set of linear extensions is not practically reachable beyond $n = 5$ and not known beyond $n = 8$, no practical expression of this probability can be obtained, and it must be estimated. Therefore, the critical issue for the precision of the IRNG algorithm is how to get these probabilities. Our proposition is to use off line some well-performing method to generate randomly in a uniform way linear extensions of $(2^N \setminus \{\varnothing, N\}, \subseteq)$, like the Markov chain method [8], generating a sufficient number of linear extensions from which $\mathbb{P}(\mathcal{R}k(S) = i)$ could be estimated, for every subset S and every rank i. Once we have obtained these probabilities, we store them in a file so that they can be used repeatedly.

——————————————— Algorithm 3———————————
Improved-Random-Node-generator (IRNG)$(P, probability)$

Input: a poset P of $2^N \setminus \{\varnothing, N\}$, a two dimensional array named $probability[S][j]$ containing the probability of element (subset) $S \in 2^N \setminus \{\varnothing, N\}$ to be at rank j.
Output: capacity μ in $\mathcal{C}(N)$ generated with approximation method
1: AssignedElement,AssignedValue $\leftarrow [\ ],[\ ]$
2: $\mu \leftarrow$ a zero array of size $2^n - 2$
    %AssignedElement and AssignedValue store the elements $S_1, \ldots, S_p$
    %and element's value $a_1, \ldots,_p$ that have been already assigned
3: $\mathcal{L} \leftarrow$ an array of elements of $2^N \setminus \{\varnothing, N\}$ in random order
4: $p \leftarrow 0$
5: **for** S in $\mathcal{L}$ **do**
6:      Compute $\mathrm{Min}_p\mu([S]), \mathrm{Max}_p\mu([S])$ and $\mathrm{Min}_p\mathcal{R}k(S), \mathrm{Max}_p\mathcal{R}k(S)$
        % $\mathrm{Min}_p\mathcal{R}k(S), \mathrm{Max}_p\mathcal{R}k(S)$ the ranking restrictions of S
        % and $\mathrm{Min}_p\mu([S]), \mathrm{Max}_p\mu([S])$ the minimum and maximum value of $\mu([S])$
7:      $beta \leftarrow 0$
8:      $\mathrm{Pr}_{min} \leftarrow \sum_{j=0}^{\mathrm{Min}_p\mathcal{R}k(\mu([s]))-1} probability[s][j]$
9:      $\mathrm{Pr}_{max} \leftarrow \sum_{j=\mathrm{Max}_p\mathcal{R}k(\mu([s]))+1}^{2^n-3} probability[s][j]$
10:     **While** $beta \geq \mathrm{Max}_p\mu([s])$ **or** $beta \leq \mathrm{Min}_p\mu([s])$ **do**
        % Capacity should obey monotonicity
11:         $r \sim U([0,1])$
12:         $r \leftarrow \mathrm{Pr}_{min} + (1 - \mathrm{Pr}_{max} - \mathrm{Pr}_{min}) * r$
13:         $Rank \leftarrow \mathrm{Min}_p\mathcal{R}k(S))$

```
14:              Pr ← Pr_min
15:              While r > Pr do
16:                   Pr ← Pr + probability[S][Rank]
17:                   Rank ← Rank + 1
             end while
18:              beta ∼ Beta(Rank, 2^n − 1 − Rank).
        end while
19:     μ[S] ← beta
20:     Append μ[s] to Assignedvalue
21:     Append S to AssignedElement
22:     p ← p + 1
   end for
```

Let us analyze the computational complexity of one run ot IRNG. The $2^n - 2$ subsets are ordered in array $\mathcal{L}$. In $l.5$, we sweep these elements with an index p from $p = 1$ to $p = 2^n - 2$. At iteration p ($l.6 - 22$), the complexity is given by the successive steps:

- $l.6$: the computation of $\mathsf{Min}_p \mu([S])$ and $\mathsf{Max}_p \mu([S])$ requires p operations;
- $l.6$: the computation of $\mathsf{Min}_p \mathcal{R}\hbar(S)$ and $\mathsf{Max}_p \mathcal{R}\hbar(S)$ requires $2^q + 2^{q'} \leq 2^p$ operations (see (2) and (3));
- $l.8 - 9$: the computation of Pr_{min} and Pr_{max} requires at most 2^n operations;
- We assume that the While loop in $l.10$ is run at most M times. The While loop in $l.15$ is run at most 2^n times. Then the complexity of $l.10 - 18$ is $M \times 2^n$.

In total, the complexity of one run of IRNG is $O(2^n)$. The main uncertainty in the computation time is the number of times M the While loop in $l.10$ is run. In the worst case, it could be large if interval $[\mathsf{Min}_p \mu([s]), \mathsf{Max}_p \mu([s])]$ is very small and $Rank$ is not well adapted to this interval. This situation occurs with a low probability.

3   Experimental Results

We compare the performance of the IRNG with the RNG and Markov Chain generator. We apply the Markov Chain method to obtain $\mathbb{P}(\mathcal{R}\hbar(S) = i)$ for all the following experiments. In the experiments, we limit ourselves to $n = 4$ in order to be able to compare the results with the ECG. Figure 4 shows the distribution of $\mu(S)$ generated by the IRNG for $n = 4$.

From Fig. 4, we notice that the distribution of μ generated by the IRNG is much closer to the exact distribution than the one generated with the classical RNG (Fig. 2), and Fig. 5 shows the distribution of μ generated by the Markov Chain generator.

Next, we further compare their performance by calculating the Kullback-Leibler divergence (also called Relative entropy) between the distributions of

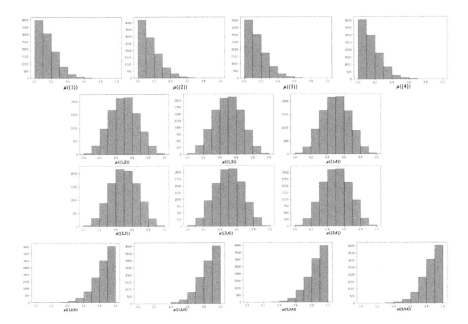

Fig. 4. Case $n = 4$. Histograms of the values of $\mu(S)$, $S \in 2^N \setminus \{N, \varnothing\}$, generated by IRNG (compare with Fig. 3 where the exact generator has been used).

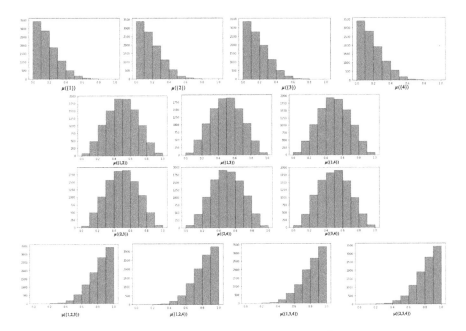

Fig. 5. Case $n = 4$. Histograms of the values of $\mu(S)$, $S \in 2^N \setminus \{N, \varnothing\}$, generated by the Markov chain generator (compare with Fig. 3).

$\mu(S)$ obtained by the exact generator and those obtained by the considered generators, which could be used to estimate the similarity of two distributions.

Recall the definition of Kullback-Leibler divergence:

$$\mathbb{D}_{KL}(p\|q) = \sum_{x \in \mathcal{X}} p(x) \log \frac{p(x)}{q(x)}$$

with p and q two discrete probability distributions defined on the same probability space $\mathcal{X}$.

In our experiments, we need to compare the distribution of $\mu(S)$ generated by the considered generators with the exact distribution of $\mu(S)$. We replace q by the exact distribution of $\mu(S)$ and p by the distribution of $\mu(S)$ obtained by one of these three generators and then compare their value. The smaller the value, the higher the similarity with the exact distribution (shown in Table 1).

Table 2 shows the CPU time of different capacity generators (we have used Python implementations of the algorithms described above and have conducted the experiments on a 3.2 GHz PC with 16 GB of RAM). For the execution time of IRNG, the time required to compute the probabilities in Eq. (5) is not taken into account, as they are computed once for all off line.

Table 1. Kullback-Leibler divergence between the histograms produced by the considered generators and those produced by the exact generator.

capacity generator	$\mu(\{1\})$	$\mu(\{2\})$	$\mu(\{3\})$	$\mu(\{4\})$
RNG	0.4220	0.3651	0.3708	0.3947
IRNG	0.0376	0.0392	0.0356	0.0367
Markov Chain	0.0115	0.0109	0.0097	0.0073

capacity generator	$\mu(\{1,2\})$	$\mu(\{1,3\})$	$\mu(\{1,4\})$	$\mu(\{2,3\})$	$\mu(\{2,4\})$	$\mu(\{3,4\})$
RNG	0.6677	0.6322	0.7401	0.6522	0.6836	0.6375
IRNG	0.0223	0.0187	0.0222	0.0253	0.0178	0.0191
Markov Chain	0.0093	0.0090	0.0110	0.0108	0.0090	0.0102

capacity generator	$\mu(\{1,2,3\})$	$\mu(\{1,2,4\})$	$\mu(\{1,3,4\})$	$\mu(\{2,3,4\})$
RNG	0.3985	0.3818	0.3691	0.3701
IRNG	0.0296	0.0270	0.0270	0.0258
Markov Chain	0.0089	0.0072	0.0081	0.0094

From Table 1, we compute the sum of the Kullback-Leibler divergences for $\mu(S)$ ($\forall S \in 2^N \setminus \{\varnothing, N\}$) for each generator. We obtain that the value for RNG is 7.086, for IRNG is 0.384 and for Markov Chain is 0.132. As can be seen from these results, compared to the RNG, the distribution of μ obtained from

Table 2. Comparison of CPU time for generating 10000 capacities.

Method	Four elements' capacity	Five elements' capacity
RNG	0.425	1.130
IRNG	2.142	16.135
Markov Chain Generator	25.270	243

the IRNG is considerably improved and does not differ significantly from the distribution obtained with the Markov chain generator.

Unlike RNG, IRNG needs to compute $\mathsf{Min_p}\mathscr{R}\hbar(S)$ and $\mathsf{Max_p}\mathscr{R}\hbar(S)$ for each S. Therefore, IRNG is theoretically more complex than RNG, and this difference is reflected in the computation time. However, from Table 2, this difference remains negligible in view of the time required by the Markov chain method, and it can be seen that IRNG is much faster than the Markov Chain Generator. This definitely shows the advantage of IRNG, whose performance is dramatically better than that of RNG, and not much different from that of the Markov Chain Generator.

4   Concluding Remarks

We have proposed an improved version of the random node generator of Havens and Pinar, by investigating in a deeper way the probability distribution of the coefficients $\mu(S)$. The results show that our algorithm yields distributions much closer to the exact ones, compared to the original random node generator, while keeping a very reasonable computation time, much smaller than the one required by the Markov Chain method.

Further studies will be devoted to the generation of special families of capacities, as well as generation under additional constraints on the capacities.

References

1. Combarro, E.F., Díaz, I., Miranda, P.: On random generation of fuzzy measures. Fuzzy Sets Syst. **228**, 64–77 (2013)
2. Combarro, E.F., Hurtado de Saracho, J., Díaz, I.: Minimals Plus: an improved algorithm for the random generation of linear extensions of partially ordered sets. Inf. Sci. **501**, 50–67 (2019)
3. Choquet, G.: Theory of capacities. Ann. Inst. Fourier **5**, 131–295 (1953)
4. Grabisch, M.: Set Functions, Games and Capacities in Decision Making, Theory and Decision Library C, vol. 46. Springer (2016). https://doi.org/10.1007/978-3-319-30690-2
5. Grabisch, M., Labreuche, C.: A decade of application of the Choquet and Sugeno integrals in multi-criteria decision aid. Ann. Oper. Res. **175**, 247–286 (2010). https://doi.org/10.1007/s10479-009-0655-8
6. Grabisch, M., Labreuche, C., Sun, P.: An approximation algorithm for random generation of capacities. arXiv:2206.04774 (2022)

7. Havens, T.C., Pinar, A.J.: Generating random fuzzy (capacity) measures for data-fusion simulations. In: IEEE Symposium Series on Computational Intelligence (IEEE SSCI2017), pp. 1–8 (2017)
8. Karzanov, A., Khachiyan, L.: On the conductance of order Markov chains. Order **8**, 7–15 (1991). https://doi.org/10.1007/BF00385809
9. Stanley, R.: Two poset polytopes. Discret. Comput. Geom. **1**, 9–23 (1986). https://doi.org/10.1007/BF02187680
10. Sugeno, M.: Theory of fuzzy integrals and its applications. Ph.D. thesis, Tokyo Institute of Technology (1974)

Full Papers: Learning

Logical Proportions-Related Classification Methods Beyond Analogy

Myriam Bounhas[1,2(✉)] and Henri Prade[3]

[1] Liwa College of Technology, Abu Dhabi, United Arab Emirates
myriam_bounhas@yahoo.fr
[2] LARODEC Laboratory, Tunis University, Tunis, Tunisia
[3] IRIT – CNRS, 118, route de Narbonne, Toulouse, France
prade@irit.fr

Abstract. This paper can be seen as a challenge to conventional ideas in classification as it proposes new procedures based on *comparative reasoning* from examples. This can be viewed as a basic case-based reasoning task where the class of new items has to be found on the basis of examples with a known class. The comparisons reveal regularities and differences in behavior that lead to solving Bongard problems (problems that amount to find a property common to a set of items but which is wrong for all the elements of another set). The approach that takes advantage of pairs (or triplets) of examples has some kinship with classifiers based on analogical proportions (and other methods using logical proportions of which analogical proportions are a special case), although it differs in important ways. Experiments on Boolean data yield competitive results with respect to standard classification approaches or methods based on logical proportions.

1 Introduction

Classification is usually regarded as a typical machine learning task. The set of examples describing items for which the class is known is generally considered to be a sampling of an unknown probability distribution whose approximation governs the prediction of the class for a new item [8]. This very successful approach has become predominant. However, in this paper we explore the possibility of another paradigm relying on a logical analysis of the data. The use of set theory-based or logic-based views of a set of data is not new and dates back at least to the version space approach [14] in concept learning. More recently, one may cite [3] that investigates the "justifiability" of rule-based classifiers and establishes that decision trees or nearest neighbor-based methods provide justifiable classifiers ; see also [7]. See [9] for an introductory discussion to logic-based approaches to classification.

Classification reasoning is a matter of exploiting and reproducing observed regularities. In this paper, we somewhat depart from the previously mentioned works by taking directly advantage of *comparative reasoning* between data. More precisely, in the following, in order to deal with a classification task, we propose and experiment a procedure that relies on a systematic analysis of the differences between the available examples and another procedure that rather looks for similarities (beyond k-nearest neighbors methods). These procedures can be respectively related to analogical proportion-based classification [4] and to another classification machinery [5] related to other logical proportions (that are quaternary logical connectives involving comparisons inside and between pairs of items). But the proposed procedures differ from these two approaches importantly, as it will be explained.

The paper is structured as follows. Section 2 explains how one can take advantage of the comparison of pieces of data for proposing classification procedures based on pairs or triplets of data. As discussed in Sect. 3 these comparative procedures have characteristics reminiscent of the use of analogical proportions in classification and of other logical proportions [17]. Section 4 details the algorithms that encode the two proposed procedures, while Sect. 5 reports the competitive results obtained and compares them to those of classifiers based on logical proportions.

2   Differences and Similarities in Classification

Let us consider a set of examples $\mathcal{E} = \{(\mathbf{x^i}, cl(\mathbf{x^i})) \mid i = 1, \cdots, m\}$, where $\mathbf{x^i} = (x^i_1, \cdots, x^i_j, \cdots, x^i_n)$ is a vector of n attributes of Boolean values. We refer to $\mathbf{x^i}$ as item i, $cl(\mathbf{x^i})$ denotes its class where $cl(\mathbf{x^i}) \in \{c_1, \cdots, c_{|C|}\})$, a finite set of class labels.

In the following attributes are assumed to be Boolean. Moreover we plan to address binary and multiple classification problems with more than two classes. What information can be obtained from the set of examples $\mathcal{E}$ which represents all we know? In order to go beyond the simple exploitation of neighborhoods as in k-nearest neighbors approaches, *we should take advantage of the examples by comparing them*, both in the case where they belong to the same class and when they are members of different classes. The comparisons will take place on pairs of examples and then on triplets, looking for regularities in the data. This is now described in the two next subsections where two new approaches, based on pairs and on triplets respectively, are presented and discussed.

2.1   Exploiting Differences and Bongard Problems

Consider two examples $\mathbf{x^i}$ and $\mathbf{x^k}$. They are equal on a subset of attributes $Equ^{i,k} = \{j \mid x^i_j = x^k_j\}$ and they differ on the subset $Dif^{i,k} = \{j \mid x^i_j \neq x^k_j\}$. Note that $Dif^{i,k} \neq \emptyset$, otherwise we would have $\mathbf{x^i} = \mathbf{x^k}$ (except in case of noisy data). There are two cases:

- If $cl(\mathbf{x^i}) = cl(\mathbf{x^k})$, this means that at least in the context defined by the values taken on $Equ^{i,k}$ (if non-empty) the difference between $\mathbf{x^i}$ and $\mathbf{x^k}$ observed on $Dif^{i,k}$ does not affect the class.

– If $cl(\mathbf{x^i}) \neq cl(\mathbf{x^k})$, it means that the change in $Dif^{i,k}$ is enough for explaining the change from $cl(\mathbf{x^i})$ to $cl(\mathbf{x^k})$ in the context defined by the values taken on $Equ^{i,k}$ (if non empty). To what extent what is true on a pair may be general?

Let $\mathbf{d} \notin \mathcal{E}$ be a new item for which $cl(\mathbf{d})$ is not known. Note that $\mathbf{d}$ differs from all items in $\mathcal{E}$, otherwise, finding the class of $\mathbf{d}$ is trivial if $\mathbf{d}$ is identical to an element in $\mathcal{E}$. So assume $\mathbf{d}$ differs from any element in $\mathcal{E}$ on at least one attribute.

This leads to first consider the items that differ from $\mathbf{d}$ in only one attribute. If no such items can be found, we may consider the items that differ from $\mathbf{d}$ in two attributes (or more if necessary). But there can be more than one element $\mathbf{c}$, differing from $\mathbf{d}$ on only one attribute, but for different attributes. Let $NN(\mathbf{d})$ be the set of these nearest neighbors of $\mathbf{d}$, and $\mathbf{c}$ be one of them. Let $dif(\mathbf{c}, \mathbf{d}) = (c_1 - d_1, \cdots, c_n - d_n) \in \{-1, 0, 1\}^n$. Let us look at all the pairs $(\mathbf{a}, \mathbf{b}) \in \mathcal{E}^2$ such that $dif(\mathbf{a}, \mathbf{b}) = dif(\mathbf{c}, \mathbf{d})$ (thus $Equ^{\mathbf{a},\mathbf{b}} = Equ^{\mathbf{c},\mathbf{d}}$) to see the effects of this difference. We have 3 cases:

case 1 $\forall(\mathbf{a}, \mathbf{b})$ such that $dif(\mathbf{a}, \mathbf{b}) = dif(\mathbf{c}, \mathbf{d})$, we have $cl(\mathbf{a}) = cl(\mathbf{b})$. Then there is no reason not to expect $cl(\mathbf{d}) = cl(\mathbf{c})$ according to the considered $\mathbf{c}$;

case 2 $\forall(\mathbf{a}, \mathbf{b})$ we have $cl(\mathbf{a}) \neq cl(\mathbf{b})$ then we are led to predict $cl(\mathbf{d}) = cl(\mathbf{b})$ according to the considered $\mathbf{c}$ if $cl(\mathbf{c}) = cl(\mathbf{a})$. Indeed in all pairs in $\mathcal{E}^2$ that present the same difference $dif(\mathbf{c}, \mathbf{d})$ there is a change of class and there is no reason not to observe the same change from $\mathbf{c}$ to $\mathbf{d}$;

case 3 We have two non-empty sets of pairs: i) the ones such that $cl(\mathbf{a}) = cl(\mathbf{b})$ and ii) the others such that $cl(\mathbf{a}) \neq cl(\mathbf{b})$.

The last case induces a new step in the procedure in order to understand why the same change inside the pairs lead to different classes or not for the items in the pairs according to the context. So the problem is to look for a property P that is true in the context of the pairs where $cl(\mathbf{a}) = cl(\mathbf{b})$ and which is false for the pairs such that $cl(\mathbf{a}) \neq cl(\mathbf{b})$. This is a Bongard problem [2] (see also [10, 11]), i.e., a problem where a set has to be separated in two subsets such that there is a property that is true for all the elements of one subset and that is wrong for all the elements of the other subset. See the example at the end of Subsect. 4.1 on how to solve a Bongard problem.

If the problem has a solution, let P be the set of properties that separates the two subsets of pairs. Note that P is expressed in terms of attributes in $Equ^{\mathbf{a},\mathbf{b}} = Equ^{\mathbf{c},\mathbf{d}}$. Then if $\mathbf{d}$ has property/ies P then $cl(\mathbf{d}) = cl(\mathbf{c})$ for this $\mathbf{c}$; otherwise $cl(\mathbf{d}) = cl(\mathbf{b})$ for this $\mathbf{c}$ if $cl(\mathbf{c}) = cl(\mathbf{a})$. If no solution P can be found, take another $\mathbf{c} \in NN(\mathbf{d})$. More generally, we may consider all the $\mathbf{c}$ that differ from $\mathbf{d}$ in one attribute. If necessary, we may consider the items $\mathbf{c}$ that differ from $\mathbf{d}$ on two properties, and so on until we succeed in making a prediction for $\mathbf{d}$.

2.2   Using Triplets of Similar Items

The previous subsection has shown how to take the best of the information provided by considering the examples by pairs. We now propose a simple approach to binary or multiple classification problems based on triplets of examples.

Let us consider all the triplets t_s made of three items $\mathbf{x^p}, \mathbf{x^q}, \mathbf{x^r}$ where $(\mathbf{x}^\ell, cl(\mathbf{x}^\ell)) \in \mathcal{E}$ for $\ell \in \{p, q, r\}$ and $cl(\mathbf{x^p}) = cl(\mathbf{x^q}) = cl(\mathbf{x^r}) =_{def} cl(t_s)$ if $t_s = \{\mathbf{x^p}, \mathbf{x^q}, \mathbf{x^r}\}$. For each triplet t_s, we can determine the attributes where $\mathbf{x^p}, \mathbf{x^q}, \mathbf{x^r}$ coincide on the same attribute values. Then it is natural to focus on triplets having enough attribute values in common. These values in common constitute a clue for being in class $cl(t_s)$. This suggests the following procedure for predicting the class of a new item $\mathbf{d}$.

$\mathbf{d}$ is compared with each triplet t_s. If $\mathbf{d}$ has also the attribute values that are in common in t_s then $\mathbf{d}$ gets a vote for being in the same class $cl(t_s)$ as the items in the triplet. Otherwise, i.e., if $\mathbf{d}$ differs on at least one attribute with the values common to the items in the triplet, then $\mathbf{d}$ gets no vote. Finally one concludes by a majority vote for predicting the class of $\mathbf{d}$.

3   Link with (ana)logical Proportions

An *analogical proportion* (AP) is a statement of the form "$\mathbf{a}$ is to $\mathbf{b}$ as $\mathbf{c}$ is to $\mathbf{d}$," connecting four items $\mathbf{a}, \mathbf{b}, \mathbf{c}, \mathbf{d}$. Given one binary attribute applied to four items, described respectively by the Boolean variables a, b, c, d, the following logical model for an AP, denoted by $a : b{::}c : d$ has been proposed and justified [13]:

$$a : b{::}c : d = [(a \wedge \neg b) \equiv (c \wedge \neg d)] \wedge [(\neg a \wedge b) \equiv (\neg c \wedge d)].$$

This formula expresses that a differs from b as c differs from d and that b differs from a as d differs from c. It is true only for 6 valuations, namely if $(a, b, c, d) \in \{(1,1,1,1), (0,0,0,0), (1,1,0,0), (0,0,1,1), (1,0,1,0), (0,1,0,1)\}$, otherwise it is false.

The items considered are represented by n attribute values, the definition of APs is extended component by component:

$\mathbf{a} : \mathbf{b}{::}\mathbf{c} : \mathbf{d}$ if and only if for all $i \in \{1, \cdots, n\}, a_i : b_i{::}c_i : d_i$.

It can be checked that each time we take two pairs $(\mathbf{a}, \mathbf{b})$ and $(\mathbf{c}, \mathbf{d})$ such that $dif(\mathbf{a}, \mathbf{b}) = dif(\mathbf{c}, \mathbf{d})$, then $\mathbf{a} : \mathbf{b}{::}\mathbf{c} : \mathbf{d}$ holds true. This establishes a link with the first procedure.

Moreover analogical inference relies on the solving of the Boolean equation in x where $a : b{::}c : x$ holds true ; the solution is unique when it exists (it may not exist, indeed $1 : 0{::}0 : x$ and $0 : 1{::}1 : x$ have no solution). When $\mathbf{a} : \mathbf{b}{::}\mathbf{c} : \mathbf{d}$ holds the analogical inference amounts to solve $cl(\mathbf{a}) : cl(\mathbf{b}){::}cl(\mathbf{c}) : x$ and then to conclude $cl(\mathbf{d}) = x$.

In case of multiple classes, one uses the extension of APs to nominal values, namely [4,15]:

$a : b{::}c : d$ holds true if and only if $(a = c$ and $b = d)$ or if $(a = b$ and $c = d)$. It clearly agrees with cases 1, 2, 3 in Sect. 2.1.

Bongard problems are related to a logical proportion called "inverse paralogy", which is also a quaternary logical connective that expresses that "what a and b have in common c and d have not it in common, and vice versa". It is defined by

$$IP(a, b, c, d) = [(a \wedge b) \equiv (\neg c \wedge \neg d)] \wedge [(\neg a \wedge \neg b) \equiv (c \wedge d)].$$

$IP(a, b, c, d)$ is true only for 6 valuations, namely $(a, b, c, d) \in \{(1, 1, 0, 0),$ $(0, 0, 1, 1), (0, 1, 1, 0), (1, 0, 0, 1), (1, 0, 1, 0), (0, 1, 0, 1)\}$, otherwise it is false. The definition of IPs is also extended to vectors componentwise. See [18] for details on how solving Bongard problems using IPs.

APs and IPs are particular cases of *logical proportions* [16]. Logical proportions are quaternary connectives whose expression has the same structure as $AP(a, b, c, d)$ or $IP(a, b, c, d)$, namely it is the conjunction of two equivalences, where each equivalence is between a comparison indicator for (a, b) and one for (c, d). By a comparison indicator, say for (a, b), we mean one of the four expressions $a \wedge b$, $\neg a \wedge \neg b$, $a \wedge \neg b$, $\neg a \wedge b$: the two first ones pertain to positive similarity and negative similarity respectively, while the last two refer to differences.

AP and IP are among the 8 existing *code-independent* logical proportions. This means that $a : b :: c : d = \neg a : \neg b :: \neg c : \neg d$ and $IP(a, b, c, d) = IP(\neg a, \neg b, \neg c, \neg d)$. In other words, APs and IPs do not depend on the positive or negative encoding of properties. Among code-independent logical proportions there are also 4 *heterogeneous* logical proportions, such as H_1 defined by

$$H_1(a, b, c, d) = [(\neg a \wedge b) \equiv (\neg c \wedge \neg d)] \wedge [(a \wedge \neg b) \equiv (c \wedge d)],$$

which is also true for 6 valuations only, namely for $(a, b, c, d) \in \{(1, 1, 1, 0), (0, 0, 0, 1), (1, 1, 0, 1), (0, 0, 1, 0), (1, 0, 1, 1), (0, 1, 0, 0)\}$. H_1 expresses that there is an intruder among $\{a, b, c, d\}$, which is not a. There are 3 other logical proportions expressing that there is an intruder which is not b (H_2), not c (H_3), not d (H_4) [17]. In the 2nd procedure, when $\mathbf{d}$ mismatches some of the attribute values that are common in a triplet t_s, then H_4 holds for some of these attributes, thus suggesting that $\mathbf{d}$ is an intruder in $cl(t_s)$.

4 Algorithms

We assume that a set of examples $\mathcal{E} = \{(\mathbf{x^i}, cl(\mathbf{x^i}))\}$ is given and that the class of a new item $\mathbf{d} \notin \mathcal{E}$ is to be predicted. In the following, we present two different classification algorithms corresponding to the procedures outlined in Sect. 2.

4.1 Algorithm 1 Based on Pairs

In the first procedure, to predict $cl(\mathbf{d})$ we first look at each close neighbor $\mathbf{c}$ of $\mathbf{d}$ in $\mathcal{E}$, one by one. In the trivial case where it exists an example $\mathbf{c}$ in $\mathcal{E}$ such that $\mathbf{c}$ is *identical* to $\mathbf{d}$, this later is then classified with the same label as $\mathbf{c}$. The general case is when $\mathbf{d}$ differs from all considered examples. For each neighbor $\mathbf{c}$, we compare the pair $(\mathbf{c}, \mathbf{d})$ to other existing pairs $(\mathbf{a}, \mathbf{b}) \in \mathcal{E}^2$ and then select the subset of pairs $(\mathbf{a}, \mathbf{b})$ such that $(\mathbf{a}, \mathbf{b})$ and $(\mathbf{c}, \mathbf{d})$ differ on the same attributes in the same way, i.e., $dif(\mathbf{a}, \mathbf{b}) = dif(\mathbf{c}, \mathbf{d})$. The main idea is to estimate how the difference between attributes influences the prediction result. Different situations may appear here:

Case 1: if for all selected pairs $(\mathbf{a}, \mathbf{b})$ we have $cl(\mathbf{a}) = cl(\mathbf{b})$, this indicates that the difference in terms of attributes of $\mathbf{a}$ and $\mathbf{b}$ has no effect on the class label (according to the examples in $\mathcal{E}^2$) and similarly $\mathbf{d}$ will be classified the same as $\mathbf{c}$ since it differs from $\mathbf{c}$ as $\mathbf{a}$ differs from $\mathbf{b}$.

Case 2: if for all previously selected pairs $(\mathbf{a}, \mathbf{b})$ we have $cl(\mathbf{a}) \neq cl(\mathbf{b})$, this means that the change in the class label may be justified by the change in terms of attributes of $\mathbf{a}$ and $\mathbf{b}$. Thus $\mathbf{d}$ will be classified differently from $\mathbf{c}$ in the same way as $\mathbf{a}$ and $\mathbf{b}$ are. Thus $cl(\mathbf{d}) = cl(\mathbf{b})$ in this case.

Case 3: if pairs $(\mathbf{a}, \mathbf{b})$ are mixed, i.e., some of them have the same class label and others not, this is an ambiguous situation that requires further analysis. Solving a Bongard problem may help for classification here. As said before, we aim to find a set of properties P that is *valid* in the context of pairs $(\mathbf{a}, \mathbf{b})$ such that $cl(\mathbf{a}) = cl(\mathbf{b})$ and *invalid* in the context of pairs $(\mathbf{a}, \mathbf{b})$ such that $cl(\mathbf{a}) \neq cl(\mathbf{b})$. If such property P could be found and if the item $\mathbf{d}$ has this property then $\mathbf{d}$ is classified as its neighbor $\mathbf{c}$ (leading to this P), otherwise $\mathbf{d}$ is classified as $\mathbf{b}$ according to this $\mathbf{c}$. In case no property P could be found, the algorithm looks for another neighbor $\mathbf{c}$.

Since many neighbors $\mathbf{c}$ may lead to different predictions, a majority vote is applied to decide for the final label for $\mathbf{d}$. The previous procedure, called *Algo*1, is described by Algorithm 1 which calls the Bongard problem solving procedure given below.

In this procedure, $getProperties(\mathcal{S}^=, \mathcal{S}^{\neq})$ is the method that searches and returns any property P of type $Attribute = Value$ satisfying the previous condition. The following example explains how $getProperties(\mathcal{S}^=, \mathcal{S}^{\neq})$ in *Algo*1 finds property(ies) P.

A small Sample from "Or" Dataset		
	$S_1^=$	$S_2^{\neq}$
Pairs (a, b)	a: 1,1,1,0,0,1,1, cl=1 b: 0,1,1,0,0,1,1, cl=1 a: 1,1,1,1,1,1,0, cl=1 b: 0,1,1,1,1,1,0, cl=1 a: 1,1,0,0,1,0,0, cl=1 b: 0,1,0,0,1,0,0, cl=1 a: 1,1,1,1,0,0,0, cl=1 b: 0,1,1,1,0,0,0, cl=1	a: 1,0,0,0,0,0,0, cl=1 b: 0,0,0,0,0,0,0, cl=0 a: 1,0,0,1,1,1,0, cl=1 b: 0,0,0,1,1,1,0, cl=0 a: 1,0,1,0,1,1,0, cl=1 b: 0,0,1,0,1,1,0, cl=0 a: 1,0,0,0,0,0,1, cl=1 b: 0,0,0,0,0,0,1, cl=0 a: 1,0,1,0,1,1,1, cl=1 b: 0,0,1,0,1,1,1, cl=0
Property P	P: (Attribute2 = 1)	$\overline{P}$: (Attribute 2 = 0)

Fig. 1. Illustrative example on How to solve a Bongard problem?.

In this example, it is clear that the only attribute/property that is valid in the context of pairs in $\mathcal{S}^=$ and not valid in the context of pairs $\mathcal{S}^{\neq}$ is P : $(Attribute2 = 1)$.

Algorithm 1. Pairs-based algorithm

Input: a set of examples $\mathcal{E} = \{(\boldsymbol{x}^i, cl(\boldsymbol{x}^i))\}$, $k > 1$
  a new item $\boldsymbol{d}$,
$N^= = 0$, $N^{\neq} = 0$, GoodNN=0, CandidateClass=$\emptyset$,
build up the set $\mathcal{S}^= = \{(\boldsymbol{a}, \boldsymbol{b}) \in |\mathcal{E}|^2 | cl(\boldsymbol{a}) = cl(\boldsymbol{b})\}$
build up the set $\mathcal{S}^{\neq} = \{(\boldsymbol{a}, \boldsymbol{b}) \in |\mathcal{E}|^2 | cl(\boldsymbol{a}) \neq cl(\boldsymbol{b})\}$
if $\exists c \in NN(\boldsymbol{d})$ such that $\boldsymbol{d} = \boldsymbol{c}$ **then**
  $cl(\boldsymbol{d}) = cl(\boldsymbol{c})$
else
  while $GoodNN \leq k$ **do**
    $\boldsymbol{c} = NN(\boldsymbol{d})$
    for each pair $(\boldsymbol{a}, \boldsymbol{b}) \in \mathcal{S}^=$ **do**
      if $dif(\boldsymbol{a}, \boldsymbol{b}) = dif(\boldsymbol{c}, \boldsymbol{d})$ **then**
        $N^= ++$
      end if
    end for
    for each pair $(\boldsymbol{a}, \boldsymbol{b}) \in \mathcal{S}^{\neq}$ **do**
      if $dif(\boldsymbol{a}, \boldsymbol{b}) = dif(\boldsymbol{c}, \boldsymbol{d})$ AND $cl(\boldsymbol{a}) = cl(\boldsymbol{c})$ **then**
        $N^{\neq} ++$
      end if
    end for
    if $N^= = 0$ AND $N^{\neq} = 0$ **then**
      {Case 0: No pairs $(\boldsymbol{a}, \boldsymbol{b})$ with the same difference as $(\boldsymbol{c}, \boldsymbol{d})$ are found}
      $predict_c = null$
    else if $N^{\neq} = 0$ **then**
      {Case 1: All pairs $(\boldsymbol{a}, \boldsymbol{b})$ (with the same difference as $(\boldsymbol{c}, \boldsymbol{d})$) are such that
      $cl(\boldsymbol{a}) = cl(\boldsymbol{b})$}
      $predict_c = cl(\boldsymbol{c})$
    else if $N^= = 0$ **then**
      {Case 2: All pairs $(\boldsymbol{a}, \boldsymbol{b})$ (with the same difference as $(\boldsymbol{c}, \boldsymbol{d})$) are such that
      $cl(\boldsymbol{a}) \neq cl(\boldsymbol{b})$}
      $predict_c = cl(\boldsymbol{b})$
    else
      {Case 3: Pairs $(\boldsymbol{a}, \boldsymbol{b})$ are such that $cl(\boldsymbol{a}) = cl(\boldsymbol{b})$ or $cl(\boldsymbol{a}) \neq cl(\boldsymbol{b})$}
      $predict_c = SolveBongardProblem(\boldsymbol{d}, \mathcal{S}^=, \mathcal{S}^{\neq})$
    end if
    if $predict_c \neq null$ **then**
      $CandidateClass.add(predict_c)$, GoodNN++
    end if
  end while
end if
$cl(\boldsymbol{d}) = Vote(CandidateClass)$
return $cl(\boldsymbol{d})$

Bongard problem solving procedure
Input: $S^=$, $S^{\neq}$, a new item d, a nearest neighbor c to d
$Properties = getProperties(S^=, S^{\neq})$
if $hasProperties(d, Properties)$ then
$\quad predict_c = cl(c)$
else
$\quad predict_c = cl(b)$
end if
return $predict_c$

4.2   Algorithm 2: Triplets-based Algorithm

The second method is quite different: we consider triplets instead of pairs. More formally, given the set C of examples in $\mathcal{E}$ having the same label, we first seek for the subset S of triplets $(a, b, c) \in C^3$ such that a, b and c agree on at least a minimum number of attributes. We first compute the *Equality* value for a given triplet defined as: $Equ(a, b, c) = \{j \mid a_j = b_j = c_j\}$ Then we select only triplets with high number of equal attributes i.e., $|Equ(a, b, c)| \geq \theta * NumberOfAttributes$ (θ is a fixed threshold). This can be done offline.

Then, for each of these previously selected triplets, if the item d also agrees with this triplet on the same attributes, this is an indication that d should be in the same class as this triplet. Thus we increment the score for this class label. Finally we allocate to d the class with the highest score.

The previous procedure, called $Algo2$ can be described with the pseudo-code of Algorithm 2.

Algorithm 2. Triplets-based algorithm

Input: a set of examples $\mathcal{E} = \{(x^i, cl(x^i))\}$, a threshold θ,
$\quad$ a new item d,
Partition $\mathcal{E}$ into sets C of examples with the same label l {l is the class label of the set C}
for each label l do $Vote(l) = 0$ end for
for each subset C do
$\quad$ for each triplet (a, b, c) in C^3 such that: $|Equ(a, b, c)| \geq \theta * NbrOfAttributes$
$\quad$ do
$\quad\quad$ if $Equ(a, b, c, d) = Equ(a, b, c)$ then
$\quad\quad\quad Vote(l) + +$
$\quad\quad$ end if
$\quad$ end for
end for
$cl(d) = argmax_l\{Vote(l)\}$
return $cl(d)$

4.3   Baseline Analogical Classifier

To evaluate the proposed algorithms previously described, we also implement a baseline analogical classifier denoted $BaselineAC$ for comparison. This classifier corresponds to the brute force AP-classifier described in [4] and looks for *all* triplets $(\mathbf{a}, \mathbf{b}, \mathbf{c})$ in the example set whose class equation $cl(\mathbf{a}) : cl(\mathbf{b})::cl(\mathbf{c}) : y$ is solvable. Then, for each of these triplets, if the AP $\mathbf{a} : \mathbf{b}::\mathbf{c} : \mathbf{d}$ is valid (an AP holds true on each attribute), the score for this class label is incremented. Finally, $BaselineAC$ assigns to $\mathbf{d}$ the class label with the highest score.

This algorithm processes as follows:

1. Look for each triplet $(\mathbf{a}, \mathbf{b}, \mathbf{c})$ in the example set.
2. Solve $cl(\mathbf{a}) : cl(\mathbf{b})::cl(\mathbf{c}) : y$.
3. If the previous analogical equation on classes has a solution l and if the analogical equation on the attributes is valid, i.e., $\mathbf{a} : \mathbf{b}::\mathbf{c} : \mathbf{d}$, increase $score(l)$ by 1.
4. Assign to $\mathbf{d}$ the class label having the highest score as $cl(\mathbf{d}) = argmax_l(score(l))$

Note that we do not consider a kNN algorithm as a baseline, since it is outperformed by the analogical classifier [4]. Still we check it in the experiments.

In terms of complexity, due to the use of triplets of examples in the sample set, the baseline analogical classifier as well as $Algo2$ have a cubic complexity. In $Algo1$, the overall complexity is quadratic due to the use of pairs. However, this approach constrains the use only to pairs $(\mathbf{a}, \mathbf{b})$ s.t.: $dif(\mathbf{a}, \mathbf{b}) = dif(\mathbf{c}, \mathbf{d})$ and $\mathbf{c} = NN(\mathbf{d})$ ($\mathbf{c}$ and $\mathbf{d}$ differs on a maximum of 1 or 2 attributes). Thus only a very small subset of these pairs $(\mathbf{a}, \mathbf{b})$ are in practical used for classification. This helps to considerably reduce the burden time during classification.

5   Experimentations

In this section, we provide experimental results obtained with the proposed algorithms. In this paper, we only consider Boolean datasets. The experimental study is based on 15 datasets: the first 8 are abstract Boolean functions (tested on random samplings of 7 Boolean variables) and the last 7 are taken from the U.C.I. machine learning repository [12]. All nominal attributes in U.C.I. ML datasets have been binarized using the free Weka software. All these datasets are binary class problems except **Balance**, **Car** and **Hayes-Roth** which are multiple classes databases. A brief description of these datasets is given in Table 1. We also provide the definition of each abstract Boolean function in the last column of this table.

Table 2 provides the experimental results for the proposed algorithms applied to these Boolean datasets. Each value in this table is the average accuracy over 5 different runs, each run apply a 10-fold cross validation. The best results are highlighted in bold.

For $Algo1$ we first consider the nearest neighbors $\mathbf{c}$ s.t: $\mathbf{c}$ differs from $\mathbf{d}$ on only one attribute. If no such $\mathbf{c}$ could exist, we then consider $\mathbf{c}$ differing from $\mathbf{d}$

Table 1. Description of datasets.

Datasets	Ins	Nom. Att	Bin. Att	Nb class	Def.:$cl(\mathbf{x}) =$
And2	128	–	7	2	$x_1 AND x_2$
Or2	128	–	7	2	$x_1 OR x_2$
Not	128	–	7	2	$x_1 AND Not(x_2)$
And7	128	–	7	2	$x_1 AND...AND x_7$
Or7	128	–	7	2	$x_1 OR...OR x_7$
XOR	128	–	7	2	$x_1 XOR x_2$
XORMin	128	–	7	2	$x_1 XOR x_2, if(Sum(x_1,...,x_7) < 6)$
					$Min(x_1,...,x_7), otherwise$
Sum7	128	–	7	2	$Sum(x1,...,x7) = 2$
Monk1	432	6	15	2	–
Monk2	432	6	15	2	–
Monk3	432	6	15	2	–
TicTacToe	521	9	27	2	–
Balance	625	4	20	3	–
Car	743	7	21	4	–
Hayes-Roth	132	5	15	3	–

on two attributes. The process finishes when k "good" nearest neighbors could be found; the ones able to predict a label for $\mathbf{d}$ (k is a tuned parameter). We use the Hamming distance to identify nearest neighbors for Boolean data.

To evaluate the proposed algorithms, we compare their efficiency to the BaselineAC, introduced before in Sect. 4.3. We also compare our algorithms to the classic kNN. For this latter as well as for *Algo*1 and *Algo*2 there is one parameter to be optimized for each classifier: the number of nearest neighbors k as well as for kNN and *Algo*1 and the parameter θ for *Algo*2. So we apply this testing protocol: in an inner cross validation and using the example set $\mathcal{E}$ only, we tuned respectively the parameters: k (with values: 1,2, ..., 11) for kNN and parameter k (with values: 1,3,5, 7) for *Algo*1 and θ (with values: 0.5,0.6,0.7,0.8) for *Algo*2. Then the best obtained value for each of them is used to predict the label for new examples in the outer cross validation (the displayed k^* and θ^* are the average values over 5 runs and 10-fold cross validation).

From these results we can derive several comments:

– If we first consider the synthetic Boolean functions in Table 2, we can see that *Algo*1 is the best classifier (see average accuracy) for all datasets except *And7* function. In particular, *Algo*1 is largely better than *Algo*2, the BaselineAC and kNN (with optimized value of k) for dataset *Sum7* for which all other classifiers achieve an accuracy of about 80% while *Algo*1 achieves 99%.
– *Algo*2 is either as good as or performs significantly better than the BaselineAC for most datasets (see the Sum7 dataset). If we compare its accuracy to kNN,

Table 2. Accuracy results (means and standard deviations).

Dataset	Algo1	k^*	Algo2	θ^*	BaselineAC	kNN	k^*	$Odd3(NN, Std, Std)$ [6]
And2	100	1	100	0.5	100	99.53 ± 1.08	1	–
Or2	100	1	99.84 ± 0.46	0.5	100	100	1	–
Not	100	1	100	0.5	100	99.69 ± 0.92	1	–
And7	98.28 ± 3.96	3	96.88 ± 4.60	0.6	96.88 ± 4.60	**99.69 ± 0.92**	1	–
Or7	**98.44 ± 3.41**	3	**98.44 ± 3.41**	0.6	**98.44 ± 3.41**	98.44 ± 3.10	1	–
XOR	100	1	100	0.5	100	99.38 ± 1.58	3	–
XORMin	96.41 ± 4.70	3	96.72 ± 4.39	0.5	**96.88 ± 4.08**	93.75 ± 6.29	1	–
Sum7	**99.06 ± 2.49**	5	83.59 ± 8.28	0.5	82.03 ± 8.27	82.50 ± 10.92	8	–
Monk1	100	1	100	0.7	99.95 ± 0.14	99.95 ± 0.14	3	99.31±3.39
Monk2	100	1	67.13 ± 6.14	0.5	99.54 ± 0.82	64.44 ± 6.99	11	60.93 ± 4.16
Monk3	100	1	100	0.7	97.36 ± 1.78	100	1	99.95 ± 0 .05
TicTacToe	100	1	97.50 ± 2.28	0.7	100	98.27 ± 1.77	1	–
Balance	**95.36 ± 2.59**	7	89.84 ± 3.06	0.5	90.05 ± 3.35	83.94 ± 4.23	11	88.62 ± 3.4
Car	**95.33 ± 2.40**	3	94.03 ± 3.03	0.8	91.22 ± 3.23	92.33 ± 3.10	1	90.93 ± 4.03
Hayes-Roth	80.30 ± 10.65	3	76.71 ± 12.74	0.5	**80.45 ± 9.22**	61.36 ± 13.46	3	79.37 ± 9.74
Average	**97.54**	–	**93.37**	–	**95.5**	**91.5**	–	–

as noted for Algo1, Algo2 has better results than kNN for all datasets except for *And7* function for which kNN is better.

- Looking at U.C.I. ML datasets results, we can see that *Algo1* still has very good accuracy rates and significantly outperforms the BaselineAC for datasets Monk3, Balance and Car and has close results for Monk 1, Monk 2, Tic.Tac. and Hayes-Roth. Moreover this algorithm shows very good results for multiple class problems Car and Balance datasets. This shows the efficiency of this first approach to deal with binary as well as multiple class problems. Algo1 also outperforms Algo2 and kNN for most datasets (see for example Monk2 and Balance). We also note that these results for *Algo1* are obtained with small values of k ($k = 1$ for most datasets)
- Now if we evaluate the second algorithm, it is clear that the best results are obtained with different values of θ for different datasets. However, as expected the classifier provides better results for small values of θ ($\theta = 0.5$) for most datasets since when θ is high, only a very few number of triplets, with similar features, can be obtained which means that several examples may remain unclassified. Contrary to all other datasets, the optimal value $\theta = 0.8$ provides very good results for Car dataset with high number of instances. We may conjuncture that for this dataset, there are enough triplets with very similar features that coincide with the examples to be classified. Thus it is clear that the optimal value of θ is highly dependent on the size and/or type of the dataset.
- Overall *Algo2* is significantly better than the k-NN for most ML datasets except Tic.tac. Especially *Algo2* largely outperforms k-NN for dataset Hayes-Roth with almost 15% of accuracy.

Based on these preliminary comments, let us try to understand how each algorithm performs on the data. We first focus on *Algo*1. Let us first note that this algorithm largely outperforms *Algo*2 and kNN for dataset Monk 2. As noted first in [4], Monk 2 dataset (which looks similar to the dataset Sum7) involves learning a binary function defined as ("having exactly two attributes with value 1") which is more complex than the two other Monk's problems since it involves all attributes while in Monk 1 and Monk 3 only 3 among 6 attributes are involved in the learning process.

Let us analyze the reasons for this success. One main difference between *Algo*1 and *Algo*2 is the type of AP-like pattern used for solving the analogical equation on class label. In *Algo*2, since the selected triplets (of similar items) are limited to those having *the same* class, only one pattern $cl(\mathbf{a}) : cl(\mathbf{b})::cl(\mathbf{c}) : y$ of type $s : s::s : y$ is exploited for predicting the class label while no such restriction is done in *Algo*1. For example, patterns $s : s::t : y$ and $s : t::s : y$ (such that s and t are two distinct values of $cl(\mathbf{x})$) are commonly useful in *Algo*1 to predict the class label. In *Algo*2, exploiting only triplets belonging to the same class may be considered as very restrictive and remains close to the spirit of classical kNN which prevents the classifier to fully benefit from a whole comparison between items in the examples set. Thus the success of *Algo*1 may be explained by the use of pairs of examples with the same/ different classes (patterns of types $s : s::t : y$ and $s : t::s : y$) which contributes to increase its performance if compared to *Algo*2.

As explained before, although *Algo*1 exploits the neighborhood of the item to be classified, it is quite different from the classical kNN. Contrary to kNN, which systematically classifies $\mathbf{d}$ as its k-nearest neighbors $\mathbf{c}$, *Algo*1 classifies $\mathbf{d}$ in the same way as its k-nearest neighbor only in one case: if for *all* pairs $(\mathbf{a}, \mathbf{b}) \in \mathcal{E}^2$ such that: $dif(\mathbf{a}, \mathbf{b}) = dif(\mathbf{c}, \mathbf{d})$, this difference in terms of attributes have no effect on the class label, i.e., $cl(\mathbf{a}) = cl(\mathbf{b})$. In the second case for which *all* pairs $(\mathbf{a}, \mathbf{b}) \in \mathcal{E}^2$ are such that $cl(\mathbf{a}) \neq cl(\mathbf{b})$, *Algo*1 classifies $\mathbf{d}$ as item(s) $\mathbf{b}$ not as $\mathbf{c}$. Thus, for binary class problems, $\mathbf{d}$ is classified in the opposite class of $\mathbf{c}$ in this second case. A deeper investigation on the relationship between the change in attribute values that may affect / not affect the change in the class label (on the example set basis) is thus shown. This may justify why *Algo*1 behaves much better than classical kNN for some datasets such as Monk 2 and *Sum*7.

If we compare *Algo*1 to the BaselineAC, the former differs from the latter mainly in terms of pairs/triplets used for prediction. In the BaselineAC, all triplets $(\mathbf{a}, \mathbf{b}, \mathbf{c}) \in \mathcal{E}^3$ building a valid analogical proportion with $\mathbf{d}$ and having a solvable class equation $cl(\mathbf{a}) : cl(\mathbf{b})::cl(\mathbf{c}) : y$ help for prediction. However in *Algo*1, only a small subset of triplets $(\mathbf{a}, \mathbf{b}, \mathbf{c}) \in \mathcal{E}^3$ is exploited, those for which $\mathbf{c}$ is very close to the item $\mathbf{d}$. Looking at the *average* results in Table 2, we may conjuncture that there is no need to use all the triplets for prediction and that the use of triplets $(\mathbf{a}, \mathbf{b}, \mathbf{c})$ such that $\mathbf{a}$ and $\mathbf{b}$ are very similar is enough for getting very good accuracy.

As said before, *Algo*2 shows good performance if compared to the kNN (see the average accuracies). It suggests that exploiting more information through the use of triplets of similar items, instead of strict similarity as in the case of k-NN, is the reason for this improvement in accuracy. We may conclude that mainly for datasets with large number of attributes and a reduced number of examples (as the case of Hayes-Roth), $Algo2$ may be a reasonable choice considering the extra computational effort. $Algo2$ may seem linked to $Odd3(NN, Std, Std)$ in [6] since both algorithms exploit triplets of examples belonging to the same class. However, $Odd3(NN, Std, Std)$ differs from $Algo2$ mainly in two respects: First, in $Odd3(NN, Std, Std)$ one element of the triplet is chosen as a nearest neighbor in the class of the item to be classified while in $Algo2$ no such restriction is applied. Second, in $Odd3(NN, Std, Std)$ an item is classified in the class where it is the least at odds w.r.t. the items already in that class; thus oddness may be considered as a dissimilarity index while in $Algo2$ we assess the similarity of the item w.r.t. other classified elements. If we compare results of $Algo2$ to the ones of $Odd3(NN, Std, Std)$ on the tested datasets, we can see that overall they have close results.

$Algo2$ is also linked to the Evenness-based classifier in [5] since both exploit triplets belonging to the same class and similarity for prediction. However in Evenness-based classifier [5], a new item is classified in a class where it should rarely be an *intruder* with respect to any triplet of items known to be in that class. This condition is less restrictive than the one in $Algo2$ since in this algorithm the new item should agree with each triplet on the same attributes while in Evenness-based classifier, the triplet is considered for vote even if the new item agrees with the *majority* of items in this triplet on a particular attribute.

Finally, to understand better how the first algorithm processes for prediction, we also investigate the Bongard problems that has been solved to achieve the prediction of new examples. For this reason we computed the average proportion (over 10-fold cross validation and 5 runs) of new examples that has been classified by solving Bongard problems. This proportion, denoted $P_{Bongard}$ is defined as:

$$P_{Bongard} = \frac{Nbr\ of\ classified\ examples\ by\ solving\ Bongard\ pbms*100}{Nbr\ of\ classified\ examples}$$

Table 3 summarizes the results. In this table we only include datasets for which classification required solving Bongard problems. For all other datasets $P_{Bongard} = 0$.

Table 3. Proportion of solved Bongard problems.

	And2	Or2	Not	Monk1	Monk2	Monk3	Car	Hayes-Roth
$P_{Bongard}$	21	21	21	1	1	1	22	1

These results first highlight that $Algo1$ may completely perform the prediction task without the need to solve any Bongard problem in some cases. For example for dataset XOR, no Bongard problem has been solved, which means that the procedure is either in case 1 or case 2 and never in case 3 (see Algorithm 1). Nevertheless, *Algo*1 makes no prediction error for this dataset.

For datasets And2, Or2 and Not, more than 20% of classified examples **d** required solving a Bongard problem (with regard to any nearest neighbor **c**) which is among the highest proportion. This shows that for many cases the procedure yields to a conflicting situation where some pairs $(\mathbf{a}, \mathbf{b})$ (with the same difference as $(\mathbf{c}, \mathbf{d})$) have the same class label and other have different class labels. For these datasets, *Algo*1 still successfully predicts class labels without making an error. This proves that the method solving Bongard problems succeeds to distinguish and resolve ambiguous situation. It is important to note that for some cases, the function $getProperties(\mathcal{S}^=, \mathcal{S}^{\neq})$ may return no properties. This means that no *true* property could be found in the context of pairs $(\mathbf{a}, \mathbf{b})$ s.t. $cl(\mathbf{a}) = cl(\mathbf{b})$ that is *false* in the context of pairs $(\mathbf{a}, \mathbf{b})$ such that $cl(\mathbf{a}) \neq cl(\mathbf{b})$. In this case, the new example remains unclassified according to the current nearest neighbor and the procedure passes to another nearest neighbor. This case will not affect the algorithm performance since a vote is applied on the predictions made by successful neighbors.

6   Conclusion

The paper has introduced two new classification methods which have some relations with logical proportions and which perform well. In particular, they rely on the processing of the examples in terms of pairs or triplets. Observe that this goes beyond standard case-based reasoning and instance-based learning [1] where examples are exploited *individually* on the basis of a similarity evaluation between a retrieved case and the item to be classified, while in the approach proposed here the information contained in the set of examples is first processed by compiling pairs or triplets.

The first procedure that uses pairs appears to be especially efficient, since in case of ambiguity of comparative reasoning results (some pairs tend to indicate that a change in attribute values causes a change of class, while other pairs suggest that there is no effect on the class) the procedure solves Bongard problems for separating the contexts. Because of the relationship between the pairwise procedure and analogical classifiers, we use the latter as a baseline and also because analogical classifiers have been shown to have competitive performance with classical classifiers such as SVMs, Bayesian, rule-based, or kNN classifiers [4]. Experiments show that the pairwise procedure outperforms the baseline. This is a clear indication in the Boolean case of the possibility of designing a classification procedure that relies on logical reasoning and especially on comparative reasoning. The extension of such a procedure to nominal attributes does not seem to raise much difficulties and is a topic for further research. Besides, the very nature of the procedure makes it a good candidate for being able to explain its results (by extracting the set of properties/attributes that are responsible for the change in class label).

Acknowledgements. This work was funded by Liwa College of Technology in Abu Dhabi (UAE) under research grant IRG-BIT-002-2020.

References

1. Aha, D.W., Muñoz-Avila, H.: Introduction: interactive case-based reasoning. Appl. Intell. **14**(1), 7–8 (2001)
2. Bongard, M.M.: Pattern Recognition. Hayden Book, Spartan Books, Rochelle Park, Russian version, p. 1967. Nauka Press, Moscow (1970)
3. Boros, E., Crama, Y., Hammer, P.L., Ibaraki, T., Kogan, A., Makino, K.: Logical analysis of data: classification with justification. Ann. Oper. Res. **188**(1), 33–61 (2011). https://doi.org/10.1007/s10479-011-0916-1
4. Bounhas, M., Prade, H., Richard, G.: Analogy-based classifiers for nominal or numerical data. Int. J. Approximate Reasoning **91**, 36–55 (2017)
5. Bounhas, M., Prade, H., Richard, G.: Oddness/evenness-based classifiers for Boolean or numerical data. Int. J. Approximate Reasoning **82**, 81–100 (2017). https://doi.org/10.1016/J.ijar.2016.12.002
6. Bounhas, M., Prade, H., Richard, G.: Oddness-based classification: a new way of exploiting neighbors. Int. J. Intell. Syst. **33**(12), 2379–2401 (2018)
7. Chikalov, I., et al.: Three Approaches to Data Analysis - Test Theory, Rough Sets and Logical Analysis of Data, Intelligent Systems Reference Library, vol. 41. Springer (2013). https://doi.org/10.1007/978-3-642-28667-4
8. Cornuejols, A., Koriche, F., Nock, R.: Statistical computational learning. In: Marquis, P., Papini, O., Prade, H. (eds.) A Guided Tour of Artificial Intelligence Research, pp. 341–388. Springer, Cham (2020). https://doi.org/10.1007/978-3-030-06164-7_11
9. Dubois, D., Prade, H.: Towards a logic-based view of some approaches to classification tasks. In: Lesot, M.-J., Vieira, S., Reformat, M.Z., Carvalho, J.P., Wilbik, A., Bouchon-Meunier, B., Yager, R.R. (eds.) IPMU 2020. CCIS, vol. 1239, pp. 697–711. Springer, Cham (2020). https://doi.org/10.1007/978-3-030-50153-2_51
10. Foundalis, H.: Phaeaco: a cognitive architecture inspired by Bongard's problems. Doctoral dissertation, Indiana University, Center for Research on Concepts and Cognition (CRCC), Bloomington (2006)
11. Hofstadter, D.R.: Gödel, Escher, Bach: an Eternal Golden Braid. Basic Books, New York (1979)
12. Mertz, J., Murphy, P.M.: UCI repository of machine learning databases (2000). ftp://ftp.ics.uci.edu/pub/machine-learning-databases
13. Miclet, L., Prade, H.: Handling analogical proportions in classical logic and fuzzy logics settings. In: Sossai, C., Chemello, G. (eds.) ECSQARU 2009. LNCS (LNAI), vol. 5590, pp. 638–650. Springer, Heidelberg (2009). https://doi.org/10.1007/978-3-642-02906-6_55
14. Mitchell, T.M.: Version spaces: A candidate elimination approach to rule learning. In: Proceedings 5th International Joint Conference on Artificial Intelligence IIJCAI, MIT, Cambridge, Ma, vol. 1, pp. 305–310 (1977)
15. Pirrelli, V., Yvon, F.: Analogy in the lexicon: a probe into analogy-based machine learning of language. In: Proceedings 6th International Symposium on Human Communication, Santiago de Cuba, 6 p (1999)
16. Prade, H., Richard, G.: From analogical proportion to logical proportions. Log. Univers. **7**(4), 441–505 (2013). https://doi.org/10.1007/s11787-013-0089-6

17. Prade, H., Richard, G.: Homogenous and heterogeneous logical proportions. IfCoLog J. Log. Appl. **1**(1), 1–51 (2014)
18. Prade, H., Richard, G.: On Different Ways to be (dis)similar to Elements in a Set. Boolean Analysis and Graded Extension. In: Carvalho, J.P., Lesot, M.-J., Kaymak, U., Vieira, S., Bouchon-Meunier, B., Yager, R.R. (eds.) IPMU 2016. CCIS, vol. 611, pp. 605–618. Springer, Cham (2016). https://doi.org/10.1007/978-3-319-40581-0_49

Learning from Imbalanced Data Using an Evidential Undersampling-Based Ensemble

Fares Grina[1,2(✉)], Zied Elouedi[1], and Eric Lefevre[2]

[1] Université de Tunis, Institut Supérieur de Gestion de Tunis, LARODEC,
Tunis, Tunisia
`grina.fares2@gmail.com, zied.elouedi@gmx.fr`
[2] Univ. Artois, UR 3926, Laboratoire de Génie Informatique et d'Automatique de
l'Artois (LGI2A), 62400 Béthune, France
`eric.lefevre@univ-artois.fr`

Abstract. In many real-world binary classification problems, one class
tends to be heavily underrepresented when it consists of far fewer observations than the other class. This results in creating a biased model with
undesirable performance. Different techniques, such as undersampling,
have been proposed to fix this issue. Ensemble methods have also been
proven to be a good strategy to improve the performance of the resulting
model in the case of class imbalance. In this paper, we propose an evidential undersampling-based ensemble approach. To alleviate the issue
of losing important data, our undersampling technique assigns soft evidential labels to each majority instance, which are later used to discard
only the unwanted observations, such as noisy and ambiguous examples.
Finally, to improve the final results, the proposed undersampling approach is incorporated into an evidential classifier fusion-based ensemble.
The comparative study against well-known ensemble methods reveal that
our method is efficient according to the G-Mean and F-Score measures.

Keywords: Imbalanced classification · Ensemble learning ·
Undersampling · Evidence theory

1 Introduction

Imbalanced classification is a common issue in modern machine learning problems. In binary classification, it is a scenario that occurs when a class, refereed to
as the minority class, is highly under-represented in the dataset, while the other
class represents the majority [14]. Due to the naturally-skewed class distributions, class imbalance has been widely observed in many real-world applications,
such as medical diagnosis [15], network intrusion detection [10], language translation [20], and fraud detection [23]. From a practical point of view, the minority
class usually yields higher interests. For example, failing to detect a fraudulent
transaction can be crucial to a banking organization.

© The Author(s), under exclusive license to Springer Nature Switzerland AG 2022
F. Dupin de Saint-Cyr et al. (Eds.): SUM 2022, LNAI 13562, pp. 235–248, 2022.
https://doi.org/10.1007/978-3-031-18843-5_16

In addition to the skewed class distribution, the complexity of the data is an important factor for classification models. Other related data imperfections include data uncertainty, i.e., class overlapping (ambiguity) and noise. The data uncertainty issue was proven to increase the difficulty for classifiers to yield good performance on imbalanced datasets [35].

In order to deal with the poor performance on imbalanced data, many strategies have been developed to deal with this issue. The proposed methods are a variety of re-sampling, classifier modifications, cost-sensitive learning, or ensemble approaches [12]. Data re-sampling is one of the most simple yet efficient strategies to deal with imbalanced classification. These methods typically aim at re-balancing the data at the preprocessing level. This gives it the advantage of versatility, for the reason that it is classifier-independent. More recently, ensemble learning is incorporated and combined with different strategies, such as resampling. Ensembles are used to improve a single classifier by combining several base classifiers (also called weak learners) that outperform every independent one.

However, most of these methods have been observed to suffer from limitations, such as the presence of other data imperfections (i.e. high class overlapping, noise and outliers).

In this paper, we propose an evidential undersampling-based ensemble, in which we incorporate an evidential undersampling method into an ensemble learning framework. Instead of randomly undersampling the data, our presented approach uses evidence theory [6, 31], which was recently used for imbalanced classification [11, 25], in order to represent majority observations with soft evidential memberships. Consequently, this gives us an idea on the location of each majority instance. Then, we eliminate the majority objects that are considered ambiguous (in overlapping regions), label noise (in the minority area), or outliers (far from both classes). The intuition behind this is to improve the visibility of the minority class, since it usually is the main learning interest in most class-imbalanced problems. The issue with this undersampling solution, is that it is rather difficult to know the exact amount of ambiguity or class overlapping present in the data. The resulting undersampled subset is heavily controlled by our assumption of how much ambiguity is present. To fix this issue, we integrate this evidential method into the process of a bagging ensemble. The goal is to train multiple base classifiers using different subsets created by our version of undersampling. Finally, we use a classifier fusion approach based on the evidence theory.

The remainder of this paper will be divided as follows. The next section presents related works in resampling and ensemble learning. The theory of evidence will be recalled in Sect. 3. Section 4 details each step of our contribution, i.e., the evidential mechanism used for undersampling and the classifier combination method. Experimental evaluation and discussion are conducted in Sect. 5. Our paper ends with a conclusion and an outlook on future work in Sect. 6.

2   Resampling and Ensemble Methods for Imbalanced Classification

In this work, we focus on binary imbalanced classification, which is the most widely studied problem in imbalanced learning. In this section, we mainly review existing works relative to resampling and ensemble learning.

2.1   Resampling

Resampling methods focus on modifying the training set to balance the class distribution. It can be categorized into 3 groups: oversampling, undersampling, or hybrid methods. Oversampling techniques aim at creating synthetic minority examples to get rid of the class imbalance. The most traditional version is to randomly replicate existing minority data. To avoid overfitting, Synthetic Minority Oversampling Technique (SMOTE) was suggested [3]. SMOTE creates minority instances by interpolating between existing observations that lie together. Nonetheless, many works [5,7,13] have proposed other versions of SMOTE, since SMOTE can cause potential amplification of noise, and overlap already present in the data.

Undersampling is another form of resampling, which eliminates examples from the majority class to re-balance the dataset. Similarly to oversampling, the traditional way of undersampling is randomly selecting majority instances to discard, which may potentially remove meaningful information from the dataset. Henceforth, other methods were presented for safer undersampling. Commonly, filtering techniques, such as the Edited Nearest Neighbors (ENN) [39] and Tomek Links (TL) [16], are occasionally used for undersampling imbalanced data. More recently, other mechanisms have been used, such as clustering [21], evolutionary algorithms [19], and evidence theory [11].

Combining oversampling and undersampling is also a solid solution to imbalanced learning. It usually consists of combining a SMOTE-like method with an undersampling approach [18,28].

2.2   Ensemble Learning in Imbalanced Classification

The main idea behind ensembles is to improve a single classifier by combining the results of multiple classifiers that outperform every independent one. This paper focuses on resampling-based ensembles, which combines ensemble learning with resampling techniques to tackles class imbalance. Most works considered the use of bagging, boosting, or a combination of the two.

Bagging builds ensembles using the concept of *independent learning*. This strategy trains the base classifiers independently from each other, and uses data re-sampling to introduce diversity into the predictions of the models. While boosting learns of the misclassification of previous iterations by adapting the importance of misclassified objects in future iterations. Random undersampling is popularly used with ensembles [36]. SMOTEBagging and UnderBagging were suggested in [37]. The former integrates SMOTE's oversampling into the bagging algorithm, with an adaptive way of computing the resampling rate, while Underbagging does the same using random undersampling. In order to optimize the model performance, a hybrid resampling technique was combined with bagging [17].

Boosting-based ensembles have also been proposed for the class imbalance issue. Similar to bagging-based ensembles, these methods merge data resampling techniques into boosting algorithms, more specifically the AdaBoost algorithm [9]. SMOTEBoost [4] performs SMOTE during each boosting iteration in order to generate minority objects. RUSBoost [30] is also similar to SMOTE-Boost, but it eliminates instances from the majority class by random undersampling in each iteration. Evolutionary algorithms were also used to create a boosting-based algorithm [19]. SMOTEWB [29] is another boosting ensemble, which combines SMOTE with a noise detection method, into a boosting framework.

Some methods have used hybrid approaches involving both boosting and bagging, such as EasyEnsemble and BalanceCascade [22].

3   Evidence Theory

The theory of evidence [6,31,33], also called belief function theory or Dempster-Shafer theory (DST), is a flexible and well-founded framework to represent and combine uncertain information. The frame of discernment denotes a finite set of M exclusive possible propositions, e.g., possible class labels for an object in a classification problem. The frame of discernment is denoted as follows:

$$\Omega = \{w_1, w_2, ..., w_M\} \tag{1}$$

A basic belief assignment (also referred to as bba) represents the amount of belief given by a source of evidence, committed to 2^Ω, that is, all subsets of the frame including the whole frame itself. Formally, a bba is represented by a mapping function $m : 2^\Omega \rightarrow [0,1]$ such that:

$$\sum_{A \in 2^\Omega} m(A) = 1 \tag{2}$$

Each mass $m(A)$ quantifies the amount of belief allocated to a event A of Ω. A bba is called unnormalized if the sum of its masses is not equal to 1, and should be normalized under a closed-world assumption [32]. A focal element is a subset $A \subseteq \Omega$ where $m(A) \neq 0$.

The *Plausibility* function is another representation of knowledge defined by *Shafer* [31] as follows:

$$Pl(A) = \sum_{B \cap A \neq \emptyset} m(B), \quad \forall \ A \in 2^\Omega \tag{3}$$

$Pl(A)$ represents the total possible support for A and its subsets.

To combine several *bbas*, *Dempster*'s rule [6] is a popular choice. Let m_1 and m_2 two BBAs defined on the same frame of discernment Ω, their combination based on *Dempster*'s rule gives the following *bba*:

$$m_1 \oplus m_2(A) = \begin{cases} \frac{\sum\limits_{B \cap C = A} m_1(B)m_2(C)}{1 - \sum\limits_{B \cap C = \emptyset} m_1(B)m_2(C)} & for\ A \neq \emptyset\ and\ A \in 2^{\Omega}. \\ 0 & for\ A = \emptyset. \end{cases} \quad (4)$$

4   Evidential Undersampling-Based Ensemble Learning

An evidential undersampling method [11] is incorporated into a bagging ensemble, to create an Ensemble-based Evidential Undersampling (E-EVUS). The main idea is to create diverse undersampled subsets using different assumptions of ambiguity. This will add diversity to the resulting model, by combining various decision boundaries created by each base learner.

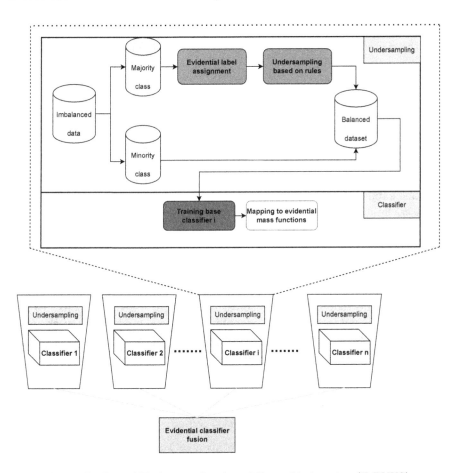

Fig. 1. Evidential Undersampling-based Ensemble learning (E-EVUS).

Our idea is detailed and illustrated in Fig 1. Before training each base classifier, the evidential undersampling process starts by assigning a soft label structure to each majority example. The amount of ambiguity present is randomly selected for each classifier. Then, the selection of instances to eliminate is made based on the location of each instance. The idea is to avoid the loss of important majority data, by only discarding unwanted observations, such as class overlapping, noise and outliers. After performing undersampling, each subset will be used to train a base model. In this paper, we use support vector machines [34] as weak classifiers. However, it is important to note that one can use any other classifier. Finally, we accomplish classifier fusion using an evidential combination, to create the final learning model.

4.1   Evidential Label Assignment

We recall the method used in [11] to create soft labels, which is based on the credal classification rule (CCR) [24]. It consists of firstly determining the center for each class by simply computing the mean value of the training data in the corresponding class. For the overlapping region, which is represented by a meta-class, the center is calculated by the barycenter of the involved class centers as follows:

$$C_U = \frac{1}{|U|} \sum_{\omega_i \in U} C_i \tag{5}$$

where U represents the meta-class, ω_i are the classes involved in U, and C_i is the corresponding center.

The evidential distribution of each majority example is represented by a *bba* over the frame of discernment $\Omega = \{\omega_0, \omega_1, \omega_2\}$ where ω_1 and ω_2 represent respectively the majority and the minority class. The element ω_0 is included in the frame explicitly to represent the outlier.

Let x_s be an observation from the majority class. Each class center represents a piece of evidence to the membership of the majority instance. The mass values for x_s should depend on $d(x_s, C)$, i.e., the distance between x_s and the corresponding class's center. The greater the distance, the lower the mass value. Henceforth, if x_s is more close to a specific class center, it means that x_s belongs very likely to the respective class. Subsequently, the initial (unnormalized) mass values should be represented by decreasing distance based functions. To deal with anisotropic datasets, the Mahalanobis distance is used in this work as recommended by [24].

The unnormalized masses are calculated as follows:

$$\hat{m}(\{\omega_i\}) = e^{-d(x_s, C_i)}, \quad i \in [1, 2] \tag{6}$$

$$\hat{m}(U) = e^{-\gamma \lambda d(x_s, C_U)}, \quad U = \{\omega_1, \omega_2\} \tag{7}$$

$$\hat{m}(\{\omega_0\}) = e^{-t} \tag{8}$$

where $\lambda = \beta \, 2^\alpha$. A recommended value for $\alpha = 1$ can be used to obtain good results on average, and β is a parameter such that $0 < \beta < 1$. The latter parameter is what gives us the ability to control the amount of overlap in the data, thus, allowing for diversity. In this ensemble framework, the value of β is randomly selected for each base classifier. The value of γ is equal to the ratio between the maximum distance of x_s to the centers in U and the minimum distance. It is used to measure the degree of distinguishability among both classes. The smaller γ indicates a poor distinguishability degree between the classes of U for x_s. The outlier class ω_0 is taken into account in order to deal with objects far from both classes, and its mass value is calculated according to an outlier threshold t.

Finally, the calculated unnormalized masses are normalized as follows:

$$m(A) = \frac{\hat{m}(A)}{\sum_{B \subseteq \Omega} \hat{m}(B)}, \quad \forall A \subseteq \Omega \tag{9}$$

4.2   Undersampling

After assigning *bbas*, each majority object will have masses in 4 focal elements namely: $m(\{\omega_1\})$ for the majority class, $m(\{\omega_2\})$ for the minority class, $m(U)$ for the overlapping region U, and $m(\{\omega_0\})$ for the outlier class. These masses are used to remove problematic samples from the majority class. There are different types of unwanted samples which could be removed namely:

- **Overlapping:** Ambiguous examples are usually present in regions where there is heavy overlap between classes as seen in Fig. 2a. This situation could be described by what is called "conflict" in Evidence Theory. In our framework, this type of examples will have a high mass value in $m(U)$. Thus, majority instances whose *bba* has the maximum mass committed to U are considered as part of an overlapping region, and are automatically discarded. The mass value assigned to U is heavily influenced by the randomly selected parameter β. Henceforth, the higher value of β will result in fewer objects committed to the ambiguous region. As for majority objects whose highest mass is not committed to U (i.e. not in overlapping region), the instance is necessarily committed to one of the singletons in Ω ($\{\omega_1\}$, $\{\omega_2\}$, or $\{\omega_0\}$). In this situation, we use the *plausibility* function defined in eq. (3) to make a decision of acceptance or rejection. Each majority instance x_s is affected to the class with the maximum plausibility $Pl_{max} = max_{\omega \in \Omega} Pl(\{\omega\})$.
- **Label noise:** Majority observations should normally have the maximum plausibility committed to ω_1 which measures the membership value towards the majority class. By contrast, having Pl_{max} committed to ω_2 signify that they are located in a minority region, as illustrated in Fig. 2c. Consequently, these objects are eliminated from the dataset.
- **Outlier:** The final scenario occurs when the sample in question is located in a region far from both classes, as shown in Fig. 2b. In our framework, this is characterized by the state of ignorance and could be discarded in the undersampling procedure. Hence, majority objects whose maximum plausibility Pl_{max} committed to ω_0 are considered as outliers and removed from the dataset.

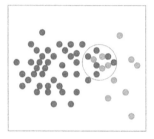
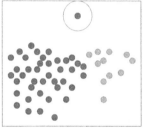
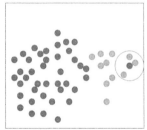

| Ambiguous samples in an overlapping area. | An outlier far from both classes. | A sample that could be characterized as label noise. |

Fig. 2. Illustrations describing the different data difficulty factors that could worsen class imbalance. Green and red colors respectively represent the majority class and the minority one. (Color figure online)

4.3   Base Classifier Learning and Combination

Our previously presented method achieved good performance in imbalanced classification tasks because it aims at improving the visibility of the minority class, by eliminating the unwanted examples [11]. However, the performance is highly influenced by the selected value for the parameter β, which controls the amount to eliminate from the ambiguous region. To tackle this issue, our evidential undersampling method is included into a bagging ensemble. For each iteration, a different value of the parameter β is randomly selected. As a result, very different subsets are created, as seen in Fig 3. The figure shows the results of undersampling performed on a real binary imbalanced example, before training a SVM classifier. As illustrated, the undersampled subsets can yield very diverse decision boundaries, depending on different ambiguity assumptions.

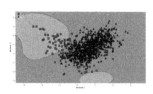
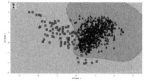
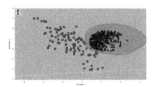

| SVM's decision boundaries on original distribution without resampling. | SVM's decision boundaries on undersampled data using our approach with $\beta = 0.7$. | SVM's decision boundaries on undersampled data using our approach with $\beta = 0.2$. |

Fig. 3. Comparing the resulted decision boundaries by SVM after performing our evidential undersampling on different amounts of overlap.

Then, each subset is used to train a base classifier. In this paper, we use the Support Vector Machine (SVM) classifier. It is a popular choice used in many imbalanced learning problems [12]. Each classifier is trained independently in bagging ensembles. Thus, we make the assumption that each model's output is an independent piece of evidence. Henceforth, we can use the Dempster's rule of combination presented in Eq. 4, as suggested in [27]. In our case, the output of each base classifier should be represented by mass functions. For this purpose, we propose to convert SVM's output into probability distributions using Platt scaling [26], before using the inverse pignistic transform [8]. As a result, a mass function is created for each base learner. Thus, the Dempster rule of combination can be applied to create a final combined mass function. Finally, the decision is made by choosing the singleton with the maximum plausibility $Pl_{max} = max_{\omega \in \Omega} Pl(\{\omega\})$.

5   Experimental Study

In this section, we will firstly detail the setup of the conducted experiments in Subsect. 5.1. Lastly, we will present the results and discuss them in Subsect. 5.2.

5.1   Setup

Datasets. We selected 14 binary imbalanced datasets from the keel repository [1]. The datasets are further detailed in Table 1. The imbalance ratio was calculated as $IR = \frac{\#majority}{\#minority}$. The variations of the different parameters (IR, features, and size) allowed for experimenting in different real world settings.

Table 1. Description of the imbalanced datasets selected from the KEEL repository.

Datasets	Imbalance ratios (IR)	Features	Samples
wisconsin	1.86	9	683
vehicle3	2.99	18	846
ecoli1	3.36	7	336
yeast3	8.1	8	1484
ecoli-0-6-7 vs 3-5	9.09	7	222
ecoli-0-2-6-7 vs 3-5	9.18	7	224
ecoli-0-1-4-7 vs 2-3-5-6	10.59	7	336
glass-0-1-4-6 vs 2	11.06	9	205
glass4	15.46	9	214
winequality-red-4	29.17	11	1599
winequality-red-8 vs 6	35.44	11	656
kr-vs-k-zero vs eight	53.07	6	1460
poker-8-9 vs 6	58.4	10	1485
abalone-20 vs 8-9-10	72.69	8	1916
poker-8 vs 6	85.88	10	1477

Reference Methods and Parameters. We compared our proposed method (E-EVUS) against well-known ensemble-based methods: EasyEnsemble (EASY) [22], RUSBoost [30], and RUSBagging [37]. For each ensemble, we use the base classifier suggested in the respective paper. In our case, we use the SVM classifier, as previously discussed. The following parameters were considered for our proposal: α was set to 1 as recommended in [24], the outlier parameter t for $m(\{\omega_0\})$ was fixed to 2 to obtain good results in average, and the number of base classifiers to train is set to 10. The other methods were set according to the suggested settings by the authors.

Metrics and Evaluation Strategy. To appropriately assess the methods in imbalanced scenarios, we use the G-Mean (GM) [2] and the F1-score, which are popular measures for evaluating classifiers in imbalanced learning. Following the confusion matrix described in Table 2, the evaluation metrics used in this paper are mathematically formulated as follows:

$$Precision = \frac{TP}{TP + FP} \tag{10}$$

$$Sensitivity = \frac{TP}{TP + FN} \tag{11}$$

$$Specificity = \frac{TN}{TN + FP} \tag{12}$$

$$\text{G-Mean} = \sqrt{sensitivity \times specificity} \tag{13}$$

$$F1 - score = \frac{2 \times sensitivity \times precision}{sensitivity + precision} \tag{14}$$

Table 2. Confusion matrix.

	Predictive Positive (P)	Predictive Negative (N)
Actual Positive	True Positive (TP)	False Negative (FN)
Actual Negative	False Positive (FP)	True Negative (TN)

In order to ensure the fairness of the observed results, we adopt a 5-fold stratified cross validation to eliminate inconsistencies. Finally, statistical comparisons were carried out using the Wilcoxon's signed rank tests [38] to further evaluate the significance of the results.

5.2 Results and Discussion

The measured scores G-Mean and F-score are reported in Table 3. The best scores are presented in bold. According to the presented experimental results, we can remark that our approach achieved relatively well for both assessment measures. In fact, the results show that our method has the best scores on G-Mean (10 out of 14) and F1-score (9 out of 14). The two chosen metrics consider the accuracy of both classes, since, as defined in Eq. 13, G-Mean is the square root of the product between the negative accuracy (i.e., specificity), and the positive accuracy (i.e., sensitivity). Meanwhile, the F-measure is based on precision and sensitivity. Therefore, we can initially argue that our proposal E-EVUS indeed improves the learning on the minority class while keeping the accuracy for the majority one.

Table 3. G-Mean and F1-score results for KEEL datasets using different ensemble techniques.

Datasets	G-Mean				F-Measure			
	EASY	RUSBagging	RUSBOOST	E-EVUS	EASY	RUSBagging	RUSBOOST	E-EVUS
wisconsin	0.962	0.971	0.945	**0.975**	0.973	**0.976**	0.962	**0.976**
vehicle3	0.736	0.768	0.719	**0.770**	0.817	**0.823**	0.822	0.822
ecoli1	0.782	0.823	0.810	**0.874**	0.905	**0.921**	0.919	0.918
yeast3	0.916	**0.922**	0.801	0.864	0.950	**0.953**	0.951	**0.953**
ecoli-0-6-7 vs 3-5	0.772	0.835	0.619	**0.879**	0.931	0.924	0.924	**0.944**
ecoli-0-2-6-7 vs 3-5	0.847	0.831	0.785	**0.874**	0.935	0.943	**0.950**	**0.950**
ecoli-0-1-4-7 vs 2-3-5-6	0.847	**0.853**	0.718	0.768	0.923	0.931	**0.956**	0.935
glass-0-1-4-6 vs 2	0.580	0.610	0.267	**0.655**	0.818	0.805	0.830	**0.872**
glass4	0.820	0.798	0.782	**0.852**	**0.971**	0.938	0.927	0.965
winequality-red-4	**0.664**	0.632	0.436	0.658	0.776	0.846	0.727	**0.890**
winequality-red-8 vs 6	0.740	0.674	0.368	**0.770**	0.875	0.854	0.893	**0.956**
poker-8-9 vs 6	0.377	0.611	0.177	**0.675**	0.510	0.872	0.881	**0.932**
abalone19	**0.753**	0.704	0.269	0.723	0.803	0.856	**0.957**	0.934
poker-8 vs 6	0.508	0.639	0.308	**0.717**	0.526	0.755	0.800	**0.882**

In the observed results, E-EVUS performed significantly better than the reference methods in highly uncertain datasets, i.e., where there are significant class overlapping, such as *poker-8-9 vs 6*, and *winequality-red-8 vs 6*. This is likely due to the fact that our method succeeded at eliminating the difficult and uncertain majority samples, which allowed for better learning of more difficult minority data examples.

In order to evaluate the significance of the comparisons, Table 4 presents the statistical analysis made by Wilcoxon's signed ranks test. $R+$ represents the sum of ranks in favor of E-EVUS, while $R-$ reflects the sum of ranks in favor of the other reference methods, and p-values are computed for each comparison. As shown in Table 4, almost all p-values are lower than 0.5. Thus, one can say that our method significantly outperformed the other techniques, for both selected metrics, with a signfgicance level of $\alpha = 0.05$.

Table 4. Wilcoxon's signed ranks test results comparing the G-Mean and F1-score metrics against the compared approaches.

Comparisons	G-Mean			F1-score		
	$R+$	$R-$	p-value	$R+$	$R-$	p-value
E-EVUS vs EASY	81.5	23.5	0.078491	101.0	4.0	0.0008544
E-EVUS vs RUSBagging	84.0	21.0	0.049438	103.0	2.0	0.004741
E-EVUS vs RUSBoost	105.0	0.0	0.000122	93.0	12.0	0.0341704

6   Conclusion

In this paper, we propose an evidential undersampling-based ensemble (E-EVUS), in which we use evidence theory to better learn from imbalanced datasets. The goal is to improve the visibility of the minority class by removing unwanted examples, such as noisy and overlapped observations. This technique is incorporated into a bagging ensemble framework, in order to diversify the created subsets. Therefore, it is more likely to improve the final decision boundary of the classifier.

In addition, our experimental study demonstrates that integrating evidential undersampling into ensemble learning, could result to diversity of base models, which facilitates the learning performance. Further investigations can include the use of hybrid resampling into our ensemble learning method.

References

1. Alcala-Fdez, J., et al.: Keel data-mining software tool: data set repository, integration of algorithms and experimental analysis framework. J. Multiple-Valued Log. Soft Comput. **17**, 255–287 (2010)
2. Barandela, R., Valdovinos, R.M., Sánchez, J.S.: New applications of ensembles of classifiers. Pattern Anal. Appl. **6**(3), 245–256 (2003). https://doi.org/10.1007/s10044-003-0192-z
3. Chawla, N.V., Bowyer, K.W., Hall, L.O., Kegelmeyer, W.P.: Smote: synthetic minority over-sampling technique. J. Artif. Intell. Res. **16**, 321–357 (2002)
4. Chawla, N.V., Lazarevic, A., Hall, L.O., Bowyer, K.W.: SMOTEBoost: improving prediction of the minority class in boosting. In: Lavrač, N., Gamberger, D., Todorovski, L., Blockeel, H. (eds.) PKDD 2003. LNCS (LNAI), vol. 2838, pp. 107–119. Springer, Heidelberg (2003). https://doi.org/10.1007/978-3-540-39804-2_12
5. Dablain, D., Krawczyk, B., Chawla, N.V.: DeepSMOTE: fusing deep learning and SMOTE for imbalanced data. IEEE Trans. Neural Netw. Learn. Syst. (2022)
6. Dempster, A.P.: A generalization of Bayesian inference. J. Roy. Stat. Soc.: Ser. B (Methodol.) **30**(2), 205–232 (1968)
7. Douzas, G., Bacao, F., Last, F.: Improving imbalanced learning through a heuristic oversampling method based on k-means and SMOTE. Inf. Sci. **465**, 1–20 (2018)
8. Dubois, D., Prade, H., Smets, P.: A definition of subjective possibility. Int. J. Approximate Reasoning **48**(2), 352–364 (2008)

9. Freund, Y., Schapire, R.E.: A decision-theoretic generalization of on-line learning and an application to boosting. J. Comput. Syst. Sci. **55**(1), 119–139 (1997)
10. Fu, Y., Du, Y., Cao, Z., Li, Q., Xiang, W.: A deep learning model for network intrusion detection with imbalanced data. Electronics **11**(6), 898 (2022)
11. Grina, F., Elouedi, Z., Lefevre, E.: Evidential undersampling approach for imbalanced datasets with class-overlapping and noise. In: Torra, V., Narukawa, Y. (eds.) MDAI 2021. LNCS (LNAI), vol. 12898, pp. 181–192. Springer, Cham (2021). https://doi.org/10.1007/978-3-030-85529-1_15
12. Haixiang, G., Yijing, L., Shang, J., Mingyun, G., Yuanyue, H., Bing, G.: Learning from class-imbalanced data: review of methods and applications. Expert Syst. Appl. **73**, 220–239 (2017)
13. Han, H., Wang, W.-Y., Mao, B.-H.: Borderline-SMOTE: a new over-sampling method in imbalanced data sets learning. In: Huang, D.-S., Zhang, X.-P., Huang, G.-B. (eds.) ICIC 2005. LNCS, vol. 3644, pp. 878–887. Springer, Heidelberg (2005). https://doi.org/10.1007/11538059_91
14. He, H., Garcia, E.A.: Learning from imbalanced data. IEEE Trans. Knowl. Data Eng. **21**(9), 1263–1284 (2009)
15. Huynh, T., Nibali, A., He, Z.: Semi-supervised learning for medical image classification using imbalanced training data. Comput. Methods Programs Biomed. 106628 (2022)
16. Ivan, T.: Two modification of CNN. IEEE Trans. Syst. Man Commun. SMC **6**, 769–772 (1976)
17. Jung, I., Ji, J., Cho, C.: EmSM: ensemble mixed sampling method for classifying imbalanced intrusion detection data. Electronics **11**(9), 1346 (2022)
18. Koziarski, M., Woźniak, M., Krawczyk, B.: Combined cleaning and resampling algorithm for multi-class imbalanced data with label noise. Knowl.-Based Syst. **204**, 106223 (2020)
19. Krawczyk, B., Galar, M., Jeleń, Ł, Herrera, F.: Evolutionary undersampling boosting for imbalanced classification of breast cancer malignancy. Appl. Soft Comput. **38**, 714–726 (2016)
20. Li, X., Gong, H.: Robust optimization for multilingual translation with imbalanced data. Adv. Neural Inf. Process. Syst. **34** (2021)
21. Lin, W.C., Tsai, C.F., Hu, Y.H., Jhang, J.S.: Clustering-based undersampling in class-imbalanced data. Inf. Sci. **409–410**, 17–26 (2017)
22. Liu, X.Y., Wu, J., Zhou, Z.H.: Exploratory undersampling for class-imbalance learning. IEEE Trans. Syst. Man Cybern. Part B (Cybern.) **39**(2), 539–550 (2008)
23. Liu, Y., et al.: Pick and choose: a GNN-based imbalanced learning approach for fraud detection. In: Proceedings of the Web Conference 2021, pp. 3168–3177 (2021)
24. Liu, Z.G., Pan, Q., Dezert, J., Mercier, G.: Credal classification rule for uncertain data based on belief functions. Pattern Recogn. **47**(7), 2532–2541 (2014)
25. Niu, J., Liu, Z.: Imbalance data classification based on belief function theory. In: Denœux, T., Lefèvre, E., Liu, Z., Pichon, F. (eds.) BELIEF 2021. LNCS (LNAI), vol. 12915, pp. 96–104. Springer, Cham (2021). https://doi.org/10.1007/978-3-030-88601-1_10
26. Platt, J.: Probabilistic outputs for SVMs and comparisons to regularized likehood methods. In: Advances in Large Margin Classifiers. MIT Press (1999)
27. Quost, B., Masson, M.H., Denœux, T.: Classifier fusion in the dempster-Shafer framework using optimized t-norm based combination rules. Int. J. Approximate Reasoning **52**(3), 353–374 (2011)

28. Sáez, J.A., Luengo, J., Stefanowski, J., Herrera, F.: SMOTE-IPF: addressing the noisy and borderline examples problem in imbalanced classification by a re-sampling method with filtering. Inf. Sci. **291**, 184–203 (2015)

29. Sağlam, F., Cengiz, M.A.: A novel smote-based resampling technique trough noise detection and the boosting procedure. Expert Syst. Appl. **200**, 117023 (2022)

30. Seiffert, C., Khoshgoftaar, T.M., Van Hulse, J., Napolitano, A.: RUSBoost: a hybrid approach to alleviating class imbalance. IEEE Trans. Syst. Man Cybern.-Part A Syst. Hum. **40**(1), 185–197 (2009)

31. Shafer, G.: A Mathematical Theory of Evidence, vol. 42. Princeton University Press, Princeton (1976)

32. Smets, P.: The nature of the unnormalized beliefs encountered in the transferable belief model. In: Uncertainty in Artificial Intelligence, pp. 292–297. Elsevier (1992)

33. Smets, P.: The transferable belief model for quantified belief representation. In: Smets, P. (ed.) Quantified Representation of Uncertainty and Imprecision. HDRUMS, vol. 1, pp. 267–301. Springer, Dordrecht (1998). https://doi.org/10.1007/978-94-017-1735-9_9

34. Vapnik, V.: The Nature of Statistical Learning Theory. Springer, Heidelberg (2013). https://doi.org/10.1007/978-1-4757-2440-0

35. Vuttipittayamongkol, P., Elyan, E., Petrovski, A.: On the class overlap problem in imbalanced data classification. Knowl.-Based Syst. **212**, 106631 (2021)

36. Wallace, B.C., Small, K., Brodley, C.E., Trikalinos, T.A.: Class imbalance, redux. In: 2011 IEEE 11th International Conference on Data Mining, pp. 754–763. IEEE (2011)

37. Wang, S., Yao, X.: Diversity analysis on imbalanced data sets by using ensemble models. In: 2009 IEEE Symposium on Computational Intelligence and Data Mining, pp. 324–331. IEEE (2009)

38. Wilcoxon, F.: Individual comparisons by ranking methods. In: Kotz, S., Johnson, N.L. (eds.) Breakthroughs in Statistics, pp. 196–202. Springer, New York (1992). https://doi.org/10.1007/978-1-4612-4380-9_16

39. Wilson, D.L.: Asymptotic properties of nearest neighbor rules using edited data. IEEE Trans. Syst. Man Cybern. **3**, 408–421 (1972)

Non-specificity-based Supervised Discretization for Possibilistic Classification

Ilyes Jenhani[1]([✉]), Ghaith Khlifi[2], Panagiotis Sidiropoulos[2,3], Henk Jansen[2], and George Frangou[2,4,5]

[1] College of Computer Engineering and Science,
Prince Mohammad Bin Fahd University, Al-Khobar 31952, Kingdom of Saudi Arabia
ijenhani@pmu.edu.sa
[2] Massive Analytic Ltd., London, UK
{ghaith.khlifi,panagiotis.sidiropoulos,henk.jansen,
george.frangou}@massiveanalytic.com
[3] Mullard Space Science Laboratory, University College London, London, UK
[4] UCL Quantum Science & Technology Institute, London, UK
{p.sidiropoulos,george.frangou.20}@ucl.ac.uk
[5] Autonomous Systems Dynamics and Control Research Group Centre for
Autonomous and Cyber Physical Systems, Cranfield University, Bedford, UK
George.Frangou@cranfield.ac.uk

Abstract. Data imperfection and information uncertainty are inevitable in many application domains, including medicine, finance, meteorology, cybersecurity, etc. Sources of uncertainty include the lack of information of the solicited experts, sensor unreliability for automatically collected data, conflicting information sources, etc.. Classification techniques, such as the non-specificity based possibilistic decision trees (NSPDT) have been proposed to deal with such uncertainty. However, most of the introduced possibilistic methods are limited to categorical features, i.e. they can not process data input that is continuous. This paper address this limitation through a supervised possibilistic discretization method, which transforms continuous features into categorical features in datasets where class labels are imperfect and represented by possibility distributions. The proposed method can be used as a pre-processing step to make it possible to use methods such as NSPDT in datasets that initially have continuous features. The proposed non-specificity based discretization algorithm has provided good quality categorical features which have led to obtain NSPDT trees showing an accuracy higher than 80% in most cases. With original datasets, where the instances have certain (i.e. non-possibilistic) class labels, the proposed possibilistic discretization method has shown a robust performance compared to the standard discretization algorithm which is the default approach in this case. The difference in accuracy has not exceeded 5% for all used datasets and all tested classifiers, and in some cases, the possibilistic discretization outperformed the standard discretization.

© The Author(s), under exclusive license to Springer Nature Switzerland AG 2022
F. Dupin de Saint-Cyr et al. (Eds.): SUM 2022, LNAI 13562, pp. 249–262, 2022.
https://doi.org/10.1007/978-3-031-18843-5_17

Keywords: Discretization · Possibility theory · Possibilistic decision trees · Non-specificity

1 Introduction

The discretization of continuous features is a very common practice in many machine learning tasks such as classification and clustering. It consists in transforming a range of numeric values of one particular feature into a finite smaller set of intervals. Interval labels are then used to replace actual numeric data values. Discretization, as a pre-processing step, helps provide datasets with less noisy, more concise and more informed features, which in turn increases interpretability and explainability of machine learning models (and results). Moreover, many machine learning techniques are restricted to categorical data, hence they cannot be used without passing the data through a pre-processing, discretization step.

Discretization algorithms can be subdivided into two groups, namely the unsupervised and the supervised methods [1], depending on whether any labels are used to guide the discretization algorithm. Unsupervised discretisation includes simple methods such as equal-width (in which each bin has the same value width) [20] and equal-frequency (in which each bin has the same number of observations) [19]. More sophisticated unsupervised discretisation techniques make use of clustering [21], or fuzzy partitions and fuzzy set intervals [22].

However, it is commonly assumed that the classification accuracy of pipelines employing unsupervised discretisation is worse than this achieved if supervised disretisation is used [23]. Hence, a number of techniques have been introduced that employ class labels in continuous features discretisation. These can be further categorised into the techniques that optimise a statistical property of the discretised signal such as its entropy [24] or inter-class statistical independence [25] and the techniques that assume a prior distribution [26].

Regardless of the specific approach, most of existing supervised discretization algorithms deal with perfectly labeled data, i.e. each instance has a certain and precise class label. However, in many application domains such as medicine, finance, meteorology, cybersecurity, etc., data imperfection and information uncertainty are inevitable. This uncertainty might be the result of: (1) a lack of information from the expert who is providing it, (2) sensor unreliability for automatically collected data, (3) conflicting information sources. Several classification algorithms such as k-nearest neighbors, decision trees, naive Bayes, etc. have been extended to deal with feature and/or class imperfections using different uncertainty theories such as probability theory [3], fuzzy set theory [5], evidence theory [7], possibility theory [4], etc. Some of these uncertain classifiers (e.g., Possibilistic decision trees [2], Naive Possibilistic Networks [8,9]) only deal with categorical features.

In this paper, we are proposing a supervised discretization method for possibilistic datasets (i.e., where instances are imperfectly labeled by possibility distributions over the possible class labels). The proposed method can be used to discretize continuous features in such datasets then train possibilisitc decision trees or any other possibilistic classifier that only handles categorical features.

The rest of the paper is organized as follows: Sect. 2 provides an overview of Possibility theory and standard discretization techniques. Section 3 describes our proposed non-specificity based discretization algorithm. Section 4 presents experiments and discusses results. Finally, Sect. 5 concludes the paper.

2   Background

In this section, we provide an overview of possibility theory and the standard discretization methods.

2.1   Possibility Theory

Possibility theory [4,6] is a simple mathematical tool which offers a natural and simple model to deal with information that is subject to imprecision, uncertainty or inconsistency, hence the term imperfection or uncertainty. The approach that is proposed in this article relies on the following elements of the possibility theory.

Possibility Distribution. One of the key elements of possibility theory is the concept of possibility distributions. A possibility distribution (denoted by π) is suitable for representing imperfect/uncertain information from the varying sources such experts and sensors. Given a state of affairs $\Omega = \{\omega_1, \omega_2, \ldots, \omega_n\}$, π represents a mapping of each element ω_i from the state of affairs to a value known as a possibility degree from the interval $[0, 1]$ that is a representation/encoding of our knowledge of the real world. By convention, $\pi(\omega_i) = 1$ means that it is fully possible that ω_i is the real world, $\pi(\omega_i) = 0$ means that ω_i cannot be the real world (is impossible). Flexibility is modeled using a possibility degree from $]0, 1[$. $\pi(\omega_i) > \pi(\omega_j)$ means that ω_i is more plausible than ω_j.

In possibility theory, we can distinguish the following two special cases of possibility distributions:

– Dogmatic possibility distribution: $\exists \omega_i \in \Omega$, $\pi(\omega_i) = 1$ and $\forall \omega_j \neq \omega_i$, $\pi(\omega_j) = 0$. In this situation of complete knowledge, one element is fully possible and all remaining elements are impossible.
– Vacuous possibility distribution: $\forall \omega_i \in \Omega$, $\pi(\omega_i) = 1$. In this situation of total ignorance, all elements are equally fully possible.

Normalization and Inconsistency. A possibility distribution π is said to be normalized if there exists at least one element $\omega_i \in \Omega$ which is fully possible ($\pi(\omega_i) = 1$). Otherwise, π is said to be inconsistent and we can measure its inconsistency degree with the following formula:

$$\text{Inc}(\pi) = 1 - \max_{\omega_i \in \Omega} \{\pi(\omega_i)\} \tag{1}$$

For normalized π, $\max_{\omega_i \in \Omega} \{\pi(\omega_i)\} = 1$, hence $\text{Inc}(\pi) = 0$. The measure Inc is very useful in assessing the degree of conflict between two information sources (i.e. two possibility distributions π_1 and π_2) which is given by $\mathrm{Inc}(\pi_1 \wedge \pi_2)$ where the conjunction $\wedge$ is taken as the minimum (min) operator:

$$\mathrm{Inc}\,(\pi_1, \pi_2) = \mathrm{Inc}\,(\pi_1 \wedge \pi_2) = 1 - \max_{\omega_i \in \Omega} \left\{ \min_{\omega_i \in \Omega} \left\{ \pi_1\,(\omega_i), \pi_2\,(\omega_i) \right\} \right\} \qquad (2)$$

Similarity in Possibility Theory. The similarity degree between imperfect information provided by two information sources (i.e. two normalized possibility distributions π_1 and π_2), could be measured by the so-called Information Affinity [10] which is given by the following formula:

$$\mathrm{InfoAff}\,(\pi_1, \pi_2) = 1 - \frac{\kappa \times d\,(\pi_1, \pi_2) + \lambda \times \mathrm{Inc}\,(\pi_1, \pi_2)}{\kappa + \lambda} \qquad (3)$$

where $\kappa > 0$ and $\lambda > 0$ are two user-defined parameters, and d is the normalized Manhattan distance defined as follows:

$$d\,(\pi_1, \pi_2) = \frac{\sum_{i=1}^{n} |\pi_1\,(\omega_i) - \pi_2\,(\omega_i)|}{n} \qquad (4)$$

Inc denotes the inconsistency measure (Eq. 2) between the two distributions π_1 and π_2.

Please note that $\mathrm{InfoAff}\,(\pi_1, \pi_2) \in [0, 1]$. $\mathrm{InfoAff}\,(\pi_1, \pi_2) = 1$ when π_1 and π_2 are identical normalized possibility distributions whereas $\mathrm{InfoAff}\,(\pi_1, \pi_2) = 0$ when π_1 and π_2 are normalized binary possibility distributions which complement each others (i.e. $\forall i, \pi_1(\omega_i) = 1 - \pi_2(\omega_i)$ or $\pi_2(\omega_i) = 1 - \pi_1(\omega_i)$ and $\pi_2(\omega_i), \pi_1(\omega_i) \in \{0, 1\}$).

Non-Specificity in Possibility Theory. Given a permutation σ of the degrees of a possibility distribution π: $[\pi_{\sigma(1)}, \pi_{\sigma(2)}, ..., \pi_{\sigma(n)}]$ s.t. $1 = \pi_{\sigma(1)} \geq \pi_{\sigma(2)} \geq ... \geq \pi_{\sigma(n)}$, the non-specificity degree of the information encoded by π is given by [11]:

$$U(\pi) = \sum_{i=1}^{n} \left(\pi_{\sigma(i)} - \pi_{\sigma(i+1)} \right) \log_2(i) \qquad (5)$$

where $\pi_{\sigma(n+1)=0}$. Note that the range of U is $[0, log_2(n)]$. $U(\pi) = 0$ is obtained for the case of complete knowledge (no uncertainty) and $U(\pi) = log_2(n)$ is obtained for the case of total ignorance.

2.2   Discretization of Continuous Features

Discretization represents a very useful pre-processing method which aims to transform continuous features into discrete ones. This is usually accomplished by splitting each feature space into a discrete number of intervals.

There are different categorizations of the discretization methods: (1) unsupervised vs. supervised, (2) local vs. global, (3) direct vs. incremental, (4) splitting (top-down) vs. merging (bottom-up). Unsupervised discretization techniques only rely on feature values and ignore the class labels assigned to each instance for labeled datasets. These algorithms divide each feature space into a fixed number of intervals having equal width intervals or equal frequency intervals, etc. On the other hand, supervised discretization tries to find the most appropriate (informative) intervals by using the mutual information between the feature values and their associated class labels.

A widely used supervised discretization technique is the Minimum Description Length Principle (MDLP) based discretization technique [14]. This technique relies on the calculation of the entropy and information gain with a predetermined stopping criteria. Local discretization techniques operate on a local region of the feature space. (i.e. a subset of instances). On the other hand, global methods use the entire feature space during their discretization process [17]. Direct discretization methods simultaneously divide the initial interval into n sub-intervals and therefore require to choose the desired number of intervals beforehand. However, incremental methods [18] start with a simple initial splitting and gradually improve the splits, until a stopping criterion is met.

Splitting techniques start with an empty list of cut-points and gradually find the cut-points to form the intervals. In contrast, merging techniques begin with C possible cut-points and, at each step of the discretization process, refine this set by removing cut-points (i.e. by the merging intervals). The technique we are proposing in this paper is a top-down, supervised, global splitting technique.

3   The Non-specificity Based Discretization Algorithm

Let us consider a dataset $D = \{I_1, I_2, ..., I_n\}$ of n possibilistic instances where each instance I_i is (1) represented by a m-tuple of m continuous features $(F_1, F_2, ..., F_m)$ and (2) labeled by a possibility distribution π_i : $[\pi_i(L_0), \pi_i(L_1), ..., \pi_i(L_{c-1})]$ where $L = \{L_0, L_1, ..., L_{c-1}\}$ is the set of the c possible class labels of the problem. An example of a possibilistic dataset is provided in Table 1.

Table 1. An example of a possibilistic dataset

F_1	F_2	...	F_m	Class $[L_i : \pi(L_i)]$
150.6	16.7	...	43	[0: 0.4; 1: 0.7; 2: 1]
141.8	33.8	...	54	[0: 0.3; 1: 1; 2 :0.6]
111.9	23.2	...	80	[0: 1; 1: 0.3; 2 :0.5]
137.2	42.5	...	20	[0: 1; 1:0; 2: 0]

A possibilistic dataset can contain both certain and uncertain instances. For example, the last instance in Table 1 is a perfect (crisp) one and its label is certainly "0" since $\pi(L_0) = 1$ and $\pi(L_j) = 0 \ \forall j \neq 0$. This is a nice property of this dataset representation since it allows to also handle crisp datasets (i.e. where all possibility distributions are dogmatic).

3.1   The Proposed Algorithm

Steps of the non-specificity based discretization algorithm (NS-Discretization) are outlined below.

Step 1. Consider all continuous features F_1, F_2, ..., F_m for Steps 2–6.

Step 2. Sort all given values of a particular continuous feature $F_i \in F$ in ascending order.

Step 3. For the current dataset partition P, generate the set of possible cut points $T = \{t_1, t_2, ..., t_k\}$. Cut points will be calculated as the average of the F_i values of two consecutive instances j and $j+1$ only when the similarity between the possibility distributions labeling both instances is smaller than a pre-defined threshold, i.e. InfoAff(π_j, π_{j+1}) $\leq \eta$. InfoAff is the similarity measure defined in Eq. 3.

Step 4. For each cut point $t \in T$, calculate the non-specificity based information gain of the cut point t for the partition P using the following equation:

$$NSGain\left(P, t\right) = U\left(\pi_{Rep}^P\right) - \left(\frac{\left|P^{F_i \leq t}\right|}{|P|} U\left(\pi_{Rep}^{P^{F_i \leq t}}\right) + \frac{\left|P^{F_i > t}\right|}{|P|} U\left(\pi_{Rep}^{P^{F_i > t}}\right)\right)$$

(6)

U denotes the non-specificity function provided by Eq. 5. $P^{F_i \leq t}$ denotes the sub-partition of P where $F_i \leq t$. $P^{F_i > t}$ denotes the sub-partition of P where $F_i > t$. $|P|$ (resp. $\left|P^{F_i \leq t}\right|$ and $\left|P^{F_i > t}\right|$) denotes the number of instances in P (resp. $P^{F_i \leq t}$ and $P^{F_i > t}$). π_{Rep}^P (resp. $\pi_{Rep}^{P^{F_i \leq t}}$ and $\pi_{Rep}^{P^{F_i > t}}$) denotes the normalized representative possibility distribution of the set of possibility distributions labeling the instances in P (resp. $P^{F_i \leq t}$ and $P^{F_i > t}$) and is calculated as:

$$\pi_{Rep}^P\left(L_i\right) = \frac{\pi_{AM}^P\left(L_i\right)}{\max_{i=1}^c \left\{\pi_{AM}^P\left(L_i\right)\right\}} , \forall i = 1..c$$

(7)

and

$$\pi_{AM}^P\left(L_i\right) = \frac{1}{|P|}\left(\sum_{j=1}^{|P|} \pi_j\left(L_i\right)\right), \forall i = 1..c$$

(8)

$\pi_{AM}^P\left(L_i\right)$ denotes the mean of the possibility degrees associated to the class label L_i in the partition P.

Step 5. Choose the cut point t_{cut} that maximizes the non-specificity gain criterion: $t_{cut} = argmax_{i=1}^k \{NSGain(P, t_i)\}$. If $NSGain(P, t_{cut}) > 0$, accept the cut point t_{cut}. Otherwise, terminate the recursion.

Step 6. Execute Steps 2–5 for the partitions $P^{F_i \leq t_{cut}}$ and $P^{F_i > t_{cut}}$ recursively and sort all cut points.

3.2   Algorithm Steps Discussion

In what follows, we provide justifications of the choices made in the main steps of the algorithm.

Cut Points Detection. For the cut point selection step (Step 3) of the algorithm, prior research [14] has demonstrated that, after sorting values of one particular feature in ascending order, cut points always occur on the boundary between two classes (i.e. when the class label of instance $i+1$ and instance i are no longer the same). In our context, since we are dealing with possibilistic labels, the boundary between two classes is not necessarily sharp and the label changes gradually. To assess the degree of change between possibilistic class labels, we used the InfoAff similarity measure between the possibility distributions labeling any two consecutive instances. We chose to assign the same weight $\kappa = \lambda = 1$ in Eq. 3. As indicated in Step 3 of the algorithm, we consider that there is a class label change, hence a possible cut point, when the similarity between two consecutive possibilitic labels falls under a threshold η. Smaller η values result in sharper and more restrictive boundaries whereas greater η values result in softer and less restrictive boundaries.

Supervised Cut Point Selection and Stopping Criterion. In Step 4 of the algorithm, we propose to use the non-specificity measure (defined in Sect. 2.1) to assess the information gain (i.e. the mutual information) when splitting a feature partition according to a given cut point. Standard discretization algorithms use entropy as the basis of the information gain relative to given cut point because each (sub-)partition can be represented by a class label probability distribution. In our context, each (sub-)partition will be represented by a set of possibility distributions which correspond to the labels of the instances reaching that (sub-)partition. Since these possibility distributions correspond to different observations which are not necessarily provided by the same source, we opted for the average as a fusion approach to aggregate the possibility degrees associated to each class label independently then we normalized the obtained possibility distribution π_{AM} to get the final possibility distribution representing the (sub-)partition P, namely π_{Rep}^P. The non-specificity measure (Eq. 5) is used to assess the "imprecision" of the (sub-)partition which is now represented by π_{Rep}^P. From the identified cut points (Step 3), the one which will maximize the information gain (i.e. the one which will result in the least imprecise sub-partitions) will be selected. For a given partition P, if all identified cut points result in negative or null information gains, we stop the recursive partitioning of P.

4   Experimental Study

In this section, we will first provide a description of the datasets we used in our experimental study. Secondly, we will describe the process we used in order to generate the possibilistic labels from the crisp (original) datasets. Finally, we will report and analyze the results of the discretization of the possibilistic datasets by using the non-specificity based possibilistic decision trees (NSPDT) [2].

4.1   Datasets

In Table 2, we provide the details of the datasets we used in our experiments. These datasets have been selected from the U.C.I. machine learning repository [12]. We selected datasets with different sizes (#instances), different number of class labels (#classes), different total number of features (#features) and different number of continuous features (#continuous features). The first five datasets have only continuous features. The last two ones have mixed (continuous and categorical) features.

Table 2. Dataset characteristics

Dataset	#instances	#classes	#features	#continuous features
Letter Recognition	20000	26	16	16
Dry Bean	13611	7	16	16
Magic Gamma Telescope	19020	2	10	10
Occupancy Detection	9752	2	5	5
Spambase	4601	2	57	57
Adult	48842	2	14	6
Bank Marketing	45211	2	20	10

4.2   Possibilistic Dataset Generation

The datasets in Table 2 are all crisp datasets where each instance is labeled by a unique, precise and certain class label. In the following, we explain how to distill the class uncertainty to generate a possibilistic dataset (from a crisp dataset) that has a structure similar to the one described in Table 1.

1. **Step 1:** In this step, we take the original crisp dataset and we feed it to a Gaussian Naive Bayes classifier [13]: a variant of the Naive Bayes classifier that supports continuous features and models each as conforming to a Gaussian (normal) distribution.
2. **Step 2:** Now we feed all instances of our original dataset to the Gaussian Naive Bayes model that was trained in Step 1 to get the predictions. For each instance, we will obtain the prediction as a probability distribution over the different possible classes.

3. **Step 3:**. For each instance, we will transform the predicted probability distribution into a possibility distribution using the following probability-possibility transformation [16]:

$$\pi\left(x_i\right) = \sum_{j=1,n} \min\left(p\left(x_i\right), p\left(x_j\right)\right) \qquad (9)$$

where p is a probability distribution over the set $X = \{x_1, x_2, ..., x_n\}$.

4. **Step 4:** Replace the crisp label of each instance in the original dataset by its corresponding computed possibility distribution.

We have implemented the possibilitic dataset generator in Python where we used the Scikit-learn implementation of the Gaussian Naive Bayes classifier[1].

4.3   Experimental Results and Analyses

In this section, we will assess the quality of the possibilistic discretization algorithm in two different settings: (1) the standard setting where class labels are known with certainty and (2) the uncertain setting where the class labels of the dataset are uncertain.

How Does the Possibilitic Discretization Perform Compared to the Standard Discretization with Certain (standard) Datasets? To answer this question, we will first discretize the original datasets using the standard supervised discretization [14] then train/test several standard classifiers on the discretized datasets. Secondly, we will discretize the original datasets using the proposed possibilistic discretization algorithm. To do so, we simply need to one-hot encode the original class label of each instance, which will result in a dogmatic possibility distribution which represents that fully known class. After performing the possibilistic discretization, each dogmatic possibility distribution will be reverted back to the original crisp class it encodes and the same standard classifiers will be trained/tested (with the same hyper-parameters setting) on the discretized datasets.

We have implemented the standard discretization algorithm [14] as well as the proposed possibilistic discretization algorithm in Python. For this experiment, we have used the Weka [15] environment to train/test different classification approaches on the original and discretized datasets, including Naive Bayes (NB), Logistic regression (LogReg), 1-Nearest neighbors (1-NN), Decision trees (J48) and Random Forests (RF). We chose these classifiers because they can deal with both continuous and categorical features.

Table 3 shows the mean accuracy of a 10-fold cross-validation performed for each classifier on (1) the original non-discretized dataset, (2) the dataset discretized with the standard discretization algorithm [14] and (3) the dataset

---

[1] https://scikit-learn.org/stable/modules/generated/sklearn.naive_bayes.Gaussian NB.html.

discretized with the possibilistic non-specificity based discretization algorithm. Please note that in this certain context, the parameter η was set to be equal to $1 - [(2 + c)/(2 * c)]$ where c denotes the number of classes of the dataset. This value corresponds to the minimum $InfoAff$ similarity degree between two possibility distributions which encode two different class labels.

From Table 3, we can notice that no method is outperforming all others on all datasets. However, we can make the following observations:

- For most of the datasets (5 out of 7), discretization has improved the accuracy of almost all classifiers.
- For the Naive Bayes classifier, which is initially designed to handle categorical features, discretization (standard or possibilistic) has improved the results with all datasets. The increase in accuracy was significant for datasets like Letter recognition (+9%), Magic Gamma Telescope (+6%), Spambase (+5%) and Occupancy detection (+4%).
- With tree based classifiers (i.e. J48 and RF) which were designed to handle both categorical and continuous features, we notice that the random forest performed the highest with 6 out of the 7 original datasets. This is not the case with decision trees (J48) where the discretization slightly improved its accuracy with 4 out of the 7 datasets. The highest increase in accuracy happened with the Spambase dataset (+10%).
- The 1-nearest neighbor with its Euclidean distance can handle continuous features easily. This classifier seems to be the one that worked the best with the non-specificity discretization method. In fact, 1-NN provided the highest accuracy with 4 out of 7 datasets.
- The Logistic regression classifier has shown high accuracy with all datasets. Moreover, this classifier is showing very close accuracy on all dataset versions (original, standard and possibilistic discretization). It seems like the one-hot encoding of the categorical features is doing a good job with this classifier (which was initially designed to handle continuous features).

Overall, we can notice that the non-specificity based discretization is providing good quality discretization but the standard discretization is more suitable when class labels are known with certainty. In fact, our proposed method was initially designed to handle class uncertainty where standard discretization is not applicable.

How Does the Possibilitic Discretization Perform with Uncertain Datasets? To answer this question, we first need to use the possibilistic dataset generation procedure described in Sect. 4.2. Secondly, we will train/test a possibilistic decision tree classifier, namely NSPDT [2] on the generated possibilistic datasets. For this experiment, we used a MATLAB implementation of the Non-specificity based possibilitic decision trees (NSPDT) [2].We used the following metrics to evaluate the possibilistic decision tree classifier performance:

- Percentage of Cautious Most Plausible-based correct classification (CMPcc):

Table 3. Mean accuracy (10-fold cross validation) of standard classifiers on different dataset versions: (1) non discretized (Non disc.), (2) discretized with the standard discretization algorithm [14] (Std. disc.) and (3) discretized with the Non-specificity discretization algorithm (NS-disc.)

Dataset	Classifier	Mean Acc. (Non disc.)	Mean Acc.(Std. disc.)	Mean Acc.(NS-disc.)
Letter recognition	NB	64.01	**73.85**	70.6
	J48	**87.92**	78.75	80.59
	RF	**96.41**	93.41	92.61
	1-NN	**95.96**	91.86	89
	LogReg	91.24	**92.84**	90.14
Dry Bean	NB	89.7	**89.94**	88.5
	J48	**91.03**	90.05	90.25
	RF	**92.5**	91.47	91.14
	1-NN	**90.2**	89.25	**90.2**
	LogReg	**92.6**	92.3	**92.6**
Magic Gamma Telescope	NB	72.68	**78.25**	75
	J48	**85.05**	84.45	77.57
	RF	**88**	84.04	77.46
	1-NN	80.93	**81.97**	77.42
	LogReg	79.11	**84.68**	77.5
Occupancy Detection	NB	95.34	99.1	**99.33**
	J48	95.86	**99.37**	**99.37**
	RF	**99.4**	**99.4**	99.37
	1-NN	94.99	**99.37**	**99.37**
	LogReg	99.24	**99.35**	**99.35**
Spambase	NB	85.24	**90.19**	85.78
	J48	82.59	**92.82**	91.58
	RF	**95.5**	94.59	93.87
	1-NN	85.28	**93.1**	92.24
	LogReg	92.41	**94.41**	91.58
Adult	NB	83.25	**83.87**	82.35
	J48	86.1	**86.67**	85.45
	RF	85.17	**85.4**	84.75
	1-NN	79.52	83.04	**84.13**
	LogReg	85.09	**87.23**	85.58
Bank Marketing	NB	88	**88.88**	**88.88**
	J48	90.31	**90.32**	88.88
	RF	**90.38**	89.92	88.87
	1-NN	86.96	88.83	**88.87**
	LogReg	90.15	**90.4**	88.87

$$CMPcc = \frac{\text{number of correctly classified instances}}{\text{total number of testing instances}} \times 100 \qquad (10)$$

A correctly classified instance is an instance whose predicted most plausible labels (i.e. labels with a possibility degree equal to 1) correspond exactly to all its initial most plausible labels. This is a rigid "all or nothing" criterion.

– Information Affinity-based criterion (InfoAffC):

$$\text{InfoAffC} = \frac{1}{n} \sum_{i=1}^{n} InfoAff\left(\pi_i^{\text{init}}, \pi_i^{\text{pred}}\right) \qquad (11)$$

This metric corresponds to the mean similarity (Information Affinity) between the initial possibility distribution labeling an instance i (π_i^{init}) and its predicted possibility distribution (π_i^{pred}) for all n testing instances.

We discretized each possibilistic dataset using the non-specificity based discretization algorithm. Then we split each dataset into a training set (80%) and a testing set (20%). Table 4 reports the Percentage of Cautious Most Plausible-based correct classification (CMPcc) and the Information Affinity-based criterion (InfoAffC) of the NSPDT trees for each dataset.

Table 4. Percentage of Cautious Most Plausible-based correct classification (CMPcc) and Mean Information Affinity criterion (InfoAffC) of the NSPDT trees on the possibilistic versions of the different used datasets

Dataset (Possibilistic version)	CMPcc (%)	InfoAffC
Letter Recognition	60.20	0.871
Dry Bean	88.47	0.963
Magic Gamma Telescope	81.65	0.836
Occupancy Detection	95.95	0.956
Spambase	79.91	0.84
Adult	96.66	0.96
Bank Marketing	86.82	0.882

The NSPDT trees are showing a high InfoAffC values (0.882 and above) for all datasets. This reflects the high similarity between the initial possibility distributions and the predicted ones. With the "all or nothing" CMPcc metric, the NSPDT trees are still showing a very good performance (between 79.91% for the Spambase dataset and 96.66% for the Adult dataset). It is important to note that the high CMPcc values obtained for the Adult and Occupancy detection datasets are not related to the inherent class label uncertainty which was distilled during the dataset transformation (from crisp to possibilistic). In fact, for the Adult (resp. Occupancy) dataset, only 0.76% (resp. 0.78%) of the instances have at least another possible class (class with a possibility degree ≥ 0.5).

The relatively low performance of 60.2% obtained with the Letter recognition dataset can be explained by the large number of class labels (26 labels) for this dataset. With larger sets of class labels, we get sparse possibility distributions and a full agreement about the most plausible classes is less likely to happen.

The high InfoAffC and CMPcc reported values in Table 4 indicate that the non-specificity discretization algorithm has provided discretized datasets with good quality. Hence, thanks to this algorithm, possibilistic classifiers, such as the Non-specificity based decision trees, can now handle classification problems where the datasets have continuous and categorical features.

5   Conclusion

In this paper, we proposed a discretization algorithm for possibilistic datasets where class labels are labeled by possibility distributions. This will extend the coverage of the possibilistic classifiers such as the possibilistic decision trees and make them applicable to problems where instances have continuous features as well. The proposed method uses the concept of non-specificity to assess the mutual information between the feature values and the possibilistic class labels. Possibilistic datasets have been generated to test the quality of the possibilitic discretization algorithm. Results have shown that the algorithm performs well with standard (certain) datasets but performs better with uncertain datasets (which is the main motivation behind its design).

In the future, we are planing to further improve the algorithm by considering feature dependency during the discretization process. We are also thinking about optimizing the algorithm to avoid getting imbalanced intervals by suggesting a better stopping criterion.

References

1. García, S., Luengo, J., Sáez, J.A., López, V., Herrera, F.: A survey of discretization techniques: taxonomy and empirical analysis in supervised learning. IEEE Trans. Knowl. Data Eng. **25**(4), 734–750 (2013)
2. Jenhani, I., Amor, N.B., Elouedi, Z.: Decision trees as possibilistic classifiers. Int. J. Approx. Reasoning. **48**(3), 784–807 (2008)
3. Kolmogorov, A.N.: Foundations of the Theory of Probability. Chelsea Pub Co., New York (1960)
4. Dubois, D., Prade, H.: Possibility theory: An approach to computerized processing of uncertainty. Plenum Press, New York (1988)
5. Zadeh, L.A.: Fuzzy sets. Inf. Control **8**, 338–353 (1965)
6. Zadeh, L.A.: Fuzzy sets as a basic for a theory of possibility. Fuzzy Sets Syst. **1**, 3–28 (1978)
7. Shafer, G.: A Mathematical Theory of Evidence. Princeton Univ. Press, Princeton (1976)
8. Haouari, B., Ben Amor, N., Elouedi, Z., Mellouli, K.: Naïve possibilistic network classifiers. Fuzzy Sets Syst. **160**(22), 3224–3238 (2009)

9. Benferhat, S., Tabia, K.: An efficient algorithm for naive possibilistic classifiers with uncertain inputs. In: Proceedings of the 2nd International Conference on Scalable uncertainty management (SUM2008),63–77 (2008)
10. Jenhani, I., Benferhat, S., Elouedi, Z.: Properties analysis of inconsistency-based possibilistic similarity measures. In: Proceedings of 12th International Conference on Information Processing and Management of Uncertainty in Knowledge-Based Systems (IPMU 2008), 173–180 (2008)
11. Higashi, M., Klir, G.J.: Measures of uncertainty and information based on possibility distributions. Int. J. Gen Syst 9(1), 43–58 (1883)
12. Murphy, P.M., Aha, D.W.: UCI repository of machine learning databases. http://www.ics.uci.edu/mlearn (1996)
13. Chan, T. F., Golub, G. H., LeVeque, R. J.: Updating formulae and a pairwise algorithm for computing sample variances, STAN-CS-79-773 Technical Report (1979)
14. Fayyad, U.M., Irani, K.B.: Multi-interval discretization of continuous-valued attributes for classification learning. In: Proceedings of the 13th International Joint Conference on Artificial Intelligence (IJCAI-93), 1022–1027 (1993)
15. Frank, E., Hall, M.A., Witten, I.W.: The WEKA Workbench. Online Appendix for Data Mining: Practical Machine Learning Tools and Techniques. Morgan Kaufmann, Fourth Edition (2016)
16. Dubois D., Prade H.: On several representations of an uncertain body of evidence. In: Fuzzy Information and Decision Processes (M.M. Gupta, E. Sanchez, eds.), North-Holland, Amsterdam, 167–181 (1982)
17. Chmielevski M.R., Grzymala-Busse J.W.: Global discretization of continuous attributes on preprocessing for machine learning. In: Third International Workshop on Rough Sets and Soft Computing, pp. 294–301 (1994)
18. Cerquides, J., Mantaras, R.L.: Proposal and empirical comparison of a parallelizable distance-based discretization method. In: KDD97. Third International Conference on Knowledge Discovery and Data Mining, 139–142 (1997)
19. Jiang, S.Y., Li, X., Zheng, Q., Wang, L.X.: Approximate equal frequency discretization method. In: 2009 IEEE WRI Global Congress on Intelligent Systems, vol. 3, pp. 514–518 (2009)
20. Dougherty, J., Kohavi, R., Sahami, M.: Supervised and unsupervised discretization of continuous features. In ICML 95, 194–202 (1995)
21. Palaniappan, S., Hong, T.K.: Discretization of continuous valued dimensions in OLAP data cubes. Int. J. Comput. Sci. Netw. Secur. 8(11), 116–126 (2009)
22. Hishamuddin, M.N.F., Hassan, M.F., Mokhtar, A.A.: Improving classification accuracy of random forest algorithm using unsupervised discretization with fuzzy partition and fuzzy set intervals. In: Proceedings of the 9th International Conference on Software and Computer Applications (ICSCA), pp. 99–104 (2020)
23. Agre, G. and Peev, S.: On supervised and unsupervised discretization. Cybern. Inf. Technol. 2(2) (2002)
24. Han, J., Pei, J., Kamber, M.: Data Mining: Concepts and Techniques. Elsevier, Amsterdam (2011)
25. Kerber, R.: ChiMerge: discretization of numeric attributes. In: Proceedings of the 10th National Conference on Artificial Intelligence (AAAI), pp. 123–128 (1992)
26. Boulle, M.: A Bayesian approach for supervised discretization. WIT Trans. Inf. Commun. Technol. 33, 1–10 (2004)

Levelwise Data Disambiguation by Cautious Superset Classification

Julian Rodemann[1]($\boxtimes$), Dominik Kreiss[1], Eyke Hüllermeier[2],
and Thomas Augustin[1]

[1] Department of Statistics, LMU Munich, Munich, Germany
{julian.rodemann,dominik.kreiss,thomas.augustin}@stat.uni-muenchen.de
[2] Department of Computer Science, LMU Munich, Munich, Germany
eyke@lmu.de

Abstract. Drawing conclusions from set-valued data calls for a trade-off between caution and precision. In this paper, we propose a way to construct a hierarchical family of subsets within set-valued categorical observations. Each subset corresponds to a level of cautiousness, the smallest one as a singleton representing the most optimistic choice. To achieve this, we extend the framework of Optimistic Superset Learning (OSL), which disambiguates set-valued data by determining the singleton corresponding to the most predictive model. We utilize a variant of OSL for classification with 0/1 loss to find the instantiations whose corresponding empirical risks are below context-depending thresholds. Varying this threshold induces a hierarchy among those instantiations. In order to rule out ties corresponding to the same classification error, we utilize a hyperparameter of Support Vector Machines (SVM) that controls the model's complexity. We twist the tuning of this hyperparameter to find instantiations whose optimal separations have the greatest generality. Finally, we apply our method on the prototypical example of yet undecided political voters as set-valued observations. To this end, we use both simulated data and pre-election polls by Civey including undecided voters for the 2021 German federal election.

Keywords: Optimistic superset learning · Set-valued data · Support vector machines · Data disambiguation · Epistemic imprecision · Undecided voters

We sincerely thank the polling institute Civey for providing the data as well as the anonymous reviewers for their valuable feedback and stimulating remarks. DK further thanks the LMU mentoring program for its support.

F. Dupin de Saint-Cyr et al. (Eds.): SUM 2022, LNAI 13562, pp. 263–276, 2022.
https://doi.org/10.1007/978-3-031-18843-5_18

1   Introduction

Within many applied learning settings, data is not available with the level of precision required for conventional methodology. This coarseness can arise from insufficient information about an existing truth as within sensor imprecision or can be due to inherently unacquaintable table structures like temporary indecisiveness between viable choice options. Either way, we are often provided with a set of viable candidates as a coarse version of one true value. Predicting the true value out of the set of candidates or training an overall model is difficult, as one has to account for the uncertainty either cautiously or has to rely on possibly untenable strong assumptions.

Technically, such data are described by so-called disjunctively or epistemically interpreted random sets (see, e.g., [3]). Without any further assumptions or underlaid structure, the empirical distribution of the underlying true values is only partially identified [16,17]. The field of *superset learning* (also known under different names, such as partial label learning) provides a methodological framework to incorporate set-valued data in the learning process, (re)interpreting and utilizing its information in different manners. The goal is predominantly to obtain one overall best model (e.g. [18]) or an optimal set of models (e.g. [4]) by incorporating the imprecise information. Different ideas building on maximum likelihood from fuzzy data were suggested by [5]. [20] show that the direct profile likelihood of set-valued categorical data naturally has a set-valued maximum, while underlying further parametric modelling structures (for instance, a non-saturated multinomial logit model) may substantially reduce imprecision in the result, even possibly leading to single-valued parameter estimates, see also [22] or the marrow region of [24].

[8] introduced Optimistic Superset Learning (OSL). Combining model identification and data disambiguation, OSL searches for and relies on the most plausible instantiation, i.e. a singleton (precise) representation of set-valued (imprecise) observations. The idea is to quantify the plausibility of possible data instantiations by the discriminative power of a given model when trained on it.

In this paper we build on OSL, constructing hierarchical set-valued variants of it: Instead of possibly over-optimistically determining only one single instantiation, we consider the set(s) of all instantiations whose empirical risk lies below a (varying) context-dependent threshold and focus on data disambiguation. To this end, we utilize a variant of OSL with the 0/1 loss, resulting in the full set of alternatives first, and narrowing down those alternatives in a hierarchical manner by decreasing the threshold in a step-wise manner. In order to rule out ties, we use a hyperparameter of Support Vector Machines that controls the model's complexity to obtain the instantiation whose separation has the most clarity. Provided with this hierarchical family of subsets, the practitioner can now choose the threshold to induce the level of conciseness desired for their application. We further provide a visual aid similar to a Scree Plot to assist the choice of the context-dependent threshold. We illustrate our method in a simulation study and later apply the new approach to undecided voters in a pre-election poll for the 2021 German federal election. Within this prototypical situation of complex inherent uncertainty, we characterize still undecided voters with their set of viable options, as suggested by [13,14,19,21], instead of neglecting them like in conventional polls.

This paper is structured as follows. After formalizing data disambiguation and discussing OSL in Sect. 2, we introduce our extensions narrowing down the supersets in Sect. 3 and resolving potential ties in Sect. 4. The proposed methodology is then applied on simulated as well as on real-world survey data in Sect. 5. Finally and in light of the presented results, we conclude by discussing some potential venues for future work in Sect. 6.

2   Data Disambiguation by Optimistic Superset Learning

Consider a set of observations $\mathcal{O} = \{(x_i, Y_i)\}_{i=1}^{n} \in (\mathcal{X} \times 2^{\mathcal{Y}})^{n}$, where $\mathbf{x} = (x_1, ..., x_n)$ are singleton observations of covariates and Y_i set-valued observations of target variables[1]. $\mathcal{X}$ is the covariate space and $\mathcal{Y}$ is the target space. Leaning on the idea of Optimistic Superset Learning (OSL) as proposed by [8], Y_i is regarded a coarse representation (a superset) of a true underlying singleton $y_i \in \mathcal{Y}$. In what follows, $\mathcal{Y}$ is assumed to be categorical. Let $\mathbf{Y} = Y_1 \times Y_2 \times \cdots \times Y_n$ be the Cartesian product of the observed supersets, and denote the number of different observed categories by q^2. Then any singleton vector $\mathbf{y} = (y_1, \ldots, y_i, \ldots, y_n)' \in \mathbf{Y}$ is called an *instantiation* of the observed set-valued data.

In practice, the set of candidate instantiations might be restricted to a subset of $\mathbf{Y}$, thereby allowing for the incorporation of domain knowledge in the form of constraints, for example, that observations with similar covariates and supersets ought to be instantiated with the same value for the target variable[3], see Sect. 5.1. We regard further research concerning the restriction of $\mathbf{Y}$ as powerful and briefly touch upon it in Sect. 6. In the following, for ease of exposition, we simply assume $\mathbf{Y}$ to be the full Cartesian product of the individual set-valued observations.

Consider an instantiation $\mathbf{y} \in \mathbf{Y}$, a loss function $L : \mathcal{Y} \times \mathcal{Y} \to \mathbb{R}$ and a model's predictive function $\hat{\mathbf{y}}^{(\mathbf{h},\mathbf{y})}(\mathbf{x})$ when trained on this instantiation $\mathbf{y}$. The latter is found by minimizing the empirical risk with a suitable loss function. Vector $\mathbf{h}$ shall denote the predictive model's hyperparameters, which are assumed to be fixed for now but will turn out to be of some relevance in Sect. 4. Now denote by $\mathbb{P}(\mathbf{x}, \mathbf{y})$ the underlying joint probability measure of $\mathbf{x}, \mathbf{y}$ and $\mathcal{R}(\mathbf{h}, \mathbf{x}, \mathbf{y}) = \int L(\hat{\mathbf{y}}^{(\mathbf{h},\mathbf{y})}(\mathbf{x}), \mathbf{y}) \, d\, \mathbb{P}(\mathbf{x}, \mathbf{y})$ the (theoretical) risk, which is estimated by the empirical risk $\mathcal{R}_{emp}(\mathbf{h}, \mathbf{x}, \mathbf{y}) = \frac{1}{n} \sum_{i=1}^{n} L(\hat{y}_i^{(\mathbf{h},\mathbf{y})}(x_i), y_i), \hat{y}_i \in \hat{\mathbf{y}}^{(\mathbf{h},\mathbf{y})}(\mathbf{x}), y_i \in \mathbf{y}, x_i \in \mathbf{x}$. Based on OSL we then consider

$$\mathbf{y}_{\mathcal{R}_{emp}}^{*} = arg\, min_{\mathbf{y} \in \mathbf{Y}} \mathcal{R}_{emp}(\mathbf{h}, \mathbf{x}, \mathbf{y}) \tag{1}$$

---

[1] Note that this formalization allows Y_i to also (partially) consist of singletons.

[2] Notably, $q = |\mathcal{Y}| - k$, where k is the number of categories in $\mathcal{Y}$ that are not present in the data.

[3] This subsetting of $\mathbf{Y}$ can be seen as a form of "data choice" similar to model choice.

for a pre-defined $\mathbf{h}$ the most plausible instantiation(s)[4]. That is, we opt for those instantiation(s) $\mathbf{y} \in \mathbf{Y}$ that make a given model the most predictive one when trained and evaluated on those instantiation(s). Its predictive function $\hat{\mathbf{y}}^{(\mathbf{h},\mathbf{y})}(\mathbf{x})$ might also output set-valued predictions as long as they can be evaluated by a real-valued loss function. In Sect. 3, we will explicitly estimate $\hat{\mathbf{y}}^{(\mathbf{h},\mathbf{y})}(\mathbf{x})$ for each instantiation $\mathbf{y} \in \mathbf{Y}$ to find $\mathbf{y}^*_{\mathcal{R}_{emp}}$ from (1), i.e. minimize the empirical risk for all $\mathbf{y} \in \mathbf{Y}$. This is in contrast to minimizing a generalized empirical risk function, the "optimistic superset loss"[5]

$$\mathrm{OSL}(\hat{\mathbf{y}}, \mathbf{Y}) = \frac{1}{n} \sum_{i=1}^{n} L^*(\hat{y}_i, Y_i) = \frac{1}{n} \sum_{i=1}^{n} \min_{y \in Y_i} L(\hat{y}_i, y) \,, \tag{2}$$

as done in the original OSL method [8, Sect. 4.1]. Our approach will allow us to hierarchically distinguish between instantiations in $\mathbf{Y}$ with regard to their $\mathcal{R}_{emp}$. Computationally, this comes at the cost of estimating up to q^n models. Solving the optimization problem in Eq. (1) thus has exponential computational complexity. However, we will suggest a variant of (1) in Sect. 5 for socio-economic applications that reduces this number by clustering observations.

Further note that OSL, in addition to the optimal instantiation, returns a predictive model with minimal risk, i.e. a model producing predictions $\hat{y}_i$ minimizing (2). Thus, OSL performs model identification and data disambiguation simultaneously [10, Sect. 2.2]: The model provides information about the data and, vice versa, the data about the model[6]. Nevertheless, model identification could be regarded as less general than data disambiguation in practical applications. This is due to the fact that the found risk-minimal instantiation(s) $\mathbf{y}^*_{\mathcal{R}_{emp}}$ can be used to train other models regardless of the one used in OSL. Theoretically, the same holds vice versa. Yet, it might be hard to access other (that is, new) data in practice. Furthermore, our approach of disambiguating data by providing subsets rather than singletons can be regarded as a way of loosening the degree to which we rely on the model. This is why we will focus on data disambiguation rather than model identification in the following.

3   Narrowing Down Supersets

As in some situations it is preferable to be cautious rather than optimistic, we attempt to narrow down the supersets in a hierarchical manner ranging from

---

[4] Criterion (1) aims at a unique minimum. In general, in the light of the next section, we understand $arg\,min$ potentially in a set-valued manner, i.e. giving the set of all elements where the minimum is attained.

[5] The loss is called optimistic due to the minimum in (2): each prediction $\hat{y}_i$ is assessed optimistically by assuming the most favorable ground-truth $y \in Y_i$.

[6] Notably, some models can be more informative on certain aspects of the data generating process than others. For instance, naive Bayes classifiers model the joint distribution $\mathbb{P}(x, y)$ as opposed to standard regression models that are typically concerned with the conditional distribution $\mathbb{P}(y|x)$.

least to most concise. Recall that for an instantiation $\mathbf{y} \in \mathbf{Y}$, criterion (1) depends on the loss function $L(\cdot)$ through the empirical risk $\mathcal{R}_{emp}(\mathbf{h}, \mathbf{x}, \mathbf{y}) = \frac{1}{n} \sum_{i=1}^{n} L(\hat{y}_i^{(\mathbf{h}, \mathbf{y})}(x_i), y_i)$, $x_i \in \mathbf{x}$, $\hat{y}_i \in \hat{\mathbf{y}}^{(\mathbf{h}, \mathbf{y})}(\mathbf{x})$, $y_i \in \mathbf{y} \in \mathbf{Y}$. Let $\hat{\mathbf{y}}^{(\mathbf{h}, \mathbf{y})}(\mathbf{x})$ be the predictive function of a specific linearly representable model with fixed hyperparameters $\mathbf{h}$ trained on $\mathbf{y} \in \mathbf{Y}$ with any suitable loss function.

For the 0/1-loss $L(\hat{y}_i^{(\mathbf{h}, \mathbf{y})}(x_i), y_i) = I(\hat{y}_i^{(\mathbf{h}, \mathbf{y})}(x_i) \neq y_i)$, I the indicator function, we can evaluate the model of an instantiation $\mathbf{y} \in \mathbf{Y}$ by $n \cdot \mathcal{R}_{emp}(\mathbf{h}, \mathbf{x}, \mathbf{y})$ the number of misclassifications. Hence, we are able to compare all instantiations with regard to their induced number of misclassifications $n \cdot \mathcal{R}_{emp}(\mathbf{h}, \mathbf{x}, \mathbf{y})$ or misclassification rate $\mathcal{R}_{emp}(\mathbf{h}, \mathbf{x}, \mathbf{y})$. Formally, we end up with a total order. This is due to $(\mathbb{N}, \leq)$ being a total order and the fact that any subset of a totally ordered set is a total order with the restriction of the order on the subset[7].

We use this very order to provide the decision-maker with a hierarchy of sets of instantiations ranging from complete ambiguity to a concise optimistic interpretation of set-valued observation. To prepare this, two definitions are given. The first one looks at the respective number of misclassifications $n \cdot \mathcal{R}_{emp}(\mathbf{h}, \mathbf{x}, \mathbf{y})$ to introduce the notion of an optimistic subset; the second one describes the resulting set on the level of individual observations.

Definition 1 ($\mathcal{E}$-Optimistic Subset). *Let $\mathbf{Y}$ be the Cartesian product of the observed supersets as above and $\mathcal{E} \in \mathbb{N}$ a pre-defined upper bound for classification errors. Then*

$$\mathbf{Y}_{\mathcal{E}} = \{\mathbf{y} \in \mathbf{Y} \mid n \cdot \mathcal{R}_{emp}(\mathbf{h}, \mathbf{x}, \mathbf{y}) \leq \mathcal{E}\} \subseteq \mathbf{Y}$$

shall be called $\mathcal{E}$-optimistic subset of $\mathbf{Y}$.

Definition 2 (i-th Consideration Function). *Let $y_i \in \mathbf{y} \in \mathbf{Y}_{\mathcal{E}}$ be the class of a fixed observation $i \in \{1, ..., n\}$ in an instantiation $\mathbf{y} \in \mathbf{Y}_{\mathcal{E}}$. For varying $\mathcal{E}$, the function*

$$f_i : \mathbb{N} \to 2^{\mathcal{Y}}$$
$$\mathcal{E} \mapsto \{y \in \mathcal{Y} \mid \exists \mathbf{y} \in \mathbf{Y}_{\mathcal{E}} : y = y_i, y_i \in \mathbf{y}\}$$

shall be called consideration function of observation i.

Verbally, $f_i(\mathcal{E})$ gives the set of possible classes of an observation i in all instantiations in $\mathbf{Y}_{\mathcal{E}}$, i.e. so-to-say the set still under consideration given an overall error $\mathcal{E}$. Note that the above described total order of $n \cdot \mathcal{R}_{emp}(\mathbf{h}, \mathbf{x}, \mathbf{y})$-values induces a partial order $(\mathbf{Y}_{\mathcal{E}}, \subseteq)$, which is part of the following proposition's proof.

Proposition 1. *Function $g_i(\mathcal{E}) = |f_i(\mathcal{E})|$ is monotonically non-decreasing.*

Proof. Let $\tilde{\mathbf{y}} \in \mathbf{Y}_{\mathcal{E}_1}$. Definition 1 directly delivers that $n \cdot \mathcal{R}_{emp}(\mathbf{h}, \mathbf{x}, \tilde{\mathbf{y}}) \leq \mathcal{E}_1$. With $\mathcal{E}_1 < \mathcal{E}_2$ by assumption, we trivially have $n \cdot \mathcal{R}_{emp}(\mathbf{h}, \mathbf{x}, \tilde{\mathbf{y}}) \leq \mathcal{E}_2 \implies \tilde{\mathbf{y}} \in \mathbf{Y}_{\mathcal{E}_2}$ Thus, for any two $\mathcal{E}_1, \mathcal{E}_2 \in \mathbb{R}$ with $\mathcal{E}_1 < \mathcal{E}_2$ it holds $\mathbf{Y}_{\mathcal{E}_1} \subseteq \mathbf{Y}_{\mathcal{E}_2}$. Since $f_i(\mathcal{E})$ only contains classes of instantiations in $\mathbf{Y}_{\mathcal{E}}$, the assertion follows.

---

[7] Note that $n \cdot \mathcal{R}_{emp}(\mathbf{h}, \mathbf{x}, \mathbf{y}) \in \mathbb{N}$.

The $\mathcal{E}$-optimistic subset $\mathbf{Y}_\mathcal{E} \subseteq \mathbf{Y}$ can be interpreted as those instantiations that are (optimistically) plausible given models that make less than $\mathcal{E}$ classification errors. Practitioners might either *a priori* select an application-dependent level of tolerable errors $\mathcal{E} \in \mathbb{N}$ and proceed with the corresponding instantiations $\mathbf{Y}_\mathcal{E} \subseteq \mathbf{Y}$. They might as well decide *a posteriori* by visual support of plotting $|\mathbf{Y}_\mathcal{E}|$ (the number of instantiations in the subset) against $\mathcal{E}$, see Sect. 5. Generally, this order will include ties for instantiations that are separable by the classifier with the same misclassification error: $\mathbf{Y}_\mathcal{E}^* \overset{def}{=} \{\mathbf{y}^* \mid n \cdot \mathcal{R}_{emp}(\mathbf{h}, \mathbf{x}, \mathbf{y}^*) = \mathcal{E}\}$, $\mathbf{Y}_\mathcal{E}^* \subseteq \mathbf{Y}$, see the weak monotonicity of $g_i(\mathcal{E})$ in Proposition 1. For a given $\mathcal{E}$, they can be thought of as equally optimistic instantiations. Instead of forcing to identify a singleton instantiation in the set-valued observations, the practitioner can make his choice how to work with this set of instantiations.

However, in some applications, it might also be beneficial to at least have the opportunity to decide for a "most optimistic" singleton from all instantiations in $\mathbf{Y}_\mathcal{E}^*$ that are *prima facie* equally optimistic with regard to their corresponding values of $n \cdot \mathcal{R}_{emp}(\mathbf{h}, \mathbf{x}, \mathbf{y})$. This option seems especially relevant for the smallest non-trivial (that is, non-empty) set in the hierarchy induced by Proposition 1, e.g. for all instantiations separable by the classifier, that is for the set $\mathbf{Y}_0^*$ ($\mathcal{E} = 0$).

In the following, we will introduce methodology to decide for such a "most optimistic" instantiation from $\mathbf{Y}_\mathcal{E}^*$ while maintaining the interpretable and intuitive number of misclassifications $n \cdot \mathcal{R}_{emp}(\mathbf{h}, \mathbf{x}, \mathbf{y}) \in \mathbb{N}$ as order criterion. Whilst the method of narrowing down supersets is generally applicable to any classifiers, we will restrict ourselves to Soft-margin Support Vector Machines (SVMs) in the following. This is due to their hyperparameter C that has an exciting interpretation, which we will utilize for a second-level-criterion. In doing so, we will seek inspiration from [9, Sect. 3.2], where the model architecture (that is, hyperparameters) is (visually) taken into account and instantiations are compared based on models of varying complexity[8].

4   Resolving Ties by Twisted Tuning of SVMs

Support Vector Machines (SVMs) [1] transform input vectors to a high-dimensional covariate space, where a linear classification hyperplane is constructed[9]. Soft-margin SVMs [2] allow violations of this hyperplane. In order to penalize such misclassifications, a hyperparameter C is used to control the trade-off between maximizing the margin M (the minimal distance from the separating hyperplane to the data) and minimizing the number of violations – or, in the original words of [2], between "complexity of decision rule and frequency of

---

[8] However, in [9, sect. 3.1] the class of models, thus the model's hyperparameters, is fixed.

[9] For multi-class classification (as in Sect. 5), hyperplanes from one-versus-all classifications are combined by a voting scheme and Platt scaling, for details see [11, pages 8–9]. When tuning with regard to C, one common C-value is used for all one-versus-all classifications.

error." To be a bit more precise, the classification hyperplane is found by minimizing a weighted sum of the margin M and the loss function that penalizes misclassifications. The hyperparameter C is the weight of that loss function.

For a given classification problem, the C that minimizes the training error can be thought of as a proxy for the clarity of optimal separation. In other words, the larger the hyperparameter C, the more sensitive the SVM is towards violations of the hyperplane; the lower C, the more the SVM focuses on finding maximal margins, respectively[10].

The latter is the starting point for our deliberations regarding hyperparameter tuning of C, which is usually not learned by the data, but set *a priori* by human choice. The emerging field of automated machine learning, however, aims at an unmanned optimal selection of hyperparameters. This is typically achieved by optimizing the generalization error through cross-validation.

We twist this tuning of C: Instead of asking for the optimal C given the observations, we ask for the instantiation of set-valued observations that leads to the lowest C when chosen in order to minimize the training error. In other words, among the set $\mathbf{Y}^*_{\mathcal{E}} = \{\mathbf{y}^* \mid n \cdot \mathcal{R}_{emp}(\mathbf{h}, \mathbf{x}, \mathbf{y}^*) = \mathcal{E}\}$, see Sect. 3, of instantiations that correspond to the same $n \cdot \mathcal{R}_{emp}(\mathbf{h}, \mathbf{x}, \mathbf{y})$ with 0/1-loss, we search for that version of the data whose optimal separation has the greatest clarity. To make things more tangible, recall the set of candidate instantiations $\mathbf{Y}$ from Sect. 2 and 3. Note that the vector of the model's hyperparameters $\mathbf{h}$ now contains, possibly among others, C, i.e. $\mathbf{h} = (C, \mathbf{h}'_r)'$. We abstract from the remaining hyperparameters $\mathbf{h}_r$ and assume them to be manually set. Among those instantiations in $\mathbf{Y}^*_{\mathcal{E}}$ we propose to select the instantiation whose most predictive model on the training data has the least complex decision rule, see Eq. (3).

$$\mathbf{y}^*_C = arg\,min_{\mathbf{y}^*} \underline{arg\,min_C} \{\mathcal{R}_{emp}(\mathbf{h}_r, C, \mathbf{x}, \mathbf{y}^*) \mid \mathbf{y}^* \in \mathbf{Y}^*_{\mathcal{E}}\} \qquad (3)$$

In other words, we perform hyperparameter-tuning[11] with 0/1-loss with regard to C of all those models that were trained on instantiations from $\mathbf{Y}^*_{\mathcal{E}} = \{\mathbf{y}^* \mid n \cdot \mathcal{R}_{emp}(\mathbf{h}_r, C, \mathbf{x}, \mathbf{y}^*) = \mathcal{E}\}$. We then choose the instantiation(s) corresponding to the model(s) with the lowest C. Notably, we fix the hyperparameters $\mathbf{h}$ including C in order to find instantiations in $\mathbf{Y}^*_{\mathcal{E}}$, see Sect. 3, only to optimize with regard to it later. We select the minimal C in the set of all C values that minimize the training or generalization error: $arg\,min_C$. This minimal C has a sound interpretation: It tells us, for a given instantiation, how general we can make the decision rule while maintaining optimal classification. Figure 1 illustrates this very idea in a specific context: Depicted are $n = 200$ singleton observations of a binary target variable in a two-dimensional covariate

---

[10] For kernelized versions of SVMs this hyperplane is generally only linear in the transformed feature space. However, we can still think of C as a proxy for the generality of optimal separation in that transformed space.

[11] We use Grid Search for solving this minimization problem. When evaluations are rather expensive, Bayesian Optimization, Simulated Annealing or Evolutionary Algorithms might be preferred. For an overview of these heuristic optimizers and their limitations, see [23, chapter 10].

space, of which 100 belong to class -1 (blue) and 100 to class 1 (red). Four observations (situated around $(5, 5)$) are set-valued and might be interpreted as indecisive between blue and red. In the upper row, all of these four observations are instantiated as 1 (red) and in the lower row as -1 (blue), respectively. Note that for both instantiations we have $\mathcal{R}_{emp}(\mathbf{h}, \mathbf{x}, \mathbf{y}) = 0$, since the corresponding data set is linearly separable in the covariate space. Each column in Fig. 1 shows the predictions of an SVM with varying C. It becomes evident that the red instantiation can be separated even for $C = 0.1$ (left), while the blue instantiation requires higher C values, i.e. more complex decision rules, in order to be classified correctly.

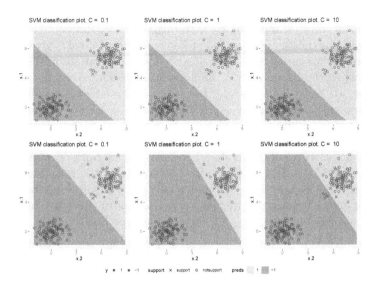

Fig. 1. Different instantiations of set-valued observations require different levels of C in order to be classified correctly.

Distinguishing between instantiations in $\mathbf{Y}_{\mathcal{E}}^*$ by (3) gives rise to the following preference function.

Definition 3 (*i-th Preference Function for level $\mathcal{E}$*). *Let $y_i \in \mathbf{y}^* \in \mathbf{Y}_{\mathcal{E}}^*$ be the class of a fixed observation $i \in \{1, ..., n\}$ in an instantiation $\mathbf{y}^* \in \mathbf{Y}_{\mathcal{E}}^*$. For a given $\mathcal{E}$, the function*

$$p_i^{(\mathcal{E})} : \mathcal{Y} \to \mathbb{R}$$
$$y \mapsto \min\{C \mid C = \underline{arg\,min_C}\{\mathcal{R}_{emp}(\mathbf{h}_r, C, \mathbf{x}, \mathbf{y}^*) \mid \mathbf{y}^* \in \mathbf{Y}_{\mathcal{E}}^* \wedge y = y_i \in \mathbf{y}^*\}\}$$

shall be called preference function of observation i for subset $\mathbf{Y}_{\mathcal{E}}^*$.

Verbally, the i-th Preference Function outputs for class y the minimal C from all those minimal C-values that correspond to such instantiations in $\mathbf{Y}_{\mathcal{E}}^*$

that assign class y to observation i. The following proposition then entitles us to provide the user with a ranking of classes according to their plausibility in $\mathbf{Y}^*_{\mathcal{E}}$ for the i-th individual. The induced total order can be used to rank all classes present in $\mathbf{Y}^*_{\mathcal{E}}$ for observation i.

Proposition 2. *For any fixed i, the element-wise composition $p_i^{(\mathcal{E})} \odot f_i$ induces a total order.*

Proof. Since $p_i^{(\mathcal{E})}$ maps to $\mathbb{R}$, we have $p_i^{(\mathcal{E})} \odot f_i(\mathcal{E}) \in \mathbb{R}^d$, where $d \leq |\mathcal{Y}|$ is the dimension of the output of $p_i^{(\mathcal{E})}$. Since any subset of the total order $(\mathbb{R}, \leq)$ is a total order with the restriction of the total order on the subset, one single output vector $p_i^{(\mathcal{E})} \odot f_i(\mathcal{E}) \in \mathbb{R}^d$ has elements that are totally ordered.

Notably, using the Hinge loss function [7] in OSL would also allow for disambiguation of instantiations in $\mathbf{Y}^*_{\mathcal{E}}$, since it accounts for margin maximization. Deploying OSL with hinge loss in the first place, however, typically does not induce ties, since then $n \cdot \mathcal{R}_{emp}(\mathbf{h}, \mathbf{x}, \mathbf{y}) \in \mathbb{R}$. What is more, the real-valued $n \cdot \mathcal{R}_{emp}(\mathbf{h}, \mathbf{x}, \mathbf{y})$ is not as interpretable as in the countable case of the 0/1-loss and thus a pre-defined and context-dependent level of acceptable errors $\mathcal{E}$ might be hard to specify for the decision maker. Still, OSL with hinge loss could be used to eventually rule out ties after having sequentially narrowed down supersets by means of 0/1-loss. However, the simultaneous model identification would not take into account C and could thus be regarded less general. In light of this, we recommend further research on the interaction of margin maximization induced by the hinge loss and the optimal level of generality represented by C.

5 Applications to Undecided Voters

5.1 Clustering

In what follows, we will abstain from considering all q^n possible instantiations (with q again as the number of different observed classes) by only considering the candidate instantiations in $\mathbf{Y}$. Instead, for the sake of both interpretability and computational convenience, we cluster all (non-singleton) set-valued observations to k groups of observations $G_1, ..., G_k$ according to their covariates[12]. Generally, for each common set of classes one would need to perform a cluster analysis separately. With q observed classes, we would have $q_c = 2^q - q - 1$ clusterings to be done, since we exclude q singletons and the empty set from the power set of observed classes. In the following application, however, we will only deal with individuals that are fully ambiguous among all options, i.e. $q_c = q$. We then disambiguate all observations in a cluster in the same way, i.e. assign all of them to the same class. This reduces $Y_1 \times Y_2 \times \cdots \times Y_n$ to $G_1 \times G_2 \times \cdots \times G_k$ with q_c^k instead of q^n possible instantiations.

---

[12] Any clustering algorithm can be used. In our applications in Sect. 5, we opt for k-means clustering as proposed by [15].

5.2   Simulations

We simulate 120 observations with two metric socio-economic covariates in the set-up of a pre-election polling survey with individuals undecided between three parties. Figure 2 illustrates the distribution of the observations in the covariate space. The 60 still undecided (among all three parties) voters hereby disaggregate in three clusters, with from now on called *Cluster I* (triangles) in the left lower corner, *Cluster II* (squares) in the upper middle and *Cluster III* (crosses) in the right upper corner. One might think of these groups as sociodemographic clusters or social milieus. With the three parties we obtain $3^3 = 27$ possible instantiations for the clusters.

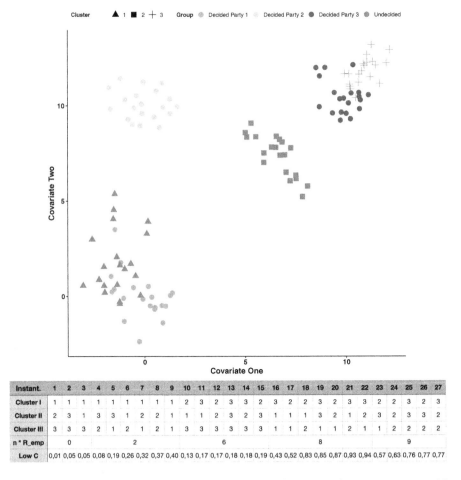

Cluster ▲ 1 ■ 2 + 3   Group ● Decided Party 1 ● Decided Party 2 ● Decided Party 3 ● Undecided

Instant.	1	2	3	4	5	6	7	8	9	10	11	12	13	14	15	16	17	18	19	20	21	22	23	24	25	26	27
Cluster I	1	1	1	1	1	1	1	1	1	1	2	3	2	3	3	2	3	2	2	3	2	3	3	2	2	3	2
Cluster II	2	3	1	3	3	1	2	2	1	1	1	2	3	2	3	1	1	1	3	2	1	2	3	2	3	3	2
Cluster III	3	3	3	2	1	2	1	2	1	3	3	3	3	3	3	1	1	2	1	1	2	1	1	2	2	2	2
n * R_emp	0					2							6							8					9		
Low C	0,01	0,05	0,05	0,08	0,19	0,26	0,32	0,37	0,40	0,13	0,17	0,17	0,18	0,18	0,19	0,43	0,52	0,83	0,85	0,87	0,93	0,94	0,57	0,63	0,76	0,77	0,77

Fig. 2. Simulation setting: 120 observations in a two-dimensional covariate space with three parties, among which 60 are undecided. Simulation results: The 27 possible instantiations are ordered by their $\mathcal{R}_{emp}$ and the lower bound of their C value.

With our approach we obtain for each instantiation its $\mathcal{R}_{emp}$ as well as a lower bound of its C value. We can thus order them as illustrated in Fig. 2.

Depending on the application, the practitioner can now decide which level of imprecision is adequate and choose the viable instantiations correspondingly. A tolerable number of misclassifications of $\mathcal{E} = 2$ would for example induce Cluster I to be always assigned to Party 1 while the other clusters might be assigned to either of the three. The resulting ties in $n \cdot \mathcal{R}_{emp}$ can furthermore be resolved by taking into account the lower bound of the C value.

5.3 German Pre-Election Polls

We are in the fortunate position of cooperating with the polling institute Civey to explicitly account for undecided voters in a set-valued manner. Hence, we have first-hand access to polling data for the 2021 German federal election two months before the election, in which all still pondering individuals are represented by the set containing their viable options. We employ our methodology to the three center-left-/ left-leaning parties *SPD*, *Greens* and *The Left*, while it could straight forwardly be generalized to overall forecasting by addressing all groups of undecided sequentially following [12, p. 245]. In the provided polling data we have 935 participants determined to vote for the Greens, 592 determined to vote for the SPD, 168 for The Left and 66 still pondering between the three parties, thus $n = 1761$. Furthermore, we are provided with 10 socioeconomic covariates capturing the socioeconomic status (education, population density of place of residence, purchasing power, employment status and the like) in an ordinal and nominal manner[13].

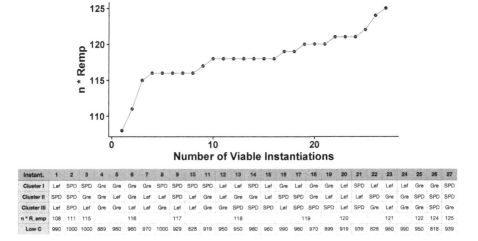

Instant.	1	2	3	4	5	6	7	8	9	10	11	12	13	14	15	16	17	18	19	20	21	22	23	24	25	26	27
Cluster I	Lef	SPD	SPD	Gre	Gre	Gre	Gre	SPD	SPD	SPD	SPD	Lef	Lef	SPD	Lef	Gre	Lef	Gre	Gre	Lef	SPD	Lef	Lef	Lef	Gre	Gre	SPD
Cluster II	SPD	SPD	Gre	Gre	Lef	Gre	Lef	Lef	SPD	Lef	Gre	Lef	Gre	Gre	Lef	SPD	SPD	Gre	Lef	Lef	Lef	SPD	Gre	Gre	SPD	SPD	SPD
Cluster III	Lef	SPD	Lef	Gre	Gre	Lef	Lef	Gre	Lef	Lef	Lef	Gre	Gre	SPD	SPD	SPD	Lef	SPD	SPD	SPD	Lef	SPD	Gre	Lef	Gre	Gre	Gre
n * R_emp	108	111	115			116			117				118						119		120			121	122	124	125
Low C	990	1000	1000	889	960	960	970	1000	929	828	919	950	950	960	960	990	960	970	899	919	939	828	980	990	950	818	939

Fig. 3. Results from the application on polling data. Party Legend: Lef = Left, Gre = Green. The 27 possible instantiations are again ordered by their $n \cdot \mathcal{R}_{emp}$ and the lower bound of their C value. (Color figure online)

---

[13] The covariates appear to be generally of rather low predictive power : Training and generalization error, even exclusively for the decided, are high.

Clustering finds three socio-economic groups. Based on the covariates they can be roughly subsumed as older population with low and medium income (1), top-earning academics on the countryside (2) and a small group of urbanites without paid employment (3). Figure 3 shows the results for all $3^3 = 27$ instantiations in the same manner as for the simulated data in Fig. 2. It also entails a plot of the number of instantiations in the $\mathcal{E}$-optimistic subsets $|\mathbf{Y}_\mathcal{E}|$ and their respective $\mathcal{E} = n \cdot \mathcal{R}_{emp}$ that can be used as decision support when opting for a level of tolerable misclassifications $\mathcal{E}$.

It becomes evident that even for realistically large datasets ($n = 1761$) we can obtain ties with OSL and the 0/1-loss. In other words, we end up with non-singleton (and non-empty) sets $\mathbf{Y}_\mathcal{E}^*$ for $\mathcal{E} \in \{116, 118, 119, 120, 121\}$. Here, twisted tuning can offer decision support. Applying a modified version of the i-th Consideration Function (Definition 2) to clusters rather than to individuals offers additional insight: The first (older population with low and middle income) and the third (unemployed townspeople) socio-economic clusters are not instantiated as Greens voters for $\mathcal{E}$ lower than 116. Rural top-earners (2), however, are. For the latter group it is more plausible to vote Green, given the model and the available covariates, than for the other two groups, which appears to be an empirical insight that is in line with socio-politological literature on previous German elections, see [6] for instance.

6   Discussion

As underpinned by the application on polling data in Sect. 5, considering several instantiations can be an attractive extension to classical OSL, as it offers additional insights into (groups of) undecided voters. Moreover, it might prevent forecasters from over-optimistic predictions. Generally, we consider our level-wise approach to data disambiguation a practically powerful alternative to exclusively relying on a singleton instantiation of set-valued data.

However, with increasing n, stronger efforts are indispensable to ensure computational feasibility. This opens up venues for further work, extending our approach of homogeneous treatment of found clusters to general approaches of "data selection". For instance, one could integrate the restrictions describing the reduced sets of instantiations $Y_1 \times Y_2 \times \cdots \times Y_n$ (see Sect. 2) as side-constraints in the minimization of the generalized empirical risk [8, Sect. 4.1] for classical Optimistic Superset Learning.

Furthermore, decision criteria beyond the total (lexicographic) order on the $\mathcal{E}$-optimistic subsets to moderate the trade-off between accuracy and generality should be investigated in detail. One could argue, for instance, that considering instantiations corresponding to higher $\mathcal{E}$ is justified if they can be separated with sufficiently lower C, i.e. more general hyperplanes. Clear recommendations for different decision rules tailored to specific applications would be of high practical value. In addition, we see potential in a more versatile approach by not forcing a precise disambiguation of inconclusive cases in $\mathbf{Y}_\mathcal{E}^*$. This could either be achieved by two-stage criteria that account for further hyperparameters of the model or by considering some interval $[C - \epsilon, C + \epsilon]$ instead of C.

References

1. Boser, B., Guyon, I., Vapnik, V.: A training algorithm for optimal margin classifiers. In: Proceedings of the Fifth Annual Workshop on Computational Learning Theory, pp. 144–152 (1992)
2. Cortes, C., Vapnik, V.: Support-vector networks. Mach. Learn. **20**(3), 273–297 (1995)
3. Couso, I., Dubois, D.: Statistical reasoning with set-valued information: Ontic vs. epistemic views. Int. J. Approximate Reasoning **55**, 1502–1518 (2014)
4. Couso, I., Sánchez, L.: Machine learning models, epistemic set-valued data and generalized loss functions: an encompassing approach. Inf. Sci. **358**, 129–150 (2016)
5. Denœux, T.: Maximum likelihood estimation from uncertain data in the belief function framework. IEEE Trans. Knowl. Data Eng. **25**(1), 119–130 (2011)
6. Faas, T., Klingelhöfer, T.: The more things change, the more they stay the same? The German federal election of 2017 and its consequences. West Eur. Polit. **42**(4), 914–926 (2019)
7. Gentile, C., Warmuth, M.: Linear hinge loss and average margin. In: Advances in Neural Information Processing Systems, vol. 11 (1998)
8. Hüllermeier, E.: Learning from imprecise and fuzzy observations: data disambiguation through generalized loss minimization. Int. J. Approximate Reasoning **55**, 1519–1534 (2014)
9. Hüllermeier, E., Cheng, W.: Superset learning based on generalized loss minimization. In: Appice, A., Rodrigues, P.P., Santos Costa, V., Gama, J., Jorge, A., Soares, C. (eds.) ECML PKDD 2015. LNCS (LNAI), vol. 9285, pp. 260–275. Springer, Cham (2015). https://doi.org/10.1007/978-3-319-23525-7_16
10. Hüllermeier, E., Destercke, S., Couso, I.: Learning from imprecise data: adjustments of optimistic and pessimistic variants. In: Ben Amor, N., Quost, B., Theobald, M. (eds.) SUM 2019. LNCS (LNAI), vol. 11940, pp. 266–279. Springer, Cham (2019). https://doi.org/10.1007/978-3-030-35514-2_20
11. Karatzoglou, A., Smola, A., Hornik, K., Zeileis, A.: kernlab-an S4 package for kernel methods in R. J. Stat. Softw. **11**(9), 1–20 (2004)
12. Kreiss, D., Augustin, T.: Undecided voters as set-valued information – towards forecasts under epistemic imprecision. In: Davis, J., Tabia, K. (eds.) SUM 2020. LNCS (LNAI), vol. 12322, pp. 242–250. Springer, Cham (2020). https://doi.org/10.1007/978-3-030-58449-8_18
13. Kreiss, D., Augustin, T.: Towards a paradigmatic shift in pre-election polling adequately including still undecided voters-some ideas based on set-valued data for the 2021 German federal election. arXiv preprint arXiv:2109.12069 (2021)
14. Kreiss, D., Nalenz, M., Augustin, T.: Undecided voters as set-valued information, machine learning approaches under complex uncertainty. In: ECML/PKDD 2020 Tutorial and Workshop on Uncertainty in Machine Learning (2020)
15. Lloyd, S.: Least squares quantization in PCM. IEEE Trans. Inf. Theor. **28**, 129–137 (1982)
16. Manski, C.: Partial Identification of Probability Distributions. Springer, Cham (2003)
17. Molchanov, I., Molinari, F.: Random Sets in Econometrics. Cambridge University Press, Cambridge (2018)
18. Nguyen, N., Caruana, R.: Classification with partial labels. In: Proceedings of the 14th ACM SIGKDD International Conference on Knowledge Discovery and Data Mining, pp. 551–559 (2008)

19. Oscarsson, H., Oskarson, M.: Sequential vote choice: applying a consideration set model of heterogeneous decision processes. Electoral Stud. **57**, 275–283 (2019)
20. Plass, J., Cattaneo, M., Augustin, T., Schollmeyer, G., Heumann, C.: Reliable inference in categorical regression analysis for non-randomly coarsened observations. Int. Stat. Rev. **87**, 580–603 (2019)
21. Plass, J., Fink, P., Schöning, N., Augustin, T.: Statistical modelling in surveys without neglecting the undecided. In: ISIPTA 15, pp. 257–266. SIPTA (2015)
22. Ponomareva, M., Tamer, E.: Misspecification in moment inequality models: back to moment equalities? Econometrics J. **14**, 186–203 (2011)
23. Rodemann, J.: Robust generalizations of stochastic derivative-free optimization. Master's thesis, LMU Munich (2021)
24. Schollmeyer, G., Augustin, T.: Statistical modeling under partial identification: distinguishing three types of identification regions in regression analysis with interval data. Int. J. Approximate Reasoning **56**, 224–248 (2015)

Full Papers: Explanation

Descriptive Accuracy in Explanations: The Case of Probabilistic Classifiers

Emanuele Albini[1], Antonio Rago[1]([✉]), Pietro Baroni[2], and Francesca Toni[1]

[1] Department of Computing, Imperial College London, London, UK
{emanuele,antonio,ft}@imperial.ac.uk
[2] Dip.to di Ingegneria dell'Informazione, Università degli Studi di Brescia, Brescia, Italy
pietro.baroni@unibs.it

Abstract. A user receiving an explanation for outcomes produced by an artificially intelligent system expects that it satisfies the key property of *descriptive accuracy* (DA), i.e. that the explanation contents are in correspondence with the internal working of the system. Crucial as this property appears to be, it has been somehow overlooked in the XAI literature to date. To address this problem, we consider the questions of formalising DA and of analysing its satisfaction by explanation methods. We provide formal definitions of *naive, structural* and *dialectical* DA, using the family of probabilistic classifiers as the context for our analysis. We evaluate the satisfaction of our given notions of DA by several explanation methods, amounting to two popular feature-attribution methods from the literature and a novel form of explanation that we propose and complement our analysis with experiments carried out on a varied selection of concrete probabilistic classifiers.

Keywords: Explainable AI · Probabilistic classifiers · Descriptive accuracy

1 Introduction

Equipping automated decision systems with explanation capabilities is a compelling need in order to achieve user *trust*, a prerequisite for acceptance, especially if the systems are based on some model or technique that is not directly understandable by the users. This need lies, in particular, at the basis of the rapid growth of the research field of explainable AI (XAI) in recent years. As pointed out in [10], trust, which is an attitude of the trustors (in our case, the systems' users), is distinguished from trustworthiness, which is a property of the trustees (in our case the explained systems). This makes the goal of achieving trust, and the role of explanations there for, a rather tricky issue. On the one hand, there can be situations where trust is achieved by explanations which are convincing but somehow deceptive. On the other hand, there can be situations

© The Author(s) 2022
F. Dupin de Saint-Cyr et al. (Eds.): SUM 2022, LNAI 13562, pp. 279–294, 2022.
https://doi.org/10.1007/978-3-031-18843-5_19

where an otherwise trustworthy system loses users' trust due to problems in its explanations' capabilities.

These considerations call for the need of identifying some basic requirements that explanations should satisfy in order to lead to (deservingly) trustworthy AI systems. In this paper, for the specific setting of *probabilistic classifiers*, we focus on the property of *descriptive accuracy* (DA) described in [19], for machine learning in general, as "the degree to which an interpretation method objectively captures the relationships learned by machine learning models". DA appears to be a crucial requirement for any explanation: its absence would lead to the risk of misleading (if not deceptive) indications for the user.

In this work we consider the issue of providing formal counterparts to the general notion of DA and then of assessing their satisfaction by both existing and suitably defined explanation approaches. Specifically, we make the following contributions.

- We introduce three formal notions of DA (Sect. 4): *naive* DA, as a precursor to *dialectical DA*, both applicable to any probabilistic classifier, and *structural DA*, applicable to probabilistic classifiers that are equipped with a *structural description*, as is the case for *Bayesian network classifiers* (BCs) and *Chain Classifiers* (CCs).
- We study whether concrete explanation methods satisfy our notions of DA (Sect. 5). We focus our analysis on existing *feature attribution methods* from the literature (LIME [24] and SHAP [15]) as well as a novel method we define.
- We evaluate our forms of DA empirically (when they cannot be guaranteed formally) on a variety of BCs and CCs (Sect. 6) showing that they are often violated in practice by LIME and SHAP.

2   Related Work

Numerous methods for providing explanations have been proposed (e.g. see the survey by [8]) and their desirable properties have been considered from a variety of perspectives (e.g. see the survey by [26]). We draw inspiration from [19] and focus, in particular, on their notion of *descriptive accuracy* (DA) for (model-based or post-hoc) interpretable machine learning. As mentioned in the introduction, DA concerns the degree to which an interpretation (in our setting, explanation) method objectively captures the relationships learned by the machine-learned models.

DA is seen, in [19], as a crucial property for achieving interpretable machine learning, alongside, in particular, *predictive accuracy*, wrt (test) data, of the predictions produced by the interpretations/explanations. Whereas DA is concerned with the inner workings of models, predictive accuracy is concerned with the input-output behaviour thereof. Predictive accuracy is thus closely linked with properties of *fidelity* or *faithfulness* which have been considered by several works (see e.g. [8,13]). In the case of explanations concerning a single instance, *local fidelity* has been defined as a measure of how well an explanation model approximates the original model in a neighbourhood of the instance in need of explaining [1, 24].

Overall, whereas formal counterparts of predictive accuracy/faithfulness/fidelity have been extensively studied in the XAI literature, to the best of our knowledge, formal counterparts of DA appear to be lacking up to now. This gap is particularly significant for the classes of post-hoc explanations methods which, *per se*, have no relations with the underlying operation of the explained model and therefore cannot rely on any implicit assumption that DA is guaranteed, in a sense, by construction. This applies, in particular, to the family of model-agnostic local explanation methods, namely methods which are designed to be applicable to any model (and hence need to treat the model itself purely as a black-box) and whose explanations are restricted to illustrate individually a single outcome of the model without aiming to describe its behaviour in more general terms. This family includes the well-known class of *additive feature attribution* methods, such as LIME [24] and SHAP [15], where the explanation for the outcome of a model basically consists in ascribing to each input feature a numerical weight. We will provide three *formal* characterisations for DA, allowing evaluation of explanation methods for satisfaction of DA in precise terms and we will study our notions of DA in the context of both LIME and SHAP, showing that they are not able to satisfy them.

3   Preliminaries

As DA is inherently related to the internal operation of a model, rather than just to its input/output behaviour, any formal notion of DA cannot be completely model-agnostic. It follows that an investigation of DA needs to find a balance between the obvious need for wide applicability and the potential advantages of model-tailored definitions. For this reason we will focus on the broad family of *probabilistic classifiers*.

We consider (discrete) probabilistic classifiers with *feature variables* $\mathbf{X} = \{X_1, \ldots, X_m\}$ ($m > 1$) and *class variables* $\mathbf{C} = \{C_1, \ldots, C_n\}$ ($n \geq 1$). Each (random) variable $V_i \in \mathbf{V} = \mathbf{X} \cup \mathbf{C}$ is equipped with a discrete set of possible *values* Ω_{V_i}: we define the *feature space* as $\mathcal{X} = \Omega_{X_1} \times \ldots \times \Omega_{X_m}$ and the *class space* as $\mathcal{C} = \Omega_{C_1} \times \ldots \times \Omega_{C_n}$. From now on, we call any vector $\mathbf{x} \in \mathcal{X}$ an *input* and denote as $\mathbf{x}(X_i)$ the value of feature X_i in $\mathbf{x}$. Given input $\mathbf{x}$, a *probabilistic classifier* $\mathcal{PC}$ computes, for each class variable C_i and value $\omega \in \Omega_{C_i}$, the probability $P(C_i = \omega | \mathbf{x})$ that C_i takes value ω, given $\mathbf{x}$. We then refer to the *resulting value* for a class variable $C_i \in \mathbf{C}$ given input $\mathbf{x}$ as $\mathcal{PC}(C_i|\mathbf{x}) = argmax_{\omega \in \Omega_{C_i}} P(C_i = \omega | \mathbf{x})$. Table 1 gives a probabilistic classifier for a (toy) financial setting where the values of class variables *problematic external event* and *drop in consumer confidence* are determined based on the feature variables *company share price trend*, *devaluation of currency*, *healthy housing market* and *negative breaking news cycle*. Here, for any variable $V_i \in \mathbf{V}$, $\Omega_{V_i} = \{+, -\}$.

For $X_i \in \mathbf{X}$, we will abuse notation as follows, to simplify some of the formal definitions later in the paper: $\mathcal{PC}(X_i|\mathbf{x}) = \mathbf{x}(X_i)$ (basically, the "resulting value"

Table 1. An example of *probabilistic classifier* with $\mathbf{X} = \{s, d, h, n\}$ and $\mathbf{C} = \{c, e\}$. Here, e.g. for $\mathbf{x}$ (highlighted in bold) such that $\mathbf{x}(s) = \mathbf{x}(d) = \mathbf{x}(h) = \mathbf{x}(n) = +$, $\mathcal{PC}(c|\mathbf{x}) = +$ (as $P(c = +|\mathbf{x}) = .60$)), and $\mathcal{PC}(e|\mathbf{x}) = +$ (as $P(e = +|\mathbf{x}) = .60$)).

s	+	+	+	+	+	+	+	+	−	−	−	−	−	−	−	−
d	+	+	+	+	−	−	−	−	+	+	+	+	−	−	−	−
h	+	+	−	−	+	+	−	−	+	+	−	−	+	+	−	−
n	+	−	+	−	+	−	+	−	+	−	+	−	+	−	+	−
c	+	−	+	+	+	−	+	−	+	−	+	+	+	−	+	−
P	.60	.65	1	.60	.60	1	1	.65	.60	.65	1	.60	.60	1	1	.65
e	+	−	+	+	+	−	+	−	+	−	+	+	+	−	+	−
P	.60	1	.60	.60	.60	1	.60	1	1	.65	1	1	1	.65	1	.65

for a feature variable, given an input, is the value assigned to that variable in the input) and $P(X_i = \mathbf{x}(X_i)) = 1$ (basically, the probability of a feature variable being assigned its value, in the given input, is 1). We will also use notation:

$$P(V = v|\mathbf{x}, set(V_i = v_i)) = \begin{cases} P(V = v|\mathbf{x}'), & \text{if } V_i \in \mathbf{X}, \\ P(V = v|\mathbf{x}, V_i = v_i), & \text{if } V_i \in \mathbf{C}, \end{cases}$$

where, in the first case, $\mathbf{x}'(V_i) = v_i$ and $\mathbf{x}'(V_j) = \mathbf{x}(V_j)$ for all $V_j \in \mathbf{X} \setminus \{V_i\}$. Basically, this notation allows to gauge the effects of changes in value for (input or class) variables on the probabilities computed by the classifiers (for assignments of values to any variables).

Various types of probabilistic classifiers exist. In Sect. 6 we will experiment with (explanations for) a variety of (discrete) *Bayesian Classifiers* (BCs, see [2] for an overview), where the variables in $\mathbf{V}$ constitute the nodes in a Bayesian network, i.e. a directed acyclic graph whose edges indicate probabilistic dependencies amongst the variables. We will also experiment with (explanations for) *chained probabilistic classifiers* (CCs, e.g. as defined by [23] for the case of BCs). These CCs result from the combination of simpler probabilistic classifiers (possibly, but not necessarily, BCs), using an ordering $\succ_C$ over $\mathbf{C}$ such that the value of any $C_i \in \mathbf{C}$ is treated as a feature value for determining the value of any $C_j \in \mathbf{C}$ with $C_j \succ_C C_i$, and thus a classifier computing values for C_i can be chained with one for computing values for C_j. For illustration, in Table 2 we re-interpret the classifier from Table 1 as a CC amounting to a chain of two classifiers, using $e \succ_C c$: the classifier (a) determines the value of c as an additional input for the classifier (b). Then, the overall classifier determines the value of c first based on the feature variables d, h and n, and then e based on s and c (treated as a feature variable in the chaining). Note that, in Table 2 and throughout the paper, we abuse notation and use inputs for overall (chained) classifiers ($\mathbf{x}$ in the caption of the table) as inputs of all simpler classifiers forming them (rather than the inputs' restriction to the specific input variables of the simpler classifiers).

For some families of probabilistic classifiers (e.g. for BCs) it is possible to provide a graphical representation which gives a synthetic view of the depen-

Table 2. An example of *chained probabilistic classifier* (CC) with (a) the first probabilistic classifier $\mathcal{PC}_1$ with $\mathbf{X}_1 = \{d, h, n\}$, $\mathbf{C}_1 = \{c\}$, and (b) the second probabilistic classifier $\mathcal{PC}_2$ with $\mathbf{X}_2 = \{s, c\}$, $\mathbf{C}_2 = \{e\}$ (both inputs highlighted in bold). Here, e.g. for **x** as in the caption of Table 1, $\mathcal{PC}(c|\mathbf{x}) = \mathcal{PC}_1(c|\mathbf{x}) = +$ and $\mathcal{PC}(e|\mathbf{x}) = \mathcal{PC}_2(e|\mathbf{x}, set(c = \mathcal{PC}_1(c|\mathbf{x}))) = +$. (c) A *structural description* for the CC in (a–b), shown as a graph.

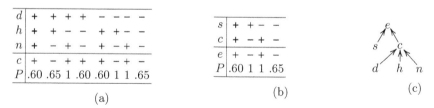

d	+	+	+	+	−	−	−	−
h	+	+	−	−	+	+	−	−
n	+	−	+	−	+	−	+	−
c	+	−	+	+	+	−	+	−
P	.60	.65	1	.60	.60	1	1	.65

(a)

s	+	+	−	−
c	+	−	+	−
e	+	−	+	−
P	.60	1	1	.65

(b)

(c)

dence and independence relations between the variables. In these cases, we will assume that the classifier is accompanied by a *structural description*, namely a set $\mathcal{SD} \subseteq \mathbf{V} \times \mathbf{V}$. The structural description identifies for each variable $V_j \in \mathbf{V}$ a (possibly empty) set of *parents* $\mathcal{PA}(V_j) = \{V_i \mid (V_i, V_j) \in \mathcal{SD}\}$ with the meaning that the evaluation of V_j is completely determined by the evaluations of $\mathcal{PA}(V_j)$ in the classifier. In the case of BCs, the parents of each (class) variable correspond to the variables in its unique *Markov boundary* [20,21] $\mathcal{M} : \mathbf{V} \to 2^{\mathbf{V}}$, where, for any $V_i \in \mathbf{V}$, $\mathcal{M}(V_i)$ is the $\subseteq$-minimal set of variables such that V_i is conditionally independent of all the other variables $(\mathbf{V} \setminus \mathcal{M}(V_i))$, given $\mathcal{M}(V_i)$. In the case of CCs, even when no information is available about the internal structure of the individual classifiers being chained, a structural description may be extracted to reflect the connections between features and classes. For illustration, for the CC in Table 2(a–b), the structural description is $\mathcal{SD} = \{(d, c), (h, c), (n, c), (s, e), (c, e)\}$, given in Table 2(c) as a graph.

We remark that similar notions have been considered earlier in the literature. For instance in [27] a notion of support graph derived from a Bayesian network has been considered. This support graph however is built with reference to a given variable of interest and is meant to support the construction of arguments which provide a sort of representation of the reasoning inside the network. In our case we provide a structural description which does not refer to a single variable of interest and is not used for building explanations but rather to verify whether they satisfy structural DA, as it will be described later. A deeper analysis of the possible connections between our proposal and argumentation-based approaches for explaining Bayesian networks is an interesting subject for future work.

In the remainder, unless specified otherwise, we assume as given a probabilistic classifier $\mathcal{PC}$ with feature variables **X** and class variables **C**, without making any assumptions.

4   Formalising Descriptive Accuracy

We aim to define DA formally, in such a way that DA, independently of any specific explanation method (but with a focus on the broad class of local explanations, and specifically feature attribution methods to obtain them). To do so we will consider different abstractions of explanation, with the capability to encompass a broad range of existing notions in the literature as instances. The abstractions are based on the combinations of alternative choices along two dimensions. First, we consider two basic elements that an explanation may refer to: (1) *input features*; (2) pairs of variables representing *relations* between variables. Second, we assume that the basic elements inside an explanation can be: (a) regarded as an undifferentiated set (we call these elements *unsigned*, in contrast with (b)); (b) partitioned into two sets according to their *positive or negative* role in the explanation. The combinations (1)-(a) and (2)-(a) will correspond respectively to the abstract notions of *unipolar* and *relational unipolar* explanations while the combinations (1)-(b) and (2)-(b) will correspond respectively to the notions of *bipolar* and *relational bipolar* explanations. We will introduce a notion of *naive* DA for all the kinds of abstract explanations we consider and a notion of *dialectical* DA tailored to the two cases of relational explanations. We see naive DA as a very weak pre-requisite for explanations (it can be regarded as related to the basic notion of relevance), and prove that it is implied by dialectical DA for both bipolar and relational bipolar explanations (Propositions 1 and 2, resp.): thus, naive DA can be seen as a step towards defining dialectical DA. (Naive and) Dialectical DA are applicable to *any* probabilistic classifiers. In the specific setting of classifiers with underlying graph structures, such as BCs and CCs, we will also define a notion of *structural* DA for relational unipolar/bipolar explanations.

4.1   Unipolar Explanations and Naive DA

We begin with a very general notion of *unipolar explanation*: we only assume that, whatever the nature and structure of the explanation, it can be regarded at an abstract level as a *set of features*:

Definition 1. *Given an input $x \in \mathcal{X}$ and the resulting value $\omega = \mathcal{PC}(C|x)$ for class $C \in \mathbf{C}$ given x, a unipolar explanation (for $C = \omega$, given x) is a triple $\langle \mathbf{F}, C, x \rangle$ where $\mathbf{F} \subseteq \mathbf{X}$.*

Intuitively, the features in a unipolar explanation are those deemed "relevant" for explaining the resulting value assigned by the classifier to a class variable, for the input under consideration. It is easy to see that it is straightforward to derive unipolar explanations from the outcomes produced by existing explanation methods when they return features accompanied by additional information (e.g. feature importance as in the case of the attribution methods LIME and SHAP): basically, in these settings the unipolar explanations disregard the additional information, and amount to (a subset of) the set of features alone (e.g. the k most important features).

The simplest form of DA, i.e. *naive DA*, matches the intuition that the inclusion of features in a unipolar explanation should play a role in the underlying model, and is formally defined as follows:

Property 1. A unipolar explanation $\langle \mathbf{F}, C, \mathbf{x} \rangle$ satisfies *naive descriptive accuracy* iff for every $X_i \in \mathbf{F}$ there exists an input $\mathbf{x}' \in \mathcal{X}$ with $\mathbf{x}'(X_j) = \mathbf{x}(X_j)$ for every $X_j \neq X_i$ and with $\mathbf{x}'(X_i) \neq \mathbf{x}(X_i)$, such that, letting $\omega = \mathcal{PC}(C|\mathbf{x})$, it holds that $P(C = \omega|\mathbf{x}) \neq P(C = \omega|\mathbf{x}')$.

Naive DA holds when, for each feature, there is at least one case (i.e. an alternative input $\mathbf{x}'$ to the input $\mathbf{x}$ being explained) where a change in the value of the feature has an effect on the probability of the value of the class variable. It is a rather weak requirement as it excludes individually "irrelevant" features from playing a role in the explanation.

For illustration, given the probabilistic classifier in Table 1 and $\mathbf{x}$ as in the table's caption, the unipolar explanation $\langle \{s, d, h, n\}, c, \mathbf{x} \rangle$ does not satisfy naive DA, given that both s and d are "irrelevant" here: changing the value of either does not affect the probability of c. Meanwhile, it is easy to see that $\langle \{h, n\}, c, \mathbf{x} \rangle$ satisfies naive DA.

4.2 Bipolar Explanations and Dialectical DA

Unipolar explanations consist of "minimal" information, i.e. just the features playing a role in explanations. At a finer level of granularity, we consider *bipolar explanations*, where the features are partitioned into two sets: those having a positive effect on the resulting value and those having a negative effect. The notions of positive and negative effect may admit different specific interpretations in different contexts, the general underlying intuition being that the corresponding features provide, resp., reasons for and against the resulting value being explained. Whatever the interpretation, we assume that positive and negative features are disjoint, as, in an explanation, a feature with a twofold role would be confusing for the user.

Definition 2. *Given an input $\boldsymbol{x} \in \mathcal{X}$ and the resulting value $\omega = \mathcal{PC}(C|\boldsymbol{x})$ for class $C \in \mathbf{C}$ given $\boldsymbol{x}$, a bipolar explanation (for $C = \omega$, given $\boldsymbol{x}$) is a quadruple $\langle \mathbf{F}_+, \mathbf{F}_-, C, \boldsymbol{x} \rangle$ where $\mathbf{F}_+ \subseteq \mathbf{X}$, $\mathbf{F}_- \subseteq \mathbf{X}$, and $\mathbf{F}_+ \cap \mathbf{F}_- = \varnothing$; we refer to features in $\mathbf{F}_+$ and $\mathbf{F}_-$ resp. as* positive *and* negative reasons.

It is easy to see that existing explanation methods can be regarded as producing bipolar explanations when those methods return features accompanied by additional positive or negative information: in these settings, as in the case of unipolar explanations, bipolar explanations disregard the additional information, and amount to (a subset of) the set of features with their polarity (e.g. the k features with the highest positive importance as positive features and the k features with the lowest negative importance as negative features).

Taking into account the distinction between positive and negative reasons, we introduce a property requiring that the role assigned to features is justified:

Property 2. A bipolar explanation $\langle \mathbf{F}_+, \mathbf{F}_-, C, \mathbf{x} \rangle$ satisfies *dialectical descriptive accuracy* iff for every $X_i \in \mathbf{F}_+ \cup \mathbf{F}_-$, for every $\mathbf{x}' \in \mathcal{X}$ with $\mathbf{x}'(X_j) = \mathbf{x}(X_j)$ for all $X_j \neq X_i$ and $\mathbf{x}'(X_i) \neq \mathbf{x}(X_i)$, letting $\omega = \mathcal{PC}(C|\mathbf{x})$, it holds that

if $X_i \in \mathbf{F}_+$ then $P(C = \omega|\mathbf{x}) > P(C = \omega|\mathbf{x}')$;
if $X_i \in \mathbf{F}_-$ then $P(C = \omega|\mathbf{x}) < P(C = \omega|\mathbf{x}')$.

In words, if a feature is identified as a positive (negative) reason for the resulting value for a class variable, given the input, the feature variable's value leads to increasing (decreasing, resp.) the posterior probability of the class variable's resulting value (with all other feature values unchanged).

For illustration, in the running example with $\mathcal{PC}$ in Table 1, the bipolar explanation $\langle \{d, n\}, \{h\}, c, \mathbf{x} \rangle$, given input $\mathbf{x}$ as in the table's caption does not satisfy dialectical DA. Indeed, d is a positive reason in the explanation but, for $\mathbf{x}'$ agreeing with $\mathbf{x}$ on all features other than d (with $\mathbf{x}'(d) = -$), we obtain $P(c = +|\mathbf{x}) = .60 \not< P(c = +|\mathbf{x}') = .60$. Instead, it is easy to see that the bipolar explanation $\langle \{n\}, \{h\}, c, \mathbf{x} \rangle$, satisfies dialectical DA.

In general, unipolar explanations can be directly obtained from bipolar explanations by ignoring the distinction between positive and negative reasons, and the property of naive DA can be lifted:

Definition 3. *A bipolar explanation* $\langle \mathbf{F}_+, \mathbf{F}_-, C, \boldsymbol{x} \rangle$ *satisfies naive descriptive accuracy iff the unipolar explanation* $\langle \mathbf{F}_+ \cup \mathbf{F}_-, C, \boldsymbol{x} \rangle$ *satisfies naive descriptive accuracy.*

It is then easy to see that dialectical DA strengthens naive DA:[1]

Proposition 1. *If a bipolar explanation* $\langle \mathbf{F}_+, \mathbf{F}_-, C, \boldsymbol{x} \rangle$ *satisfies dialectical DA then it satisfies naive DA.*

4.3   Relational Unipolar Explanations and Naive DA

Moving towards a richer explanation notion, we pursue the idea of providing a detailed view of the relations between variables of a probabilistic classifier, reflecting influences possibly occurring amongst the variables. To this purpose we first introduce *relational unipolar explanations* as follows.

Definition 4. *Given* $\boldsymbol{x} \in \mathcal{X}$ *and the resulting value* $\omega = \mathcal{PC}(C|\boldsymbol{x})$ *for* $C \in \mathbf{C}$ *given* $\boldsymbol{x}$, *a relational unipolar explanation (for* $C = \omega$, *given* $\boldsymbol{x}$) *is a triple* $\langle \mathcal{R}, C, \boldsymbol{x} \rangle$ *where* $\mathcal{R} \subseteq \mathbf{V} \times \mathbf{V}$.

In words, a relational unipolar explanation includes a set $\mathcal{R}$ of pairs of variables (i.e. a relation between variables) where $(V_i, V_j) \in \mathcal{R}$ indicates that the value of V_i has a role in determining the value of V_j, given the input.

For illustration, for $\mathcal{PC}$ in Table 1, $\langle \{(s, e), (c, e)\}, e, \mathbf{x} \rangle$ may be a relational unipolar explanation for $\mathbf{x}$ in the table's caption, indicating that s and c both influence (the value of) e. Note that relational unipolar explanations admit unipolar explanations as special instances: given a unipolar explanation $\langle \mathbf{F}, C, \mathbf{x} \rangle$, it is straightforward to see that $\langle \mathbf{F} \times \{C\}, C, \mathbf{x} \rangle$ is a relational unipolar explanation. However, as demonstrated in the illustration, relational unipolar explanations may include relations besides those between feature and class variables found in unipolar explanations.

The notion of naive DA can be naturally extended to relational unipolar explanations:

---

[1] All proofs are omitted due to space limitations.

Property 3. A relational unipolar explanation $\langle \mathcal{R}, C, \mathbf{x} \rangle$ satisfies *naive descriptive accuracy* iff for every $(V_i, V_j) \in \mathcal{R}$, letting $v_i = \mathcal{PC}(V_i|\mathbf{x})$ and $v_j = \mathcal{PC}(V_j|\mathbf{x})$, there exists $v_i' \in \Omega_{V_i}$, $v_i' \neq v_i$, such that $P(V_j = v_j|\mathbf{x}) \neq P(V_j = v_j|\mathbf{x}, set(V_i = v_i'))$.

For illustration, for $\mathcal{PC}$ in Table 1, $\langle \{(s, e), (n, e)\}, e, \mathbf{x} \rangle$ satisfies naive DA for $\mathbf{x}$ in the table's caption, but $\langle \{(s, e), (d, e)\}, e, \mathbf{x} \rangle$ does not, as changing the value of d to $-$ (the only alternative value to $+$), the probability of $e = +$ remains unchanged.

It is easy to see that, for relational unipolar explanations $\langle \mathbf{F} \times \{C\}, C, \mathbf{x} \rangle$, corresponding to unipolar explanations $\langle \mathbf{F}, C, \mathbf{x} \rangle$, Property 3 implies Property 1.

4.4   Relational Bipolar Explanations and Dialectical DA

Bipolar explanations and dialectical DA can also be naturally extended to accommodate relations, as follows:

Definition 5. *Given an input* $\mathbf{x} \in \mathcal{X}$ *and the resulting value* $\omega = \mathcal{PC}(C|\mathbf{x})$ *for class* $C \in \mathbf{C}$ *given* $\mathbf{x}$, *a relational bipolar explanation (RX) is a quadruple* $\langle \mathcal{R}_+, \mathcal{R}_-, C, \mathbf{x} \rangle$ *where:*
$\mathcal{R}_+ \subseteq \mathbf{V} \times \mathbf{V}$, *referred to as the set of* positive reasons;
$\mathcal{R}_- \subseteq \mathbf{V} \times \mathbf{V}$, *referred to as the set of* negative reasons;
$\mathcal{R}_+ \cap \mathcal{R}_- = \varnothing$.

Property 4. An RX $\langle \mathcal{R}_+, \mathcal{R}_-, C, \mathbf{x} \rangle$ satisfies *dialectical descriptive accuracy* iff for every $(V_i, V_j) \in \mathcal{R}_+ \cup \mathcal{R}_-$, letting $v_i = \mathcal{PC}(V_i|\mathbf{x})$, $v_j = \mathcal{PC}(V_j|\mathbf{x})$, it holds that, for every $v_i' \in \Omega_{V_i} \setminus \{v_i\}$:

if $(V_i, V_j) \in \mathcal{R}_+$ then $P(V_j = v_j|\mathbf{x}) > P(V_j = v_j|\mathbf{x}, set(V_i = v_i'))$;
if $(V_i, V_j) \in \mathcal{R}_-$ then $P(V_j = v_j|\mathbf{x}) < P(V_j = v_j|\mathbf{x}, set(V_i = v_i'))$.

An RX can be seen as a graph of variables connected by edges identifying positive or negative reasons. Examples of RXs for the running example are shown as graphs in Fig. 1 (where the nodes also indicate the values ascribed to the feature variables in the input $\mathbf{x}$ and to the class variables by any of the toy classifiers in Tables 1 and 2). Here, (iii) satisfies dialectical DA, since setting to $-$ the value of any variable with a positive (negative) reason to another variable will reduce (increase, resp.) the probability of the latter's value being $+$, whereas (ii) does not, since setting d to $-$ does not affect the probability of c's value being $+$ and (i) does not since setting d to $-$ does not affect the probability of e's value being $+$.

Similarly to the case of unipolar/bipolar explanations, relational unipolar explanations can be obtained from RXs by ignoring the distinction between positive and negative reasons, and the property of dialectical DA can be lifted:

Definition 6. *An RX* $\langle \mathcal{R}_+, \mathcal{R}_-, C, \mathbf{x} \rangle$ *satisfies naive DA iff the relational unipolar explanation* $\langle \mathcal{R}_+ \cup \mathcal{R}_-, C, \mathbf{x} \rangle$ *satisfies naive DA.*

It is then easy to see that dialectical DA strengthens naive DA:

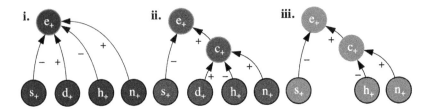

Fig. 1. Example RXs (shown as graphs, with positive and negative reasons given by edges labelled + and −, resp.) with input $\mathbf{x}$ such that $\mathbf{x}(s) = \mathbf{x}(d) = \mathbf{x}(h) = \mathbf{x}(n) = +$ (represented as s_+, d_+, h_+, n_+) and (resulting) class values $c = +$ (represented as c_+) and $e = +$ (represented as e_+).

Proposition 2. *If an RX* $\langle \mathcal{R}_+, \mathcal{R}_-, C, \boldsymbol{x} \rangle$ *satisfies* dialectical DA *then it satisfies* naive DA.

Note that bipolar explanations $\langle \mathbf{F}_+, \mathbf{F}_-, C, \mathbf{x} \rangle$ can be regarded as special cases of RXs, i.e. $\langle \{(X,C)|X \in \mathbf{F}_+\}, \{(X,C) \mid X \in \mathbf{F}_-\}, C, \mathbf{x} \rangle$ (indeed, the RX in Fig. 1(i) is a bipolar explanation). Thus, from now on we will often refer to all forms of bipolar explanation as RXs.

4.5   Relational Bipolar Explanations and Structural DA

When a classifier is equipped with a structural description, one can require that the relations used for explanation purposes in RXs are subsets of those specified by the structural description, so that the RXs correspond directly to (parts of) the inner working of the model. This leads to the following additional form of DA:

Property 5. Given a probabilistic classifier $\mathcal{PC}$ with structural description $\mathcal{SD}$:

- a relational unipolar explanation $\langle \mathcal{R}, C, \mathbf{x} \rangle$ satisfies *structural descriptive accuracy* iff $\mathcal{R} \subseteq \mathcal{SD}$; and
- an RX $\langle \mathcal{R}_+, \mathcal{R}_-, C, \mathbf{x} \rangle$ satisfies *structural descriptive accuracy* iff $\mathcal{R}_+ \cup \mathcal{R}_- \subseteq \mathcal{SD}$.

For instance, suppose that $\mathcal{SD}$ is the structural description in Table 2(c). Then, the RXs in Fig. 1(ii-iii) satisfy structural DA, while the RX in Fig. 1(i) does not, since the relations from d, h and n to e are not present in the structural description.

5   Achieving DA in Practice

Here, we study the satisfaction of the proposed properties by explanation methods. We focus in particular on two existing methods in the literature (LIME [24] and SHAP [15]). After showing that these methods do not satisfy the properties introduced in Sect. 4, we introduce a novel form of explanation guaranteed to satisfy them. Thus, this novel form of explanation can be seen as a "champion" for our proposed forms of DA, showing that they can be satisfied in practice.

We start with LIME and SHAP. The explanations they produce (given an input $\mathbf{x}$ and a classifier, computing $C=\omega$, given $\mathbf{x}$) basically consist in computing, for each feature $X_i \in \mathbf{X}$, a real number $w(\mathbf{x}, X_i, C)$ indicating the importance of X_i, which has assigned value $\mathbf{x}(X_i)$ in the given input $\mathbf{x}$, towards the probability of the class variable C being assigned value $\omega = \mathcal{PC}(C|\mathbf{x})$ by the classifier, in the context of $\mathbf{x}$.[2] The absolute value of this number can be interpreted as a measure of the feature importance in the explanation, while its sign, in the context of explaining probabilistic classifiers, indicates whether the feature has a positive or negative role wrt the classifier's resulting value for the explained instance. Features which are assigned a value of zero can be regarded as irrelevant. Clearly, such explanations correspond to bipolar explanations $\langle \mathbf{F}_+, \mathbf{F}_-, C, \mathbf{x} \rangle$ as in Definition 2, with

- $\mathbf{F}_+ = \{ X_i \in \mathbf{X} \mid w(\mathbf{x}, X_i, C) > 0 \}$ and
- $\mathbf{F}_- = \{ X_i \in \mathbf{X} \mid w(\mathbf{x}, X_i, C) < 0 \}$.

In the remainder, with an abuse of terminology, we call these bipolar explanations *LIME/SHAP explanations*, depending on whether w is calculated using, resp., the method of LIME/SHAP. For illustration, consider the classifier in Table 1 and $\mathbf{x}$ such that $\mathbf{x}(s) = \mathbf{x}(d) = \mathbf{x}(h) = \mathbf{x}(n) = +$, as in the caption of Fig. 1, for which the classifier computes $e = +$. In this simple setting, SHAP computes $w(\mathbf{x}, s_+, e_+) = -0.20$, $w(\mathbf{x}, d_+, e_+) = 0.03$, $w(\mathbf{x}, h_+, e_+) = -0.05$, and $w(\mathbf{x}, n_+, e_+) = 0.25$ (adopting here the same conventions on variable assignments as in the caption of the figure). This results in the SHAP explanation in Fig. 1(i). Thus features d and n (with their current values) are ascribed positive roles and s and h are ascribed negative roles in determining the outcome $\mathcal{PC}(e|\mathbf{x}) = +$. However, as stated earlier, for feature d this is in contrast with the property of naive DA. In fact, by inspection of Table 1, it can be noted that in changing the value of this variable individually we would still have $P(e = +|\mathbf{x}) = 1$. To put it in intuitive terms, assigning a positive importance to this variable suggests to the user that its current value (namely +) has a role in determining the outcome $e = +$ (though minor), which is misleading. The following proposition generalizes these considerations:

Proposition 3. *In general, LIME and SHAP explanations are not guaranteed to satisfy naive nor dialectical DA.*

The illustration above proves this result for SHAP explanations, by providing a counterexample to naive (and hence dialectical) DA in the context of the classifier in Table 1. As to LIME, we built counterexamples by introducing spurious features within trained probabilistic classifiers and showing that they are assigned non-null importance.

Concerning structural DA, LIME and SHAP explanations may in general satisfy it only if $\mathbf{X} \times \mathbf{C} \subseteq \mathcal{SD}$, i.e. if the structural description includes all the

---

[2] We omit the formal definitions of how these well-known methods compute w, as not essential for the considerations on property satisfaction drawn in this paper.

possible relations from feature variables to class variables. This is for instance the case for naive BCs [16], but not for more general BCs or CCs.

To guarantee the missing properties too, we define novel *dialectically accurate relational explanations (DARXs)*:

Definition 7. *Given a probabilistic classifier with structural description SD, a* dialectically accurate relational explanation *(DARX) is a relational bipolar explanation $\langle \mathcal{R}_+, \mathcal{R}_-, C, \boldsymbol{x} \rangle$ where, letting $v_x = \mathcal{PC}(V_x|\mathbf{x})$ for any $V_x \in \mathbf{V}$:*

- $\mathcal{R}_+ = \{(V_i, V_j) \in SD | \forall v_i' \in \Omega_{V_i} \setminus \{v_i\}$ *it holds that* $P(V_j = v_j|\mathbf{x}) > P(V_j = v_j|\mathbf{x}, set(V_i = v_i'))\};$
- $\mathcal{R}_- = \{(V_i, V_j) \in SD | \forall v_i' \in \Omega_{V_i} \setminus \{v_i\}$ *it holds that* $P(V_j = v_j|\mathbf{x}) < P(V_j = v_j|\mathbf{x}, set(V_i = v_i'))\}.$

Proposition 4. *DARXs are guaranteed to satisfy naive, structural and dialectical DA.*

For illustration, suppose SD corresponds exactly to the links in Fig. 1(iii). Then, this figure shows the DARX for e given the input in the figure's caption and the classifier in Table 1 (or Table 2). Here, the satisfaction of naive DA ensures that no spurious reasons, i.e. where the corresponding variables do not, in fact, influence one another, are included in the DARX. Note that, when explaining e with the same input, SHAP may draw a positive reason from d to e (as in Fig. 1(i)) when, according to SD, d does not directly affect e. Further, the satisfaction of dialectical DA means that each of the reasons in the DARX in Fig. 1(iii) is guaranteed to have the desired dialectical effect. Note that DARXs are local explanations, meaning that they are meant to explain the behaviour of the classifier given a specific input, not the behaviour of the classifier in general. In other words, they assign a positive or negative role to variables with reference to the specific input considered and it may of course be the case that, given a different input, the same variable has a different role.

6 Empirical Evaluation

As mentioned in Sect. 3, we experiment with (chains of) BCs as well as chains (in the form of trees) of tree-based classifiers (referred to as *C-DTs* below). As far as BCs are concerned, we experiment with different types, corresponding to different restrictions on the structure of the underlying Bayesian network and conditional dependencies: naive BCs (*NBC*) [16]; tree-augmented naive BCs (*TAN*) [7]; and *chains* of BCs [29], specifically in the form of chains of NBCs (*CNBC*) and of the unrestricted BCs suggested in [22] (*CUBC*). We choose C-DTs and (chains of) BCs as they are endowed with a natural structural description, allowing us to evaluate structural DA, while they are popular methods with tabular data, e.g. in the case of BCs, for medical diagnosis [14,17].[3]

---

[3] We use several datasets or (pre-computed) Bayesian networks, and deploy the best-performing type of the chosen type of classifier for each. As structural descriptions, we use those described in Sect. 3. When training classifiers on datasets, we split them into train/test sets (with 75/25% ratio) and optimise the hyper-parameters.

Table 3. Average percentages of reasons (over 100 samples) *violating* DA (i.e. $|\{(V_i, V_j) \in \mathcal{R}_- \cup \mathcal{R}_+ \text{ such that}(V_i, V_j) \text{ violates DA}\}|/|\mathcal{R}_- \cup \mathcal{R}_+|)$ for several instantiated RXs. (∗) NBC (Naive BC), TAN (Tree-Augmented NBC), CUBC (Chain of Unrestricted BCs), C-DTs (Chain of Decision Trees); (†) results must be 0.0% due to the BC type.

Dataset	Source	Classifier*	SHAP			LIME		
			Naive	Structural	Dialectical	Naive	Structural	Dialectical
Shuttle	[28]	NBC	0%	0%†	16.43%	0%	0%†	17.14%
German	[28]	NBC	0%	0%†	54.56%	0%	0%†	49.55
California	[11]	TAN	0%	0%†	16.75%	0%	0%†	16.75%
Child	[3]	CUBC	0%	70.97%	75.35%	63.74%	89.59%	91.16%
Insurance	[3]	CUBC	0%	67.07%	78.77%	59.56%	89.26%	93.07%
HELOC	[5]	C-DTs	51.77%	100%	94.42%	62.21%	100%	97.87%
LendingClub	[4]	C-DTs	16.19%	100%	94.47%	72.95%	100%	98.57%

Our experiments aim to evaluate the satisfaction/violation of structural and dialectical DA empirically for various concrete RXs (i.e. LIME, SHAP and their structural variants) when they are not guaranteed to satisfy the properties, as shown in Sect. 5. The main questions we aim to address concern *actual DA* and *efficiency*, as follows.

Actual DA. While some approaches may not be guaranteed to satisfy DA in general, they may for the most part in practice. *How much DA is achieved in the concrete settings of SHAP, and LIME explanations?* We checked the average percentages of reasons in LIME and SHAP explanations which do not satisfy our notions of descriptive accuracy. The results are in Table 3. We note that: **(1)** LIME often violate *naive descriptive accuracy*, e.g. in the *Child* and *Insurance* BCs, whereas SHAP does not; **(2)** LIME and SHAP systematically violate *structural descriptive accuracy*; **(3)** LIME and SHAP often violate *dialectical descriptive accuracy*.

Efficiency. We have defined DARXs so that they are guaranteed to satisfy structural and dialectical DA. *Is the enforcement of these properties viable in practice, i.e. how expensive is it to compute DARXs?* Formally, the computational cost for DARXs can be obtained as follows. Let t_p be the time to compute a prediction and its associated posterior probabilities.[4] The upper bound of the time complexity to compute a DARX is $T_{DARX}(\Omega) = O\left(t_p \cdot \sum_{V_i \in \mathbf{V}} |\Omega_{V_i}|\right)$, which is *linear* with respect to the sum of the number of variables' values, making DARXs *efficient*, while the time required by LIME is exponential with respect to the number of variables' values for discrete variables, while it requires a large (by default 5000) number of sample in the case of continuous variables.

---

[4] In our experiments, using a machine with *Intel i9-9900X* at 3.5 Ghz and 32 GB of RAM (no GPU acceleration) t_p ranges from $3\mu s$ to $436ms$ depending on the classifier.

7   Discussion and Conclusions

We have introduced a three-fold notion of DA for explanations of probabilistic classifiers, which, despite its intuitiveness, is often not satisfied by prominent explanation methods, and shown that it can be satisfied, by design, by the novel explanation concept of DARXs.

A variety of approaches devoted in particular to the explanation of Bayesian networks exist in the literature [12,18]. At a high level these approaches can be partitioned into three main families [12]: explanation of evidence (which concerns explaining observations by abducing the value of some unobserved variables), explanation of model (which aims at presenting the entire underlying model to the user), and explanation of reasoning. Explanation of reasoning is the closest to our approach and, according to [12] is in turn divided into: (i) explanation of the results obtained by the system and the reasoning process that produced them; (ii) explanation of the results not obtained by the system, despite the user's expectations; (iii) hypothetical reasoning, i.e. what results the system would have returned if one or more given variables had taken on different values from those observed. Our approach is mainly related to point (i), even if it may support some form of hypothetical reasoning too. We remark anyway that the spirit of DARX is not advancing the state of the art in explanations for Bayesian networks but rather providing a concrete example of a method satisfying the DA properties we introduced and showing that even with this baseline approach we can get improvements with respect to popular model-agnostic methods.

Our work opens several avenues for future work. It would be interesting to experiment with other forms of probabilistic classifiers, including (chained) neural networks, possibly in combination with methods for extracting *causal models* from these classifiers to provide structural descriptions for satisfying structural DA. It would also be interesting to study the satisfaction of (suitable variants of) DA by other forms of explanations, including *minimum cardinality* explanations [25] and set-based explanations [6,9].

Acknowledgements. Toni was partially funded by the European Research Council (ERC) under the European Union's Horizon 2020 research and innovation programme (grant agreement No. 101020934). Rago and Toni were partially funded by J.P. Morgan and by the Royal Academy of Engineering under the Research Chairs and Senior Research Fellowships scheme. Any views or opinions expressed herein are solely those of the authors listed.

References

1. Alvarez-Melis, D., Jaakkola, T.S.: A causal framework for explaining the predictions of black-box sequence-to-sequence models. In: EMNLP (2017)
2. Bielza, C., Larrañaga, P.: Discrete Bayesian network classifiers: a survey. ACM Comput. Surv. **47**(1), 5:1–5:43 (2014)
3. BNlearn: Bayesian network repository - an R package for Bayesian network learning and inference (2020). https://www.bnlearn.com/bnrepository

4. Club, L.: Lending Club Loans (2019). https://kaggle.com/wordsforthewise/lending-club
5. FICO Community: Explainable Machine Learning Challenge (2019). https://community.fico.com/s/explainable-machine-learning-challenge
6. Dhurandhar, A., et al.: Explanations based on the missing: towards contrastive explanations with pertinent negatives. In: NeurIPS (2018)
7. Friedman, N., Geiger, D., Goldszmidt, M.: Bayesian network classifiers. Mach. Learn. **29**(2–3), 131–163 (1997). https://doi.org/10.1023/A:1007465528199
8. Guidotti, R., Monreale, A., Ruggieri, S., Turini, F., Giannotti, F., Pedreschi, D.: A survey of methods for explaining black box models. ACM Comput. Surv. **51**(5), 93:1–93:42 (2019)
9. Ignatiev, A., Narodytska, N., Marques-Silva, J.: Abduction-based explanations for machine learning models. In: AAAI (2019)
10. Jacovi, A., Marasovic, A., Miller, T., Goldberg, Y.: Formalizing trust in artificial intelligence: Prerequisites, causes and goals of human trust in AI. In: FAccT (2021)
11. Kelley Pace, R., Barry, R.: Sparse spatial autoregressions. Stat. Probab. Lett. **33**(3), 291–297 (1997)
12. Lacave, C., Díez, F.J.: A review of explanation methods for Bayesian networks. Knowl. Eng. Rev. **17**(2), 107–127 (2002). https://doi.org/10.1017/S026988890200019X
13. Lakkaraju, H., Kamar, E., Caruana, R., Leskovec, J.: Faithful and customizable explanations of black box models. In: AIES (2019)
14. Lipovetsky, S.: Let the evidence speak - using Bayesian thinking in law, medicine, ecology and other areas. Technometrics **62**(1), 137–138 (2020)
15. Lundberg, S.M., Lee, S.: A unified approach to interpreting model predictions. In: NeurIPS (2017)
16. Maron, M.E., Kuhns, J.L.: On relevance, probabilistic indexing and information retrieval. J. ACM **7**(3), 216–244 (1960)
17. McLachlan, S., Dube, K., Hitman, G.A., Fenton, N.E., Kyrimi, E.: Bayesian networks in healthcare: distribution by medical condition. Artif. Intell. Medicine **107**, 101912 (2020)
18. Mihaljevic, B., Bielza, C., Larrañaga, P.: Bayesian networks for interpretable machine learning and optimization. Neurocomputing **456**, 648–665 (2021)
19. Murdoch, W.J., Singh, C., Kumbier, K., Abbasi-Asl, R., Yu, B.: Definitions, methods, and applications in interpretable machine learning. Proc. Natl. Acad. Sci. **116**(44), 22071–22080 (2019)
20. Neapolitan, R.E., Jiang, X.: Probabilistic Methods for Financial and Marketing Informatics. Elsevier, Amsterdam (2010)
21. Pearl, J.: Probabilistic Reasoning in Intelligent Systems - Networks of Plausible Inference. Morgan Kaufmann, Burlington (1989)
22. Provan, G.M., Singh, M.: Learning Bayesian networks using feature selection. In: AISTATS (1995)
23. Read, J., Pfahringer, B., Holmes, G., Frank, E.: Classifier chains for multi-label classification. In: Buntine, W., Grobelnik, M., Mladenić, D., Shawe-Taylor, J. (eds.) ECML PKDD 2009. LNCS (LNAI), vol. 5782, pp. 254–269. Springer, Heidelberg (2009). https://doi.org/10.1007/978-3-642-04174-7_17
24. Ribeiro, M.T., Singh, S., Guestrin, C.: "Why should i trust you?": explaining the predictions of any classifier. In: ACM SIGKDD (2016)
25. Shih, A., Choi, A., Darwiche, A.: A symbolic approach to explaining Bayesian network classifiers. In: IJCAI (2018)

26. Sokol, K., Flach, P.A.: Explainability fact sheets: a framework for systematic assessment of explainable approaches. In: FAT* (2020)

27. Timmer, S.T., Meyer, J.-J.C., Prakken, H., Renooij, S., Verheij, B.: Explaining Bayesian networks using argumentation. In: Destercke, S., Denoeux, T. (eds.) ECSQARU 2015. LNCS (LNAI), vol. 9161, pp. 83–92. Springer, Cham (2015). https://doi.org/10.1007/978-3-319-20807-7_8

28. UCI, C.: Machine Learning Repository (2020). https://archive.ics.uci.edu/ml/datasets.php

29. Zaragoza, J.H., Sucar, L.E., Morales, E.F., Bielza, C., Larrañaga, P.: Bayesian chain classifiers for multidimensional classification. In: IJCAI (2011)

Explanation of Pseudo-Boolean Functions Using Cooperative Game Theory and Prime Implicants

Christophe Labreuche[1,2]([⊠]) (iD)

[1] Thales Research and Technology, Palaiseau, France
christophe.labreuche@thalesgroup.com
[2] SINCLAIR AI Lab, Palaiseau, France

Abstract. Explanation methods can be formal or heuristic-based. Many explanation methods have been developed. Formal methods provide principles to derive sufficient reasons (prime implicants) or necessary reasons (counterfactuals, causes). These approaches are appealing but require to discretize the input and output spaces. Heuristic-based approaches such as feature attribution (such as the Shapley value) work in any condition but the relation to explanation is less clear. We show that they cannot distinguish between conjunction and disjunction, which is not the case with sufficient explanations. This work is an initial work that aims at combining some idea of prime implicants into feature attribution, in order to measure sufficiency of the features. We apply it to two values - the proportional division and the Shapley value.

Keywords: Explainable AI · Prime implicant · Cooperative Game Theory · Proportional division · Shapley value

1 Introduction

Generating relevant explanations is crucial in many applications such as safety critical domains (e.g. medicine, autonomous car, train or aircraft monitoring) [2]. Explainable AI (XAI) has thus emerged as an important question in AI. There is a variety of XAI techniques, as depicted in the following section.

1.1 Related Works

The first category of XAI methods provide formal definition of explanation. Counterfactual methods look at the minimal change in the characteristics of the instance that switches the outcome [23]. Actual causes aim at finding a causal explanation, that is the minimal characteristics of the instance that would change the outcome if it were changed [9]. Prime Implicants (PI) aims at finding the minimum information to keep in order be to get the same outcome of the model, whatever the other piece of information [3]. They define sufficient interpretation in first-order logic [16]. They can be used to explain a particular instance, which yields the concepts of *sufficient reason* [7],

© The Author(s), under exclusive license to Springer Nature Switzerland AG 2022
F. Dupin de Saint-Cyr et al. (Eds.): SUM 2022, LNAI 13562, pp. 295–308, 2022.
https://doi.org/10.1007/978-3-031-18843-5_20

PI-explanation [22] and *abductive explanation* [11]. An explanation is a subset of the literals of the instance that entails the same conclusion. A sufficient cause is a subset of literals such that if they were modified, the conclusion would have been different [10]. Prime implicants are sufficient reasons whereas actual causes are necessary reasons.

Some other methods are less formal and for instance simply aim at allocating an importance to each feature (feature attribution methods) [19]. The Shapley value has recently become popular in Machine Learning (ML) to estimate the level of contribution of each feature to the prediction [8, 14, 15, 17, 24]. What distinguishes these methods is the game on which the Shapley value is computed. A major difficulty in assessing the game is to take into account the interdependencies among the features [1].

Feature-attribution and counterfactual methods are unified in [18] based on the concepts of sufficiency and necessary explanations. However counterfactual explanations are interpreted as necessary explanations and feature-attributions are interpreted as sufficient explanations. This latter is not justified and we believe that feature attributions fail to recover sufficient reasons.

1.2   Contribution

We are interested in explaining a decision function over a set of discrete attributes with feature attribution techniques based on game theory, thanks to their ability to adapt to a wide range of situations and especially numerical models. These methods require transforming the decision function into a game. In Game Theory, a *game* is a set function and corresponds to a function defined on a set of Boolean variables (also called *pseudo-Boolean function*). Even though game theoretical feature attribution techniques can capture the contribution of each individual feature to the overall score, they cannot grasp the idea of sufficiency. More precisely, they cannot distinguish between a situation where all features are necessary (they are linked in a conjunctive way) and another one where only a subset of features is sufficient (they are linked in a disjunctive way). On the other hand, prime implicants are designed to provide sufficient explanations, as they identify the minimal subsets of characteristics that are sufficient to yield the outcome. Based on this remark, the main contribution of this paper is to extend feature-attribution – and especially the ones based on Cooperative Game Theory – to incorporate some sufficiency measures. In order to account for sufficient reasons in feature-attribution, we consider each subset of features (as being a potential prime implicant) and share the importance of all variables within this subset. Then the importance of a feature is the largest attribution of this variable over all possible subsets including it. We show some preliminary properties on this new imputation.

2   Problem at Stake and Preliminaries

Consider a set of variables (also called features) $M = \{1, \ldots, m\}$ taking values in discrete domains $X_1, \ldots, X_m$. The set of instances is $X = X_1 \times \cdots \times X_m$. Our aim is to explain a decision function $F : X \to \mathbb{R}$.

Feature attribution methods such as SHAP typically work on a binary feature space. The explanation of F will thus be done through a function defined on a set $N = \{1, \ldots, n\}$ of binary variables. Such a function is called pseudo-Boolean function.

Definition 1. *A* pseudo-Boolean function (PBF) *on N is a function $f : D \to \mathbb{R}$ where $D = \{0, 1\}^N$.*

We assume that f is monotone in all its coordinates. This hypothesis is relevant in domains such as decision [5] or many situations of classification [6]. Most of our results can be easily extended to the non-monotonic case. Without loss of generality, we assume that f is normalized in the sense that $f(0, \ldots, 0) = 0$ and $f(1, \ldots, 1) = 1$.

Several binarization techniques are presented in Sect. 2.1 to derive f defined on D from F defined on X. We then recall Cooperative Game Theory which applies on a set of Boolean variables (Sect. 2.2). Finally we describe in Sect. 2.3 another explanation approach, based on prime implicants.

2.1 Explanation Through Binarization of the Feature Space

Function f can be constructed in different ways.

Local explanation of F: In local explanation, we wish to explain $F(x)$ for a particular instance $x \in X$. Here, $N = M$. A first way to binarize the set of features is to compare x to a particular reference element $r \in X$ [12, 17]. For $d \in D$, we define the composite instance $z(x, r, d) \in X$ by $z_i(x, r, d) = x_i$ if $d_i = 1$ and $z_i(x, r, d) = r_i$ if $d_i = 0$. Then $f(d) = F(z(x, r, d))$.

A second way is to define $f(d)$ as the conditional expected output of F when features in $S_d = \{i \in M : d_i = 1\}$ take value x [12,17]: $f(d) = \frac{1}{K} \sum_{k=1}^{K} F(x_{S_d}, r^k_{M \setminus S_d})$, where $r^k \in X$ (for $k = 1, \ldots, K$) are elements of a dataset, and $(x_{S_d}, r^k_{M \setminus S_d})$ is the compound option taking value of x in S_d and of r^k in $M \setminus S_d$.

Global explanation of F: The aim of global explanation is to explain F in general (not on a particular instance). One can then use one-hot encoding to transform the feature spaces $X_1, \ldots, X_m$ into n Boolean variables, where $n = \sum_{i=1}^{n} |X_i|$.

2.2 Feature Attribution Techniques Based on Cooperative Game Theory

The aim of Cooperative Game Theory is to determine how to share among the players the wealth obtained by all players together. The set of players is N. A *Transferable Utility (TU) game* (game in short) is a set function $v : 2^N \to \mathbb{R}$ satisfying $v(\emptyset) = 0$, where $v(S)$ for $S \subseteq N$ is the wealth produced by players S when they form a coalition. We denote by $\mathcal{G}(N)$ the set of games on N. A $0--1$ game is a game that can only take values 0 and 1. We denote by $\mathcal{G}^+(N)$ the set of games $v \in \mathcal{G}(N)$ such that $v(S) > 0$ for all $S \subseteq N$ with $S \neq \emptyset$. The *dual* of a game v is a game $\bar{v}$ defined by $\bar{v}(S) = v(N) - v(N \setminus S)$. A game is *monotone* if $v(S \cup \{i\}) \geq v(S)$ for all $i \in N$ and $S \subseteq N \setminus \{i\}$. For $S \subseteq N$, we define the *restricted game* $v_{|S} \in \mathcal{G}(S)$ defined on S by $v_{|S}(T) = v(T)$ for all $T \subseteq S$.

Given a PBF f, we define a game v_f by

$$v_f(S) = f(1_S, 0_{N \setminus S}) \qquad \forall S \subseteq N. \tag{1}$$

Explaining f is equivalent to explaining v_f. The idea of feature attribution is to identify the contribution level of each feature to outcome $f(1, \ldots, 1) = v_f(N)$.

A *value* is a function that allocates a worth to each player. It is defined as a function $\phi : N \times \mathcal{G}(N) \to \mathbb{R}^N$, where $\phi_i(N, v)$ is what is given to player $i \in N$. We denote by $\Phi(N)$ the set of values on N. The basic property of a value – called *efficiency* – tells that it shares the wealth $v(N)$ obtained by the grand coalition N among its members:

$$\sum_{i \in N} \phi_i(N, v) = v(N).$$

Several values have been defined. One of the simplest one is the *proportional division (PD)*, which allocates $v(N)$ proportionally to each player's solo wealth [25]

$$\phi_i^{\text{PD}}(N, v) = \begin{cases} \frac{v(\{i\})}{\sum_{j \in N} v(\{j\})} v(N) & \text{if } \exists j \in N \text{ s.t. } v(\{j\}) \neq 0 \\ \frac{v(N)}{n} & \text{if } \forall j \in N \ v(\{j\}) = 0 \end{cases} \tag{2}$$

The second line considers the case where the worth of all singletons is zero, which is often the case of $0 - -1$ games.

The *proportional allocation of nonseparable contributions (PANSC)* is [13]

$$\phi_i^{\text{PANSC}}(N, v) = \begin{cases} \frac{SC_i(N,v)}{\sum_{j \in N} SC_j(N,v)} v(N) & \text{if } \exists j \in N \text{ s.t. } SC_j(N, v) \neq 0 \\ \frac{v(N)}{n} & \text{if } \forall j \in N \ SC_j(N, v) = 0 \end{cases} \tag{3}$$

where

$$SC_i(N, v) = \overline{v}(\{i\}) = v(N) - v(N \setminus \{i\})$$

is the *Separable Contribution* of player i. One can readily see that PD and PANSC are dual concepts as $\phi_i^{\text{PANSC}}(N, v) = \phi_i^{\text{PD}}(N, \overline{v})$.

The Shapley value is a fair share of the global wealth $v(N)$ [21]:

$$\phi_i^{\text{Sh}}(N, v) = \sum_{S \subseteq N \setminus i} \frac{(n - |S| - 1)! |S|!}{n!} \left[v(S \cup \{i\}) - v(S) \right]. \tag{4}$$

Many other values exist such as the Banzhaf value [4] or the nucleolus [20].

The importance of feature i to $f(1, \ldots, 1) = v_f(N)$ is then $\phi_i(N, v_f)$. We note that the Shapley value has been widely used for feature attribution. To the best of our knowledge, PD and PANSC have never been used in feature attribution. However we will show some interests of these concepts in this paper.

2.3   Prime Implicants

In order to use more formal explanation methods than feature attribution, we need to discretize the output. We assume a binary output.

Definition 2. A Boolean function (BF) *on N is a function* $f : D \to \{0, 1\}$.

We wish to understand where value $f = 1$ can come from in general for a BF f. A *sufficient* explanation (of $f = 1$) is an instanciation of a subset S of variables such that fixing the variables S to these values yields the same conclusion whatever the value on the other features.

Definition 3 *([16]). An* implicant (I) *of f is a conjunction of literals* $(1_S, 0_T)$ *such that* $f(1_S, 0_T, x_{N\setminus(S\cup T)}) = 1$ *for all* $x_{N\setminus(S\cup T)} \in D_{N\setminus(S\cup T)}$. *The* prime implicants (PI) *of f are the minimal elements of the set of implicants in the sense of* $\subseteq$.

Let $\mathcal{I}_f$ be the set of implicants of f and $\mathcal{PI}_f$ be the set of prime implicants of f. As f is monotone, the PI are of the form 1_S, and they are the minimal subsets $S \subseteq N$ such that $f(1_S, 0_{N\setminus S}) = 1$.

Definition 4 *([3]). A variable is* irrelevant *if changing the value on this variable never modifies the outcome f. A variable is* mandatory *for a prediction f* $= 1$, *if every instance having this prediction takes value 1 on this attribute.*

Example 1. Let f be defined on $N = \{1, 2, 3, 4\}$ by $f(x) = (x_1 \wedge x_2) \vee (x_1 \wedge x_3)$. Then $\mathcal{I}_f = \{1_{\{1,2\}}, 1_{\{1,3\}}, 1_{\{1,2,3\}}, 1_{\{1,2,4\}}, 1_{\{1,3,4\}}, 1_{\{1,2,3,4\}}\}$ and $\mathcal{PI}_f = \{1_{\{1,2\}}, 1_{\{1,3\}}\}$. Hence feature 4 is irrelevant and 1 is mandatory to obtain $f = 1$.   ∎

3   Global Explanation for a Pseudo-Boolean Function

We are interested in the global explanation of a PBF f defined on a set N of Boolean variables, through an index $I_i(f)$ measure the level of influence of variable i in f. We will indifferently define the influence on f or on the corresponding game v_f (see (1)) – yielding $I_i(N, v_f)$. We will extend the values defined in Sect. 2.2.

3.1   Motivating Example and Proposal on Boolean Functions

The main argument of this work is that standard feature attribution techniques fail to provide sufficient explanations, unlike PI. We aim thus at defining sufficient feature attribution. We need first to formally define the concept of sufficiency for a value. To this end, we start with BF as sufficiency can be more easily defined from PIs, and PIs are defined for BFs. We show that sufficiency is not satisfied for standard values. We then propose a new value dedicated to BFs, that fulfills sufficiency.

Definition 5. *A value I on BFs is said to satisfy the* sufficiency *property if the following properties are satisfied:*

  (i) *if i is irrelevant for f, then* $I_i(f) = 0$,
 (ii) *If* $\{i\} \in \mathcal{PI}_f$ *then* $I_i(f) = 1$,
(iii) *If for all* $S \in \mathcal{PI}_f$ *with* $i \in S$, *there exists* $T \in \mathcal{PI}_f$ *with* $j \in T$ *and* $|S| \geq |T|$, *then* $I_i(f) \leq I_j(f)$,
 (iv) *If i is mandatory for f, then its influence cannot be smaller than that of any other player.*

The influence is a number between 0 (null importancve) and 1 (maximal importance). A variable that is not in any PI has no importance in the game. Property (i) thus says that the influence is null for a variable that is irrelevant. The maximal value $I_i(f) = 1$ for a variable that is a PI alone. Such a variable is sufficient to get $f = 1$.

For (iii), generalizing this example, for a variable i, we look at the PI including i of the smallest cardinality. A variable is all the more important if this cardinality is small. Lastly, (iv) says that an attribute that belongs to all PIs shall be the more important feature.

Let us now give an illustrative example showing that standard values do not fulfill sufficiency.

Example 2. For $N = \{1, 2\}$, let us define

$$f_\wedge(x_1, x_2) = x_1 \wedge x_2 \quad \text{and} \quad f_\vee(x_1, x_2) = x_1 \vee x_2.$$

Applying any value fulfilling symmetry and efficiency (e.g. the Shapley value, the PD or the PANSC), we obtain the same influence for both games:

$$\phi_1(N, v_{f_\wedge}) = \phi_2(N, v_{f_\wedge}) = \phi_1(N, v_{f_\vee}) = \phi_2(N, v_{f_\vee}) = \frac{1}{2}.$$

However, these two situations are quite different as any variable is sufficient in $f_\vee$ whereas the two variables are necessary in $f_\wedge$. This is well depicted by PI as $\mathcal{PI}_{f_\wedge} = \{1_{\{1,2\}}\}$ and $\mathcal{PI}_{f_\vee} = \{1_{\{1\}}, 1_{\{2\}}\}$. The Shapley value or the PD cannot distinguish between $f_\wedge$ and $f_\vee$. ∎

Following this example, we wish to define the influence of variables incorporating the idea behind PI. Instead of computing the value of a feature i on the BF f, we shall consider all PIs of f that include i. Let us consider $1_S \in \mathcal{PI}_f$ with $S \ni i$. Each feature j in S is decisive in the sense that S is no more an implicant if j is removed, and deserves thus the same influence. Hence each feature $j \in S$ is allocated to $\frac{1}{|S|}$ from S, by efficiency. Then the influence of feature i shall be its largest influence among all PI it belongs to:

$$I_i(f) := \max_{1_S \in \mathcal{PI}_f : S \ni i} \frac{1}{|S|}. \tag{5}$$

Example 3. (Ex. 2 cont.). We obtain that

$$I_1(f_\wedge) = I_2(f_\wedge) = \frac{1}{2} \quad \text{and} \quad I_1(f_\vee) = I_2(f_\vee) = 1.$$

In $f_\vee$ any feature is sufficient to get $f = 1$ so that any feature deserves influence 1. On the other hand, the two features are complementary in $f_\wedge$ and deserve only half of the total influence 1. ∎

The next result shows that properties (i)-(iv) of Definition 5 are fulfilled.

Lemma 1. *The value defined by (5) is sufficient.*

Proof. *As feature i is irrelevant, i does not belong to any PI. Hence $I_i(f) = 0$. Hence (i) holds. Property (ii) is also trivial. Under the assumptions of (iii), $\max_{1_S \in \mathcal{PI}_f : S \ni i} |S| \geq \max_{1_T \in \mathcal{PI}_f : T \ni j} |T|$. Hence $I_i(f) \leq I_j(f)$.*

If i is mandatory then i belongs to all PIs. Let $1_{S^\star}$ be the PI with $S^\star$ having the smallest cardinality. All $j \in S^\star$ have the smallest value of $I_j(f)$. All mandatory features belong to $S^\star$. Hence $I_i(f) = \frac{1}{|S^\star|} = \max_{1_S \in \mathcal{PI}} \frac{1}{|S|} = \max_{j \in N} I_j(f)$. ∎

For convenience, we can rewrite (5) in the context of game theory. To this end, we consider a $0-1$ game v. The concept of PI for a BF is equivalent to the minimal winning coalitions of such a game. The set of *winning coalitions* of v is $\mathcal{W}_f = \{S \subseteq N : v(S) = 1\}$, and the set $\mathcal{MW}_f$ of *minimum winning coalitions* are the minimal elements of $\mathcal{W}_f$. Then

$$I_i^{0-1}(N, v) = \max_{S \in \mathcal{MW}_f : S \ni i} \frac{1}{|S|}. \tag{6}$$

3.2 Proposal on PBF

Following the correspondence between PBF and games, let us extend (6) to general games. We need to extend (6) in two ways. Firstly, in (6), all players of a coalition S are assumed to be symmetric and are thus allocated the same worth $\frac{1}{|S|}$. For a non-Boolean game, players are not in general symmetric in a coalition S and shall not be allocated the same worth. In order to set what player i shall be allocated in coalition $S \ni i$, we naturally consider the restricted game $v_{|S}$ on S. Then i shall get what $v_{|S}$ gives, that is $\phi_i(S, v_{|S})$, where ϕ is a standard value to be chosen. Hence $\frac{1}{|S|}$ shall be replaced by $\phi_i(S, v_{|S})$ in (6). Secondly, the concept of MW or PI is not defined for a non-Boolean game. We generalize the use of the minimum winning coalitions by taking the max over all coalitions.

Definition 6. *The* sufficient value *defined from a value ϕ is given by:*

$$I_i^\phi(N, v) = \max_{S \ni i} \phi_i(S, v_{|S}). \tag{7}$$

The next result shows that (7) subsumes to (6) for $0-1$ games and the PD or PANSC value. Hence (7) is a suitable generalization of (6).

Lemma 2. *For any $0-1$ game v, we have*

$$I_i^{\phi^{PD}}(N, v) = I_i^{\phi^{PANSC}}(N, v) = I_i^{0-1}(N, v).$$

Proof. *Let us start with ϕ^{PD}. We first note that for $S \in \mathcal{MW}$, $\phi_i^{PD}(S, v_{|S}) = \frac{1}{|S|}$. We use the top equation in (2) when S is a singleton and the bottom equation in (2) otherwise.*

For $T \subseteq N$ including no subset $S \in \mathcal{MW}$ (i.e. $v(T) = 0$), then every element of T is null in T so that $\phi_i^{PD}(T, v_{|T}) = 0$ for all $i \in T$.

Let $T \subseteq N$ including at least one $S \in \mathcal{MW}$ (i.e. $v(T) = 1$). Let $S^\star \in \mathcal{MW}$ of minimal cardinality s.t. $i \in S^\star$. We have the following cases:

- $S^\star = \{i\}$. Then $\phi_i^{PD}(\{i\}, v_{|i}) = 1$. Moreover,

$$\phi_i^{PD}(T, v_{|T}) = \frac{1}{1 + \sum_{j \in T \setminus \{i\} : \{j\} \in \mathcal{MW}} 1} v(T) \le v(T) = 1 = \phi_i^{PD}(\{i\}, v_{|i}).$$

- $\{i\} \notin \mathcal{MW}$ but there exists $j \in T$ s.t. $\{j\} \notin \mathcal{MW}$. Then $\phi_i^{\mathrm{PD}}(T, v_{|T}) = 0 \leq \phi_i^{\mathrm{PD}}(S^\star, v_{|S^\star})$
- There is no $j \in T$ s.t. $\{j\} \notin \mathcal{MW}$. Then $\phi_i^{\mathrm{PD}}(T, v_{|T}) = \frac{v(T)}{|T|}$ But $\phi_i^{\mathrm{PD}}(S^\star, v_{|S^\star}) = \frac{v(N)}{|S^\star|}$ as there is no $j \in S^\star$ s.t. $\{j\} \notin \mathcal{MW}$. Hence $\phi_i^{\mathrm{PD}}(S^\star, v_{|S^\star}) \geq \phi_i^{\mathrm{PD}}(T, v_{|T})$.

Then we have $\phi_i^{\mathrm{PD}}(T, v_{|T}) \leq \max_{S \in \mathcal{MW} : S \supseteq T} \frac{1}{|S|}$. Hence we have shown that $I_i^{\phi^{\mathrm{PD}}}(N, v) = I_i^{0-1}(N, v)$.

The proof works in a similar way with ϕ^{PANSC} and is skipped. ∎

Lemma 2 is not fulfilled for the Shapley value, as illustrated in the following example.

Example 4. Let $N = \{1, 2, 3\}$. For 0−1 game v defined by $v(\{1, 2\}) = v(\{1, 3\}) = v(\{1, 2, 3\}) = 1$ and $v(\{2, 3\}) = v(\{1\}) = v(\{2\}) = v(\{3\}) = v(\emptyset) = 0$, we note that $\mathcal{MW} = \{\{1, 2\}, \{1, 3\}\}$. Then

$$\phi_1^{\mathrm{Sh}}(N, v) = \frac{2}{3},$$

$$\phi_1^{\mathrm{Sh}}(\{1, 2\}, v_{|\{1,2\}}) = \frac{1}{2}.$$

Hence $I_1^{\phi^{\mathrm{Sh}}}(N, v) = \frac{2}{3} > \frac{1}{2} = I_1^{0-1}(N, v)$. ∎

Eventhough Lemma 2 is not fulfilled for the Shapley value, it is still possible to use expression $I^{\phi^{\mathrm{Sh}}}$. It still represents some ideas of sufficiency.

3.3   Some Properties of I_i

The aim of this section is to provide some interesting properties that I_i satisfies.

Let us first try to extend Definition 5 to PBF. Property (i) says that if feature i does not belong to any important coalition, then the influence of i shall be small. In Definition 5-(i), we assume that i does not belong to any PI. This implies that if $S \in \mathcal{I}$ with $S \ni i$, then $S \setminus \{i\} \in \mathcal{I}$. In terms of game, this gives $v(S) = v(S \setminus \{i\})$ for all coalition S. This corresponds to a *null player* in the terminology of Game Theory.

Definition 7. *A player $i \in N$ is said to be* null *if $v(S \cup \{i\}) = v(S)$ for all $S \subseteq N \setminus \{i\}$.*

According Definition 5-(i), the influence of such a player shall be zero. A null player does not contribute at all to the game and shall get thus a zero reward. We note that this property is very well-know in Game Theory and is called *Null Player*.

Null Player (NP): A value $\phi \in \Phi(N)$ satisfies **NP** if $\phi_i(N, v) = 0$ whenever i is null for v.

Let us review the other properties in Definition 5. Item (ii) says that if singleton i is a PI, then its influence shall be maximal. In terms of game, this means that if $v(\{i\}) = 1$ then $\phi_i(N, v) = 1$.

Essential Singleton (ES): A value $\phi \in \Phi(N)$ satisfies **ES** if $\phi_i(N, v) = 1$ whenever $v(\{i\}) = 1$.

This property represents well the idea of sufficiency as if a feature alone is very important, then its importance is very large.

Property (iii) in Definition 5 is related to the cardinality of subsets and is not necessarily key for PBFs. Finally, property (iv) is in fact a corollary of (ii).

Let us now give some classical properties of values in Cooperative Game Theory.

The value shall treat each player in a similar manner. So, permuting the labels of the players shall not change their worth. For a permutation σ on N, we define the game $\sigma(v)$ (for $v \in \mathcal{G}(N)$) by $\sigma(v)(S) = v(\sigma(S))$.

Symmetry (S): A value $\phi \in \Phi(N)$ satisfies **S** if, for every permutation σ on N, $\phi_i(N, v) = \phi_{\sigma(i)}(\sigma(N), \sigma(v)))$.

The next property is a variant of **S** saying that if the added value of two players to any coalition is the same, then they shall get the same value.

Equal Treatment Property (ETP): A value $\phi \in \Phi(N)$ satisfies **ETP** if $\phi_i(N, v) = \phi_j(N, v)$ whenever $v(S \cup \{i\}) = v(S \cup \{j\})$ for all $S \subseteq N \setminus \{i, j\}$.

Efficiency means that the value given to players shall share the worth $v(N)$ of the grand coalition.

Efficiency (E): A value $\phi \in \Phi(N)$ satisfies **E** if $\sum_{i \in N} \phi_i(N, v) = v(N)$ for all $v \in \mathcal{G}(N)$.

The Shapley value is characterized by four properties: *NP, S, E* and *Additivity* ($\phi_i(N, v + w) = \phi_i(N, v) + \phi_i(N, w)$) [21]. The PD value satisfies *NP, S, E* but not *Additivity*. It satisfies other properties such as *proportional-balanced treatment* ($\frac{\phi_i(N,v)}{v(\{i\})} = \frac{\phi_j(N,v)}{v(\{j\})}$ for all i, j being weak symmetric, i.e. $v(S \cup \{i\}) = v(S \cup \{j\})$ for all $S \subseteq N \setminus \{i, j\}, S \neq \emptyset$) [25].

We now introduce some properties more specific for I^ϕ.

Efficiency is not desirable for I^ϕ as we look for sufficient explanations. If a small subset S of variables is sufficient, then its member will certainly get a larger influence than what they would get from a larger coalition (as the total worth will be shared among more members). As a result, if there are several sufficient subsets, the total value allotted to all players exceeds $v(N)$.

Super Efficiency (SE): A value $\phi \in \Phi(N)$ satisfies **E** if $\sum_{i \in N} \phi_i(N, v) \geq v(N)$ for all $v \in \mathcal{G}(N)$.

If the influence is viewed as the impact of a variable on a coalition S, but also on all subsets of S (as a subset of S might be sufficient), then the influence shall be monotone in S.

Subset Dominance (SD): A value $\phi \in \Phi(N)$ satisfies **SD** if $\phi_i(S, v) \geq \phi_i(S', v)$ for all $S' \subseteq S$.

All previous properties are satisfied by I^ϕ.

Lemma 3.

- If ϕ satisfies **NP**, so does I^ϕ;
- If ϕ satisfies **E**, then I^ϕ satisfies **ES**;
- If ϕ satisfies **S**, so does I^ϕ;
- If ϕ satisfies **ETP**, so does I^ϕ;
- If ϕ satisfies **E**, then I^ϕ satisfies **SE**;
- I^ϕ satisfies **SD**.

The proof of this result is trivial and is skipped.

3.4   Identification of the Subsets Realizing the Maximum I_i

We fix $i \in N$. An essential ingredient in (7) is the maximum over all $S \ni i$. The following concept

$$\mathcal{S}_i(N,v) = \{S \ni i \text{ such that } \phi_i(S, v_{|S}) \geq \phi_i(T, v_{|T}) \, \forall T \ni i\} \tag{8}$$

is the set of subsets realizing the maximum (7).

In order to better characterize expression (7), we need to be able to identify (at least some) elements of $\mathcal{S}_i(N,v)$ without explicitly using the expression of $I_i^\phi(N,v)$. We assume thus that we are given a value $I_i \in \Phi(N)$, which follows relation (7) with some given value ϕ. The basic idea is to identify $\mathcal{S}_i(N,v)$ from I_i only by observing how I_i evolves when we change game v. This modification is performed by a *reduction* operator by $\mathcal{R}^{i,S} : \mathcal{G}(N) \rightarrow \mathcal{G}(N)$ defined for $S \subseteq N$ with $S \ni i$. This operator will be defined for each value ϕ.

We define thus

$$\mathcal{T}_i(N,v) = \{T \ni i \text{ s.t. } I_i(N, \mathcal{R}^{i,T}(v)) = I_i(N,v)\}. \tag{9}$$

Let $\underline{\mathcal{T}}_i(N,v)$ be the minimal elements of $\mathcal{T}_i(N,v)$ in the sense of $\subseteq$.

Lemma 4. *Assume that for all $S \subseteq N$ with $S \ni i$, we have*

$$\forall T \subseteq S \text{ with } T \ni i, \quad \phi_i(T, \mathcal{R}^{i,S}(v)_{|T}) = \phi_i(T,v) \tag{10}$$

$$\forall T \not\subseteq S \text{ with } T \ni i, \quad \phi_i(T, \mathcal{R}^{i,S}(v)_{|T}) < \phi_i(T,v) \tag{11}$$

Then

$$\underline{\mathcal{T}}_i(N,v) \subseteq \mathcal{S}_i(N,v) \subseteq \mathcal{T}_i(N,v). \tag{12}$$

Proof. *Let $S \in \mathcal{S}_i(N,v)$. Then $I_i(N,v) = \phi_i(S, v_{|S})$. By (10) and (11), setting $v' = \mathcal{R}^{i,S}(v)$, we have*

$$I_i(N,v') = \max_{T \ni i} \phi_i(T, v'_{|T}) = \underbrace{\max_{T \subseteq S : T \ni i} \phi_i(T, v'_{|T})}_{=\phi_i(S,v_{|S})} \vee \underbrace{\max_{T \not\subseteq S : T \ni i} \phi_i(T, v'_{|T})}_{<\phi_i(S,v_{|S})}$$

$$= \phi_i(S, v_{|S}) = I_i(N,v)$$

so that $S \in \mathcal{T}_i(N,v)$. Hence $\mathcal{S}_i(N,v) \subseteq \mathcal{T}_i(N,v)$.

Secondly let $S \in \underline{\mathcal{T}}_i(N, v)$. Then

$$I_i\big(N, \mathcal{R}^{i,S}(v)\big) = I_i(N, v) \tag{13}$$

$$\forall T \subsetneq S \quad I_i\big(N, \mathcal{R}^{i,T}(v)\big) < I_i(N, v) \tag{14}$$

Assume by contradiction that for all $T \subseteq S$ with $T \ni i$, we have $\phi_i(T, v_{|T}) < I_i(N, v)$. Then by (10) and (11), we have for $v' = \mathcal{R}^{i,S}(v)$

$$I_i(N, v') = \underbrace{\max_{T \subseteq S \,:\, T \ni i} \phi_i(T, v'_{|T})}_{\leq \max_{T \subseteq S \,:\, T \ni i} \phi_i(T, v_{|T}) < I_i(N,v)} \quad \vee \quad \underbrace{\max_{T \not\subseteq S \,:\, T \ni i} \phi_i(T, v'_{|T})}_{<\max_{T \not\subseteq S \,:\, T \ni i} \phi_i(T, v_{|T}) = I_i(N,v)}$$

$$< I_i(N, v)$$

which contradicts (13). Hence there exists $T \subseteq S$ with $T \ni i$, we have $\phi_i(T, v_{|T}) = I_i(N, v)$.

If $S \notin \mathcal{S}_i(N, v)$, then there exists $T \subsetneq S$ with $T \ni i$ such that $T \in \mathcal{S}_i(N, v)$. By the first part of the proof, we obtain $T \in \mathcal{T}_i(N, v)$, which contradicts (14). Hence $S \in \mathcal{S}_i(N, v)$. We have shown that $\underline{\mathcal{T}}_i(N, v) \subseteq \mathcal{S}_i(N, v)$. ∎

The previous lemma proves that, under (10) and (11), we can construct some elements of $\mathcal{S}_i(N, v)$ without knowing the exact expression of $I_i(N, v)$, simply thanks to $\underline{\mathcal{T}}_i(N, v)$.

Let us instantiate this approach for value $\phi = \phi^{\mathrm{PD}}$. In order to avoid unimportant cumbersome particular cases when the expression of ϕ^{PD} is ill-defined, we restrict ourselves to games in $\mathcal{G}^+(N)$. Consider a game $v \in \mathcal{G}^+(N)$. Let ϑ be any number strictly larger than $\max_{j \in N} v(\{j\})$. For $S \subseteq N \setminus \{i\}$ fixed, let us define another game v' on N by

$$v'(T) = \begin{cases} \vartheta & \text{if } T \subseteq N \setminus S \text{ and } |T| = 1 \\ v(T) & \text{otherwise} \end{cases} \tag{15}$$

Then we define the *reduction* operator by

$$\mathcal{R}^{i,S} : v \mapsto v',$$

where v' is defined by (15).

Lemma 5. *Let $S \subseteq N$ with $S \ni i$. Then (10) and (11) hold for $\phi = \phi^{\mathrm{PD}}$.*

Proof. Let $S \subseteq N$ with $S \ni i$. Set $v' = \mathcal{R}^{i,S}(v)$.

For $T \subseteq S$ with $T \ni i$, $\phi_i^{\mathrm{PD}}(T, v'_{|T}) = \phi_i^{\mathrm{PD}}(T, v_{|T})$ as $v'(K) = v(K)$ for all $K \subseteq S$.

For $T \not\subseteq S$ with $T \ni i$, we have $|T| \geq 2$ (since otherwise $T = \{i\} \subseteq S$). Hence

$$\phi_i^{\mathrm{PD}}(T, v'_{|T}) = \frac{v'(\{i\})}{\sum_{j \in T \cap S} v'(\{j\}) + \sum_{j \in T \setminus S} v'(\{j\})} v'(T)$$

$$= \frac{v(\{i\})}{\sum_{j \in T \cap S} v(\{j\}) + \sum_{j \in T \setminus S} V} v(T)$$

$$\leq \frac{v(\{i\})}{\sum_{j \in T \cap S} v(\{j\}) + \sum_{j \in T \setminus S} v(\{j\})} v(T) = \phi_i^{\mathrm{PD}}(T, v_{|T}).$$

The last inequality is strict if $v(\{i\}) > 0$ and $v(S) > 0$.   ■

Combining Lemmas 4 and 5, relation (12) holds for $\phi = \phi^{\mathrm{PD}}$.

We do not have an equality in the left part of (12) in Lemma 4, as shown in the following example.

Example 5. Let $N = \{1, 2, 3\}$ and a game v defined on N by: $v(\emptyset) = 0$, $v(\{1\}) = v(\{2\}) = v(\{3\}) = v(\{1,2\}) = v(\{2,3\}) = v(\{1,2,3\}) = 1$ and $v(\{1,2\}) = 2$. Then $I_1^{\phi^{\mathrm{PD}}}(\{1,2\}, v_{\{1,2\}}) = I_1^{\phi^{\mathrm{PD}}}(\{1\}, v_{|1}) = 1$. Then $\mathcal{S}_1(N, v) = \{\{1\}, \{1, 2\}\}$.

Moreover, $\mathcal{T}_1(N, v) = \{\{1\}, \{1,2\}, \{1,3\}, \{1,2,3\}\}$ and $\underline{\mathcal{T}}_1(N, v) = \{\{1\}\}$. We have thus $\underline{\mathcal{T}}_1(N, v) \subset \mathcal{S}_1(N, v) \subset \mathcal{T}_1(N, v)$.   ■

Let us instantiate this approach for value $\phi = \phi^{\mathrm{Sh}}$. We need to define the reduction operator $\mathcal{R}^{i,S}$ (with $i \in N$ and $S \subseteq N \setminus \{i\}$) for the Shapley value. Given a game v, let us define another game v' by

$$\text{For } T \subseteq S \quad \begin{cases} v'(T \cup \{i\}) = v(T \cup \{i\}) \\ v'(T) = v(T) \end{cases} \tag{16}$$

$$\text{For } T \nsubseteq S \quad \begin{cases} v'(T \cup \{i\}) = v(T \cup \{i\}) \\ v'(T) = v(T \cup \{i\}) \end{cases} \tag{17}$$

We define the *reduction* operator by $\mathcal{R}^{i,S} : v \mapsto v'$, where v' is defined by (16) and (17). The added-values $v'(T \cup \{i\}) - v'(T)$ of game v' wrt player i are equal to that of the original game when $T \subseteq S$ and are equal to 0 otherwise.

Lemma 6. *Let $S \subseteq N$ with $S \ni i$. Then (10) and (11) hold for $\phi = \phi^{\mathrm{Sh}}$.*

Proof. *Let $S \subseteq N$ with $S \ni i$. Set $v' = \mathcal{R}^{i,S}(v)$.*

By (7), we have $I_i(N, v) = \phi_i(S, v_{|S})$. For $T \supseteq S$, operator $\mathcal{R}^{i,T}$ has the effect of setting the added value $v(K \cup \{i\}) - v(K)$ to 0 for all subsets K that are not included in T. This has no effect on $I_i(N, v) = \phi_i(S, v_{|S})$. This proves (10).

One can prove (11) in a similar way.   ■

Combining lemmas 4 and 6 that we can construct elements of $\mathcal{S}_i(N, v)$ without knowing the exact expression of $I_i(N, v)$, simply thanks to $\underline{\mathcal{T}}_i(N, v)$.

4   Conclusion and Future Works

We have first considered Boolean Functions and defined prime implicants (sufficient explanations) and causes (necessary explanations). For PBF, the use of these concepts require to discretize, which introduce some arbitrariness. We start from feature-attribution methods, and especially the ones based of cooperative game theory. We note that these concepts cannot distinguish between a conjunction and a disjunction, and thus cannot capture sufficient reasons. For a BF, a natural way to define an influence level to a feature would consist in considering all prime implicants including this feature and assign an important based on the cardinality of the prime implicant. A natural way to extend this to PBF is to assign to a feature the largest value for this feature over all subsets of variables. This allows us to capture the idea of sufficiency. We show that this formula subsumes to the previous one for the proportional division but not for the Shapley value. In order to characterize such value, we look at way to identify the subset realizing the maximum without taking into account directly the expression. The idea is to identify the subsets only by testing modification of the initial game. Finally, we provide some properties that are satisfied by the new index.

For future work, extension to more complex input domains will be considered. We will also consider other value concepts such as Banzhaf value.

References

1. Aas, K., Jullum, M., Løland, A.: Explaining individual predictions when features are dependent: more accurate approximations to Shapley values. In: arXiv preprint arXiv:1903.10464 (2019)
2. Arrieta, A.B., et al.: Explainable artificial intelligence (XAI): concepts, taxonomies, opportunities and challenges toward responsible AI. Inf. Fusion **58**, 82–115 (2020)
3. Audemard, G., Koriche, F., Marquis, P.: On tractable XAI queries based on compiled representations. In: Proceedings of the 17th International Conference on Principles of Knowledge Representation and Reasoning (KR 2020), pp. 838–849. Rhodes, Greece (2020)
4. Banzhaf, J.: Weighted voting doesn't work: a mathematical analysis. Rutgers Law Rev. **19**, 317–343 (1965)
5. Bisdorff, R., Dias, L.C., Meyer, P., Mousseau, V., Pirlot, M. (eds.): Evaluation and Decision Models with Multiple Criteria. IHIS, Springer, Heidelberg (2015). https://doi.org/10.1007/978-3-662-46816-6
6. Cano, J.R., Gutiérrez, P., Krawczyk, B., Woźniak, M., García, S.: Monotonic classification: an overview on algorithms, performance measures and data sets. arXiv:1811.07155 (2018)
7. Darwiche, A., Hirth, A.: On the reasons behind decisions. In: Proceedings of the European Conference on Artificial Intelligence (ECAI 2020), pp. 712–720. Santiago, Spain (2020)
8. Datta, A., Sen, S., Zick, Y.: Algorithmic transparency via quantitative input influence: theory and experiments with learning systems. In: IEEE Symposium on Security and Privacy. San Jose, CA (2016)
9. Halpern, J.Y., Pearl, J.: Causes and explanations: a structural-model approach - Part I: causes. In: Proceedings of the Seventeenth Conference on Uncertainty in Artificial Intelligence (UAI), pp. 194–202. San Francisco, CA (2001)
10. Halpern, J.Y., Pearl, J.: Causes and explanations: a structural-model approach - Part II: explanations. Br. J. Philos. Sci. **56**(4), 889–911 (2005)
11. Ignatiev, A., Narodytska, N., Marques-Silva, J.: Abduction-based explanations for machine learning models. In: AAAI, pp. 1511–1519. Honolulu, Hawai (2019)
12. Kumar, I., Venkatasubramanian, S., Scheidegger, C., Friedler, S.: Problems with Shapley-value-based explanations as feature importance measures. In: 37th International Conference on Machine Learning (ICML 2020), pp. 5491–5500 (2020)
13. Lemaire, J.: An application of game theory: cost allocation. ASTIN Bull.: J. IAA **14**, 61–81 (1984)
14. Lundberg, S., Enrion, G., Lee, S.: Consistent individualized feature attribution for tree ensembles. arXiv preprint arXiv:1802.03888 (2018)
15. Lundberg, S., Lee, S.: A unified approach to interpreting model predictions. In: Guyon, I., Luxburg, U.V., Bengio, S., Wallach, H., Fergus, R., Vishwanathan, S., Garnett, R. (eds.) 31st Conference on Neural Information Processing Systems (NIPS 2017), pp. 4768–4777. Long Beach, CA (2017)

16. Marquis, P.: Consequence finding algorithms. In: Handbook of Defeasible Reasoning and Uncertainty Management Systems, pp. 41–145 (2000)
17. Merrick, L., Taly, A.: The explanation game: explaining machine learning models with cooperative game theory. arXiv preprint arXiv:1909.08128 (2018)
18. Mothilal, R.K., Mahajan, D., Tan, C., Sharma, A.: Towards unifying feature attribution and counterfactual explanations: different means to the same end. In: Proceedings of the 2021 AAAI/ACM Conference on AI, Ethics, and Society (AIES 2021), pp. 652–663 (2021)
19. Ribeiro, M., Singh, S., Guestrin, C.: Why should i trust you?: explaining the predictions of any classifier. In: KDD 2016 Proceedings of the 22nd ACM SIGKDD International Conference on Knowledge Discovery and Data Mining, pp. 1135–1144. San Francisco, California (2016)
20. Schmeidler, D.: The nucleolus of a characteristic function game. SIAM J. Appl. Math. **17**(6), 1163–1170 (1969)
21. Shapley, L.S.: A value for n-person games. In: Kuhn, H.W., Tucker, A.W. (eds.) Contributions to the Theory of Games, Vol. II, pp. 307–317, no. 28 in Annals of Mathematics Studies, Princeton University Press (1953)
22. Shih, A., Choi, A., Darwiche, A.: A symbolic approach to explaining Bayesian network classifiers. In: Proceedings of the Twenty-Seventh International Joint Conference on Artificial Intelligence (IJCAI 2018), pp. 5103–5111. Stockholm, Sweden (2018)
23. Verma, S., Dickerson, J., Hines, K.: Counterfactual explanations for machine learning: a review. arXiv preprint arxiv:2010.10596 (2020)
24. Štrumbelj, E., Kononenko, I.: An efficient explanation of individual classifications using game theory. J. Mach. Learn. Res. **11**, 1–18 (2010)
25. Zou, Z., van den Brink, R., Chun, Y., Funaki, Y.: Axiomatizations of the proportional division value. Soc. Choice Welfare **57**, 35–62 (2021)

Using Analogical Proportions for Explanations

Suryani Lim[1], Henri Prade[2(✉)], and Gilles Richard[2]

[1] Federation University, Churchill, Australia
`suryani.lim@federation.edu.au`
[2] IRIT, CNRS & Université Paul Sabatier, Toulouse, France
`{prade,richard}@irit.fr`

Abstract. In this article, we offer an introduction to the notion of analogical explanations. Because analogical reasoning is a widely used type of reasoning, we take the view that analogy-based explanations will be acceptable for humans. The cornerstone of the approach is the concept of analogical proportion (i.e., statements of the form "a is to b as c is to d"), comparing 2 pairs of items. Analogical proportions are not simply based on similarity but also involve differences between items. The approach applies to the explanation of the label of an item in a repository, whether the couple (item, label) belongs to a sample of a given population or the label is predicted via an algorithm. The output can be in terms of abductive/factual explanations (answering a "why?" question and providing examples having the same label) or contrastive/counterfactual (answering a "why not?" question and providing examples having a different label). For preliminary experiments, we build Boolean data sets where relevant attributes are known. Our results show that analogical proportion-based explanations can be effective.

1 Introduction

Explanation is an old theme of research in artificial intelligence. Indeed we have the right to expect from an "intelligence", even an artificial one, that it can explain its conclusions or predictions. "What is an explanation?", "What must be explained and how?" are questions that have been discussed for a long time by psychologists or philosophers; see for example [6,44], and for a recent account in an AI perspective, see [32]. A little more than thirty years ago, the success of systems based on rules encoding expert knowledge had led to the development of systems capable of explaining their conclusions in the face of questions from a user; see [7] for a retrospective overview of the subject and references. More recently, the study of causality [8] has contributed to renew the interest for explanations [15] in AI.

The success of learning methods based on neural networks has rekindled interest, over the last five years, in the problem of explanation, by raising the problem of explaining the outcome of "black box" methods; see for example [11,13,16–18,24]. Explanation in neural networks is often seen as a problem of sensitivity analysis [39,41], even if a logical analysis is possible in terms of abductive explanations (answering a "why?" question) or contrastive (answering a "why not?" question) [29]. Note that both in expert systems and in machine learning, we have the knowledge about the process that led to the conclusion to be explained. Namely, we respectively know the set of rules used and the classification function that has been learnt, on which the prediction relies. Such knowledge is no longer necessary in the approach proposed here.

Our understanding of the world is deeply based on comparisons. Often, for finding what to do in a given situation, we compare it to another situation, similar to the first one in many respects and differing in other respects. Then when a solution associated to the latter situation is known, this solution can be adapted to the first situation by addressing their differences. This is the basis of case-based reasoning that exploits the parallel between the situation under consideration and a case in a repertory (gathering a collection of experienced situations with their solution). This means that the cases are considered *one by one* (according to their similarity with the situation under consideration).

Analogical reasoning based on analogical proportions (APs) offers a more sophisticated and powerful way of exploiting data. Indeed, APs are statements of the form "a is to b as c is to d" that involve four items (i.e., cases, or examples) [37]. They state an identity between two comparisons pertaining to two pairs of items. Then it is possible to infer d from a, b and c (under some condition), thus exploiting the items *three by three* [36].

The comparison of two items, may also be used for an explanation or an argumentation purpose. Moreover the didactic, explanatory value of analogies is well known to pedagogues. There is an analogy between two situations insofar as one can put them in parallel, and establish a correspondence, not only between the elements of the respective situations but also between the relations which link them [10,47]. Such a parallel may be stated under the form of APs, "a is to b as c is to d", where a and b refer to first situation and c and d to the second one. Thus, "the calf is to the cow as the foal is to the mare", makes a parallel between bovidae and equidae.

In this paper we investigate a new line of research on explanation, based on the use of APs: this approach also has the merit of being directly applicable to data, without assuming an underlying machine learning process. The paper is structured as follows. Section 2 provides a background on APs and analogical inference. Section 3 discusses a reading of APs, as a parallel between pairs of items described in terms of Boolean or nominal attributes, and suggests how this can be useful for explanations. In Sect. 4, we present the process for building explanations and reports experiments showing the effectiveness of the approach. Section 5 is devoted to related work.

2   Analogical Proportions

An analogical proportion (AP) is a statement of the form "a is to b as c is to d", linking four items a, b, c, d. The considered items are supposed to be represented by vectors of n attributes. The values of the attributes may be Boolean (binary attributes) or nominal (discrete attributes with finite attribute domains having more than two values). The APs are defined component-wise. We start with the case of one Boolean attribute applied to four items. We limit ourselves here to the essential reminders for the understanding of the rest of the article. For a detailed introduction, please consult [36].

Boolean and Nominal Modeling. Given a binary attribute applied to four items, described by Boolean variables a, b, c, d, the following logical expression has been proposed and justified for an AP, denoted by $a : b :: c : d$ [31]:

$$a : b :: c : d = ((a \wedge \neg b) \equiv (c \wedge \neg d)) \wedge ((\neg a \wedge b) \equiv (\neg c \wedge d))$$

This formula expresses that a *differs from* b *as* c *differs from* d *and* b *differs from* a *as* d *differs from* c. It is only true for 6 valuations, namely $0 : 0 :: 0 : 0$; $1 : 1 :: 1 : 1$; $0 : 1 :: 0 : 1$; $1 : 0 :: 1 : 0$; $0 : 0 :: 1 : 1$; $1 : 1 :: 0 : 0$.
     This easily extends to nominal or categorical values where a, b, c, d belong to a finite attribute domain $\mathcal{A}$. In that case, $a : b :: c : d$ holds true only for the three following patterns $(a, b, c, d) \in \{(g, g, g, g), (g, h, g, h), (g, g, h, h)\}, g, h \in \mathcal{A}, g \neq h$. This generalizes the Boolean case where $\mathcal{A} = \{0, 1\}$. When items are represented by n attribute values: e.g., $a = (a_1, \cdots, a_n)$, APs are defined componentwise:

$a : b :: c : d$ holds true if and only if $\forall i \in \{1, \cdots, n\}, a_i : b_i :: c_i : d_i$ holds true

Example. Consider the AP "the `calf` is to the `cow` as the `foal` is to the `mare`", with the items described in terms of 4 relevant Boolean attributes: *mammal*, *carnivore*, *young*, *adult* and one nominal attribute *family* whose domain is the list of mammal families: equidae, bovidae, felidae, canidae, etc. Note that each of the four items is represented by a horizontal vector in Table 1:

Table 1. AP: example with Boolean and nominal attributes

	mammal	*carnivore*	*young*	*adult*	*family*
calf	1	0	1	0	bovidae
cow	1	0	0	1	bovidae
foal	1	0	1	0	equidae
mare	1	0	0	1	equidae

Properties of APs. Observe in Table 1 that, vertically, for each attribute we have a valid valuation for the AP. If we swap b (i.e., `cow`) and c (i.e., `foal`), $a : c :: b : d$ is still a true AP; besides if we swap the pairs (a, b) and (c, d), $c : d :: a : b$ remains true. These are two characteristic properties of APs:

1. $a : b :: c : d \Rightarrow c : d :: a : b$ (*symmetry*);
2. $a : b :: c : d \Rightarrow a : c :: b : d$ (*central permutation*).

which along with $a\!:\!b :: a\!:\!b$ (*reflexivity*), are the basic AP postulates (e.g., [35]).

Boolean APs enjoy a code independence property: $a : b :: c : d \Rightarrow \neg a : \neg b :: \neg c : \neg d$. In other words, encoding truth (resp. falsity) with 1 or with 0 (resp. with 0 and 1) is just a matter of convention, and does not impact the AP.

Analogical Inference. Assuming that the AP $a : b :: c : d$ is true, note also in Table 1 that we can recalculate d from a, b, c. This is a general fact, not specific to the example. In the Boolean (and nominal) case, the equation $a : b :: c : x$ where x is unknown does not always have a solution. Indeed neither $0 : 1 :: 1 : x$ nor $1 : 0 :: 0 : x$ have a solution (since 0111, 0110, 1000, 1001 are not valid patterns for an AP). Similarly, $g : h :: h : x$ has no solution in the nominal case when $g \neq h$. The Boolean solution exists if and only if $(a \equiv b) \vee (a \equiv c)$ is true. If the solution exists, it is unique and given by $x = c \equiv (a \equiv b)$. Analogical inference [5,34] amounts to an analogical jump stating that if an AP holds between four items for n attributes, an AP may also hold for attribute $n + 1$:

$$\frac{\forall i \in \{1, ..., n\}, \quad a_i : b_i :: c_i : d_i \text{ holds}}{a_{n+1} : b_{n+1} :: c_{n+1} : d_{n+1} \text{ holds}}$$

Classification. Classification is an immediate application of the above inference principle where $a_{n+1}, b_{n+1}, c_{n+1}$ are class labels and one has to predict a label d_{n+1} (viewed as a nominal value) for a new item d. Then one looks for triplets (a, b, c) of items with a known class, for which equation $a_{n+1} : b_{n+1} :: c_{n+1} : x$ is solvable, and for which analogical proportions hold with d on the attributes describing the items. In practice there are usually many such triplets, which may lead to different predictions and a majority vote should take place for choosing among them. Such a mechanism has been successively applied to Boolean, nominal, and even numerical attributes (using a multiple-valued logic extension of the definition of an AP in the latter case) [5,30], yielding competitive results with respect to more traditional classifiers. In the following, we do not deal with classification (i.e., the process of allocating a label to an item), but with explanation (i.e., the process of giving explanation to a known label). Thus, we do not assume that we know the classifier or a learned classification function. We only suppose we have a sample set providing examples of items with their class.

3   Explanation Power of APs

We first show that an AP can always be viewed as a pair of pairs of items such that the items of the two pairs are identical on the same subset of attributes and differ in the same way on the other attributes. The four items are supposed to be associated with a conclusion or a class whose values also form an AP that holds. We then examine the situations where the attribute(s) on which the items of two pairs differ is/are associated, or not, with a change in the conclusion value. This suggests to read pairs as potential rules. A motivating example is presented, before recalling what abductive and contrastive explanations are, and then discussing how such types of explanation can be produced with APs. In order to exploit the fact that APs are both about similarity and difference, we need to define agreement and disagreement between two elements.

Definition 1. *Given two Boolean vectors a and b, their* agreement set $Ag(a, b)$ *is the set of attributes* $Ag(a, b) =_{def} \{i \in \{1, ..., n\} \mid a_i = b_i\}$. *Their* disagreement set $Dis(a, b)$ *is the set of attributes* $Dis(a, b) =_{def} \{i \in \{1, ..., n\} \mid a_i \neq b_i\}$.

Note that the Hamming distance $H(a, b)$ between a and b is $|Dis(a, b)|$.

An AP as a Pair of Pairs. In order to show the potential of APs for explainability, we need to look at the joint structure of a quadruplet of items forming an AP. See Table 2 where, in all generality, the attributes have been grouped and ordered in such a way that for the attributes from A_1 to A_{j-1}, a, b, c, d are all equal, for the attributes from A_j to $A_{\ell-1}$, a and b are equal, and so are c and d (but not in the same way), i.e., $Ag(a, b) = Ag(c, d) = \{1, \ldots, \ell - 1\}$. For the remaining attributes from A_ℓ to A_n, a differs from b in the same way as c differs from d. The conditions $Ag(a, b) = Ag(c, d)$ and $Dis(a, b) = Dis(c, d)(= \{\ell, \ldots, n\})$ are not enough for ensuring $a : b :: c : d$, which also requires that the differences between a and b and between c and d are in the same sense. We can easily see that $a : b :: c : d$ is true on the attributes from A_1 to A_n (Table 2 exhibits vertically the 6 patterns that make an AP true), and that any situation where $a : b :: c : d$ is true can be described in this way. We use Boolean attributes in Table 2 for attributes A_1 to A_n. Replacing some attribute values 1 into g and 0 into h corresponding to the case of nominal attributes, would change nothing in the above analysis.

Table 2. AP: Pairing pairs

	$A_1 - A_{i-1}$	$A_i - A_{j-1}$	$A_j - A_{k-1}$	$A_k - A_{\ell-1}$	$A_\ell - A_{m-1}$	$A_m - A_n$	C
a	1	0	1	0	1	0	p
b	1	0	1	0	0	1	q
c	1	0	0	1	1	0	r
d	1	0	0	1	0	1	s

Thus in Table 2, a and b on the one hand, and c and d on the other hand are paired in the same way: the items of each pair are equal on the same attributes (A_1 to $A_{\ell-1}$), and a and b differ from each other exactly as c and d differ (attributes A_ℓ to A_n). Observe that if we swap b and c, the APs are preserved (as expected), but now a and c (resp. b and d) are equal on attributes A_1 to A_{j-1} and A_ℓ to A_n, while they differ on attributes A_j to $A_{\ell-1}$.

Changes in Pairs. In Table 2, suppose that the attributes from A_1 to A_n are used to describe situations for which a conclusion, a decision, or a class $\mathcal{C}$ is associated to them. $\mathcal{C}$ may be a Boolean or a nominal attribute. It is also assumed that the AP $p : q :: r : s$ is true, which means that $p = q$ and $r = s$, or that $p = r$ and $q = s$, in column $\mathcal{C}$. This fits with the analogical prediction of $\mathcal{C}(d)$ from $\mathcal{C}(a)$, $\mathcal{C}(b)$, and $\mathcal{C}(c)$ when $a : b :: c : d$ holds on attributes A_1 to A_n.

These considerations allow a reading of the data turned toward explanation. Indeed, let us first examine the case where $p = r$ and $q = s$ with $p \neq q$. The tilting of the $\mathcal{C}$ value from p to q between a and b and between c and d can be explained, in view of the attributes considered, only by the change of values of the attributes from A_ℓ to A_n (which is the same for pair (a, b) and pair (c, d)).

Pairs as Rules. These two pairs, which correspond to different contexts (described by the attributes A_1 to $A_{\ell-1}$, and differentiated by values of attributes A_j to $A_{\ell-1}$), suggest to see these pairs as instances of a *rule* expressing that the change on the attributes A_ℓ to A_n determines the change on $\mathcal{C}$ *whatever* the context. However, this rule may have exceptions in the data set. Indeed nothing forbids that there exist items a' and b' such that $a' : b' :: c : d$ holds on attributes A_1 to A_n and $\mathcal{C}(a') = \mathcal{C}(b') = p$, which would lead to the analogical prediction $\mathcal{C}(d) = s = r = p$ (remember we assumed $p = r$), which contradicts the fact that $s = q$ (since $p \neq q$). So we may calculate the confidence and the support of the rule associated with pair (a, b) and pair (c, d), in the data set. This reflects the *competence* of the pairs [26]. As in classification, it may seem preferable to use only competent pairs, i.e., with at least a confidence greater than 50% (we opt for the prediction supported by the largest number of triplets). Besides, in practice, we should prefer the rules where the number $n - \ell + 1$ of attributes that change is small, since this should lead to more concise explanations. This means that d is a "close" neighbor of c in the sense of the Hamming distance.

No Change in Conclusions. We continue to assume $p = r$ and $q = s$. If there is no change in the value of $\mathcal{C}$ between a and b and between c and d, namely we have $p = q$ (and $r = s$), this indicates that the change on the attributes A_ℓ to A_n has no impact on $\mathcal{C}$, and that the equality on the other attributes leads for a pair to the equality on $\mathcal{C}$. This means that the attributes A_ℓ to A_n are *not relevant* (at least in the context of the two pairs) for determining the $\mathcal{C}$ values.

In the particular case where $n - \ell + 1$ is small, d is a close neighbor of c as already said, which is a reason to have $s = r$. Since $p = q = r$, the same difference between a and b as between c and d does not lead to any change in the value of $\mathcal{C}$, which supports the prediction $s = r$ $(= p = q)$[1].

The case where $p = q$ and $r = s$ could be analyzed in a similar way, but would not bring anything essential, given that $a : b :: c : d$ is true if and only if $a : c :: b : d$ is true.

---

[1] We can however notice that in the extreme case where $a = c$ and $b = d$, we have on $\mathcal{C}$ the AP $p : q :: p : q$ where q is unknown, which leaves open the possibility that $q \neq p$ (expressing that a change on a small number of attributes may be enough to change the value of $\mathcal{C}$), or that $q = p$ (as the neighborhood reasoning tends to conclude).

Motivating Example. Let us further illustrate different kinds of AP-based explanation with an example of a decision with multiple options [3]. The decision is whether to serve a coffee with or without sugar (option 1), with or without milk (option 2) to a person in a medical facility. As shown in the table below, in situation sit_1 with contraindication $(c. - i.)$, it is recommended to serve coffee alone, in situation sit_1 without $c. - i.$, coffee with sugar, while in situation sit_2 with $c. - i.$ we serve coffee with milk. What can be done in sit_2 without $c. - i.$? Common sense suggests coffee with sugar and milk. This is what the analogical inference gives: in fact $\delta : \delta :: \delta : x$, $0 : 1 :: 0 : y$ and $0 : 0 :: 1 : z$ have as solutions $(x, y, z) = (\delta, 1, 1)$, as in Table 3.

Table 3. A suggestive example

case	situation	$c. - i.$	dec.	opt. 1	opt. 2
a	sit_1	yes	δ	0	0
b	sit_1	no	δ	1	0
c	sit_2	yes	δ	0	1
d	sit_2	no	δ	1	1

Thus, to the question "why milk and sugar for d?", we can answer "because we are in sit_2 (and not in sit_1)" for milk, and "because there is no $c. - i.$" for sugar. To the question "why no milk for b?", we get the answer "because we are in sit_1 (and not in sit_2)". As can be seen, the switching of opt. 1 (resp. opt. 2) from 0 to 1 is associated with the change of $c. - i.$ from yes to no, (resp. the change of situation from sit_1 to sit_2). This example suggests that APs have an explanatory potential from data, for answering "why" and "why not" questions.

Abductive and Contrastive Explanations. In a logical setting, one distinguishes between *abductive* and *contrastive* explanations (see, e.g., [29]). Let us recall these notions. Let $\mathcal{A}$ be a set of n attributes $i = 1, \cdots, n$. x_i denotes an attribute value of i, v_i a constant in $\mathcal{D}_i$, the domain of attribute i, $\mathcal{D} = \mathcal{D}_1 \times \cdots \times \mathcal{D}_n$, and cl is a classification function. Given $cl(v) = c_0$ for $v = (v_1, \cdots, v_n)$, a prime implicant (or *abductive*) explanation is any *minimal* set $\mathcal{X} \subseteq \mathcal{A}$ such that

$$\forall x \in \mathcal{D}.[\bigwedge_{i \in \mathcal{X}} (x_i = v_i)] \rightarrow (cl(x) = c_0)$$

It means that it is enough to set the value of attributes x_i in $\mathcal{X}$ to v_i for ensuring that cl takes the value c_0. In other words, using our notations, we have $\forall x \in \mathcal{D}.[(Ag(x, v) = \mathcal{X}) \rightarrow (cl(x) = c_0)]$. This corresponds to explain *why* some prediction (here $cl(v) = c_0$) is made for some point in the attribute space $\mathcal{D}$. Given $cl(v) = c_0$, a *contrastive* explanation is any *minimal* set $\mathcal{Y} \subseteq \mathcal{A}$ such that

$$\exists x \in \mathcal{D}.[\bigwedge_{j \in \mathcal{A}\backslash\mathcal{Y}} (x_j = v_j)] \wedge (cl(x) \neq c_0)$$

It expresses that it is possible to find an x, no longer in class c_0, which coincides with v on a maximal set of attributes, or if we prefer, it is possible to perform a minimal change on v in order to get an x no longer in class c_0. This corresponds to an answer to the question "Why not $cl(v) \neq c_0$?", i.e., we point out what attribute value(s) has/have to be changed to change the prediction. In our notations, one can write $\exists x \in \mathcal{D}.[Dis(x, v) = \mathcal{Y}] \wedge (cl(x) \neq c_0)$.

In our case, we do not assume the knowledge of a classification function cl. We still have examples v such that $cl(v) = c_0$ (for different pairs (v, c_0) for some unknown function cl), and counterexamples v' such that $cl(v') \neq c_0$. Thus answers to "why?" questions can only be based on examples and answers to "why not?" questions rely on counterexamples. In fact we have to replace $\forall x \in \mathcal{D}$ and $\exists x \in \mathcal{D}$ in the above expressions by $\forall x \in \mathcal{S}$ and $\exists x \in \mathcal{S}$ respectively, where $\mathcal{S} \subset \mathcal{D}$ is the sample set of items with known classes we have at our disposal.

What Is an AP-based Explanation? Let us abstract the Table 3 of the previous example. Focusing on *opt.* 1, we obtain the basic situation for analogical explanations, as depicted in Table 4. The other table (see Table 5), obtained by focusing on *opt.* 2, is nothing but Table 4, exchanging *context* and *change* attributes and swapping b and c, as can be checked.

Table 4. Schematic situation of analogical explanation

case	context	change	cl
a	sit_1	yes	p
b	sit_1	no	q
c	sit_2	yes	p
d	sit_2	no	q

Table 5. Another view of Table 4 (up to permutations)

case	context	change	cl
a	sit_1	yes	p
b	sit_1	no	p
c	sit_2	yes	q
d	sit_2	no	q

Let us consider Table 4. It should be clear that *context* and *change* in Tables 4 (and 5) denote subsets of attributes, while sit_1, sit_2, yes, no respectively refer to instantiations of these subsets. We assume $p \neq q$. In Table 4 the class change from p to q is necessarily associated to the *change* attributes, while attributes in *context* play no role in the change from p to q (at least for a, b, c, d).

So the answer to the question "why d is not in class p?" is to be found in the values taken by the *change* attributes for d. Note that when c is a close neighbor of d, the number of *change* attributes is small. This looks like the above definition of a *contrastive* explanation, namely we have

$$\exists x = c \in \mathcal{S}.[\bigwedge_{j \in \mathcal{A} \backslash change} (x_j = c_j = d_j)] \wedge (cl(d) \neq p)$$

Such a c will be termed as an *adverse example* in the sequel. But the analogy-based explanation is richer, we know at least another pair (here (a, b)), with another *context* value, where the same change of attribute values leads to the same change of class, as in pair (c, d), which suggests the possibility of a rule

$$\forall \ sit, (context = sit) \wedge (change = no) \rightarrow cl((sit, no)) = q$$

However, nothing forbids that $\exists \ (a', b') \in \mathcal{S}^2$ such that $a' = (sit', yes)$, $b' = (sit', no)$ with $cl(a') = cl(b') = p$, which would provide an exception to the rule. Similarly we have the tentative rule

$$\forall \ sit, (context = sit) \wedge (change = yes) \rightarrow cl((sit, yes)) = p$$

Note that these two rules provide a reading of Table 4 with an *abductive* explanation flavor. They answer why the item is in class p (or in class q).

As already said, for a given d, there may exist several close neighbors c, and several pairs (a, b), such that $a : b :: c : d$ holds. Since rules associated with pairs may have exceptions, it is cautious to restrict ourselves to *competent* pairs, namely the pairs with two different classes should correspond to at least a majority of cases where the class change takes place.

4   Experiments

Using artificial data, we focus on adverse example-based explanations[2] Still the same type of computation could be done for abductive explanations. AP has never been used for explanations, so artificial data provides a good start to provide a proof of concept.

4.1   Attribute Relevance

As mentioned in Sect. 3, we would like to provide to the end user explanations using only *relevant* attributes. Relevant means that they have an impact on the final class. In the literature, the task of finding a subset U of relevant attributes appears under the umbrella term of "feature selection". There is a huge amount of works on this topic in the field of machine learning but also in the general field of data analysis - see [40]. In the case of artificial data, the set U is known in advance, but this is generally not the case for real datasets. For real datasets, feature selection is required; the 3 main methods which deal with categorical attributes and categorical classes are chi-square [22], mutual information [42] and Relief family algorithms [45].

---

[2] Python code available from https://github.com/simplyanalogy/AXAI.git. UCI is https://archive.ics.uci.edu/ml/.

Algorithm 1. Pseudo-algorithm to provide explanations

Input: U all relevant attributes, $\mathcal{S}$ sample set, $d \in \mathcal{S}$
Output: c satisfying Condition 1 and confidence

1: $c = get\_nearest\_neighbor(U, \mathcal{S}, d)$ with $cl(c) \neq cl(d)$
2: $pairs = compute\_all\_pairs(\mathcal{S})$
3: $L = pairs\_with\_matching\_profile(pairs, c, d, U)$
4: $\alpha = length(compute\_pair\_with\_diff\_class(L))$
5: $\beta = length(L)$
6: **return** $(c, \frac{\alpha}{\beta})$

4.2 Adverse Example-Based Explanations

In the context of binary classification, given $d \in \mathcal{S}$ with allocated class $cl(d)$, the question could be: why is the class of d, $cl(d)$, not in class 1, i.e., why is d in the other class? This is where our analogy-based method can provide adverse examples-based explanations using a set U of relevant attributes:

1. Condition 1: $\exists c \in \mathcal{S}$ such that $Dis(c, d) \cap U$ is small and such that $cl(c) \neq cl(d)$ (c is a small perturbation of d w.r.t. U).
2. Condition 2: $\forall a, b \in \mathcal{S}, [Dis(a, b) \cap U = Dis(c, d) \cap U \implies cl(a) \neq cl(b)]$

Condition 1 defines what an adverse example is (c). It tells us that c slightly disagrees from d on U, but it should be clear that the Hamming distance $H(c, d)$ can be huge because c and d can differ on irrelevant attributes. We call $Dis(c, d) \cap U$ the profile of the pair (c, d): this indicates how c and d differ on relevant attributes.

Condition 2 tells us that, as soon as a pair $(a, b) \in \mathcal{S} \times \mathcal{S}$ has the profile of (c, d), then there is the same class change. Due to the universal quantifier, this is quite a strong requirement. We can relax the constraint on the universal quantifier: the bigger the number of such pairs (a, b), the more convincing is the explanation. In that case, such an example (a, b), having the profile of (c, d) with the class change, can be used for explaining why c is in $cl(c)$ and not in the other class. To summarize, we would like to "explain" $cl(d)$ by:

- Providing an element c satisfying Condition 1
- Providing a ratio related to the relaxed Condition 2

$$\frac{|\{a, b \in \mathcal{S}[Dis(a, b) \cap U = Dis(c, d) \cap U | cl(a) \neq cl(b)\}|}{|\{a, b \in \mathcal{S}[Dis(a, b) \cap U = Dis(c, d) \cap U\}|}$$

which is an indication of how "confident" we can be of why $cl(d)$ differs from $cl(c)$. We call this number *pair-based confidence*. The higher its value, the more difficult it is to challenge the explanation by exhibiting pairs violating Condition 2. This leads us to a simple Algorithm 1 to explain $cl(d)$ for a given d.

4.3   Examples

We have created a full dataset of Boolean vectors of dimension 10 (1024 elements). The classes are defined by a Boolean formula so that the set U of relevant attributes is known. We have tested 7 different formulas:

1. $g_1 : (x_1 \wedge (x_2 \vee x_3))$, $g_2 : xor(x_1, x_2)$
2. $g_3 : xor(xor(x_1, x_2), x_3)$, $g_4 : \Sigma_1^{10} x_i = 3$
3. $g_5 : (x_1 \vee x_2 \vee x_3) \wedge (x_4 \vee \neg(x_5) \vee x_6)$
4. $g_6 : (x_1 \wedge (x_2 \vee \neg(x_3)))$, $g_7 : \Sigma_1^3 x_i = 2.$

The size of the sample S is 200 so that the total number of candidate pairs is $200 \times 199 = 39800$.

In Table 6, 7, and 8, we provide some summary examples of what we provide for 3 different formulas, g_1, g_4, g_5, among the 7 we have tested. For each function, the relevant attributes constituting U are in bold font.

Table 6. A sample of adverse examples for g_1

$g_1 : x_1 \wedge (x_2 \vee x_3)$						conf = 0.63				
	a₁	**a₂**	**a₃**	a₄	a₅	a₆	a₇	a₈	a₉	a₁₀	cl
d	**0**	**1**	**0**	1	0	0	1	0	0	1	0
c	**1**	**1**	**0**	0	0	0	0	0	0	0	1
g_1						conf = 0.58				
d	**0**	**0**	**1**	1	1	1	1	0	0	0	0
c	**1**	**0**	**1**	0	0	0	0	0	0	0	1
g_1						conf = 0.72				
d	**0**	**0**	**1**	1	1	1	0	0	0	0	0
c	**1**	**0**	**1**	0	0	0	0	0	0	0	1

When the set of relevant attributes is small and because we deal with binary datasets at this stage, the candidate variations are small: for instance, when we have p relevant attributes among a total of n, we have only 2^p different profiles. Regarding the case where none of the attributes is more relevant than the others, we have a high volatility: providing a c close to d can lead to very low confidence. Note that c is just one of the nearest neighbors of d in a different class: so c can be close ($H(c, d) = 1$) but can also be a bit further (for instance in g_5 example 2, $H(c, d) = 2$). Finally, if we fix a limit k to the Hamming distance between c and d, we can enumerate all the c in the Hamming ball around d, s. t. $cl(c) \neq cl(d)$ and we will get different confidences associated with each of these c's. Each of these c's associated with its confidence level, is an adverse example for d. On a practical level, for function g_1, our code provides an output such as:

Table 7. A sample of adverse examples for g_4

$g_4 : \Sigma_1^{10} x_i = 3$							conf $= 0.4$			
	a_1	a_2	a_3	a_4	a_5	a_6	a_7	a_8	a_9	a_{10}	cl
d	1	0	1	0	0	1	1	0	1	1	0
c	0	0	0	0	0	0	1	0	1	1	1
g_4							conf $= 0.2$			
d	1	1	1	0	0	1	1	1	0	0	0
c	0	1	1	0	0	0	0	1	0	0	1
g_4							conf $= 0.33$			
d	1	1	0	1	1	1	0	1	1	0	0
c	0	0	0	1	1	0	0	1	0	0	1

Table 8. A sample of adverse examples for g_5.

$g_5 : (x_1 \vee x_2 \vee x_3) \wedge (x_4 \vee \neg(x_5) \vee x_6)$					conf $= 0.16$					
	a_1	a_2	a_3	a_4	a_5	a_6	a_7	a_8	a_9	a_{10}	cl
d	0	0	1	0	0	0	1	0	1	1	1
c	0	0	1	0	1	0	0	0	0	0	0
g_5						conf $= 0.39$				
d	0	1	1	0	0	1	0	0	1	0	1
c	0	1	0	1	0	0	0	0	0	0	0
g_5						conf $= 0.46$				
d	1	1	0	0	0	1	1	0	1	0	1
c	0	0	0	0	1	0	0	0	0	0	0

```
Why vector D: [0. 0. 1. 0. 0. 0. 0. 0. 1. 0. 0.] is in class 0:
- C [1. 0. 1. 0. 0. 0. 0. 0. 0. 0. 1.]: one of its nearest neighbours.
- C is in class 1 and the relevant attributes are [1, 2, 3] .
- 61% of confidence that attribute(s) [1] cause(s) change of class.
```

For function g_5, our code provides exactly an output such as:

```
Why vector D: [0. 1. 1. 1. 1. 1. 1. 0. 0. 0. 1.] is in class 1:
- C [0. 1. 1. 0. 1. 0. 0. 0. 0. 0. 0.]: one of its nearest neighbours.
- C is in class 0 and the relevant attributes are [1, 2, 3, 4, 5, 6] .
- 23% of confidence that attribute(s) [4, 6] cause(s) change of class.
```

Because our explanations only rely on the concept of agreement/disagreement sets, the process remains valid when dealing with nominal or categorical attributes. With such attributes, it makes sense to use a Hamming distance: this distance allows to provide a clear focus on the attributes which differ and consequently, are useful for the explanations. Moreover, because we have a definition of AP in a non Boolean context, having more classes will not change the validity of the approach.

When dealing with real data, feature selection methods generally provide a ranking of relevant attributes via a weight indicating the importance of the attribute in the definition of the final label. A natural next step in our work would be to integrate these weights in the explanations we provide.

5   Related Work and Prospects for Further Development

Hüllermeier [20] was the first to recently write a plea for the explanatory use of APs in classification and preference learning. He advocates that similarity-based explanations establish a relationship between two items, whereas an AP involves four items, which allows for richer explanations. In addition, [2] discusses how one can do feature selection in conjunction with AP-based learning. However, the pair-based view of AP's extensively used in the present paper is not explicitly considered. More recently, two of the authors of this paper wrote a short note in French for a workshop [38], where this pair-based view play a central role.

The literature on Explain'AI has grown rapidly over the past five years. The main research trend concerns approaches to understanding why a classifier makes a particular prediction. Explanations based on Shapley values have become popular (e.g., [28,46]). Shapley values[3], originally designed for evaluating the importance of a player in a coalition in game theory [25,43], provides an estimate of the impact of an attribute (feature) on the model output. However these approaches suppose to know the classifier. Our approach only assumes the knowledge of a sample of data with their class, and the attribute relevance ratio we compute requires less information.

Since pairs of items can be read as (potential) rules, what we propose has some resemblance with LORE (Local Rule-Based explanations) system [14]. Still in our approach pairs are not organised as a set of rules. Moreover, as explained above, we are close to the ideas of abductive / contrastive explanations in logic. We also privilege the role of "adverse" examples in explanation [21]. The look for contrastive cases in case-based reasoning for explanation purposes has been convincingly explored in [23]. In the analogical approach proposed here a competent pair-based evaluation assesses the strength of the explanations. It may be also applied to abductive explanations.

Besides, APs themselves may have an explanatory value [19] (even if we do not use it here): For example, looking for APs in the data of a movie recommendation system can allow us to find analogies such as "Star Wars" is to "Raiders of the Lost Ark" as "Return of the Jedi" is to "Indiana Jones and the Last Crusade", to explain why the latter film is recommended, especially if we know that the user likes the three other films (for what they have in common). A more elaborate explanation of the merits of the last film can also be added using differences between the first two films that are also found between the last two.

The use of APs in relation with explanation concerns may take many paths. we now briefly review some perspectives and possible further developments.

---

[3] We may also wonder if an interaction index of the same style between two attributes [12,33] would not be of interest for explanation.

Enriching the Approach with Statistics. In this paper, we are not taking into account any existing non uniform distribution on the universe $\mathcal{D}$. So, it would be natural to take this information into account in the explanation process in order, e.g., to ensure we exhibit an adverse example c which is not an outlayer.

Numerical Attributes. Graded APs can be defined for numerical attributes [9]. Still, their handling raises the point that we have to judge not only if $a_i = b_i$ or $a_i \neq b_i$, but also to consider the amount of change. How to do it properly is a topic for further research.

Explaining Preferences. Hüllermeier [20] also proposes the use of analogy in preference learning, an area where APs have been shown to perform well [1,4]. The approach proposed here would also apply to preferences. Indeed, analogical inference concludes from "a is to b as c is to d" (i.e., $a : b :: c : d$ holds) and from "a is preferred to b", that "c is preferred to d". The explanation of this conclusion thus rests on the differences between a and b (which also exist between c and d), which make that a is preferred to b.

Case-Based Reasoning and Explanation. Suppose we have a repertory of cases with their class, and an explanation for it, we might think of adapting explanations associated to similar items for getting an explanation of the class of a new item. CBR adaptation can be managed by AP-based inference [27].

6   Concluding Remarks

This paper proposes a new approach using analogical proportions to adverse example-based explanations with a pair-based confidence index. It applies to any categorical data sets and is classifier agnostic. It heavily relies on the comparison of items inside pairs and to the pairing of pairs exhibiting identical changes on relevant attributes, supposed to be selected by an external method. Then, comparisons are performed with regard to such attributes. One of the next steps, beyond the lines for further research listed at the end of previous section, is to investigate real datasets where the relevant attributes are given via an external feature selection process.

References

1. Ahmadi Fahandar, M., Hüllermeier, E.: Learning to rank based on analogical reasoning. In: Proceedings 32nd AAAI Conference on AI, pp. 2951–2958. AAAI Press (2018)
2. Ahmadi Fahandar, M., Hüllermeier, E.: Feature selection for analogy-based learning to rank. In: Kralj Novak, P., Šmuc, T., Džeroski, S. (eds.) DS 2019. LNCS (LNAI), vol. 11828, pp. 279–289. Springer, Cham (2019). https://doi.org/10.1007/978-3-030-33778-0_22
3. Billingsley, R., Prade, H., Richard, G., Williams, M.-A.: Towards analogy-based decision - a proposal. In: Christiansen, H., Jaudoin, H., Chountas, P., Andreasen, T., Legind Larsen, H. (eds.) FQAS 2017. LNCS (LNAI), vol. 10333, pp. 28–35. Springer, Cham (2017). https://doi.org/10.1007/978-3-319-59692-1_3

4. Bounhas, M., Pirlot, M., Prade, H., Sobrie, O.: Comparison of analogy-based methods for predicting preferences. In: Ben Amor, N., Quost, B., Theobald, M. (eds.) SUM 2019. LNCS (LNAI), vol. 11940, pp. 339–354. Springer, Cham (2019). https://doi.org/10.1007/978-3-030-35514-2_25

5. Bounhas, M., Prade, H., Richard, G.: Analogy-based classifiers for nominal or numerical data. Int. J. Approx. Reason. **91**, 36–55 (2017)

6. Bromberger, S. (ed.): On What we Know we Don't Know: Explanation, Theory, Linguistics, and How Questions Shape Them. University of Chicago Press, Chicago (1992)

7. Charnay, L., Dibie, J., Loiseau, S.: Validation and explanation. In: Marquis, P., Papini, O., Prade, H. (eds.) A Guided Tour of Artificial Intelligence Research, pp. 707–731. Springer, Cham (2020). https://doi.org/10.1007/978-3-030-06164-7_22

8. Dubois, D., Prade, H.: A glance at causality theories for artificial intelligence. In: Marquis, P., Papini, O., Prade, H. (eds.) A Guided Tour of Artificial Intelligence Research, pp. 275–305. Springer, Cham (2020). https://doi.org/10.1007/978-3-030-06164-7_9

9. Dubois, D., Prade, H., Richard, G.: Multiple-valued extensions of analogical proportions. Fuzzy Sets Syst. **292**, 193–202 (2016)

10. Gentner, D., Holyoak, K.J., Kokinov, B.N.: The Analogical Mind: Perspectives from Cognitive Science. Cognitive Science, and Philosophy, MIT Press, Cambridge (2001)

11. Gilpin, L.H., Bau, D., Yuan, B.Z., Bajwa, A., Specter, M., Kagal, L.: Explaining explanations: an overview of interpretability of machine learning. In: Bonchi, F., et al. (eds.) Proceedings of 5th IEEE International Conference on Data Science and Advanced Analytics (DSAA 2018), Turin, 1–3 October 2018, pp. 80–89. IEEE (2018)

12. Grabisch, M.: Subjective evaluation. In: Bouyssou, D., Dubois, D., Pirlot, M., Prade, H. (eds.) Decision Making Process: Concepts and Methods, pp. 723–777. Wiley-ISTE (2009)

13. Guidotti, R.: Evaluating local explanation methods on ground truth. Artif. Intell. **291**, 103428 (2021)

14. Guidotti, R., Monreale, A., Ruggieri, S., Pedreschi, D., Turini, F., Giannotti, F.: Local rule-based explanations of black box decision systems. CoRR abs/1805.10820, 1–10 (2018)

15. Halpern, J.Y., Pearl, J.: Causes and explanations: a structural-model approach - part II: explanations. In: Nebel, B. (ed.) Proceedings of 17th International Joint Conference on Artificial Intelligence (IJCAI 2001), Seattle, 4–10 August 2001, pp. 27–34. Morgan Kaufmann (2001)

16. Hoffman, R.R., Klein, G.: Explaining explanation, part 1: theoretical foundations. IEEE Intell. Syst. **32**(3), 68–73 (2017)

17. Hoffman, R.R., Miller, T., Müller, S.T., Klein, G., Clancey, W.J.: Explaining explanation, part 4: a deep dive on deep nets. IEEE Intellig. Syst. **33**(3), 87–95 (2018)

18. Hoffman, R.R., Müller, S.T., Klein, G.: Explaining explanation, part 2: empirical foundations. IEEE Intell. Syst. **32**(4), 78–86 (2017)

19. Hug, N., Prade, H., Richard, G., Serrurier, M.: Analogical proportion-based methods for recommendation. First Invest. Fuzzy Sets Syst. **366**, 110–132 (2019)

20. Hüllermeier, E.: Towards analogy-based explanations in machine learning. In: Torra, V., Narukawa, Y., Nin, J., Agell, N. (eds.) MDAI 2020. LNCS (LNAI), vol. 12256, pp. 205–217. Springer, Cham (2020). https://doi.org/10.1007/978-3-030-57524-3_17

21. Ignatiev, A., Narodytska, N., Marques-Silva, J.: On relating explanations and adversarial examples. In: Wallach, H.M., Larochelle, H., Beygelzimer, A., d'Alché-Buc, F., Fox, E.B., Garnett, R. (eds.) Proceedings of 32nd Annual Conference on Neural Information Processing System (NeurIPS 2019), Vancouver, pp. 15857–15867 (2019)

22. Jin, X., Xu, A., Bie, R., Guo, P.: Machine learning techniques and chi-square feature selection for cancer classification using SAGE gene expression profiles. In: Li, J., Yang, Q., Tan, A.-H. (eds.) BioDM 2006. LNCS, vol. 3916, pp. 106–115. Springer, Heidelberg (2006). https://doi.org/10.1007/11691730_11

23. Keane, M.T., Smyth, B.: Good counterfactuals and where to find them: a case-based technique for generating counterfactuals for explainable AI (XAI). In: Watson, I., Weber, R. (eds.) ICCBR 2020. LNCS (LNAI), vol. 12311, pp. 163–178. Springer, Cham (2020). https://doi.org/10.1007/978-3-030-58342-2_11

24. Klein, G.: Explaining explanation, part 3: the causal landscape. IEEE Intell. Syst. **33**(2), 83–88 (2018)

25. Laruelle, A., Valenciano, F.: Shapley-Shubik and Banzhaf indices revisited. Math. Oper. Res. **26**, 89–104 (2001)

26. Lieber, J., Nauer, E., Prade, H.: Improving analogical extrapolation using case pair competence. In: Bach, K., Marling, C. (eds.) ICCBR 2019. LNCS (LNAI), vol. 11680, pp. 251–265. Springer, Cham (2019). https://doi.org/10.1007/978-3-030-29249-2_17

27. Lieber, J., Nauer, E., Prade, H.: When revision-based case adaptation meets analogical extrapolation. In: Sánchez-Ruiz, A.A., Floyd, M.W. (eds.) ICCBR 2021. LNCS (LNAI), vol. 12877, pp. 156–170. Springer, Cham (2021). https://doi.org/10.1007/978-3-030-86957-1_11

28. Lundberg, S.M., Lee, S.: A unified approach to interpreting model predictions. In: Guyon, I., et al. (eds.) Advances in Neural Information Processing System 30: Proceedings on Annual Conference (NIPS 2017). 4–9 December 2017, pp. 4765–4774. Long Beach (2017)

29. Marques-Silva, J., Gerspacher, T., Cooper, M.C., Ignatiev, A., Narodytska, N.: Explanations for monotonic classifiers. In: Meila, M., Zhang, T. (eds.) Proceedings of 38th International Conference on Machine Learning (ICML 2021). PMLR, vol. 139, pp. 7469–7479 (2021)

30. Miclet, L., Bayoudh, S., Delhay, A.: Analogical dissimilarity: definition, algorithms and two experiments in machine learning. JAIR **32**, 793–824 (2008)

31. Miclet, L., Prade, H.: Handling analogical proportions in classical logic and fuzzy logics settings. In: Sossai, C., Chemello, G. (eds.) ECSQARU 2009. LNCS (LNAI), vol. 5590, pp. 638–650. Springer, Heidelberg (2009). https://doi.org/10.1007/978-3-642-02906-6_55

32. Miller, T.: Explanation in artificial intelligence: insights from the social sciences. Artif. Intell. **267**, 1–38 (2019)

33. Murofushi, T., Someda, S.: Techniques for reading fuzzy measures (iii): interaction index. In: Proceedings of 9th Fuzzy System Symposium, Sapporo, pp. 693–696. in Japanese (1993)

34. Pirrelli, V., Yvon, F.: Analogy in the lexicon: a probe into analogy-based machine learning of language. In: Proceedings of 6th International Sympsium on Human Communication, Cuba (1999)

35. Prade, H., Richard, G.: From analogical proportion to logical proportions. Logica. Univers. **7**, 441–505 (2013)

36. Prade, H., Richard, G.: Analogical proportions and analogical reasoning - an introduction. In: Aha, D.W., Lieber, J. (eds.) ICCBR 2017. LNCS (LNAI), vol. 10339, pp. 16–32. Springer, Cham (2017). https://doi.org/10.1007/978-3-319-61030-6_2

37. Prade, H., Richard, G.: Analogical proportions: why they are useful in AI. In: Zhou, Z.H. (ed.) Proceedings of 30th International Joint Conference on AI (IJCAI-21), pp. 4568–4576 (2021)

38. Prade, H., Richard, G.: Explications analogiques. In: Workshop EXPLAIN'AI'22 @ EGC conference, Blois, 25, January 2022

39. Ribeiro, M.T., Singh, S., Guestrin, C.: "Why should I trust you?": explaining the predictions of any classifier. In: Proceedings of 22nd ACM SIGKDD International Conference on Knowledge Discovery and Data Mining, San Francisco, 13–17 August, pp. 1135–1144 (2016)

40. Sánchez-Maroño, N., Alonso-Betanzos, A., Tombilla-Sanromán, M.: Filter methods for feature selection – a comparative study. In: Yin, H., Tino, P., Corchado, E., Byrne, W., Yao, X. (eds.) IDEAL 2007. LNCS, vol. 4881, pp. 178–187. Springer, Heidelberg (2007). https://doi.org/10.1007/978-3-540-77226-2_19

41. Selvaraju, R.R., Cogswell, M., Das, A., Vedantam, R., Parikh, D., Batra, D.: Gradcam: visual explanations from deep networks via gradient-based localization. Int. J. of Comput. Vis. **128**(2), 336–359 (2019)

42. Shannon, C.E.: A mathematical theory of communication. Bell Syst. Tech. J. **27**(3), 379–423 (1948)

43. Shapley, L.S.: A value for n-person games. Ann. Math. Stud. **28**, 307–317 (1953)

44. Thagard, P.R.: The best explanation: criteria for theory choice. J. Philos. **75**(2), 76–92 (1978)

45. Urbanowicz, R.J., Meeker, M., LaCava, W., Olson, R.S., Moore, J.H.: Reliefbased feature selection: introduction and review (2017). https://doi.org/10.48550/ARXIV.1711.08421, https://arxiv.org/abs/1711.08421

46. Van den Broeck, G., Lykov, A., Schleich, M., Suciu, D.: On the tractability of SHAP explanations. In: Proceedings of 35th AAAI Conference, pp. 6505–6513. AAAI Press (2021)

47. Winston, P.H.: Learning and reasoning by analogy. Com. ACM **23**, 689–703 (1980)

Short Papers: Non-classical Reasoning

Towards a Unified View on Logics for Uncertainty

Esther Anna Corsi[1]([✉])(ID), Tommaso Flaminio[2](ID), and Hykel Hosni[1](ID)

[1] Department of Philosophy, University of Milan,
Via Festa del Perdono 7, 20122 Milano, Italy
{esther.corsi,hykel.hosni}@unimi.it
[2] Artificial Intelligence Research Institute (IIIA - CSIC),
Campus UAB, Bellaterra 08193, Spain
tommaso@iiia.csic.es

Abstract. In the present paper, we propose a general logical approach for reasoning about probability functions, belief functions, lower probabilities and the corresponding duals. The logical setting we consider combines the modal logic S5, Łukasiewicz logic and an additional modality P that applied to boolean formulas formalises probability functions. The modality P together with an S5 modal $\Box$ provides a language rich enough to characterise probability, belief and lower probability theories.

Keywords: Fuzzy logic · Dempster-Shafer belief functions · Probability functions · Imprecise probabilities · Modal logic

1 Introduction

This paper aims at presenting some ideas on our ongoing research project on modal logics for uncertainty. More in detail, we aim to show how most of the uncertainty measures known in the literature can be defined by the interplay of a propositional many-valued logic and only two modalities that we add to its language: one denoted by P for "probably" and a modal necessity $\Box$ operator.

The use of modal logic to define probability functions is not new [6,8,10], see also [5] for a survey. In [7], the same approach used in the just mentioned papers has been generalized to represent belief functions. In [12,13], lower and upper probabilities have been formalized in a similar setting.

In the present work, we introduce a class of both measure-based and relational-based models that allow to represent several uncertainty measures at the same time and in a "minimal" way. In fact, by combining only two modalities, one denoted by P for "probably" and a normal modal $\Box$ (together with its dual $\Diamond$) based on a many-valued setting, we can define probability functions, belief functions, lower probabilities and the corresponding duals. More specifically, probabilities can be represented by formulas of the form $P(\varphi)$; belief functions by formulas such as $P(\Box\varphi)$, plausibility functions by formulas like $P(\Diamond\varphi)$; lower

F. Dupin de Saint-Cyr et al. (Eds.): SUM 2022, LNAI 13562, pp. 329–337, 2022.
https://doi.org/10.1007/978-3-031-18843-5_22

probabilities by formulas of the form $\Box P(\varphi)$ and upper probabilities by formulas like $\Diamond P(\varphi)$.

The construction of a general framework that characterizes the above-mentioned uncertainty measures opens up to a systematic comparison of such measures. The "minimality" of the modalities used in these class of models, is key to investigating the relations between the uncertainty measures considered that are obtained as theorems of the system.

The rest of this paper is organized as follows: In the next Sect. 2 we will briefly recall our logical and measure-theoretical settings. Section 3 is dedicated to define the measure-based and relational-based models that allow to represent uncertainty measures as a whole. Besides the basic definition, we will explain the main ideas of this current research line by means of some examples. Then we conclude with Sect. 4 in which we briefly present the next step we intend to go through.

2 Modal Logics and Uncertainty Measures

2.1 Logical Preliminaries

The propositional logic on which our whole approach is grounded is Łukasiewicz calculus. Let us briefly recall that Łukasiewicz infinite-valued logic Ł is a fuzzy logic, in the sense of [8], whose algebraic semantics is the variety of *MV-algebras*. Those are structures of the form $\mathbf{A} = (A, \oplus, \neg, 1)$ where A is a nonempty set, $\oplus$ is a binary and $\neg$ a unary operation on A, while 1 is a constant. Thus, an algebra in that signature is an MV-algebra iff $(A, \oplus, 1)$ is a commutative monoid, and the following equations are satisfied: $\neg\neg x = x$; $\neg(\neg x \oplus y) \oplus y = \neg(\neg y \oplus x) \oplus x$. These algebras forms a variety, denoted by $\mathbb{MV}$, that is the equivalent algebraic semantics for Ł. This implies, among other things, that formulas of Łukasiewicz logic can be regarded as terms in the language of MV-algebras and we will henceforth use this convention without danger of confusion. $\mathbb{MV}$ is generated, both as a variety and a quasivariety by the so called *standard MV-algebra*, $[0, 1]_{MV} = ([0, 1], \oplus, \neg, 1)$ where $[0, 1]$ denotes the real unit interval, and for all $a, b \in [0, 1]$, $a \oplus b = \min\{1, a + b\}$ and $\neg a = 1 - a$.

As shown by Chang in [4], Łukasiewicz logic, whose axiomatization can be found in [8] (see also [14]) turns out to be sound and complete with respect to evaluations to $[0, 1]_{MV}$, i.e., with respect to maps e from the variables to $[0, 1]$ that interpret connectives by the operations of $[0, 1]_{MV}$ recalled above. The notion of *theorem* $(\models \varphi)$ and *deduction from a theory* $(T \models \varphi)$ are defined as usual in algebraic logic.

Theorem 1. *For every finite set of formulas $T \cup \{\varphi\}$ in Łukasiewicz language, $T \models \varphi$ iff for every evaluation e to $[0, 1]_{MV}$ that maps all $\psi \in T$ to 1, $e(\varphi) = 1$ as well.*

In recent years the community of fuzzy logicians has put forward several attempts to extend modal logic from the classical to the many-valued setting.

The approach followed by that community is mainly semantic-based and, for instance, the generalization of the modal logic S5 to the Łukasiewicz setting have been proposed by defining its relational semantics as Kripke-like models of the form $(W, R, \{e_w\}_{w \in W})$ where W is nonempty, R is the total relation on W and for every Łukasiewicz formula φ, and every $w \in W$, $e_w(\varphi)$ is evaluated in the standard MV-algebra $[0,1]_{MV}$.

As shown by Hájek, the following Hilbert-style calculus, denoted by S5Ł and based on a language that expands that of Ł by a unary modality $\square$, is sound and complete w.r.t. the above defined class of relational models.

$(\square 1)$ $\square \varphi \to \varphi$; $(\lozenge 1)$ $\varphi \to \lozenge \varphi$

$(\square 2)$ $\square(\psi \to \varphi) \to (\psi \to \square \varphi)$; $(\lozenge 2)$ $\square(\varphi \to \psi) \to (\lozenge \varphi \to \psi)$;

$(\square 3)$ $\square(\psi \vee \varphi) \to (\psi \vee \square \varphi)$; $(\lozenge 3)$ $\lozenge(\varphi \& \psi) \equiv \lozenge \varphi \& \lozenge \psi$;

(MP) the modus ponens rule; $(N\square)$ the necessitation rule $\varphi \vdash \square \varphi$.

Some comments on the S5 axioms:

(1) As we already recalled above, Hájek proved in [9] (see also [3]) S5Ł to be sound and complete w.r.t. the class of Kripke models $(W, R, \{e_w\}_{w \in W})$ where W is nonempty, R is the total relation on W and for every Łukasiewicz formula φ, and every $w \in W$, $e_w(\varphi)$ is evaluated in the standard MV-algebra $[0,1]_{MV}$. We will henceforth denote the class of these models by $\mathcal{M}^t$. The truth value of a modal formula $\square \varphi$ at w is

$$\inf\{e_{w'}(\varphi) \mid wRw'\} = \inf\{e_{w'}(\varphi) \mid w' \in W\}.$$

(2) If we add the axiom $\varphi \vee \neg \varphi$ to S5Ł we get the classical modal logic S5 [2]. Thus, it turns out to be sound and complete w.r.t. both the class of Kripke models $(W, R, \{e_w\}_{w \in W})$ where now e_w is a classical evaluation for all $w \in W$ and R is the total relation (as above), but also w.r.t. the class of Kripke models in which R is an equivalence relation, i.e., it is reflexive, symmetric and transitive.

We can easily extend the result recalled in (1) above and proving that S5Ł is sound and complete w.r.t. to the class of those Kripke models in which each e_w evaluates propositional formulas in $[0,1]_{MV}$ and R is an equivalence relation.

Definition 1. $\mathcal{M}^e$ is the class of models $(W, R, \{e_w\}_{w \in W})$ where W is nonempty, R is an equivalence relation on W and for all $w \in W$, e_w is a $[0,1]_{MV}$-evaluation of Łukasiewicz formulas.

If ϕ is any formula in the language of S5Ł, $\mathcal{K} = (W, R, \{e_w\}_{w \in W}) \in \mathcal{M}^e$ and $w \in W$, the truth value of ϕ in $\mathcal{K}$ at w, denoted $\|\phi\|_{\mathcal{K}, w}$, is defined as usual.

Lemma 1. The classes $\mathcal{M}^t$ and $\mathcal{M}^e$ have the same tautologies.

Proof. Since every total relation on any W is in particular en equivalence relation, if ϕ is a tautology of $\mathcal{M}^e$, ϕ also is a tautology of $\mathcal{M}^t$. Conversely, assume that ϕ is not a tautology of $\mathcal{M}^e$, i.e., assume there exists $\mathcal{K} = (W, R, \{e_w\}_{w \in W}) \in \mathcal{M}^e$ and $w \in W$ such that $\|\phi\|_{\mathcal{K},w} < 1$. Since R is an equivalence relation, the restriction of R to $R[w] = \{w' \in W \mid wRw'\}$ is total. Thus, take $W' = R[w]$ (where w is the same as above), $R' = W' \times W'$ and for all $w^* \in W'$, e_{w*} is as in $\mathcal{K}$. Call $\mathcal{K}' = (W', R', \{e_{w^*}\}_{w^* \in W'})$. Since $w \in W'$, $\|\phi\|_{\mathcal{K}',w} = \|\phi\|_{\mathcal{K},w} < 1$ (easy to see by induction). It then follows that ϕ is not a tautology of $\mathcal{M}^e$.

Thus, the following immediately follows.

Theorem 2. *The logic S5L is sound and complete with respect to the class $\mathcal{M}^e$.*

2.2   Uncertainty Measures

As we assume the reader to be familiar with finitely additive probability measures (for otherwise, see for instance [11]), this section is meant to recall more general measures for uncertainty, namely belief functions [15] and lower probabilities [16]. Along the whole paper we will always work on finite boolean algebras. Here below we just recall the definitions of belief functions and lower probabilities.

Definition 2 (Belief functions [15]). *A belief function on an algebra $\mathbf{A}$ is a $[0, 1]$-valued map $\mathbf{B}$ satisfying:*

(B1) $B(\top) = 1$, $B(\bot) = 0$;

(B2) $B \left(\bigvee_{i=1}^{n} \psi_i \right) \geq \sum_{i=1}^{n} \sum_{\{J \subseteq \{1,\ldots,n\}:|J|=i\}} (-1)^{i+1} B \left(\bigwedge_{j \in J} \psi_j \right)$, *for $n \in \mathbb{N}$.*

An element φ of a boolean algebra $\mathbf{A}$ is said to be *covered m times by a multiset* $\{\{\psi_1, \ldots, \psi_n\}\}$ *of elements of A* if every homomorphisms of $\mathbf{A}$ to $\{0,1\}$ that maps φ to 1, also maps to 1 at least m propositions from $\psi_1, \ldots, \psi_n$ as well. An (m, k)-cover of $(\varphi, \top)$ is a multiset $\{\{\psi_1, \ldots, \psi_n\}\}$ that covers $\top$ k times and covers φ $n + k$ times.

Definition 3 (Lower Probability functions [16]). *A Lower probability on an algebra $\mathbf{A}$ is a monotone $[0, 1]$-valued map $\underline{P}$ satisfying:*

(L1) $\underline{P}(\top) = 1$, $\underline{P}(\bot) = 0$;

(L2) For all natural numbers n, m, k and all $\psi_1, \ldots, \psi_n$, if $\{\{\psi_1, \ldots, \psi_n\}\}$ is an (m, k)-cover of $(\varphi, \top)$, then $k + m\underline{P}(\varphi) \geq \sum_{i=1}^{n} \underline{P}(\psi_i)$.

Although this definition does not make the name *Lower probabilities* particularly obvious, [1, Theorem 1] puts forward the following enlightening characterisation, anticipated by [16]. Let $\underline{P} : \mathbf{A} \to [0,1]$ be a Lower probability and denote with $\mathcal{M}(\underline{P})$ the set of probability functions which bound $\underline{P}$ from above, i.e. $\mathcal{M}(\underline{P}) = \{P \in \mathbb{P} \mid \underline{P}(\psi) \leq P(\psi), \forall \psi \in A\}$. Then, for all $\psi \in A$,

$$\underline{P}(\psi) = \min_{P \in \mathcal{M}(\underline{P})} P(\psi).$$

3   A Unified Logic for Uncertainty

Let us start from $\mathscr{L}$, the language of Łukasiewicz logic over finitely many (say n) propositional variables. We now expand $\mathscr{L}$ by two additional unary modalities: $\Box$ and P. Formulas are defined by the following classes.

(CF). The set of *classical formulas*. Those are definable in $\mathscr{L}$ from variables, constants $\top$ and $\bot$, and the connectives $\wedge, \vee, \neg$.

(CMF). The set of *classical modal formulas* is defined by closing CF by the unary modality $\Box$ as usual in a modal language. Notice that in CMF, for every $\varphi \in CMF$, $\Diamond\varphi$ stands for $\neg\Box\neg\varphi$.

(PMF). The set of *probabilistic modal formulas* is obtained by the following two steps: (1) *atomic probabilistic formulas* are all those in the form $P(\varphi)$ for $\varphi \in CMF$; (2) *compound probabilistic formulas* are defined by composing atomic ones with connectives of Łukasiewicz language.

(UMF). Finally, the set of *uncertain modal formulas* is the smallest set of formulas that contains PMF and is closed under $\Box$ and connectives of Łukasiewicz logic.

In order to clarify with what formulas we will deal with, let consider a pair of classical formulas φ and ψ. Then, $\varphi \to \Box\psi$, $\Box\varphi \wedge \Diamond\psi$ and $\Box(\Box\varphi \wedge \Diamond\psi)$ are examples of formulas in CMF; $P(\varphi \to \Box\psi)$, $P(\varphi) \to P(\Box\psi)$ belongs to PMF, but neither $\Box\varphi \to P(\psi)$, nor $P(P(\varphi) \to P(\Box\psi))$ are examples of probabilistic modal formulas because we ask no interaction between classical modal and probabilistic modal formulas and P cannot occur nested. Finally, $\Box P(\varphi)$, $\Box P(\varphi) \to P(\Diamond\psi)$, $\Box(P(\varphi) \to P(\Diamond\psi))$ and $\Box(\Box P(\varphi) \to P(\Diamond\psi))$ are examples of uncertain modal formulas.

Now, let us define a semantics for the language defined above.

Definition 4. *A* uniform uncertain model *is a tuple*

$$\mathcal{U} = (W, R, \{e_w\}_{w\in W}, \{p_w\}_{w\in W})$$

where:

1. *(W, R) is a (non empty) S5-Kripke frame;*
2. *For all $w \in W$, $e_w : CF \to \{0,1\}$ is a classical evaluation;*
3. *For all $w \in W$, p_w is a probability distribution on W.*

If $\mathcal{U} = (W, R, \{e_w\}_{w\in W}, \{p_w\}_{w\in W})$ is an uncertain model, $w \in W$ is any world and φ is a formula, we define the truth-value of φ in $\mathcal{U}$ at w (denoted $\|\varphi\|_{\mathcal{U},w}$) in the following way:

(1) If $\varphi \in CF$, $\|\varphi\|_{\mathcal{U},w} = e_w(\varphi)$;
(2) If $\varphi \in CMF$ then, if $\varphi = \Box\psi$, then $\|\varphi\|_{\mathcal{U},w} = \inf\{\|\psi\|_{\mathcal{U},w'} \mid wRw'\}$. If φ is compound then $\|\varphi\|_{\mathcal{U},w}$ is computed by the truth-functionality of classical connectives.

(3) If $\varphi \in PMF$ and φ is atomic, i.e., $\varphi = P(\psi)$, then $\psi \in CMF$ and

$$\|\varphi\|_{\mathcal{U},w} = \sum\{p_w(w') \mid \|\psi\|_{\mathcal{U},w'} = 1\}.$$

If $\varphi \in PMF$ and is compound, then its truth-values is computed by the truth-functionality of Lukasiewicz connectives.

(4) If $\varphi \in UMF$ and $\varphi = \Box\psi$, then $\psi \in PMF$ and

$$\|\varphi\|_{\mathcal{U},w} = \inf\{\|\psi\|_{\mathcal{U},w'} \mid wRw'\}.$$

Again, if φ is compound than we will compute $\|\varphi\|_{\mathcal{U},w}$ by the truth-functionality of Lukasiewicz connectives.

The cases (1) and (2) above are indeed as usual. Let us hence provide some examples for the possibly less clear cases (3) and (4).

Let us start with the case (3) and let φ be the formula $P(\psi)$ for $\psi \in CF$. Then, $\|P(\psi)\|_{\mathcal{U},w} = \sum\{p_w(w') \mid \|\psi\|_{\mathcal{U},w'} = 1\}$, i.e., $\sum\{p_w(w') \mid e_{w'}(\psi) = 1\}$. In other words $\|P(\psi)\|_{\mathcal{U},w}$ is the probability, computed in w, of ψ.

If $\varphi = P(\Box\psi)$ and again $\psi \in CF$, then $\|P(\Box\psi)\|_{\mathcal{U},w}$ is, by definition, $\sum\{p_w(w') \mid \|\Box\psi\|_{\mathcal{U},w'} = 1\}$. In this case, notice that $\|\Box\psi\|_{\mathcal{U},w'} = 1$ iff $\|\psi\|_{\mathcal{U},w''}$ for all $w'Rw''$. Therefore, if we denote by μ_w the probability function on 2^W induced by the distribution p_w,

$$\|P(\Box\psi)\|_{\mathcal{U},w} = \mu_w(\{w^* \in W \mid \forall w' \in W \; (w^*Rw' \Rightarrow \|\psi\|_{\mathcal{U},w'} = 1)\}).$$

Finally, let us consider the case of $\varphi \in UMF$. Again, if φ is atomic, i.e., of the form, for instance $\Box P(\psi)$ and $\psi \in CF$,

$$\|\Box P(\psi)\|_{\mathcal{U},w} = \inf\{\|P(\psi)\|_{\mathcal{U},w'} \mid wRw'\} = \inf\{\mu_{w'}(\psi) \mid wRw'\}.$$

Clearly, more complex formulas can be considered.

Let us now deal with a more concrete example. Consider a language with three propositional variables p, q, r and the S5L Kripke frame as in Fig. 1. Let the evaluations e_w be as follows: $w_1 \models p, q, r$; $w_2 \models p, \neg q, r$; $w_3 \models \neg p, q, \neg r$; $w_4 \models p, \neg q, \neg r$; $w_5 \models \neg p, \neg q, \neg r$. The probability distributions are as follows: $p_1(w_i) = 1/5$ for all $i = 1, \ldots, 5$; $p_2(w_1) =$

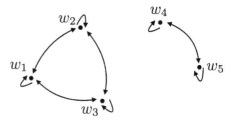

Fig. 1. An S5 Kripke frame on 5 possible worlds.

$p_2(w_2) = p_2(w_3) = 1/3$ and $p_2(w_4) = p_2(w_5) = 0$; $p_3(w_1) = p_3(w_5) = 0$, $p_3(w_2) = p_3(w_3) = 1/4$ and $p_3(w_4) = 1/2$; $p_4(w_1) = p_4(w_3) = 0$ and $p_4(w_2) = p_4(w_4) = p_4(w_5) = 1/3$; $p_5(w_3) = 0$ and $p_5(w_1) = p_5(w_2) = p_5(w_4) = p_5(w_5) = 1/4$. Thus, let $\mathcal{U} = (W, R, \{e_1, \ldots, e_5\}, \{p_1, \ldots, p_5\})$ and $\varphi = r \to (p \wedge q)$. Its models are w_1, w_3, w_4, w_5. Then, for every $i = 1, \ldots, 5$, it is easy to compute $\|P(\varphi)\|_{\mathcal{U},w_i}$

as $p_i(w_1) + p_i(w_3) + p_i(w_4) + p_i(w_5)$. For instance, $\|P(\varphi)\|_{\mathcal{U},w_1} = 4/5$ and $\|P(\varphi)\|_{\mathcal{U},w_2} = 2/3$.

Now, consider the slightly more complicated formula $P(\Box\varphi)$. In order to compute $\|P(\Box\varphi)\|_{\mathcal{U},w_i}$, we first need to notice that the models of $\Box\varphi$, are w_4 and w_5. Indeed, for all $i = 1, 2, 3$, $w_i R w_2$ and $w_2 \not\models \varphi$. Thus, for all $i = 1, \ldots, r$,

$$\|P(\Box\varphi)\|_{\mathcal{U},w_i} = p_i(w_4) + p_1(w_5).$$

Thus, $\|P(\Box\varphi)\|_{\mathcal{U},w_1} = 2/5$, $\|P(\Box\varphi)\|_{\mathcal{U},w_2} = 0$ and $\|P(\Box\varphi)\|_{\mathcal{U},w_5} = 1/2$. Note that, for all $i = 1, \ldots, 5$, $\|P(\Box\varphi)\|_{\mathcal{U},w_i} \leq \|P(\varphi)\|_{\mathcal{U},w_i}$, i.e. the PFM formula $P(\Box\varphi) \to P(\varphi)$ is valid in $\mathcal{U}$.

Finally, let us consider $\Box P(\varphi)$. In this case the $\Box$ is external to P, thus the above is an uncertain modal formula. For all $i = 1, \ldots, 5$,

$$\|\Box P(\varphi)\|_{\mathcal{U},w_i} = \min\{\|P(\varphi)\|_{\mathcal{U},w_j} \mid w_i R w_j\}.$$

For instance, $\|\Box P(\varphi)\|_{\mathcal{U},w_1} = \min\{\|P(\varphi)\|_{\mathcal{U},w_1}, \|P(\varphi)\|_{\mathcal{U},w_2}, \|P(\varphi)\|_{\mathcal{U},w_3}\} = \min\{4/5, 2/3, 3/4\} = 2/3$. Again, since R is reflexive in all S5 Kripke frames, one has that $\Box P(\varphi) \to P(\varphi)$ is valid in $\mathcal{U}$. From this observation, together with the fact that $x \to y$ and $z \to y$ imply, in Łukasiewicz logic, that $(x \wedge z) \to y$,

$$(P(\Box\varphi) \wedge \Box P(\varphi)) \to P(\varphi)$$

holds in $\mathcal{U}$. In the following table, we summarize the evaluations of $\|P(\varphi)\|_{\mathcal{U},w_i}$, $\|\Box\varphi\|_{\mathcal{U},w_i}$, $\|P(\Box\varphi)\|_{\mathcal{U},w_i}$, $\|\Box P(\varphi)\|_{\mathcal{U},w_i}$ computed on all worlds in the given model $\mathcal{U}$.

	w_1	w_2	w_3	w_4	w_5
$\|P(\varphi)\|_{\mathcal{U},w_i}$	4/5	2/3	3/4	2/3	3/4
$\|\Box\varphi\|_{\mathcal{U},w_i}$	0	0	0	1	1
$\|P(\Box\varphi)\|_{\mathcal{U},w_i}$	2/5	0	1/2	2/3	1/2
$\|\Box P(\varphi)\|_{\mathcal{U},w_i}$	2/3	2/3	2/3	2/3	2/3

In this example, $\|\Box P(\varphi)\|_{\mathcal{U},w_i}$, the modal formula representing the "lower probability degree of φ" is always greater or equal to $\|P(\Box\varphi)\|_{\mathcal{U},w_i}$, the modal formula standing for the "belief of φ". However, this is not always the case and by changing the probability distributions on W there are cases in which $\|\Box P(\varphi)\|_{\mathcal{U},w_i} \leq \|P(\Box\varphi)\|_{\mathcal{U},w_i}$.

4   Future Work

Our future work on the subject that we briefly presented in this short paper, aims at presenting an axiomatization for the logic of the class of uniform uncertain models we went through in the previous section. A proposal is given by the following Hilbert-style calculus:

(CPL). The axioms and rules of classical propositional logic for formulas in (CF);

(S5). The axioms and rules for S5L, i.e., those of Łukasiewicz calculus plus the modal axioms we recalled in Sect. 2.1;

(P). The following axioms are rules for the modality P:

(P1) $P(\varphi \to \psi) \to (P(\varphi) \to P(\psi))$; (P3) $P(\varphi \lor \psi) \equiv [(P(\varphi) \to P(\varphi \land \psi)) \to P(\psi)]$;
(P2) $\neg P(\varphi) \equiv P(\neg\varphi)$;   (NP) necessitation: from φ infer $P(\varphi)$.

The above axiom schema **(P)**, has already been shown to define a complete calculus for (finitely additive) probability functions [5,8], while the interaction between P and an S5 $\Box$ in formulas like $P(\Box\varphi)$ gives a way to represent belief functions [7]. Of course, a first step to make is to prove that the axioms **(S5)**, together with **(P)** combined as $\Box P(\varphi)$ actually captures lower probabilities. Furthermore, it remains to show a completeness theorem of the whole above system with respect to the class of uniform uncertain models. Interestingly, the class of models presented here might result in the definition of possibly new ways for the uncertain quantification that can be identified first on a syntactic level, e.g. a formula of the form $\Box(P(\Box\varphi))$ might represent a *lower belief function*.

Acknowledgements. The authors thank the anonymous referees for their comments and suggestions. Corsi and Hosni acknowledge funding by the Department of Philosophy "Piero Martinetti" of the University of Milan under the Project "Departments of Excellence 2018–2022" awarded by the Ministry of Education, University and Research (MIUR). Flaminio acknowledges partial support by the Spanish project PID2019-111544GB-C21 and by the MOSAIC project (EU H2020-MSCA-RISE-2020 Project 101007627). Hosni also acknowledges funding from the Deutsche Forschungsgemeinschaft (DFG, grant LA 4093/3-1).

References

1. Anger, B., Lembcke, J.: Infinitely subadditive capacities as upper envelopes of measures. Zeitschrift für Wahrscheinlichkeitstheorie und verwandte Gebiete **68**(3), 403–414 (1985)
2. Blackburn, P., de Rijke, M., Venema, Y.: Modal Logic. Cambridge University Press, Cambridge (2002)
3. Castaño, D., Cimadamore, C., Varela, J.P.D., Rueda, L.: Completeness for monadic fuzzy logics via functional algebras. Fuzzy Sets Syst. **407**, 161–174 (2021)
4. Chang, C.C.: A new proof of the completeness of the lukasiewicz axioms. Trans. Am. Math. Soc. **95**(1), 74–80 (1959)
5. Flaminio, T., Godo, L., Marchioni E.: Reasoning about uncertainty of fuzzy events: an overview. In: Understanding Vagueness - Logical, Philosophical, and Linguistic Perspectives, Cintula, P., et al. (Eds.), College Publications, pp. 367–400 (2011)
6. Godo, L., Esteva, F., Hájek, P.: Reasoning about probability using fuzzy logic. Neural Netw. World **10**, 811–824 (2000)
7. Godo, L., Hájek, P., Esteva, F.: A fuzzy modal logic for belief functions. Fundam. Inf. **57**(2–4), 127–146 (2003)
8. Hájek, P.: Metamathematics of Fuzzy Logic, vol. 4. Springer, Heidelrberg (1998). https://doi.org/10.1007/978-94-011-5300-3
9. Hájek, P.: On fuzzy modal logics s5 (c). Fuzzy Sets Syst. **161**(18), 2389–2396 (2010)
10. Hájek, P., Godo, L., Esteva, F.: Fuzzy logic and probability. Inst. Compu. Sci. (ICS) (1995)
11. Halpern, J.Y.: Reasoning About Uncertainty. MIT press, Cambridge (2003)
12. Marchioni, E.: Uncertainty as a modality over t-norm based logics. In: EUSFLAT Conference, vol. 1, pp. 169–176 (2007)

13. Marchioni, E.: Representing upper probability measures over rational Lukasiewicz logic. Mathware Soft Comput. **15**(2), 159–174 (2008)
14. Mundici, D.: Advanced Lukasiewicz Calculus and MV-Algebras, vol. 35. Springer, Heidelberg (2011). https://doi.org/10.1007/978-94-007-0840-2
15. Shafer, G.: A Mathematical Theory of Evidence. Princeton University Press, Princeton (1975)
16. Smith, C.: Consistency in statistical inference and decision. J. Royal Stat. Soc. Series B (Methodological) **23**(1), 1–37 (1961)

Extending the Macsum Aggregation to Interval-Valued Inputs

Yassine Hmidy[1], Agnès Rico[2], and Olivier Strauss[1(✉)]

[1] LIRMM, Université de Montpellier, CNRS, Montpellier, France
olivier.strauss@lirmm.fr
[2] LIRIS, Université Claude Bernard Lyon 1, CNRS, Écully, France

Abstract. Due to a lack of information or access to the data, or simply due to the imprecise nature of the data, there are cases where a function that maps interval-valued inputs is more appropriate to model a system. With the concern to keep the advantageous properties of the Choquet integral, we propose here a model that maps interval-valued inputs onto interval-valued outputs whose upper and lower bounds are Choquet integrals with respect to a parametric set function. This model is an extension to interval-valued inputs of the macsum aggregation proposed in [16]. In this article, we show that this extension can be easily computed thanks to some properties of the macsum parametric set function.

Keywords: Interval system · Choquet integral · Macsum aggregation

1 Introduction

As mentioned by Grabisch in [7], the linear model is the main tool for modeling dependencies among data. The Choquet integral can be viewed as a generalization of this modeling. It is widely used as a flexible aggregation function in many fields, such as multiple criteria decision making [6], classification [3], regression [10] or data fusion [1]. Its main advantage is that it allows to quantify the importance of each variable and the interaction between groups of variables. Therefore it is an aggregation function that offers interpretability on the top of flexibility.

In a recent paper, Strauss et al. [16] were interested in the use of the Choquet integral to model incoherent systems. An incoherent system is a system which, for the same inputs, can have different outputs. This kind of behavior can be due, for example, to unmeasured inputs, to a partially random behavior of the modeled system or to partial lack of knowledge on the system.

There are many works interested in this type of modeling [11,15–17]. The originality of the approach proposed by Strauss et al. is that it aims at providing the convex envelope of all the values that should have been outputted by the considered incoherent system for the same inputs. The modeling they propose, under the name of macsum, is an aggregation function that maps a vector of precise inputs onto an interval-valued output. The upper and lower bounds of this interval is computed respectively by the Choquet integral w.r.t. a particular submodular set function, called the macsum operator, and its conjugate. As stated in [16], this modeling can be thought of as an imprecise linear model, thus representing a lack of knowledge about the input-output relationship of the modeled system. It has the major advantage over most of the other Choquet integral based approaches in that it depends only on a small number of parameters leading to very simple computation.

However, the inaccuracy may not be due solely to scant knowledge of the system. It can also be due to an imprecise measurement of the inputs [4,13,14]. One can therefore be interested in modeling a system that is imprecisely known and whose inputs are imprecise too. For example, in [12], Lacerda and Crespo propose to extend their interval predictor model to the case where inputs are interval-valued.

In this article, we are interested, as Lacerda and Crespo, in extending the macsum model to the case where the inputs are interval-valued. One of the difficulties of this kind of extension is that it can lead to very complex computations, thus losing the advantage of the simplicity of the macsum model. We show in this paper that extending the macsum model to interval-valued inputs leads to computation whose complexity is equivalent to that of the macsum model with precise inputs. As mentioned by Dubois and Prade [2], a minimal requirement for those extensions should be to be monotonically increasing in the wide sense with respect to each argument. We propose here two extensions. The first extension is disjunctive. It aims at dealing with the case where some sets to be aggregated cannot be considered as reliable. It presents the advantage of containing all the information but can lead to too broad intervals. The second extension is conjunctive. It aims at dealing with consonant sets of information. It would lead to more narrow intervals, giving the minimal set of common information in the considered sets.

This article is organized as follows. Section 2 gives the background needed to understand the following. Section 3 is a reminder of the macsum aggregation. Section 4 introduces the disjunctive extension and Sect. 5 the conjunctive extension of the macsum aggregation to interval-valued inputs we propose. In Sect. 6, an example is given to illustrate the low complexity calculation of the bounds of these extensions. We then conclude in Sect. 7.

2   Background

- $\Omega = \{1, \ldots, N\} \subset \mathbb{N}$.
- A vector is a function $\boldsymbol{x} : \Omega \to \mathbb{R}$ defined by an element of $\mathbb{R}^N$ denoted $\boldsymbol{x} = (x_1, \cdots, x_N) \in \mathbb{R}^N$.
- Let $\boldsymbol{x} \in \mathbb{R}^N$, we define $\boldsymbol{x}^+, \boldsymbol{x}^- \in \mathbb{R}^N$ such that $\forall i \in \Omega$, $x_i^+ = \max(0, x_i)$ and $x_i^- = \min(0, x_i)$.
- $\overline{\underline{x}} = [\underline{x}, \overline{x}]$ is a real interval whose lower bound is $\underline{x}$ and upper bound is $\overline{x}$.
- $\mathbb{IR}$ is the set of real intervals.
- A vector of real intervals is an element of $\mathbb{IR}^N$ denoted $\overline{\underline{\boldsymbol{x}}} = (\overline{\underline{x}}_1, \overline{\underline{x}}_2, .., \overline{\underline{x}}_N)$.

- We say that $\boldsymbol{x} \in \overline{\boldsymbol{x}}$ if $\forall i \in \Omega$, $x_i \in \overline{x}_i$.
- An aggregation function $f : \mathbb{R}^N \to \mathbb{R}$ maps several input values onto a single real value.
- An interval aggregation function $f : \mathbb{IR}^N \to \mathbb{IR}$ maps several interval-valued inputs onto a single interval-valued output.
- A set function is a function $\mu : 2^\Omega \to \mathbb{R}$ that maps any subset of Ω onto a real value. To a set function μ is associated a complementary set function μ^c: $\forall A \subseteq \Omega$, $\mu^c(A) = \mu(\Omega) - \mu(A^c)$, with $\mu(\varnothing) = 0$.
- A set function μ is said to be submodular if $\forall A, B \subseteq \Omega$, $\mu(A \cup B) + \mu(A \cap B) \leq \mu(A) + \mu(B)$.
- A set function μ is said to be supermodular if $\forall A, B \subseteq \Omega$, $\mu(A \cup B) + \mu(A \cap B) \geq \mu(A) + \mu(B)$.
- The asymmetric Choquet integral of $\boldsymbol{x} \in \mathbb{R}^N$ w.r.t. a set function μ, denoted $\check{\mathbb{C}}_\mu$ [9], can be defined by:

$$\check{\mathbb{C}}_\mu(\boldsymbol{x}) = \sum_{k=1}^{N} x_{(k)} . (\mu(A_{(k)}) - \mu(A_{(k+1)})) = \sum_{k=1}^{N} (x_{(k)} - x_{(k-1)}) . \mu(A_{(k)}),$$

where $(.)$ is the permutation that sorts the element of $\boldsymbol{x}$ in increasing order: $x_{(1)} \leq x_{(2)} \leq \cdots \leq x_{(N)}$ with $x_{(0)} = 0$ and $A_{(i)}$ $(i \in \Omega)$ being the coalition of Ω such that $A_{(i)} = \{(i), \ldots, (N)\}$ with $A_{(N+1)} = \varnothing$.

- $\forall \overline{x}, \overline{y} \in \mathbb{IR}$, the natural union between $\overline{x}$ and $\overline{y}$ and the natural intersection between $\overline{x}$ and $\overline{y}$ are respectively defined as: $\overline{x} \cup \overline{y} = \{z \in \mathbb{R}| z \in \overline{x} \text{ or } z \in \overline{y}\}$ and $\overline{x} \cap \overline{y} = \{z \in \mathbb{R}| z \in \overline{x} \text{ and } z \in \overline{y}\}$.
- $\forall \overline{x}, \overline{y} \in \mathbb{IR}$, the extensive union between $\overline{x}$ and $\overline{y}$ and the extensive intersection between $\overline{x}$ and $\overline{y}$ are respectively defined as: $\overline{x} \tilde{\cup} \overline{y} = [\min(\underline{x}, \underline{y}), \max(\overline{x}, \overline{y})]$ and $\overline{x} \tilde{\cap} \overline{y} = [\max(\underline{x}, \underline{y}), \min(\overline{x}, \overline{y})]$.

Remark 1. The natural and extensive unions of two intervals $\overline{x}$ and $\overline{y}$ are equal if $\overline{x} \cap \overline{y} \neq \varnothing$.

Remark 2. $\overline{x} \tilde{\cup} \overline{y}$ is the convex envelope of $\overline{x} \cup \overline{y}$.

Remark 3. If $\overline{x} \cap \overline{y} \neq \varnothing$, then $\overline{x} \cap \overline{y} = \overline{x} \tilde{\cap} \overline{y}$.

3   The Macsum Aggregation

A set function is said to be parametric when its computing involves values of a predefined set of parameters. The macsum operator is a parametric set function denoted ν_φ where φ stands for the vector of parameters. This set function was introduced in [16], and is defined as $\forall \varphi \in \mathbb{R}^N$, $\forall A \subseteq \Omega$:

$$\nu_\varphi(A) = \max_{i \in A} \varphi_i^+ + \min_{i \in \Omega} \varphi_i^- - \min_{i \in A^c} \varphi_i^-,$$

$$\nu_\varphi^c(A) = \min_{i \in A} \varphi_i^- + \max_{i \in \Omega} \varphi_i^+ - \max_{i \in A^c} \varphi_i^+.$$

Let $\varphi \in \mathbb{R}^N$, the macsum aggregation is defined by using the macsum operator ν_φ as:

$$\mathcal{A}_{\nu_\varphi}(\boldsymbol{x}) = [\check{\mathbb{C}}_{\nu_\varphi^c}(\boldsymbol{x}), \check{\mathbb{C}}_{\nu_\varphi}(\boldsymbol{x})]. \tag{1}$$

Let $\psi \in \mathbb{R}^N$, $\forall A \subseteq \Omega$, we denote λ_ψ the linear parametric set function defined by:

$$\lambda_\psi(A) = \sum_{i \in A} \psi_i.$$

Let $\psi \in \mathbb{R}^N$, the linear aggregation is defined by using the linear operator λ_ψ as:

$$\mathcal{A}_{\lambda_\psi}(\boldsymbol{x}) = \check{\mathbb{C}}_{\lambda_\psi}(\boldsymbol{x}) = \sum_{i \in \Omega} \psi_i.x_i.$$

Contrarily to the macsum aggregation, the linear aggregation is precise-valued. It can easily be extended to interval valued inputs by $\forall \overline{\boldsymbol{x}} \in \mathbb{IR}$:

$$\mathcal{A}_{\lambda_\psi}(\overline{\boldsymbol{x}}) = \{\check{\mathbb{C}}_{\lambda_\psi}(\boldsymbol{x})/\boldsymbol{x} \in \overline{\boldsymbol{x}}\} = \left[\inf_{\boldsymbol{x} \in \overline{\boldsymbol{x}}} \mathcal{A}_{\lambda_\psi}(\boldsymbol{x}), \sup_{\boldsymbol{x} \in \overline{\boldsymbol{x}}} \mathcal{A}_{\lambda_\psi}(\boldsymbol{x})\right],$$

this set being convex due to the fact that $\overline{\boldsymbol{x}}$ is convex and $\mathcal{A}_{\lambda_\psi}$ is linear.

The macsum core of a vector φ of $\mathbb{R}^N$ is a convex subset of $\mathbb{R}^N$ defined as:

$$\mathcal{M}(\varphi) = \left\{\psi \in \mathbb{R}^N / \forall A \subseteq \Omega, \nu_\varphi^c(A) \leq \lambda_\psi(A) \leq \nu_\varphi(A)\right\}.$$

Since the macsum operator is submodular, as proven in [16], the macsum core of a vector of $\mathbb{R}^N$ is never empty. Moreover, Eq. (1) can be interpreted as:

$$\mathcal{A}_{\nu_\varphi}(\boldsymbol{x}) = \left\{\mathcal{A}_{\lambda_\psi}(\boldsymbol{x})/\psi \in \mathcal{M}(\varphi)\right\},$$

this set being convex [16]: $\forall \psi \in \mathcal{M}(\varphi), \exists y \in \mathcal{A}_{\nu_\varphi}(\boldsymbol{x})$ such that $y = \mathcal{A}_{\lambda_\psi}(\boldsymbol{x})$ and $\forall y \in \mathcal{A}_{\nu_\varphi}(\boldsymbol{x}), \exists \psi \in \mathcal{M}(\varphi)$ such that $y = \mathcal{A}_{\lambda_\psi}(\boldsymbol{x})$.

4   Disjunctive Extension to Interval-Valued Inputs

Extending the macsum aggregation to interval valued inputs consists in considering aggregating the set of all $\mathcal{A}_{\nu_\varphi}(\boldsymbol{x})$ with $\boldsymbol{x} \in \overline{\boldsymbol{x}}$. In this section, we consider a very conservative aggregation consisting in keeping all the aggregated interval-valued outputs of the macsum aggregations for each $\boldsymbol{x}$ of $\overline{\boldsymbol{x}}$. This can be defined, $\forall \overline{\boldsymbol{x}} \in \mathbb{IR}^N$, by:

$$\mathcal{D}_{\nu_\varphi}(\overline{\boldsymbol{x}}) = \bigcup_{\boldsymbol{x} \in \overline{\boldsymbol{x}}} \mathcal{A}_{\nu_\varphi}(\boldsymbol{x}) = \bigcup_{\boldsymbol{x} \in \overline{\boldsymbol{x}}} \left[\check{\mathbb{C}}_{\nu_\varphi^c}(\boldsymbol{x}), \check{\mathbb{C}}_{\nu_\varphi}(\boldsymbol{x})\right] = \{\mathcal{A}_{\lambda_\psi}(\boldsymbol{x})/\boldsymbol{x} \in \overline{\boldsymbol{x}}, \psi \in \mathcal{M}(\varphi)\}. \tag{2}$$

Remark 4. Given the Choquet integral w.r.t. the macsum operator is continuous as proven in [8] (Propostion 5.39) and $\overline{\boldsymbol{x}}$ is a compact subspace of $\mathbb{R}^N$, we have that $\bigcup_{\boldsymbol{x} \in \overline{\boldsymbol{x}}}[\check{\mathbb{C}}_{\nu_\varphi^c}(\boldsymbol{x}), \check{\mathbb{C}}_{\nu_\varphi}(\boldsymbol{x})] = \tilde{\bigcup}_{\boldsymbol{x} \in \overline{\boldsymbol{x}}}[\check{\mathbb{C}}_{\nu_\varphi^c}(\boldsymbol{x}), \check{\mathbb{C}}_{\nu_\varphi}(\boldsymbol{x})]$.

Thus Eq. (2) can be rewritten, $\forall \overline{\boldsymbol{x}} \in \mathbb{IR}^N$:

$$\mathcal{D}_{\nu_\varphi}(\overline{\boldsymbol{x}}) = \widetilde{\bigcup}_{\boldsymbol{x} \in \overline{\boldsymbol{x}}} \left[\check{\mathbb{C}}_{\nu_\varphi^c}(\boldsymbol{x}), \check{\mathbb{C}}_{\nu_\varphi}(\boldsymbol{x}) \right] = \left[\inf_{\boldsymbol{x} \in \overline{\boldsymbol{x}}} \check{\mathbb{C}}_{\nu_\varphi^c}(\boldsymbol{x}), \sup_{\boldsymbol{x} \in \overline{\boldsymbol{x}}} \check{\mathbb{C}}_{\nu_\varphi}(\boldsymbol{x}) \right]. \tag{3}$$

Due to the definition of the disjunctive extension given in Eq. (2), and the fact that the $\mathcal{A}_{\nu_\varphi}(\boldsymbol{x})$ are convex sets of $\mathbb{R}$, the bounds of $\mathcal{D}_{\nu_\varphi}(\overline{\boldsymbol{x}})$ are reached, i.e. $\exists \boldsymbol{y} \in \overline{\boldsymbol{x}}$ and $\exists \psi \in \mathcal{M}(\varphi)$ such that $\sup_{\boldsymbol{x} \in \overline{\boldsymbol{x}}} \check{\mathbb{C}}_{\nu_\varphi}(\boldsymbol{x}) = \mathcal{A}_{\lambda_\psi}(\boldsymbol{y})$ and $\exists \boldsymbol{y}' \in \overline{\boldsymbol{x}}$ and $\exists \psi' \in \mathcal{M}(\varphi)$ such that $\inf_{\boldsymbol{x} \in \overline{\boldsymbol{x}}} \check{\mathbb{C}}_{\nu_\varphi^c}(\boldsymbol{x}) = \mathcal{A}_{\lambda_{\psi'}}(\boldsymbol{y}')$.

The two following propositions are needed to compute the disjunctive extension.

Proposition 1. *(Proposition 5.1 in [16]). Let $\varphi \in \mathbb{R}^N$, let $\psi \in \mathcal{M}(\varphi)$, $\forall i \in \Omega$, $\varphi_i > 0 \Rightarrow \psi_i \geq 0$ and $\varphi_i < 0 \Rightarrow \psi_i \leq 0$.*

Proposition 2. *Let $\varphi \in \mathbb{R}^N$, let $\psi \in \mathcal{M}(\varphi)$, $\forall i \in \Omega$, $\varphi_i = 0 \Rightarrow \psi_i = 0$.*

Proof. Let $j \in \Omega$ such that $\varphi_j = 0$. We have $\nu_\varphi(\{j\}) = 0 + \min_{i \in \Omega} \varphi_i^- - \min_{i \in \Omega \setminus j} \varphi_i^-$.

As $\varphi_j = 0$, either $\min_{i \in \Omega} \varphi_i^- < 0$ and then $\min_{i \in \Omega} \varphi_i^- = \min_{i \in \Omega \setminus j} \varphi_i^-$ which gives $\nu_\varphi(\{j\}) = 0$, or $\min_{i \in \Omega} \varphi_i^- = \varphi_j = \min_{i \in \Omega \setminus j} \varphi_i^- = 0$, which also gives $\nu_\varphi(\{j\}) = 0$.

Furthermore, we have $\nu_\varphi^c(\{j\}) = 0 + \max_{i \in \Omega} \varphi_i^+ - \max_{i \in \Omega \setminus j} \varphi_i^+$. Proving that $\max_{i \in \Omega} \varphi_i^+ = \max_{i \in \Omega \setminus j} \varphi_i^+$ and consequently $\nu_\varphi^c(\{j\}) = 0$ can be done in the same manner.

As $\psi \in \mathcal{M}(\varphi)$, we have $\forall A \subseteq \Omega, \nu_\varphi^c(A) \leq \lambda_\psi(A) \leq \nu_\varphi(A)$, therefore $\nu_\varphi^c(\{j\}) \leq \lambda_\psi(\{j\}) \leq \nu_\varphi(\{j\})$, thus $0 \leq \psi_j \leq 0$ i.e. $\psi_j = 0$.

Therefore the non-negativity (resp. non-positivity) of an element of a parameter entails the non-negativity (resp. non-positivity) of the corresponding element of any parameter of its macsum core.

Proposition 3. *(Proposition 2.2 in [16]) Let $\varphi \in \mathbb{R}^N$, let $\psi \in \mathcal{M}(\varphi)$, $\forall \boldsymbol{x} \in \mathbb{R}^N$ we have*
$$\mathcal{A}_{\lambda_\psi}(\boldsymbol{x}) = \check{\mathbb{C}}_{\lambda_\psi}(\boldsymbol{x}) \in \mathcal{A}_{\nu_\varphi}(\boldsymbol{x}) = \left[\check{\mathbb{C}}_{\nu_\varphi^c}(\boldsymbol{x}), \check{\mathbb{C}}_{\nu_\varphi}(\boldsymbol{x}) \right].$$

Considering that $\forall \boldsymbol{x} \in \mathbb{IR}$, $\check{\mathbb{C}}_{\nu_\varphi^c}(\boldsymbol{x}) = \inf_{\psi \in \mathcal{M}(\varphi)} \check{\mathbb{C}}_\psi(\boldsymbol{x})$ and $\check{\mathbb{C}}_{\nu_\varphi}(\boldsymbol{x}) = \sup_{\psi \in \mathcal{M}(\varphi)} \check{\mathbb{C}}_\psi(\boldsymbol{x})$ Eq. (3) can be rewritten:

$$\mathcal{D}_{\nu_\varphi}(\overline{\boldsymbol{x}}) = \left[\inf_{\boldsymbol{x} \in \overline{\boldsymbol{x}}} \inf_{\psi \in \mathcal{M}(\varphi)} \check{\mathbb{C}}_{\lambda_\psi}(\boldsymbol{x}), \sup_{\boldsymbol{x} \in \overline{\boldsymbol{x}}} \sup_{\psi \in \mathcal{M}(\varphi)} \check{\mathbb{C}}_{\lambda_\psi}(\boldsymbol{x}) \right] \tag{4}$$

$$= \left[\inf_{\psi \in \mathcal{M}(\varphi)} \inf_{\boldsymbol{x} \in \overline{\boldsymbol{x}}} \check{\mathbb{C}}_{\lambda_\psi}(\boldsymbol{x}), \sup_{\psi \in \mathcal{M}(\varphi)} \sup_{\boldsymbol{x} \in \overline{\boldsymbol{x}}} \check{\mathbb{C}}_{\lambda_\psi}(\boldsymbol{x}) \right]. \tag{5}$$

Now, let $\overline{\underline{x}} \in \mathbb{IR}^N$ be a vector of real intervals and let $\varphi \in \mathbb{R}^N$. Let us define $x^* \in \mathbb{R}^N$ the vector such that $\forall i \in \Omega$, $x_i^* = \overline{x}_i$ if $\varphi_i \geq 0$ and $x_i^* = \underline{x}_i$ if $\varphi_i < 0$. Let us also define $x_* \in \mathbb{R}^N$ the vector such that $\forall i \in \Omega$, $x_{*i} = \underline{x}_i$ if $\varphi_i \geq 0$ and $x_{*i} = \overline{x}_i$ if $\varphi_i < 0$.

Proposition 4. $\forall \overline{\underline{x}} \in \mathbb{IR}^N$, $\forall \varphi \in \mathbb{R}^N$, $\forall \psi \in \mathcal{M}(\varphi)$, $\sup_{x \in \overline{\underline{x}}} \check{C}_{\lambda_\psi}(x) = \check{C}_{\lambda_\psi}(x^*)$ and $\inf_{x \in \overline{\underline{x}}} \check{C}_{\lambda_\psi}(x) = \check{C}_{\lambda_\psi}(x_*)$.

Proof. Given Propositions 1 and 2, we know that $\forall i \in \Omega$, if $\varphi_i \geq 0$ then $\psi_i \geq 0$ and if $\varphi_i < 0$ then $\psi_i \leq 0$. Furthermore, by construction $\check{C}_{\lambda_\psi}(x) = \sum_{i \in \Omega} \psi_i^+ . x_i + \sum_{i \in \Omega} \psi_i^- . x_i$. Thus $\forall x \in \overline{\underline{x}}$ we have: $\check{C}_{\lambda_\psi}(x) = \sum_{i \in \Omega} \psi_i . x_i \leq \sum_{i \in \Omega} \psi_i^+ . \overline{x}_i + \sum_{i \in \Omega} \psi_i^- . \underline{x}_i = \check{C}_{\lambda_\psi}(x^*)$. Consequently $\sup_{x \in \overline{\underline{x}}} \check{C}_{\lambda_\psi}(x) = \check{C}_{\lambda_\psi}(x^*)$. Proving that $\inf_{x \in \overline{\underline{x}}} \check{C}_{\lambda_\psi}(x) = \check{C}_{\lambda_\psi}(x_*)$ can be done by the same way. $\square$

Proposition 5. $\forall \overline{\underline{x}} \in \mathbb{IR}^N$, $\forall \varphi \in \mathbb{R}^N$, $\mathcal{D}_{\nu_\varphi}(\overline{\underline{x}}) = [\check{C}_{\nu_\varphi^c}(x_*), \check{C}_{\nu_\varphi^c}(x^*)]$.

Proof. We know from [16] that $\forall x \in \mathbb{R}^N$, $\forall \varphi \in \mathbb{R}^N$, $\check{C}_{\nu_\varphi}(x) = \sup_{\psi \in \mathcal{M}(\varphi)} \check{C}_{\lambda_\psi}(x)$, and from Proposition 4 that $\sup_{x \in \overline{\underline{x}}} \sup_{\psi \in \mathcal{M}(\varphi)} \check{C}_{\lambda_\psi}(x) = \sup_{\psi \in \mathcal{M}(\varphi)} \check{C}_{\lambda_\psi}(x^*)$. Thus, $\sup_{x \in \overline{\underline{x}}} \check{C}_{\nu_\varphi}(x) = \check{C}_{\nu_\varphi}(x^*)$. We can prove that $\inf_{x \in \overline{\underline{x}}} \check{C}_{\nu_\varphi^c}(x) = \check{C}_{\nu_\varphi^c}(x_*)$ in the same way. $\square$

Thus the relation between the parameter of the macsum operator and the vectors of its core allows to compute the macsum aggregation on interval-valued inputs with a linear complexity.

5 Conjunctive Extension to Interval-Valued Inputs

In this section, we consider the conjunctive aggregation that can be viewed as the antonymous version of the previously defined disjunctive aggregation. Where disjunctive aggregation is conservative and tries not to reject any information, conjunctive aggregation tries to reduce the set of values to those for which each set being aggregated agrees.

There are two possible ways to create this conjunctive aggregation: either by making the conjunction on the input vectors x belonging to the interval-valued input vector $\overline{\underline{x}}$, thus taking the conjunctive counterpart of Eq. (4), or by making the conjunction on the vectors ψ belonging to the macsum core of the macsum parameter φ, thus taking the conjunctive counterpart of Eq. (5).

The first approach leads to:

$$C_{\nu_\varphi}^{\triangleleft}(\overline{\underline{x}}) = \bigcap_{x \in \overline{\underline{x}}} A_{\nu_\varphi}(x) = \bigcap_{x \in \overline{\underline{x}}} \{A_{\lambda_\psi}(x)/\psi \in \mathcal{M}(\varphi)\}, \tag{6}$$

while the second approach leads to:

$$C_{\nu_\varphi}^{\triangleright}(\overline{\underline{x}}) = \bigcap_{\psi \in \mathcal{M}(\varphi)} A_{\lambda_\psi}(\overline{\underline{x}}) = \bigcap_{\psi \in \mathcal{M}(\varphi)} \{A_{\lambda_\psi}(x)/x \in \overline{\underline{x}}\}. \tag{7}$$

Let us consider the computation of Eq. (6). If $\mathcal{C}^{\lhd}_{\nu_\varphi}(\overline{\boldsymbol{x}}) \neq \varnothing$, then:

$$\mathcal{C}^{\lhd}_{\nu_\varphi}(\overline{\boldsymbol{x}}) = \tilde{\bigcap}_{x \in \overline{\boldsymbol{x}}} \mathcal{A}_{\nu_\varphi}(x) = \tilde{\bigcap}_{x \in \overline{\boldsymbol{x}}} \left[\check{\mathbb{C}}_{\nu^c_\varphi}(x), \check{\mathbb{C}}_{\nu_\varphi}(x) \right] \tag{8}$$

$$= \left[\sup_{x \in \overline{\boldsymbol{x}}} \check{\mathbb{C}}_{\nu^c_\varphi}(x), \inf_{x \in \overline{\boldsymbol{x}}} \check{\mathbb{C}}_{\nu_\varphi}(x) \right] = \left[\sup_{x \in \overline{\boldsymbol{x}}} \inf_{\psi \in \mathcal{M}(\varphi)} \check{\mathbb{C}}_{\lambda_\psi}(x), \inf_{x \in \overline{\boldsymbol{x}}} \sup_{\psi \in \mathcal{M}(\varphi)} \check{\mathbb{C}}_{\lambda_\psi}(x) \right].$$

In the same way, computation of Eq. (7), if $\mathcal{C}^{\rhd}_{\nu_\varphi}(\overline{\boldsymbol{x}}) \neq \varnothing$, leads to:

$$\mathcal{C}^{\rhd}_{\nu_\varphi}(\overline{\boldsymbol{x}}) = \tilde{\bigcap}_{\psi \in \mathcal{M}(\varphi)} \mathcal{A}_{\lambda_\psi}(\overline{\boldsymbol{x}}) = \left[\sup_{\psi \in \mathcal{M}(\varphi)} \inf_{x \in \overline{\boldsymbol{x}}} \check{\mathbb{C}}_{\lambda_\psi}(x), \inf_{\psi \in \mathcal{M}(\varphi)} \sup_{x \in \overline{\boldsymbol{x}}} \check{\mathbb{C}}_{\lambda_\psi}(x) \right]. \tag{9}$$

Proposition 6. $\forall \overline{\boldsymbol{x}} \in \mathbb{IR}^N$, $\forall \varphi \in \mathbb{R}^N$, the upper bound of $\mathcal{C}^{\rhd}_{\nu_\varphi}(\overline{\boldsymbol{x}})$ equals the lower bound of $\mathcal{C}^{\lhd}_{\nu_\varphi}(\overline{\boldsymbol{x}})$ and vice versa.

Proof. Lets remind that $\forall \varphi \in \mathbb{R}^N$, $\forall \psi \in \mathcal{M}(\varphi)$, we have that $\sup_{x \in \overline{\boldsymbol{x}}} \check{\mathbb{C}}_{\lambda_\psi}(x) = \check{\mathbb{C}}_{\lambda_\psi}(\boldsymbol{x}^*)$ and that $\forall \boldsymbol{x} \in \mathbb{R}^N$, $\inf_{\psi \in \mathcal{M}(\varphi)} \check{\mathbb{C}}_{\lambda_\psi}(\boldsymbol{x}) = \check{\mathbb{C}}_{\nu^c_\varphi}(\boldsymbol{x})$.
Therefore, $\inf_{\psi \in \mathcal{M}(\varphi)} \sup_{x \in \overline{\boldsymbol{x}}} \check{\mathbb{C}}_{\lambda_\psi}(x) = \inf_{\psi \in \mathcal{M}(\varphi)} \check{\mathbb{C}}_{\lambda_\psi}(\boldsymbol{x}^*) = \check{\mathbb{C}}_{\nu^c_\varphi}(\boldsymbol{x}^*)$.
Moreover, $\sup_{x \in \overline{\boldsymbol{x}}} \inf_{\psi \in \mathcal{M}(\varphi)} \check{\mathbb{C}}_{\lambda_\psi}(x) = \sup_{x \in \overline{\boldsymbol{x}}} \check{\mathbb{C}}_{\nu^c_\varphi}(x) = \check{\mathbb{C}}_{\nu^c_\varphi}(\boldsymbol{x}^*)$.
Thus, $\inf_{\psi \in \mathcal{M}(\varphi)} \sup_{x \in \overline{\boldsymbol{x}}} \check{\mathbb{C}}_{\lambda_\psi}(x) = \sup_{x \in \overline{\boldsymbol{x}}} \inf_{\psi \in \mathcal{M}(\varphi)} \check{\mathbb{C}}_{\lambda_\psi}(x)$, i.e. the upper bound of $\mathcal{C}^{\rhd}_{\nu_\varphi}(\overline{\boldsymbol{x}})$ equals the lower bound of $\mathcal{C}^{\lhd}_{\nu_\varphi}(\overline{\boldsymbol{x}})$. By the same reasoning we obtain that the lower bound of $\mathcal{C}^{\rhd}_{\nu_\varphi}(\overline{\boldsymbol{x}})$ equals the upper bound of $\mathcal{C}^{\lhd}_{\nu_\varphi}(\overline{\boldsymbol{x}})$. $\square$

If we refer to the theory of generalized intervals [5], we can say that if $\mathcal{C}^{\rhd}_{\nu_\varphi}(\overline{\boldsymbol{x}})$ is proper then $\mathcal{C}^{\lhd}_{\nu_\varphi}(\overline{\boldsymbol{x}})$ is improper and conversely. In other words, $\mathcal{C}^{\lhd}_{\nu_\varphi}(\overline{\boldsymbol{x}}) = \varnothing \Rightarrow \mathcal{C}^{\rhd}_{\nu_\varphi}(\overline{\boldsymbol{x}}) \neq \varnothing$ and $\mathcal{C}^{\rhd}_{\nu_\varphi}(\overline{\boldsymbol{x}}) = \varnothing \Rightarrow \mathcal{C}^{\lhd}_{\nu_\varphi}(\overline{\boldsymbol{x}}) \neq \varnothing$. In that sense those two approaches can be considered as dual. We thus have:

$$\mathcal{C}^{\lhd}_{\nu_\varphi}(\overline{\boldsymbol{x}}) = \left[\check{\mathbb{C}}_{\nu^c_\varphi}(\boldsymbol{x}^*), \check{\mathbb{C}}_{\nu_\varphi}(\boldsymbol{x}_*) \right], \text{ if } \check{\mathbb{C}}_{\nu^c_\varphi}(\boldsymbol{x}^*) \leq \check{\mathbb{C}}_{\nu_\varphi}(\boldsymbol{x}_*), \text{ and}$$

$$\mathcal{C}^{\rhd}_{\nu_\varphi}(\overline{\boldsymbol{x}}) = \left[\check{\mathbb{C}}_{\nu_\varphi}(\boldsymbol{x}_*), \check{\mathbb{C}}_{\nu^c_\varphi}(\boldsymbol{x}^*) \right], \text{ if } \check{\mathbb{C}}_{\nu^c_\varphi}(\boldsymbol{x}^*) \geq \check{\mathbb{C}}_{\nu_\varphi}(\boldsymbol{x}_*).$$

We thus propose to consider, for the conjunctive extension of the macsum aggregation to interval-valued inputs, the following expression:

$$\mathcal{C}_{\nu_\varphi}(\overline{\boldsymbol{x}}) = \left[\min\left(\check{\mathbb{C}}_{\nu^c_\varphi}(\boldsymbol{x}^*), \check{\mathbb{C}}_{\nu_\varphi}(\boldsymbol{x}_*) \right), \max\left(\check{\mathbb{C}}_{\nu^c_\varphi}(\boldsymbol{x}^*), \check{\mathbb{C}}_{\nu_\varphi}(\boldsymbol{x}_*) \right) \right].$$

This formula gathers in the same expression the two conjunctive counterparts (i.e. Eqs. (8) and (9)) of the disjunctive extension. As in the disjunctive case, this extension only needs computation of two Choquet integrals.

6   Example

In this section, we give a simple example illustrating the simplicity of the computation of the macsum aggregation of interval-valued inputs. Let $\overline{\boldsymbol{x}} = ([-2, 3], [0, 1], [-5, 8]) \in \mathbb{IR}^3$ and let $\varphi = (-2, 3, -1) \in \mathbb{R}^3$. Let us compute $\mathcal{D}_{\nu_\varphi}(\overline{\boldsymbol{x}})$ and $\mathcal{C}_{\nu_\varphi}(\overline{\boldsymbol{x}})$. We have $\boldsymbol{x}^* = (-2, 1, -5)$ and $\boldsymbol{x}_* = (3, 0, 8)$. Now lets sort $\boldsymbol{x}^*$ in increasing order: $\boldsymbol{x}^*_{(.)} = (x^*_3, x^*_1, x^*_2) = (-5, -2, 1)$.

Therefore $\boldsymbol{\varphi}_{(.)} = (\varphi_3, \varphi_1, \varphi_2) = (-1, -2, 3)$.

Remember that $\nu_\varphi(A_{(k)}) = \max_{i \in A_{(k)}} \varphi_i^+ - \min_{i \in A_{(k)}} \varphi_i^- + \min_{i \in \Omega} \varphi_i^-$, with $A_{(k)} = \{(k), \ldots, (N)\}$, thus $\nu_\varphi(A_{(k)}) = \max_{i=k}^{N} \varphi_{(i)}^+ - \min_{i=1}^{k-1} \varphi_{(i)}^- + \min_{i \in \Omega} \varphi_i^-$ (by convention $\min_{i=1}^{0} \varphi_{(i)}^- = 0$).

Thus:

$$\check{\mathbb{C}}_{\nu_\varphi}(\boldsymbol{x}^*) = \sum_{k=1}^{3} (x_{(k)}^* - x_{(k-1)}^*) . \nu_\varphi(A_{(k)}),$$

$$= \sum_{k=1}^{3} (x_{(k)}^* - x_{(k-1)}^*) . \left(\max_{i=k}^{3} \varphi_{(i)}^+ - \min_{i=1}^{k-1} \varphi_{(i)}^- + \min_{i \in \Omega} \varphi_i^- \right),$$

$$= (x_{(1)}^* - x_{(0)}^*) . \left(\max_{i=1}^{3} \varphi_{(i)}^+ - \min_{i=1}^{0} \varphi_{(i)}^- + \min_{i \in \Omega} \varphi_i^- \right)$$

$$+ (x_{(2)}^* - x_{(1)}^*) . \left(\max_{i=2}^{3} \varphi_{(i)}^+ - \min_{i=1}^{1} \varphi_{(i)}^- + \min_{i \in \Omega} \varphi_i^- \right)$$

$$+ (x_{(3)}^* - x_{(2)}^*) . \left(\max_{i=3}^{3} \varphi_{(i)}^+ - \min_{i=1}^{2} \varphi_{(i)}^- + \min_{i \in \Omega} \varphi_i^- \right),$$

$$= -5. (3 - 2) + (-2 + 5). (3 + 1 - 2) + (1 + 2). (3 + 2 - 2),$$

$$= -5 + 6 + 9 = 10.$$

Lets now sort $\boldsymbol{x}_*$ in increasing order: $\boldsymbol{x}_{*(.)} = (x_{*2}, x_{*1}, x_{*3}) = (0, 3, 8)$.

Therefore $\boldsymbol{\varphi}_{(.)} = (\varphi_2, \varphi_1, \varphi_3) = (3, -2, -1)$.

Remember that $A_{(k)}^c = \{(1), \ldots (k-1)\}$, we have $\nu_\varphi^c(A_{(k)}) = \min_{i=k}^{N} \varphi_{(i)}^- - \max_{i=1}^{k-1} \varphi_{(i)}^+ + \max_{i \in \Omega} \varphi_i^+$ (by convention $\min_{i=1}^{0} \varphi_{(i)}^- = 0$).

Then:

$$\check{\mathbb{C}}_{\nu_\varphi^c}(\boldsymbol{x}^*) = \sum_{k=1}^{3} (x_{*(k)} - x_{*(k-1)}) . \nu_\varphi^c(A_{(k)}),$$

$$= \sum_{k=1}^{3} (x_{*(k)} - x_{*(k-1)}) . \left(\min_{i=k}^{3} \varphi_{(i)}^- - \max_{i=1}^{k-1} \varphi_{(i)}^+ + \max_{i \in \Omega} \varphi_i^+ \right),$$

$$= (x_{*(1)} - x_{*(0)}) . \left(\min_{i=1}^{3} \varphi_{(i)}^- - \max_{i=1}^{0} \varphi_{(i)}^+ + \max_{i \in \Omega} \varphi_i^+ \right)$$

$$+ (x_{*(2)} - x_{*(1)}) . \left(\min_{i=2}^{3} \varphi_{(i)}^- - \max_{i=1}^{1} \varphi_{(i)}^+ + \max_{i \in \Omega} \varphi_i^+ \right)$$

$$+ (x_{*(3)} - x_{*(2)}) . \left(\min_{i=3}^{3} \varphi_{(i)}^- - \max_{i=1}^{2} \varphi_{(i)}^+ + \max_{i \in \Omega} \varphi_i^+ \right),$$

$$= 0. (-2 + 3) + (3 - 0). (-2 - 3 + 3) + (8 - 3). (-1 - 3 + 3),$$

$$= 0 - 6 - 5 = -11.$$

Finally, $\mathcal{D}_{\nu_\varphi}(([-2, 3], [0, 1], [-5, 8])) = [-11, 10]$.

By the same way we show that $\mathcal{C}_{\nu_\varphi}(([-2, 3], [0, 1], [-5, 8])) = [-6, 7]$.

7 Discussion

The macsum aggregation, as introduced in [16], allows to model incoherent systems. Aggregating precise inputs within the macsum approach leads to interval-valued outputs. In contrast to a simple linear model, it gives a convex set of linear models which makes it more flexible, while preserving the simplicity of use of linear model, as it depends only on N parameters, N being the number of inputs. A promising path would be to use this extension of the macsum aggregation as a simple and flexible learning model. This gives rise to other theoretical issues on its ability to approximate any functions that maps interval-valued inputs onto interval-valued outputs. Moreover, as the macsum operator needs the separation of the positive and negative elements of its parameter, further work could go towards the definition of a simpler submodular parametric set function in order to facilitate the computations during a learning process.

References

1. Abichou, B., Voisin, A., Iung, B., Kosayyer, N.: Choquet integral capacities-based data fusion for system health monitoring. In: 8th IFAC Symposium on Fault Detection, Supervision and Safety of Technical Processes (2012)
2. Dubois, D., Prade, H.: On the use of aggregation operations in information fusion processes. Fuzzy Sets Syst. **142**, 143–161 (2004)
3. Fallah Tehrani, A., Cheng, W., Dembczy, K., Hüllermeier, E.: Learning monotone nonlinear models using the Choquet integral. Mach. Learn. **89**, 414–429 (2011)
4. Floquet, P., Hétreux, G., Thery, R., Payet, L.: Analysis of operational heat exchanger network robustness via interval arithmetic. Comput. Aided Chem. Eng. **38**, 1401–1406 (2016)
5. Goldsztejn, A.: Modal intervals revisited part 1: A generalized interval natural extension. Reliable Comput. **16** (2012)
6. Grabisch, M.: The application of fuzzy integrals in multicriteria decision making. Eur. J. Oper. Res. **89**(3), 445–456 (1996)
7. Grabisch, M.: Modelling data by the Choquet integral. Inf. Fusion Data Min. **123**, 135–148 (2003)
8. Grabisch, M., Marichal, J., Mesiar, R., Pap, E.: Aggregation Functions. Encyclopedia of Mathematics and its Applications, Cambridge University Press, Cambridge (2009)
9. Grabisch, M., Sugeno, M., Murofushi, T.: Fuzzy Measures and Integrals: Theory and Applications. Physica, Heidelberg (2000)
10. Havens, T., Anderson, D.: Machine learning of Choquet integral regression with respect to a bounded capacity (or non-monotonic fuzzy measure). IEEE Int. Conf. Fuzzy Syst. **28**, 1–6 (2019)
11. Kieffer, M., Jaulin, L., Walter, E.: Guaranteed recursive nonlinear state estimation using interval analysis. In: Conference in decision and control, vol. 37. no. 19, pp. 3966–3971 (1998)
12. Lacerda, J., Crespo, G.: Interval predictor models for data with measurement uncertainty. Am. Control Conf. **25**, 1487–1492 (2017)
13. Lamberto, R.: Autocatalytic reactions as dynamical systems on the interval. J. Math. Phys. **34**, 5238–5251 (1993)

14. Lin, W., González-Rivera, G.: Interval-valued time series models: estimation based on order statistics exploring the agriculture marketing service data. Comput. Stat. Data Anal. **100**, 694–711 (2016)
15. Milan, H., Černý, M.: Interval regression by tolerance analysis approach. Fuzzy Sets Syst. **193**, 85–107 (2012)
16. Strauss, O., Rico, A., Hmidy, Y.: Macsum: a new interval-valued linear operator. Int. J. Approx. Reasoning **145**, 121–138 (2022)
17. Troffaes, M.: Learning and optimal control of imprecise Markov decision processes by dynamic programming using the imprecise Dirichlet model. Soft Methodol. Random Inf. Syst. **26**, 141–148 (2004)

Short Papers: Explanation

Analogical Proportions, Multivalued Dependencies and Explanations

Sebastian Link[1], Henri Prade[2]([⊠]), and Gilles Richard[2]

[1] School of Computer Science, The University of Auckland, Auckland, New Zealand
`s.link@auckland.ac.nz`
[2] IRIT, CNRS & Université Paul Sabatier, Toulouse, France
`{prade,richard}@irit.fr`

Abstract. Analogical proportions are statements of the form "a is to b as c is to d". They deal simultaneously with the similarities and differences between items, and they may be considered as a building block of analogical inference. This short paper establishes the existence of a close linkage between analogical proportions and (weak) multivalued dependencies in databases, thus providing an unexpected bridge between two distant areas of research: analogical reasoning and database design. (Weak) multivalued dependencies express a form of contextual logical independence. Besides, analogical proportions, which heavily rely on the comparison of items inside pairs and to the pairing of pairs exhibiting identical changes on attributes, are also a tool for providing adverse example-based explanations. Lastly, it is suggested that this may be applied to a data set reporting decisions in order to detect if some decision is unfair with respect to a sensitive variable (fairness being a matter of independence).

1 Introduction

It is always interesting to discover that the same concept has been introduced independently and for different purposes in two unrelated fields. It is the topic of the present paper where we establish that analogical proportions and analogical inference are at work in (weak) multivalued dependencies.

Analogical proportions are statements of the form a is to b as c is to d that relate two pairs of items on a comparative basis. Analogical proportions have proved to be instrumental in the formalization of analogical inference [2, 13]. They started to receive a mathematical formalization about two decades ago [7,12,19,20], although analogical reasoning has long been regarded more as a heuristic way of making a plausible inference on the basis of a parallel between two situations deemed to be analogous. Recently, it has been shown that analogical proportions are a tool for building explanations about the value taken by some attribute of interest using examples and counterexamples.

A multivalued dependency [3] is a constraint between two sets of attributes in a relation in database theory. It states that when such a dependency holds if two tuples are equal on the first set of attributes then there exist two other tuples

F. Dupin de Saint-Cyr et al. (Eds.): SUM 2022, LNAI 13562, pp. 351–360, 2022.
https://doi.org/10.1007/978-3-031-18843-5_24

satisfying some particular constraints involving the two sets of attributes. It expresses that two sets of attributes take values that are logically independent of each other. When multivalued dependencies hold in a database, some redundancy takes place, which can be handled through an appropriate normalisation. In weak multivalued dependencies [4–6] the existence of three tuples satisfying some conditions entails the existence of a fourth tuple satisfying some other particular conditions.

The two fields of research, analogical reasoning and databases have in common to deal with data, still in very different perspectives: plausible inference on the one hand and design, updating and querying on the other hand. In the following, after bridging analogical proportions and multivalued dependencies, we discuss some synergy between the explanatory capabilities of analogical proportions and the idea of independence underlying multivalued dependencies, and we apply it to the evaluation of fairness.

The paper is organized as follows. First, a double background on analogical proportions and on multivalued dependencies is given in Sect. 2 and in Sect. 3 respectively. Then Sect. 4 establishes the bridge between the two concepts. Lastly, in Sect. 5, we make use of analogical proportions for providing adverse example-based explanations, and thanks to the independence semantics, we use it for discussing fairness. In Sect. 6, concluding remarks suggest lines for further research.

2   Analogical Proportions

An analogical proportion (AP) is a statement of the form "a is to b as c is to d", linking four items a, b, c, d. It is denoted by $a : b :: c : d$. APs are supposed to satisfy the following properties:

1. $a : b :: c : d \Rightarrow c : d :: a : b$ (*symmetry*);
2. $a : b :: c : d \Rightarrow a : c :: b : d$ (*central permutation*).

which along with $a : b :: a : b$ (*reflexivity*), are the basic AP postulates (e.g., [14]). These properties mimic the behavior of arithmetic proportions (i.e., $a - b = c - d$) or geometric proportions (i.e., $\frac{a}{b} = \frac{c}{d}$) between numbers. Easy consequences of postulates are i) $a : a :: b : b$ (*identity*); ii) $a : b :: c : d \Rightarrow d : b :: c : a$ (*extreme permutation*); iii) $a : b :: c : d \Rightarrow b : a :: d : c$ (*internal reversal*); iv) $a : b :: c : d \Rightarrow d : c :: b : a$ (*complete reversal*).

The items a, b, c, d considered in the following are tuples of n attribute values. The values of the attributes may be Boolean (binary attributes) or nominal (discrete attributes with finite attribute domains having more than two values). The APs are defined component-wise. We first consider the case of one Boolean attribute applied to four items. Given a binary attribute applied to four items, described by Boolean variables a, b, c, d respectively, the following logical expression has been proposed for an AP [12]:

$$a : b :: c : d = ((a \wedge \neg b) \equiv (c \wedge \neg d)) \wedge ((\neg a \wedge b) \equiv (\neg c \wedge d))$$

This formula expresses that a *differs from* b *as* c *differs from* d *and* b *differs from* a *as* d *differs from* c. It is only true for 6 valuations, namely $0 : 0 :: 0 : 0$;

$1:1 :: 1:1$; $0:1 :: 0:1$; $1:0 :: 1:0$; $0:0 :: 1:1$; $1:1 :: 0:0$. This is the minimal Boolean model agreeing with the three postulates of an AP [15]. Boolean APs enjoy a code independence property: $a:b :: c:d \Rightarrow \neg a : \neg b :: \neg c : \neg d$. In other words, encoding truth (resp. falsity) with 1 or with 0 (resp. with 0 and 1) is just a matter of convention, and does not impact the AP.

This easily extends to nominal or categorical values where a, b, c, d belong to a finite attribute domain $\mathcal{A}$. In that case, $a:b :: c:d$ holds true only for the three following patterns $(a, b, c, d) \in \{(g, g, g, g), (g, h, g, h), (g, g, h, h)\}, g, h \in \mathcal{A}, g \neq h$. This generalizes the Boolean case where $\mathcal{A} = \{0, 1\}$.

In the following, items are represented by tuples of n attribute values: e.g., $a = (a_1, \cdots, a_n)$, where a_i is the value of attribute i for the considered item, APs are defined componentwise:

$a:b :: c:d$ holds true if and only if $\forall i \in \{1, \cdots, n\}, a_i : b_i :: c_i : d_i$ holds true.

In the Boolean (and nominal) case, the equation $a:b :: c:x$ where x is unknown does not always have a solution. Indeed neither $0:1 :: 1:x$ nor $1:0 :: 0:x$ have a solution (since 0111, 0110, 1000, 1001 are not valid patterns for an AP). Similarly, $g:h :: h:x$ has no solution in the nominal case when $g \neq h$. The Boolean solution exists if and only if $(a \equiv b) \vee (a \equiv c)$ is true. If the solution exists, it is unique and given by $x = c \equiv (a \equiv b)$. In the nominal case, the solution exists (and is unique) if $a = b$ (then $d = c$) or if $a = c$ (then $d = b$) [13].

Table 1 provides an example of an AP with nominal attributes (with a database flavor!). Note that, assuming that the AP $a:b :: c:d$ is true, one can indeed recalculate d from a, b, c. This corresponds to the case of a weak multivalued dependency as we shall see in the next section.

Table 1. AP: example with nominal attributes

	Course	Teacher	Time
a	Maths	Peter	8 am
b	Maths	Peter	2 pm
c	Maths	Mary	8 am
d	Maths	Mary	2 pm

More generally, analogical inference amounts to an analogical jump stating that if an AP holds between four items for n attributes, an AP may also hold for an attribute $n + 1$ (see [2] for the relation with the analogical jump: from $P(x), Q(x), P(y)$ infer $Q(y)$):

$$\frac{\forall i \in \{1, ..., n\}, \quad a_i : b_i :: c_i : d_i \text{ holds}}{a_{n+1} : b_{n+1} :: c_{n+1} : d_{n+1} \text{ holds}}$$

If $a_{n+1}, b_{n+1}, c_{n+1}$ are known, this enables the prediction of d_{n+1}, provided that $a_{n+1} : b_{n+1} :: c_{n+1} : x$ is solvable. This is the basis for analogical proportion-based classification [2].

3   Multivalued Dependencies

In the following, we use standard database notations. Let R be a relation schema viewed as a set of attributes; X and Y denote subsets of attributes. A tuple t is a complete instantiation of the attributes in R describing some existing item. A relation $\mathbf{r}$ over R is a finite set of tuples over R. The restriction of a tuple t to the attributes in $X \subseteq R$ is denoted by $t[X]$. $t[XY]$ is short for $t[X \cup Y]$.

Functional dependencies and multivalued dependencies play an important role in the design of databases. A functional dependency $X \to Y$ ($X \subseteq R$ and $Y \subseteq R$) states that for any pair of tuples t_1 and t_2 obeying the relational schema R, if $t_1[X] = t_2[X]$ then $t_1[Y] = t_2[Y]$, which reads "X determines Y".

Departing from a functional dependency, the definition of a multivalued dependency requires the existence of particular tuples in the database, under some conditions: The *multivalued dependency* [1,3] (see also [5]) $X \twoheadrightarrow Y$ (which can be read as "X multidetermines Y") holds on R if, for all pairs of tuples t_1 and t_2 in $\mathbf{r}$ such that $t_1[X] = t_2[X]$, there exists some tuple t_3 in $\mathbf{r}$ such that $t_3[XY] = t_1[XY]$ and $t_3[X(R\backslash Y)] = t_2[X(R\backslash Y)]$. Note that, as a consequence of the definition there also exists a tuple t_4 in $\mathbf{r}$ such as $t_4[XY] = t_2[XY]$ and $t_4[X(R\backslash Y)] = t_1[X(R\backslash Y)]$ (swapping the roles of t_1 and t_2).

Thus altogether, when $X \twoheadrightarrow Y$ holds, for all pairs of tuples t_1 and t_2 in $\mathbf{r}$ such that $t_1[X] = t_2[X]$, there exist tuples t_3 and t_4 in $\mathbf{r}$ such that

- $t_1[X] = t_2[X] = t_3[X] = t_4[X]$
- $t_1[Y] = t_3[Y]$
- $t_2[Y] = t_4[Y]$
- $t_1[R\backslash(X \cup Y)] = t_4[R\backslash(X \cup Y)]$
- $t_2[R\backslash(X \cup Y)] = t_3[R\backslash(X \cup Y)]$

A more simple, equivalent version of the above conditions can be expressed as follows: if we denote by (x, y, z) the tuple having values x, y, z for subsets X, Y, $R\backslash(X \cup Y)$ respectively, then whenever the tuples (p, q, r) and (p, s, u) exist in $\mathbf{r}$, the tuples (p, q, u) and (p, s, r) should also exist in $\mathbf{r}$. Note that in the definition of $X \twoheadrightarrow Y$, not only the attributes in X and in Y are involved, but also those in $R\backslash(X \cup Y)$, which departs from functional dependencies (where only the attributes in X and in Y are involved).

A multivalued dependency $X \twoheadrightarrow Y$ is trivial if Y is a subset of X, or if $X \cup Y$ is the whole set of attributes of the relation (then $R\backslash(X \cup Y)$ is empty).

In Table 2, the two multivalued dependencies $\{course\} \twoheadrightarrow \{teacher\}$ and $\{course\} \twoheadrightarrow \{time\}$ hold, as can be checked.

Note that Table 2 can be rewritten more compactly as in Table 3. This acknowledges the fact that $r = \{Maths\} \times \{Peter, Mary, Paul\} \times \{8am, 2pm\} \cup \{Comp.Sci.\} \times \{Peter, Mary\} \times \{8am\}$. Indeed the teachers attached to the course and the time attached to the course are *logically independent* of each other. Indeed, a multivalued dependency exists in a relation when there are at least three attributes, say X, Y and Z, and for a value of X there is a defined set of values of Y and a defined set of values of Z. Then, the set of values of Y is *independent* of set Z and vice versa.

Table 2. Multivalued dependencies: {course} $\twoheadrightarrow$ {teacher}; {course} $\twoheadrightarrow$ {time}

Course	Teacher	Time
Maths	Peter	8 am
Maths	Peter	2 pm
Maths	Mary	8 am
Maths	Mary	2 pm
Maths	Paul	8 am
Maths	Paul	2 pm
Comp. Sci	Peter	8 am
Comp. Sci	Mary	8 am

Table 3. Compact writing of Table 2

Course	Teacher	Time
Maths	{Peter, Mary, Paul }	{8 am, 2 pm }
Comp. Sci	{Peter, Mary}	{8 am}

Moreover the following properties holds:

If $X \rightarrow Y$, then $X \twoheadrightarrow Y$.

If $X \twoheadrightarrow Y$, then $X \twoheadrightarrow R\backslash Y$

If $X \twoheadrightarrow Y$ and $Z \subseteq U$, then $XU \twoheadrightarrow YZ$

If $X \twoheadrightarrow Y$ and $Y \twoheadrightarrow Z$, then $X \twoheadrightarrow Z\backslash Y$.

Multivalued dependencies are of interest in databases since decomposition of a relation R into (X, Y) and $(X, R\backslash Y)$ is a lossless-join decomposition if and only if $X \twoheadrightarrow Y$ holds in R. Multivalued dependencies are involved in the 4th normal form in database normalization.

A multivalued dependency, given two particular tuples, requires the existence of other tuples. Its weak form only requires the existence of one tuple given three particular tuples.

A *weak multivalued dependency* [4] $X \twoheadrightarrow_w Y$ holds on R if, for all tuples t_1, t_2, t_3 in $\mathbf{r}$ such that $t_1[XY] = t_2[XY]$ and $t_1[X(R\backslash Y)] = t_3[X(R\backslash Y)]$ there is some tuple t_4 in $\mathbf{r}$ such that $t_4[XY] = t_3[XY]$ and $t_4[X(R\backslash Y)] = t_2[X(R\backslash Y)]$. It can be checked that if $X \twoheadrightarrow Y$ then $X \twoheadrightarrow_w Y$.

The existence of the weakmultivalued dependency $X \twoheadrightarrow_w Y \;/\; Z$ is sufficient for ensuring the commutativity of Y and Z in the nesting process that enables us to rewrite Table 2 into Table 3 [5].

4   Analogical Proportion and Multivalued Dependency: the Link

Let us go back to analogical proportions. As for multivalued dependencies they involved four tuples, which are taken by pairs. Let us consider the Boolean case first. When one considers a pair of tuples (a, b), one can distinguish between the attributes where the two tuples are equal and the attributes where the two tuples disagree. If we take two pairs (a, b) and (c, d) whose tuples are equal on the same attributes and which disagree *in the same way* on the other attributes (when $(a_i, b_i) = (1, 0)$ (resp. $(0, 1)$), $(c_i, d_i) = (1, 0)$ (resp. $(0, 1)$)), these two pairs form an AP; see Table 4 where attributes A_1 to A_n have been suitably ordered and where all the possible situations are exhibited. As can be seen, we recognize the six valuations, vertically, which make a Boolean AP true. Conversely, any AP can be put under this form (with possibly some empty columns) [18].

Table 4. AP: Pairing pairs

	$A_1 - A_{i-1}$	$A_i - A_{j-1}$	$A_j - A_{k-1}$	$A_k - A_{\ell-1}$	$A_\ell - A_{m-1}$	$A_m - A_n$
a	1	0	1	0	1	0
b	1	0	1	0	0	1
c	1	0	0	1	1	0
d	1	0	0	1	0	1

This can be easily generalized to nominal attributes, as shown in Table 5, where a, b, c, d are equal on the subset of attributes X, where $a = b \neq c = d$ on the subset of attributes Y, and where the same change take place between a and b and between c and d for attributes in Z. Note that by central permutation, we can exchange the roles of Y and Z.

Table 5. AP: the nominal case

	X (full identity)	Y (pair identity)	Z (change)
a	s	t	v
b	s	t	w
c	s	u	v
d	s	u	w

Let us now first examine the weak multivalued dependency: for all tuples t_1, t_2, t_3 in $\mathbf{r}$ such that $t_1[XY] = t_2[XY]$ and $t_1[X(R\backslash Y)] = t_3[X(R\backslash Y)]$ there is some tuple t_4 in $\mathbf{r}$ such that $t_4[XY] = t_3[XY]$ and $t_4[X(R\backslash Y)] = t_2[X(R\backslash Y)]$.

Then if $t_1[XY] = t_2[XY] = (s, t)$ and $t_1[X(R\backslash Y)] = t_3[X(R\backslash Y)] = (s, v)$ there exists a tuple t_4 in $\mathbf{r}$ such that $t_4[XY] = t_3[XY] = (s, u)$ and $t_4[X(R\backslash Y)] = t_2[X(R\backslash Y)] = (s, w)$. We recognize Table 5 with $t_1 = a$, $t_2 = b$, $t_3 = c$, $t_4 = d$. Thus there is a perfect match between a weak multivalued dependency and an analogical proportion. In fact, the existence of t_4 in $\mathbf{r}$ amounts to the existence of a (unique) solution for $a : b :: c : x$ in Table 5.

The case of a multi-valued dependency is slightly different, as we are going to see. Indeed $X \twoheadrightarrow Y$ holds as soon as whenever the tuples (p, q, r) and (p, s, u) exist in $\mathbf{r}$ on subsets $X, Y, R\backslash(X \cup Y)$, the tuples (p, q, u) and (p, s, r) also exist in $\mathbf{r}$ on subsets $X, Y, R\backslash(X \cup Y)$. This corresponds to Table 6 where (r, u, u, r) is not a valid valuation for an AP. So $t_1 : t_2 :: t_3 : t_4$ does not hold (in fact, this corresponds to another logical proportion called "paralogy" [14]).

Table 6. Multivalued dependency and the failure of the AP

	X	Y	$R\backslash(X \cup Y)$
t_1	p	q	r
t_2	p	s	u
t_3	p	q	u
t_4	p	s	r

Fortunately, it is possible to reorder the tuples for obtaining a valid AP. Indeed $t_1 : t_4 :: t_3 : t_2$ does hold. See Table 7.

Table 7. Multivalued dependency and the AP recovered

	X	Y	$R\backslash(X \cup Y)$
t_1	p	q	r
t_4	p	s	r
t_3	p	q	u
t_2	p	s	u

5   Explanations and Fairness

We now go back to Table 5 which describes what is an AP in the nominal case. Moreover, we have singled out a (nominal) attribute called *Result*, supposed to depend on the other attributes, it may be the class to which the tuple belongs, or the result of an evaluation/selection for each tuple. We have also identified the roles plaid by each subset of attributes: attributes X having the same values for the four tuples, attributes Y stating the different contexts of pairs (a, b) and (c, d), attributes Z describing the change(s) inside the pairs, which may be associated or not with a change on the value of *Result*. This is Table 8.

Table 8. Results associated with tuples

	X (shared values)	Y (context)	Z (change)	Result
a	s	t	v	p
b	s	t	w	q
c	s	u	v	p
d	s	u	w	?

We recognize the schema of analogical inference in Table 8 ($p : q :: p : x$ always has a (unique) solution $x = q$; see the end of Sect. 2; we do not consider the case $p : p :: q : x$ which can be obtained by central permutation, exchanging Y and Z). We leave aside the case $p = q$, which suggests that the rule $X = s \rightarrow Result = p$ may hold, and even that a functional dependency $X \rightarrow Result$ might hold. Referring to notations in Table 8, if for all a, b, c in **r** there exists d in **r**, $X \twoheadrightarrow_w Y$ and $X \twoheadrightarrow_w Z$ hold in **r**; if for all a, d in **r** there exist b, c in **r**, $X \twoheadrightarrow Y$ and $X \twoheadrightarrow Z$ hold in **r**. It is also true changing Z in *Result*.

Table 8 is also a basis for presenting analogical proportion-based explanations [8,17]. Indeed the answer to the question "why *Result*(d) is not p?" is to be found in the values taken by the *change* attributes for d. Note that when c is a close neighbor of d, the number of *change* attributes is small. This looks like the definition of a *contrastive* explanation [10], namely we have

$$\exists x = c \in r. \left[\bigwedge_{j \in R \setminus change} (x_j = c_j = d_j) \right] \wedge (Result(d) \neq p)$$

where c_j is the value of tuple c for attribute j. Such a c could be termed as an *adverse example*. But the analogy-based explanation is richer, we know at least another pair (here (a, b)), with another *context* value, where the same change of attribute values leads to the same change of *Result* value as in pair (c, d), which suggests the possibility of the following rule (with an abductive flavor)

$$\forall\, t, (context = t) \wedge (change = w) \rightarrow Result((s, t, w)) = q$$

However, nothing forbids that $\exists\, a' \in r$, $\exists\, b' \in r$ such that $a' = (s, t', v)$, $b' = (s, t', w)$ with $Result(a') = Result(b') = p$, which would provide an exception to the rule. The strength of the explanation would depend on the relative cardinalities of pairs such as (a, b) and (a', b').

Table 9. Is *Result* for d fair (and if no, why)?

	X (shared values)	Y (diploma)	Z (sex)	Result
a	s	yes	M	P
b	s	yes	F	P
c	s	no	M	N
d	s	no	F	P

Estimating fairness is a matter of conditional stochastic independence [11]. However we have seen that multi-valued dependencies and thus analogical proportions exhibit logical independence relations. Thus the violation of an AP (and thus of a multivalued dependency) in Table 9 suggests that the value of $Result(d)$ is unfair.

6   Concluding Remarks

The link established in this paper between analogical proportions and multivalued dependencies should lead to further developments, besides explanation and fairness. One may wonder if the axiomatic characterization of dependencies may bring some new light on analogical proportions. Other questions worth of interest are: What might be the impact on explanation capabilities [8] on analogical querying [16]? Can we handle uncertain data with analogical proportions, as in database design [9]?

References

1. Beeri, C., Fagin, R., Howard, J.H.: A complete axiomatization for functional and multivalued dependencies in database relations. In: Smith, D.C.P. (ed.) Proceedings of ACM SIGMOD International Conference on Management of Data, Toronto, 3–5 August, pp. 47–61 (1977)
2. Bounhas, M., Prade, H., Richard, G.: Analogy-based classifiers for nominal or numerical data. Int. J. Approx. Reason. **91**, 36–55 (2017)
3. Fagin, R.: Multivalued dependencies and a new normal form for relational databases. ACM Trans. Database Syst. **2**(3), 262–278 (1977)
4. Fischer, P.C., Van Gucht, D.: Weak multivalued dependencies. In: Proceedings of 3rd ACM SIGACT-SIGMOD Symposium on Principles of Database Systems, 2–4 April 1984, Waterloo, Ontario, pp. 266–274 (1984)
5. Hartmann, S., Link, S.: On inferences of weak multivalued dependencies. Fundam. Inform. **92**(1–2), 83–102 (2009)
6. Jaeschke, G., Schek, H.J.: Remarks on the algebra of non first normal form relations. In: Proceedings of the ACM Symposium on Principles of Database Systems, 29–31 March Los Angeles, pp. 124–138 (1982)
7. Lepage, Y.: Analogy and formal languages. In: Proceedings of FG/MOL 2001, pp. 373–378 (2001)
8. Lim, S., Prade, H., Richard, G.: Using analogical proportions for explanations. In: Dupin de Saint-Cyr, F., Öztürk, M., Potyka, N. (eds.) SUM 2022, LNCS, vol. 13562, pp. 309–325. Springer, Cham (2022)
9. Link, S., Prade, H.: Relational database schema design for uncertain data. Inf. Syst. **84**, 88–110 (2019)
10. Marques-Silva, J., Gerspacher, T., Cooper, M.C., Ignatiev, A., Narodytska, N.: Explanations for monotonic classifiers. In: Meila, M., Zhang, T. (eds.) Proceedings of 38th International Conference on Machine Learning, (ICML 2021), 18–24 July 2021, Virtual Event Proceedings of Machine Learning Research, vol. 139, pp. 7469–7479. PMLR (2021)
11. Mehrabi, N., Morstatter, F., Saxena, N., Lerman, K., Galstyan, A.: A survey on bias and fairness in machine learning. ACM Comput. Surv. **54**(6), 115:1–35 (2021)

12. Miclet, L., Prade, H.: Logical definition of analogical proportion and its fuzzy extensions. In: Proceedings of Annual Meeting of the North American Fuzzy Information Processing Society (NAFIPS), New-York, 19–22 May 2008, IEEE (2008)

13. Pirrelli, V., Yvon, F.: Analogy in the lexicon: a probe into analogy-based machine learning of language. In: Proceedings of 6th International Symposium. on Human Communication, Cuba (1999)

14. Prade, H., Richard, G.: From analogical proportion to logical proportions. Logica Univers. **7**, 441–505 (2013)

15. Prade, H., Richard, G.: Analogical proportions: from equality to inequality. Int. J. Approx. Reason. **101**, 234–254 (2018)

16. Prade, H., Richard, G.: Analogical querying? In: Andreasen, T., De Tré, G., Kacprzyk, J., Legind Larsen, H., Bordogna, G., Zadrożny, S. (eds.) FQAS 2021. LNCS (LNAI), vol. 12871, pp. 17–28. Springer, Cham (2021). https://doi.org/10.1007/978-3-030-86967-0_2

17. Prade, H., Richard, G.: Explications analogiques. Bul. l'AFIA **116**, 17–18 (2022)

18. Prade, H., Richard, G.: Multiple analogical proportions. AI Commun. **34**(3), 211–228 (2021)

19. Stroppa, N., Yvon, F.: Du quatrième de proportion comme principe inductif?: une proposition et son application à l'apprentissage de la morphologie. Traitement Automatique Lang. **47**(2), 1–27 (2006)

20. Yvon, F., Stroppa, N., Delhay, A., Miclet, L.: Solving analogical equations on words. Technical report, Ecole Nationale Supérieure des Télécommunications (2004)

Explaining Robust Classification Through Prime Implicants

Hénoïk Willot, Sébastien Destercke[(⊠)], and Khaled Belahcene

Heudiasyc, Université de Technologie de Compiègne, Compiègne, France
{henoik.willot,sebastien.destercke,khaled.belahcene}@hds.utc.fr

Abstract. In this paper, we investigate how robust classification results can be explained by the notion of prime implicants, focusing on explaining pairwise dominance relations. By robust, we mean that we consider imprecise models that may abstain to classify or to compare two classes when information is insufficient. This will be reflected by considering (convex) sets of probabilities. By prime implicants, we understand a minimal number of attributes whose value needs to be known before stating that one class dominates/is preferred to another.

1 Introduction

Two important aspects of trustworthy AI are the ability to provide robust and safe inferences or predictions, and the ability to be able to provide explanations as of why those have been made.

Regarding explainability, the notion of prime implicants corresponds to provide minimal sufficient condition to make a given prediction, e.g., the attributes that need to be instantiated to make a classification. They have been successfully proposed as components of explanations for large classes of models such as graphical ones [12], with very efficient procedure existing for specific structures such as the Naive one [11]. In contrast with other methods such as SHAP [6] that tries to compute the average influence of attributes, prime implicants have the advantage to be well-grounded in logic, and to provide certifiable explanation (in the sense that the identified attributes are logical, sufficient reasons).

However, explainable AI tools have been mostly if not exclusively applied to precise models, at least in the machine learning domain (this is less true, e.g., in preference modelling [4]). Yet, in some applications involving sensitive issues or where the decision maker wants to identify ambiguous cases, it may be preferable to use models that will return sets of classes in some cases where information is missing rather than always returning a point-valued prediction. Several frameworks such as conformal prediction [3], indeterminate classifiers [9] or imprecise probabilistic models [7] have been proposed to handle such issue.

The later have the interest that they are direct extensions and generalisations of probabilistic classifiers, hence one can directly try to transport well-grounded explanation principles existing for precise probabilistic classifier to this setting. This is what we intend to do in this paper for prime implicant explanations.

© The Author(s), under exclusive license to Springer Nature Switzerland AG 2022
F. Dupin de Saint-Cyr et al. (Eds.): SUM 2022, LNAI 13562, pp. 361–369, 2022.
https://doi.org/10.1007/978-3-031-18843-5_25

We will start by introducing how the idea of prime implicants can be adapted to classifiers considering sets of probabilities as their uncertainty models. This will be done in Sect. 2. As the formulated problem is likely to be computationally challenging for generic models, we focus in Sect. 3 on the naive credal classifier, that generalise the naive Bayes classifier. We show that for such a model, computing and enumerating prime implicants can be done in polynomial time, thanks to its independence assumption and decompositional properties. We also provide an example illustrating our approach.

2 Setting and General Problem Formulation

In this section, we lay down our basic notations and provide necessary reminders about imprecise probabilities. We also introduce the idea of prime implicants applied to classifiers, and particular to imprecise probabilistic classifiers.

2.1 Robust Classification: Setting

We consider a usual discrete multi-class problem, where we must predict a variable Y taking values in $\mathcal{Y} = \{y_1, \ldots, y_m\}$ using n input variables $X_1, \ldots, X_n$ that respectively takes values in $\mathcal{X}_i = \{x_i^1, \ldots, x_i^{k_i}\}$. We note $\mathcal{X} = \times_{i=1}^n \mathcal{X}_i$ and $\mathbf{x} \in \mathcal{X}$ a vector in this space. When considering a subset $E \subseteq \{1, \ldots, n\}$ of dimensions, we will denote by $\mathcal{X}_E = \times^{i \in E} \mathcal{X}_i$ the corresponding domain, and by $\mathbf{x}_E$ the values of a vector on this sub-domain. We will also denote by $-E := \{1, \ldots, n\} \setminus E$ all dimensions not in E, with $\mathcal{X}_{-E}, \mathbf{x}_{-E}$ following the same conventions as $\mathcal{X}_E, \mathbf{x}_E$. We will also denote by $(\mathbf{x}_E, \mathbf{y}_{-E})$ the concatenation of two vectors whose values are given for different elements.

When considering precise probabilistic classifiers, a class y is said to weakly dominate[1] y', written $y \succeq_p y'$, upon observing a vector $\mathbf{x}$ when the condition[2]

$$\frac{p(y|\mathbf{x})}{p(y'|\mathbf{x})} \geq 1 \tag{1}$$

is met, or in other words when $p(y|\mathbf{x}) \geq p(y'|\mathbf{x})$. However, probabilistic classifiers can be deceptively precise, for instance when only a small number of data are available to estimate them, or when data become imprecise.

This is why, in this paper, we consider generalised probabilistic settings, and more specifically imprecise probability theory, where one considers that the probability p belongs to some subset $\mathcal{P}$, often assumed to be convex (this will be the case here). One then needs to extend the relation $\succeq_p$ to such a case, and a common and robust way to do so is to require $\succeq_p$ to be true for all elements

---

[1] We work in a non cost-sensitive framework, but most of our discussion easily transfer to such cases.

[2] Using dominance expressed this way will be useful in the sequel.

$p \in \mathcal{P}$. In this case, y is said to robustly dominate y', written $y \succeq_p y'$, upon observing a vector $\mathbf{x}$ when the condition

$$\inf_{p \in \mathcal{P}} \frac{p(y|\mathbf{x})}{p(y'|\mathbf{x})} \geq 1 \tag{2}$$

is met, or in other words when $p(y|\mathbf{x}) \geq p(y'|\mathbf{x})$ for all $p \in \mathcal{P}$. Note that the relation $\succeq_{\mathcal{P}}$ can be a partial pre-order with incomparabilities, whereas $\succeq_p$ is a pre-order.

2.2   Explaining Robust Classification Through Prime Implicants

Explaining the conclusion or deduction of an algorithm, and in particular of a learning algorithm, has become an important issue. A notion that can play a key role in explanation mechanisms is the one of prime implicants, i.e., which elements are sufficient before drawing a given conclusion. When observing a vector $\mathbf{x}^o$ and making a prediction about whether y dominates y', the idea of prime implicant roughly translates as the values of $\mathbf{x}^o$ that are sufficient to know to state that y dominates y', and that are minimal with this property.

   With this idea in mind, we will say that a subset $E \subseteq \{1, \ldots, n\}$ of attributes (where E are the indices of the considered attributes) is an *implicant* of $y \succeq_{\mathcal{P}} y'$ iff

$$\inf_{p \in \mathcal{P}, \mathbf{x}^a_{-E} \in X_{-E}} \frac{p(y|(\mathbf{x}^o_E, \mathbf{x}^a_{-E}))}{p(y'|(\mathbf{x}^o_E, \mathbf{x}^a_{-E}))} \geq 1, \tag{3}$$

that is if dominance holds for any values of attributes whose indices are outside E, and any probability $p \in \mathcal{P}$. This means that knowing $\mathbf{x}^o_E$ alone is sufficient to deduce $y \succeq_{\mathcal{P}} y'$. A set E is a *prime implicant* iff we satisfy (3) and for any $i \in E$, we have

$$\inf_{p \in \mathcal{P}, \mathbf{x}^a_{-E \cup \{i\}} \in X_{-E \cup \{i\}}} \frac{p(y|(\mathbf{x}^o_{E \setminus \{i\}}, \mathbf{x}^a_{-E \cup \{i\}}))}{p(y'|(\mathbf{x}^o_{E \setminus \{i\}}, \mathbf{x}^a_{-E \cup \{i\}}))} \leq 1, \tag{4}$$

that is if removing any attribute from E makes our deduction invalid, so that E is a minimal sufficient condition for $y \succeq_{\mathcal{P}} y'$ to hold. In the sequel, it will prove useful to consider the function $\phi(E)$ that associates to each possible subset the value

$$\phi(E) := \inf_{p \in \mathcal{P}, \mathbf{x}^a_{-E} \in X_{-E}} \frac{p(y|(\mathbf{x}^o_E, \mathbf{x}^a_{-E}))}{p(y'|(\mathbf{x}^o_E, \mathbf{x}^a_{-E}))}. \tag{5}$$

$\phi(E)$ being inclusion-monotonic (for $E \subseteq F$, $\phi(E) \leq \phi(F)$), it can be seen as a value function associated to E, and finding a prime implicant can then be seen as the task of finding a minimal "bundle of items"[3] E such that $\phi(E) \geq 1$, therefore allowing us to map the finding of robust prime implicants to an item selection problem. Also note that, in general, $\phi(E)$ will not be additive, as we will not have $\phi(E \cup \{i\}) = \phi(E) + \phi(\{i\})$.

---

[3] Each index of an attribute being associated to an item.

Note that when sets $\mathcal{P}$ reduce to singletons, that is when we consider precise classifiers instead of robust ones, then our notion of prime implicant reduces to previously proposed ones [11], and our approach is therefore a formal generalisation of those.

3   The Case of the Naive Credal Classifier

We now study the specific case of the Naive classifier, and show that in this case, computing prime implicants become easy, as such a computation can be brought back to selecting items with an additive value functions, or equivalently to a very simple knapsack problem.

3.1   Generic Case

The basic idea of the Naive classifier is to assume that attributes are independent of each other given the class. This modelling assumption means that

$$p(y|\mathbf{x}) = \frac{\prod_{i=1}^{n} p_i(x_i|y) \times p_{\mathcal{Y}}(y)}{p(\mathbf{x})}$$

once we apply the Naive assumption and Bayes rule. This means in particular that

$$\frac{p(y|\mathbf{x})}{p(y'|\mathbf{x})} = \frac{p_{\mathcal{Y}}(y)}{p_{\mathcal{Y}}(y')} \prod_{i=1}^{n} \frac{p_i(x_i|y)}{p_i(x_i|y')}$$

with every $p_i(\cdot|y)$ independent of $p_i(\cdot|y')$, and every $p_i(\cdot|y), p_j(\cdot|y)$ independent for i, j. When switching to credal models, one has sets of conditional distributions $\mathcal{P}_i(\cdot|y)$ and a set $\mathcal{P}_{\mathcal{Y}}$ of priors.

Let us now see how Eq. (3) transform in this case. We do have

$$\inf_{\substack{p \in \mathcal{P} \\ \mathbf{x}^a_{-E} \in X_{-E}}} \frac{p(y|(\mathbf{x}^o_E, \mathbf{x}^a_{-E}))}{p(y'|(\mathbf{x}^o_E, \mathbf{x}^a_{-E}))} =$$

$$\inf_{\substack{p \in \mathcal{P} \\ \mathbf{x}^a_{-E} \in X_{-E}}} \frac{p_{\mathcal{Y}}(y)}{p_{\mathcal{Y}}(y')} \underbrace{\prod_{i \in E} \frac{p_i(x_i^o|y)}{p_i(x_i^o|y')}}_{Part A} \underbrace{\prod_{i \notin E} \frac{p_i(x_i^a|y)}{p_i(x_i^a|y')}}_{Part B}. \tag{6}$$

In Eq. (6), we can treat the minimization problem of parts A and B completely separately, due to two principal observations. First, the sets $\mathcal{P}_i(\cdot|y)$ are all independent when i (the attribute) or y (the conditioning element) changes. This implies that part A and B are minimised over independent convex sets of probabilities (as they are over distinct i's), and that the numerator and denominator of each fraction within the two parts can also be treated separately (being conditioned on different y, y'). Second, E and $-E$ are disjoint, which means that the value $\mathbf{x}^a_{-E}$ for which part B is minimised only depends on part B, hence in this case it makes sense to define a unique "worst case" vector $\mathbf{x}^{a*}$ which minimises part B for any E. Also, since conditional laws with different conditional classes are independent, we get that Eq. (6) becomes

$$\inf_{p_y \in \mathcal{P}_y} \frac{p_y(y)}{p_y(y')} \prod_{i \in E} \frac{\underline{p}_i(x_i^o|y)}{\overline{p}_i(x_i^o|y')} \inf_{\mathbf{x}_{-E}^a \in X_{-E}} \prod_{i \notin E} \frac{\underline{p}_i(x_i^a|y)}{\overline{p}_i(x_i^a|y')}. \tag{7}$$

where $\underline{p}(x) = \inf_{p \in \mathcal{P}} p(x)$ and $\overline{p}(x) = \sup_{p \in \mathcal{P}} p(x)$. If we consider the vector $\mathbf{x}_{-E}^{a*}$, we finally have

$$\inf_{\substack{p \in \mathcal{P} \\ \mathbf{x}_{-E}^a \in X_{-E}}} \frac{p(y|(\mathbf{x}_E^o, \mathbf{x}_{-E}^a))}{p(y'|(\mathbf{x}_E^o, \mathbf{x}_{-E}^a))} = \inf_{p_y \in \mathcal{P}_y} \frac{p_y(y)}{p_y(y')} \prod_{i \in E} \frac{\underline{p}_i(x_i^o|y)}{\overline{p}_i(x_i^o|y')} \prod_{i \notin E} \frac{\underline{p}_i(x_i^{a*}|y)}{\overline{p}_i(x_i^{a*}|y')} \tag{8}$$

Let us now go back to our idea of selecting minimal bundle of items (or attribute) making $\phi(E) > 1$ or equivalently $\log \phi(E) > 0$. Let us first note by

$$C = \log \inf_{p_y \in \mathcal{P}_y} \frac{p_y(y)}{p_y(y')} \prod_{i \in \{1, \dots, n\}} \frac{\underline{p}_i(x_i^{a*}|y)}{\overline{p}_i(x_i^{a*}|y')} \tag{9}$$

the value of $\log \phi(\emptyset)$, and by

$$G_i = (\log \underline{p}_i(x_i^o|y) - \log \overline{p}_i(x_i^o|y')) - (\log \underline{p}_i(x_i^{a*}|y) - \log \overline{p}_i(x_i^{a*}|y')) \tag{10}$$

the positive[4] gain obtained by adding element i to E. Developing Eq. (7), one can check that

$$\log \phi(E) = C + \sum_{i \in E} G_i$$

has an additive form. Finding a smallest prime implicant is then computationally easy, as it amounts to order the $G_i's$ in decreasing order, and add them until $\sum_{i \in E} G_i \geq -C$. The whole procedure is summarised in Algorithm 1.

The complexity of Algorithm 1 is obviously linear over the ordered contributions, in number of attributes. Computing the contributions remains easy as the only complexity is to compute the "worst case" vector $\mathbf{x}^{a*}$, whose components x_i^{a*} requires $|X_i| = k_i$ evaluations on each dimensions. As sets $\mathcal{P}$ are typically polytopes defined by linear constraints, finding the values $\underline{p}$ and $\overline{p}$ amounts to solve linear programs, something that can be done in polynomial time. For some specific cases such as probability intervals [8] (induced, e.g., by the classical Imprecise Dirichlet Model [5]), this can even be done in linear time. Therefore, the overall method is clearly polynomial, with a linear pre-treatment over the sum of k_i's, followed by a sorting algorithm, after which Algorithm 1 is linear over the number of attributes.

---

[4] As $\log \underline{p}_i(x_i^{a*}|y) - \log \overline{p}_i(x_i^{a*}|y') < \log \underline{p}_i(x_i^o|y) - \log \overline{p}_i(x_i^o|y')$ by definition.

Algorithm 1: Compute first available prime implicants explanation

---

Input: $C : log(\phi(\emptyset))$; G : Contributions of criteria in decreasing order;
Output: $Xpl = (E, \mathbf{x}_E)$: explanation in terms of attribute
1 Order G in decreasing order, with σ the associated permutation
2 $i \leftarrow 1$
3 **while** $\phi(E) + C < 0$ **do**
4 | $i \leftarrow i + 1$
5 | $E \leftarrow E \cup \{\sigma^{-1}(i)\}$
6 | $\phi(E) \leftarrow \phi(E) + G_{\sigma(i)}$
7 $Xpl \leftarrow (E, \mathbf{x}_E^o)$
8 **return** (Xpl)

3.2 Illustrative Case

We will present a small illustrative example using categorical data and probability intervals. Those later could, for instance, be obtained through the use of the classical Imprecise Dirichlet Model [5], possibly with some regularisation to avoid zero probabilities, or in the case of continuous variable, by parametric [1] or non-parametric models [10].

In this example we want to predict the class of animal from its physical characteristics. We have data concerning the set $\mathcal{Y} = \{$D(og), C(at), H(orse), B(unny)$\}$ of animals and observe the length of their $\mathcal{X} = \{$E(ars), T(ail), H(air)$\}$. Each of these criteria can have a value in $\{L(ong), A(verage), S(hort)\}$. To identify easily variables in the example, we will use the notation LE for long ears, and similarly for all other attribute combinations. The prior probabilities are presented in Table 1 and the conditioned probabilities in Table 2, 3 and 4.

Table 1. Probability intervals of each animal class

Dog	Cat	Horse	Bunny
$[0.25, 0.26]$	$[0.29, 0.31]$	$[0.20, 0.22]$	$[0.25, 0.26]$

Assume that we observe the vector $\mathbf{x}^o = $ (Long Ear, Short Tail, Long Hair) or (LE, ST, LH) for short. As we are using an imprecise classification model, the predicted classes will correspond to the non dominated classes, and our explanations will mostly be used to understand why we rejected the other classes. For every pair (y,y') of animals we compare $\inf_{p \in \mathcal{P}} \frac{p(y|\mathbf{x})}{p(y'|\mathbf{x})}$ to 1 to build the partial order between them. In our specific case, this comes down to compare

$$log\ \underline{p}(y) - log\ \overline{p}(y') + \sum_{i=1}^{3} log\ \underline{p}(\mathbf{x}_i^o \mid y) - \sum_{i=1}^{3} log\ \overline{p}(\mathbf{x}_i^o \mid y')$$

Table 2. Conditional probabilities of the length of the ears knowing the animal

		Animal			
		Dog	Cat	Horse	Bunny
	Long	[0.33,0.40]	[0.02,0.08]	[0.10,0.19]	[0.58,0.65]
Length	Average	[0.30,0.37]	[0.55,0.61]	[0.66,0.75]	[0.26,0.33]
	Short	[0.30,0.37]	[0.37,0.43]	[0.15,0.23]	[0.09,0.16]

Table 3. Conditional probabilities of the length of the tail knowing the animal

		Animal			
		Dog	Cat	Horse	Bunny
	Long	[0.54,0.61]	[0.31,0.37]	[0.66,0.75]	[0.02,0.09]
Length	Average	[0.23,0.30]	[0.61,0.67]	[0.23,0.32]	[0.30,0.37]
	Short	[0.16,0.23]	[0.02,0.08]	[0.02,0.10]	[0.61,0.69]

Table 4. Conditional probabilities of the length of hair knowing the animal

		Animal			
		Dog	Cat	Horse	Bunny
	Long	[0.40,0.47]	[0.46,0.52]	[0.23,0.32]	[0.02,0.09]
Length	Average	[0.26,0.33]	[0.17,0.22]	[0.10,0.19]	[0.19,0.26]
	Short	[0.26,0.33]	[0.31,0.37]	[0.58,0.66]	[0.72,0.79]

to 0. As we have probability intervals, the bound $\underline{p}$ (resp. $\overline{p}$) can be read directly from the tables. Taking the pair (Dog, Horse) or $(\overline{D}, H)$ as an example, we have

$$log\ \underline{p}(D) - log\ \overline{p}(H) + \sum_{i=1}^{3} log\ \underline{p}(\mathbf{x}_i^o \mid D) - \sum_{i=1}^{3} log\ \overline{p}(\mathbf{x}_i^o \mid H) = 0.58 > 0$$

We then have that $D \succeq_{\mathcal{P}} H$. Repeating this for all pairs, we obtain the partial order in Fig. 1. The cautious prediction will be $\{D, B\}$, and each arc of Fig. 1 can be explained with prime implicants.

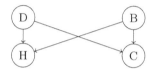

Fig. 1. Class dominance for prediction of $\mathbf{x}^o = $ (LE, ST, LH)

We detail the computation only for $D \succeq_{\mathcal{P}} H$. First we need to compute the worst opponent $\mathbf{x}^a$ that minimises $log \; \underline{p}(x_i^{a*} \mid D) - log \; \overline{p}(x_i^a \mid H)$ for each variable i. We obtain $\mathbf{x}^{a*} = (AE, AT, SH)$. Applying Eq. (9), we obtain

$$C = log \; \underline{p}(D) - log \; \overline{p}(H) + \sum_{i=1}^{3} log \; \underline{p}(\mathbf{x}_i^{a*} \mid D) - log \; \overline{p}(\mathbf{x}_i^{a*} \mid H) = -0.90$$

The contributions of the criteria required by Algorithm 1 are :

$$G_i = log \; \underline{p}(\mathbf{x}_i^o \mid D) - log \; \overline{p}(\mathbf{x}_i^o \mid H) - (log \; \underline{p}(\mathbf{x}_i^{a*} \mid D) - log \; \overline{p}(\mathbf{x}_i^{a*} \mid H))$$
$$G_{Ears} = log(0.33) - log(0.19) - (log(0.30) - log(0.75)) = 0.65$$
$$G_{Tail} = log(0.16) - log(0.10) - (log(0.23) - log(0.32)) = 0.33$$
$$G_{Hair} = log(0.40) - log(0.32) - (log(0.26) - log(0.66)) = 0.50$$

We can now apply Algorithm 1 and we obtain the explanation {(Ears, Long), (Hair, Long)} as $(0.65 + 0.50) - 0.90 > 0$, but with an enumeration algorithm we would find a second prime implicant explanation with {(Ears, Long), (Tail, Short)}, as $(0.65+0.33) - 0.90 > 0$, that is less important in terms of gain, but maybe intuitively more satisfying. Similarly we can compute explanations for other dominances, like {(Ears, Long), (Tail, Short)} for Dog $\succeq_{\mathcal{P}}$ Cat, {(Ears, Long), (Tail, Short)} for Bunny $\succeq_{\mathcal{P}}$ Cat and {(Ears, Long), (Tail, Short)} for Bunny $\succeq_{\mathcal{P}}$ Horse.

4   Conclusion

This paper proposes to explain robust classification by prime implicants, extending notions proposed so far in the precise setting. We show that, as for the precise case, this task is easy for the Naive classifier. To our knowledge, this is the first attempt to combine imprecise probabilistic classification with explanation.

In the future, we would like to focus on various questions not investigated here, such as: does enumerating all prime implicants remain easy for the naive credal classifier? For which robust models (e.g., including some dependence statements) do computations remain tractable? What happens with interaction between attributes ? Can we explain incomparabilities with similar notions? When trying to explain the complete partial order, should we use pairwise or holistic (i.e., prime implicants explaining the non-dominated classes at once) explanations? There are also several other explanation mechanisms we could consider [2].

References

1. Alarcón, Y.C.C., Destercke, S.: Imprecise gaussian discriminant classification. Pattern Recogn. **112**, 107739 (2019)
2. Audemard, G., Koriche, F., Marquis, P.: On tractable XAI queries based on compiled representations. In: Proceedings of the International Conference on Principles of Knowledge Representation and Reasoning, vol. 17, pp. 838–849 (2020)

3. Balasubramanian, V., Ho, S.S., Vovk, V.: Conformal Prediction for Reliable Machine Learning: Theory, Adaptations and Applications. Newnes, London (2014)
4. Belahcene, K., Labreuche, C., Maudet, N., Mousseau, V., Ouerdane, W.: Explaining robust additive utility models by sequences of preference swaps. Theor. Decis. **82**(2), 151–183 (2017)
5. Bernard, J.M.: An introduction to the imprecise Dirichlet model for multinomial data. Int. J. Approximate Reasoning **39**(2–3), 123–150 (2005)
6. Van den Broeck, G., Lykov, A., Schleich, M., Suciu, D.: On the tractability of SHAP explanations. In: Proceedings of the 35th AAAI (2021)
7. Corani, G., Antonucci, A., Zaffalon, M.: Bayesian networks with imprecise probabilities: theory and application to classification. In: Data Mining: Foundations and Intelligent Paradigms, vol. 23, pp. 49–93. Springer, Heidelberg (2012) https://doi.org/10.1007/978-3-642-23166-7_4
8. De Campos, L.M., Huete, J.F., Moral, S.: Probability intervals: a tool for uncertain reasoning. Int. J. Uncertain. Fuzziness Knowl.-Based Syst. **2**(02), 167–196 (1994)
9. Del Coz, J.J., Díez, J., Bahamonde, A.: Learning nondeterministic classifiers. J. Mach. Learn. Res. **10**(10) (2009)
10. Dendievel, G., Destercke, S., Wachalski, P.: Density estimation with imprecise kernels: application to classification. In: Destercke, S., Denoeux, T., Gil, M.Á., Grzegorzewski, P., Hryniewicz, O. (eds.) SMPS 2018. AISC, vol. 832, pp. 59–67. Springer, Cham (2019). https://doi.org/10.1007/978-3-319-97547-4_9
11. Marques-Silva, J., Gerspacher, T., Cooper, M.C., Ignatiev, A., Narodytska, N.: Explaining naive bayes and other linear classifiers with polynomial time and delay. In: NeurIPS 2020, 6–12 December 2020, virtual
12. Shih, A., Choi, A., Darwiche, A.: A symbolic approach to explaining Bayesian network classifiers. arXiv preprint arXiv:1805.03364 (2018)

Author Index

Printed in the United States
by Baker & Taylor Publisher Services